Arabic-English
English-Arabic
Practical
Dictionary

قاموس

إنكليزي – عربي

عربي – إنكليزي

Arabic
Practical
Dictionary

Arabic-English by
N. Awde

English-Arabic by
N. Awde & K. Smith

HIPPOCRENE BOOKS, INC.
NEW YORK

Typeset & designed by Desert ❤ Hearts, London

For information, address:
HIPPOCRENE BOOKS, INC.
171 Madison Avenue
New York, NY 10016
www.hippocrenebooks.com

Library of Congress Cataloging-in-Publication Data

Awde, Nicholas.
    Arabic-English/English-Arabic practical dictionary / Arabic-
English by N. Awde ; English-Arabic by N. Awde & K. Smith.
        p. cm.
    ISBN-10: 0-7818-1045-0
    ISBN-13: 978-0-7818-1045-6
    1. Arabic language--Dictionaries--English. 2. English--language-
-Dictionaries--Arabic. I. Title: Arabic-English practical dictionary.
II. Title: English-Arabic practical dictionary. III. Title: Half title:
Qamus Inklizi-'Arabi/'Arabi-Inklizi. IV. Smith, K. (Kevin), 1956-
V. Title.

PJ6640.A934 2004
92.7'321--dc24

                                                            2004042469

Printed in the United States of America.

Contents

Foreword

We hope the modern approach of this new dictionary will make it a useful resource to all those speakers of English and Arabic who wish to deepen their knowledge and use of these languages. The dictionary is intended to cover their needs with the most up-to-date entries in a handy reference form, and it should especially prove to be an aid in navigating the ever-growing global vocabulary of politics, telecommunications, computers, business and travel.

مقدّمة

نرجو أن يشكّل هذا القاموس مصدراً مفيداً لمتكلّمي اللغتين الإنكليزية والعربية الذين يريدون تعميق معرفتهم واستعمالهم لهاتين اللغتين. والقصد ان يغطّي هذا القاموس حاجاتهم باستعمال أحدث المعاني والإصطلاحات وعلى وجه الخصوص سبر أغوار المصطلحات في السياسة والإتّصالات والكمبيوتر والإنترنت والسياحة والتجارة وكذلك الرحلات وقد تمّ ترتيب هذا القاموس بطريقة تسهل الإستعمال.

Thanks to Peter Davies for his invaluable technical contributions and suggestions in the final stages of completing this volume.

Thanks also to the following for their contributions and encouragement: Thea Khitarishvili, Fred James Hill, Farouque Abdela, Ian 'Knox' Carnochan, Amanallah Abdel Azim, the Arabic Section of the BBC World Service, George and Ludmilla Blagowidow, Nicholas Williams, and Caroline Gates.

Abbreviations

أكاديمي	*acad*	academic
صفة	*adj*	adjective
مسيحي	*Chr*	Christian
إقتصادي	*ec*	economic
تجاري	*com*	commerce
كمبيوتر	*comp*	computer
تعليمي	*ed*	education
مؤنّث	*f*	feminine
مالي	*fin*	finance
إسلامي	*Isl*	Islamic
قانوني	*leg*	legal
مذكّر	*m*	masculine
بحري	*mar*	marine
طبّي	*med*	medical
عسكري	*mil*	military
موسيقي	*mus*	music
اسم	*n*	noun
جمع	*pl*	plural
سياسي	*pol*	political
حرف جرّ	*prep*	preposition
ديني	*rel*	religion
عامّي	*sl*	slang
شخص ما	*so*	someone
شيء ما	*sth*	something
رياضي	*spor*	sports
تكنولوجي	*tech*	technology
الإتصالات	*tel*	telecommunications
الإنكليزي البريطاني	*UK*	British English
الإنكليزي الأمريكي	*US*	American English
فعل	*v*	verb

Notes on the entries

1. Brackets following an English verb contain its past tense and past participle.

2. Brackets following an Arabic verb contain its imperfect vowelling and its verbal noun.

3. Brackets following a noun contain other noun forms and/or its plural.

4. Long vowels in Arabic are marked with a macron: ā, ē, ī, ō, ū.

5. Emphatic or 'dark' consonants in Arabic are marked with a dot: ḍ, ṣ, ṭ, ẓ.

6. ع is transliterated as ᶜ.

7. ء is transliterated as '. It is omitted at the beginnings of words. Note that ' is also used to indicate where vowels have been dropped before the l of al 'the', and therefore should not be pronounced.

8. Following modern standards, Arabic grammatical endings in nouns (**tanwīn**) has been omitted except in exceptional cases.

زائد zā'id 1. extra 2. plus

زائر zā'ir (-ūn; زوّار zuwwār) 1. visitor 2. guest

زائف zā'if 1. imitation 2. counterfeit 3. pseudo-

- Innovative, clear presentation
- Instantly accessible transliteration
- Meanings clearly signposted
- Modern, authoritative language

زاحف zāḥif (زواحف zawāḥif) reptile

plural forms

زاد zāda (i; زيادة ziyāda) 1. to increase 2. to boost 3. زاد على zāda 'alā; زاد عن zāda 'an to be more than 4. زاد في zāda fī to extend 5. زاده ثلاثة أضعاف zādah thalāthat aḍ'āf to treble

expressions and idioms

زار zāra (u; زيارة ziyāra) to visit

verbal forms

زارع zāri' (-ūn) grower

زال zāla (يزال yazāl) 1. to cease 2. لا يزال lā yazāl still

easy-to-use transliteration

زامل zāmala to associate

زاوية zāwiya (زوايا zawāyā) 1. angle 2. corner

زبادي zabādī: لبن زبادي laban zabādī yoghurt

زبالة zubāla litter; rubbish

زبدة zubda 1. butter 2. الزبدة النباتية az-zubda an-nabātīya margarine

زبون zabūn (زبائن zabā'in) 1. customer 2. client

easy-to-read phonetics

grammatical forms

numbers for different senses

cross-references

conversation [konvə'seishən] n ḥadīth حديث; محادثة muḥādatha

conversion [kən'və:shən] n (fin.) taḥwīl تحويل; taḥawwul تحول

convert [kon'və:t] v (fin.) ḥawwala حول; taḥawwala تحول

convey [kən'vei] v naqala نقل (u; نقل naql)

convict ['konvikt] n sajīn سجين (sujanā' سجناء)

convict [kən'vikt] v adāna أدان

convince [kən'vins] v aqna'a أقنع

convoy ['konvoi] n qāfila قافلة (qawāfil قوافل)

cook [kuk] 1. n ṭabbākh طباخ (-ūn) 2. v ṭabakha طبخ (u/a; ṭabkh طبخ)

cooker ['kukə] n jihāz li 'ṭ-ṭabkh جهاز للطبخ

cool [ku:l] 1. adj bārid بارد 2. ghayr munfa'il غير منفعل 3. v barrada برد

cooperate [kəu'opəreit] v ta'āwana تعاون

cooperation [kəuopə'reishən] n ta'āwun تعاون

copier ['kopiə] see photocopier

The Arabic alphabet

Arabic letter	Roman equivalent	Name of letter	Arabic letter	Roman Equivalent	Name of letter
ا، آ	ā	alif	ط	ṭ	ṭā'
ب	b	bā'	ظ	ẓ	ẓā'
ت	t	tā'	ع	ʿ	ʿayn
ث	th	thā'	غ	gh, g	ghayn
ج	j	jīm	ف	f	fā'
ح	ḥ	ḥā'	ق	q	qāf
خ	kh	khā'	ك	k, g	kāf
د	d	dāl	ل	l	lām
ذ	dh, z	dhāl	م	m	mīm
ر	r	rā'	ن	n	nūn
ز	z	zā'	و	w, ū, ō	wāw
س	s	sīn	ه	h	hā'
ش	sh	shīn	ى ، ي	y, ī, ē	yā'
ص	ṣ	ṣād			
ض	ḍ	ḍād	ء	'	hamza

Final letters

ة	-a, -h, -at	tā' marbūṭa
ى	-ā	alif maqṣūra

Short vowels

َ	a	fatḥa
ِ	i, e	kasra
ُ	u, o	ḍamma

Note: In the alphabetical order used in this dictionary, ء and ى have the same value as ا, and ة has the same value as ت. آ comes after ا and before ب.

Numbers

٠	١	٢	٣	٤	٥	٦	٧	٨	٩	١٠
0	1	2	3	4	5	6	7	8	9	10

Arabic-English

عربي - إنكليزي

أ

أ **a** 1. *interrogative particle* 2. ؟كذلك أليس و
laysa kadhālik? isn't that so?

إئتلاف **i'tilāf** coalition

آب **āb** August

آت **ātin** 1. forthcoming 2. future

آثار **āthār** *pl* 1. remains 2. trail 3. ruins 4.
الآثار علم **'ilm al-āthār** archeology 5.
and see أثر

آثر **āthara** to prefer (على **'alā** to)

آجلاً **ājilan:** آجلاً أو عاجلاً **'ājilan aw ājilan**
sooner or later

آخر **ākhar** (أخرى **ukhrā;** *pl* أخر **ukhar**) 1.
other 2. another 3. آخر مكان **makān**
ākhar elsewhere 4. أخرى مرّةً **marratan**
ākhar once more 5. الآخر بعد الواحد **al-**
wāḥid ba'd al-ākhar one after the other

آخِر **ākhir** (-ūn/-āt/أواخر **awākhir**) 1. last 2.
end 3. آخره إلى **ilā ākhirih** etc.; et
cetera 4. لحظة آخر في **fī ākhir laḥza** in
the nick of time 5. الأخبار آخر **ākhir al-**
akhbār the latest news

آداب **ādāb** *pl* manners

آذار **ādhār** March

آرق **āriq** sleepless

آسف **āsif** sorry

آسيا **āsiyā** Asia

آسيوي **āsiyawī** Asian

آلة **āla** (-āt) 1. machine 2. instrument 3.
tool 4. الكاتبة الآلة **al-āla al-kātiba**
typewriter 5. تصوير آلة **ālat taṣwīr** camera
6. حاسبة آلة **āla ḥāsiba** computer 7.
تصنّت آلة **ālat taṣannut** electronic bug
8. الخياطة آلة **ālat al-khiyāṭa** sewing
machine 9. الشعر لتنشيف آلة **āla li**
tanshīf ash-sha'r hairdryer

آلات **ālāt** *pl* machinery

آلم **ālama** 1. to pain 2. to ache

آلي **ālī** 1. mechanical 2. آلي إنسان **insān ālī**
robot 3. آلي رشّاش **rashshash ālī**
(آلية رشّاشات **rashshashāt ālīya**)
machine-gun

آلية **ālīya** (-āt) mechanism

آمن **āmin** 1. safe 2. secure

آمن **āmana** to believe (ب **bi** in)

الآن **al-ān** 1. now 2. الآن بعد **ba'd al-ān**
anymore 3. الآن حتّى **ḥatta al-ān** still 4.
الآن قبل **qabl al-ān** already

آنذاك **ānadhāk** then; at that time

آنسة **ānisa** Miss (-āt)

آني **ānī** momentary

آنية **āniya:** الطعام آنية **āniyat aṭ-ṭa'ām**
crockery

آهة **āha** (-āt) sigh

آوى **āwā** to retire (إلى **ilā** to)

آية āya (-āt) verse of the Qur'an

أب ab ءآبآ(ء) abā') 1. father 2. أبوان abawān parents

أبى abā (يأبى ya'bā; إبا ء ibā') to refuse

أباد abāda to exterminate

إبادة ibāda genocide

ابتدأ ibtada'a to begin (ب bi with)

إبتدائي ibtidā'ī 1. initial 2. elementary 3. primary 4. مدرسة إبتدائية madrasa ibtidā'īya elementary school; primary school

ابتزّ ibtazza to blackmail

إبتسام ibtisām smile

ابتسم ibtasama to smile

ابتعد ibta'ada 1. to go away (عن 'an from) 2. to keep away (عن 'an from)

ابتكر ibtakara to devise

ابتلع ibtala'a 1. to swallow 2. to devour

ابتهج ibtahaja to be happy (ب bi at/with)

إبحار ibḥār sailing

أبحر abḥara 1. to sail 2. to set sail

أبد abad: إلى الأبد ilā 'l-abad forever

أبداً abadan 1. ever 2. never

أبدى abdā to show; to express

إبداع ibdā' 1. creation 2. originality

أبدع abda'a to create

أبدي abadī perpetual

إبرة ibra (إبر ibar) needle

أبراج abrāj: دائرةالأبراج dā'irat al-abrāj zodiac

أبروي obrawī see أوبروي

إبريق ibrīq (أباريق abārīq) 1. الشاي jug 2. إبريق الشاي ibrīq ash-shāy teapot

أبريل abrīl April

أبطأ abṭa'a to slow down

إبعاد ib'ād 1. exile 2. deportation

أبعد ab'ada 1. to exile 2. to deport

أبعد ab'ad 1. further 2. ultimate

أبغض abghaḍa to detest

أبكم abkam 1. mute 2. أصمّ أبكم aṣamm abkam deaf-mute

أبلغ ablagha to inform; to notify (ه so; ب bi/عن 'an of)

أبله ablah simple

ابن ibn (ء أبنا abnā'; بنون banūn) 1. son 2. ابن أخ ibn akh nephew 3. ابن أخت ibn ukht nephew 4. إبن خال ibn khāl; ابن خالة ibn khāla cousin 5. ابن عم ibn 'amm; إبن عمة ibn 'amma cousin 6. زوجة الإبن zawjat al-ibn daughter-in-law 7. ابن البلد ibn al-balad native 8. ابن مقرض ibn miqraḍ ferret 9. ابن عرس ibn 'irs بنات عرس) banāt 'irs) weasel 10. ابن عرس أبيض ibn 'irs abyaḍ stoat 11. and see ابن

ابنة ibna (بنات banāt) daughter

إبهام ibhām (أباهيم abāhīm) thumb

أبوان abawān 1. parents 2. see أب

أبوي abawī paternal

أبيض abyaḍ (f ء بيضا bayḍā'; pl بيض bīḍ) 1. white 2. البحر الأبيض المتوسّط al-baḥr al-abyaḍ al-mutawassiṭ Mediterranean Sea

أتاح atāḥa to permit (ه *sth*; ل li to)

أتباع atbā' *pl* مجموعة أتباع majmū'at atbā' following

اتّبع ittaba'a 1. to follow 2. اتّبع راصداً ittaba'a rāṣidan to stalk

إتّجاه ittijāh 1. direction 2. trend 3. شارع واحد الإتّجاه shāri' wāḥid al-ittijāh one-way street

اتّجه إلى ittajaha ilā to head for

إتّحاد ittiḥād 1. union 2. federation 3. combination 4. الإتّحاد الأوروبي al-ittiḥād al-ūrūbī European Union (E.U.)

إتّحادي ittiḥādī federal

اتّحد ittaḥada to unite

اتّخذ ittakhadha 1. to take 2. to adopt 3. اتّخذ إجراءات ittakhadha ijrā'āt to take measures

إتّزان ittizān balance

إتّساع ittisā' expansion

إتّساق ittisāq proportion

اتّسع ittasa'a to expand

إتّصال ittiṣāl (-āt) 1. communication 2. contact 3. interface 4. وسائل إتّصال wasā'il ittiṣāl communications 5. الإتّصال الجنسي al-ittiṣāl al-jinsī sex 6. شبكة إتّصالات shabakat ittiṣālāt communications network

اتّصل ittaṣala 1. to be connected (ب bi to) 2. to communicate (ب bi with) 3. to continue (ب bi with)

إتّفاق ittifāq agreement

إتّفاقي ittifāqī occasional

إتّفاقية ittifāqīya (-āt) 1. agreement 2. convention 3. treaty

اتّفق ittafaqa 1. to agree (على 'alā on) 2. to happen (by chance)

اتّكأ على ittaka'a 'alā to lean on

أتمّ atamma to complete

إتّهام ittihām (-āt) 1. accusation 2. *(leg.)* charge

اتّهم ittahama 1. to accuse (ه so; ب bi of) 2. *(leg.)* to charge (ه so; ب bi with)

أتّون attūn أتاتين atātīn furnace

أوتوستراد otostrād (-āt) motorway

أتى atā (i) 1. to come 2. to arrive (إلى\ه ilā) 3. to produce (ب bi) 4. to finish off (على 'alā)

إتقان itqān proficiency

أتمّ atamma to complete

أتوبيس otobīs (-āt) 1. bus 2. موقف الأتوبيس mawqif al-otobīs bus-stop

أوتوماتيكي otomatīkī automatic

أثاث athāth *pl* 1. furniture 2. طقم أثاث ṭaqm athāth suite

أثار athāra 1. to excite 2. to thrill 3. to agitate 4. to stir up 5. to stimulate 6. أثار الإهتمام athāra 'l-ihtimām to intrigue 7. أثار الإستياء athāra al-istiyā' to displease 8. أثار المشاعر athāra al-mashā'ir to move

إثارة ithāra 1. excitement 2. thrill 3. agitation 4. stimulation

إثبات **ithbāt 1.** proof **2.** إثبات الهوية **ithbāt al-huwīya** identification

أثبت **athbata 1.** to prove **2.** to verify **3.** to demonstrate **4.** أثبت الهوية **athbata al-huwīya** to identify **5.** أثبت بلولب **athbata bi lawlab** to screw

أثر **aththara 1.** to impress **2.** to influence **3.** أثر في\على **aththara fi/ʻalā** to affect

أثر **athar** (آثار **āthār**) **1.** trace **2.** relic **3.** antique **4.** work of art **5.** and see أثر

إثر **ithra** straight after

أثري **atharī 1.** antique **2.** (-ūn) archeologist

أثقل **athqala** to burden

إثم **ithm** (آثام **āthām**) sin

أثم **athima** (a; إثم **ithm**) to sin

أثناء **athnā'**; في أثناء **fī athnā'** during

إثنا عشر **ithnā ashar** twelve

إثنان **ithnān** two

الإثنين **al-ithnayn**; يوم الإثنين **yawm al-ithnayn** Monday

أجاب **ajāba** to reply; to answer (ه **so**; إلى **ilā**/على **ʻalā** about)

إجابة **ijāba** (-āt) response

إجازة **ijāza** (-āt) **1.** holiday **2.** leave

أجاز **ajāza** to sanction

أجانب **ajānib** pl **1.** foreigners **2.** الأجانب كره **kurh al-ajānib** xenophobia

إجباري **ijbārī** compulsory

أجبر **ajbara** to compel

اجتاز **ijtāza** to go through

اجتثّ **ijtaththa** to uproot

اجتماع **ijtimāʻ** (-āt) **1.** meeting **2.** congress **3.** مكان الإجتماع **makān al-ijtimāʻ** assembly point **4.** وقائع إجتماع **waqā'iʻ ijtimāʻ** minutes of a meeting **5.** عقد إجتماعاً **ʻaqada ijtimāʻan** (i; عقد **ʻaqd**) to hold a meeting **6.** إجتماع حاشد **ijtimāʻ ḥāshid** mass meeting; rally **7.** إجتماع الشمل **ijtimāʻ ash-shaml** reunion **8.** علم الإجتماع **ʻilm al-ijtimāʻ** sociology

إجتماعي **ijtimāʻī 1.** social **2.** مركز إجتماعي **markaz ijtimāʻī** position **3.** خدمات إجتماعية **khidmāt ijtimāʻīya** welfare

اجتمع **ijtamaʻa 1.** to collect **2.** to assemble **3.** اجتمع ب **ijtamaʻa bi** to meet **4.** اجتمع بعد فراق **ijtamaʻa baʻd firāq** to reunite

اجتهد **ijtahada** to work hard

أجّر **ajjara 1.** to hire **2.** to rent **3.** to lease

أجر **ajr** (أجور **ujūr**) **1.** wage **2.** salary **3.** fee

أجرى **ajrā 1.** to carry out **2.** to apply **3.** أجرى إستفتاء **ajrā istiftā'** poll **4.** أجرى إنتخابات **ajrā intikhābāt** to hold elections **5.** أجرى عملية جراحية **ajrā ʻamalīya jarāḥīya** (med.) to operate

إجراء **ijrā'** (-āt) **1.** procedure **2.** اتّخذ إجراءات **attakhadha ijrā'āt** to take measures

إجرامي **ijrāmī** criminal

أجرة **ujra 1.** hire **2.** rent **3.** charge; rate **4.** أجرة السفر **ujrat as-safar** fare **5.**

سيّارة أجرة sayyārat ujra taxi

أجرح ajraḥa: أجرح مشاعر غيره ajraḥa mashāʿir ghayrih to offend

أجّل ajjala 1. to delay 2. to postpone

أجل ajl 1. term 2. sake 3. قصير الأجل qaṣīr al-ajal short-term 4. من أجل min ajl; لأجل li ajl for the sake of 5. من أجلي min ajlī for my sake

أجلى ajlā to evacuate

إجماعي ijmāʿī unanimous

إجمال ijmāl: بالإجمال bi 'l-ijmāl altogether

إجمالاً ijmālan on the whole

إجمالي ijmālī mass

أجمع ajmaʿ all

أجناس ajnās pl: متعدّد الأجناس mutaʿaddid al-ajnās multi-racial

أجنبي ajnabī (أجانب ajānib) 1. foreign 2. foreigner 3. alien 4. عملة أجنبية ʿumla ajnabīya foreign currency

إجهاض ijhāḍ (med.) miscarriage

أجهزة ajhiza pl 1. equipment 2. (pol.) machinery

أجهض ajhaḍa (med.) to miscarry

أجود ajwad better

أحاط ب aḥāṭa bi 1. to surround 2. to contain 3. أحاط به علماً aḥāṭa bih ʿilman to have in-depth knowledge of

أحال aḥāla to refer (إلى to)

أحبّ aḥabba 1. to love 2. to like

إحباط iḥbāṭ frustration

أحبط aḥbaṭa to frustrate

احتاج إلى iḥtāja ilā to need

احتال iḥtāla to swindle

احتبس iḥtabasa to withhold

احتجّ iḥtajja 1. to protest (على ʿalā against) 2. احتجّ ب to put forward as an argument

إحتجاج iḥtijāj protest

إحتجاجي iḥtijājī protest

إحتجاز iḥtijāz detention

احتذى iḥtadhā to set an example

إحترام iḥtirām (-āt) 1. respect 2. إحترام النفس iḥtirām an-nafs self-respect 3. عدم إحترام ʿadm iḥtirām disrespect

إحترامات iḥtirāmāt pl respects

احترس iḥtarasa to beware

احترق iḥtaraqa to burn

احترم iḥtarama to respect

إحتشام iḥtishām decency

إحتفال iḥtifāl 1. celebration 2. ceremony 3. إحتفال شعبي iḥtifāl shaʿbī carnival

احتفظ ب iḥtafaẓa bi to retain

احتفل iḥtafala to celebrate

إحتقار iḥtiqār contempt

احتقر iḥtaqara to despise

إحتكار iḥtikār (-āt) monopoly

إحتكاك iḥtikāk contact

احتلّ iḥtalla (mil.) to occupy

إحتلال iḥtilāl (mil.) occupation

إحتمال iḥtimāl 1. potential 2. قدرة على الإحتمال qudra 'alā 'l-iḥtimāl stamina

إحتمالي iḥtimālī potential

إحتمل iḥtamala 1. to bear; to put up with 2. يحتمل yuḥtamalu passive to be possible

إحتوى iḥtawā to contain

إحتياط iḥtiyāṭ (-āt) precaution

إحتياطي iḥtiyāṭī 1. spare 2. reserve

إحتيال iḥtiyāl 1. fraud 2. عمل احتيالي 'amal iḥtiyālī racket

أحد aḥad 1. one 2. someone; anyone 3. لا أحد lā aḥad no one; none 4. يوم الأحد yawm al-'aḥad Sunday 5. and see أحد عشر

أحداث aḥdāth pl 1. ملي‘ بالأحداث malī' bi 'l-aḥdāth eventful 2. رهن الأحداث rahn al-aḥdāth at stake 3. and see حدث

أحدث aḥdatha to bring about

أحد عشر aḥad 'ashar eleven

أحذية aḥdhiya: أحذية رياضية aḥdhiya riyāḍiya pl trainers; tennis shoes

أحرى aḥrā: بالأحرى bi 'l-aḥrā rather

إحراق iḥrāq burn

أحرز aḥraza to attain

أحزاب aḥzāb 1. متعدّد الأحزاب muta'addid al-aḥzāb multi-party 2. and see حزب

أحزن aḥzana to sadden

إحساس iḥsās (-āt; أحاسيس aḥāsīs) feeling

إحسان iḥsān charity

أحسن aḥsan better; best

أحشاء aḥshā' pl guts

أحصى aḥṣā 1. to count 2. لا يحصى lā yuḥṣā passive countless

إحصاء iḥṣā' 1. علم الإحصاء 'ilm al-iḥṣā' statistics 2. إحصاء السكان (-āt) iḥṣā' as-sukkān census

إحصائي iḥṣā'ī statistical

إحصائيات iḥṣā'īyāt statistics

أحكّ aḥakka i to itch

أحلّ aḥalla to dissolve

أحمر aḥmar (f حمراء ḥamrā'; pl حمر ḥumr) 1. red 2. أحمر زهري aḥmar zahrī pink 3. أحمر الشفاه aḥmar ash-shifāh lipstick

احمرّ iḥmarra 1. to go red 2. احمرّ الوجه iḥmarra al-wajh to blush

أحمق aḥmaq (حمق ḥumq) 1. stupid 2. idiot

أحيا aḥyā 1. to bring to life 2. to vitalise

أحياء aḥyā' pl: علم الأحياء 'ilm al-aḥyā' biology

إحياء iḥyā' revival

أحيان aḥyān pl: معظم الأحيان mu'aẓẓam al-aḥyān for the most part

أحياناً aḥyānan sometimes

أخ akh (إخوة ikhwa; إخوان ikhwān) 1. brother 2. ابن أخ ibn akh nephew 3. بنت أخ bint akh niece

أخاف akhāfa to frighten

أخبار akhbār pl 1. news 2. نشرة الأخبار nashrat al-akhbār newscast 3. مذيع نشرة الأخبار mudhī' nashrat al-akhbār newscaster; newsreader 4. آخر الأخبار ākhir al-akhbār the latest news 5. نشرة الأخبار الأخيرة nashrat al-akhbār al-akhīra the late news

إخباري ikhbārī news; information

أخبر akhbara to inform (ﻫ so; ب bi of)

أخت ukht (أخوات akhawāt) 1. sister 2. ابن أخت ibn ukht nephew 3. بنت أخت bint ukht niece

اختار ikhtāra to choose

إختبار ikhtibār (-āt) 1. test 2. experiment 3. إختبار المعلومات ikhtibār al-maʿlūmāt quiz

إختباري ikhtibārī experimental

اختبر ikhtabara to test

اختتم ikhtatama to finish

إختراع ikhtirāʿ invention

اخترع ikhtaraʿa to invent

اخترق ikhtaraqa 1. to penetrate 2. to cross

اختصّ ikhtaṣṣa to be distinguished (ب bi with/by) 2. to concern

اختصار ikhtiṣār 1. abbreviation 2. بالإختصار bi ʾl-ikhtiṣār in short

إختصاص ikhtiṣāṣ speciality

إختصاصي ikhtiṣāṣī (-yūn) specialist

اختصر ikhtaṣara to outline

إختطاف ikhtiṭāf 1. kidnapping 2. hijacking

اختطف ikhtaṭafa 1. to kidnap 2. to hijack

اختطف ikhtaṭafa 1. to snatch; to grab 2. to kidnap 3. to hijack

اختفى ikhtafā 1. to disappear 2. to hide

إختفاء ikhtifāʾ disappearance

إختلاف ikhtilāf 1. difference 2. في الرأي ikhtilāf fi ʾl-raʾy disagreement

اختلط ikhtalaṭa 1. to mix; to be mixed (ب bi with) 2. to associate (ب bi with)

اختلف ikhtalafa 1. to be different (عن ʿan to); to differ (عن ʿan from) 2. اختلف في الرأي ikhtalafa fi ʾr-raʾy disagree

أختم akhtama to conclude

اختنق ikhtanaqa 1. to choke 2. to suffocate

إختيار ikhtiyār 1. choice 2. selection

إختياري ikhtiyārī 1. optional 2. voluntary

أخجل akhjala to shame

أخذ akhadha (u; أخذ akhdh) 1. to take 2. to begin to 3. إذا أخذنا في عين الإعتبار idhā akhadhnā fī ʿayn al-iʿtibār considering 4. أخذ صورة الأشعّة akhadha ṣurat al-ashiʿʿa to take an x-ray 5. أخذ حمّام شمس akhadha ḥammām shams to sunbathe

أخدود ukhdūd (أخاديد akhādīd) groove

أخّر akhkhara to delay

أخرى ukhrā ƒ 1. other 2. another 3. see آخر

أخرج akhraja 1. to take out 2. to extract 3. to direct 4. to dismiss (عن ʿan from) 5. to expel (عن ʿan from) 6.

أخرج القابس من المأخذ akhraja al-qābis min al-ma'khadh to unplug

إخراج ikhrāj 1. extraction 2. film direction

أخرس akhras mute

أخرق akhraq awkward

أخصّائي akhiṣṣā'ī specialist

أخضر akhḍar (f خضراء khaḍrā'; pl خضر khuḍr) green

أخطأ akhṭa'a 1. to make a mistake 2. أخطأ التقدير akhṭa'a at-taqdīr to misjudge 3. أخطأ الحساب akhṭa'a al-ḥisāb to miscalculate

أخطبوط ukhṭabūṭ collective octopus

أخفى akhfā to hide (عن 'an/على 'alā from)

إخفاق ikhfāq 1. failure 2. misfire 3. (spor.) miss

أخفق akhfaqa 1. to fail 2. to fire 3. to flap 4. (spor.) to miss

إخلاص ikhlāṣ devotion

أخلاق akhlāq pl 1. manners 2. morals 3. دمث الأخلاق damith al-akhlāq good-tempered

أخلاقي akhlāqī 1. moral 2. لا أخلاقي lā akhlāqī immoral

أخلاقية akhlāqīya morality

أخمص akhmaṣ: أخمص القدم akhmaṣ al-qadam sole

أخوي akhawī fraternal

أخير akhīr 1. last 2. final 3. latest 4. latter 5. موعد أخير maw'id akhīr

نشرة الأخبار الأخيرة nashrat al-akhbār al-akhīra the late news 7. كملاذ أخير ka malādh akhīr as a last resort 8. المحطة الأخيرة al-maḥaṭṭat al-akhīra terminus

أخيراً akhīran 1. at last 2. finally 3. recently

أدّى addā 1. to carry out 2. to take an exam 3. أدى إلى addā ilā to cause

أداة adāt (أدوات adawāt) 1. tool 2. device 3. article 4. instrument 5. أداة صغيرة adāh ṣaghīra gadget 6. أداة لحمل شيء adāh li ḥaml shay' holder

أداء adā' (-āt) performance

أدار adāra 1. to direct 2. to manage 3. to administer 4. to run 5. أدار الأوركسترا adāra al-orkestrā (mus.) to conduct

إدارة idāra (-āt) 1. management 2. administration 3. مجلس الإدارة majlis al-idāra board of directors 4. سوء الإدارة sū' al-idāra mismanagement 5. رئيس مجلس الإدارة ra'is majlis al-idāra (com.) president 6. الإدارة الحكومية al-idāra al-ḥukūmīya civil service

إداري idārī 1. administrative 2. الشؤون الإدارية ash-shu'ūn al-idārīya personnel 3. دائرة إدارية كنيسية dā'ira idārīya kanīsīya parish

أدان adāna 1. to convict 2. to condemn

أدّب addaba 1. to discipline 2. to educate

أدب adab (آداب ādāb) 1. literature 2. culture 3. courtesy 4. أدب قصصي adab qaṣaṣī fiction

أدبي adabī literary

ادّخر iddakhara 1. to save 2. to store

أدخل adkhala 1. to let in 2. to insert 3. to include 4. to introduce 5. to tuck in 6. أدخل القابس في المأخذ adkhala al-qābis fī 'l-ma'khadh to plug in

إدراك idrāk perception

أدرك adraka to realize

ادّعى idda'ā to claim; to allege

ادّعاء iddi'ā' claim; allegation

إدماج idmāj integration

إدمان idmān 1. addiction 2. الإدمان بالكحول alcoholism al-idmān bi 'l-kuḥūl

أدمج admaja to incorporate

أدنى adnā 1. bottom 2. lowest 3. الحدّ الأدنى al-ḥadd al-adnā minimum

أدهش adhasha to astonish

أدوات adawāt pl 1. tackle 2. أدوات المائدة adawāt al-mā'ida cutlery

إذ idh 1. when; as; (and) then 2. إذ أنّ idh anna since; because 3. إذ ذلك idh dhālik then; at that time

أذّى adhdhā 1. to harm 2. to damage

إذا idhā 1. if; whether 2. ما إذا mā idhā whether 3. إذا أخذنا في عين الإعتبار idhā akhadhnā fī 'ayn al-i'tibār considering

إذاً idhan then; in that case

أذى adhan 1. harm 2. damage

أذاب adhāba to dissolve

أذاع adhā'a to broadcast

إذاعة idhā'a 1. broadcast 2. broadcasting 3. هيئة الإذاعة البريطانية hay'at al-idhā'a al-brīṭānīya British Broadcasting Corporation (BBC)

أذعر adh'ara to alarm

أذلّ adhalla to humiliate

أذن udhun (آذان ādhān) ear

إذن idhn 1. permission 2. permit

إذن idhan see إذاً

أذن adhina (a; إذن idhn) to permit

إذهال idhhāl amazement

أذهل adhhala to amaze

ذهوب dhuhūb 1. going 2. departure

أرى arā to show; to demonstrate

أراح arāḥa to relieve

أراد arāda to want

إرادة irāda 1. will 2. wish

إرادي irādī 1. voluntary 2. غير إرادي ghayr irādī involuntary 3. إنعكاس لا إرادي in'ikās lā irādī (-āt) reflex

أراضٍ arādin pl 1. ملاك أراضٍ mallāk arādin landowner 2. مبنىّ والأراضي التابعة له mabnan wa 'l-arāḍī at-tābi'a lah premises 3. استصلح أراضٍ istaṣlaḥa arādin to reclaim land 4. and see أرض

أربعة arba'a four

الأربعاء al-arba'ā'; 1. يوم الأربعاء yawm al-arba'ā' Wednesday

أربعة عشر arba'ata 'ashar fourteen

أربعون arba'ūn forty

أربك arbaka 1. to confuse 2. to embarrass

إرتاب irtāba to mistrust

إرتاح irtāḥa 1. to rest 2. to relax 3. to be happy (إلى/ل li about)

إرتباط irtibāṭ connection

إرتباك irtibāk 1. confusion 2. embarrassment

إرتبط irtabaṭa 1. to be tied (ب bi to) 2. to be linked (ب bi to)

إرتبك irtabaka 1. to be confused 2. to be embarrassed

إرتجح irtajaḥa to swing

إرتجف irtajafa 1. to tremble 2. to shiver

إرتدادي irtidādī reverse

إرتري iritarī (-yūn) Eritrean

إرتريا iritariyā Eritrea

إرتشى irtashā to bribe

إرتشاء irtishā' bribery

إرتعش irta'asha to shiver

إرتفاع irtifā' 1. altitude 2. height 3. (fin.) rise 4. إرتفاع الصوت irtifā' aṣ-ṣawt loudness

إرتفع irtafa'a 1. to rise 2. to climb 3. to increase

إرتقاء irtiqā' progress

إرتكب irtakaba 1. to commit 2. إرتكب جريمة irtakaba jarīma to commit a crime 3. إرتكب جرائم حرب irtakaba jarā'im ḥarb to commit a war crime

إرتياب irtiyāb 1. mistrust 2. suspicion

إرتياح irtiyāḥ relief

إرث irth legacy

رثا rathā; رثي (i) rathw (u; رثو (i) rithā'; مرثاة marthiya; مرثية marthāh) 1. to lament 2. رثى ل rathā li to mourn 3. يرثى له yurthā lah pitiful

أرجأ arja'a 1. to put off 2. إرجاء تنفيذ حكم arja'a tanfidh ḥukm (leg.) to suspend 3. إرجاء تنفيذ حكم irjā' tanfidh ḥukm (leg.) suspension 4. أرجأ تنفيذ حكم بالاعدام arja'a tanfidh ḥukm bi 'l-i'dām (leg.) to reprieve

أرجح arjaḥa to prefer

أرجع arja'a 1. to send back 2. to replace

الأرجنتين al-arjantīn Argentinia

أرجنتيني arjantīnī (-yūn) Argentinian

أرجواني urjuwānī purple

أرجوك! arjūk! please!

أرخى arkhā to relax

إرخاء irkhā' relaxation

الأردن al-urdunn Jordan

أردني urdunnī Jordanian

أرزّ aruzz rice

إرسال irsāl transmission

إرسالية irsālīya: إرسالية تبشيرية irsālīya tabshīrīya (rel.) mission

أرسل arsala 1. to send (إلى/ل li to) 2. dispatch 3. to forward 4. to transmit 5. أرسل بالبريد arsala bi 'l-barīd to post; to mail

إرشاد irshād (-āt) guidance

إرشادات irshādāt *pl* directions

أرشد arshada 1. to direct 2. to guide

أرشيف arshīf (-āt) archive(s)

أرض arḍ *f* (أراضٍ arāḍin) 1. ground 2. land 3. floor 4. الأرض al-arḍ the earth 5. سطح الأرض saṭḥ al-arḍ ground 6. قطعة أرض qiṭ'at arḍ lot; plot 7. تحت سطح الأرض ;تحت الأرض taḥta l-arḍ; taḥta saṭḥ al-arḍ underground 8. إنهيال الأرض inhiyāl al-arḍ landslide 9. *and see* أراضٍ ;أرضي

أرضى arḍā 1. to satisfy 2. to please 3. to suit

أرضي arḍī 1. earth 2. الكرة الأرضية al-kura al-arḍīya the globe

أرعب ar'aba 1. to scare 2. to alarm

أرغن urghun (أراغن arāghin) *(mus.)* organ

أرفع arfa' 1. higher 2. finer 3. رتبةً\منزلةً أرفع arfa' rutbatan/manzilatan superior

أرق araq insomnia

أرق ariq sleepless

أوركسترا orkestrā 1. orchestra 2. مدير الأوركسترا mudīr al-orkestrā *(mus.)* conductor 3. أدار الأوركسترا adāra al-orkestrā *(mus.)* to conduct

أرملة armala (أرامل arāmil) widow

أرمل armal (أرامل arāmil) widower

أرنب arnab (أرانب arānib) rabbit

إرهاب irhāb 1. terror 2. terrorism

إرهابي irhābī (-ūn) terrorist

إرهاق irhāq exhaustion

أرهب arhaba to terrify

أرهق arhaqa to exhaust

أريكة arīka (أرائك arā'ik) couch; sofa

أزال azāla 1. to end 2. to remove 3. to eliminate

إزالة izāla elimination

ازداد izdāda to increase

إزدحام izdiḥām 1. overcrowding 2. المرور izdiḥām al-murūr traffic jam

إزدهار izdihār 1. flourishing 2. heyday(s) 3. إزدهار إقتصادي izdihār iqtiṣādī *(ec.)* boom

ازدهر izdahara to flourish

ازدياد izdiyād increase

أزرق azraq (*f* زرقا ، زرقا zurqā'; *pl* زرق zuruq) blue

إزعاج iz'āj 1. irritation 2. disturbance

أزعج az'aja 1. to irritate 2. to disturb 3. الرجاء عدم الإزعاج ar-rajā' 'adm al-iz'āj please do not disturb

أزمة azma (أزمات azamāt) crisis

أسىً asan grief

أساء asā'a: أساء إستعمال asā'a isti'māl to abuse

أساس asās (أسس usus) 1. base 2. foundation 3. basis

أساساً asāsan primarily

أساسي asāsī 1. fundamental 2. primary

أساطير asāṭīr *pl*: علم الأساطير 'ilm al-asāṭīr mythology

أساقفة asāqifa pl رئيس الأساقفة ra'īs al-asāqifa archbishop

أسباب asbāb pl (leg.) 1. grounds 2. and see سبب

إسباني isbānī Spanish

إسبانيا isbānyā Spain

أسبوع usbū' (أسابيع asābī') 1. week 2. بعد أسبوع ba'd usbū' in a week 3. نهاية الأسبوع nihāyat al-usbū' weekend 4. منتصف الأسبوع muntaṣif al-usbū' midweek

أسبوعان usbū'ān fortnight

أسبوعي usbū'ī weekly

أسبوعياً usbū'īyan weekly

استأجر ista'jara 1. to hire out 2. to rent out 3. to lease 4. to charter

استأنف ista'nafa 1. to resume 2. (leg.) to appeal

استأهل ista'halla to deserve

إستاد istād stadium

أستاذ ustādh (أساتذة asātidha) (acad.) 1. doctor; professor 2. أستاذ جامعي ustādh jāmi'ī lecturer

إستبدال istibdāl 1. exchange 2. (spor.) substitution 3. متعذر إستبداله muta'adhdhir istibdāluh irreplaceable

استبدل istabdala 1. to replace 2. to substitute

استبقى istabqā 1. to retain 2. to spare

إستثمار istithmār investment

استثمر istathmara to invest

إستثناء istithnā' 1. exception 2. إستثناء دون istithnā' without exception دون إستثناء

إستثنائي istithnā'ī exceptional

استجاب istajāba 1. to respond (ل li to) 2. to oblige

إستجمام istijmām recreation

إستجواب istijwāb 1. questioning 2. interrogation

استجوب istajwaba 1. to question 2. to interrogate

استحى istaḥā 1. to be shy (من min of) 2. to be embarrassed (من min about)

إستحالة istaḥāla impossibility

استحق istaḥaqqa to deserve

إستحقاق istiḥqāq: فات موعد إستحقاقه fāt maw'id istiḥqāquh overdue

استحم istaḥamma to bathe

استحيا istaḥyā 1. to let live 2. to be shy 3. to be embarrassed

إستخبارات istikhbārāt pl (mil.) intelligence

استخدم istakhdama 1. to use 2. to employ

استخرج istakhraja to mine

استخف istakhaffa to underestimate

استدعى istad'ā to summon

إستراتيجي istrātījī strategic

إستراتيجية istrātījīya strategy

إستراحة istirāḥa (-āt) 1. rest 2. break 3. relaxation

استراح istarāḥa 1. to rest 2. to take a break 3. to relax

أسترالي usturālī (-ūn) Australian

أستراليا usturāliyā Australia

إسترجاع istirjā‘ recovery

استرجع istarja‘a to retrieve

استرخى istarkhā to relax

إسترخاء istirkhā’ relaxation

استرداد istirdād recovery

استردّ istaradda 1. to take back 2. to get back 3. to retrieve 4. to reclaim 5. to recall

إسترليني istarlīnī (fin.) sterling

إستريو isteriyō 1. stereo 2. جهاز إستريو jihāz isteriyō stereo set

استسلم istaslama 1. to give in 2. to surrender 3. استسلم ل istaslama li resign

استشار istashāra to consult

إستشارة istishāra consultation

استصدر istaṣdara (leg.) to obtain a verdict/judgement

استصلح istaṣlaḥa: استصلح أراض istaṣlaḥa arāḍin to reclaim land

استضاف istaḍāfa to entertain

استطاع istaṭā‘a to be able (to); can

إستطلاع istiṭlā‘ 1. investigation 2. إستطلاع رأي istiṭlā‘ ra’y questionnaire 3. حبّ الإستطلاع ḥubb al-istiṭlā‘ curiosity

استعاد ista‘āda to recover; to regain

استعار ista‘āra to borrow

استعجل ista‘jala to hurry; to hurry up

استعداد isti‘dād preparation

استعدّ ista‘adda to prepare; to get ready (ل li for)

إستعراض isti‘rāḍ 1. parade 2. cabaret 3. (mil.) review 4. إستعراض عامّ isti‘rāḍ ‘āmm spectacle 5. إستعراض مسرحي isti‘rāḍ masraḥī show

استعرض ista‘raḍa (mil.) to review

إستعلاء isti‘lā’ superiority

إستعلام isti‘lām inquiry

استعلم ista‘lama to inquire (عن ‘an about)

إستعمال isti‘māl 1. use 2. operation 3. application 4. ساء الإستعمال sā’a al-isti‘māl misuse 5. عدم الإستعمال ‘adm al-isti‘māl disuse 6. أفرط في إستعمال شيء afraṭa fī isti‘māl shay’ to overuse 7. أعاد إستعمال a‘āda isti‘māl to recycle

استعمل ista‘mala 1. to use 2. to apply 3. to operate 4. استعمل حقّ النقض ista‘mala ḥaqq an-naqḍ to veto

استغرق istaghraqa 1. to take up; to occupy 2. to last 3. to sink (في fī into)

استغلّ istaghalla 1. to utilize 2. to exploit 3. to manipulate

إستغلال istighlāl exploitation

إستغلالي istighlālī exploitative

إستفاد istafāda 1. to benefit (من/ب bi/min from) 2. to make a profit

إستفتا ء istiftā' 1. poll 2. إستفتاء الشعب istiftā' al-sha'b referendum 3. إستفتاء، أجرى istiftā' to poll

إستفزّ istafazza to provoke

إستفزازي istifzāzī provocative

إستفهام istifhām (-āt) 1. query 2. علامة إستفهام 'alāmat istifhām question mark

إستفهم istafhama to question

إستقال istaqāla to resign; to quit

إستقالة istiqāla (-āt) resignation

إستقبال istiqbāl 1. reception 2. موظّف الإستقبال muwaẓẓaf al-istiqbāl receptionist 3. إستقبال الفندق istiqbāl al-funduq hotel lobby

إستقبل istaqbala 1. to meet 2. to receive

إستقرّ istaqarra to settle; to stabilise

إستقرار istiqrār 1. stability 2. عدم إستقرار 'adm istiqrār instability

إستقلال istiqlāl 1. independence 2. self-rule

إستكشاف istikshāf exploration

إستكشف istakshafa to explore

إستلام istilām 1. receipt 2. وصل إستلام waṣl istilām receipt

إستلقى istalqā to lie down

إستلم istalama to receive

إستمارة istimāra (-āt) form

إستماع istimā': جلسة إستماع jalsat istimā' tribunal

إستمتع ب istamta'a bi to savour

إستمدّ istamadda to take; to derive (ه sth; من min from)

إستمرّ istamarra 1. to continue 2. إستمرّ ب istamarra bi to keep up with 3. إستمرّ في\على istamarra fī/'alā keep on

إستمرار istimrār 1. بإستمرار bi istimrār continually 2. دواماً وإستمراراً dawāman wa istimrāran incessantly

إستنتاج istintāj conclusion

إستنفد istanfada to exhaust

إستنكار istinkār disapproval

إستهدف istahdafa 1. to aim (at) 2. to have in mind

إستهزأ istahza'a to scorn

إستهزاء istihzā' scorn

إستهلاك istihlāk consumption

إستهلك istahlaka to consume

إستهلاكي istihlākī consumer

إستواء istiwā' 1. straightness 2. equality 3. خطّ الإستواء khaṭṭ al-istiwā' equator

إستوائي istiwā'ī 1. tropical 2. المناطق الإستوائية al-manāṭiq al-istiwā'iya pl tropics

إستودع istawda'a to deposit

إستوديو istudiyō (إستوديوهات istudiyōhāt) studio

إستورد istawrada to import

إستوطن istawṭana to settle

إستولى على istawlā 'alā to capture

إستولد istawlada to breed

إستياء istiyā' 1. dissatisfaction 2. أثار الإستياء athāra al-istiyā' displease

إستيراد istīrād (-āt) import

استيقظ istayqaẓa to wake; to wake up

أسد asad (أسود usūd) lion

أسر asara (i; أسر asr) to capture

أسرّ asarra to please

إسرائيل isrā'īl Israel

إسرائيلي isrā'īlī (-yūn) Israeli

أسرة usra (أسر usar) family

أسرع asra'a to hurry; to speed (في fī with; إلى ilā to)

أسبرين asparīn aspirin

أسّس assasa 1. to found 2. to establish

أسطوانة usṭuwāna (-āt) 1. cylinder 2. (mus.) record

أسطورة usṭūra (أساطير asāṭīr) 1. legend 2. myth

أسطوري usṭūrī 1. legendary 2. mythical

أسطول usṭūl (أساطيل asāṭīl) fleet

إسعاف is'āf 1. سيّارة إسعاف sayyārat is'āf ambulance 2. الإسعاف الأولي al-is'āf al-awwalī first aid

أسف asaf 1. regret 2. للأسف li 'l-asaf unfortunately

أسف asifa (a; أسف asaf) to regret

أسف li 'l-asaf see أسف

أسفر عن asfara 'an 1. to disclose 2. to yield 3. to result in

أسفل asfal 1. lower; lowest 2. bottom 3. إلى أسفل ilā asfal down; downhill 4. underneath 5. الطابق الأسفل aṭ-ṭābiq al-asfal downstairs 6. الجانب الأسفل al-jānib al-asfal underside

أسقط asqaṭa to drop

أسقف usquf (أساقفة asāqifa) 1. bishop 2. رئيس الأساقفة ra'īs al-asāqifa archbishop

إسكان iskān housing

اسكتلندا iskotlandā Scotland

اسكتلندي iskotlandī 1. Scot 2. Scottish

الإسكواش al-iskwāsh (spor.) squash

أسلاك aslāk pl: أسلاك شائكة aslāk shā'ika barbed wire

الإسلام al-islām Islam

إسلامي islāmī Islamic

أسلحة asliha pl arms; weapons

أسلوب uslūb (أساليب asālīb) 1. method 2. style 3. أسلوب الحياة uslūb al-ḥayāh way of life; lifestyle 4. أسلوب الطبخ uslūb aṭ-ṭabkh cuisine

اسم ism (أسماء asmā'; أسامٍ asāmin) 1. name 2. noun 3. اسم أوّل ism awwal first name 4. اسم العائلة ism al-'ā'ila surname 5. اسم مستعار ism musta'ār alias 6. إسمي فريد ismī fred My name is Fred.

إسمنت ismant 1. cement 2. concrete

إسمنتي ismantī 1. cement 2. concrete

أسنان asnān pl 1. teeth 2. طبيب الأسنان ṭabīb al-asnān dentist 3. فرشاة الأسنان furshāt al-asnān toothbrush 4. معجون الأسنان ma'jūn al-asnān toothpaste 5. and see سن

أسناني asnānī dental

أسهم ashum pl (fin.) 1. stock 2. سمسار الأسهم simsār al-ashum stockbroker

أسوأ aswa' worse; worst

أسود aswad (f سوداء sūdā'; pl سود sūd) black

أسي asiya (u; أسًى asan) to grieve

أسير asīr (أسرى asrā) 1. prisoner 2. الحرب أسير asīr al-ḥarb prisoner of war; P.O.W.

أشار ashāra 1. to point (إلى ilā at) 2. to refer (إلى ilā to) 3. to signal 4. to publicize 5. أشار إلى ashāra ilā to indicate

إشارة (-āt) ishāra 1. sign 2. signal 3. indication 4. إشارة يد ishārat yad gesture 5. إشارة طريق ishārat ṭarīq road sign 6. إشارة ضوئية ishāra ḍaw'īya traffic lights 7. وضع إشارة waḍa'a ishāra to tick

إشاعة ishā'a (-āt) rumour

أشبه ashbaha to resemble; to be like

اشتاق إلى ishtāqa ilā to long for

إشتباه ishtibāh suspicion

اشتبه ishtabaha to suspect

اشتدّ ishtadda 1. to become stronger 2. to intensify

اشترى ishtarā to buy

إشتراك ishtirāk 1. participation (في fī in) 2. subscription

إشتراكي ishtirākī socialist

إشتراكية ishtirākīya socialism

اشترك ishtaraka 1. to share 2. to subscribe 3. to take part (في fī in) 4. اشترك في حملة ishtaraka fī ḥamla campaign

اشتعل ishta'ala to burn

اشتكى ishtakā to complain (من min about; إلى/ل ilā/li to)

إشتهاء ishtihā' desire

الأشراف al-ashrāf nobility

إشراف ishrāf supervision

أشرف على ashrafa 'alā to supervise

أشرق ashraqa to brighten

أشعّ asha''a to radiate

إشعاع ish'ā' 1. radiation 2. إشعاع الليزر ish'ā' al-layzer laser

أشعة ashi''a pl 1. rays 2. x-rays 3. أخذ صورة الأشعّة akhadha ṣūrat al-ashi''a to take an x-ray 4. أشعّة الشمس ashi''at al-shams sunshine

أشعل ash'ala 1. to light 2. to set fire to 3. to ignite

أشغل ashghala 1. to occupy 2. أشغل جهاز الكمبيوتر ashghala jihāz al-kombyūtar to log in

أشفق ashfaqa to pity

أشقر ashqar blond; blonde

أشلّ ashalla 1. to cripple 2. to paralyze

إشمئزاز ishmi'zāz 1. disgust 2.

مثير للاشمئزاز muthir li 'l-ishmi'zāz disgusting

أشياء ashyā' *pl* 1. things 2. articles 3. stuff 4. أشياء قيمة ashyā' qayyima valuables

أصاب aṣāba 1. to attain 2. *see* أصيب

إصابة iṣāba (-āt) (*spor.*) 1. score 2. سجل إصابة sajjala iṣāba score 3. مسجل إصابة musajjil iṣāba scorer 4. عدم إصابة 'adm iṣāba miss 5. مجموع الإصابات majmū' al-iṣābāt score

أصبح aṣbaḥa to become; to get

إصبع iṣba' (أصابع aṣābi') 1. finger 2. digit 3. اصبع (القدم) iṣba' (al-qadam) toe

أصدر aṣdara 1. to issue 2. to export

أصرّ aṣarra 1. to insist (على 'alā on) 2. to persist (على 'alā in)

اصطاد iṣṭāda 1. to hunt 2. اصطاد السمك iṣṭāda as-samak to fish

اصطاف iṣṭāfa to spend the summer

إصطبل iṣṭabl (-āt) stable

اصطحب iṣṭaḥaba to accompany

إصطدام iṣṭidām 1. crash 2. clash 3. shock

اصطدم iṣṭadama 1. to crash 2. to clash 3. to shock

إصطناعي iṣṭinā'ī 1. artificial 2. synthetic 3. بحيرة إصطناعية buḥayra iṣṭinā'īya reservoir

إصطياد iṣṭiyād 1. hunting 2. إصطياد السمك iṣṭiyād as-samak fishing

أصغر aṣghar 1. smaller; smallest 2. kid

3. أصغر سناً aṣghar sinnan junior

أصفر aṣfar yellow

أصل aṣl (أصول uṣūl) 1. origin 2. stock 3. principle; element 4. basis

أصلاً aṣlan originally

إصلاح iṣlāḥ (-āt) 1. repair 2. reform 3. renovation 4. reconciliation 5. متعذر إصلاحه muta'adhdhir iṣlāḥuh irreparable

أصلح aṣlaḥa 1. to mend; to repair 2. to reform 3. to renovate 4. to reconcile 5. أصلح ل aṣlaḥa li to serve

أصلع aṣla' bald

أصلي aṣlī 1. original 2. fundamental 3. basic 4. native 5. الوطن الأصلي al-waṭan al-aṣlī native country

أصمّ aṣamm 1. deaf 2. أصمّ أبكم aṣamm abkam deaf-mute

أصولي uṣūlī fundamentalist

أصولية uṣūlīya fundamentalism

أصيب ب uṣība bi *passive* 1. to suffer; to be struck by 2. to have *an illness* 3. أصيب بصدمة uṣība bi ṣadma to be in shock 4. أصيب بالذعر uṣība bi 'dh-dhu'r to panic 5. أصيب ببرد uṣība bi bard. He caught a cold. 6. *and see* أصاب

أصيل aṣīl afternoon

أضاء aḍā'a 1. to light 2. to illuminate 3. to turn on

إضاءة iḍā'a 1. lighting 2. illumination 3. عمود الإضاءة 'amūd al-'iḍā'a lamp-post

أضاع aḍā'a to misplace

أضاف aḍāfa 1. to add (إلى ilā to) 2. to suffix

إضافة iḍāfa 1. addition 2. بالإضافة إلى bi 'l-iḍāfati ilā in addition to

إضافي iḍāfī 1. extra; additional 2. spare 3. supplementary 4. subsidiary

إضراب iḍrāb; إضراب عن العمل iḍrāb ‘an al-‘amal (pol.) strike

أضرب aḍraba: أضرب عن العمل aḍraba ‘an al-‘amal (pol.) to strike

إضطراب iḍṭirāb 1. disturbance 2. excitement

اضطرّ iḍṭarra to compel (ه so; إلى ilā to)

إضطرب iḍṭiraba 1. to be disturbed 2. to be excited

إضطهاد iḍṭihād persecution

إضطهد iḍṭahada to persecute

أضعاف aḍ‘āf pl: زاده ثلاثة أضعاف zādah thalāthat aḍ‘āf (ه i; زيادة ziyāda) to treble

أضعف aḍ‘afa 1. to weaken 2. أضعف المكانة aḍ‘afa al-makāna to undermine

أضواء aḍwā’ pl: تحت الأضواء taḥt al-aḍwā’ in the limelight

إطار iṭār (-āt) 1. tyre 2. frame 3. frame-work 4. إطار داخلي iṭār dākhilī inner tube

أطاع aṭā‘a 1. to obey 2. أطاع القانون aṭā‘a al-qānūn to observe the law

أطاق aṭāqa: لا يطاق lā yuṭāq unbearable

أطرش aṭrash deaf

أطروحة uṭrūḥa (-āt) dissertation; thesis

أطعم aṭ‘ama to feed

أطفأ aṭfa’a to put out; to extinguish

إطفاء iṭfā’ 1. سيّارة الإطفاء sayyārat al-iṭfā’ fire engine 2. محطّة الإطفاء maḥaṭṭat al-iṭfā’ fire station

إطفائي iṭfā’ī (-yūn) fireman; firefighter

إطفائية iṭfā’īya fire brigade

أطفال aṭfāl pl 1. children 2. مربّية أطفال murabbīyat aṭfāl nanny 3. حفاظة الأطفال ḥifāẓat al-aṭfāl nappy 4. and see طفل

إطلاق iṭlāq 1. release 2. على الإطلاق ‘alā ‘l-iṭlāq absolutely 3. إطلاق النار iṭlāq an-nār shooting 4. وقف إطلاق النار waqf iṭlāq an-nār cease-fire 5. أطلق اسماً على aṭlaqa isman ‘alā to apply a term to

أطلس aṭlas atlas

أطلق aṭlaqa 1. to set free 2. to release 3. to launch 4. to shoot; to fire 5. أطلق النار على aṭlaqa an-nār ‘alā to fire at

اطّلع iṭṭala‘a to be informed (على ‘alā about); to know (على ‘alā about)

اطمأنّ iṭma’anna 1. to be calm 2. to be confident (من min/إلى ilā about)

أطوار aṭwār pl 1. غريب الأطوار gharīb al-aṭwār peculiar; strange 2. and see طور

أظلم aẓlama to darken

إظهار iẓhār show

أظهر aẓhara to show; to reveal

أعاد a‘āda 1. to give back 2. to bring back 3. to send back 4. to restore 5. to repeat 6. أعاد الضبط a‘āda ‘ḍ-ḍabṭ to reset 7. أعاد ترتيب المناصب a‘āda tartīb al-manāṣib *(pol.)* to shuffle 8. أعاد إستعمال a'āda isti'māl to recycle 9. أعاد الشريط a'āda 'sh-shariṭ to rewind 10. أعاد البناء a'āda al-binā' to rebuild; to reconstruct 11. أعاد الترتيب a'āda al-tartīb to rearrange 12. أعاد الطبع a'āda al-ṭab' to reprint 13. أعاد الكتابة a'āda 'l-kitāba to rewrite 14. أعاد الملء a'āda al-mal' to refill 15. أعاد النظر في a'āda al-naẓar fī to reconsider 16. أعاد مالاً a'āda mālan to refund 17. أعاد انتخاب a'āda intikhāb to re-elect 18. أعاد التنظيم a'āda at-tanẓīm to reorganize

إعادة i'āda 1. restoration 2. إعادة مال i'ādat māl refund 3. إعادة تنظيم i'ādat tanẓīm shake-up 4. إعادة البناء i'ādat al-binā' reconstruction

إعاقة i'āqa 1. hitch 2. handicap

أعان a'āna to help; to aid (ه so; في fī in; على 'alā to)

إعانة i'āna (-āt) 1. relief 2. إعانة مالية i'āna mālīya benefit; subsidy

إعتبار i'tibār 1. consideration 2. بالإعتبار جدير bi 'l-i'tibār jadīr considerable 3. إذا أخذنا في عين الإعتبار idhā akhadhnā fī 'ayn al-i'tibār considering

إعتبر i'tabara to consider (ه\ه so/sth; ه as)

إعتداء i'tidā' 1. assault 2. violation

إعتدى على i'tadā 'alā 1. to assault 2. to violate

إعتذار i'tidhār apology

إعتذر i'tadhara to apologize

إعتراض i'tirāḍ 1. objection 2. protest

إعتراف i'tirāf 1. acknowledgement 2. admission 3. *(pol.)* recognition

إعترض i'taraḍa 1. to object (على 'alā to) 2. to protest (على 'alā to) 3. إعترض سبيل i'taraḍa sabīl to intercept

إعترف ب i'tarafa 1. to admit 2. إعترف ب i'tarafa bi to acknowledge 3. *(pol.)* to recognize

إعتزم i'tazama to be determined (على 'alā/ه; to)

إعتقال i'tiqāl to arrest

إعتقد i'taqada to believe

إعتمد i'tamada to depend (على 'alā on)

إعتنى ب i'tanā bi 1. to look after 2. to mind

إعتيادي i'tiyādī 1. common 2. regular

إعجاب i'jāb 1. admiration 2. تكلم بإعجاب شديد عن takallama bi i'jāb shadīd 'an to rave about

أعجب a'jaba 1. to please 2. to appeal to 3. يعجب ب (أعجب ب yu'jabu bi) to admire

أعجوبة a'jūba (أعاجيب a'ājīb) wonder

أعدّ a'adda to prepare

إعداء i'dā' infection

إعداد i'dād preparation

إعدادي i'dādī preparatory

إعدام i'dām 1. execution 2. حكم الإعدام ḥukm al-i'dām death sentence 3. أرجأ تنفيذ حكم بالاعدام arja'a tanfīdh ḥukm bi 'l-i'dām *(leg.)* to reprieve

أعدم **a'dama 1.** to execute **2.** أعدم بالكهرباء **a'dama bi 'l-kahrabā' electrocute 3.** أعدم بدون محاكمة **a'dama bidūn muḥākama** to lynch

أعدى **a'dā** to infect

أعراض **a'rāḍ:** أعراض نقص المناعة المكتسبة **a'rāḍ naqṣi 'l-manā'ati 'l-muktasaba AIDS**

أعرب **a'raba** to express (عن **'an** *sth*); to make clear

أعزب **a'zab 1.** unmarried; single **2.** bachelor

أعزل **a'zal 1.** unprotected **2.** unarmed

أعسر **a'sar** left-handed

أعصاب **a'ṣāb** *pl* **1.** متوتّر الأعصاب **mutawattir al-a'ṣāb** nervous **2.** توتّر الأعصاب **tawattur al-a'ṣāb** nervousness **3.** *and see* عصب

إعصار **a'ṣār** (*pl* أعاصير **a'āṣīr**) hurricane

أعضاء **a'ḍā'** *pl:* أعضاء التناسل **a'ḍā' at-tanāsul** genitals

أعطى **a'ṭā 1.** to give **2.** to present **3.** أعطى سعراً **a'ṭā sa'ran** to bid **4.** أعطى الطريق **a'ṭā aṭ-ṭarīq** to give way **5.** أعطى إفادة **a'ṭā ifāda** to make a statement

أعظم **a'ẓam 1.** great; greatest **2.** super-

أعفى عن **a'fā 'an** to let off

أعقاب **a'qāb 1.** في أعقاب **fī a'qāb** straight after **2.** *see* عقب

أعلى **a'lā** (*f* عليا **'ulyā;** *pl* أعال **a'āl/** 'ulan **'ulan**) **a'ālin** 1.** higher; highest **2.** top **3.** upper **4.** up **5.** on **6.** senior **7.**

باتّجاه الأعلى **bi ittijāh al-a'lā** upward, upwards **8.** أعلى مكانةً **a'lā makānatan** senior **9.** المحكمة العليا **al-maḥkama al-'ulyā** high court; supreme court

إعلام **i'lām 1.** notice **2.** media **3.** تعدّد وسائل الإعلام **ta'addud wasā'il al-i'lām** multimedia

إعلان **i'lān (-āt) 1.** notice **2.** announce-ment **3.** advert; advertisement **4.** لوحة الإعلانات **lawḥat al-i'lānāt** notice-board **5.** ألصق إعلاناً **alṣaqa i'lānan** to post a notice

أعلم **a'lama 1.** to notify **2.** to inform

أعلن **a'lana 1.** to announce **2.** to publicize **3.** to advertise **4.** أعلن الحرب **a'lana al-ḥarb** to declare war

أعمى **a'mā** (*f* عمياء **'amyā'**; *pl* عمي **'umy**) blind

أعماق **a'māq** *pl:* أعماق البحر **a'māq al-baḥr** deep-sea

أعمال **a'māl** *pl* **1.** business **2.** رجل أعمال **rajul a'māl** businessman **3.** ستّ أعمال **sitt a'māl** businesswoman

أغاظ **aghāẓa** to vex

أغاني **aghān 1.** كلمات أغاني **kalimāt aghānī** lyrics **2.** مؤلّف كلمات الأغاني **mu'allif kalimāt al-aghānī** lyricist

اغتاظ **ightāẓa** to rage

اغتصاب **ightiṣāb** rape

اغتصب **ightaṣaba** to rape

إغتيال **ightiyāl (-āt)** assassination

أغذية aghdhiya *see* غذا ء

إغراء ighrā' temptation

أغرم ب ughrima bi *passive* to be fond of

أغرى aghrā 1. to tempt 2. to lure 3. to seduce

أغسطس aghustus August

أغضب aghḍaba to make angry

أغفل aghfala to overlook

أغلال aghlāl *pl* handcuffs

أغلب aghlab 1. majority 2. most 3. في الأغلب aghlab al-amr mostly; في الأغلب fī 'l-aghlab; أغلب الأمر

أغلبية aghlabīya majority

أغلق aghlaqa 1. to close 2. to switch off 3. to lock 4. أغلق بقوة aghlaqa bi qūwa slam

أغمي ughmiya *passive*: أغمي عليه ughmiya 'alayh to faint

أغنية ughniya (أغان aghānin) 1. song 2. أغنية دينية ughniya dīnīya hymn

أفاد afāda 1. to be of help to 2. to benefit

إفادة ifāda 1. statement 2. أعطى إفادة a'ṭā ifāda to make a statement

إفتتاح iftitāḥ opening

إفتتاحي iftitāḥī opening

إفتتاحية iftitāḥīya editorial

افتتح iftataḥa 1. to open 2. to inaugurate

إفتخار iftikhār boast

افتخر iftakhara to boast (ب bi about)

افتدى iftadā to ransom

افترس iftarasa to devour

افترض iftaraḍa to suppose

افترق iftaraqa 1. to part 2. to separate

افتقد iftaqada 1. to miss 2. to look for 3. to study

أفتن aftana to fascinate

إفراط ifrāṭ: حمّل بإفراط ḥammala bi ifrāṭ overload

أفرض afraḍa أفرض حصاراً على: afraḍa ḥiṣāran 'alā to lay/set siege to

أفرط في afraṭa fī 1. to overdo 2. أفرط في إستعمال شيء afraṭa fī isti'māl shay' to overuse

أفرغ afragha to unload

أفريقي afrīqī; إفريقي ifrīqī (-ūn) African

إفريقيا afrīqiyā; أفريقيا afrīqīya; إفريقيا ifrīqīyā Africa

أفزع afza'a 1. to scare 2. to shock

أفسد afsada 1. to spoil 2. to go sour

أفضل afḍal best

أفظع afẓa'a to outrage

أفعى af'an (أفاع afā'in) snake

أفق ufuq (آفاق āfāq) 1. horizon 2. ضيّق الأفق ḍayyiq al-ufuq narrow-minded

أفقي ufuqī horizontal

أفلت aflata get away (من min from)

أفلح aflaḥa to succeed

أقام aqāma 1. to set up 2. to found 3. to erect 4. to stay 5. to live (ب bi in)

إقامة iqāma 1. stay 2. residence

إقتباس iqtibās (-āt) quote; quotation

اقتبس iqtabasa to quote

إقتحام iqtiḥām intrusion

إقتحامي iqtiḥāmī intrusive

اقتحم iqtaḥama 1. to raid 2. to storm

إقتراح iqtirāḥ (-āt) 1. suggestion 2. proposal 3. (pol.) motion

إقتراع iqtirā' ballot; poll

أقترب من iqtaraba min to approach

اقترح iqtaraḥa 1. to propose 2. to suggest

اقترع على iqtara'a 'alā to take a vote on

إقتصاد iqtiṣād 1. economy 2. علم الإقتصاد 'ilm al-iqtiṣād economics

إقتصادي iqtiṣādī 1. economic 2. economical 3. عالم إقتصادي 'ālim iqtiṣādī economist 4. إزدهار إقتصادي izdihār iqtiṣādī (ec.) boom 5. ركود اقتصادي rukūd iqtiṣādī (ec.) recession 6. هبوط إقتصادي hubūṭ iqtiṣādī (ec.) slump

إقتصاديات iqtiṣādīyāt pl 1. economic affairs 2. economy

إقتضى iqtaḍā to require (ه sth; ٥ from)

اقتلع iqtala'a to pluck

أقدام aqdām pl 1. feet 2. على الأقدام 'alā 'l- aqdām on foot 3. and see قدم

أقرّ aqarra 1. to agree (ب bi to) 2. to acknowledge (ب bi sth)

أقرض aqraḍa to lend; to loan

أقسم aqsama 1. to swear 2. to vow

أقصى aqṣā 1. maximum 2. extreme 3. بأقصى سرعة bi aqṣā sur'a at top speed

أقضى على aqḍā 'alā to wipe out

أقعد aq'ada to sit down; to seat

أقفل aqfala 1. to shut 2. to lock 3. to switch off

أقلّ aqall 1. less 2. lesser; least 3. أقلّ من aqall min below 4. على الأقلّ 'alā 'l- aqall at least

أقلع aqla'a to take off

أقلق aqlaqa to worry

أقلّية aqallīya (-āt) 1. minority 2. أقلّية عرقية aqallīya 'irqīya ethnic minority

إقليم iqlīm (أقاليم aqālīm) 1. territory 2. province 3. region 4. country; countryside

إقليمي iqlīmī 1. territorial 2. regional

إقناع iqnā' persuasion

أقنع aqna'a to persuade

نشر أقوال nashr aqwāl pl 1. نشر أقوال قذفية nashr aqwāl qadhfīya libel 2. نشر أقوال قذفية nashara aqwāl qadhfīya (u; nashr نشر) to libel 3. and see قول

أكاديمي akādīmī 1. academic 2. جودة أكاديمية jawda akādīmīya scholarship

أكاديمية akādīmīya (-āt) academy

أكازيون okāzyūn sale

أكبر akbar 1. great; greater; greatest 2. elder; eldest 3. senior 4. super- 5. أكبر سنّاً akbar sinnan senior 6. أكبر من المألوف akbar min al-ma'lūf outsize

إكتئاب ikti'āb (med.) depression

اكتساب iktisāb acquisition

اكتسب iktasaba to acquire

إكتشاف iktishāf discovery

اكتشف iktashafa to discover

أكتوبر oktōbir October

أكثر akthar 1. more 2. most 3. أكثر من akthar min more than; above 4. أكثر بكثير akthar bi kathīr much more 5. أكثر ممّا ينبغي akthar mimmā yanbaghī too 6. أكثر من أيّ وقت مضى akthar min ayy waqt maḍā more than ever 7. صمد أكثر ṣamida akthar (u; صمود ṣumūd) to outlast 8. أنفق أكثر من اللازم anfaqa akthar min al-lāzim to overspend 9. مكث أكثر من اللازم makatha akthar min al-lāzim (u; مكث makth) to overstay 10. طلب ثمناً أكثر من اللازم ṭalaba thamanan akthar min al-lāzim to overcharge 11. عمل أكثر من اللازم 'amala akthar min al-lāzim to overwork

أكثريّة aktharīya majority

أكّد akkada 1. to assure (ل li so; ه of) 2. to confirm 3. to emphasize 4. to highlight

أكذوبة ukdhūba (أكاذيب akādhīb) lie

أكر akr acre

إكرام ikrām: إكراماً لي ikrāman lī for my sake

أكسجين oksizhen oxygen

أكل akala (u; أكل akl) 1. to eat 2. صالح للأكل ṣāliḥ li 'l-akl edible

أكل akl food

أكمل akmala 1. to complete 2. to perfect

أكيد akīd certain

ال al the

آل āl family

إلى ilā 1. to 2. up to 3. towards 4. into 5. for 6. إلى الأبد ilā 'l-abad forever 7. إلى الأمام ilā 'l-amām forwards 8. إلى الوراء ilā 'l-warā' backwards 9. إلى ما بعد ilā mā ba'd beyond 10. إلى أسفل ilā asfal down; downhill 11. إلى آخره ilā ākhirih; وما إليه wa mā ilayh; إلى أن ilā an until 12. وما إلى ذلك wa mā ilā dhālik etc; et cetera 13. إلى هذا الحدّ ilā hādhā 'l-ḥadd so 14. إلى حدّ ما ilā ḥaddin mā somewhat 15. إلى أمد غير محدّد ilā amad ghayr muḥaddad indefinitely

ألّا allā that... not

إلّا illā 1. except (for) 2. إلّا و illā wa unless 3. وإلّا wa illā otherwise 4. إلّا أن illā an only 5. إلّا أنّ illā anna however 6. ليس إلّا laysa illā merely 7. ماذا وإلّا mādhā wa illā otherwise 8. ليس إلّا laysa illā simply 9. وما هو\هي إلّا أن wa mā huwa/hiya illā an it was not long until 10. وما هو\هي إلّا... حتّى wa mā huwa/hiya illā... ḥattā no sooner had... than

الآن al'ān 1. now 2. بعد الآن ba'd al'ān anymore 3. حتّى الآن ḥatta al'ān still 4. من الآن فصاعداً min al'ān faṣā'idan henceforth 5. قبل الآن qabl al'ān already

ألباني albānī (-ūn; الألبان al-albān) Albanian

ألبانيا albāniyā Albania

أبيض abyaḍ (f بيضاء bayḍā'; pl بيض bīḍ) 1. white 2. البحر الأبيض المتوسّط al-baḥr al-abyaḍ al-mutawassiṭ Mediterranean Sea

إتّصالات al-ittiṣālāt pl: الإتّصالات الهاتفية ittiṣālāt al-hātifīya telecommunications

التحق iltaḥaqa bi to join

التزم iltazama 1. to stick to 2. to persist in

التصق iltaṣaqa to stick (بـ bi to)

التفّ iltaffa to coil

التقط iltaqaṭa 1. to pick up 2. to receive 3. التقط صورةً iltaqaṭa ṣūratan to take a photo

التقى iltaqā to meet (بـ bi with)

إلتهاب iltihāb 1. inflammation 2. سريع الإلتهاب sarī' al-iltihāb inflammable (burnable) 3. إلتهاب المفاصل iltihāb al-mafāṣil arthritis

التي allatī see الذي

ألجأ alja'a to shelter

ألحّ alaḥḥa to urge

إلحاح ilḥāḥ urgency

ألحق alḥaqa 1. to append 2. to suffix

الّذي alladhī m; الّتي allatī f; الّذين alladhīn pl 1. who 2. whose 3. what 4. which 5. that

ألصق alṣaqa 1. to stick 2. ألصق بطاقة على alṣaqa biṭāqa 'alā to label 3. ألصق إعلاناً alṣaqa i'lānan to post; to advertise

ألعاب al'āb pl 1. games 2. ألعاب نارية al'āb nārīya fireworks 3. ألعاب رياضية al'āb riyāḍīya athletics 4. الألعاب المائية al-al'āb al-mā'īya watersports 5. and see لعب

ألغى alghā to cancel

إلغاء ilghā' 1. cancellation 2. متعذّر إلغاؤه muta'adhdhir ilghā'ihi irreversible

ألغام alghām pl: 1. حقل الألغام ḥaql al-alghām minefield 2. جهاز الكشف عن الألغام jihāz al-kashf 'an al-alghām mine detector 3. التخلّص من الألغام at-takhalluṣ min al-alghām mine disposal 4. and see لغم

ألّف allafa 1. to form 2. to write 3. to compose

ألف alf (آلاف ālāf; ألوف ulūf) thousand

ألفة ulfa intimacy

ألفباء alifbā' alphabet

ألفت alfata to attract

ألفية alfiya (-āt) millennium

ألقى alqā 1. to throw 2. to deliver 3. ألقى نظرة على alqā naẓra 'alā look over 4. ألقى خطاباً alqā khiṭāban to make a speech

ألكتروني alaktrūnī/iliktrōnī 1. electronic 2. بريد ألكتروني barīd alaktrūnī e-mail 3. لوحة مفاتيح إلكترونية lawḥat mafātīḥ alaktrōnīya synthesizer

ألكترونيات alaktrūnīyāt pl electronics

اللاتي allā'ī mpl; اللاتي allātī fpl 1. who 2. whose 3. what 4. which 5. that

اللذان alladhān masculine dual; اللتان allatān feminine dual 1. who 2. whose 3. what 4. which 5. that

الله allāh God

اللواتي allawātī fpl 1. who 2. whose 3. what 4. which 5. that

ألم alam (آلام ālām) 1. pain 2. ache 3. suffering 4. ألم ظهر alam ẓahar backache

ألماس almās diamond

ألمان almān pl Germans

ألماني almānī (-yūn) German

ألمانيا almānya Germany

ألمح إلى almaḥa ilā to glance at

إله ilāh (إلاه ilāh; آلهة āliha) god

إلهة ilāha (-āt) goddess

إلهام ilhām inspiration

ألهم alhama to inspire

إلهي ilāhī divine

ألهى alhā to amuse

ألومنيوم alūminyūm aluminium

أليف alīf domestic

أليم alīm sore

أم am 1. or 2. أم... أ a...am whether... or

أمّ umm (أمّهات ummahāt) 1. mother 2. اللغة الأمّ al-lughat al-umm mother-tongue 3. وطن الأمّ al-waṭan al-umm mainland

إمّا immā 1. either 2. إمّا... إمّا immā... immā; أو... إمّا immā... aw either... or

إمارة imāra (-āt) 1. emirate 2. principality

أمام amām/amāma 1. opposite 2. in front of; before 3. إلى الأمام ilā 'l-amām ahead 4. خطوة إلى الأمام khaṭwa ilā 'l-amām a step forward

إمام imām (أئمة a'imma) imam

أمامي amāmī forward

أمان amān 1. safety 2. security 3. الأمن والأمان al-amn wa 'l-amān law and order 4. حزام الأمان ḥizām al-amān seatbelt; (mar.) lifebelt

أمانة amāna 1. honesty 2. secretariat

أمانع umāniʻ; لا أمانع! lā umāniʻ! I don't mind!

إمبراطور imbarāṭūr emperor

إمبراطوري imbarāṭūrī imperial

إمبراطورية imbarāṭūrīya empire

إمبريالي imbiriyālī 1. imperial 2. (-yūn) imperialist

إمبريالية imbiriyālīya imperialism

أمّة umma (أمم umam) nation

إمتحان imtiḥān (-āt) (ed.) 1. examination 2. test 3. سقط في إمتحان saqaṭa fī imtiḥān (u) to fail an exam

امتحن imtaḥana (ed.) 1. to examine 2. to test

امتدّ imtadda to extend; to stretch

إمتداد imtidād span

امتصّ imtaṣṣa to absorb

أمتعة amti‘a 1. luggage 2. belongings

إمتعاض imti‘āḍ resentment

امتعض imta‘aḍa to resent

امتلك imtalaka to own

إمتنان imtinān gratitude

امتنع imtana‘a 1. to refrain (عن ‘an from) 2. to keep away (عن ‘an from) 3. to keep out of (عن ‘an from) 4. to be impssible (على ‘alā for)

إمتياز imtiyāz (-āt) 1. distinction 2. privilege 3. franchise

أمثال amthāl such as

أمثل amthal pl optimum

أمد amad (آماد āmād) 1. duration 2. period 3. distance 4. قصير الأمد qaṣīr al-amad short-term 5. بعيد الأمد ba‘īd al-amad; طويل الأمد ṭawīl al-amad long-term 6. إلى أمد غير محدّد ilā amad ghayr muḥaddad indefinitely

أمر amara (u; أمر amr) 1. to order (ب so; ه bi to) 2. to command 3. to instruct

أمرّ amarra to pass

أمر amr (أمور umūr; أوامر awāmir) 1. order 2. command 3. instruction 4. matter; issue 5. الأمر إليك al-amr ilayk it's up to you 6. ما الأمر؟ mā al-amr? What's the matter? 7. أمر بالإنصراف amara bi

'l-inṣirāf to dismiss 8. and see أمرين

إمرؤ imru' man

إمرأة imra'a (نساء nisā'; نسوان niswān; نسوة niswa) 1. woman 2. wife

أمراض amrāḍ pl 1. طبيب أمراض النساء ṭabīb amrāḍ an-nisā' gynaecologist 2. طبّ أمراض النساء ṭibb amrāḍ an-nisā' gynaecology 3. مستشفى الأمراض العقلية mustashfā 'l-amrāḍ al-‘aqlīya mental hospital 4. and see أمراض

أمرض amraḍa to sicken

أمريكان amrīkān pl Americans

أمريكا amrīkā America

أمريكي amrīkī (-yūn) American

أمرين amrayn dual 1. كلا الأمرين kilā al-amrayn neither 2. and see أمر

أمس ams; amsi 1. yesterday 2. ليلة الأمس laylat al-ams last night 3. أول أمس awwal ams; أمس الأول ams al-awwal the day before yesterday

أمضى amḍā 1. to sign 2. to spend; to pass (time)

إمضاء imḍā' signature

أمعاء am‘ā' pl tripe

إمكان imkān 1. possibility 2. ability 3. على قدر الأمكان ‘alā qadr al-imkān as much as possible; as far as possible

إمكانية imkānīya (-āt) 1. possibility 2. potential 2. إمكانيات مالية imkānīyāt mālīya means

أمكن amkana to be possible; can; may

أمل amal (آمال āmāl) 1. hope 2. مفعم بالأمل

خائب الأمل muf'am bi 'l-amal hopeful 3.
khā'ib al-amal disappointed 4.
خيبة الأمل khaybat al-amal
disappointment 5. خيّب الأمل
khayyaba al-amal to disappoint

أمل amala (a; أمل amal) to hope (في fī for)

أملى amlā to dictate

إملاء imlā' dictation

أمّم ammama to nationalize

أمم umam pl 1. الأمم المتحدة al-umam
al-muttahida United Nations (UN)
2. and see أمّة

أمّن ammana 1. to make safe 2. to secure
3. to insure

أمن amn 1. safety 2. security 3. حزام الأمن
ḥizām al-amn seatbelt; (mar.) lifebelt
4. الأمن والأمان al-amn wa 'l-amān law
and order 5. مجلس الأمن majlis al-amn
Security Council

أمني amnī security

أمنية umnīya (أمان amānīn) wish

الأموات al-amwāt pl 1. the dead 2.
غرفة الأموات ghurfat al-amwāt
mortuary

أموال amwāl pl 1. funds 2. gear

أمومة umūma maternity

أمومي umūmī maternal

أمّي ummī maternal

أمّية ummīya illiteracy

أمير amīr (أمراء umarā') 1. prince 2. emir
3. commander

أميرة amīra (-āt) princess

أميركا amīrikā America

أميركي amīrikī (-yūn) American

أمين amīn 1. safe 2. honest 3. (أمناء)
umanā') warden 4. أمين الصندوق amīn
aṣ-ṣandūq cashier 5. treasurer 6.
أمين عامّ amīn 'āmm secretary general

أن an 1. that 2. على وشك أن ' alā washk an
on the verge of

أنّ anna 1. that 2. كأنّ ka anna as though
3. رغم أنّ raghma إلى أنّ ilā anna until 4.
anna though 5. بما أنّ bi mā anna since

أنّ anna (i; أنين anīn) to moan

إن wa in if وإن in

إنّ inna particle beginning a nominal sentence

أنا ana I

إناء ināʼ (آنية āniya) container

أنابيب anābīb pl 1. خطّ أنابيب khaṭṭ anābīb
pipeline 2. and see أنبوبة

أنار anāra to light

أناقة anāqa elegance

أناني anānī 1. selfish 2. egotistical 3.
غير أناني ghayr anānī unselfish

أنانية anānīya selfishness

أنباء anbāʼ pl 1. news 2. وكالة الأنباء
wikālat al-anbāʼ press agency; news
agency

إنبغى inbaghā see ينبغي

أنابيب anbūb; أنبوبة unbūba) أنبوب
anābīb). 1. tube 2. pipe 3. and see
أنابيب

أنت anta m you

أنت anti f you

إنتاج intāj 1. production 2. output 3. produce 4. وفير الإنتاج wafir al-intāj prolific 5. الإنتاج الجملي al-intāj al-jumlī mass production

إنتاجية intājīya productivity

إنتباه intibāh 1. attention 2. ملفت الإنتباه mulfit al-intibāh conspicuous 3. صرف الإنتباه ṣarf al-intibāh distraction

إنتبه intabaha 1. to pay attention (إلى ilā to) 2. to take notice (ل li of) 3. !إنتبه intabih! look out!

أنتج antaja 1. to produce 2. أنتج فلماً antaja filman to produce a film

إنتحار intiḥār suicide

إنتخاب intikhāb (-āt) 1. election 2. أعاد انتخاب a'āda intikhāb to re-elect 3. تلاعب بإنتخاب talā'aba bi intikhāb to rig an election 4. and see إنتخابات

إنتخابات intikhābāt pl 1. elections 2. أجرى إنتخابات ajrā intikhābāt to hold elections 3. and see إنتخاب

إنتخابي intikhābī 1. electoral 2. دائرة إنتخابية dā'ira intikhābiya (pol.) ward

إنتخب intakhaba to elect

إنترنيت internet 1. internet 2. متصل بالإنترنيت muttaṣil bi 'l-internet on-line

إنتزع intaza'a to snatch

إنتشى intashā to get high (sl.)

إنتشر intashara to spread

إنتصار intiṣār victory; triumph

إنتصافي intiṣāfī: فاصل إنتصافي fāṣil intiṣāfī (spor.) half-time

إنتصر intaṣara 1. to triumph 2. to win

إنتظام intiẓām regularity

إنتظر intaẓara 1. to wait; wait for 2. to expect

إنتفع intafa'a to profit

إنتقى intaqā to select

إنتقاء intiqā' selection

إنتقائي intiqā'ī selective

إنتقادي intiqādī critical

إنتقالي intiqālī transitional

إنتقام intiqām revenge

إنتقد intaqada to criticize

إنتقل intaqala to move (إلى ilā to)

إنتكاس intikās (med.) relapse

أنتم antum mpl you

أنتما antumā dual you

إنتمى intamā to belong (إلى ilā to)

أنتنّ antunna fpl you

إنتهى intahā 1. to finish (من min with) 2. to end up (إلى ilā at) 3. لا ينتهي lā yantahī never-ending

إنتهاك intihāk violation

إنتهز intahaza: انتهز الفرصة intahaza al-furṣa to make the most of

إنتهك intahaka 1. to violate 2. انتهك القانون intahaka al-qānūn to break the law

أنثى unthā (إناث ināth) 1. female 2. feminine

أنثوي unthawī female

إنجاز injāz (-āt) achievement

إنجراح injirāḥ 1. قابل للإنجراح qābil li 'l-injirāḥ vulnerable 2. قابلية للإنجراح qābiliya li 'l-injirāḥ vulnerability

أنجز anjaza to achieve

أنحاز anḥāza to take sides (ل/إلى li/ilā with)

إنحدار inḥidār 1. slope 2. شديد الإنحدار shadīd al-inḥidār steep

انحدر inḥadara to slope

انحنى inḥanā 1. to bend 2. to curve

إنحياز inḥiyāz 1. bias 2. غيار الإنحياز ghiyār al-inḥiyāz non-alignment

إنخفض inkhafaḍa 1. to sink 2. to grow less 3. to be reduced

إندفاع indifāʿ rush

اندفع indafaʿa to rush

اندمج indamaja to merge

إندونيسي indūnīsī Indonesian

إندونيسيا indūnīsīya Indonesia

إنذار indhār 1. warning 2. صفارة الإنذار ṣaffārat al-indhār siren 3. إنذار بخطر indhār bi khaṭar alarm 4. جرس الإنذار بالحريق jaras al-indhār bi 'l-ḥarīq fire alarm 5. إنذار أخير indhār akhīr ultimatum

أنذر andhara to warn

أنزل anzala 1. to descend 2. أنزل بالمظلّة

anzala bi 'l-miẓalla to parachute

انزلق inzalaqa to slide

إنسان insān 1. human; human being 2. إنسان آلي insān ālī robot 3. إنسان العين insān al-ʿayn pupil 4. علم الإنسان ʿilm al-insān anthropology 5. حقوق الإنسان ḥuqūq al-insān human rights

إنساني insānī 1. human 2. humane 3. غير إنساني ghayr insānī inhumane 4. الفطرة الإنسانية al-fiṭrat al-insānīya human nature

إنساني insānī humanitarian

إنسانية insānīya humanity

انسجم insajama to get on

إنسحاب insiḥāb 1. withdrawal 2. retreat 3. walk-out 4. secession

انسحب insaḥaba 1. to withdraw 2. to retreat 3. to walk out 4. to secede 5. to stand down

إنسداد insidād (med.) obstruction

إنسلال insilāl stealth

إنسيابي insiyābī streamlined

أنشأ anshaʾa to set up

أنشأ عن anshaʾa ʿan to derive

إنشائي inshāʾī structural

إنشقاق inshiqāq dissent

انشقّ inshaqqa to split

إنصاف inṣāf 1. justice 2. بإنصاف bi inṣāf fairly

إنصراف inṣirāf 1. dismissal 2. بالإنصراف amara bi 'l-inṣirāf to dismiss أمر

انصرف inṣarafa 1. to go away (عن 'an from) 2. to concentrate (إلى ilā on) 3. انصرف عن inṣarafa 'an to leave

انضباط inḍibāṭ discipline

إنطباع intibā' impression

انطلق intalaqa to go ahead

أنعش an'asha to refresh

إنعقاد ; دور الإنعقاد dawr al-in'iqād session in'iqād

انعقد in'aqada to be held

إنعكاس in'ikās (-āt) 1. reflection 2. إنعكاس لا إرادي in'ikās lā irādī reflex

أنغولا angōla Angola

أنغولي angōlī Angolan

أنف anf (أنوف unūf ; آناف ānāf) 1. nose 2. فتحة الأنف fatḥat al-anf nostril

أنفى anfā to banish

أنفاق ; مترو الأنفاق metro al-anfāq the Underground; subway; metro

إنفجار infijār(-āt) 1. explosion 2. bomb blast 3. eruption

انفجر infajara 1. to burst 2. to explode 3. to erupt

أنفسك anfus(u)ka m; anfus(u)ki f yourself

أنفسكم ; anfus(u)kum mpl yourselves

أنفسكنّ ; anfus(u)kunna fpl yourselves

أنفسنا anfus(u)nā ourselves

أنفسهم ; anfus(u)hum mpl themselves

أنفسهنّ anfus(u)hunna fpl themselves

إنفصالي infiṣālī separatist

انفصل infaṣala to separate (عن 'an from)

أنفق anfaqa 1. to spend 2. أنفق أكثر من اللازم anfaqa akthar min al-lāzim to overspend

إنفلونزا influwanza flu; influenza

إنقاذ inqādh 1. rescue 2. salvation 3. salvage

أنقذ anqadha 1. to save 2. to rescue 3. to salvage

انقرض inqaraḍa to become extinct

إنقسام inqisām division

انقسم inqasama 1. to be split 2. to be divided

انقضّ inqaḍḍa 1. to dive 2. to swoop

انقضى inqaḍā to expire

انقطع inqaṭa'a 1. to stop; to be stopped 2. to be cut off 3. انقطع فجأة inqaṭa'a faj'atan to snap

أنقع anqa'a to soak

إنقلاب inqilāb coup; coup d'état

انقلب ; انقلب ضدّ inqalaba ḍidda to turn against inqalaba:

إنكار inkār 1. denial 2. disbelief 3. لا يمكن إنكاره lā yumkin inkāruh undeniable

أنكر ankara to deny

إنكلترا ingilterā England

الإنكليز al-inglīz pl the English

إنكليزي inglīzī (-yūn) 1. English 2. بالإنكليزي bi 'l-inglīzī in English

إنّما innamā 1. but 2. only

إنماء inmā' increase

أنهى‬ anhā to finish

انهار‬ inhāra to collapse

إنهيار‬ inhiyār 1. breakdown 2. collapse 3. *(ec.)* crash

إنهيال‬ inhiyāl: إنهيال الأرض inhiyāl al-arḍ landslide

أنيق‬ anīq 1. smart 2. elegant

أنين‬ anīn moan

أهاج‬ ahāja to agitate

أهان‬ ahāna to insult

إهانة‬ ihāna insult

أهبل‬ ahbal (هبل hubl) idiot

اهتزّ‬ ihtazza 1. to shake 2. to quake

اهتمّ‬ ihtamma 1. to be concerned (ب bi about) 2. to pay attention (ب bi to) 3. to be interested (ب bi in)

إهتمام‬ ihtimām 1. interest (ب bi in) 2. care (ب bi over/of) 3. attention (ب bi to) 4. أثار الإهتمام athāra 'l-ihtimām to intrigue

أهدى‬ ahdā to dedicate

إهداء‬ ihdā' dedication

أهّل‬ ahhala to qualify

أهل‬ ahl (أهالٍ ahālin; أهلون ahlūn) 1. people 2. family 3. أهل البيت ahl al-bayt household 4. أهل ل\ب ahl li/bi worthy of

أهلاً وسهلاً!‬ ahlan! 1. hello! 2. ahlan wa sahlan! hello!; welcome!

أهلك‬ ahlaka to destroy

أهلي‬ ahlī 1. family 2. domestic 3.

national 4. native 5. أهلي ahlī; حرب ḥarb أهلية ahlīya; حرب أهلية ḥarb ahlīya *f* civil war

أهلية‬ ahlīya 1. competence 2. حرّم من الأهلية ḥarrama min al-ahlīya to disqualify

أهمّ‬ ahamma 1. to matter 2. لا يهمّ lā yuhimm. It doesn't matter.

إهمال‬ ihmāl 1. neglect 2. negligence

أهمل‬ ahmala 1. to neglect 2. to disregard

أهمّية‬ ahammīya (-āt) 1. importance 2. قلّل من أهمّية... qallala min ahammīyat... underestimate

أو‬ aw 1. or 2. أو... أو immā... aw either... or

أوى‬ awā (i) to take shelter

أوّى‬ awwā to shelter

أوان‬ awān: سابق الأوان sābiq al-awān premature

أوبرا‬ ōbrā 1. opera 2. دار الأوبرا dār al-ōbrā opera house

أوبروي‬ ōbrawī opera

أتوبيس‬ otobīs *see* أوتوبيس

أتوماتيكي‬ otomātīkī *see* أوتوماتيكي

أوجب‬ awjaba 1. to oblige 2. to make necessary (على 'alā for)

أوجع‬ awja'a to hurt

أودع‬ awda'a to deposit

أوروبا‬ ūrūbā; أوروبّا ūrubbā Europe

أوروبي‬ ūrūbī; أوروبّي ūrubbī (-yūn) 1. European 2. Euro-

إوزّة iwazza (collective إوزّ iwazz) goose

أوساط awsāṭ pl 1. circles; quarters 2. and see وسط

أوسط awsaṭ (f وسطى wusṭā; pl وسط wusaṭ) 1. middle 2. central 3. الشرق الأوسط ash-sharq al-awsaṭ the Middle East

أوضح awḍaḥa to make clear

أوفد awfada 1. to send 2. to delegate

أوقات awqāt pl 1. بعض الأوقات ba‘ḍ al-awqāt; في بعض الأوقات fī ba‘ḍ al-awqāt sometimes 2. see وقت

أوقظ awqaẓa to arouse

أوقع awqa‘a to drop

أوقف awqafa to halt

أومأ awma’a: أومأ بالرأس awma’a bi ’r-ra’s to nod

أونس awns ounce

أوّل awwal (f أولى ūlā) 1. first 2. اسم أوّل ism awwal first name 3. الأمس الأوّل ams al-awwal the day before yesterday 4. أوّل الأمر awwal al-amr at first

أولى ūlā 1. f الدرجة الأولى ad-daraja al-ūlā first-class 2. and see أوّل

أوّلاً awwalan at first

أولئك ūlā’ik; ūlā’ika those

أولمبياد olimbiyād Olympic games

أولوية awlawīya (-āt) priority

أوّلي awwalī 1. primary 2. elementary 3. raw 4. الإسعاف الأوّلي al-is‘āf al-awwalī first aid 5. نموذج أوّلي namūdhaj awwalī prototype

أوّه awwaha to sigh

أي ay that is; i.e.

أيّ ayy 1. any 2. which 3. أيّ شخص ayy shakhṣ anybody 4. أيّ شيء ayy shay’ anything 5. أيّ يوم ayy yawm anyday 6. أيّ مكان ayy makān anywhere 7. أيّاً كان ayyan kān whoever; whosoever; whatever 8. أيّ وقت ayy waqt anytime 9. أيّما ayyumā whichever 10. على أيّة حال ‘alā ayyati ḥāl at any rate 11. أكثر من أيّ وقت مضى akthar min ayy waqt maḍā more than ever

إيّا iyyā: إيّاك أن... iyyāka an... take care not to...

أيّام ayyām pl 1. أيّام زمان ayyām zamān olden times 2. في هذه الأيّام fī hādhihi ’l-ayyām nowadays 3. بعد عدّة أيّام ba‘d ‘iddat ayyām in a few days 4. قبل عدّة أيّام qabl ‘iddat ayyām the other day 5. and see يوم

أيتام aytām pl 1. دار الأيتام dār al-aytām orphanage 2. and see يتيم

إيجابي ījābī positive

إيجار ījār 1. hire 2. rent 3. lease 4. للإيجار li ’l-ijār for hire etc

إيجاز ījāz 1. brevity 2. بالإيجاز bi ’l-ījāz briefly

أيّد ayyada 1. to back up 2. to support 3. to further 4. to uphold

إيراد īrād (-āt) income

إيران īrān Iran

إيراني īrānī (-yūn) Iranian; Persian

أيّل ayyil (أيائل ayā'il) deer

أيلول aylūl September

أيّما ayyumā whichever

إيماءة īmā'a gesture

إيمان īmān (rel.) belief; faith

أيمن ayman 1. right 2. right-hand

أين ayn; ayna 1. where 2. من أين min ayn from where?

أينما aynamā wherever

إيهاب īhāb 1. granting 2. تذكرة ذهاب إيهاب tadhkirat dhihāb īhāb return ticket

آيرلندا āyrlandā 1. Ireland 2. آيرلندا الشمالية āyrlandā ash-shamālīya Northern Ireland

آيرلندي āyrlandī (-yūn) Irish

إيصال īṣāl (-āt) voucher

أيضاً ayḍan 1. also; too; as well 2. ليس فقط... لكن... أيضاً laysa faqaṭ... lākin... ayḍan not only... but also

إيضاح īḍāḥ illustration

إيطالي iṭālī (-yūn) Italian

إطاليا iṭāliyā Italy

إيقاع īqā' (-āt) 1. harmony 2. rhythm

ب

ب bi 1. by 2. with 3. at 4. in 4. through 5. of 6. أصيب ببرد uṣiba bi bard. He caught a cold. 7. بالبريد الجوّي bi 'l-barid al-jawwī by airmail 8. بالقطار bi 'l-qiṭār by train 9. بالإنكليزي bi 'l-inglīzī in English 10. بالمئة bi 'l-mi'a per cent 11. بالدور bi 'd-dawr in turn 12. بالإجمال bi 'l-ijmāl altogether 13. مخفّض بخمسين بالمئة mukhaffaḍ bi khamsīn bi 'l-mi'a; بنصف السعر bi niṣf as-si'r (at) half price 14. بصحتك! bi ṣiḥḥatik! cheers! 15. بكثير bi kathīr much 16. أكثر بكثير akthar bi kathīr much more 17. بالطبع bi ṭ-ṭab'

naturally 18. بسبب bi sabab because of 19. بشأن bi sha'n about 20. بالقرب من bi 'l-qurb min near (to) 21. بواسطة bi wāsiṭa through 22. بالنسبة إلى bi 'n-nisbati ilā regarding 23. بالإضافة إلى bi 'l-iḍāfati ilā as well as 24. بالأخرى bi 'l-akhrā rather 25. بما في bi mā fī including 26. بما أنّ bi mā anna since 27. بالرغم من bi 'r-raghm; بالرغم من bi 'r-raghmi min despite 28. بالنيابة عن bi 'n-niyāba 'an on behalf of 29. بإنصاف bi inṣāf fairly 30. بالكاد bi 'l-kād hardly 31. بجانب bi jānib beside 32. بخصوص bi khuṣūṣ with reference to 33. بخير

bikhayr alright 34. بالصدفة bi 'ṣ-ṣudfa by chance 35. بالضبط bi 'ḍ-ḍabṭ precisely 36. بالإيجاز bi 'l-ijāz briefly 37. بهدوء bi hudū' quietly 38. بسرعة bi sur'a quickly 39. بأقصى سرعة bi aqṣā sur'a at top speed 40. باستمرار bi istimrār continually 41. بشكل كامل bi shakl kāmil perfectly 42. بقسوة bi qaswa roughly 43. بوضوح bi wuḍūḥ clearly 44. بالتأكيد bi 't-ta'kīd certainly 45. بالعكس bi 'l-'aks on the contrary 46. بالإختصار bi 'l-ikhtiṣār in short 47. بالمقلوب bi 'l-maqlūb inside-out 48. بانتظام bi intiẓām regularly 49. بالتتابع bi 't-tatābi' in succession 50. بالتحديد bi 't-taḥdīd specifically 51. بإخلاص bi ikhlāṣ sincerely 52. *and see* بلا ;بدون

بائس bā'is (بؤساء bu'asā') miserable

بائع bā'i' (-ūn; باعة bā'a) 1. seller 2. vendor 3. dealer 4. salesman 5. بائع بالتجزئة bā'i' bi 't-tajzi'a a retailer 6. بائع الزهور bā'i' al-zuhūr florist

بائعة bā'i'a (-āt) 1. saleswoman 2. *and see* بائع

باب bāb (أبواب abwāb; بيبان bībān) 1. door 2. gate

بابا bābā (بابوات bābawāt) pope

بابوي bābawī papal

بات bāta (i; مبيت mabīt) to spend the night

باحث bāḥith (-ūn) researcher

باخرة bākhira (بواخر bawākhir) cruise liner

بادئ bādi': في بادئ الأمر fī bādi' al-amr at first

بادل bādala 1. to swap 2. to exchange

باذنجانة bādhinjāna (*collective* باذنجان bādhinjān; *pl* -āt) aubergine; eggplant

بار bār (-āt) bar

بئر bi'r (آبار ābār; بئار bi'ār) 1. well 2. بئر نفط bi'r nafṭ oil well 3. بئر غاز bi'r ghāz gas well

بارئ bāri' 1. skilled 2. غير بارئ ghayr bāri' unskilled

بارد bārid 1. cold 2. cool 3. الحرب الباردة al-ḥarb al-bārida the Cold War

بارز bāriz outstanding

بارع bāri' skilful

بارك bāraka to bless

بأس ba's: لا بأس! lā ba's! 1. never mind! 2. no problem!

بؤس bu's misery

باشر bāshara to put into effect

باص bāṣ (-āt) 1. bus 2. موقف باص mawqif bāṣ bus stop 3. محطة باصات maḥaṭṭat bāṣāt bus station

باض bāḍa (i; بيض bayḍ) to lay an egg

باطل bāṭil invalid

باع bā'a (i; بيع bay'; مبيع mabī') 1. to sell 2. to deal 3. باع بالتجزئة bā'a bi 't-tajzi'a retail

باعث bā'ith (بواعث bawā'ith) 1. motive 2. incentive

باق bāqin lasting

باكستاني bākistānī Pakistani

باكياً bākiyan in tears

بالغ bālagha 1. to exaggerate 2. بالغ في bālagha fī overdo

بالغ bāligh (-ūn) 1. mature 2. grown-up 3. extensive; considerable 4. سنّ الرشد bāligh sinn ar-rushd adult 5. الذروة بالغ bāligh adh-dharwa peak

بالكون bālkōn (-āt) balcony

بالوعة bālū'a (-āt; بواليع bawālī') 1. drain 2. sewer

بالون bālūn balloon

باليه bālēh ballet

بان bāna (i; بيان bayān) to materialize

باهى bāhā to show off

باهت bāhit 1. faint 2. dull

باوند bawnd (-āt) pound (sterling)

بايسكل bāysikil bicycle

باينت bāynt (-āt) pint

ببغاء babghā' (ببغوات babghawāt) parrot

بتّة batta: البتّة al-batta none

بتر batara (u; بتر batr) to amputate

بترول bitrōl petrol

بتروكيماويات bitrōkīmāwiyāt pl petrochemicals

بثّ baththa (u; بثّ baththth) 1. to spread 2. to broadcast

بثّ baththth 1. broadcast 2. بثّ حيّ baththth ḥayy live broadcast

بحار biḥār pl 1. عبر البحار 'abr al-biḥār overseas 2. and see بحر

بحّار baḥḥār (-ūn) 1. sailor 2. seaman

بحث baḥatha (a; بحث baḥth) 1. to search (عن 'an for) 2. to look up 3. to research 4. to study 5. to discuss 6. بحث في baḥatha fī to look into

بحث baḥth (بحوث buḥūth; أبحاث abḥāth) 1. search 2. research 3. study

بحّر baḥḥara to set sail

بحر baḥr (بحار biḥār; بحور buḥūr; أبحر abḥur) 1. sea 2. على البحر 'alā 'l-baḥr at sea 3. سطح البحر saṭḥ al-baḥr; مستوى سطح البحر mustawā saṭḥ al-baḥr sea-level 4. أعماق البحر a'māq al-baḥr deep-sea 5. تحت سطح البحر taḥta saṭḥ al-baḥr submarine; underwater 6. دوار البحر duwār al-baḥr seasick 7. سرطان البحر saraṭān al-baḥr crab 8. and see بحار

بحراً baḥran by sea

بحري baḥrī 1. marine 2. nautical 3. naval 4. رحلة بحرية riḥla baḥrīya cruise 5. القوات البحرية al-qūwāt al-baḥrīya navy 6. جندي البحرية jundī 'l-baḥrīya (mil.) marine 7. قطع بحرية qiṭa' baḥrīya navyal ships

بحرية baḥrīya navy

بحوث buḥūth pl 1. research 2. مركز للبحوث markaz li 'l-buḥūth research centre

بحيرة buḥayra (-āt) 1. lake 2. pond 3. بحيرة إصطناعية buḥayra iṣṭinā'īya reservoir

بخار bukhār 1. steam 2. smoke 3. vapour 4. بخار المحرّك bukhār al-muḥarrik exhaust

بخيل bakhīl mean; miserly

بدّ budd 1. way out 2. escape 3. لا بدّ lā budd inevitably; definitely 4. لا بدّ من lā budd min it is inevitable (أن an that); it is necessary (أن an that)

بدا badā (u) 1. to appear (لـ li to) 2. فيما يبدو fī mā yabdū apparently

بدأ bada'a (a; بد bad') to begin

بدائي bidā'ī primitive

بداية bidāya (-āt) beginning; start

بدّد baddada 1. to scatter 2. to waste

بدّل baddala 1. to change 2. to switch

بدل badal: بدله badaluh in his stead 2. بدلاً badalan instead (من min of)

بدلة badla (بدل bidal) suit

بدن badan (أبدان abdān; أبدن abdun) body

بدني badanī physical

بدون bidūn 1. without 2. -less 3. بدون توقّف bidūn tawaqquf non-stop 4. بدون كحول bi dūn kuḥūl alcohol-free 5. and see دون

بديل badīl (بدلا budalā') 1. replacement; alternative 2. (spor.) substitute

بذرة badhra (collective بذر badhr; بذور budhūr) 1. seed 2. pip

بذل badhala (u/i; بذل badhl) 1. to spend (freely); to give freely 2. to expend

برّ barr 1. land 2. continent 3. البرّ الرئيسي al-barr ar-ra'īsī mainland

برّاً barran by land; overland

برّأ barra'a 1. to clear 2. برّأ من barra'a min to acquit from

براءة barā'a innocence

براعة barā'a (-āt) skill

برتغال burtughāl Portugal

برتقالة burtuqāla (collective برتقال burtuqāl) orange

برتغالي burtughālī 1. (-yūn) Portuguese 2. orange

برج burj (بروج burūj; أبراج abrāj); tower

برّد barrada to cool

برد bard 1. cold 2. أصيب ببرد uṣība bi bard. He caught a cold.

برّر barrara 1. to justify 2. to vindicate

برز baraza/bariza (u) to stand out

برطمان barṭamān (-āt) jar

برعم bur'um (براعم barā'im) shoot; bud

برغر burghar burger

برغوث burghūth (براغيث baraghīth) flea

برق baraqa (u; برق barq) to flash

برق barq lightning

برقوقة barqūqa (collective برقوق barqūq) plum

بركان burkān (براكين barākīn) 1. volcano 2. حمم البركان ḥumam al-burkān lava

بركة birka (برك birak) 1. pool 2. pond 3. lake 4. reservoir

برلمان barlamān 1. parliament 2. نائب برلمان nā'ib barlamān (نوّاب nuwwāb) member of parliament (M.P.)

برلماني barlamānī parliament

برمج barmaja to programme

برميل barmīl (براميل barāmīl) barrel; drum

برنامج barnāmij (برامج barāmij) 1. programme 2. schedule 3. agenda 4. *(comp.)* application 5. برنامج تلفزيوني barnāmij tiliviziyōnī television show 6. علة في برنامج 'illa fī barnāmij computer bug

برهن barhana 1. to prove (على *sth*) 2. to demonstrate

برهان burhān (براهين barāhīn) proof

برهنة barhana demonstration

بروتستانتي brotostantī (-yūn) Protestant

بروتين brōtīn (-āt) protein

بري barrī 1. overland 2. continental

بريء barī' innocent

بريد barīd 1. cold 2. post; mail 3. بريد ألكتروني barīd alaktrūnī e-mail 4. بريد جوي barīd jawwī airmail 5. بالبريد الجوي bi 'l-barīd al-jawwī by airmail 6. ساعي البريد sā'i 'l-barīd postman 7. صندوق البريد ṣundūq al-barīd (صناديق ṣanādīq) postbox; P.O. box 8. مكتب البريد maktab al-barīd (مكاتب makātib) post office 9. أرسل بالبريد arsala bi 'l-barīd to post

بريدي barīdī 1. post; postal 2. طابع بريدي ṭābi' baridī (طوابع ṭawābi') postage stamp 3. بطاقة بريدية biṭāqa barīdīya postcard 4. رمز بريدي ramz barīdī (رموز rumūz) post code

بريطاني brīṭānī (-yūn) 1. British 2. Briton

بريطانيا brīṭāniyā Britain

بريطانيا العظمى brīṭāniyā al-'uẓmā Great Britain

بريق barīq flash

بزر bizr *collective* (بزور buzūr) seed

بزغ bazagha (u) to dawn

بساط bisāṭ (-āt; بسط busuṭ) carpet

بساطة basāṭa simplicity

بستان bustān (بساتين basātīn) 1. orchard 2. garden

بستاني bustānī 1. horticultural 2. gardener

بسط basaṭa (u; بسط basṭ) 1. to spread 2. to unroll

بسّط bassaṭa to simplify

بسط basṭ spread

بسكويت biskit; بسكوت baskawīt biscuit

بسيط basīṭ (بسطاء busaṭā') simple

بشر bashar human being

بشري basharī 1. human 2. فوق البشري fawq al-basharī superhuman 3. القوة البشرية al-qūwa al-basharīya manpower

بشرية basharīya mankind; humankind

بشع bashi' hideous

بصر baṣar (أبصار abṣār) 1. vision; sight; eyesight 2. insight 3. حسير البصر ḥasir al-baṣar short-sighted

بصري baṣarī 1. visual 2. optical

بصق baṣaqa (a) to spit

بصقة baṣqa spit

بصلة baṣala (collective بصل baṣal) onion

بصيرة baṣīra foresight

بضائع baḍā'i' pl 1. goods 2. stock 3. بضائع بقالية baḍā'i' baqqālīya groceries 4. زوّد بالبضائع zawwada bi 'l-baḍā'i' stock

بضع biḍ' some; several

بضعة biḍ'a some

بطء buṭ' 1. slowness 2. بطء bi buṭ' slow

بطّأ baṭṭa'a to slow down

بطاطس baṭāṭis collective 1. potato(es) 2. بطاطس مقلية baṭāṭis maqlīya chips

بطاقة biṭāqa (-āt) بطائق baṭā'iq) 1. card 2. ticket 3. label 4. tag 5. بطاقة بريدية biṭāqa barīdīya postcard 6. بطاقة سخصية biṭāqa shakhṣīya identity card; I.D. 7. بطاقة معونة biṭāqa ma'awna voucher 8. ألصق بطاقة على alṣaqa biṭāqa 'alā to label

بطالة biṭāla unemployment

بطالون pl: البطالون al-baṭṭālūn the unemployed

بطّارية baṭṭārīya (-āt) battery

بطّانية baṭṭānīya (-āt) blanket

بطّة baṭṭa (collective بطّ baṭṭ) 1. duck 2. بطّة الساق baṭṭat as-sāq calf

بطل baṭal (أبطال abṭāl) 1. champion 2. hero

بطلة baṭala (-āt) heroine

بطن baṭn (بطون buṭūn) stomach

بطولة buṭūla (-āt) (spor.) 1. championship 2. title

بطيء baṭi' slow

بطّيخة baṭṭīkha (collective بطّيخ baṭṭīkh) watermelon

بعث ba'atha (a; بعث ba'th) 1. to send 2. بعث فاكس ba'atha fāks to fax

بعثة ba'tha/bu'tha (بعثات ba'athāt) 1. delegation 2. mission 3. expedition 4. scholarship trip 5. revival 6. بعثة دبلوماسية bu'tha diblomāsīya diplomatic mission

بعثر ba'thara to scatter

بعد ba'd 1. after 2. afterwards 3. post- 4. still; yet 5. past 6. بعد أن ba'd an after 7. بعد الظهر ba'd aẓ-ẓuhr afternoon; p.m. 8. بعد غد ba'd ghad the day after tomorrow 9. بعد ذلك ba'd dhālik; فى ما بعد fī mā ba'd afterwards 10. بعد أسبوع ba'd usbū' in a week 11. يوم بعد يوم yawm ba'da yawm every other day 12. بعد عدّة أيّام ba'd 'iddat ayyām in a few days 13. بعد قليل ba'd qalīl soon 14. بعد لحظة ba'd laḥẓa in a moment 15. بعد الآن ba'd al-'ān anymore 16. إلى ما بعد ilā mā ba'd beyond 17. الواحد بعد الآخر al-wāḥid ba'd al-ākhar one after the other 18. اجتمع بعد فراق ijtama'a ba'd firāq to reunite

بعد bu'd (أبعاد ab'ād) 1. dimension 2. distance

بعدئذ ba'da'idhin afterwards

بعدما ba'damā after

بعض ba'ḍ 1. some; one 2. part 3. بعضهم
ba'ḍahum; البعض بعضهم ba'ḍuhum al-
ba'ḍ each other 4. الشيء بعض ba'ḍ ash-
shay' somewhat 5. ...بعض ba'ḍ...
بعض... بعضاً ba'ḍ some... others 6.
ba'ḍ...; البعض بعض ba'ḍ... al-
ba'ḍ one... another

بعوض ba'ūḍ collective mosquito

بعيد ba'īd 1. far; distant (عن 'an from) 2.
بعيد عهد منذ mundhu 'ahd ba'īd long
ago 3. الأمد بعيد ba'īd al-amad long-
term 4. المدى بعيد ba'īd al-madā long-
range 5. النظر بعيد ba'īd an-naẓar far-
sighted

بعير ba'īr (بعران ;أبعرة ab'ira; bu'rān) camel

بغيض baghīḍ dreadful

بقاء baqā' survival

بقّال baqqāl (-ūn) grocer

بقّالي baqqālī: بقالية بضائع baḍā'i'
baqqālīya groceries

بقايا baqāyā remains

بقبقة baqbaqa bubble

بقر baqar collective cattle

بقرة baqara (collective بقر baqar) 1. cow 2.
البقر راعي ;بقر لحم laḥam baqar beef 3.
rā'i 'l-baqar cowboy

بقشيش baqshīsh tip; gratuity

بقّع baqqa'a to stain

بقعة baq'a/buq'a (بقع buqa') 1. stain 2.
(med.) spot 3. بقعة دون dūn buq'a
stainless

بقي baqiya (يبقى yabqā; بقاء baqā') 1. to

بقي baqiya (بقي ḥayyan stay; to remain 2.
ḥayyan to survive

بقية baqiya (بقايا baqāyā) remainder; rest

بكى bakā (i; بكاء bukā') to cry; to weep

بكالوريوس bakālūriyūs bachelor's
degree

بكتيري baktīrī bacterial

بكتيريا baktīrīya bacteria

بلّ balla (u; بلّ ball) to wet

بل bal 1. indeed; even 2. but; rather;
however

بلا bilā 1. without 2. -less 3. شكّ بلا bilā
shakk without doubt 4. معنى بلا bilā
ma'nan senseless 5. جدوى بلا bilā jadwā
futile 6. حيا بلا bilā ḥayā' shameless

بلى balā yes, indeed

بلاء balā' curse

بلاد bilād (بلدان buldān) 1. country 2. and
see بلاد

بلاستيك blāstīk plastic

بلاستيكي blāstīkī plastic

بلاطة balāṭa (collective بلاط balāṭ) tile

بلاغ balāgh: سرّي بلاغ balāgh sirrī tip-off

بلجيكا beljīkā Belgium

بلجيكي beljīkī Belgian

بلح balaḥ collective date(s)

بلد balad (بلاد bilād; بلدان buldān) 1. town
2. place 3. country 4. البلد ابن ibn al-
balad native; national 5. and see بلاد

بلدة balda (-āt) town

بلدي baladī 1. municipal 2. indigenous

بلدية baladiya (-āt) 1. town council; city council 2. municipality 3. دار البلدية dār al-baladiya town hall; city hall 4. عضو بلدية 'uḍw baladiya (أعضاء a'ḍā') councillor 5. رئيس البلدية ra'īs al-baladiya mayor

بلغ balagha (u; بلوغ bulūgh) 1. to reach 2. to arrive at 3. بلغ الذروة balagha adh-dharwa to peak

بلغ عن ballagha 'an to report

بلط ballaṭa to tile

بلوز blūz; بلوزة blūza (-āt) blouse

بلوط ballūṭ oak

بلي baliya (a; بلى bilan) to wear out

بليد balīd (sl.) dumb

بليغ balīgh eloquent

بن bin 1. son of 2. and see ابن

بنى banā (i; بناء binā'; بنيان bunyān) 1. to build 2. to establish

بناء binā' (أبنية abniya) 1. building 2. structure 3. construction 4. مواد بناء mawādd binā' building materials 5. بناء الجملة binā' al-jumla syntax 6. إعادة البناء i'ādat al-binā' rebuilding; reconstruction 7. أعاد البناء a'āda al-binā' to rebuild; to reconstruct 8. بناء على ذلك binā'an 'alā dhālik consequently

بنّاء bannā' (-ūn) 1. builder 2. constructive

بنائي binā'ī 1. construction 2. structural

بناية bināya (-āt) building

بنت bint (بنات banāt) 1. girl 2. daughter 3. بنت خال bint khāl; بنت خالة bint khāla; بنت عمّ bint 'amm; بنت عمّة bint 'amma cousin 4. بنت أخ bint akh; بنت أخت bint ukht niece

بنّج bannaja to anaesthetise

بند band (بنود bunūd) (leg.) article

بندقية bunduqīya (-āt) rifle

بنزين binzīn 1. petrol 2. محطة بنزين maḥaṭṭat binzīn petrol station 3. خزّان البنزين khazzān al-banzīn petrol tank

بنسيون bansiyūn pension

بنطلون banṭalōn; banṭalūn (-āt) 1. trousers 2. بنطلون قصير banṭalōn qaṣīr shorts 3. بنطلون الجينز banṭalōn al-jīnz jeans

بنك bank (بنوك bunūk) 1. bank 2. البنك الدولي al-bank ad-dawalī World Bank

بني bunnī brown

بنيان bunyān construction

بنية bunya 1. structure 2. البنية التحتية al-bunya at-taḥtīya infrastructure

بهجة bahja delight

بهيج bahīj festive

بوّاب bawwāb (-ūn) porter; doorman

بوزة bōza ice cream

بورصة būrṣa (-āt) 1. stock exchange 2. stock market 3. سمسار البورصة simsār al-būrṣa stockbroker

بوصة būṣa (-āt) inch

بوفيه **būfēh** buffet

بوق (أبواق abwāq; -āt) **būq** trumpet

بول **bawl** urine

بوليس **būlīs** 1. police 2. بوليس سري **būlīs sirrī** secret police

بوليسي **būlīsī** 1. police 2. محقّق بوليسي **muḥaqqiq būlīsī** detective

بوم **būm** *collective* owl

بيئة **bay'a** 1. environment 2. علم البيئة **'ilm at-bay'a** ecology

بيئي **bay'ī** 1. environmental 2. ecological

بياض **bayāḍ** 1. whiteness 2. blank

بيان **bayān** 1. statement; announcement 2. communiqué 3. بيان صحفي **bayān ṣaḥafī** press release 4. بيان آخر التطوّرات **bayān ākhir at-taṭawwurāt** update

بيانو **biyānū** piano

رسم بياني **rasm bayānī** 1. explanatory 2. رسم بياني **rasm bayānī** diagram

بيبة **bība** (-āt) pipe

بيت **bayt** 1. (بيوت buyūt) house 2. home 3. (أبيات abyāt) verse 4. في البيت **fi 'l-bayt** at home; indoors 5. مصنوع في البيت **maṣnū' fi 'l-bayt** homemade 6. أهل البيت **ahl al-bayt** household 7. صاحب بيت **ṣāḥib al-bayt** landlord 8. صاحبة بيت **ṣāḥibat al-bayt** landlady 9. علّية البيت **'ullīyat al-bayt** attic 10. بيت زجاجي **bayt zujājī** greenhouse 11. بيت كبير **bayt kabīr** mansion 12. بيت الشباب **bayt ash-shabāb** hostel

بيتروكيميائي **bītrūkīmyā'ī** petrochemical

بيتسا **bītsa** pizza

بيجاما; بيجامة **bījāmā; bījāma** pyjamas

بيرة **bīra** beer

بيروقراطي **bīrūqrātī** 1. bureaucratic 2. bureaucrat

بيروقراطية **bīrūqrātīya** bureaucracy

بيضا ء **bayḍā'** *see* أبيض بيض **bīḍ**

بيضة **bayḍa** (*collective* بيض **bayḍ**) egg

بيطري **bayṭarī** 1. veterinary 2. الطبّ البيطري **aṭ-ṭibb al-bayṭarī** veterinary medicine 3. طبيب بيطري jarrāḥ bayṭarī; **ṭabīb bayṭarī** veterinary surgeon

بيع **bay'** 1. sale 2. للبيع **li 'l-bay'** for sale 3. بيع بالتجزئة **bay' bi 't-tajzi'a** retail 4. سلع للبيع **sila' li 'l-bay'** *pl* wares

بين **bayn; bayna** 1. among 2. between 3. بين بين **bayn bayn** so-so 4. بين العرقات **bayn al-'irqāt** interracial 5. بين الولايات **bayn al-wilāyāt** interstate 6. بين القارّات **bayn al-qārrāt** intercontinental

بيّن **bayyana** 1. to clarify; to explain 2. to indicate

بيّن **bayyin** 1. distinct 2. obvious

بينما **baynamā** while

بيولوجية **biyūlūjīya** biology

ت

تآمر ta'āmara (pol.) to plot

تأثر ta'aththara to be affected (ب bi by)

تأثير ta'thīr effect

تأخر ta'akhkhara 1. to be late (عن 'an for) 2. تأخروا عن الطائرة ta'akhkharū 'an aṭ-ṭā'ira They missed the plane.

تأخير ta'khīr delay

تأرجح ta'arjaḥa to rock

تأسف ta'assafa 1. to regret (على/ل 'alā/li) 2. to be sorry (على/ل 'alā/li for)

تأسف ta'assuf 1. regret; 2. being sorry

تأسيس ta'sīs (-āt) 1. institution 2. foundation

تأسيسي ta'sīsī 1. founding 2. fundamental 3. مجلس تأسيسي majlis ta'sīsī constituent assembly

تأشيرة ta'shīra (-āt) visa

تأكد ta'akkada to be sure (من min of)

تأكيد ta'kīd 1. confirmation 2. emphasis 3. بالتأكيد bi 't-ta'kīd certainly

تألف ta'allafa to consist of

تأمل ta'ammala 1. to study 2. to consider

تأميم ta'mīm nationalization

تأمين ta'mīn 1. insurance 2. تأمين سياحي ta'mīn siyāḥī travel insurance 3. 4. تأمين على الحياة ta'mīn 'alā 'l-ḥayāh life insurance 5. تأمين صحّي ta'mīn

ṣiḥḥī healthcare 6. life insurance

تأوه ta'awwaha to groan

تأييد ta'yīd (leg.) support

تابع tābi' 1. following 2. تابع ل tābi' li belonging to; of 3. (أتباع atbā') follower 4. subject 5. (تبعة tuba'a; تبّاع tubbā') dependant 6. subordinate 7. مبنى والأراضي التابعة له mabnan wa 'l-arāḍī at-tābi'a lah premises

تابل tābil (توابل tawābil) spice

تابوت tābūt (توابيت tawābīt) coffin

تاج tāj (تيجان tījān) crown

تاجر tājir (تجّار tujjār) 1. merchant; trader 2. businessman

تاريخ tārīkh (تواريخ tawārikh) 1. history 2. date 3. ما قبل التاريخ mā qabl at-tārīkh pre-history

تاريخي tārīkhī historical

تاسع tāsi' 1. ninth 2. تاسع عشر tāsi' 'ashar nineteenth

تافه tāfih trivial

تاكسي tāksī (-āt) 1. taxi 2. سواق تاكسي sawwāq tāksī (-ūn) taxi driver

تال tālin 1. following; subsequent 2. بالتالي bi 't-tālī later; subsequently

تام tāmm 1. complete 2. entire 3. full 4. توقف تام tawaqquf tāmm standstill

تايوان **tāywān** Taiwan

تبادل **tabādala** to swap; to exchange

تبرّع **tabarraʿa** to contribute; to donate

تبرّع **tabarruʿ** (-āt) contribution; donation

تبع **tabiʿa** (a; تبع tabaʿ; تباعة tabāʿa) 1. to follow 2. to belong to 3. ما يتبع **mā yatbaʿ** sequel

تبع **tabaʿ** 1. following 2. subordinate (ل **li** to) 3. بالتبع **bi 't-tabaʿ** consecutively 4. تبعاً ل **tabaʿan li** according to 5. أتباع (**atbāʿ**) follower 6. citizen

تبغ **tibgh** (تبوغ **tubūgh**) tobacco

تبنّ **tabannin** adoption *of a child*

تبنّى **tabannā** to adopt *a child*

تبيّن **tabayyana** 1. to be clear 2. to see clearly; to recognize

تتابع **tatābiʿ**: بالتتابع **bi 't-tatābiʿ** in succession

تثاءب **tathā'aba** to yawn

تثاؤب **tathā'ub** yawn

تثليج **tathlīj** refrigeration

تجارة **tijāra** trade; business; commerce

تجاري **tijārī** 1. commercial; trade 2. مجمّع تجاري **mujammaʿ tijārī** shopping centre; shopping mall 3. معرض تجاري **maʿraḍ tijārī** (معارض **maʿāriḍ**) trade fair

تجاعيد **tajāʿīd** *pl* wrinkles

تجاه **tujāh; tujāha** 1. facing 2. regarding

تجاهل **tajāhala** to ignore

تجاوز **tajāwaza** 1. to exceed 2. to overtake

تجديد **tajdīd** 1. renewal 2. restoration 3. refurbishment

تجر **tajara** (u; تجارة **tijāra**) to trade (ب **bi** in)

تجربة **tajriba** (تجارب **tajārib**) 1. attempt 2. test 3. practice 4. rehearsal 5. experiment 6. trial 7. experience

تجزئة **tajzi'a**: 1. بيع بالتجزئة **bayʿ bi 't-tajzi'a** retail 2. بائع بالتجزئة **bā'iʿ bi 't-tajzi'a** a retailer 3. باع بالتجزئة **bāʿa bi 't-tajzi'a** (i; بيع **bayʿ**) to retail

تجزئي **tajzi'ī** retail

تجسّس **tajassasa** to spy

تجسّس **tajassus** spying

تجمّد **tajammud** 1. freezing 2. solidification 3. تجمّد الرواتب **tajammud ar-rawātib** wage freeze

تجمّع **tajammaʿa** to mass together

تجمّع **tajammuʿ** 1. تجمّع تجاري **tajammuʿ tijārī** shopping centre; shopping mall 2. تجمّع سكني **tajammuʿ sakanī** housing estate

تجميل **tajmīl** 1. making beautiful 2. making handsome 3. مادة للتجميل **mādda li 't-tajmīl** cosmetic 4. مسحوق تجميل للجلد **mashūq tajmīl li 'l-jild** moisturizing cream

تجميلي **tajmīlī** 1. cosmetic 2. مستحضر تجميلي **mustaḥḍar tajmīlī** cream

تجنّب **tajannaba** to avoid

تجنيد **tajnīd** recruitment

تجوّل tajawwala to wander

تحت taḥt/taḥta 1. below 2. under; underneath 3. down 4. تحت الأرض taḥta al-arḍ; تحت سطح الأرض taḥta saṭḥ al-arḍ underground; subterranean 5. تحت سطح الماء taḥt saṭḥ al-mā' underwater 6. تحت سطح البحر taḥta saṭḥ al-baḥr submarine 7. تحت الضغط taḥt al-ḍaġh under pressure 8. تحت الأضواء taḥt al-aḍwā' in the limelight 9. تحت القذف taḥta al-qadhf under fire 10. رسم خطّاً تحت rasima khaṭṭan taḥta (a) to underline

تحتاني taḥtānī 1. lower 2. دور تحتاني dūr taḥtānī basement

تحتي taḥtī: البنية التحتية al-bunya at-taḥtīya infrastructure

تحدّ taḥaddin (تحدّيات taḥaddiyāt) challenge

تحدّى taḥaddā to challenge

تحدّث taḥaddatha to chat

تحدّد taḥaddada 1. to be limited 2. to be defined

تحديد taḥdīd 1. limitation 2. definition 3. بالتحديد bi 't-taḥdīd specifically

تحذير taḥdhīr warning

تحرّك taḥarraka 1. to move 2. تحرّك إلى الوراء taḥarraka ilā 'l-warā' to reverse

تحرير taḥrīr 1. liberation 2. release 3. editing 4. writing 5. (-āt; تحارير taḥārīr) document; record 6. رئيس التحرير ra'īs al-taḥrīr newspaper editor

تحريري taḥrīrī editorial

تحريم taḥrīm ban

تحسّن taḥassana to improve

تحسّن taḥassun; تحسين taḥsīn improvement

تحطّم taḥaṭṭama to break up

تحقّق taḥaqqaqa 1. to be realised 2. to prove true

تحقيق taḥqīq 1. realisation 2. execution 3. precision 4. (-āt) check; check-up 5. investigation

تحكّم taḥakkum 1. control 2. تحكّم في النفس taḥakkum fi 'n-nafs self-control

تحليل taḥlīl 1. analysis 2. تحليل الدم taḥlīl ad-dam blood test

تحمّل taḥammala to endure; to put up with

تحمّل taḥammul endurance

تحوّل taḥawwala to convert (إلى ilā into)

تحوّل taḥawwul 1. conversion 2. transition

تحويل taḥwīl 1. transformation 2. conversion 3. diversion 4. مفتاح تحويل miftāḥ taḥwīl switch 5. لوحة التحويل الهاتفي lawḥat at-taḥwīl al-hātifī telephone switchboard 6. سعر تحويل العملة si'r taḥwīl al-'umla rate of exchange

تحية taḥīya (تحيّات taḥayyāt) 1. greeting(s) 2. salute

تخريب takhrīb sabotage

تخصّص takhaṣṣaṣa to specialize (بـ/لـ li/bi في fī in)

تخطّى takhaṭṭā 1. to step 2. قافزاً تخطى takhaṭṭā qāfizan skip

تخطّب takhaṭṭaba to get engaged

تخطيط takhṭīṭ 1. planning; lay-out 2. design 3. town planning

تخطيطي takhṭīṭī 1. planning 2. رسم تخطيطي rasm takhṭīṭī sketch; draft design 3. الفنون التخطيطية al-funūn at-takhṭīṭīya graphic arts

تحفيض takhfīḍ reduction

تخلّى takhallā to renounce (عن 'an sth)

تخلّص takhallaṣa to dispose (من min of)

تخلّص takhalluṣ 1. disposal 2. التخلّص من الألغام at-takhalluṣ min al-alghām mine disposal

تخلّل takhallala to penetrate

تخمين takhmīn guess

تخويف takhwīf intimidation

تخيّل takhayyala 1. to imagine 2. لا يتخيّل lā yutakhayyal inconceivable

تخيّل takhayyul 1. imagination 2. fiction

تدحنج tadaḥnaja to roll along

تدخّل tadakhkhala 1. to interfere (في fī in) 2. to intervene (في fī in) 3. لا تتدخّل! lā tatadakhkhal! Mind your own business!

تدخّل tadakhkhul 1. interference 2. intervention

تدخين tadkhīn 1. smoking 2.

ممنوع التدخين mamnūʻ at-tadkhīn no smoking!

تدرّب tadarrub practice

تدريب tadrīb 1. training 2. practice

تدريجي tadrījī gradual

تدريجياً tadrījīyan gradually

تدريس tadrīs 1. teaching 2. training

تدفئة tadfiʼa heating

تدليك tadlīk massage

تدمير tadmīr 1. destruction 2. demolition

تدهور tadahwara to deteriorate

تدوين tadwīn (fin.) entry

تذاكر tadhākir pl 1. tickets 2. شبّاك التذاكر shubbāk at-tadhākir; مكتب التذاكر maktab at-tadhākir ticket office; box office 3. قاطع التذاكر qāṭiʻ at-tadhākir; مفتّش التذاكر mufattish at-tadhākir ticket inspector 4. and see تذكرة

تذبذب tadhabdhaba 1. to vibrate 2. to fluctuate

تذكار tadhkār 1. memory 2. souvenir

تذكاري tadhkārī 1. memorial 2. نصب تذكاري nuṣub tadhkārī memorial; monument

تذكّر tadhakkara to remember

تذكرة tadhkara (تذاكر tadhākir) 1. ticket 2. تذكرة المرور tadhkirat al-murūr pass 3. تذكرة للذهاب فقط tadhkara li 'dh-dhihāb faqa single ticket 4. تذكرة ذهاب إياب tadhkirat dhihāb īhāb return ticket 5. and see تذاكر

تذوّق tadhawwaqa to savour

تراب turāb soil; earth; dirt

تراث turāth heritage

تراجع tarāja'a 1. to retreat (عن 'an from) 2. to withdraw (عن 'an from) 3. to retract

تراجع tarāju' 1. retreat 2. withdrawal

ترأّس tara''asa to head

تراكم tarākama to accumulate

تراموای trāmwāy tram

تربة turba (تراب turāb) soil; earth; dirt

تربوي tarbawī educational

تربية tarbiya 1. education 2. upbringing

ترتة turta (-āt) 1. cake 2. tart

ترتيب tartīb 1. arrangement 2. order 3. أعاد الترتيب a'āda al-tartīb to rearrange 4. أعاد ترتيب المناصب a'āda tartīb al-manāṣib (pol.) to reshuffle

ترجم tarjama 1. to translate (من min from; إلى ilā into) 2. to interpret

ترجمة tarjama (-āt تراجم tarājim) 1. translation 2. interpretation 3. version 4. biography 5. ترجمة فلم tarjamat film subtitles 6. ترجمة شخصية tarjama shakhṣīya profile

ترجيح tarjīḥ preference

ترحيب tarḥīb; ترحاب tarḥāb welcome

ترحيل tarḥīl deportation

تردّد taraddada 1. to hesitate 2. to come and go

تردّد taraddud 1. hesitation 2. frequency

ترس turs (أتراس atrās) shield

ترس tirs (تروس turūs) gear

ترشّح tarashshaḥa to stand for election

ترشيح tarshīḥ nomination

ترف taraf luxury

ترفيه tarfīh 1. comfort 2. leisure

ترقية tarqīya promotion

ترك taraka (u; ترك tark) 1. to let 2. to leave 3. to quit 4. to abandon 5. to give up

تركّز tarakkaza to concentrate; to centre

تركي turkī 1. Turkish 2. (أتراك atrāk) Turk

تركيا at-turkiya; التركية turkiyā Turkey

تركيب tarkīb 1. installation 2. combination 3. composition

تركيز tarkīz concentration

ترميم tarmīm 1. repair 2. restoration

ترنزيت tranzīt transit

ترويج tarwīj (com.) 1. promotion 2. باشر ترويج (سلعة ما) bāshara tarwīj (sil'atin mā) to launch

ترياز tiryāz antidote

تزايد tazāyada to increase

تزحلق tazaḥlaqa 1. to slide 2. تزحلق على الثلج tazaḥlaqa 'alā 'th-thalj to ski

تزحلق at-tazaḥluq 1. sliding 2. التزحلق على الثلج at-tazaḥluq 'alā 'th-thalj skiing

تزلّج tazallaja 1. to slide 2. تزلّج على الجليد tazallaja 'alā 'l-jalīd to skate

تزوّج tazawwaja 1. to get married 2. to mate

تزوير tazwīr forgery

تساءل tasā'ala to wonder (هل hal whether)

تسامح tasāmaḥa to tolerate

تسامح tasāmuḥ toleration

تساوى tasāwā to match

تسجّل tasajjala 1. to register 2. to check in

تسجيل tasjīl 1. registration 2. check-in 3. (mus.) recording

تسديد tasdīd (fin.) settlement

تسرّب tasarraba to leak

تسرّب tasarrub leak

تسريحة tasrīḥa hairstyle

تسع tus' (أتساع atsā') ninth

تسعة tis'a 1. nine 2. تسعة عشر tis'at 'ashar nineteen

تسعون tis'ūn ninety

تسلّح tasallaḥa to arm

تسلّح tasalluḥ 1. arming 2. سباق التسلح sibāq al-tasalluḥ arms race

تسلسل tasalsul sequence

تسلّق tasallaqa to climb

تسلّق tasalluq climbing

تسلّل tasallala to sneak

تسلّم tasallama to receive

تسلية tasliya 1. entertainment 2. pastime

تسليم taslīm delivery

تسهيلات tashīlāt pl facilities

تسوّق tasawwaqa to shop

تسوّق tasawwuq shopping

تسوية taswiya settlement

تسويق taswīq marketing

تشاؤم tashā'um pessimism

تشابه tashābuh similarity

تشاد chād Chad

تشاور tashāwara to consult (مع ma'a with; في fī about)

تشاور tashāwur consultation

تشجيع tashjī' encouragement

تشخيص tashkhīṣ diagnosis

تشريع tashrī' 1. legislation 2. legalization

تشريعي tashrī'ī legislative

تشرين الأوّل tishrīn al-awwal October

تشرين الثاني tishrīn ath-thānī November

تشكيل tashkīl formation

تشوّش tashawwush muddle

تشويش tashwīsh 1. mix-up 2. mutilation

تشيكي chekī (-yūn) Czech

تصادم taṣādama to collide

تصادم taṣādum collision

تصالح taṣālaḥa to make up

تصبح tuṣbiḥ: تصبح على خير! tuṣbiḥ 'alā khayr! good night!

تصحيح taṣḥīḥ correction

تصدير taṣdīr (-āt) export

تصرّف taṣarrafa to behave

تصرّف taṣarruf 1. behaviour 2. سوء التصرّف saw' at-taṣarruf misbehaviour 3. تحت تصرّف taḥt taṣarruf at the disposal of 4. ساء التصرّف sā'a at-taṣarruf (i) to misbehave

تصريح taṣrīḥ statement

تصفيق taṣfīq applause

تصميم taṣmīm determination

تصنّت taṣannut: آلة تصنّت ālat taṣannut electronic bug

تصنّت taṣannata (tech.) to bug

تصنيفات taṣnīfāt pl listings

تصوّر taṣawwara to conceive

تصويت taṣwīt 1. ballot 2. حقّ التصويت ḥaqq al-taṣwīt franchise

تصوير taṣwīr 1. photography 2. آلة تصوير ālat taṣwīr camera 3. جهاز التصوير jihāz at-taṣwīr photocopier

تضارب taḍārub conflict

تضاعف taḍā'afa to double

تضامن taḍāmun 1. solidarity 2. joint liability

تضحية taḍḥiya sacrifice

تضخّم taḍakhkhum (ec.) inflation

تضمّن taḍammana 1. to include 2. to imply

تضمّن taḍammun 1. inclusion 2. implication

تضمين taḍmīn inclusion

تضييق taḍyīq restriction

تطرّق taṭarraqa ilā 1. to reach; to arrive at 2. to go into; to touch on

تطعيم taṭ'īm immunization

تطفّل taṭafful intrusion

تطفّلي taṭaffulī intrusive

تطلّب taṭallaba to require

تطلّع taṭalla'a to look forward (إلى ilā to); to look out (إلى ilā for)

تطهير taṭhīr: تطهير عرقي taṭhīr 'irqī ethnic cleansing

تطوّر taṭawwara 1. to develop 2. to evolve

تطوّر taṭawwur (-āt) 1. development 2. evolution 3. بيان آخر التطوّرات bayān ākhir at-taṭawwurāt update

تطوّع taṭawwa'a to volunteer

تطوّعي taṭawwa'ī voluntary

تطوير taṭwīr development

تظاهر taẓāhara 1. (pol.) to demonstrate 2. تظاهر ب taẓāhara bi to pretend 3. to simulate

تظاهر taẓāhur 1. (pol.) demonstratation 2. pretence 3. simulation

تعادل ta'ādala (spor.) to draw; to tie

تعادل ta'ādul (spor.) draw; tie

تعارض ta'āruḍ 1. conflict 2. opposition

تعاطف ta'āṭafa to sympathize

تعاطف ta'āṭuf sympathy

تعال! ta'āl! come on!

تعامل ta'āmala to deal (مع ma'a with)

تعاون ta'āwana to cooperate

تعاون ta'āwun cooperation

تعاوني ta'āwanī cooperative

تعاونية ta'āwanīya cooperation

تعب ta'iba (a; تعب ta'ab) to get tired; to be tired

تعبان ta'bān tired

تعبير ta'bīr 1. expression 2. حرّية التعبير ḥurrīyat at-ta'bīr freedom of speech

تعجّب ta'ajjaba to be amazed

تعجّب ta'ajjub amazement

تعدّد ta'addud 1. multitude; great number 2. variety 3. تعدّد وسائل الإعلام ta'addud wasā'il al-i'lām multimedia

تعديل ta'dīl (-āt) 1. modification 2. regulation

تعدين ta'dīn mining

تعديني ta'dīnī mining

تعذيب ta'dhīb torture

تعرّض ta'arraḍa 1. to face (ل li sth) 2. to be exposed (ل li to) 3. to incur (ل li sth)

تعرّف ta'arrafa to get to know (على 'alā so)

تعرّق ta'arruq perspiration

تعرية ta'riya erosion

تعريف ta'rīf introduction

تعزيزات ta'zīzāt pl (mil.) reinforcements

تعصّب ta'aṣṣub intolerance

تعطّل ta'aṭṭala 1. to fail; to stop 2. to

break down 3. تعطّل عن العمل ta'aṭṭala 'an al-'amal to be unemployed

تعطيل ta'ṭīl disruption

تطعيم taṭ'īm vaccination

تعفّن ta'affana to decay

تعفّن ta'affun decay

تعقّب ta'aqqaba 1. to pursue 2. to trace

تعلّق ta'allaqa 1. to be attached (ب bi to) 2. to be related (ب bi to) 3. to depend (ب bi on) 4. to concern 5. فيما يتعلق ب fīmā yata'allaq bi concerning

تعلّم ta'allama to learn; to learn how

تعليق ta'līq 1. suspension 2. remark

تعليم ta'līm (-āt; تعاليم ta'ālīm) 1. education 2. instruction 3. منهج التعليم manhaj at-ta'līm (مناهج manāhij) syllabus

تعليمات ta'līmāt pl instructions

تعليمي ta'līmī 1. educational 2. دورة تعليمية dawra ta'līmīya (-āt) course 3. دورة تعليمية مصغرة dawra ta'līmīya muṣaghghara seminar 4. منحة تعليمية minḥa ta'līmīya scholarship; grant

تعهّد ب ta'ahhada bi 1. to undertake 2. to make a commitment to

تعهّد ta'ahhud commitment

تعوّد على ta'awwada to get used to

تعوّض ta'awwuḍ repayment

تعويض ta'wīḍ (leg.) 1. compensation 2. damages

تعيين ta'yīn appointment

تغاير taghāyur contrast

تغدّى taghaddā to have lunch

تغذية taghdhiya 1. nutrition 2. feeding 3. (tech.) charging 4. سوء التغذية sū' at-taghdhiya malnutrition

تغلّب taghallaba 1. to manage 2. تغلب على taghallaba 'alā to overcome 3. to beat *an opponent*

تغيّب taghayyaba 1. to be absent 2. تغيب بدون إذن taghayyaba bidūn idhn to skip

تغيّر taghayyara 1. to change 2. لا يتغير lā yataghayyar set; fixed

تغيّر taghayyur change

تغيير taghyīr change

تفاؤل tafā'ul optimism

تفّاحة (*collective* تفّاح tuffāḥ) apple

تفاهم tafāhama 1. to understand one another (مع ma'a with; على 'alā about/over) 2. to come to an understanding

تفاهم tafāhum 1. understanding 2. سوء التفاهم sū' at-tafāhum misunderstanding 3. ساء التفاهم sā'a at-tafāhum to misunderstand

تفاوض tafāwaḍa to negotiate (مع ma'a with; فى fī about/over)

تفتيش taftīsh 1. inspection 2. *official* search 3. نقطة تفتيش nuqṭat taftīsh checkpoint

تفحّص tafaḥḥuṣ scrutiny

تفرّج على tafarraja 'alā 1. to watch 2.

تفرّج على تلفزيون tafarraja 'alā 't-tilivizyōn to watch television

تفسير tafsīr (تفاسير tafāsīr) interpretation

تفصيل tafṣīl (تفاصيل tafāṣīl) detail

تفضّل! tafaḍḍal! please!

تفّاحة tuffāḥa apple

تفكّر tafakkara 1. to speculate 2. to reflect

تفكّر tafakkur 1. speculation 2. reflection

تفوّق tafawwaqa to excel

تفهّم tafahhama 1. to try to understand 2. to come to understand

تفوّق tafawwuq excellence

تقابل taqābala 1. to meet (مع ma'a with) 2. to face one another

تقاضى taqāḍā :ثمناً taqāḍā thamanan (com.) to charge

تقاطع taqāṭu' interchange

تقاعد taqā'ada to retire

تقاعد taqā'ud retirement

تقدّم taqaddama 1. to progress 2. to advance 3. تقدّم ب taqaddama bi to submit

تقدّم taqaddum 1. progress 2. advance

تقدّمي taqaddumī progressive

تقدير taqdīr 1. estimate 2. recognition 3. أخطأ التقدير akhṭa'a at-taqdīr to misjudge

تقديم taqdīm presentation

تقرّر taqarrara to be decided

تقريب taqrīb: تقريباً taqrīban; بالتقريب bi 't-taqrīb approximately

تقريبي taqrībī approximate

تقرير taqrīr (تقارير taqārīr) report

تقسيم taqsīm 1. division 2. تقسيم كهرباء taqsīm kahrabā' electric adaptor

تقطر taqaṭṭara to drip

تقلب taqallaba to fluctuate

تقليد taqlīd (تقاليد taqālīd) 1. tradition 2. convention 3. imitation 4. simulation

تقليدي taqlīdī 1. traditional 2. conventional

تقني tiqnī technical

تقنية tiqniya technique

تقويم taqwīm calendar

تقي taqī pious

تقيّأ taqayya'a to vomit

تقيّد ب taqayyada bi to adhere to

تقييد taqyīd (-āt) restriction

تكاليف takālīf pl 1. expenses 2. costs

تكامل takāmul integration

تكبّر takabbur arrogance

تكتّل takattala to group together

تكتك taktaka to tick

تكتكة taktaka tick

تكتيك taktīk (-āt) tactic

تكتيكي taktīkī tactical

تكرار takrār repetition

تكراراً takrāran frequently

تكرّر takarrara to recur

تكرّر takarrur recurrence

تكلّف takallafa to cost

تكلّم takallama to talk; to speak

تكليف taklīf cost

تكنولوجي tiknolozhī technological

تكنولوجية tiknōlōzhiya technology

تكوّن takawwana 1. to be formed 2. to consist (من min of)

تكوين takwīn composition

تكيّف takayyafa to adapt

تكييف takyīf: تكييف الهواء takyīf al-hawā' airconditioning 2. تكييف هوائي takyīf hawā'ī airconditioner

تلّ tall (تلال tilāl) hill

تلا talā (u; تلو tulūw) to recite

تلاعب talā‘aba bi: تلاعب بإنتخاب talā‘aba bi intikhāb to rig an election

تلاكمة talākama (spor.) boxing

تلألأ tala'la'a to glitter; to twinkle

تلاوة tilāwa recital

تلبية talbiya: تلبيةً ل talbiyatan li in response to

تلسكوب tiliskūb telescope

تلطخ talaṭṭakha: لا يتلطخ lā yatalaṭṭakh stainless

تلفزيون tilivizyōn (-āt) 1. television 2. جهاز تلفزيون jihāz tilifizyōn television set 3. برنامج تلفزيوني barnāmij tiliviziyōnī television show 4.

تفرّج على تلفزيون tafarraja 'alā 't-tilivizyōn to watch television

تلفزيوني tilivizyōnī 1. television 2. televisual

تلفّظ talaffaẓa to pronounce

تلفّظ talaffuẓ pronunciation

تلفن talfana 1. to telephone (ل li so) 2. to dial (ل li so)

تلفون tilifōn (-āt) 1. telephone 2. التلفون النقّال al-tilifūn an-naqqāl mobile phone 3. متحدث بالتلفون mutaḥaddith bi 't-tilifūn caller 4. مكالمة تلفونية mukālama tilifōniya telephone call 5. خطّ تلفوني khaṭṭ tilifūnī telephone line 6. كشك التلفون kushk at-tilifōn; صندوق التلفون sundūq at-tilifōn telephone booth

تلفوني tilifōnī 1. telephone 2. telephonic

تلقّى talaqqā 1. to receive 2. to take a lesson

تلقائي tilqā'ī spontaneous

تلقيح talqīḥ vaccination

تلك tilka f 1. that 2. those

تلميح talmīḥ 1. hint 2. implication

تلميذ tilmīdh (تلاميذ talāmīdh; تلامذة talāmidha) 1. pupil 2. student 3. تلميذ مدرسي tilmīdh madrasi schoolboy 4. تلميذة مدرسية tilmīdha madrasīya schoolgirl

تلهّب talahhaba to blaze

تلهّف talahhuf: بتلهّف bi talahhuf eagerly

تلوّى talawwā to wriggle

تلوّث talawwuth pollution

تمّ tamma (i) 1. to be finished 2. to happen 3. لم يتمّ lam yatimm unfinished

تماثل tamāthala to match

تمام tamām 1. complete 2. okay

تماماً tamāman 1. completely 2. جديد تماماً jadīd tamāman brand new

تمتّع ب tamatta'a bi to enjoy

تمثال timthāl (تماثيل tamāthīl) 1. statue 2. sculpture 3. قاعدة تمثال qā'idat timthāl pedestal

تمثيل tamthīl 1. performance 2. representation

تمدّد tamaddada to lie down

تمديد tamdīd extension

تمر tamr collective date

تمرّد tamarrada 1. to disobey 2. to rebel (على 'alā against) 3. to mutiny (على 'alā against)

تمرّد tamarrud 1. disobedience 2. rebellion 3. mutiny

تمركز tamarkaza to establish oneself

تمرّن tamarrana to exercise

تمريض tamrīḍ (med.) nursing

تمرين tamrīn (-āt) 1. exercise 2. rehearsal 3. حجرة للتمرينات الرياضية ḥujra li 't-tamrīnāt ar-riyāḍīya gym

تمسّك tamassaka to cling (ب bi to)

تمطّى tamaṭṭā to stretch

تمكّن tamakkana 1. to be able 2. to be skilled (من min at) 3. to possess

تمنّى tamannā to hope for; to wish

تمنّيات tamannīyāt *pl* regards

تمهيدي tamhīdī preliminary

تموز tammūz July

تمويل tamwīl funding

تموين tamwīn 1. supply 2. حصّة تموين ḥiṣṣat tamwīn ration

تميّز tamayyaza to be distinguished

تمييز tamyīz discrimination

تنازل tanāzala to abandon (عن 'an *sth*)

تناسق tanāsuq symmetry

تناسل tanāsul 1. sex; reproduction 2. أعضاء التناسل a'ḍā' at-tanāsul genitals

تناسلي tanāsulī 1. sexual 2. مرض تناسلي maraḍ tanāsulī venereal disease

تنافس مع tanāfasa ma'a to compete

تناقض مع tanāqaḍa ma'a to clash

تناوب tanāwaba to rotate

تناول tanāwala 1. to take 2. to accept 3. to eat 4. to deal with

تنبّأ tanabba'a 1. to predict; to forecast 2. (*fin.*) to project

تنبّؤ tanabbu' (-āt) 1. prediction; forecast 2. (*fin.*) projection 3. يمكن التنبّؤ به yumkin at-tanabbu' bih predictable 4. لا يمكن التنبّؤ به lā yumkin at-tanabbu' bih unpredictable

تنس tanis 1. tennis 2. مضرب التنس miḍrab at-tanis (مضارب maḍārib) tennis racket

تنشّق tanashshaqa to sniff

تنشيف tanshīf 1. drying 2. آلة لتنشيف الشعر

آلة لتنشيف الشعر ālat li tanshīf ash-sha'r hairdryer

تنظيف tanẓīf cleaning

تنظيم tanẓīm 1. organization 2. regulation 3. إعادة تنظيم i'ādat tanẓīm reorganization; shake-up 4. أعاد التنظيم a'āda at-tanẓīm to reorganize; to shake up

تنفيذ tanfīdh (*leg.*) 1. execution; implementation 2. إرجاء تنفيذ حكم irjā' tanfīdh ḥukm suspension 3. أرجأ تنفيذ حكم arja'a tanfīdh ḥukm to suspend 4. أرجأ تنفيذ حكم بالاعدام arja'a tanfīdh ḥukm bi 'l-i'dām to reprieve

تنفّس tanaffasa to breathe

تنفيذي tanfīdhī executive

تنقيح tanqīḥ revision

تنكّر tanakkur disguise

تنمية tanmiya development

تنّورة tannūra (-āt) skirt

تنّين tinnīn (تنانين tanānīn) dragon

تنوّع tanawwu' variety

تنوير tanwīr illumination

تهانئ tahāni' congratulations

تهجّى tahajjā to spell

تهجية tahjiya spelling

تهديد tahdīd (-āt) threat

تهرّب taharraba to evade

تهريب tahrīb smuggling

تهزّأ من tahazza'a min to make fun of

تهكّم tahakkum irony

تهمة **tuhma** (تهم **tuham**) 1. accusation 2. charge

تهوية **tahwiya** ventilation

توّاً **tawwan** straightaway

توائم **tawā'im** (singular توأم/توءم **taw'am**) twins

توازن **tawāzun** balance

تواضع **tawāḍu'** modesty

توافق مع **tawāfaqa ma'a** to conform to

توالد **tawālada** to sexually reproduce

توالد **tawālud** sexual reproduction

توت **tūt** collective 1. mulberries 2. توت العليق **tūt al-'ullayq** raspberries

توتّر **tawattur** 1. tension 2. توتر الأعصاب **tawattur al-a'ṣāb** nervousness

توجّه **tawajjaha** to go (إلى **ilā** to)

توجيه **tawjīh** direction

توحيد **tawḥīd** union

تورّط **tawarruṭ** involvement

توزيع **tawzī'** distribution

توسّط **tawassaṭa** to mediate

توسّط **tawassuṭ** mediation

توسّع **tawassa'a** to expand

توسّع **tawassu'** expansion

توسّعي **tawassu'ī** expansionist

توسيع **tawsī'** expansion

توصّل **tawaṣṣala** to reach (إلى **ilā** somewhere)

توصيلة **tawṣīla** lift

توصية **tawṣīya** recommendation

توظيف **tawẓīf** employment

توفير **tawfīr** economy

توقّع **tawaqqa'a** to expect

توقّع **tawaqqu'** 1. expectation 2. (fin.) projection

توقّف **tawaqquf** 1. halt 2. توقّف تام **tawaqquf tāmm** standstill 3. بدون توقّف **bidūn tawaqquf** non-stop 4. توقّف قصير **tawaqquf qaṣīr** pause

توقّف **tawaqqafa** 1. توقّف عن to cease 2. توقّف فجأةً **tawaqqafa faj'atan** to stall 3. توقّف على to depend on 4. توقّف قصيراً **tawaqqafa qaṣīran** to pause

توقير **tawqīr** reverence

توقيع **tawqī'** signature

تولّى **tawallā** 1. to occupy an office 2. to take over

تونس **tūnis** 1. Tunisia 2. Tunis

تونسي **tūnisī** (-yūn) Tunisian

توهّج **tawahhaja** 1. to glow 2. to blaze

تيّار **tayyār** 1. current 2. تيّار هوائي **tayyār hawā'ī** draught

تيسّر **tayassur** availability

تي شرت **tī shirt** (-āt) T-shirt

تينة **tīna** (collective تين **tīn**) fig

ث

ثائر tha'ir (ثوّار thuwwār) 1. revolutionary 2. rebel

ثابت thābit 1. firm 2. fixed 3. stable 4. constant 5. غير ثابت ghayr thābit unstable

ثابر thābara to persist

ثأر tha'r vengeance

ثار thāra (u) 1. to be stirred up 2. to arise 3. to rise على 'alā against) 4. to rage 5. to break out

ثالث thālith third

ثالث عشر thālith 'ashar thirteenth

ثامن thāmin eighth

ثامن عشر thāmin 'ashar eighteenth

ثان thānin 1. second 2. كانون الثاني kānūn ath-thānī January 3. الدرجة الثانية ad-daraja 'th-thānīya second class

ثانوي thānawī 1. secondary 2. subsidiary 3. مدرسة ثانوية madrasa thānawīya secondary school

ثانياً thānīyan secondly

ثانية thānīya (ثوان thawānin) second

ثانيةً thānīyatan 1. again 2. ثانيةً وحد waḥḥada thānīyatan to reunite

ثاني عشر thānī 'ashar twelfth

ثبت thabata (u; ثبوت thubūt; ثبات thabāt) 1. to be fixed 2. to be established

ثبّت thabbata 1. to fix 2. to fasten 3. to stabilise

ثدي thady breast

ثديي thadyī (ثدييات thadyīyāt) mammal

ثروة tharwa wealth; fortune

ثري tharī prosperous

ثعلب tha'lab (ثعالب tha'ālib) fox

ثقافة thaqāfa (-āt) culture

ثقافي thaqāfī cultural

ثقب thaqaba (u; ثقب thaqb) 1. to pierce 2. to puncture 3. to bore 4. to drill

ثقب thaqb (ثقب thuqab; ثقوب thuqūb) 1. hole 2. puncture

ثقة thiqa 1. trust 2. confidence 3. الثقة بالنفس ath-thiqa bi 'n-nafs self-confidence 4. جدير بالثقة jadīr bi 'th-thiqa reliable 5. جدارة بالثقة jidāra bi 'th-thiqa reliability 6. غير جدير بالثقة ghayr jadīr bi 'th-thiqa unreliable

ثقل thuql/thiql 1. heaviness 2. جاذبية الثقل jādhibīyat ath-thiql gravity

ثقيل thaqīl 1. heavy 2. ثقيل الدم thaqīl ad-dam unpleasant

ثكنة thukna (-āt) garrison

ثلاث thulāth: ضاعف ثلاث مرات ḍā'afa thulāth marrāt to triple

الثلاثاء ath-thalāthā'; يوم الثلاثاء yawm ath-thalāthā' Tuesday

ثلاثة thalātha 1. three 2. زاده ثلاثة أضعاف zādah thalāthat aḍ'āf (i; زيادة ziyāda) to treble

ثلاثة عشر thalāthat 'ashar thirteen

ثلاثون thalāthūn thirty

ثلاثي thulāthī tripartite

ثلث thulth third

ثلج thalaja (u) to snow

ثلج thalj (ثلوج thulūj) 1. snow 2. تزحلق على الثلج tazaḥlaqa 'alā 'th-thalj ski 3. متزحلق على الثلج mutazaḥliq 'alā 'th-thalj skier 4. التزحلق على الثلج at-tazaḥluq 'alā 'th-thalj skiing

ثلج thalij icy

ثلاجة thallāja (-āt) 1. refrigerator 2. freezer

ثمّ thamma 1. there... 2. من ثمّ min thamma therefore

ثمّ thumma then

ثمانون thamānūn eighty

ثمانية thamāniya eight

ثمانية عشر thamāniyat 'ashar eighteen

تمّت\ثمّة thammata there is/are...

ثمن thaman (أثمان athmān) 1. price 2. cost 3. charge 4. تقاضى ثمناً taqāḍā thamanan to charge 5. طلب ثمناً أكثر من اللازم ṭalaba thamanan akthar min al-lāzim to overcharge

ثمين thamin valuable

ثمن thumn (أثمان athmān) one eighth

ثنائي thunā'ī 1. bipartite 2. binary

ثنائية thunā'īya duo

ثوب نسائي thawb nisā'ī gown

ثوب thawb (ثياب thiyāb; أثواب athwāb) 1. dress 2. gown 3. clothing 4. costume

ثور thawr (ثيران thīrān) bull

ثورة thawra (-āt) (pol.) 1. revolution 2. revolt; uprising

ثوري thawrī (-yūn) revolutionary

ثوم thūm garlic

ج

جاء jā'a (i; مجيء majī') 1. to come 2. to be said; to be mentioned (في fi in) 3. jā'a bi to bring

جائر jā'ir oppressive

جائزة jā'iza (جوائز jawā'iz) prize

جاحد jāḥid ungrateful

جادّة jādda (-āt) avenue

جادل jādala to argue

جاذبية jādhibīya 1. charm 2. attraction 3. جاذبية الثقل jādhibīyat ath-thiql gravity

جار jār (جيران jīrān) neighbour

جارح jāriḥ 1. injuring 2. painful 3. جارح مشاعر الغير jāriḥ mashā'ir al-ghayr offensive

جاري jārī 1. underway 2. current 3. topical 4. جاري العمل فيه jāri al-'amal fīh in process

جاز jāza (u) to be allowed

جاسوس jāsūs (جواسيس jawāsīs) spy

جاع jā'a (u; جوع jaw'/jū') to starve

جاف jāff dry

جاكتة jāketa; jākitta (-āt) jacket

جال jāla (u; جولة jawla). 1. to tour 2. to roam

جالية jālīya (-āt) community

جامع jāma'a to make love

جامع jāmi' 1. universal 2. (جوامع jawāmi') mosque

جامعة jāmi'a (-āt) 1. university 2. league 3. رئيس الجامعة ra'īs al-jāmi'a (acad.) chancellor

جامعي jāmi'ī 1. university 2. academic 3. أستاذ جامعي ustādh jāmi'ī lecturer 4. شهادة جامعية shahāda jāmi'īya degree

جانب jānib (جوانب jawānib) 1. side 2. الجانب الأسفل al-jānib al-asfal underside 3. من جانب إلى آخر min jānib ilā ākhar across 4. من جانب... ومن جانب آخر min jānib... wa

min jānib ākhar on the one hand... and on the other

جانباً jāniban apart; aside

جانبي jānibī 1. side 2. partial 3. مظهر جانبي maẓhar jānibī profile

جانبياً jānibīyan sideways

جاهد jāhada 1. to try hard 2. to strive

جاهز jāhiz ready

جاهل jāhil (جهلة jahala; ء juhalā') ignorant

جاوب jāwaba to reply; to answer

جاور jāwara to border

جبّار jabbār mighty

جبال jibāl pl 1. سلسلة جبال silsilat jibāl mountain range 2. متسلق الجبال mutasalliq al-jibāl (-ūn) mountaineer 3. see جبل

جبان jubān (ء جبناء jubanā') coward

جبر jabr might

جبل jabal (جبال jibāl) mountain

جبلي jabalī mountainous

جبن jubn; جبنة jubna cheese

جبهة jabha (جبهات jabahāt) front

جبين jabīn (أجبنة ajbina) forehead

جثّ jaththa (u; جثّ jathth) to uproot

جثّة juththa (جثث juthath) corpse

جثمان juthmān pl remains

جحيم jaḥīm hell

جدّ jadd (أجداد ajdād) 1. grandfather 2. ancestor

جدّاً jiddan 1. very; too 2. قليل جدّاً qalīl jiddan next to nothing 3. صغير جدّاً saghīr jiddan tiny 4. مشغول جدّاً mashghūl jiddan hectic 5. دقيق جدّاً daqīq jiddan rigorous 6. شخص مهم جدّاً shakhṣ muhimm jiddan V.I.P.

جدار jidār (جدران judrān) wall

جدارة jadāra/jidāra 1. worthiness 2. suitability 3. جدارة بالثقة jadāra bi 'th-thiqa reliability

جدال jidāl dispute

جدّة jadda (-āt) grandmother

جدجد judjud (جداجد jadājid) cricket

جدّد jaddada 1. to renew 2. to modernize 3. to renovate 4. to restore 5. جدّد المعلومات jaddada al-ma'lūmāt update

جدل jadala (u; جدل jadl) to twist

جدل jadal 1. argument 2. dispute 3. مثير للجدل muthīr li 'l-jadal controversial

جدوى jadwā: بلا جدوى bilā jadwā futile

جدول jadwal (جداول jadāwil) 1. chart 2. جدول مواعيد jadwal mawā'īd timetable

جدّي jiddī serious

جديد jadīd (جدد judud) 1. new 2. neo- 3. incoming 4. جديد تماماً jadīd tamāman brand new 5. من جديد min jadīd again 6. جديد وغريب jadīd wa gharīb novel 7. قادم جديد qādim jadīd newcomer 8. مولود جديد mawlūd jadīd newborn 9. عضو جديد 'uḍw jadīd (أعضاء a'ḍā')

recruit 10. مجنّد جديد mujannad jadīd (-ūn) (mil.) recruit

جدير jadīr 1. worthy (ب bi of) 2. suitable (ب bi for) 3. جدير بالثقة jadīr bi 'th-thiqa reliable 4. غير جدير بالثقة ghayr jadīr bi 'th-thiqa unreliable 5. جدير بالاعتبار jadīr bi 'l-i'tibār considerable 6. جدير بالملاحظة jadīr bi 'l-mulāḥaẓa; جدير بالذكر jadhīr bi 'dh-dhikr noteworthy

جذّاب jadhdhāb 1. attractive 2. غير جذّاب ghayr jadhdhāb unattractive

جذّب jadhdhaba to attract

جذب jadhb attraction

جذر jidhr (جذور judhūr) root

جذري jidhrī radical

جذع jidh' (جذوع judhū'; أجذاع ajdhā') trunk

جذف jadhdhafa (mar.) to row

جرّ jarr (u; جرّ jarr) 1. to pull 2. to drag 3. to draw 4. to tow

جرّ jarr genitive

جرى jarā (i; جري jary) 1. to flow 2. to run 3. to happen 4. to proceed (على 'alā with) 5. جرى ب jarā bi to entail

جرؤ jaru'a (u; جرأة jur'a; جراءة jarā'a) to dare

جرائم jarā'im pl 1. جرائم حرب jarā'im ḥarb war crime 2. ارتكب جرائم حرب irtakaba jarā'im ḥarb to commit a war crime 3. مرتكب جرائم حرب murtakib jarā'im ḥarb (-ūn) war criminal 4. see جريمة

جرثوم jurthūm (singular جرثومة jurthūma; pl جراثيم jarāthīm) germs; bacteria

جراثيم *pl* jarāthīm bacteria

جرّاح jarrāḥ (-ūn) 1. surgeon 2. جرّاح بيطري jarrāḥ bayṭarī veterinary surgeon

جراحة jirāḥa surgery

جراحي jarāḥī 1. surgical 2. أجرى عملية جراحية ajrā ʻamalīya jarāḥīya *(med.)* to operate

جرّارة jarrāra (-āt) tractor

جرّب jarraba 1. to try 2. to try out; to test

جرجر jarjara 1. to drag 2. to trail

جرح jaraḥa (a; جرح jarḥ) 1. to hurt 2. to injure 3. to wound

جرح juriḥa *passive* 1. to get hurt 2. to be injured 3. to get wounded

جرح jurḥ (جروح jurūḥ) 1. hurt 2. injury 3. wound 4. جرح المشاعر jurḥ al-mashāʻir offence

جرّد jarrada 1. to strip 2. to bare

جرذ juradh (جرذان jirdhān) rat

جرس jaras (أجراس ajrās) 1. bell 2. جرس الإنذار بالحريق jaras al-indhār bi 'l-ḥariq fire alarm

جرسية jirsīya (-āt) sweater; jersey

جرعة jurʻa/jarʻa (-āt; جرع jurʻa) 1. dose 2. جرعة مفرطة jurʻa mufriṭa (-āt) overdose

جرف jurf (أجراف ajrāf) cliff جروف jurūf) cliff

جرّم jarrama to incriminate

جرم jurum 1. body 2. mass

جرو jarw (جراء jirāʼ) puppy

جريء jarīʼ bold

جريب فروت graypfrūt grapefruit

جريح jarīḥ (جرحى jarḥā) 1. wounded 2. casualty

جريدة jarīda (جرائد jarāʼid) 1. newspaper 2. gazette 3. جريدة شعبية jarīda shaʻbīya tabloid

جريمة jarīma (جرائم jarāʼim) 1. crime 2. ارتكب جريمة irtakaba jarīma to commit a crime 3. *and see* جرائم

جزى jazā (i; جزا ، jazāʼ) to compensate

جزء juzʼ (أجزاء ajzāʼ) 1. part; section 2. portion

جزاء jazāʼ 1. compensation 2. ضربة الجزاء ḍarbat al-jazāʼ *(spor.)* penalty

الجزائر al-jazāʼir 1. Algeria 2. Algiers

جزائري jazāʼirī Algerian

جزّار jazzār (-ūn) butcher

جزئي juzʼī partial

جزئياً juzʼīyan partly

جزر jazr: المدّ والجزر al-madd wa ʼl-jazr tide

جزرة jazra carrot

جزري jazrī: مد وجزري madd wa jazrī tidal

جزمة jazma (-āt; جزم jizam) boot

جزيء juzayʼ (جزيئات juzayʼāt) molecule

جزيرة jazīra (جزر juzur) 1. island 2. شبه جزيرة shibh jazīra peninsula

جسر jisr (جسور jusūr) bridge

جسم jism (أجسام ajsām) body

جسور jasūr bold

جصّ jiṣṣ plaster

جصّص jaṣṣaṣa to plaster

جعالة ju'āla (fin.) royalty

جعل ja'ala (a; جعل ja'l) 1. to make; to do 2. to begin to 3. جعل غير مستقرّ ja'ala ghayr mustaqirr destabilize

جغرافية zhoghrāfīya ؛جغرافيا geography

جغرافي zhoghrāfī geographic; geographical

جفّف jaffafa to dry

جفن jafn (أجفان ajfān) eyelid

جلا jalā (u); جلي jalā (i; جلي jaly) 1. to clean 2. to clarify

جلاتي jalātī ice cream

جلّاد jallād (-ūn) hangman

جلب jalaba (i/u; جلب jalb) 1. to bring 2. to fetch

جلد jalada (i; جلد jald) to freeze

جلّد jallada to freeze

جلد jild (جلود julūd) 1. skin 2. leather

جلس jalasa (i; جلوس julūs) to sit down (إلى ilā at على alā on)

جلسة jalsa (-āt) 1. session 2. sitting 3. (leg.) hearing 4. جلسة إستماع jalsat istimā' tribunal

جلوس julūs 1. sitting 2. غرفة الجلوس ghurfat al-julūs; حجرة الجلوس hujrat al-julūs sitting-room

جليد jalīd 1. ice 2. الهوكي على الجليد al-hōkī 'alā 'l-jalīd ice hockey 3. تزلج على الجليد tazallaja 'alā 'l-jalīd to skate

جلي jalī evident

جلياً jalīyan evidently

جليل jalīl stately

جماع jimā' sexual intercourse

جمع jama'a (a; جمع jam') to gather

جماعة jamā'a (-āt) 1. group 2. pack 3. troop

جماعي jamā'ī 1. group 2. mass; collective 3. رحلة جماعية rihla jamā'īya package tour

جمال jamāl 1. beauty 2. فائق الجمال fā'iq al-jamāl gorgeous

جماهيري jamāhīrī mass

جماهيرية jamāhīrīya republic

جمجمة jumjuma (جماجم jamājim) skull

جمرك gumruk (جمارك gamārik) customs

جمع jama'a (a; جمع jam') 1. to collect 2. to group 3. to total 4. to raise

جمع jam' 1. gathering 2. group 3. plural 4. جمع الشمل jam' ash-shaml reunion

الجمعة al-jum'a; يوم الجمعة yawm al-jum'a Friday

جمعي jam'ī plural

جمعية jam'īya (-āt) 1. association 2. society 3. assembly 4. الجمعية العامّة al-jam'īya al-'āmma general assembly

جمل jamala (u; جمل jaml) to sum up

جمل jamula (u; جمال jamāl) 1. to be beautiful 2. to be handsome 3. to be suitable

جمّل jammala 1. to make beautiful 2. to make handsome

جمل jamal (جمال jimāl; أجمال ajmāl) camel

جملة jumla (جمل jumal) 1. whole 2. sum 3. group 4. crowd 5. sentence 6. clause 7. بناء الجملة binā' al-jumla syntax

جملةً jumlatan altogether

جملي jumlī 1. mass 2. الإنتاج الجملي al-intāj al-jumlī mass production

جمنازي zhimnāzī gymnast

الجمنازية zhimnāziya: رياضة الجمنازية riyāḍat azh-zhimnāziya gymnastics

جمنازيوم zhimnāziyūm gym; gymnasium

جمهور jumhūr (جماهير jumāhīr) 1. community 2. public 3. audience 4. multitude

جمهوري jumhūrī (-yūn) republican

جمهورية jumhūrīya (-āt) republic

جميع jamī' 1. all 2. everybody 3. everything

جميل jamīl beautiful

الجنة al-janna 1. heaven 2. paradise

جناح janāḥ (أجنحة ajniḥa) 1. wing 2. suite 3. (med.) ward

جنازة janāza (-āt) funeral

جناية jināya (-āt) felony

جنب janb (أجناب ajnāb) 1. side 2. next to 3. جنب البيت janb al-bayt by the house 4. جنباً إلى جنب janban ilā janb; جنباً لجنب janban li janb side by side

جنّد jannada to recruit

جند jund pl 1. troops 2. جند المظليين jund al-miẓalliyīn paratroops

جندي jundī (جنود junūd؛ جند jund) 1. soldier 2. private 3. جندي البحرية jundī 'l-baḥrīya marine

جنرال jinrāl general

جنّس jannasa to naturalize

جنس jins (أجناس ajnās) 1. gender; sex 2. species 3. race 4. kind; sort

جنساني jinsānī (-yūn) sexist

جنسانية jinsānīya 1. sexuality 2. sexism

جنسي jinsī 1. sexual 2. racial

جنسية jinsīya (-āt) 1. citizenship 2. nationality 3. متعدّد الجنسيات muta'addid al-jinsīyāt multinational

جنّن jannana to madden

جنوب janūb 1. south 2. نحو الجنوب naḥw al-janūb southwards 3. الجنوب الشرقي al-janūb al-sharqī southeast 4. الجنوب الغربي al-janūb al-gharbī southwest

جنوباً janūban southwards

جنوبي janūbī 1. south; southern 2. southerly 3. (-yūn) southerner 4. جنوبي شرقي janūbī sharqī southeast 5. جنوبي غربي janūbī gharbī southwest

جنود junūd pl 1. سكن الجنود sakan al-junūd (mil.) quarters 2. and see جند

جنوسية junūsīya sexuality

جنون junūn 1. madness; insanity 2. mania

جنينة junayna (-āt؛ جنائن janā'in) yard

جهارة jahāra: جهارة الصوت jahārat aṣ-ṣawt volume; loudness

جهاز jihāz (أجهزة ajhiza) 1. piece of equipment 2. set; apparatus 3. appliance 4. device 5. gear 6. receiver 7. جهاز للطبخ jihāz li 'ṭ-ṭabkh cooker 8. جهاز تلفزيون jihāz tilifizyōn television set 9. جهاز إستريو jihāz isteriyō stereo 10. جهاز الفيديو jihāz al-vīdiyo video recorder 11. جهاز طباعة الليزر jihāz ṭibā'at al-layzer laser printer 12. جهاز كمبيوتر jihāz kombyūtar computer terminal 13. جهاز وسيط jihāz wasīṭ modem 14. جهاز التصوير jihāz at-taṣwīr photocopier 15. جهاز العرض jihāz al-'arḍ projector 16. جهاز الكشف عن الألغام jihāz al-kashf 'an al-alghām mine detector

جهة jiha (-āt) 1. side 2. direction 3. area 4. district 5. quarter 6. إلى جهة ilā jiha in the direction of; toward 7. من جهة min jiha from; on the part of 8. من جهة... ومن جهة أخرى min jiha... wa min jiha ukhrā on the one hand... on the other

جهد jahada (a; جهد jahd) 1. to try 2. to make an effort 3. to strain

جهد jahd; juhd (جهود juhūd) 1. effort 2. strain 3. لا جهد له lā juhd lah effortless

جهراً jahran publicly

جهّز jahhaza 1. to equip (ب bi with) 2. to furnish (ب bi with)

جهل jahl ignorance

جهنّم jahannam hell

جوّ jaww 1. air 2. atmosphere 3. weather

جواب jawāb (أجوبة ajwiba) answer; reply

جوار jiwār 1. بجوار bi jiwār in the vicinity of 2. في هذا الجوار fī hādhā 'l-jiwār hereabouts

جواز jawāz 1. authorization 2. passing 3. جواز سفر jawāz safar (-āt) passport

جواهر jawāhir pl jewellery

جودة jūda 1. goodness 2. متوسّط الجودة muta-wassiṭ al-jūda mediocre 3. جودة أكاديمية jūda akādīmīya scholarship

جورب jawrab (جوارب jawārib) sock

جوزة jawza (collective جوز jawz; pl -āt) 1. walnut 2. جوزة الهند jawzat al-hind coconut

جوع jū' 1. hunger 2. starvation

جوعان jaw'ān hungry (جياع jiyā')

جوقة jawqa (أجواق ajwāq) choir

جولة jawla (-āt) 1. tour 2. round of talks

جولف gōlf 1. golf 2. ملعب الجولف mal'ab al-gōlf golf course

جوهر jawhar (جواهر jawāhir) 1. essence 2. substance 3. core

جوهرة jawhara (جواهر jawāhir) jewel

جوهري jawharī (-yūn) 1. jeweller 2. essential

جوّي jawwī 1. air; aerial 2. atmospheric 3. weather 4. خطوط جوّية khuṭūṭ jawwīya airline; airways 5. بريد جوّي barīd jawwī airmail 6. بالبريد الجوّي bi 'l-barīd al-jawwī by airmail 7. منخفض جوّي munkhafaḍ jawwī turbulence

جيّداً jayyidan well

جير jīr lime

جيشتا وذهاباً jay'atan wa dhihāban to and fro جيئة jay'a:

جيش jaysh (جيوش juyūsh) army

جيب jīp: سيّارة جيب sayyārat jīp jeep

جيل jīl (أجيال ajyāl) generation

جيب jayb (جيوب juyūb) pocket

جيولوجيا zhiyolōzhiya geology

جيّد jayyid 1. good 2. fine; excellent 3. مزاج جيّد mizāj jayyid a good mood

جينز jīnz: بنطلون الجينز banṭalōn al-jīnz jeans

ح

حائر ḥā'ir 1. puzzling 2. uncertain

حادي عشر ḥādī 'ashar eleventh

حائط ḥā'iṭ (حيطان ḥīṭān) wall

حارّ ḥārr hot

حاجب ḥājib (حواجب ḥawājib) 1. eyebrow 2. brow

حارس ḥāris (حرّاس ḥurrās) 1. guard 2. حارس المرمى ḥāris al-marmā goalkeeper

حاجة ḥāja (-āt) 1. need 2. عند الحاجة 'inda 'l-ḥāja in case of need 3. سدّ حاجة sadda ḥāja to meet a need

حاسّة ḥāssa (حواسّ ḥawāss) sense

حاجز ḥājiz (حواجز ḥawājiz) 1. screen 2. barrier

حاسب ḥāsib 1. calculator 2. صندوق حاسب ṣundūq ḥāsib cash till; cash register

حاخام ḥākhām (-ūn) (rel.) rabbi

حاسد ḥāsid envious

حادّ ḥādd 1. sharp 2. acute 3. fierce 4. غير حادّ ghayr ḥādd blunt

حاسم ḥāsim 1. conclusive 2. غير حاسم ghayr ḥāsim inconclusive

حادث ḥādith (حوادث ḥawādith) 1. event; happening 2. incident 3. accident 4. episode

حاشد ḥāshid 1. mass 2. إجتماع حاشد ijtimā' ḥāshid mass meeting; rally

حادثة ḥāditha (حوادث ḥawādith) event; happening

حاصر ḥāṣara 1. to surround 2. to lay/set siege to

حاضر ḥāḍara to lecture

حاضر **ḥāḍir** 1. present 2. ready 3. الحاضر al-ḥāḍir the present

حافة **ḥāfa** (-āt; حواف ḥawāfin) 1. edge 2. border 3. rim 4. fringe 5. حافة الرصيف ḥāfat ar-raṣīf curb 6. حافة الطريق ḥāfat aṭ-ṭarīq road verge; road shoulder

حافز **ḥāfiz** (حوافز ḥawāfiz) motivation

حافظ **ḥāfaẓa** 1. to preserve 2. to protect (على ʿalā so/sth)

حافظ **ḥāfiẓ** (حفّاظ ḥuffāẓ) 1. keeper 2. warden

حافلة **ḥāfila** 1. coach 2. carriage

حاقد **ḥāqid** spiteful

حاك **ḥāka** (u; حياك ḥiyāk) to knit

حاكم **ḥākama** to prosecute

حاكم **ḥākim** 1. ruling 2. (-ūn; حكّام ḥukkām) ruler 3. governor 4. judge

حال **ḥāl** (أحوال aḥwāl) 1. state 2. condition 3. circumstance 4. adverb 5. في حاله fī ḥālih private 6. على كل حال ʿalā kull ḥāl; على أية حال ʿalā ayyati ḥāl anyway 7. كيف حالك؟ kayf al-ḥāl?; كيف حالك؟ kayf ḥālak? how are you?

حالاً **ḥālan** immediately

حالة **ḥāla** (-āt) 1. state 2. condition 3. case

حالما **ḥālamā** as soon as

حالي **ḥālī** 1. present; current 2. existing

حالياً **ḥālīyan** at present; presently

حام **ḥāmin** (حماة ḥumāh) protector

حامض **ḥāmiḍ** 1. acid 2. ليمون حامض laymūn ḥāmiḍ collective lime(s)

حامض **ḥāmiḍ** sour

حامل **ḥāmil** 1. pregnant 2. carrier 3. حاملة الطائرات ḥāmilat aṭ-ṭāʾirāt aircraft carrier

حانة **ḥāna** (-āt) bar; pub

حاول **ḥāwala** to try

حبّ **ḥabba** (i; حبّ ḥubb) 1. to love 2. to like

حبّ **ḥubb** 1. love 2. affection 3. قصّة حبّ qiṣṣat ḥubb romance 4. حبّ الإستطلاع ḥubb al-istiṭlāʿ curiosity 5. وقع في الحبّ waqaʿa fī 'l-ḥubb to fall in love (مع maʿa with)

حبّة **ḥabba** (collective حبّ ḥabb; pl حبوب ḥubūb) 1. grain 2. seed 3. tablet; 4. pill 5. (med.) boil 6. حبّة منوّمة ḥabba munawwima sleeping pill 7. حبّ منع الحمل ḥabb manʿ al-ḥaml contraceptive pill

حبر **ḥibr** ink

حبس **ḥabasa** (i; حبس ḥabs) 1. to confine 2. to imprison

حبط **ḥabaṭa** (u/i; حبوط ḥubūṭ) 1. to descend 2. to sink 3. to land

حبل **ḥabila** (i; حبل ḥabal) to conceive

حبل **ḥabl** (حبال ḥibāl) 1. rope 2. cord 3. line 4. حبل السير ḥabl as-sīr lead; leash

حبيب **ḥabīb** (أحبّا ʾ aḥibbāʾ; أحباب aḥbāb) 1. darling 2. sweetheart 3. beloved

حتّى **ḥattā** 1. until 2. as far as; up to 3. so (that); in order to 4. حتّى الآن ḥattā 'l-ān still 5. حتّى لو ḥattā law even if 6. وما أن/إن... حتّى wa mā an/in... ḥattā no sooner... than

حتماً ḥatman without fail

حث ḥaththa (u; حث ḥathth) 1. to urge (ه so; على 'alā to) 2. to prompt

حجّة ḥujja (حجج ḥujaj) argument

حجاب ḥijāb (أحجبة aḥjiba; حجب ḥujub) 1. veil 2. seclusion

حجب ḥajaba (u; حجب ḥajb) to shield

حجر ḥajar (أحجار aḥjār; حجارة ḥijāra) stone

حجرة ḥujra (حجرات ḥujarāt; حجر ḥujar) 1. room 2. compartment 3. chamber 4. حجرة الطعام ḥujrat aṭ-ṭaʿām dining room 5. حجرة الجلوس ḥujrat al-julūs lounge 6. حجرة النوم ḥujrat an-nawm bedroom 7. حجرة لحفظ الطعام ḥujra li ḥifẓ aṭ-ṭaʿām larder 8. حجرة الدراسة ḥujrat ad-dirāsa classroom 9. حجرة للتمرينات الرياضية ḥujra li 't-tamrīnāt ar-riyāḍīya gym; gymnasium

حجري ḥajarī stony

حجز ḥajaza (u/i; حجز ḥajz) 1. to reserve 2. to book

حجز ḥajz 1. reservation 2. booking

حجم ḥajm (أحجام aḥjām) 1. size 2. dimension 3. volume 4. bulk 5. متوسط الحجم mutawassiṭ al-ḥajm medium-sized

حدّ ḥadda (u; حدّ ḥadd) 1. to mark off 2. to limit

حدّ ḥadd (حدود ḥudūd) 1. edge 2. boundary 3. frontier; border 4. extent; degree 5. limit 6. حدّ عمري ḥadd 'umarī age limit 7. الحدّ المسموح به للسرعة al-ḥadd

al-masmūḥ bih li 's-surʿa speeding 8. حدّ النسل ḥadd an-nasl birth control 9. الحدّ من الأسلحة al-ḥadd min al-asliḥa arms control 10. الحدّ الأدنى al-ḥadd al-adnā minimum 11. الحدّ الأقصى al-ḥadd al-aqṣā maximum 12. لا حدّ له lā ḥadd lah limitless 13. إلى هذا الحدّ ilā hādhā 'l-ḥadd so 14. لحدّ ما li ḥaddin mā; إلى حدّ ما ilā ḥaddin mā rather; quite

حدّة ḥidda 1. sharpness 2. fierceness 3. anger

حداد ḥidād mourning

حدث ḥadatha (u; حدوث ḥudūth) to happen; to take place

حدّث ḥaddatha to modernize

حدث ḥadath (أحداث aḥdāth) 1. event; happening 2. novelty 3. youth

حدّد ḥaddada 1. to limit 2. to fix 3. to define 3. to sharpen 4. حدّد مواعيداً ḥaddada mawāʿīd to schedule

حدّق ḥaddaqa to gaze; to stare (في/إلى ilā/ fī at)

حديث ḥadīth 1. recent 2. modern 3. up-to-date; new 4. talk 5. conversation 6. narrative

حديثاً ḥadīthan recently

حديد ḥadīd 1. iron 2. خطّ سكّة الحديد khaṭṭ sikkat al-ḥadīd railtrack

حديدة اللجام ḥadīdat al-lijām ḥadīda bridle bit

حديدي ḥadīdī 1. iron 2. السكّة الحديدية as-sikka al-ḥadīdīya railway

حديقة **ḥadīqa** (حدائق ḥadā'iq) 1. garden park 2. حديقة الحيوانات ḥadīqat al-ḥayawānāt zoo

حذاء **ḥidhā'** (أحذية aḥdhiya) shoe(s)

حذر **ḥadhira** (a; حذر ḥidhr/ḥadhar) 1. to be cautious 2. to beware

حذّر **ḥadhdhara** to warn

حذر **ḥadhar** 1. caution 2. على حذر ‘alā ḥadhar on one's guard

حذر **ḥadhir** 1. careful 2. cautious 3. discreet

حذف **ḥadhafa** (i; حذف ḥadhf) 1. to omit 2. to delete 3. *(ec.)* to cut

حذف **ḥadhf** omission

حرّ **ḥurr** (أحرار aḥrār) 1. free 2. *(pol.)* liberal 3. عامل حرّ ‘āmil ḥurr freelance; freelancer

حرارة **ḥarāra** 1. heat 2. درجة الحرارة darajat al-ḥarāra temperature 3. ميزان الحرارة mīzān al-ḥarāra thermometer

حرب **ḥarb** *f* (حروب ḥurūb) 1. war 2. زمن الحرب zaman al-ḥarb wartime 3. أعلن الحرب a‘lana al-ḥarb to declare war 4. الحرب الباردة al-ḥarb al-bārida the Cold War 5. حرب أهلية ḥarb ahlīya civil war 6. حرب صليبية ḥarb ṣalībīya crusade 7. أسير الحرب asīr al-ḥarb (أسرى asrā) prisoner of war (POW) 8. جرائم حرب jarā'im ḥarb war crime 9. ارتكب جرائم حرب irtakaba jarā'im ḥarb to commit a war crime 10. مرتكب جرائم حرب murtakib jarā'im ḥarb (-ūn) war criminal

حربي **ḥarbī** war

حربية **ḥarbīya** 1. وزير الحربية wazīr al-ḥarbīya war minister 2. وزارة الحربية wizārat al-ḥarbīya war ministry

حرث **ḥaratha** (i/u; حرث ḥarth) to plough

حرج **ḥarij** awkward

حرّر **ḥarrara** 1. to free 2. to edit

حرس **ḥaras** 1. guard 2. bodyguard

حرس **ḥarasa** (u; حراسة ḥirāsa) to guard

حرشف **ḥarshaf** (حراشف ḥarāshif) fish scale(s)

حرّض **ḥarraḍa** 1. to stir up 2. to incite

حرف **ḥarf** (حروف ḥurūf) 1. letter 2. حرف ساكن ḥarf sākin consonant 3. حرف جرّ ḥarf jarr preposition

حرفة **ḥirfa** (حرف ḥiraf) 1. craft 2. trade 3. صاحب الحرفة ṣāḥib al-ḥirfa craftsman

حرفياً **ḥarfiyan** literally

حرّق **ḥarraqa** to burn

حرق **ḥarq** burn

حرّك **ḥarraka** 1. to move 2. to stir

حركة **ḥaraka** (-āt) 1. movement 2. motion 3. vowel 4. قابل للحركة qābil li 'l-ḥaraka mobile 5. قابلية للحركة qābilīya li 'l-ḥaraka mobility

حرم **ḥarama** (i; حرم ḥirm; حرمان ḥirmān) to deprive (من min of)

حرّم **ḥarrama** 1. to prohibit 2. حرّم من الأهلية ḥarrama min al-ahlīya to disqualify

حروف **ḥurūf** *pl* 1. print 2. الحروف المائلة al-ḥurūf al-mā'ila italics

حُرِّية ḥurrīya (-āt) 1. freedom 2. حرِّية التعبير ḥurrīyat at-ta'bīr freedom of speech 3. حرِّية الصحافة ḥurrīyat aṣ-ṣaḥāfa freedom of the press

حرير ḥarīr silk

حريق ḥarīq (حرائق ḥarā'iq) 1. fire 2. bonfire 3. blaze 4. جرس الإنذار بالحريق jaras al-indhār bi 'l-ḥarīq fire alarm 5. سلم الحريق sullam al-ḥarīq fire escape; fire exit

حزام ḥizām (-āt; أحزمة aḥzima) 1. belt 2. حزام الأمان ḥizām al-amān seatbelt 3. lifebelt

حزب ḥizb (أحزاب aḥzāb) (pol.) 1. party 2. حزب معارض ḥizb mu'āriḍ opposition party 3. حزب العمّال ḥizb al-'ummāl Labour Party 4. حزب الأحرار ḥizb al-aḥrār Liberal party 5. حزب المحافظين ḥizb al-muḥāfiẓīn Conservative party

حزم ḥazama (i; حزم ḥazm) to pack

حزّن ḥazzana to sadden

حزن ḥuzn (أحزان aḥzān) sadness

حزيران ḥazīrān June

حزيرة ḥazīra (حزائر ḥazā'ir) shed

حزين ḥazīn 1. sad 2. sorry

حسّ ḥassa (u; حسّ ḥass) to feel

حسّ ḥiss feeling

حساء ḥasā' soup

حساب ḥisāb (-āt) (fin.) 1. bill 2. calculation 3. account 4. علم الحساب 'ilm al-ḥisāb arithmetic 5. كشف الحساب kashf al-ḥisāb bank statement

حسّاس ḥassās 1. sensitive 2. غير حسّاس ghayr ḥassās insensitive

حسّاسي ḥassāsī allergic

حسّاسية ḥassāsīya 1. sensitivity 2. allergy

حسب ḥasaba (u; حسب ḥasb; حساب ḥisāb; حسبان hisbān/ḥusbān) 1. to reckon 2. to calculate

حسبان ḥusbān calculation

حسد ḥasada (u; حسد ḥasad) to envy

حسد ḥasad envy

حسم ḥasm 1. deduction 2. discount

حسم ḥasama (i; حسم ḥasm) to make up one's mind

حسّن ḥassana to improve

حسن ḥasan 1. good 2. nice 3. good-looking

حسن ḥusn 1. excellence 2. beauty 3. حسن النية ḥusn an-nīya goodwill 4. حسن الضيافة ḥusn aḍ-ḍiyāfa hospitality 5. لحسن الحظّ li ḥusn al-ḥaẓẓ fortunately

حسناً ḥasanan well; good; all right

حسود ḥasūd envious

حسير ḥasīr 1. tired 2. حسير البصر ḥasīr al-baṣar short-sighted

حشا ḥashā (u; حشو ḥashw) to stuff

حشد ḥashd (حشود ḥushūd) 1. crowd 2. horde

حشرة ḥashara (-āt) 1. insect 2. عضّة حشرة 'aḍḍat ḥashara insect bite

حشيش ḥashīsh (حشائش ḥashā'ish) 1. grass 2. herbs 3. marijuana

حصّة ḥiṣṣa (حصص ḥiṣaṣ) 1. share 2. portion 3. quota 4. *(ed.)* period 5. حصّة تموين ḥiṣṣat tamwīn ration

حصاد ḥaṣād harvest

حصار ḥiṣār 1. blockade 2. embargo 3. siege 4. أفرض حصاراً على afraḍa ḥiṣāran 'alā to lay/set siege to

حصان ḥiṣān (أحصنة aḥṣina) 1. horse 2. حصان السباق ḥiṣān as-sibāq race horse 3. راكب الحصان rākib al-ḥiṣān on horseback

حصاني ḥiṣānī 1. equine 2. قدرة حصانية qudra ḥiṣānīya horsepower

حصد ḥaṣada (i; حصاد ḥaṣād) to harvest

حصل ḥaṣala (u; حصول ḥuṣūl) 1. to happen (ل li to) 2. to get; to obtain (على 'alā *sth*)

حصن ḥiṣn (حصون ḥuṣūn) fort

حصير ḥaṣīr (حصر ḥuṣur) mat

حضارة ḥaḍāra (-āt) civilisation

حضانة ḥiḍāna (-āt) 1. nursery 2. دار الحضانة dār al-ḥiḍāna kindergarten

حضر ḥaḍara (u; حضور ḥuḍūr) 1. to be present (إلى\ه ilā at) 2. to attend (إلى\ه ilā *sth*)

حضن ḥaḍana (u; حضن ḥaḍn; حضانة ḥaḍāna) to hug

حضن ḥiḍn (أحضان aḥḍān) lap

حضور ḥuḍūr 1. presence 2. attendance

حطب ḥaṭab firewood

حطّم ḥaṭṭama 1. to smash 2. قياسياً رقماً ḥaṭṭama raqman qiyāsīyan to break a record

حظّ ḥaẓẓ 1. luck; fortune 2. chance 3. سوء الحظّ sū' al-ḥaẓẓ misfortune 4. لحسن الحظّ li ḥusn al-ḥaẓẓ luckily

حظر ḥaẓara (u; حظر ḥaẓr) to outlaw

حظّر ḥaẓẓara to prohibit

حظيرة ḥaẓīra: حظيرة الطائرات ḥaẓīrat aṭ-ṭā'irāt hangar

حفاظ ḥifāẓ; حفاظة ḥifāẓa: حفاظ الطفل ḥifāẓ aṭ-ṭifl; حفاظة الأطفال ḥifāẓat al-aṭfāl nappy

حفر ḥafara (i; حفر ḥafr) to dig

حفرة ḥufra (حفر ḥufar) pit

حفظ ḥafiẓa (a; حفظ ḥifẓ) 1. to keep 2. to preserve 3. to memorize 4. *(comp.)* to save

حفظ ḥifẓ conservation

حفلة ḥafla (-āt) 1. party 2. festivity; festival 3. حفلة موسيقية ḥafla mūsiqīya concert

حفيد ḥafīd (أحفاد aḥfād) 1. grandson 2. grandchild

حفيدة ḥafīda (-āt) granddaughter

حقّ ḥaqq (حقوق ḥuqūq) 1. right 2. truth 3. duty 4. حقّ المؤلف ḥaqq al-mu'allif; 5. حقّ الناشر ḥaqq an-nāshir copyright 5. حقّ التصويت ḥaqq at-taṣwīt franchise 6. حقّ النقض ḥaqq an-naqḍ veto 7. استعمل حقّ النقض ist'amala ḥaqq an-naqḍ to veto 8. *and see* حقوق

حقّ **ḥuqq** socket

حقّاً **ḥaqqan** really

حقائب **ḥaqā'ib** *pl* baggage; luggage

حقبة **ḥiqba** (حقب **ḥiqab**) period; long time

حقد **ḥiqd** (أحقاد **aḥqād**) 1. spite 2. malice

حقّق **ḥaqqaqa** 1. to realize; to make come true 2. to investigate

حقل **ḥaql** (حقول **ḥuqūl**) 1. field 2. حقل نفط **ḥaql nafṭ** oilfield 3. حقل الألغام **ḥaql al-alghām** minefield

حقن **ḥaqana** (i; حقن **ḥaqn**) 1. to pierce 2. to inject

حقنة **ḥuqna** (حقن **ḥuqan**) injection

حقود **ḥaqūd** venomous

حقوق **ḥuqūq** *pl* 1. rights 2. الحقوق المدنية **ḥuqūq al-ḥuqūq al-madanīya** civil rights 3. حقوق الإنسان **ḥuqūq al-insān** human rights 4. *and see* حقّ

حقيبة **ḥaqība** (حقائب **ḥaqā'ib**) 1. bag 2. suitcase 3. حقيبة اليد **ḥaqībat al-yad** briefcase 4. فرّغ الحقيبة **farragha al-ḥaqība** to unpack

حقير **ḥaqīr** mean

حقيقة **ḥaqīqa** (حقائق **ḥaqā'iq**) 1. truth 2. fact

حقيقةً **ḥaqīqatan** truly

حقيقي **ḥaqīqī** 1. right 2. true 3. real 4. authentic

حكّ **ḥakka** (u; حكّ **ḥakk**) to rub

حكى **ḥakā** (i; حكاية **ḥikāya**) 1. to tell 2. to narrate

حكاية **ḥikāya** (-āt) story

حكم **ḥakam** (حكّام **ḥukkām**) 1. referee; umpire 2. arbitrator

حكم **ḥakama** (u; حكم **ḥukm**) 1. to rule 2. to govern 3. *(leg.)* to sentence 4. حكم على **ḥakama 'alā** to judge

حكم **ḥukm** (أحكام **aḥkām**) 1. rule 2. government 3. judgement 4. *(leg.)* sentence 5. الحكم الذاتي **al-ḥukm adh-dhāti** autonomy; self-government 6. خلع عن الحكم **khala'a 'an al-ḥukm** (a; خلع **khal'**) to depose 7. أرجأ تنفيذ حكم **arja'a tanfīdh ḥukm** *(leg.)* suspend 8. إرجاء تنفيذ حكم **irjā' tanfīdh ḥukm** *(leg.)* suspension 9. حكم سبقي **ḥukm sabaqī** prejudice 10. حكم الإعدام **ḥukm al-i'dām** death sentence 11. أرجأ تنفيذ حكم بالإعدام **arja'a tanfīdh ḥukm bi 'l-i'dām** *(leg.)* to reprieve

حكمة **ḥikma** wisdom

حكومة **ḥukūma** (-āt) government

حكومي **ḥukūmī** 1. state; public; civil 2. governmental 3. موظف حكومي **muwaẓẓaf ḥukūmī** civil servant 4. الروتين الحكومي **al-rūtīn al-ḥukūmī** red tape 5. الإدارة الحكومية **al-idāra al-ḥukūmīya** civil service

حكيم **ḥakīm** wise

حلّ **ḥalla** (u; حلّ **ḥall**) 1. to work out; to solve 2. to dissolve 3. to settle (ب **bi** at/in) 4. to stay (ب **bi** at/in; على **'alā** with) 5. to untie 6. to undo 7. حلّ محل شخص **ḥalla maḥall shakhṣ** to relieve someone 8. حلّ مشكلة ḥalla mushkila to solve a problem

حلّ ḥall (حلول ḥulūl) 1. solution 2. resolution 3. *(leg.)* settlement

حلّاق ḥallāq (-ūn) 1. barber 2. hairdresser

حلاقة ḥilāqa 1. shaving 2. شفرة الحلاقة shafrat al-ḥilāqa razor-blade

حلاوة ḥalāwa sweetness

حلبة ḥalba (حلبات ḥalabāt) *(spor.)* track

حلزون ḥalazūn collective snail

حلف ḥallafa to swear

حلف ḥilf (أحلاف aḥlāf) 1. alliance 2. pact

حلق ḥalaq earrings

حلق ḥalaqa (i; حلق ḥalq) to shave

حلقة ḥalaqa (-āt) 1. link 2. loop 3. episode 4. instalment

حلّل ḥallala 1. to dissolve 2. to analyse

حلم ḥalama (u; حلم ḥulm) to dream (ب bi/ عن ʿan of; في أن fī an of being)

حلم ḥulm (أحلام aḥlām) dream

حلمة ḥalama (-āt) nipple

حلو ḥulw 1. sweet 2. nice 3. pretty

حلوى ḥalwā (حلاوى ḥalāwā) sweet(s)

حلويات ḥalwayāt pl 1. sweets 2. dessert

حليب ḥalīb milk

حليف ḥalīf (حلفا ḥulafāʾ) ally

حليم ḥalīm mild

حم ḥam (أحماء aḥmāʾ) father-in-law

حمى ḥamā (i; حماية ḥimāya) to protect

حمّى ḥummā (حمّيات ḥummayāt) fever

حماة ḥamāh (حموات ḥamawāt) mother-in-law

حمار ḥimār (حمير ḥamīr) donkey

حماس ḥamās 1. enthusiasm 2. fanaticism

حماقة ḥamāqa stupidity

حمّال ḥammāl (-ūn) porter

حمّام ḥammām (-āt) 1. bath 2. bathroom 3. lavatory 4. حمّام سباحة ḥammām sibāḥa swimming pool 5. أخذ حمّام شمس akhadha ḥammām shams (u; أخذ akhdh) to sunbathe

حمامة ḥamāma (collective حمام ḥamām) pigeon

حماية ḥimāya 1. protection 2. defence

حمرا ḥamrāʾ; حمر ḥumr see أحمر

حمرة ḥumra redness

حمّص ḥammaṣa to toast

حمّص ḥummuṣ chickpeas

حمض ḥamuḍa (u; حموضة ḥumūḍa) to be sour

حمض ḥamḍ (أحماض aḥmāḍ) acid

حمل ḥamala (i; حمل ḥaml) 1. to carry 2. to conceive 3. to win over (على ʿalā; ه so to) 4. حمل على ḥamala ʿalā to attack

حمّل ḥammala 1. to load 2. to download 3. to impose 4. حمّل بإفراط ḥammala bi ifrāṭ to overload

حمل ḥaml 1. carrying 2. pregnancy 3. قابل للحمل qābil li 'l-ḥaml portable 4. حبّ منع الحمل ḥabb manʿ al-ḥaml contraceptive pill 5. منع الحمل manʿ

مانع الحمل al-ḥamal contraception **6.** mānić al-ḥamal contraceptive **7.** وسيلة منع الحمل wasīlat manć al-ḥamal contraceptive; contraception

حملة ḥamla **1.** campaign **2.** crusade **3.** اشترك في حملة ishtaraka fī ḥamla to campaign

حمم ḥumam: حمم البركان ḥumam al-burkān lava

حمولة ḥumūla cargo

حمية ḥimya diet

حنان ḥanān affection; tenderness

حنجرة ḥanjara (حناجر ḥanājir) throat

حنفية ḥanafīya (-āt) tap; faucet

حنو ḥinw (أحناء aḥnā') bend

حنون ḥanūn loving; tender

حنين ḥanīn: الحنين إلى الماضي al-ḥanīn ilā 'l-māḍī nostalgia

حوار ḥiwār dialogue

حوالى ḥawālā about; some

حوت ḥūt whale

حوض ḥawḍ (أحواض aḥwāḍ; حياض ḥiyāḍ) **1.** sink **2.** trough **3.** cistern; tank **4.** حوض السفن ḥawḍ as-sufun dock, docks

حول ḥawl around

حوّل ḥawwala **1.** to change **2.** to divert **3.** (fin.) to convert **4.** حوّل إلى ḥawwala ilā to turn into

حيّ ḥayya (يحيا yaḥyā; حياة ḥayāh) **1.** to live **2.** see حيي

حيّ ḥayy **1.** alive **2.** animate **3.** (أحياء aḥyā') neighbourhood **4.** quarter **5.** كائن حيّ kā'in ḥayy (-āt) organism **6.** بثّ حيّ bathth ḥayy live broadcast **7.** حيّ الفقراء ḥayy al-fuqarā' slum

حيّا ḥayyā **1.** to greet **2.** to salute

حيّاً ḥayyan **1.** live **2.** بقي حيّاً baqiya ḥayyan (a; بقاء baqā') to survive

حياء ḥayā' **1.** shame **2.** بلا حياء bi lā ḥayā' shameless

حياة ḥayāh **1.** life **2.** مدى الحياة mada 'l-ḥayāh lifetime **3.** أسلوب الحياة uslūb al-ḥayāh lifestyle **4.** تأمين على الحياة ta'mīn ćalā 'l-ḥayāh life insurance **5.** علم الحياة ćilm al-ḥayāh biology

حيادي ḥiyādī neutral

حياض ḥiyāḍ menstruation

حيّة ḥayya (-āt) snake

حيث ḥayth **1.** where **2.** since; as **3.** من حيث min ḥayth with regard to **4.** حيث أنّ ḥayth anna due to the fact that **5.** حيث كان ḥayth kān whereas **6.** من حيث المبدأ min ḥayth al-mabda' as a matter of principle

حيّر ḥayyara to puzzle

حيران ḥayrān (حيارى ḥayārā) confused

حيطان ḥīṭān: ورق الحيطان waraq al-ḥīṭān wallpaper

حيلة ḥīla (حيل ḥiyal) **1.** trick **2.** deceit

حين ḥīn **1.** (أحيان aḥyān) time **2.** when **3.** في ذلك الحين ḥīnadhāk then **4.** في ذلك الحين fī dhālik al-ḥīn already **5.** أحياناً aḥyānan; في بعض الأحيان fī baćḍ al-aḥyān sometimes **6.** في كثير من الأحيان

fī kathīr min al-aḥyān often 7. بين حين وحين ;bayna ḥīn wa ḥīn بين الحين والحين bayna 'l-ḥīn wa 'l-ḥīn from time to time 8. ;ʻalā ḥīn على حين fī ḥīn whereas في حين

حينئذ ḥīna'idhin at that time

حيوان ḥayawān (-āt) 1. animal 2. حيوان فقري ḥayawān fiqrī vertebrate 3.

حيوانات صدفية ḥayawānāt ṣadafīya shellfish 4. حديقة الحيوانات ḥadīqat al-ḥayawānāt ZOO

حيوي ḥayawī 1. vital 2. active 3. مضاد حيوي muḍādd ḥayawī antibiotics

حيوية ḥayawīya vitality

حيي ḥayiya (يحيى yaḥyā; حياء ، ḥayā') 1. to be shy 2. see حي

خ

خائب khā'ib 1. unsuccessful 2. خائب الأمل khā'ib al-amal disappointed

خائف khā'if afraid

خائن khā'in (خونة khawana) traitor

خاتم khātim (خواتم khawātim) ring

خادع khāda'a to fool

خادم khādim (خدّام khuddām; خدمة khadama) servant; domestic

خارج khārij 1. outside; exterior 2. الخارج fī 'l-khārij outside; outdoors 3. abroad 4. نحو الخارج naḥw al-khārij outwards 5. خارج البلد khārij al-balad abroad 6. خارج نطاق الرقابة khārij niṭāq ar-raqāba offshore

خارجي khārijī 1. exterior 2. external 3. outdoor 4. outer 5. الفضاء الخارجي al-faḍā' al-khārijī outer space

خارجية khārijīya 1. وزير الخارجية wazīr al-khārijīya foreign minister 2. وزارة الخارجية wizārat al-khārijīya foreign ministry

خارق khāriq 1. unusual 2. للعادة khāriq li 'l-'āda extraordinary 3. خارق الطبيعة khāriq aṭ-ṭabī'a supernatural

خاسر khāsir loser

خاص khāṣṣ 1. special 2. particular 3. exclusive 4. relevant (ب bi to) 5. private 6. محقّق خاصّ muḥaqqiq khāṣṣ private detective; private investigator 7. قوة خاصّة qūwa khāṣṣa task force

خاصّة khāṣṣatan 1. especially 2. وأنّ khāṣṣatan wa anna especially as/when

خاض **khāḍa** (u; خوض khawḍ) 1. to wade 2. to plunge

خاطئ **khāṭi'** wrong

خاطب **khāṭaba** to address; to speak to

خاطب **khāṭib** fiancé

خاطر **khāṭara** to risk

خاطف **khāṭif** 1. momentary 2. (-ūn) kidnapper 3. hijacker 4. لحظة خاطفة laḥẓa khāṭifa flash

خاف **khāfa** (a; خوف khawf) to fear

خال **khālin** 1. empty 2. bare 3. vacant 4. blank 5. خال من الفوائد **khālin min al-fawā'id** (fin.) interest-free

خال **khāl** 1. uncle 2. إبن خال **ibn khāl** male cousin 3. بنت خال **bint khāl** female cousin

خالة **khāla** 1. aunt 2. إبن خالة **ibn khāla** male cousin 3. بنت خالة **bint khāla** female cousin

خالد **khālid** 1. eternal 2. immortal

خالص **khāliṣ** pure

خالف **khālafa** to disagree

خالق **khāliq** creator

خام **khām** 1. crude 2. مواد خام **mawādd khām** raw materials

خامس **khāmis** fifth

خامس عشر **khāmis 'ashar** fifteenth

خان **khāna** (u; خيانة khiyāna) to betray

خان **khān** (-āt) inn

خباز **khabbāz** (-ūn) baker

خبر **khabar** (أخبار akhbār) news; news item

خبراء **khubarā'** pl 1. مؤتمر خبراء **mu'tamar khubarā'** seminar 2. and see خبير

خبرة **khibra** 1. experience 2. expertise

خبز **khabaza** (i; خبز khabz) to bake

خبز **khubz** 1. bread 2. خبز محمّص **khubz muḥammaṣ** toast

خبيث **khabīth** malignant

خبير **khabīr** (خبراء khubarā') 1. expert 2. consultant 3. and see خبراء

ختام **khitām** conclusion

ختم **khatama** (i; ختم khatm) 1. to stamp 2. to seal 3. to complete 4. to terminate

ختم **khatm** (أختام akhtām; ختام khitām) 1. stamp 2. seal 3. ختم مطاطي **khatm maṭṭāṭī** rubber stamp

خجّل **khajjala** 1. to shame 2. to embarrass

خجل **khajl** 1. shame 2. embarrassment

خجل **khajil** 1. ashamed 2. embarrassed

خجلان **khajlān** 1. ashamed 2. embarrassed

خجول **khajūl** 1. shy 2. timid

خدّ **khadd** (خدود khudūd) cheek

خدّام **khaddām** (-ūn) domestic; servant

خدر **khadir** numb

خدع **khada'a** (a; خدعة khud'a) 1. to deceive 2. to trick 3. to cheat 4. to hoax 5. to betray

خدعة **khud'a** (-āt; خدع khuda') 1. deception 2. trick 3. cheating 4. hoax 5. betrayal

خدم **khadama** (i/u; خدمة khidma) to serve

خدمة **khidma** (خدمات khidmāt/khadamāt) 1. employment 2. service 3. favour 4. خدمات إجتماعية **khidmāt ijtimā'īya** welfare

خذل **khadhala** (u; خذل khadhl) to let down

خراب **kharāb** ruin; ruins

خرافة **khurāfa** (-āt) superstition

خرافي **khurāfī** 1. fabulous 2. superstitious

خرّب **kharraba** 1. to ruin 2. to wreck 3. to sabotage

خربش **kharbasha** to scratch

خرج **kharaja** (u; خروج khurūj) 1. to go out; to come out (من min of) 2. to leave; exit (من min from) 3. to get out (من min of) 4. خرج ب **kharaja bi** to take out

خرز **kharaz** *collective* beads

خرطوم **khurṭūm** (خراطيم kharāṭīm) 1. hose 2. trunk

خرفان **kharfān**; خرف **kharif** senile

خرق **kharaqa** (i/u; خرق kharq) 1. to tear 2. to breach 3. to pierce

خرق **kharq** (خروق khurūq) 1. tear 2. breach 3. hole

خروف **kharūf** (خرفان khirfān) lamb

خريطة **kharīṭa** (خرائط kharā'iṭ) 1. map 2. chart

خريف **kharīf** autumn

خزّان **khazzān** (-āt; خزازين khazāzīn) 1. tank 2. خزان البنزين **khazzān al-banzīn** gas tank

خزانة **khizāna** (خزائن khazā'in) 1. cupboard 2. wardrobe 3. treasury 4. safe 5. خزانة للملابس **khizāna li 'l-malābis** wardrobe

خزفي **khazafī** ceramic

خزن **khazana** (u; خزن khazn) to store

خزن **khazn** storage

خسائر **khasā'ir** *pl (mil./fin.)* losses

خسارة **khasāra** (خسائر khasā'ir) 1. loss 2. يا خسارة! **yā khasāra** what a pity!

خسر **khasira** (a; خسر khasr) to lose

خسيس **khasīs** squalid

خشب **khashab** (أخشاب akhshāb) 1. wood 2. timber 3. log 4. لوح خشب **lawḥ khashab** board

خشبة **khashaba** piece of wood

خشبي **khashabī** wooden

خشخش **khashkhasha** to rattle

خشن **khashin** crude; rough

خشية **khashya** awe

خصّب **khaṣṣaba** to fertilize

خصب **khiṣb** fertility

خصر **khaṣr** (خصور khuṣūr) waist

خصم **khaṣm** (خصوم khuṣūm) 1. discount 2. opponent

خصوصاً **khuṣūṣan** especially; in particular

خصوصي **khuṣūṣī** 1. special 2. particular 3. private

خصومة **khuṣūma** feud

خصيب khaṣīb fertile

خصّيصاً khiṣṣīṣan expressly

خضر khuḍr see أخضر

خضر khuḍar pl vegetables

خضراء khaḍrā see أخضر

خضرة khuḍra 1. vegetation 2. green; greenness

خضروات khaḍrawāt pl greens

خضع khaḍa'a (a; خضوع khuḍū') 1. to submit 2. لـ khaḍa'a li to undergo

خضوع khaḍū' submissive

خطّ khaṭṭ (خطوط khuṭūṭ) 1. line 2. خطّ تلفوني khaṭṭ tilifūnī telephone line 3. خطّ سكّة الحديد khaṭṭ sikkat al-ḥadīd railtrack 4. خطّ الرحلة khaṭṭ ar-riḥla itinerary 5. خطّ كفافي khaṭṭ kifāfī outline 6. خطّ عمودي khaṭṭ 'amūdī vertical 7. خطّ أنابيب khaṭṭ anābīb pipeline 8. رسم خطّاً تحت rasima khaṭṭan taḥta (a) to underline 9. خطّ الطول khaṭṭ aṭ-ṭūl longitude 10. خطّ العرض khaṭṭ al-'arḍ latitude 11. خطّ الإستواء khaṭṭ al-istiwā' equator 12. and see خطوط

خطّة khuṭṭa; khiṭṭa (خطط khiṭaṭ) plan; project

خطا khaṭā (u; خطو khaṭw) 1. to step 2. to pace

خطأ khaṭa' (أخطاء akhṭā') 1. mistake 2. خطأ مطبعي khaṭa' maṭba'ī misprint

خطأً khaṭa'an by mistake

خطاب khiṭāb (أخطبة akhṭiba) speech 2. letter 3. ألقى خطاباً alqā khiṭāban to make a speech

خطبة khuṭba (خطب khuṭab) speech

خطبة khiṭba engagement

خطر khaṭar (أخطار akhṭār) 1. danger 2. risk 3. إنذار بخطر indhār bi khaṭar alarm 4. عرّض للخطر 'arraḍa li 'l-khaṭar to endanger; to jeopardize

خطر khaṭir 1. dangerous 2. risky 3. serious 4. (med.) critical

خطّط khaṭṭaṭa to plan

خطف khaṭafa (i; خطف khaṭf) 1. to kidnap 2. to hijack 3. to grab

خطف khaṭf 1. kidnapping 2. hijacking

خطوة khaṭwa/khuṭwa (خطوات khaṭawāt; خطىً khuṭan) 1. step 2. pace 3. move 4. خطوة فخطوة khaṭwa fa khaṭwa step by step 5. خطوة إلى الأمام khaṭwa ilā 'l-amām a step forward

خطورة khuṭūra seriousness

خطوط khuṭūṭ pl 1. خطوط جوية khuṭūṭ jawwīya; خطوط الطيران khuṭūṭ aṭ-ṭayarān airline, airways 2. and see خطّ

خطيئة khaṭī'a (خطايا khaṭāyā) sin

خطير khaṭir 1. dangerous 2. serious 3. major 4. (med.) critical 5. غير خطير ghayr khaṭir minor

خفّاش khuffāsh (خفافيس khafāfish) bat

خفّة khiffa lightness

خفض khafaḍa (i; خفض khafḍ) to lower

خفّض khaffaḍa 1. to reduce 2. خفّض تخفيضاً كبيراً khaffaḍa takhfīḍan kabīran (fin.) to slash

خفق khafaq (i/u; خفق khafq) to beat

خفي khafī 1. invisible 2. دافع خفي dāfiʿ khafī (دوافع خفية dawāfiʿ khafīya) ulterior motive

خفيف khafīf 1. light 2. وجبة خفيفة wajba khafīfa snack 3. خفيف الدم khafīf ad-dam pleasant

خلّ khall vinegar

خلاء khalāʾ vacancy

خلاص khalāṣ salvation

خلّاط khallāṭ (-āt) mixer

خلاف khilāf 1. disagreement 2. difference 3. على خلاف ʿalā khilāf unlike

خلافاً ل khilāfan li contrary to

خلافة khilāfa succession

خلال khilāl 1. during 2. across 3. من خلال min khilāl through 4. on the basis of

خلّص khallaṣa to rid

خلط khalaṭa (i; خلط khalṭ) to mix

خلع khalaʿa (a; خلع khalʿ) 1. to remove 2. خلع عن الحكم khalaʿa ʿan al-ḥukm to depose

خلف khalafa (u; خلافة khilāfa) to succeed

خلف khalf behind

خلفي khalfī rear

خلفية khalfiya background

خلق khalaqa (u; خلق khalq) to create

خلق khalq creation

خلق khuluq (أخلاق akhlāq) character

خلل khalal (خلال khilāl) defect

خلود khulūd eternity

خلية khalīya (خلايا khalāyā) 1. cell 2. honeycomb 3. beehive

خليج khalīj (خلج khuluj) 1. bay 2. gulf

خليط khalīṭ 1. mixture 2. mixed 3. خليط من معدنين khalīṭ min maʿdanayn alloy

خليفة khalīfa (خلفا khulafāʾ) successor

خمد khamada (u; خمود khumūd) 1. to die down 2. خمدت النار khamadat an-nār The fire's gone out.

خمر khamr (خمور khumūr) wine

خمس khums (أخماس akhmās) fifth

خمسة khamsa five

خمسة عشر khamsata ʿashar fifteen

خمسون khamsūn 1. fifty 2. مخفّض بخمسين بالمئة mukhaffaḍ bi khamsīn bi 'l-miʾa half-price

خمّن khammana to guess

يوم الخميس yawm al-khamīs; الخميس al-khamīs; al-khamīs Thursday

خنجر khanjar (خناجر khanājir) dagger

خندق khandaq (خنادق khanādiq) ditch

خنزير khinzīr (خنازير khanāzīr) pig

خنق khanaqa (u; خنق khanq) 1. to strangle 2. to suffocate

خنوع khanūʿ meek

خوخة khawkha (collective خوخ khawkh) peach

خوذة khūdha (-āt) helmet

خوف khawf fear (من min of)

خيار khiyār 1. (-āt) choice 2. *collective* cucumber

خياري khiyārī optional

خيّاط khayyāṭ (-ūn) tailor

خياطة khiyāṭa 1. sewing 2. آلة الخياطة ālat al-khiyāṭa sewing machine

خيال khayāl 1. imagination 2. fantasy

خيالي khayālī imaginary

خيانة khiyāna treason

خيّب khayyaba: خيّب الظنّ khayyaba aẓ-ẓann; خيّب الأمل khayyaba al-amal to disappoint

خيبة khayba 1. failure 2. خيبة الأمل khaybat al-amal disappointment

خير khayr (أخيار akhyār) 1. good 2. بخير bi

khayr well 3. مبشر بالخير mubashshir bi 'l-khayr promising 4. صباح الخير! ṣabāḥ al-khayr! good morning! 5. مساء الخير! masā' al-khayr good evening! 6. تصبح على خير! tuṣbiḥ 'alā khayr! good night!

خيري khayrī 1. good 2. مؤسسة خيرية mu'assasa khayrīya charity

خيط khayṭ (خيوط khuyūṭ) 1. thread 2. string 3. fibre

خيّل إلى\ل khuyyila ilā/li *passive* to imagine

خيل khayl *collective* 1. horses 2. cavalry 3. سباق الخيل sibāq al-khayl horse racing 4. راكب الخيل rākib al-khayl jockey

خيّط khayyaṭa to sew

خيّم khayyama to camp

خيمة khayma (خيم khiyam) tent

د

دائخ dā'ikh 1. dizzy 2. nauseous

دائرة dā'ira (دوائر dawā'ir; دائرات dā'irāt) 1. circle 2. circuit 3. department; office 4. دائرة رسمية dā'ira rasmīya bureau; department 5. دائرة إنتخابية dā'ira intikhābiya (*pol.*) ward 6. دائرة إدارية كنيسية dā'ira idārīya kanīsīya parish 7. دائرة الأبراج dā'irat al-abrāj zodiac

دائري dā'irī circular

دائم dā'im 1. long-lasting 2. permanent

دائماً dā'iman 1. always 2. permanently

داخل 1. dākhil inside; interior 2. dākhila inside; within

داخلي dākhilī 1. inner 2. interior 3. internal 4. indoor 5. إطار داخلي iṭār dākhilī inner tube 6. ملابس داخلية malābis dākhilīya underwear

داخلية dākhilīya 1. وزير الداخلية wazīr ad-dākhilīya home secretary; minister of the interior 2. وزارة الداخلية wizārat ad-dākhilīya home office; ministry of the interior

دارج dārij 1. in vogue 2. colloquial

دار dāra (u; دور dawr) 1. to turn (على 'alā/حول ḥawla around) 2. to revolve 3. to orbit

دار dār f (دور dūr; ديار diyār) 1. house; building 2. دار البلدية dār al-baladiya town hall 3. دار الحضانة dār al-ḥaḍāna kindergarten 4. دار الأوبرا dār al-ūbrā opera house 5. دار الأيتام dār al-aytām orphanage 6. دار سك العملة dār sakk al-'umla (fin.) mint

داس dāsa (u; دوس daws) to tread

داع dā'in 1. propagandist 2. cause 3. لا داعي ل lā dā'iya li there is no cause to

داعب dā'aba to tease

داعر dā'ir obscene

داعرة dā'ira (-āt) prostitute

دافئ dāfi' warm

دافع dāfi' (دوافع dawāfi') 1. urge 2. impetus 3. دافع خفي dāffi khafī دوافع خفية dawāfi' khafīya) ulterior motive

دافع dāfa'a 1. to resist 2. دافع عن dāfa'a 'an to defend 3. to advocate

دام dāma (u; دوام dawām) 1. to last 2. ما دام mā dāma as long as; while

داه dāhin resourceful

دب dubb (أدباب adbāb) bear

دبابة dabbāba (-āt) (mil.) tank

دباسة dabbāsa stapler

دبر dabbara 1. to plan 2. دبر مكيدة dabbara makīda to scheme

دبس dabbasa to staple

دبغ dabagha (a; دبغ dabgh) to tan

دبلوم diblōm; دبلومة diblōma (-āt) diploma

دبلوماسي diblōmāsī (-yūn) 1. diplomat 2. diplomatic 3. بعثة دبلوماسية bu'tha diblōmāsīya diplomatic mission 4. العلاقات الدبلوماسية al-'alāqāt ad-diblōmāsīya diplomatic relations

دبور dabbūr (دبابير dabābīr) wasp

دبوس dabbūs (دبابيس dabābīs) pin

دجاجة dajāja (دجاج dajāj) chicken; hen

دخان dukhān (أدخنة adkhina) smoke

دخل dakhala (u; دخول dukhūl) 1. to go in; to enter 2. to penetrate

دخل dakhl 1. income 2. revenue

دخن dakhana (u) to smoke

دخّن dakhkhana to smoke

دخول dukhūl entry

درى darā (i; دراية dirāya) to know

دراجة darrāja (-āt) 1. bicycle 2. دراجة الرجل darrājat ar-rijl scooter 3. دراجة نارية darrāja nārīya motorcycle 4. ركب الدراجة rakiba ad-darrāja (a; ركوب rukūb) to cycle

دراسة dirāsa 1. study 2. حجرة الدراسة ḥujrat

منهاج الدراسة 3. **ad-dirāsa** classroom. **minhāj ad-dirāsa** curriculum

دراسي **dirāsī** 1. study 2. academic 3. فصل دراسي **faṣl dirāsī** (ed.) term

دراما **drāmā** drama

درامي **drāmī** dramatic

درب **darb** (دروب **durūb**) track

درّب **darraba** 1. to practise 2. to train

درج **durj** (أدراج **adrāj**) drawer

درجات **darajāt** pl stairs

درجة **daraja** (-āt) 1. class 2. degree 3. grade 4. step 5. stair 6. درجة الحرارة **darajat al-ḥarāra** temperature 7. درجة النغم **darajat an-naghm** (mus.) pitch 8. الدرجة الأولى **ad-daraja al-ūlā** first class 9. الدرجة الثانية **ad-daraja 'th-thānīya** second class 10. لهذه الدرجة **li hādhihi 'd-daraja** so

نظام درجي **niẓām darajī** scale: درجي **darajī** scale

درز **daraza** (u; درز **darz**) to stitch

درس **darasa** (u; درس **dars**) to study

درّس **darrasa** to teach

درس **dars** (دروس **durūs**) (ed.) 1. class 2. lesson 3. seminar 4. study

دزّينة **dazzīna** dozen

دستور **dustūr** (pol.) constitution

دستوري **dustūrī** constitutional

ديسكو **disko** disco

دعا **daʿā** (u; دعاء **duʿāʾ**) 1. to call; to invite (ل/إلى **ilā/li** to) 2. to pray (ه **so**)

دعاء **duʿāʾ** (أدعية **adʿiya**) prayer

دعامة **diʿāma** (-āt) support

دعاية **diʿāya** (-āt) 1. publicity 2. propaganda

دعم **daʿama** (a; دعم **daʿm**) 1. to support 2. to strengthen 3. to consolidate

دعّم **daʿʿama** to support

دعنا **daʿnā** 1. let's... 2. and see ودع

دعوى **daʿwā** (دعاوى **daʿāwā**; دعاوٍ **daʿāwin**) (leg.) 1. lawsuit 2. action 3. رفع دعوى على **rafaʿa daʿwā ʿalā** (a; رفع **rafʿ**) to sue

دعوة **daʿwā** (دعوت **daʿawāt**) 1. invitation (إلى **ilā** to) 2. call 3. summons 4. prayer

دغدغ **daghdagha** to tickle

دغل **daghal** (أدغال **adghāl**) jungle

دفء **difʾ** warmth

دفّأ **daffaʾa** to warm

دفاع **difāʿ** 1. defence 2. الدفاع عن النفس **ad-difāʿ ʿan an-nafs** self-defence 3. وزير الدفاع **wazīr ad-difāʿ** defence secretary; minister of defence 4. وزارة الدفاع **wizārat ad-difāʿ** ministry of defence

دفّاية **daffāya** heater

دفتر **daftar** 1. notebook 2. register 3. ledger 4. دفتر شيكات **daftar shīkāt** cheque book

دفع **dafʿ** 1. payment 2. قوة الدفع **qūwat ad-dafʿ** momentum

دفع **dafaʿa** (a; دفع **dafʿ**) 1. to pay 2. to push 3. دفع الضرائب **dafaʿa aḍ-ḍarāʾib** to pay tax

دفن **dafana** (i; دفن **dafn**) to bury

دفن **dafn** burial

دقّ **daqqa** (u; دقّ daqq) to tap

دقّة **diqqa** 1. accuracy 2. punctuality

دقيق **daqīq** 1. flour 2. accurate 3. proper 4. punctual 5. دقيق جداً **daqīq jiddan** rigorous

دقيقة **daqīqa** (دقائق daqā'iq) minute

دكّان **dukkān** (دكاكين dakākīn) 1. shop; store 2. صاحب دكّان **ṣāḥib dukkān** shopkeeper 3. منضدة دكّان **minḍadat dukkān** shop counter

دكتاتور **diktātūr** dictator

دكتاتورية **diktātūrīya** dictatorship

دكتور **duktūr** (دكاترة dakātira) doctor

دلّ **dalla** (u; دلالة dalāla) to show (ه so; إلى ilā/على 'alā to)

دلفين **dulfīn** (دلافين dalāfīn) dolphin

دلّك **dallaka** to massage

دلّل **dallala** indulge

دلو **dalw** usually f (أدلاء adlā') bucket

دليل **dalīl** (أدلة adilla; دلائل dalā'il) 1. evidence; proof 2. indication 3. clue 4. directory 5. guidebook 6. manual 7. prospectus

دم **dam** (دماء dimā') 1. blood 2. فصيلة دم **faṣīlat dam** blood group 3. تحليل الدم **taḥlīl ad-dam** blood test 4. نقل الدم **naql ad-dam** blood transfusion 5. فقر الدم **faqr ad-dam** anaemia 6. خفيف الدم **khafīf ad-dam** pleasant 7. ثقيل الدم **thaqīl ad-dam** unpleasant 8. and see دماء

دماء **dimā'** pl 1. سفك الدماء **safaka 'd-dimā'** (i/u; سفك safk) to shed blood 2.

مصّاص الدماء **maṣṣāṣ ad-dimā'** vampire 3. and see دم

دمار **damār** destruction

دماغي **dimāghī** 1. brain 2. سكتة دماغية **sakta dimāghīya** (med.) stroke

دمث **damith:** دمث الأخلاق **damith al-akhlāq** good-tempered

دمج **damaja** (u; دموج dumūj) to integrate

دمج **damj** integration

دمّر **dammara** 1. to destroy 2. to demolish

دمعة **dam'a** (دموع dumū') 1. tear; tear drop 2. and see دموع

دمغة **damgha** stamp

دموع **dumū'** pl 1. الغاز المسيّل للدموع **al-ghāz al-musayyil li 'd-dumū'** tear gas 2. and see دمعة

دموي **damawī** 1. blood 2. وعاء دموي **wi'ā' damawī** blood vessel

دمية **dumya** (دمى duman) 1. doll 2. dummy

الدنمارك **ad-danmārk** Denmark

دنماركي **danmārkī** (-yūn) 1. Dane 2. Danish

دنيء **danī'** low

دهان **dihān** (أدهنة adhina) 1. paint 2. دهان الطلاء **dihān aṭ-ṭilā'** varnish

دهّان **dahhān** (-ūn) painter

دهن **duhn** (دهون duhūn) 1. fat 2. lubricant 3. قليل الدهن **qalīl ad-duhn** lean

دواء **dawā'** (أدوية adwiya) 1. medicine 2. medication; drug 3. cure

دواجن **dawājin** pl poultry

دوار duwār 1. nausea 2. دوار البحر duwār al-baḥr seasick

دوارة dawwāra roundabout

دواسة dawwāsa (-āt) pedal

دوام dawāman wa istimrāran incessantly دواماً وإستمراراً

دوّخ dawwakha to stun

دوخة dawkha nausea

دودة dūda (دود dūd; ديدان dīdān) worm

دور dawr (أدوار adwār) 1. turn 2. part 3. role 4. storey 5. period 6. (spor.) league 7. بالدور bi 'd-dawr in turn 8. دورك dawruk It's your turn. 9. دور تحتاني dūr taḥtāni basement 10. دور الإنعقاد dawr al-in'iqād session 11. دور اللاعب dawr al-lā'ib (spor.) move

دوران dawarān circulation

دورة dawra (-āt) 1. cycle 2. revolution 3. rotation 4. session 5. patrol 6. (spor.) round 7. lap 8. دورة تعليمية dawra ta'līmīya (ed.) course 9. دورة تعليمية مصغرة dawra ta'līmīya muṣaghghara seminar 10. الدورة الشهرية للنساء ad-dawra ash-shahrīya li 'n-nisā' (med.) period

دورية dawrīya (-āt) 1. patrol 2. قام بدورية qāma bi dawrīya (u) to patrol

دوش dūsh shower

دولاب dūlāb (دواليب dawālīb) cupboard

دولار dōlār (-āt) dollar

دولة dawla (دول duwal) 1. state 2. رجل دولة rajul dawla statesman 3. دولة عظمى dawla 'uẓmā superpower

دولي duwalī 1. international 2. البنك الدولي al-bank ad-dawalī World Bank

دوّن dawwana to record

دون dūn; dūna 1. without 2. between 3. on this side of 4. before 5. below 6. من دون min dūn without preposition 7. دون أن dūn an; بدون أن bi dūn an; من دون أن min dūn an without conjunction 8. دون ما dūna mā without any 9. دون شك dūna shakk without a doubt 10. دون إستثناء dūn istithnā' without exception 11. دون المستوى dūn al-mustawā unsatisfactory 12. دون بقعة dūn buq'a stainless 13. and see بدون

ديزل dīzal diesel

ديسمبر disimbir December

ديك dīk (ديوك duyūk) 1. cock; cockerel 2. ديك رومي dīk rūmī turkey

ديمقراطي dimuqrāṭī 1. democratic 2. democrat

ديمقراطية dīmuqrāṭīya democracy

دين dayn (ديون duyūn) 1. debt 2. وفاء الدين wafā' ad-dayn repayment 3. وفى ديناً wafā daynan (i; وفي wafiy) to repay

دين dīn (أديان adyān) religion

دينار dīnār (دنانير danānīr) dinar

ديناصور dīnāṣūr dinosaur

ديناميكي dīnāmīkī dynamic

ديني dīnī 1. religious 2. أغنية دينية ughniya dīnīya (rel.) hymn

ذ

ذئب dhi'b (ذئاب dhi'āb) 1. wolf 2. رجل ذئب rajul dhi'b werewolf

ذاب dhāba (u; ذوب dhawb; ذويان dhawabān) 1. to melt 2. to thaw

ذات dhāt f 1. self 2. ذاته dhātuh himself 3. identical 4. بالذات bi 'dh-dhāt in itself possessing; possessor of 5. ذات الرئة dhāt ar-ri'a pneumonia 6. see ذو

ذاتي dhātī 1. self; auto- 2. سيرة ذاتية sīra dhātīya autobiography 3. الحكم الذاتي al-ḥukm adh-dhāti autonomy; self-government 4. مكتف ذاتياً muktafin dhātīyan self-sufficient 5. see ذو

ذاق dhāqa (u; ذوق dhawq) to taste

ذا dhā (pl أولا، أولا ūlā'i) this; this one

ذاك dhāk (f تاك tāk/تيك tīk; pl أولئك ūlā'ika) this; this one

ذاكرة dhākira memory

ذبابة dhubāba (collective ذباب؛ dhubāb؛ pl ذبان dhibbān) fly

ذبح dhabaḥa (a; ذبح dhabḥ) 1. to slaughter 2. to massacre

ذبح dhabḥ 1. slaughter 2. massacre

ذبذبة dhabdhaba (-āt) vibration

ذخيرة dhakhīra (ذخائر dhakhā'ir) 1. store 2. (mil.) magazine

ذراع dhirā' m/f (ذرعان dhur'ān؛ أذرع adhru') arm

ذرة dharra (collective ذرّ dharr) particle

ذرة dhurra corn

ذروة dharwa; dhurwa; dhirwa (ذرى dhuran) 1. peak 2. climax 3. highlight 4. بالغ الذروة bāligh adh-dharwa peak 5. بلوغ الذروة balagha 'l-dharwa (u; بلوغ bulūgh) to peak

ذرور dharūr powder

ذروري dharūrī powdered

ذعر dhu'r 1. alarm 2. panic 3. أصيبة بالذعر uṣība bi 'dh-dhu'r to panic

ذكاء dhakā' intelligence

ذكر dhakara (u; ذكر dhikr/تذكار tadhkār) 1. to mention 2. to remember

ذكّر dhakkara to remind

ذكر dhakar (ذكور dhukūr) male

ذكر dhikr 1. mention 2. recollection

ذكرى dhikrā (ذكريات dhikrayāt) 1. memory 2. anniversary

ذكري dhakarī 1. male 2. العضو الذكري al-'uḍw adh-dhakarī penis

ذكي dhakī (أذكيا، adhkiyā') clever

ذلّ dhull humiliation

ذلك dhālik m 1. that 2. ومع ذلك wa ma'a

ذهب dhahab gold

ذهبي dhahabī 1. gold; golden 2. ظلاء ذهبي ṭilā' dhahabī gold plate

ذهنية dhihnīya mentality

ذو dhū m 1. possessing; possessor of 2. ذو خبرة dhū khibra experienced 3. ذو قيمة dhū qīma worthwhile 4. ذو معنى dhū ma'nā significant 5. ذو نفوذ dhū nufūdh influential 6. ذو وجهين dhū wajhayn two-faced 7. see ذاتي ;ذات

ذوى dhawā (i) to fade

ذوّب dhawwaba 1. to melt 2. to dissolve

ذوبان dhawabān thaw

ذوق dhawq (أذواق adhwāq) 1. taste 2. رفيع الذوق rafī' adh-dhawq tasteful

ذيل dhayl (ذيول dhuyūl) tail

ورغم ذلك wa raghma dhālik however 3. علاوةً على ذلك 'ilāwatan 'alā dhālik nevertheless 4. 'ilāwatan 'alā dhālik moreover 5. في ذلك الوقت fī dhālika 'l-waqt at that time

ذنب dhanb (ذنوب dhunūb) fault

ذنب dhanab (أذناب adhnāb) tail

ذهاب dhihāb 1. going 2. تذكرة للذهاب فقط tadhkara li 'dh-dhihāb faqaṭ one-way ticket; single ticket 3. تذكرة ذهاب إياب tadhkirat dhihāb īhāb return ticket 4. جيئةً وذهاباً jay'atan wa dhihāban to and fro

ذهب dhahaba (a; ذهاب dhihāb; مذهب madhhab) 1. to go 2. ذهب بـ (إلى ilā to) dhahaba bi to take (away) 3. اذهب عني! idhhab 'annī! go away!

ر

رائد rā'id (رواد ruwwād) 1. explorer 2. leader 3. (mil.) major 4. رائد الفضاء rā'id al-faḍā' spaceman

رائع rā'i' 1. fantastic 2. extraordinary

رابطة rābita (روابط rawābiṭ) bond

رابح rābiḥ : صفقة رابحة ṣafqa rābiḥa bargain

رابطة rābiṭa (روابط rawābiṭ) 1. relation 2. tie 3. connection; link

---

رأى ra'ā (يرى yarā; رأي ra'y; رؤية ru'ya) 1. to see 2. to think; to consider

رئاسة ri'āsa 1. presidency 2. leadership

رئاسي ri'āsī presidential

رائج rā'ij best-seller

رائحة rā'iḥa (روائح rawā'iḥ) 1. smell 2. رائحة كريهة rā'iḥa karīha stink

رابع rābi' 1. fourth 2. رابع عشر rābi' 'ashar fourteenth

رئة ri'a (pl. رئون ri'ūn; رئات ri'āt) 1. lung 2. ذات الرئة dhāt ar-ri'a pneumonia

راتب rātib (رواتب rawātib) pay

راجع rāja'a 1. to check 2. (ed.) to revise 3. (media) to review 4. to refer (إلى ilā to)

راحة rāha 1. comfort 2. rest 3. leisure

رادار rādār radar

راديكالي rādikālī (pol.) radical

راديو rādiyo 1. radio 2. على الراديو 'alā 'r-rādiyō on the radio

رأس ra's (رؤوس ru'ūs) 1. head 2. point 3. cape 4. مسقط الرأس masqaṭ ar-ra's birthplace 5. أومأ بالرأس awma'a bi 'r-ra's to nod 6. رأس السنة ra's as-sana New Year 7. ليلة رأس السنة laylat ra's as-sana New Year's Eve

راسخ rāsikh stable

رأسمال ra'smāl (fin.) 1. capital 2. stock

رأسمالي ra'smālī capitalist

رأسمالية ra'smālīya capitalism

رأسي ra'sī head

راشد rāshid (-ūn) grown-up

راصد rāṣid: اتبع راصداً ittaba'a rāṣidan to stalk

راضٍ rāḍin (ب bi with; في fī) 1. satisfied 2. غير راضٍ ghayr rāḍin dissatisfied

راعٍ rā'in (رعاة ru'āh) 1. patron 2. sponsor 3. shepherd 4. راعي البقر rā'ī 'l-baqar cowboy 5. كلب الراعي kalb ar-rā'ī sheepdog 6. راعي كنيسة rā'ī kanīsa (rel.) minister

راعى rā'ā 1. to sponsor 2. to tend

رافعة rāfi'a (روافع rawāfi') 1. lever 2. crane

رافق rāfaqa 1. to accompany 2. to escort

راقٍ rāqin 1. high-class 2. posh

راقب rāqaba to observe; to watch

راقص rāqiṣ (-ūn) dancer

راكب rākib (ركّاب rukkāb) 1. passenger 2. rider 3. راكب الحصان rākib al-ḥiṣān on horseback 4. راكب الخيل rākib al-khayl jockey

راكض rākiḍ (-ūn) runner

راهب rāhib (رهبان ruhbān) monk

راهبة rāhiba (-āt) nun

راهن rāhana to bet

راهن rāhin current

راوغ rāwagha to dodge

راوند rāwand rhubarb

رأي ra'y (آراء ārā') 1. opinion; point of view 2. idea 3. في رأيي fī ra'yī in my opinion 4. إستطلاع رأي istiṭlā' ra'y questionnaire 5. إختلاف في الرأي ikhtilāf fi 'l-ra'y disagreement 6. إختلف في الرأي ikhtalafa fi 'r-ra'y to disagree 7. غيّر رأيه ghayyara ra'yah to change one's mind

رؤيا ru'yā (رؤى ru'an) (rel.) vision

راية rāya (-āt) standard

رؤية ru'ya looking

رئيس (ء رؤساء) ra'īs 1. head; boss 2. chief 3. leader 4. chancellor 5. president 6. رئيس الوزراء ra'īs al-wuzarā' prime minister 7. نائب الرئيس nā'ib ar-ra'īs vice-president 8. رئيس البلدية ra'īs al-baladīya mayor 9. رئيس التحرير ra'īs al-taḥrīr newspaper editor 10. رئيس الجامعة ra'īs al-jāmi'a (acad.) chancellor 11. رئيس الأساقفة ra'īs al-asāqifa archbishop 12. رئيس المجلس ra'īs al-majlis chairman 13. رئيس مجلس الإدارة ra'īs majlis al-idāra (com.) president 14. رئيس شركة ra'īs sharika chief executive officer (CEO)

رئيسي ra'īsī 1. principal; main 2. staple 3. البر الرئيسي al-barr ar-ra'īsī mainland

رب rabb 1. lord 2. رب منزل rabb manzil landlord

ربى rabbā 1. to raise; to bring up 2. to educate 3. to rear

ربة rabba: ربة منزل rabbat manzil 1. landlady 2. housewife

رباعي rubā'ī four-part

ربت rabbata to pat

ربح rabiḥa (i; ربح ribḥ) 1. to win 2. to gain

ربح ribḥ (أرباح arbāḥ) 1. gain 2. profit

ربط rabaṭa (u/i; ربط rabṭ) 1. to tie up 2. to connect; to link

ربط rabṭ 1. connection 2. مفتاح ربط miftāḥ rabṭ spanner

ربطة rabṭa (-āt): ربطة العنق rabṭa 'l-'unq tie

ربع rub' (أرباع arbā') 1. quarter; fourth 2. ربع سنوياً rub' sanawīyan quarterly

ربما rubbamā 1. perhaps 2. sometimes

ربو rabw asthma

ربيع rabī' spring

رتب rattaba 1. to arrange 2. to tidy 3. رتب سفرة rattaba sufra to set a table

رتبة rutba (رتب rutab) (mil.) 1. rank 2. أرفع رتبة arfa' rutbatan superior

رجا rajā (u; رجاء rajā') 1. to hope (for) 2. to ask (for) 3. to plead

رجاء rajā' 1. hope 2. على رجاء 'alā rajā' in the hope of 3. رجاء العلم rajā' al-'ilm for your information 4. ...الرجاء ar-rajā'... please... 5. الرجاء عدم الإزعاج ar-rajā' 'adam al-iz'āj please do not disturb

رجح rajjaḥa to prefer

رجع raja'a (a/i; رجوع rujū') to return (إلى ilā to)

رجعي raj'ī 1. reactionary 2. retroactive

رجعية raj'īya (pol.) reaction

رجفة rajfa (-āt) 1. shiver 2. tremor

رجل rajul (رجال rijāl) 1. man 2. رجل دولة rajul dawla statesman 3. رجل ذئب rajul dhi'b werewolf 4. رجل أعمال rajul a'māl businessman 5. رجل الصناعة rajul aṣ-ṣinā'a industrialist

رجل rijl (أرجل arjul) leg

رجم rajama (u; رجم rajm) to stone

رجوع rujū' return

رجولة **rujūla** virility

رحّب **raḥḥaba** to welcome (ب bi *so*)

رحل **raḥala** (a; رحيل **raḥīl**) to depart; to set off

رحّل **raḥḥala** 1. to deport 2. to evacuate 3. to transfer 4. to convey

رحلة **riḥla** (-āt) 1. journey 2. voyage 3. trip; excursion 4. travel 5. رحلة بالطائرة **riḥla bi 'ṭ-ṭā'ira** flight 6. رحلة بحرية **riḥla baḥrīya** cruise 7. رحلة جماعية **riḥla jamā'īya** package tour 8. خط الرحلة **khaṭṭ ar-riḥla** itinerary 9. رحلة صيد **riḥlat ṣayd** hunting trip 10. بدأ رحلة **bada'a riḥla** to set off on a trip

رحم **raḥim** f (أرحام **arḥām**) womb

رحم **raḥima** (a; رحمة **raḥma**) 1. to spare 2. to have mercy on

رحمة **raḥma** mercy

رحيل **raḥīl** departure

رخاء **rakhā'** prosperity

رخام **rukhām** marble

رخّص **rakhkhaṣa** to license

رخصة **rukhṣa** (رخص **rukhaṣ**) 1. licence 2. permit 3. رخصة قيادة السيّارات **rukhṣat qiyādat as-sayyārāt** driving licence

رخيص **rakhīṣ** cheap

ردّ **radda** (u; ردّ **radd**) 1. to send back 2. to take back 3. to give back 4. to put back 5. to resist 6. to refuse 7. to reply (على **'alā** to) 8. to restore 9. to restrain 10. ردّني الكتاب **raddanī al-kitāb** He gave me the book back.

ردّ **radd** (ردود **rudūd**) 1. return 2. reply 3. restoration 4. reaction 5. rejection 6. reflection 7. ردّ الفعل **radd al-fi'l** reaction 8. كان ردّ فعله **kāna radd fi'luh** to react

رداء **ridā'** (أردية **ardiya**) 1. robe 2. cape

ردود **rudūd**: ردود الفعل **rudūd al-fi'l** reaction

رديء **radī'** 1. bad 2. wicked 3. على نحو رديء **'alā naḥw radī'** badly 4. رديء القلب **radī' al-qalb** nasty

رذيلة **radhīla** (رذائل **radhā'il**) vice

رزمة **rizma** (رزم **rizam**) 1. package; parcel 2. packet

رسالة **risāla** (رسائل **rasā'il**) 1. letter 2. message 3. mission

رسّام **rassām** (-ūn) 1. illustrator 2. painter

رسم **rasama** (u; رسم **rasm**) 1. to draw; to illustrate 2. to paint 3. رسم خطًّا تحت **rasama khaṭṭan taḥta** to underline

رسم **rasm** (رسوم **rusūm**; رسومات **rusūmāt**) 1. drawing; illustration 2. painting 3. graph 4. *(ed.)* fee 5. customs duty 6. رسم بياني **rasm bayānī** diagram 7. رسم كاريكاتوري **rasm kārīkatūrī** cartoon 8. *and see* رسوم

رسمي **rasmī** (-ūn) 1. formal 2. official 3. غير رسمي **ghayr rasmī** informal 4. unofficial 5. زي رسمي **ziyy rasmī** uniform 6. غداء رسمي **ghadā' rasmī** luncheon 7. مقابلة رسمية **muqābila rasmīya** audience 8. دائرة رسمية **dā'ira rasmīya** bureau

رسمياً rasmīyan officially

رسمية rasmīya (-āt) formality

رسول rasūl (رسل rusul) messenger

رسوم rusūm pl 1. زوّد برسوم zawwada bi rusūm illustrate 2. معفاة من الرسوم mu'fāh min ar-rusūm duty-free 3. and see رسم

رشّ rashsha (u; رشّ rashsh) 1. to splash 2. to spray 3. to sprinkle

رشّ rashsh 1. splash 2. spray

رشاش rashāsh spray

رشّاشة rashshāsha (-āt); رشّاش آلي rashshāsh ālī رشّاشات آلية rashshāshāt ālīya) machine-gun

رشاقة rashāqa agility

رشّح rashshaha to nominate

رشد rushd: بالغ سنّ الرشد bāligh sinn ar-rushd (-ūn) adult

رشوة rashwa/rishwa/rushwa (رشا\رشى rishan/rushan; رشاوي rashāwī) bribe

رشيق rashīq graceful

رصاص raṣāṣ 1. lead 2. قلم رصاص qalam raṣāṣ (أقلام aqlām) pencil

رصاصة raṣāṣa bullet; bullets

رصيد raṣīd (fin.) balance

رصيف raṣīf (أرصفة arṣifa) 1. pavement 2. حافة الرصيف ḥāfat ar-raṣīf curb

رضىً riḍan satisfaction

رضي raḍiya 1. to be satisfied (ب bi with) 2. to agree (ب bi to) 3. to accept 4. to be pleased (عن 'an with)

رطّب raṭṭaba 1. to water 2. to moisturize

رطب raṭb 1. damp 2. humid 3. moist

رطوبة ruṭūba 1. damp 2. humidity 3. moisture

مرعى ri'āya (مرعى mar'an) 1. to tend 2. to nurse 3. to mind رعى ra'ā (a; رعي ra'y; رعاية

رعب ru'b terror

رعد ra'd (رعود ru'ūd) thunder

رعشة ra'sha shiver

رغب raghiba (a; رغبة raghba; رغب raghab) 1. رغب في raghiba fī to want; to want to 2. to desire 3. رغب عن raghiba 'an to not want to 4. to dislike

رغبة raghba (رغبات raghabāt) wish; desire

رغبي rughbī rugby

رغم raghm; raghma 1. despite 2. بالرغم من bi 'r-raghm min despite 2. على الرغم من 'alā 'r-raghm min despite 3. ورغم ذلك wa raghma dhālik nevertheless 4. رغم أن raghma an; though 5. رغم أنّ raghma anna though 5. رغماً عن raghman 'an despite

رغيف raghīf (أرغفة arghifa) loaf

رفّ raff (رفوف rufūf) shelf

رفاهة rafāha welfare; well-being

رفاهية rafāhīya comfort

رفس rafasa (u; رفس rafs) to kick

رفسة rafsa kick

رفض rafḍ refusal

رفض rafaḍ (i/u; رفض rafḍ) to refuse

رفع rafa'a (a; رفع raf') 1. to raise; to lift 2.

رفع الصوت rafaʻa aṣ-ṣawt to turn up the volume 3. رفع دعوى على rafaʻa daʻwā ʻalā to sue

رفّع raffaʻa 1. to lift 2. to celebrate

رفيع rafīʻ: رفيع الذوق rafīʻ adh-dhawq tasteful

رفيق rafīq (رفاق rifāq; رفقاء rufaqāʼ) 1. companion 2. friend 3. boyfriend 4. comrade 5. accomplice

رقّى raqqā to promote

رقابة raqāba 1. supervision 2. censorship 3. خارج نطاق الرقابة khārij niṭāq ar-raqāba offshore

رقبة raqaba (-āt) neck

رقّة riqqa 1. delicacy 2. tact

رقص raqaṣa (u; رقص raqṣ) to dance

رقص raqṣ 1. dance 2. dancing

رقعة ruqʻa (رقع ruqaʻ) patch

رقم raqm (أرقام arqām) 1. number 2. numeral 3. رقم قياسي raqm qiyāsī record 4. رقم قياس عالمي raqm qiyās ʻālamī world record 5. حطم رقماً قياسياً ḥaṭṭama raqman qiyāsīyan (i; كسر kasr) to break a record

رقيب raqīb sergeant

رقية ruqya (رقى ruqan) spell

رقيق raqīq 1. thin 2. delicate; fine 3. subtle

ركب rakiba (a; ركوب rukūb) 1. to ride 2. to travel 3. to get on 4. to mount 5. to board 6. ركب الدراجة rakiba ad-darrāja cycle

ركّب rakkaba 1. to assemble 2. to compose 3. to install

ركبة rukba (-āt; ركب rukab) knee

ركض rakaḍa (u; ركض rakḍ) 1. to run 2. to jog

ركض rakḍ 1. running 2. jogging

ركع rakaʻa (a; ركوع rukūʻ) to kneel

ركّز rakkaza to concentrate; to focus

ركم rakama (u; ركم rakm) to accumulate

ركن rakana (u; ركون rukūn) to park

ركوب rakūb mount; riding animal

ركوب rukūb 1. travelling 2. ride; riding 3. boarding

ركود rukūd: ركود اقتصادي rukūd iqtiṣādī (ec.) recession

رمى ramā (i; رمي ramy) 1. to throw 2. to throw away

رمادي ramādī grey

رمح rumḥ (رماح rimāḥ) spear

رمز ramz (رموز rumūz) 1. sign 2. symbol 3. رمز بريدي ramz barīdī post code

رمل raml (رمال rimāl) sand

رملي ramlī sandy

رمّم rammama to restore

رنّ ranna (i; رنين ranīn) to ring

رهان rihān bet

رهن rahn: رهن الأحداث rahn al-aḥdāth at stake

رهيب rahīb terrible

رهينة rahīna (رهائن rahāʼin) hostage

روى rawā (i; رواية riwāya) 1. to narrate 2. روى رواية rawā riwāya to tell a story

روائي riwā'ī (-yūn) novelist

رواتب rawātib pl 1. wages 2. تجمّد الرواتب tajammud ar-rawātib wage freeze

رواق riwāq (أروقة arwiqa) porch

رواية riwāya (-āt) 1. novel 2. story 3. plot 4. narration 5. version 6. account 7. رواية مثيرة riwāya muthīra thriller

روبوط rōbōṭ robot

روتين rūtīn 1. routine 2. الروتين الحكومي ar-rūtīn al-ḥukūmī red tape

روتيني rūtīnī routine

روث rawth dung

روح rūḥ (أرواح arwāḥ) soul; spirit

روحاني rūḥānī spiritual

روس rūs Russians

روسي rūsī (-yūn) Russian

روسيا rūsiyā Russia

روع raw' awe

روعة raw'a splendour

رومان rūmān Romans

رومانتكي rōmāntikī romantic

رومانس rōmāns romance

روماني rōmānī (-yūn) Romanian

رومي rūmī 1. Roman 2. Byzantine 3.

ديك رومي dīk rūmī turkey

راو rawin (راويون rawiyūn; رواة ruwāh) narrator

روّى rawwā to irrigate

روّج rawwaja (com.) to promote

روّع rawwa'a to terrify

ري riyy/rayy irrigation

رياضة riyāḍa 1. sport; sports 2. رياضة الجمنازية riyāḍat azh-zhimnāziya gymnastics

رياضي riyāḍī 1. athletic 2. sport; sports 3. (-ūn) athlete 4. sportsman 5. ألعاب رياضية al'āb riyāḍīya athletics 6. مدرّب رياضي mudarrib riyāḍī coach; trainer 7. ملابس رياضية malābis riyāḍīya sportswear 8. حجرة للتمرينات الرياضية ḥujra li 't-tamrīnāt ar-riyāḍīya gym; gymnasium

رياضية riyāḍīya (-āt) sportswoman

رياضيات riyāḍīyāt pl maths; mathematics

ريب rayb 1. doubt 2. بلا ريب bilā rayb without doubt 3. لا ريب فيه lā rayb fīh doubtless

ريح rīḥ (رياح riyāḥ) usually f wind

ريشة rīsha (collective ريش rīsh) feather

ريف rīf 1. country 2. countryside

ريفي rīfī 1. rural 2. provincial

زائد zā'id 1. extra 2. plus

زائر zā'ir (-ūn; زوّار zuwwār) 1. visitor 2. guest

زائف zā'if 1. imitation 2. counterfeit 3. pseudo-

زاحف zāḥif (زواحف zawāḥif) reptile

زاد zāda (i; زيادة ziyāda) 1. to increase 2. to boost 3. زاد على zāda 'alā; زاد عن zāda 'an to be more than 4. زاد في zāda fi to extend 5. زاده ثلاثة أضعاف zādah thalāthat aḍ'āf to treble

زار zāra (u; زيارة ziyāra) to visit

زارع zāri' (-ūn) grower

زال zāla (i; يزال yazāl) 1. to cease 2. لا يزال lā yazāl still

زامل zāmala to associate

زاوية zāwiya (زوايا zawāyā) 1. angle 2. corner

زبادي zabādī: لبن زبادي laban zabādī yoghurt

زبالة zubāla litter; rubbish

زبد zabad scum

زبدة zubda 1. butter 2. الزبدة النباتية az-zubda an-nabātīya margarine

زبدية zabdīya (زبادي zabādī) bowl

زبون zabūn (زبائن zabā'in) 1. customer 2. client

زجاج zujāj glass

زجاجة zujāja (-āt) 1. bottle 2. مفتاح زجاجة miftāḥ zujāja bottle-opener

زجاجي zujājī 1. glass 2. بيت زجاجي bayt zujājī greenhouse

زحام ziḥām squash

زحف zaḥf march

زحف zaḥafa (a; زهف zaḥf) 1. to crawl 2. (mil.) to march

زخرف zakhrafa to decorate

زخرفة zukhruf (زخارف zakhārif); زخرف zakhrafa (-āt) ornament; decoration

زخرفي zukhrufī ornamental

زرّ zirr (أزرار azrār; زرور zurūr) 1. knob 2. button

زراعة zirā'a 1. agriculture 2. farming 3. cultivation 4. sowing 5. planting

زراعي zirā'ī agricultural

زرع zara'a (a; زرع zar') 1. to farm 2. to cultivate 3. to plant 4. to sow

زرع zar' planting

أزرق zurq see أزرق

زرقة zurqa blue; blueness

زرقاء zarqā' see أزرق

زريبة zarība pen; corral

زعزع za'za'a to shake

زعل za'ila (a; زعل za'al) to be upset

زعّل za‘‘ala to upset

زعلان za‘lān 1. upset (من min about) 2. angry

زعم za‘ama (u; زعم za‘m) to allege

زعيم za‘īm (زعماء zu‘amā’) 1. leader 2. زعيم فتنة za‘īm fitna ringleader

زفاف zifāf wedding

زفر zafara (i; زفير zafīr) to exhale

زقاق zuqāq (أزقّة aziqqa) 1. alley 2. lane

زكام zukām (med.) cold

زلاقة zallāqa (-āt) sled, sledge

زلزال zilzāl (زلازل zalāzil) earthquake

زلق zaliq slippery

زمان zamān 1. time 2. من زمان min zamān long ago 3. أيام زمان ayyām zamān olden times 4. see زمن

زمّر zammara to honk

زمرة zumra (زمر zumar) faction

زمن zaman (أزمان azmān; أزمنة azmina) 1. time 2. tense 3. زمن الحرب zaman al-ḥarb wartime 4. عدا عليه الزمن ‘adā ‘alayh az-zaman out of date 5. زمناً zamanan for a time 6. see زمان

زميل zamīl (زملاء zumalā’) 1. colleague 2. 3. associate fellow worker 4. زميل في الصف zamīl fi ṣ-ṣaff classmate

زنا zinā adultery

زناد zinād (أزندة aznida) trigger

زنبرك zanbarak (زنابك zanābik) metal spring

زنزانة zinzāna (-āt) cell

زهر zuhr dice

زهرة zahra (collective زهر zahr; pl زهور zuhūr) flower

زهرية zuhriya (-āt) vase

زهق (a) zahaqa to be fed up

زهقان zahqān fed up

زهور zuhūr pl 1. بائع الزهور bā‘i‘ az-zuhūr florist 2. see زمن

زواج zawāj marriage

زوج zawj (أزواج azwāj) 1. pair 2. husband 3. mate

زوّج zawwaja to marry

زوجان zawjān dual couple

زوجة zawja (-āt) 1. wife 2. زوجة الإبن zawjat al-ibn daughter-in-law

زوجي zawjī 1. marital 2. paired

زوّد zawwada 1. to provide 2. to raise 3. زوّد بالوقود zawwada bi ’l-wuqūd to fuel 4. زوّد بالبضائع zawwada bi ’l-baḍā‘i‘ stock 5. زوّد برسوم zawwada bi rusūm to illustrate

زيّ ziyy/zayy (أزياء azyā’) 1. costume 2. dress 3. outfit 4. زيّ رسمي ziyy rasmī uniform 5. زيّ المدارس ziyy al-madāris school uniform

زيادة ziyāda (-āt) increase

زيارة ziyāra (-āt) 1. visit 2. زيارة المعالم ziyārat al-ma‘ālim sightseeing

زيت zayt (زيوت zuyūt) oil

زيتونة zaytūna (collective زيتون zaytūn) olive

زيتي zaytī 1. oil 2. لوحة زيتية lawḥa zaytīya oil painting

زيف zayf (زيوف zuyūf) fake

زينة zīna (-āt) ornament

س

سَ sa will; shall

سَاء ساء sā'a (i) 1. to be bad 2. to do badly 3. ساء التفاهم sā'a at-tafāhum; ساء الفهم sā'a al-fahm to misunderstand 4. ساء التصرف sā'a at-taṣarruf to misbehave 5. ساء الإستعمال sā'a al-isti'māl to misuse

سؤال su'āl (أسئلة as'ila) question

سائح sā'iḥ (-ūn) (سواح suwwāḥ) 1. traveller 2. tourist 3. tripper

سائس sā'is (سادة sāda) groom; stablehand

سائق sā'iq (-ūn) 1. driver 2. chauffeur

سائل sā'il (سوائل sawā'il) 1. liquid 2. fluid 3. solution 4. سائل الجمال sā'il al-jamāl lotion 5. السائل المنوي as-sā'il al-manawī sperm

سابح sābiḥ (-ūn) swimmer

سابع sābi' 1. seventh 2. سابع عشر sābi' 'ashar seventeenth

سابق sābaqa 1. to race 2. to compete with

سابق sābiq 1. previous 2. former 3. سابق الأوان sābiq al-awān premature 4. في السابق fi 's-sābiq previously

سابقاً sābiqan previously

ساحة sāḥa (-āt) 1. yard 2. ساحة عامّة sāḥa 'āmma plaza

ساحر sāḥir 1. enchanting 2. (-ūn) (سحرة saḥara; سحّار suḥḥār) magician

ساحرة sāḥira (-āt) witch

ساحل sāḥil (سواحل sawāḥil) coast

ساحلي sāḥilī coastal

ساخن sākhin hot

ساد sāda (u; سيادة siyāda) 1. to prevail over 2. to rule over 3. to be master of

سادس sādis 1. sixth 2. سادس عشر sādis 'ashar sixteenth

سادي sādī sadistic

ساذج sādhij naive

سار sāra (i; سير sayr) 1. to go 2. to move 3. to head (إلى ilā for)

سارّ sārr 1. pleasing; nice 2. سارّ للغاية sārr li 'l-ghāya delightful

سار sārin: ساري المفعول sāri 'l-maf'ūl valid

سارق sāriq (-ūn) (سرقة saraqa) robber; thief

ساطع sāṭi' bright

ساع sā'in (ساعون sā'ūn) 1. courier 2. ساعي البريد sā'i 'l-barīd postman

ساعة sā'a (-āt) 1. hour 2. time 3. clock 4. watch 5. الساعة as-sā'a o'clock 5. نصف ساعة niṣf sā'a half an hour, half-hour 6. في كل ساعة fī kull sā'a hourly 7. هذه الساعة متأخرة hādhihi 's-sā'a muta'akhkhira This clock is slow. 8. كيلومتر بالساعة kīlōmitr bi 's-sā'a kilometres per hour (k.p.h.) 9. ميل في الساعة mīl fi 's-sā'a miles per hour (m.p.h.)

ساعد sā'ada to help

سافر sāfara to travel

ساق sāqa (u; سياقة siyāqa) to drive

ساق sāq f (سوق sūq; سيقان sīqān) 1. leg 2. thigh 3. بطّة الساق baṭṭat as-sāq calf

ساكن sākin (سكّان sukkān) 1. inhabitant 2. resident 3. occupant 4. motionless 5. حرف ساكن ḥārf sākin consonant 6. *and see* سكّان

سأل sa'ala (a; سؤال su'āl) to ask (عن 'an about)

سال sāla (i; سيلان sayalān) 1. to flow 2. to flood

سالم sālim safe

سالماً sāliman safely

سامّ sāmm 1. poisonous 2. toxic

ساند sānada 1. to support; to back 2. to prop; to prop up 3. to sustain 4. *(pol.)* to second

ساهم sāhama 1. to share 2. to particpate (في fī in)

ساوى sāwā to equal

ساير sāyara 1. to travel 2. to get on with

سبّ sabba (u; سبّ sabb) to swear

سباحة sibāḥa 1. swim; swimming 2. حمّام سباحة ḥammām sibāḥa swimming pool

سباق sibāq *(spor.)* 1. race 2. meet 3. مجرى السباق majra 's-sibāq course 4.

سباق سيّارات sibāq sayyārāt rally 5. حصان السباق ḥuṣān as-sibāq racehorse 6. سباق الخيل sibāq al-khayl horse racing 7. سباق المرثون sibāq al-marathōn marathon 8. سباق التسلح sibāq at-tasalluḥ arms race

سبّاك sabbāk (-ūn) plumber

سبّب sabbaba to cause

سبب sabab (أسباب asbāb) 1. cause; reason 2. بسبب bi sabab because of

السبت al-sabt 1. Saturday 2. sabbath 3. يوم السبت yawm as-sabt Saturday

سبتمبر sibtambir September

سبح sabaḥa (a; سبح sabḥ; سباحة sibāḥa) to swim

سبع sub' seventh

سبعة sab'a 1. seven 2. سبعة عشر sab'at 'ashar seventeen

سبعون sab'ūn seventy

سبق sabaqa (i/u; سبق sabq) to precede

سبقي sabaqī: حكم سبقي ḥukm sabaqī prejudice

سبيل sabīl (سبل subul) 1. way 2. path 3. means 4. في سبيل fī sabīl for; for the sake of 5. اعترض سبيل i'taraḍa sabīl to intercept

ستّ sitt 1. lady 2. ستّ أعمال sitt a'māl businesswoman

ستارة sitāra (ستائر satā'ir) 1. curtain 2. screen 3. veil 4. ستارة النافذة sitārat an-nāfidha blind

ستّة sitta six

ستّة عشر sittat 'ashar sixteen

سُترة sutra/sitra (-āt; ستر sutar) 1. jacket 2. waistcoat 3. سترة النجاة sitrat an-najāh life jacket

سِتّون sittūn sixty

سجّادة sajjāda (سجاجيد sajājīd) 1. carpet 2. rug 3. mat

سجارة sigāra (سجائر sagā'ir) 1. cigarette 2. منفضة سجاير minfaḍat sagāyir ashtray

سجّان sajjān (-ūn) jailer

سجّل sajjala 1. to record 2. to register 3. to tape 4. سجّل على الفيديو sajjala 'alā al-vīdiyo to video-tape 5. سجّل هدفاً sajjala hadafan; سجّل إصابة sajjala iṣāba to score a goal

سجق sujuq collective sausage(s)

سجِلّ sijill (-āt) 1. register 2. record

سجن sajana (u; سجن sajn) to imprison

سجن sijn (سجون sujūn) prison

سجين sajīn (سجناء sujanā') prisoner

ناطحة سحاب nāṭiḥat saḥāb (نواطح nawāṭiḥ) skyscraper

سحابة saḥāba (سحب suḥub; سحائب saḥā'ib) cloud

سحاق siḥāq lesbianism

سحاقي siḥāqī lesbian

سحاقية siḥāqīya (-āt) lesbian

سحب saḥaba (a; سحب saḥb) 1. to take out 2. سحب نقداً saḥaba naqdan to withdraw money

سحّاب saḥḥāb zip

سحر siḥr magic

سحري siḥrī magic; magical

سحق saḥaqa (a; سحق saḥq) 1. to crush 2. to pound 3. to grind

سحلية siḥlīya (سحالي saḥālin) lizard

سخّن sakhkhana to heat

سخر sakhira (a; سخر sukhr) to make fun (من\ب min/bi of)

سخري sukhrī 1. sarcastic 2. محاكاة سخرية muḥākā sukhrīya parody

سخرية sukhrīya irony

سخط sukhṭ indignation

سخيف sakhīf ridiculous

سدّ sadda (u; سدّ sadd) 1. to block 2. to plug 3. to dam 4. سدّ حاجةً sadda ḥājatan to meet a need

سدّ sadd (سدود sudūd) 1. dam 2. dyke

سدادة sidāda (-āt) plug

سدس suds (أسداس asdās) sixth

سديم sadīm (سدم sudum) mist

سديمي sadīmī misty

سذاجة sadhāja naivety/naivete

سرّ sarra (u; سرور surūr) to make happy

سرّ sirr (أسرار asrār) 1. secret 2. سرّ عسكري sirr 'askarī military secret

سرّاً sirran 1. in secret 2. privately

سرى sarā (i; سريان sarayān) to take effect (على 'alā on)

سرب sirb (أسراب asrāb) 1. herd 2. flock

سرداب sirdāb (سراديب saradīb) vault

سرداني sardānī (-yūn) Sardinian

سردانية sardāniya Sardinia

سردين sardīn *collective* sardine(s)

سرّح sarraḥa 1. to send off 2. to release 3. to style 4. سرّح عن العمل sarraḥa ʿan al-ʿamal to lay off from work

سرطان saraṭān 1. (med.) cancer 2. (zodiac) Cancer 3. سرطان البحر saraṭān al-baḥr crab

سرّع sarraʿa to speed up

سرعة surʿa 1. speed 2. pace 3. بسرعة bi surʿa rapidly 4. بأقصى سرعة bi aqṣā surʿa at top speed 5. حدّ السرعة ḥadd as-surʿa speed limit 6. الحدّ المسموح به للسرعة al-ḥadd al-masmūḥ bih li 's-surʿa speeding

سرعان ما surʿān mā; surʿāna mā (very) quickly; (very) soon

سرق saraqa (i; سرقة saraqa/sariqa) 1. to steal (من min from) 2. to rob 3. to mug 4. سرق الصيد\السمك saraqa aṣ-ṣayd/as-samak to poach 5. سرق من الدكاكين saraqa min ad-dakākīn to shoplift

سرقة sariqa (-āt) 1. theft 2. robbery 3. mugging 4. poaching 5. السرقة من الدكاكين as-sariqa min ad-dakākīn shoplifting

سرك sirk circus

سروال sirwāl (سراويل sarāwīl) 1. trousers 2. سروال داخلي sirwāl dākhilī underpants

سرور surūr 1. happiness 2. pleasure 3. بكلّ سرور bi kull surūr gladly

سرّي sirrī 1. secret 2. private 3. undercover 4. underground 5. عميل سرّي ʿamīl sirrī secret agent 6. بوليس سرّي būlīs sirrī secret police 7. بلاغ سرّي balāgh sirrī tip-off

سرّياً sirrīyan 1. in secret 2. privately

سرّية sirrīya secrecy

سرير sarīr (سرر surur; أسرّة asirra) 1. bed 2. نهض عن السرير nahaḍa ʿan as-sarīr (a; نهوض nuhūḍ) to get up

سريع sarīʿ 1. fast; quick 2. express 3. سريع الإلتهاب sarīʿ al-iltihāb inflammable; burnable

سطح saṭḥ (سطوح suṭūḥ) 1. surface 2. roof 3. سطح الأرض saṭḥ al-arḍ ground 4. تحت سطح الأرض taḥta saṭḥ al-arḍ underground 5. سطح البحر saṭḥ al-baḥr; مستوى سطح البحر mustawā saṭḥ al-baḥr sea-level 6. تحت سطح البحر taḥta saṭḥ al-baḥr underwater

سطحي saṭḥī shallow

سطع saṭʿ brightness

سطو saṭw burglary

سطيح saṭīḥ flat

سعة saʿa/siʿa 1. space 2. capacity

سعى saʿā (يسعى yasʿā; سعي saʿy) 1. to run 2. to strive; to work (إلى ilā for)

سعادة saʿāda happiness

سعال suʿāl cough

سعد saʿida (a; سعود suʿūd) to scale *a mountain*

سعّر saʿʿara to price

سعر si‘r (أسعار as‘ār) (fin./com.) 1. price 2. rate 3. quote 4. بنصف السعر bi niṣf as-si‘r at half price 5. سعر تحويل العملة si‘r taḥwīl al-‘umla rate of exchange 6. أعطى سعراً a‘ṭā sa‘ran to bid

سعل sa‘ala (u; سعلة su‘la; سعال su‘āl) to cough

سعودي sa‘ūdī Saudi

سعيد sa‘īd (سعداء su‘adā’) happy (ب bi about)

معكرونة السبغيتي: spaghītī ماكرونة 's-spaghītī spaghetti

سفارة sifāra (-āt) embassy

سفر safar (أسفار asfār) 1. journey 2. trip 3. travel 4. departure 5. أجرة السفر ujrat as-safar fare 6. جواز سفر jawāz safar passport 7. وكالة السفر wikālat as-safar travel agency

شفرة safra (شفرات shafarāt) blade

سفرة sufra: رتّب سفرة rattaba sufra to set a table

سفع saf‘: سفع الشمس saf‘ ash-shams 1. suntan 2. sunburn

سفك safaka (i/u; سفك safk): سفك الدماء safaka 'd-dimā’ to shed blood

سفن sufun pl 1. shipping 2. حوض السفن ḥawḍ as-sufun dock, docks 3. and see سفينة

سفير safīr (سفراء sufarā’) ambassador

سفينة safīna (سفن sufun; سفائن safā’in) 1. ship 2. boat 3. craft 4. سفينة شحن safīnat shaḥn freighter 5. سفينة الفضاء safīnat al-faḍā’ spacecraft 6.

ظهر السفينة ẓahr as-safina ship's deck 7. سفينة غارقة safina ghāriqa wreck 8. نزل من السفينة nazala min as-safina (i; نزول nuzūl) to disembark 9. and see سفن

سقط saqaṭa (u; سقوط suqūṭ) 1. to fall 2. to drop 3. سقط فجأة saqaṭa faj’atan (com.) to slump 4. سقط في إمتحان saqaṭa fī imtiḥān (ed.) to fail an exam

سقف saqf (سقوف suqūf; أسقف asquf) 1. roof 2. ceiling

سكّ sakka (u; سكّ sakk) (fin.) to mint

سكّ sakk: دار سكّ العملة dār sakk al-‘umla (fin.) mint

سكّان sukkān pl 1. inhabitants 2. عدد السكّان ‘adad al-sukkān population 3. إحصاء السكّان iḥṣā’ as-sukkān (-āt) census 4. and see ساكن

سكّاني sukkānī population

سكب sakaba (u; سكب sakb) to pour

سكّة sikka 1. rail 2. السكّة الحديدية al-sikka al-ḥadīdīya railway 3. خطّ سكّة الحديد khaṭṭ sikkat al-ḥadīd railtrack

سكت sakata (u; سكت sakt; سكوت sukūt) to be quiet

سكتة sakta: سكتة دماغية sakta dimāghīya (med.) stroke

سكّر sukkar 1. sugar 2. مرض السكّر maraḍ as-sukkar diabetes

سكران sakrān 1. drunk 2. غير سكران ghayr sakrān sober

سكرتير sikritīr (-ūn) secretary

سكرتيرة sikritīra (-āt) secretary

سكرتيري sikritīrī secretarial

سكرتيرية sikritīrīya secretariat

سكن sakana 1. (u; سكن sakn) to live (in) to dwell; to inhabit 2. (u; سكون sukūn) to be calm

سكّن sakkana to relieve

سكن sakan 1. accommodation 2. سكن الجنود sakan al-junūd (mil.) quarters

سكني sakanī 1. residential 2. تجمّع سكني tajammuʿ sakanī housing estate

سكّينة sikkīna (سكاكين sakākīn) 1. knife 2. سكّين القلم sikkīn al-qalam penknife 3. طعن بسكّينة ṭaʿana bi sikkīna (a; طعن ṭaʿn) to stab

سلّى sallā to entertain

سلاح silāḥ (أسلحة asliḥa) 1. weapon 2. سلاح الطيران silāḥ aṭ-ṭayarān airforce 3. سلاح ناري silāḥ nārī (أسلحة نارية asliḥa nārīya) firearm 4. نزع السلاح nazʿ as-silāḥ disarmament

سلاسة salāsa: بسلاسة bi salāsa smoothly

سلالة sulāla descent

سلام salām 1. peace 2. greeting 3. السلام عليكم as-salām ʿalaykum Muslim greeting, to which the response is وعليكم السلام wa ʿalaykum as-salām

سلامة salāma 1. safety 2. سلامة العقل salāmat al-ʿaql sanity 3. معاهدة السلام muʿāhadat as-salām peace treaty 4. مع السلامة! maʿ as-salāma! goodbye! 5. الحمد لله على السلامة! al-ḥamdu lillāhi

على السلامة! ʿalā 's-salāma! greeting to someone returning from a journey

سلبي salbī negative

سلة sila (-āt) tie; link

سلّة salla (سلال silāl) 1. basket 2. كرة السلة kurat as-salla basketball

سلّح sallaḥa to arm

سلخ salakha (a/u; سلخ salkh) to skin

سلس salis 1. smooth 2. fluent

سلسلة silsila (-āt; سلاسل salāsil) 1. chain 2. succession 3. series 4. range 5. سلسلة جبال silsilat jibāl mountain range

سلطات sulaṭāt pl authorities

سلطة sulṭa 1. authority 2. power 3. jurisdiction 4. في السلطة fī 's-sulṭa in power

سلطة salaṭa (-āt) 1. salad 2. lettuce

سلع silaʿ pl 1. merchandise 2. stock 3. سلع للبيع silaʿ li 'l-bayʿ wares

سلعة silʿa (سلع silaʿ) 1. commodity 2. سلعة رئيسية silʿa raʾīsīya staple

سلف salaf (أسلاف aslāf) ancestor

سلّف sallafa (fin.) to advance

سلفة sulfa (fin.) advance

سلق salaqa (u; سلق salq) to poach

سلك salaka (u; سلوك sulūk) 1. to follow 2. to behave

سلك silk (أسلاك aslāk) 1. wire 2. cable 3. سلك هوائي silk hawāʾī aerial

سلّم sallama 1. to deliver 2. to hand (over) 3. to surrender

سلم sullam (سلالم salālim) 1. stairs 2. ladder 3. سلم متحرك sullam mutaḥarrik escalator 4. سلم الحريق sullam al-ḥarīq fire escape; fire exit 5. سلم موسيقي sullam mūsīqī (mus.) scale

سلم silm peace

سلمي silmī 1. peace 2. peaceful

سلوك sulūk 1. behaviour 2. manners

سليل salīl descendant

سليم salīm 1. safe 2. fit 3. healthy 4. intact 5. sound 6. uninjured 7. سليم العقل salīm al-'aql sane 8. غير سليم ghayr salīm unsafe

سمك سليمان samak sulaymān: سليمان sulaymān salmon

سمّ samm (سموم sumūm) 1. poison 2. toxin

سمّى sammā to call

سماء samā' (سموات samawāt; أسماء asmā') 1. sky 2. heaven

سماد samād (أسمدة asmida) manure

سمّاعة sammā'a (-āt) 1. headphones 2. earphones 3. receiver

سماوي samāwī 1. sky 2. heavenly

سمح samaḥa (a; سماح samāḥ); samuḥa (u; سمح samḥ; سماح samāḥ) 1. to allow; to let (ل so; ل do sth) 2. to admit

سمّر sammara to nail

سمسار simsār 1. dealer 2. سمسار عقاري simsār 'aqārī estate agent; realtor 3. سمسار البورصة simsār al-būrṣa; سمسار الأسهم simsār al-ashum stockbroker

سمع sam' hearing

سمع sami'a (a; سمع sam'; سماع samā') 1. to hear 2. to listen 3. to assemble 4. سمع مصادفةً sami'a muṣādafatan to overhear

سمعة sum'a reputation

سمفونية simfōnīya symphony

سمكة samaka (سمك samak; أسماك asmāk) 1. fish 2. صياد السمك ṣayyād as-samak (-ūn) fisherman 3. إصطياد السمك iṣṭiyād as-samak fishing 4. صنّارة لصيد السمك ṣinnāra li ṣayd as-samak (صنانير ṣanānīr) fishing rod 5. اصطاد السمك iṣṭāda as-samak to fish

سمّم sammama to poison

سمين samīn fat

سناء sanā' splendour

سنترال santrāl telephone exchange

سنّ sinn f (أسنان asnān) 1. tooth 2. age 3. صغير السنّ ṣaghīr as-sinn young 4. أكبر سنّاً akbar sinnan junior 5. أصغر سناً aṣghar sinnan senior 6. بالغ سنّ الرشد bāligh sinn ar-rushd (-ūn) adult 7. سنّ المراهقة sinn al-murāhaqa teens

سنة sana (سنوات sanawāt; سنون sinūn) 1. year 2. السنة الماضية al-sanat al-māḍīya last year 3. طوال السنة ṭiwāl as-sana all year round 4. سنة كبيسة sana kabīsa leap year 5. رأس السنة ra's as-sana New Year 6. ليلة رأس السنة laylat ra's as-sana New Year's Eve

سنّة sunna (سنن sunan) 1. custom 2. tradition 3. السنّة as-sunna the Sunna of the Prophet **4.** Sunnism **5.** أهل السنّة **ahl as-sunna** the Sunnis

سنت **sant** cent

سنتمتر **santimitr** (-āt) centimetre

سند **sanad** (-āt) (fin.) **1.** bond **2.** security

صندوق **ṣandūq/sundūq** (صناديق **ṣanādīq**) **1.** box **2.** chest **3.** صندوق التلفون **sundūq at-tilifōn** telephone booth

سندويتش **sandwīch** (-āt) sandwich

سنغال **sinighāl** Senegal

سنونو **sunūnū** swallow

سنوي **sanawī 1.** annual **2.** ربع سنوياً **rub' sanawīyan** quarterly

سنّي **sunnī** (-ūn) Sunni

سنّي **sinnī** dental

سهاد **suhād** insomnia

سهّل **sahhala 1.** to ease (ه sth; على **'alā** for) **2.** to simplify

سهل **sahl; sahil 1.** easy **2.** smooth **3.** level **4.** (سهول **suhūl**) plain; plains

سهم **sahm** (سهام **sihām**; أسهم **ashum**) **1.** arrow **2.** (fin.) share

سهولة **suhūla 1.** ease **2.** بسهولة **bi suhūla** easily

سوّى **sawwā 1.** to equalize **2.** to straighten

سوى **siwā** except

سوء **sū' 1.** evil **2.** offence **3.** سوء التصرف **sū' at-taṣarruf** misbehaviour **4.** سوء التفاهم **sū' at-tafāhum;** سوء الفهم **sū' al-fahm** misunderstanding **5.** سوء التغذية **sū' at-taghdhiya** malnutrition **6.** سوء الحظ **sū' al-ḥaẓẓ** misfortune **7.** سوء الإدارة

سوء الإدارة **sū' al-idāra** mismanagement **8.** سوء المعاملة **sū' al-mu'āmala** mistreatment

سواء **sawā' 1.** equal **2.** على حدّ سواء **'alā ḥadd sawā'** equally **3.** أم...سواء **sawā' a-... am** (no matter) whether... or

سواد **sawād** blackness

سوار **siwār/suwār** (أسورة **aswira;** أساور **asāwir**) bracelet

سوبرماركت **sūpermārket** supermarket

سوداء **sūdā'** f; سود **sūd** pl **1.** black **2.** السوق السوداء **as-sūq as-sūdā'** black market **3.** and see أسود

السودان **as-sūdān** Sudan

سوداني **sūdānī** Sudanese

سوري **sūrī** Syrian

سوريا **sūriyā;** سورية **sūriya** Syria

سوف **sawfa** will; shall

سوفيتي **sūfiyatī** soviet

سوّق **sawwaqa** to market

سوق **sūq** f/m (أسواق **aswāq**) **1.** market **2.** bazaar

سوقي **sūqī** vulgar

سوّاق **sawwāq** (-ūn) **1.** driver **2.** سوّاق تاكسي **sawwāq tāksī** taxi driver

السويد **as-suwīd** Sweden

سويدي **suwīdī 1.** Swedish **2.** (-yūn) Swede

سويسرا **suwīsrā** Switzerland

سويسري **suwīsrī** (-yūn) Swiss

سويقة **suwayqa** (-āt) stalk; stem

سيّء sayyi' 1. bad 2. evil 3. worse 4.
مزاج سيّئ mizāj sayyi' bad mood 5.
بطريقة سيّئة bi ṭarīqa sayyi'a poorly

سياج siyāj (-āt) fence

سياحة siyāḥa 1. travel 2. tourism 3.
شركة السياحة sharikat as-siyāḥa tour
operator 4. قطاع السياحة qiṭāʿ as-siyāḥa
travel industry

سياحي siyāḥī 1. travel 2. tourist 3.
مرشد سياحي murshid siyāḥī (-ūn) tour
guide 4. تأمين سياحي taʾmīn siyāḥī
travel insurance 5. الشيك السياحي ash-
shīk as-siyāḥī traveller's cheque 6.
قرية سياحية qarya siyāḥīya holiday
resort 7. الموسم السياحي al-mawsim as-
siyāḥī tourist season

سيادة siyāda 1. supremacy 2. sovereignty

سيّار sayyār 1. circulating 2. planet 3.
جرائد سيّارة jarāʾid sayyāra daily
newspapers; dailies

سيّارة sayyāra (-āt) 1. car 2. vehicle 3.
هاتف السيّارة hātif as-sayyāra car phone
4. سيّارة أسعاف sayyārat isʿāf
ambulance 5. سيّارة الإطفاء sayyārat al-
iṭfāʾ fire engine 6. سيّارة أجرة sayyārat
ujra taxi 7. سيّارة جيب sayyārat jīp jeep
8. سيّارة سحن sayyārat shaḥn truck 9.
سباق سيّارات sibāq sayyārāt (spor.) rally
10. مكان وقوف السيّارات makān wuqūf
as-sayyārāt parking space 11. موقف سيّارات
mawqif sayyārāt; مرأب السيّارات mirʾab
al-sayyārāt carpark 12. رخصة قيادةالسيّارات
rukhṣat qiyādat as-sayyārāt driving
licence 13. صندوق سيّارة ṣandūq

sayyāra car boot/trunk

سيّد sayyid (سادة sāda) 1. master 2.
gentleman 3. lord 4. السيّد as-sayyid
Mr; sir

سيّدة sayyida (-āt) 1. mistress 2. lady 3.
السيّدة as-sayyida Mrs; Ms; madam

سياسة siyāsa (-āt) 1. politics 2. policy

سياسي siyāsī 1. political 2. (-yūn؛ ساسة
sāsa) politician

سياقة siyāqa driving

سيجارة sīgāra see سجارة

سي دي sī-dī (سي ديهات sī-dīhāt) compact
disc

سير sīr 1. course 2. حبل السير ḥabl as-sīr
lead

سيرة sīra 1. life; biography 2. سيرة ذاتية
sīra dhātīya autobiography

سيطر على sayṭara ʿalā 1. to control 2. to
dominate

سيطرة sayṭara 1. control 2. domination

سيف sayf (سيوف suyūf) sword

سيكولوجي sīkolūjī psychological

سيل sayl (سيول suyūl) 1. flood 2. torrent

سيّل sayyala to shed

سيلان sayalān flow

سيّما siyyamā: (و)لا سيّما (wa) lā siyyamā
especially

سينما sīnamā (سينماهات sīnamāhāt) cinema

سينمائي sīnamāʾī 1. film; cinema 2.
منتج سينمائي muntij sīnamāʾī film
producer

ش

شاء shā'a (يشاء yashā'; مشيئة mashī'a) 1. to want 2. to wish 3. إن شاء الله in shā' allāh God willing

شائبة shā'iba (شوائب shawā'ib) drawback

شائك shā'ik: أسلاك شائكة aslāk shā'ika pl barbed wire

شابّ shābb (شباب shubbān; شباب shabāb) 1. young 2. youth; teenager

شابه shābaha to resemble

شابه shābih 1. resembling 2. شابه الواقع shābih al-wāqi' virtual

شاجر shājara to quarrel (مع ma'a with)

شاحب shāḥib pale

شاحنة shāḥina (-āt) 1. truck 2. شاحنة صغيرة shāḥina ṣaghīra van

شار shārin (-ūn) buyer

شارب shārib (شوارب shawārib) moustache

شارع shāri' (شوارع shawāri') 1. street 2. مصباح الشارع miṣbāḥ ash-shāri' streetlamp 3. شارع واحد الإتجاه shāri' wāḥid al-ittijāh one-way street

شارك shāraka 1. to share 2. to take part (في fī in) 3. to be a partner (ه with; في fī in)

شاروقة shārūqa (-āt) drinking straw

شاشة shāsha (-āt) 1. glass 2. screen

شاطئ shāṭi' (شواطئ shawāti') 1. beach 2.

shore 3. قرب الشاطئ qurb al-shāṭi' offshore

شاطر shāṭir smart

شاعر shā'ir (شعراء shu'arā') poet

شاغب shāghaba to riot

شاغر shāghir vacant

شاقّ shāqq laborious

شاكر shākir grateful

شاكّ shākk 1. doubtful 2. suspicious 3. sceptic

الشام ash-shām 1. Syria 2. Damascus

شامبانية shāmbānya champagne

شامبو shāmbū shampoo

شامل shāmil 1. total 2. thorough

شامي shāmī (-ūn) Syrian

شأن sha'n (شؤون shu'ūn) 1. matter 2. affair 3. consequence 4. importance 5. الشؤون الإدارية ash-shu'ūn al-idārīya personnel 6. بشأن bi sha'n concerning 7. كبير الشأن kabīr ash-sha'n of great importance

شاهد shāhada 1. to witness 2. to observe; to see

شاهد shāhid (شهود shuhūd; شواهد shawāhid) 1. witness 2. evidence 3. شاهد عيان shāhid 'iyān eyewitness

شاور shāwara to consult

شاويش **shāwīsh** sergeant

شاي **shāy** 1. tea 2. كيس الشاي **kīs ash-shāy** (أكياس **akyās**) teabag 3. إبريق الشاي **ibrīq ash-shāy** (أباريق **abārīq**) teapot 4. ملعقة شاي **milʿaqat shāy** teaspoon

شباب **shabāb** 1. youth 2. بيت الشباب **bayt ash-shabāb** hostel

شباط **shubāṭ** February

شبّاك **shubbāk** (شبابيك **shabābīk**) 1. window 2. شبّاك التذاكر **shubbāk at-tadhākir** ticket office

شبح **shabaḥ** (أشباح **ashbāḥ**) ghost

شبر **shibr** (أشبار **ashbār**) span

شبكة **shabaka** (-āt) 1. net 2. mesh 3. network 4. grid 5. شبكة إتّصالات **shabakat ittiṣālāt** communications network

شبه **shabah** (أشباه **ashbāh**) similarity

شبه **shibh** (أشباه **ashbāh**) 1. similarity 2. semi- 3. شبه نهائي **shibh nihāʾī** semi-final 4. شبه جزيرة **shibh jazīra** peninsula

شبهة **shubha** (شبهات **shubuhāt**) suspicion

شبيبة **shabība** youth

شبيه **shabīh** like; similar (بـ **bi** to)

شتاء **shitāʾ** winter

شتم **shatama** (i/u; شتم **shatm**) to swear

شجاعة **shajāʿa** courage

شجاع **shujāʿ**; شجّاع **shajjāʿ** brave

شجب **shajjaba** to denounce

شجرة **shajara** (-āt; collective شجر **shajar**) tree

شجّع **shajjaʿa** 1. to encourage 2. to promote

شجيرة **shujayra** (-āt) bush

شحت **shaḥata** (a; شحت **shaḥt**) to beg

شحم **shaḥm** (شحوم **shuḥūm**) 1. fat 2. grease

شحن **shaḥana** (a; شحن **shaḥn**) 1. to load 2. to ship

شحن **shaḥn** 1. freight 2. shipping 3. صندوق الشحن **ṣundūq ash-shaḥn** freight container 4. سيّارة شحن **sayyārat shaḥn** truck 5. سفينة شحن **safīnat shaḥn** freighter

شحنة **shaḥna** (شحنات **shaḥanāt**) 1. load 2. (electricity) charge

شخر **shakhara** (i; شخير **shakhīr**) to snore

شخّص **shakhkhaṣa** to diagnose

شخص **shakhṣ** (أشخاص **ashkhāṣ**) 1. person 2. أيّ شخص **ayy shakhṣ** anybody 3. شخص ما **shakhṣ mā** somebody 4. شخص مشهور **shakhṣ mashhūr** celebrity 5. شخص مهمّ جدّاً **shakhṣ muhimm jiddan** VIP 6. منظّم شخصي **munaẓẓim shakhṣī** personal organizer

شخصي **shakhṣī** 1. personal 2. بطاقة شخصية **biṭāqa shakhṣīya** I.D. card; identity card 3. ترجمة شخصية **tarjuma shakhṣīya** profile 4. المصلحة الشخصية **al-maṣlaḥa 'sh-shakhṣīya** self-interest

شخصياً **shakhṣīyan** personally

شخصية **shakhṣīya** (-āt) 1. character 2. personality

شدّ shadda (i/u; shadd شدّ) 1. to pull 2. to tighten 3. شدّ بقوة shadda bi qūwa to tug

شذا shadhan fragrance

شدّة shidda intensity

شديد shadīd 1. strong 2. acute 3. harsh 4. intense 5. شديد الإنحدار shadīd al-inḥidār steep

شرّ sharr (أشرار ashrār) evil

شراء shirā' purchase

شرائح sharā'iḥ pl 1. slices 2. sections 3. قطع شرائح qaṭṭa'a sharā'iḥ; شرّح شرائح sharraḥa sharā'iḥ to slice 4. and see شريحة

شراب sharāb (أشربة ashriba) 1. drink 2. syrup

شرارة sharāra (-āt) spark

شراع shirā' (أشرعة ashri'a) 1. sail 2. مركب شراعي markab shirā'ī sailing-boat; sailing-ship

شراكة shirāka partnership

شرب shariba (a; شرب shurb) 1. to drink 2. شرب نخبه shariba nakhbah to toast someone's health

شرح sharḥ explanation

شرح sharaḥa (a; شرح sharḥ) to explain

شرّح sharraḥa: شرّح شرائح sharraḥa sharā'iḥ to slice

شرخ sharkh (أشراخ ashrākh) 1. slice 2. crack

شرّع sharra'a to legalize

شرّف sharrafa to honour

شرس sharis vicious

شرط sharṭ (شروط shurūṭ) (leg/pol.) 1. condition 2. provision 3. من غير شرط min ghayr sharṭ unconditional 4. على شرط أن 'alā sharṭ an on condition that 5. and see شروط

شرطة shurṭa 1. police 2. police force 3. مركز الشرطة markaz ash-shurṭa police station

شرطي shurṭī 1. police 2. (-yūn) policeman 3. ضابط شرطي ḍābiṭ sharṭī police inspector

شرطية shurṭiya (-āt) policewoman

شرعي shar'ī 1. legal 2. غير شرعي ghayr shar'ī illegal 3. مقيم غير شرعي muqīm ghayr shar'ī illegal alien 4. وضع شرعي waḍ' shar'ī (leg.) status

شرعية shar'īya legitimacy

شرغوف sharghūf collective tadpole

شرف sharaf honour

شرفة shurfa (شرفات shurafāt; شرف shuruf) veranda

شرق sharq 1. east 2. الشرق الأوسط ash-sharq al-awsaṭ Middle East

شرقاً sharqan east; eastwards

شرقي sharqī 1. east; eastern 2. oriental 3. (-yūn) easterner 4. الشمال الشرقي ash-shamāl al-sharqī northeast 5. الجنوب الشرقي al-janūb al-sharqī southeast

شركة sharika (-āt) 1. company; firm 2. corporation 3. شركة السياحة sharikat

as-siyāḥa tour operator 4. شركة نقل
sharikat naql (com.) carrier 5.
شركة محدودة sharika maḥdūda limited
company 6. شركة رئيس ra'īs sharika
chief executive officer (C.E.O.)

شروال shirwāl شراويل sharāwīl 1. trousers
2. شروال نسائي ضيّق shirwāl nisā'ī ḍayyiq
tights

شروط shurūṭ pl 1. terms 2. and see شرط

شروق shurūq sunrise

شريان shiryān شرايين sharāyīn) artery

شريحة sharīḥa شرائح sharā'iḥ) 1. slice 2.
شريحة لحم sharīḥat laḥm steak 3. and see
شرائح

شرير sharīr 1. evil 2. vicious

شريط sharīṭ (أشرطة ashriṭa; شرائط sharā'iṭ)
1. band 2. strap 3. tape 4. ribbon 5.
cassette 6. شريط الفيديو sharīṭ al-vīdiyo
video tape 7. أعاد الشريط a'āda ash-
sharīṭ to rewind

شريطة sharīṭa see شرط

شريف sharīf 1. noble 2. honourable

شريك sharīk (شركاء shurakā') 1. partner 2.
associate

شطب shaṭaba (u; شطب shaṭb) to delete

شطرنج shaṭranj chess

شظية shaẓiya (شظايا shaẓāyā) chip

شعائري sha'ā'irī ritual

شعار shi'ār (-āt) 1. slogan 2. logo

شعاعة shu'ā'a (collective شعاع shu'ā'; plural
أشعّة ashi''a) ray

شعب sha'b (شعوب shu'ūb) 1. people; folk
2. nation

شعب shi'b (شعاب shi'āb) mountain pass

شعبة shu'ba (شعب shu'ab) 1. branch 2.
department

شعبي sha'bī 1. folk 2. popular 3.
إحتفال شعبي iḥtifāl sha'bī carnival

شعبية sha'bīya 1. popularity 2. لا
شعبية lā sha'bīya unpopularity 3. جريدة شعبية
jarīda sha'bīya tabloid

شعر sha'ara (u; شعور shu'ūr) to feel

شعر sha'r collective 1. hair 2. قصّ شعر qass
sha'r haircut 3. فرشاة شعر furshāt sha'r
hairbrush 4. آلة لتنشيف الشعر ālat li
tanshīf ash-sha'r hairdryer

شعر shi'r (أشعار ash'ār) 1. poetry 2. poem

شعراني sha'rānī hairy

شعرة sha'ra (collective شعر sha'r; pl أشعار
ash'ār) hair

شعري sha'rī hairy

شعري shi'rī poetic

شعشع sha'sha'a to dilute

شعور shu'ūr 1. feeling 2. ...لدي شعور أن
laday shu'ūr an... I have a hunch that...

شعيرة sha'īra (شعائر sha'ā'ir) ritual

شغب shaghab 1. unrest 2. riot

شغّل shaghghala to operate

شغف shaghaf passion

شغف shaghif passionate

شغل shaghala (a; شغل shughl) 1. to be
busy (ب bi with) 2. to occupy; to

engage 3. to distract (عن 'an from) 4. to occupy/hold *a position*

شغل shughl (أشغال ashghāl) 1. job; work 2. occupation

شغور shughūr vacancy

شغوف shaghūf 1. passionate (ب bi about) 2. هو شغوف بكرة القدم huwa shaghūf bi kurat al-qadam. He's mad about football.

شفى shafā (i; شفاء shifā') 1. to cure (so; عن 'an of) 2. recover 3. to recuperate

شفاء shifā' 1. cure 2. recovery 3. recuperation

شفر shafr (أشفار ashfār) edge

شفرة shafra 1. edge 2. blade 3. شفرة الحلاقة shafrat al-ḥilāqa razor-blade

شفرة shifra code

شفة shafa (شفاه shifāh) 1. lip 2. أحمر الشفاه aḥmar ash-shifāh lipstick 3. قرأ الشفاه qara'a ash-shifāh to lip-read

شفّاف shaffāf transparent

شفّافية shaffāfiya transparency

شفقة shafaqa 1. pity 2. مثير للشفقة muthīr li 'sh-shafaqa pathetic

شفهي shafahī 1. oral 2. verbal

شفوق shafūq humane

شفوي shafawī oral

شقّ shaqqa (u; شقّ shaqq) 1. to split 2. to crack 3. شقّ بالطول shaqqa bi 'ṭ-ṭūl to slash

شقّ shaqq (شقوق shuqūq) 1. split 2. crack 3. slot

شقّة shaqqa (شقق shiqaq) flat; apartment

شقّق shaqqaqa to split

شقي shaqī mischievous

شكّ shakk (شكوك shukūk) 1. doubt 2. suspicion 3. mistrust 4. لا شكّ lā shakk; بلا شكّ bilā shakk; دون شكّ dūna shakk undoubtedly 5. لا شكّ أن lā shakka an there is no doubt that 6. من غير شكّ min ghayr shakk surely 7. مرض الشكّ maraḍ ash-shakk paranoia 8. مصيب بمرض الشكّ muṣīb bi maraḍ al-shakk paranoid

شكّ shakka (u; شك shakk) 1. to doubt 2. to mistrust 3. to question

شكا shakā (u; شكوى shakwā; شكاية shikāya) to complain

شكر shakara (u; شكر shukr; شكران shukrān) to thank (so; على\ل 'alā/li for)

شكر shukr gratitude

شكراً shukran 1. thank you! 2. شكراً جزيلاً! shukran jazīlan! many thanks!

شكّل shakkala to form

شكل shakl (أشكال ashkāl) 1. form; figure; shape 2. pattern 3. kind; sort 4. manner 5. بشكل كامل bi shakl kāmil perfectly

شيكولاته shikolāta chocolate

شكوى shakwa (شكوات shakawāt); شكوة shakwā (شكاوى shakāwā) 1. complaint

2. accusation 3. شكوة قدّم qaddama shakwa to lodge a complaint

شلال shallāl (-āt) waterfall

شمّ shamma (u; شمّ shamm) to smell

شمال shamāl/shimāl 1. north 2. نحو الشمال naḥw ash-shamāl northwards 3. الشمال الغربي ash-shamāl al-gharbī northwest 4. الشمال الشرقي ash-shamāl al-sharqī northeast

شمالاً shamālan northwards

شمالي shamālī/shimālī 1. north; northern 2. (-yūn) northerner 3. آيرلندا الشمالية āyrlandā ash-shamālīya Northern Ireland

شمس shams (شموس shumūs) sun

شمسي shamsī solar

شمسية shamsiya (-āt) umbrella

شمع shamʿ wax

شمعة shamʿa (collective شمع shamʿ) candle

شمل shamila (a; شمل shaml) 1. to include 2. to affect

شمل shaml 1. union 2. إجتماع الشمل ijtimāʿ ash-shaml; جمع الشمل jamʿ ash-shaml reunion

شمّام shammām collective melon

شنّ shanna (u; شنّ shann) 1. شنّ الحرب shanna al-ḥarb to wage war (على ʿalā on/against) 2. شنّ غارة على shanna ghāra ʿalā to raid

شنطة shanṭa (شنط shunaṭ) 1. bag 2. suitcase

شنق shanaqa (u; شنق shanq) to hang

شنيع shanīʿ awful

شهاب shihāb (شهب shuhub) meteor

شهادة shahāda (-āt) 1. testimony 2. statement 3. certificate 4. diploma 5. (Isl.) creed 6. شهادة جامعية shahāda jāmiʿīya degree 7. شهادة ميلاد shahādat mīlād birth certificate

شهد shahida (a; شهود shuhūd) 1. to testify (على ʿalā against; لِ li on behalf of) 2. to be present at

شهر shahr (شهور shuhūr; أشهر ashhur) 1. month 2. شهر العسل shahr al-ʿasal honeymoon

شهرة shuhra fame

شهري shahrī monthly

شهق shahiqa (a; شهيق shahīq) 1. to inhale 2. to breathe

شهوة shahwa (شهوات shahawāt) 1. desire 2. lust 3. appetite

شهيد shahīd (شهداء shuhadāʾ) martyr

شهير shahīr famous

شهية shahīya appetite

شوى shawā (i; شيّ shayy) 1. to roast 2. to grill

شوّر shawwara to signal

شوق shawq (أشواق ashwāq) longing

شوكة shawka (شوك shawk) fork

شوكي shawkī spinal

شوّه shawwaha 1. to distort 2. to mutilate

شوي shawī 1. roasted 2. grilled

شيء shayʾ (أشياء ashyāʾ) 1. thing 2. item;

شيء muz'ij pest 4. مزعج article 3.
كل شيء kull shay' everything 5. لا شيء
lā shay' nothing 6. قبل كلّ شيء qabl kull
shay' primarily 7. ما شيء shay' mā
something 8. أيّ شيء ayy shay'
anything 9. whatever

شيخ (شيوخ shuyūkh) shaykh 1. elder 2.
chief 3. senator 4. religious scholar
5. old man 6. and see شيوخ

شيخوخة shaykhūkha old age

شيطان (شياطين shayāṭīn) shayṭān 1. devil
2. الشيطان ash-shayṭān Satan

الشيعة ash-shī'a 1. Shi'ism 2. the Shi'is

شيعي shī'ī (-ūn) Shi'i

شيك (-āt) 1. cheque 2. الشيك السياحي
ash-shīk as-siyāḥī traveller's cheque 3.
دفتر شيكات daftar shīkāt cheque book

شيوخ shuyūkh pl 1. مجلس الشيوخ majlis
ash-shuyūkh senate; upper house 2.
مجلس الشيوخ البريطاني majlis ash-
shuyūkh al-brīṭānī House of Lords 3.
and see شيخ

شيوعي shuyū'ī communist

شيوعية shuyū'īya communism

صبّ ṣabba (u/i; صبّ ṣabb) to pour

صابر ṣābir patient

صابون ṣābūn soap

صاحب (أصحاب aṣḥāb) ṣāḥib 1. owner 2.
possessor 3. friend; companion 4.
associate 5. صاحب البيت ṣāḥib al-bayt
landlord 6. صاحب دكان ṣāḥib dukkān
shopkeeper 7. صاحب دكّان ṣāḥib
dukkān storekeeper 8. صاحب الحرفة
ṣāḥib al-ḥirfa craftsman 9. صاحب العمل
ṣāḥib al-'amal employer 10. ملايين
ṣāḥib malāyīn millionaire

صاحبة (-āt) f ṣāḥiba 1. صاحبة بيت ṣāḥibat al-

bayt landlady 2. see صاحب

صاح (i; صيح ṣayḥ; صيحة ṣayḥa; صياح
ṣiyāḥ) ṣāḥa 1. to shout 2. to crow

صادر ṣādir (-āt) export

صادف ṣādafa to encounter

صادق ṣādiq 1. honest 2. truthful 3.
sincere 4. غير صادق ghayr ṣādiq
dishonest

صار ṣāra (i; صير ṣayr) to become

صارم ṣārim 1. severe 2. strict 3. rigorous

صاروخ (صواريخ ṣawārīkh) ṣārūkh 1.
rocket 2. missile

صاعد ṣā'id 1. uphill 2. صاعداً ṣā'idan upward; upwards

صاف ṣāfin 1. clear 2. *(fin.)* net

صافح ṣāfaḥa to shake hands

صالح ṣāliḥ: صالح للأكل ṣāliḥ li 'l-akl edible

صالون ṣālōn living-room; lounge

صام ṣāma (u; صيام ṣiyām) to fast

صامت ṣāmit silent

صان ṣāna (u; صيانة ṣiyāna) to maintain

صانع ṣāni' (صنّاع ṣunnā') 1. maker 2. manufacturer 3. صانع الفخّار ṣāni' al-fakhkhār potter

صباح ṣabāḥ 1. morning 2. في الصباح fi 'ṣ-ṣabāḥ in the morning 3. صباح الخير! ṣabāḥ al-khayr! good morning! 4. صباح اليوم ṣabāḥ al-yawm this morning 5. غداً في الصباح ghadan fī 'ṣ-ṣabāḥ tomorrow morning

صبر ṣabr 1. patience 2. endurance 3. نافد الصبر nāfid aṣ-ṣabr impatient 4. نفاد الصبر nafād aṣ-ṣabr impatience

صبغ ṣabagha (a/i/u; صبغ ṣabgh/ṣibagh) to dye

صبغ ṣibgh (أصباغ aṣbāgh) dye

صبي ṣabī (صبيان ṣibyān/ṣubyān; صبية ṣibya) 1. boy 2. youth; teenager

صبية ṣabīya (-āt) 1. girl 2. teenager

صحّة ṣiḥḥa 1. health 2. correctness 3. علم الصحّة 'ilm aṣ-ṣiḥḥa hygiene 4. ضار بالصحّة ḍārr bi 'ṣ-ṣiḥḥa unhealthy 5. صيانة الصحّة العامّة ṣiyānat aṣ-ṣiḥḥa al-'āmma sanitation 6. الصحّة النفسانية aṣ-

ṣiḥḥa an-nafsānīya mental health 7. بصحّتك! bi ṣiḥḥatik! cheers!

صحافة ṣaḥāfa; ṣiḥāfa 1. the press 2. journalism 3. حرّية الصحافة ḥurrīyat aṣ-ṣaḥāfa freedom of the press 4. منع حرّية الصحافة mana'a ḥurrīyat aṣ-ṣaḥāfa (a; منع man') to gag the press

صحافي ṣaḥāfī; ṣiḥāfī 1. press 2. journalist; journalistic

صحح ṣaḥḥaḥa 1. to correct 2. to mark

صحراء ṣaḥrā' (صحارى ṣaḥārin; صحار ṣaḥārā; صحروات ṣaḥrawāt) desert

صحراوي ṣaḥrāwī 1. desert 2. أراضٍ صحراوية arāḍin ṣaḥrāwīya desert areas

صحف ṣuḥuf pl 1. كشك الصحف kushk aṣ-ṣuḥuf newsstand 2. *see* صحيفة

صحفي ṣaḥafī/ṣuḥufī 1. press 2. (-yūn) journalist 3. بيان صحفي bayān ṣaḥafī press release 4. معتمر صحفي mu'tamar ṣaḥafī press conference

صحن ṣaḥn (صحون ṣuḥūn) 1. plate 2. saucer

صحي ṣiḥḥī 1. healthy 2. hygienic 3. health 4. sanitary 5. غير صحي ghayr ṣiḥḥī unhealthy 6. تأمين صحّي ta'mīn ṣiḥḥī healthcare

صحيح ṣaḥīḥ 1. true 2. correct 3. right 4. okay 5. healthy 6. غير صحيح ghayr ṣaḥīḥ untrue 7. بطريقة صحيحة bi ṭarīqa ṣaḥīḥa right; correctly

صحيفة ṣaḥīfa (صحف ṣuḥuf; صحائف ṣaḥā'if) 1. newspaper 2. page 3.

surface 4. صحيفة يومية ṣaḥīfa yawmīya daily 5. عمود في صحيفة 'amūd fī ṣaḥīfa newspaper column 6. صحيفة من الورق ṣaḥīfa min al-waraq a sheet of paper

صخرة ṣakhra (collective صخر ṣakhr; plural صخور ṣukhūr) 1. rock 2. صخر رملي ṣakhr ramlī sandstone

صخري ṣakhrī rocky

صدّ ṣadda (u; صدّ ṣadd) 1. to block 2. to stem 3. to repel

صدى ṣadā (ء أصدا aṣdā') echo

صداع ṣudā' 1. headache 2. صداع نصفي ṣudā' niṣfī migraine

صداقة ṣadāqa friendship

صدد ṣadad 1. في هذا الصدد fī hādhā 'ṣ-ṣadad; بهذا الصدد bi hādhā 'ṣ-ṣadad in this respect 2. بصدد bi ṣadad with regard to

صدر ṣadara (i/u; صدور ṣudūr) 1. to appear 2. to be issued

صدّر ṣaddara to export

صدر ṣadr (صدور ṣudūr) 1. chest 2. breast 3. bust

صدرة ṣudra waistcoat

صدف ṣadaf collective shell(s)

صدفة ṣudfa (صدف ṣudaf) 1. chance; coincidence 2. بالصدفة bi 'ṣ-ṣudfa by chance

صدفي ṣadafī 1. shell 2. حيوانات صدفية ḥayawānāt ṣadafīya shellfish

صدق ṣidq 1. honesty 2. عدم الصدق 'adm aṣ-ṣidq dishonesty

صدّق ṣaddaqa 1. to believe 2. to trust 3. صدّق على ṣaddaqa 'alā to approve 4. لا يصدّق lā yuṣaddaq unbelievable

صدقة ṣadaqa charity

صدمة ṣadma (صدمات ṣadamāt) 1. shock 2. مسبّب الصدمة musabbib aṣ-ṣadma traumatic 3. صدمة كهربائية ṣadma kahrabā'īya electric shock 4. (med.) أصيب بصدمة uṣība bi ṣadma to be in shock

صدىء ṣadi' rusty

صديرية ṣudayrīya brassiere; bra

صديق ṣadīq (ء أصدقا aṣdiqā') 1. friend 2. boyfriend

صديقة ṣadīqa (-āt) 1. friend 2. girlfriend

صرّة ṣurra (صرر ṣurar) package pack

صراحة ṣarāḥa 1. clarity 2. صراحةً ṣarāḥatan; بصراحة bi ṣarāḥa frankly

صراع ṣirā' (-āt) 1. struggle 2. conflict

صرّاف ṣarrāf (-ūn) 1. banker 2. cashier 3. bureau de change

صرّافة ṣarrāfa bureau de change

صرامة ṣarāma severity

صرّح ṣarraḥa 1. to state; to declare 2. to make a statement (ب bi about) 3. to explain

صرخة ṣarkha (-āt) cry; scream; yell

صرخ ṣarakha (u; صراخ ṣurākh) to cry; to scream; to yell

صرّف ṣarrafa 1. to drain 2. (fin.) to cash 3. to change

صرصور صُرْصُور (صراصير şarāṣīr) cockroach

صرف şarafa 1. (i; صرف şarf) to distract (عن 'an from) 2. (i; صريف şarīf) to squeak

صرف şarf 1. grammatical inflection 2. turning away 3. expenditure 4. drainage 5. سعر الصرف si'r aṣ-ṣarf exchange rate 6. صرف الإنتباه şarf al-intibāh distraction 7. بصرف النظر عن bi ṣarf an-naẓar 'an regardless of 8. النحو والصرف an-naḥw wa 'ṣ-ṣarf grammar

صرف şirf sheer

صريح şarīḥ 1. direct 2. outspoken

صعب şa'b hard

صعد şa'ida (a; صعود şu'ūd) 1. to go up 2. to climb

صعدة şa'da (-āt) rise; slope

صعوبة şu'ūba difficulty

صغر şaghr 1. smallness 2. youthfulness

صغير şaghīr (صغار şighār) 1. little; small 2. minor 3. (السنّ) صغير şaghīr (as-sinn) young 4. حاملة ركّاب صغيرة ḥāmilat rukkāb şaghīra minibus 5. موظّف صغير muwaẓẓaf şaghīr minor official

صفّ şaff (صفوف şufūf) 1. row 2. queue 3. tier 4. (ed.) class; grade; form 5. زميل في الصفّ zamīl fi 'ṣ-ṣaff classmate

صفّى şaffā to filter

صفّارة şaffāra 1. whistle 2. صفارة الإنذار şaffārat al-indhār siren

صفة şifa (-āt) 1. quality 2. adjective

صفحة şafḥa (صفحات şafaḥāt) page

صفر şafara (i; صفير şafīr) to whistle

صفر şifr (أصفار aşfār) zero

صفع şafa'a (a; صفع şaf') to slap

صفعة şaf'a slap

صفّف şaffafa 1. to line up 2. to align

صفق şafaqa (i; صفق şafq) to smack

صفّق şaffaqa to clap

صفق şafq smack

صفقة şafqa (صفقات şafaqāt) 1. deal 2. صفقة رابحة şafqa rābiḥa bargain

صلاة şalāh (صلوات şalawāt) ritual prayer

صلب şulb 1. hard 2. stiff 3. rigid 4. solid 5. steel 6. مادّة صلبة mādda ṣulba solid

صلة şila (-āt) 1. relation; relationship 2. مرتبط بصلة القرابة murtabiṭ bi ṣilat al-qarāba related 3. وثاقة الصلة wathāqat aṣ-ṣila relevance; relevancy 4. وثيق الصلة wathīq aṣ-ṣila relevant

صلّح şallaḥa to repair; to fix

صلصة şalşa (-āt) 1. sauce 2. صلصة المايونيز şalşat al-mayūnīz mayonnaise

صلّى şallā to pray

صليب şulīb (صلبان şulbān) cross

صمّ şumm: لغة الصمّ lughat al-şumm sign language

صمام şimām (-āt) valve

صمت şamt silence

صمد şamida (u; صمود şumūd): صمد أكثر

şamida akthar to outlast

صمّم şammama 1. to resolve (على 'alā to) 2. to design

صموت şumūt silence

صناعة şanā'a (-āt) 1. manufacture 2. industry 3. make

صناعي şanā'ī 1. manufactured 2. industrial 3. industrialized 4. قمر صناعي qamar şinā'ī communications satellite 5. عالج صناعياً 'ālaja şinā'īyan to process

صندوق şundūq (صناديق şanādīq) 1. box 2. case 3. trunk 4. صندوق البريد şundūq al-barīd postbox 5. صندوق سيّارة şandūq sayyāra car boot 6. صندوق حاسب şundūq ḥāsib cash till; cash register 7. أمين الصندوق amīn aş-şandūq cashier; treasurer 8. صندوق الشحن şundūq ash-shaḥn freight container 9. صندوق القمامة şundūq al-qumāma dustbin

صنع şana'a (a; صنع şan'/صنع şun') 1. to make; to do 2. to manufacture 3. to produce

صنّع şanna'a to industrialise

صنف şanf/şinf (أصناف aşnāf) 1. kind; sort 2. category

صنم şanam idol (أصنام aşnām)

صنّارة لصيد السمك şannāra (صنانير şanānīr): şinnāra li şayd as-samak fishing rod

صنّف şannafa 1. to sort 2. to classify

صحن şaḥn (صحون şuḥūn) dish

صوّى şawwā to squeak

صوّان şawwān granite

صوّب şawwaba to aim (نحو naḥw at)

صوب şawb; şawba towards

صوّت şawwata to vote (ل li for)

صوت şawt (أصوات aşwāt) 1. voice 2. sound 3. vote 4. بصوت عال bi şawtin 'ālin loudly 5. جهارة الصوت jahārat aş-şawt volume 6. مرتفع الصوت murtafi' aş-şawt loud 7. إرتفاع الصوت irtifā' aş-şawt loudness 8. مكبّر الصوت mukabbir aş-şawt loudspeaker 9. رفع الصوت rafa'a aş-şawt (a; رفع raf') to turn up the volume

صوتي şawtī vocal

صوّر şawwara 1. to photograph 2. to film 3. صوّر على الفيديو şawwara 'alā 'l-vīdiyo to video

صورة şūra (صور şuwar) 1. image 2. picture 3. photograph 4. portrait 5. form; shape 6. صورة فتوغرافية şūra fotōghrāfiya snapshot 7. أخذ صورة الأشعة akhadha şūrat al-ashi''a to take an x-ray 8. بصورة خاصّة bi şūra khāşşa especially 9. بصورة عامّة bi şūra 'āmma generally

صوف şūf wool

صيام şiyām fast; fasting

صيانة şiyāna (-āt) 1. service 2. maintenance 3. conservation 4. صيانة الصحّة العامّة şiyānat aş-şiḥḥa al-'āmma sanitation

صيحة şayḥa (-āt) shout

صيد **şayd 1.** hunting **2.** رحلة صيد riḥlat şayd shoot; shooting trip **3.** صنّارة لصيد السمك şinnāra li şayd as-samak (صنانير şanānīr) fishing rod

صيدلي **şaydalī 1.** pharmaceutical **2.** (-yūna) chemist; pharmacist

صيدلية **şaydalīya (-āt)** chemist's; pharmacy

صيغة **şīgha (صيغ şiyagh)** formula

صيف **şayf (أصياف aşyāf)** summer

صين **şīn 1.** China **2.** الصين الشعبية aş-şīn ash-shu'bīya People's Republic of China

صيني **şīnī 1.** Chinese **2.** porcelain; china معكرونة شعرية صينية ma'karūna shi'rīya şīnīya noodles

صيّاد **şayyād (-ūn)** hunter **2.** صيّاد السمك şayyād as-samak fisherman

ضائع **ḍā'i' 1.** lost **2.** missing

ضابط **ḍābiṭ (ضبّاط ḍubbāṭ) 1.** officer **2.** ضابط شرطي ḍābiṭ sharṭī police inspector **3.** ضابط شرطي ḍābiṭ shurṭī sheriff

ضاجّ **ḍājj** noisy

ضارّ **ḍārr 1.** harmful **2.** threatening **3.** ضارّ بالصحّة ḍārr bi 'ṣ-ṣiḥḥa unhealthy

ضارب **ḍāraba (fin.)** to speculate

ضاعف **ḍā'afa 1.** to multiply **2.** to double **3.** ضاعف ثلاث مرات ḍā'afa thulāth marrāt to triple

ضالّ **ḍāll** astray

ضأن **ḍa'n collective 1.** sheep **2.** لحم الضأن laḥm aḍ-ḍa'n mutton

ضايق **ḍāyaqa 1.** to bother **2.** to annoy

ضباب **ḍabāb 1.** mist **2.** fog

ضبابي **ḍabābī 1.** misty **2.** foggy

ضبّط **ḍabbaṭa** to adjust; to set

ضبط **ḍabṭ 1.** control **2.** setting **3.** بالضبط bi 'ḍ-ḍabṭ exactly **4.** ضبط النفس ḍabṭ an-nafs self-control **5.** أعاد الضبط a'āda 'ḍ-ḍabṭ to reset

ضجّة **ḍajja; ضجيج ḍajīj** noise

ضحّى **ḍaḥḥā** to sacrifice

ضحك **ḍaḥika (a; ضحك ḍaḥk)** to laugh

ضحك **ḍaḥk** laugh; laughter

ضحل **ḍaḥl** shallow

ضحية **ḍaḥīya (ضحايا ḍaḥāyā)** victim

ضخّ ḍakhkha (u; ضخّ ḍakhkh) to pump

ضخم ḍakhm huge

ضدّ ḍidd; ḍidda 1. against 2. versus 3. واقٍ ضدّ المطر wāqin ḍidd al-maṭar waterproof 4. انقلب ضدّ inqalaba ḍidd turn against

ضرّ ḍarra (u; ضرّ ḍarr) 1. to harm 2. to damage

ضرائب ḍarā'ib pl 1. taxes 2. معافى من الضرائب mu'āfan min aḍ-ḍarā'ib tax-free 3. دفع الضرائب dafa'a aḍ-ḍarā'ib to pay tax 4. and see ضريبة

ضرب ḍaraba (i; ضرب ḍarb) 1. to hit 2. to beat 3. to strike 4. to bang 5. to bump 6. to multiply (ﻫ sth; في fī by)

ضرب ḍarb (ضروب ḍurūb) 1. kind; sort 2. blow 3. multiplication

ضربة ḍarba (ﺍت ḍarabāt) 1. blow 2. stroke 3. bang 4. bump 5. (mil.) strike 6. ضربة الجزاء ḍarbat-al-jazā' (spor.) penalty

ضرّر ḍarrara 1. to harm 2. to damage

ضرر ḍarar 1. harm 2. damage 3. prejudice

ضرّم ḍarrama 1. to light 2. ضرّم النار في ḍarrama al-nār fī to set fire to

ضرورة ḍurūra (-āt) 1. need 2. necessity

ضروري ḍurūrī 1. necessary 2. indispensable 3. غير ضروري ghayr ḍurūrī unnecessary

ضرورياً ḍurūrīyan necessarily

ضريبة ḍarība (ضرائب ḍarā'ib) 1. tax 2.

ضريبة الطرق ḍarībat aṭ-ṭuruq toll duty 3. ضريبة القيمة المضافة ḍarībat al-qīmat al-muḍāfa value added tax (VAT) 5. فرض الضريبة على faraḍa aḍ-ḍarība 'alā (i) to tax 6. and see ضرائب

ضريبي ḍarībī tax

ضعف ḍu'f weakness

ضعيف ḍa'īf (ﺀ ضعفا ḍu'afā') weak

ضغط ḍaghaṭa (u; ضغط ḍaghṭ) 1. to squeeze 2. to push 3. to compress to pressurise 4. to stress 5. (pol.) to lobby

ضغط ḍaghṭ (ضغوط ḍughūṭ) 1. pressure 2. stress 3. (pol.) lobby

ضفّة/ضفّ ḍiffa/ḍaffa (ضفاف ḍifāf) 1. river bank 2. shore

ضفدع ḍafda'/ḍifda' (ﻉ ضفادع ḍafādi') 1. frog 2. toad

ضلع ḍil' (ﺀ أضلاع aḍlā'; ضلوع ḍulū') 1. rib 2. chop

ضلّ ḍalla (i; ضلالة ḍalāla) to stray

ضمّ ḍamma (u; ضمّ ḍamm) 1. to add 2. to bring together 3. to contain

ضمان ḍamān (-āt) guarantee

ضمن ḍamina (a; ضمان ḍamān) 1. to ensure 2. to guarantee

ضمن ḍimn; ḍimna within

ضمير ḍamīr (ﺭ ضمائ ḍamā'ir) 1. pronoun 2. conscience

ضهر ḍahr (ضهور ḍuhūr) summit

ضوء ḍaw' (ﺀ أضوا aḍwā') 1. light 2. ضوء الشمس ḍaw' ash-shams sunlight 3.

ضوء القمر ḍaw' al-qamar moonlight 4. على ضوء 'alā ḍaw' in the light of 5. أشعل الضوء ash'ala aḍ-ḍaw' to turn the light on

ضوئي ḍaw'ī 1. light 2. إشارة ضوئية ishāra ḍaw'īya traffic lights

ضواحٍ ḍawāḥin pl 1. suburbs 2. متعلّق بالضواحي muta'alliq bi 'ḍ-ḍawāḥī suburban

حسن الضيافة: ضيافة ḥusn aḍ-ḍiyāfa hospitality

ضيّع ḍayya'a 1. to lose; to misplace 2. ضيّع الوقت ḍayya'a al-waqt to waste time

ضيف (ضيوف ḍuyūf) guest

ضيّق ḍayyiq 1. narrow 2. tight 3. ضيّق الأفق ḍayyiq al-ufuq narrow-minded

طائرة ṭā'ira (-āt) 1. aeroplane/airplane 2. aircraft 3. رحلة بالطائرة riḥla bi 'ṭ-ṭā'ira flight 4. طائرة عمودية ṭā'ira 'umūdīya helicopter 5. طائرة نفّاثة ṭā'ira naffāthīya; طائرة نفّاثة ṭā'ira naffātha jet plane 6. طائرة مقاتلة ṭā'ira muqātila fighter plane 7. طائرة قاذفة ṭā'ira qādhifa bomber 8. طائرة ورقية ṭā'ira waraqīya kite 9. حظيرة الطائرات ḥaẓīrat aṭ-ṭā'irāt hangar 10. قاد طائرة qāda ṭā'ira (u; qawd ;قود qiyāda قيادة) to fly a plane

طائش ṭā'ish 1. thoughtless 2. reckless

طائفة ṭā'ifa (طوائف ṭawā'if) sect

طابع بريدي :طابع ṭābi' (طوابع ṭawābi') 1. طابع ṭābi' barīdī postage stamp 2.

طابع على الآلة الكاتبة ṭābi' 'alā 'l-ālati 'l-kātiba typist

طابق طوابق ṭābiq (ṭawābiq) 1. floor 2. الطابق الأسفل aṭ-ṭābiq al-asfal downstairs

طابور طوابير ṭābūr (ṭawābir) 1. queue 2. يقف في الطابور waqafa fi 'ṭ-ṭābūr يقف waqf) to queue وقف ;yaqifu

طار ṭāra (i; طيران ṭayarān) to fly

طارئة ṭāri'a (طوارئ ṭawāri') emergency

طارد ṭārada to chase

طازج ṭāzaj 1. fresh 2. غير طازج ghayr ṭāzij stale

طاعة ṭā'a obedience

طاقة ṭāqa 1. energy; power 3. capacity 4.

طبع ṭab' 1. printing 2. بالطبع bi 't-ṭab' naturally 3. أعاد الطبع a'āda al-ṭab' to reprint

طبعاً ṭab'an certainly

طبعة ṭab'a (-āt) edition

طبّق ṭabbaqa 1. to put into practice 2. to implement

طبق ṭabaq (أطباق aṭbāq) 1. dish 2. plate

طبقة ṭabaqa (-āt) 1. layer 2. storey 3. class 4. الطبقة الوسطى aṭ-ṭabaqa 'l-wusṭā middle class 5. متعدّد الطبقات muta'addid al-ṭabaqāt multistorey

طبلة ṭabla drum

طبّي ṭibbī 1. medical 2. medicinal 3. فحص طبّي faḥṣ ṭibbī check-up; physical 4. قطن طبّي quṭn ṭibbī cotton wool 5. مستحضر طبّي mustaḥḍar ṭibbī cream; ointment 6. لفافة طبّية lifāfa ṭibbīya (-āt) bandage 7. وصفة طبّية waṣfa ṭibbīya prescription

طبيب ṭabīb (أطبّاء aṭibbā') 1. doctor 2. طبيب بيطري ṭabīb bayṭarī vet 3. طبيب الأسنان ṭabīb al-asnān dentist 4. طبيب العيون ṭabīb al-'uyūn optician 5. طبيب أمراض النساء ṭabīb amrāḍ an-nisā' gynaecologist 6. طبيب نفساني ṭabīb nafsānī therapist 7. طبيب نفسي ṭabīb nafsī psychiatrist

طبيعة ṭabī'a 1. nature 2. ما وراء طبيعة mā warā' aṭ-ṭabī'a metaphysics 3. بطبيعة الحال bi ṭabī'at al-ḥāl naturally

طبيعي ṭabī'ī 1. natural 2. غير طبيعي ghayr ṭabī'ī unnatural 3. خارق الطبيعة khāriq

---

capability 5. محطّة الطاقة maḥaṭṭat aṭ-ṭāqa power plant; power station

طاقم ṭāqim crew

طالب ṭālaba 1. to demand (ب bi sth; ه from) 2. (fin.) to claim

طالب ṭālib (طلّاب ṭullāb) 1. student 2. طالب غير متخرّج ṭālib ghayr mutakharrij undergraduate

طالما ṭālamā so long as

طاهر ṭāhir 1. pure 2. غير طاهر ghayr ṭāhir impure

طاولة ṭāwula (-āt) table

طبّ ṭibb 1. medicine 2. كلية الطبّ kulliyat aṭ-ṭibb medical school 3. طبّ الأطفال ṭibb al-aṭfāl pediatrics 4. طبّ أمراض النساء ṭibb amrāḍ an-nisā' gynaecology 5. طبّ نفسي ṭibb nafsī psychiatry

طباشير ṭabāshīr chalk

طبّاخ ṭabbākh (-ūn) 1. cook 2. chef

طبّاع ṭabbā' (-ūn) printer

طبّاعة ṭabbā'a (-āt) (comp.) printer

طباعة ṭibā'a 1. printing 2. جهاز طباعة الليزر jihāz ṭibā'at al-layzer laser printer

طبّال ṭabbāl (-ūn) drummer

طبخ ṭabakha (u/a; طبخ ṭabkh) to cook

طبخ ṭabkh 1. cuisine 2. جهاز للطبخ jihāz li 't-ṭabkh cooker

طبع ṭaba'a (a; طبع ṭab') 1. print 2. طبع على الآلة الكاتبة ṭaba'a 'alā l-ālati 'l-kātiba type

at-ṭabī'a supernatural 4. منظر طبيعي
manẓar ṭabī'ī landscape 5. العلاج الطبيعي
al-'ilāj al-ṭabī'ī physiotherapy

طحن ṭaḥana (a; طحن ṭaḥn) to grind

طرّاد ṭarrād; طرّادة ṭarrāda cruiser

طراز ṭirāz (طرز ṭuruz) 1. type; kind 2. style
3. model 4. عتيق الطراز 'atīq aṭ-ṭarāz
out of date

طرح ṭaraḥa (a; طرح ṭarḥ) 1. to subtract 2.
to throw away 3. to put a question

طرح ṭarḥ subtraction

طرد ṭarada (u; طرد ṭard) 1. to throw out 2.
to eject 3. to expel (من min from) 4.
طرده من منصبه ṭaradah min manṣibih to
sack someone; to fire someone

طرد ṭard (طرود ṭurūd) parcel

طرف ṭaraf (أطراف aṭrāf) 1. side 2. part
3. (leg.) party 4. من طرف min ṭaraf by
5. الأطراف المعنية al-aṭrāf al-ma'nīya the
parties concerned; the interested
parties

طرق ṭaraqa (u; طرق ṭarq) to knock

طرّق ṭarraqa to hammer

طرق ṭuruq pl 1. مفترق الطرق muftaraq al-
ṭuruq crossroads 2. ضريبة الطرق ḍarībat
aṭ-ṭuruq toll 3. and see طريقة;

طريد ṭarīd outlaw

طريف ṭarīf quaint

طريق ṭarīq (طرق ṭuruq) 1. road 2. route 3.
way 4. path 5. في الطريق fī 'ṭ-ṭarīq on
the way; en route 6. عن طريق 'an ṭarīq
by way of; via 7. منتصف الطريق

muntaṣif aṭ-ṭarīq midway 8. طريق عامّ
ṭarīq 'āmm highway 9. حافة الطريق
ḥāfat aṭ-ṭarīq road verge/shoulder 10.
طريق مختصرة ṭarīq mukhtaṣira short cut
11. قاطع طريق qāṭi' ṭarīq bandit
12. إشارة طريق ishārat ṭarīq road sign
13. عن طريق الفم 'an ṭarīq al-fam oral
14. أعطى الطريق a'ṭā aṭ-ṭarīq to give
way

طريقة ṭarīqa (طرائق ṭarā'iq; طرق ṭuruq) 1.
manner 2. method 3. (rel.) sufi order
4. بطريقة سيئة bi ṭarīqa sayyi'a poorly 5.
بطريقة صحيحة bi ṭarīqa ṣaḥīḥa right 6.
بطريقة غير قانونية bi ṭarīqa ghayr
qānūnīya illegally 7. بطريقة أو بأخرى bi
ṭarīqa aw bi 'ukhrā somehow

طعام ṭa'ām (أطعمة aṭ'ima) 1. food 2.
قائمة الطعام qā'imat aṭ-ṭa'ām menu 3.
آنية الطعام āniyat aṭ-ṭa'ām crockery 4.
حجرة الطعام ḥujrat aṭ-ṭa'ām dining
room 5. حجرة لحفظ الطعام ḥujra li ḥifẓ
aṭ-ṭa'ām larder

طعّم ṭa''ama 1. to vaccinate 2. to immunize

طعم ṭa'm (طعوم ṭu'ūm) 1. taste; flavour 2.
لا طعم له lā ṭa'm lah tasteless

طعم ṭu'am bait

طعن ṭa'ana (a/u; طعن ṭa'n) to stab

طغيان ṭughyān tyranny

طفحة ṭafḥa rash

طفل ṭifl (أطفال aṭfāl) 1. baby 2. infant 3.
child 4. حفاظ الطفل ḥifāẓ aṭ-ṭifl nappy;
diaper 5. and see أطفال

طفلة ṭifla (-āt) 1. baby 2. infant 3. child

طفولة ṭufūla 1. infancy 2. childhood

طفيلي ṭufaylī 1. intruder 2. parasite

طقس ṭaqs 1. weather 2. (طقوس ṭuqūs) ritual 3. طقس عاصف ṭaqs 'āṣif rough weather 4. طقس ديني ṭaqs dīnī (rel.) service

طقسي ṭaqsī ritual; ritualistic

طقطقة ṭaqṭaqa click

طقم ṭaqm (طقوم ṭuqūm) 1. set 2. kit 3. suit 4. طقم شاي ṭaqm shāy tea set 5. طقم أثاث ṭaqm athāth suite

طلى ṭalā (i; طلي ṭaly) to paint

طلاء ṭilā' 1. paint 2. فرشاة طلاء furshāt ṭilā' paintbrush 3. طلاء ذهبي ṭilā' dhahabī gold plate 4. دهان الطلاء dihān aṭ-ṭilā' varnish

طلاق ṭalāq divorce

طلب ṭalaba (u; طلب ṭalab) 1. to request 2. طلب من ṭalaba min to ask for 3. to look for 4. (com.) order (إلى\ه ilā from)

طلب ṭalab (-āt) 1. request 2. application 3. (com.) order 4. العرض والطلب al-'arḍ wa 'ṭ-ṭalab supply and demand 5. قدّم طلباً qaddama ṭalaban to apply

طلع ṭala'a (a; طلوع ṭulū'; مطلع maṭla') 1. to rise 2. to turn out

طلق ṭalq: بالهواء الطلق bi 'l-hawā' aṭ-ṭalq open-air

طلّق ṭallaqa to divorce (من min from)

طلقة ṭalaqa (-āt) 1. shot 2. round of ammunition

طليق ṭalīq loose

طماطة ṭamāṭa (طماطم ṭamāṭim) tomato

طمّاع ṭammā' greedy

طمأن ṭam'ana to reassure

طمع ṭama' (أطماع aṭmā') 1. greed 2. ambition

طموح ṭamūḥ ambitious

طنّ ṭunn (أطنان aṭnān) 1. ton 2. طن متري ṭunn mitrī tonne

طنّان ṭannān buzzer

طهارة ṭahāra purity

طهّر ṭahhara to purify

طوى ṭawā (i; طي ṭayy) to roll up

طوّاق ṭawwāq eager (إلى ilā for)

طوال ṭiwāl 1. throughout; during 2. along; alongside 3. طوال السنة ṭiwāl as-sana all year round

طوفان ṭūfān flood

طول ṭūl 1. length 2. height 3. throughout; during 4. خطّ الطول khaṭṭ aṭ-ṭūl longitude 5. شقّ بالطول shaqqa bi 'ṭ-ṭūl (u; شق shaqq) to slit

طوّر ṭawwara to develop

طوّق ṭawwaqa to enclose

طوّل ṭawwala to lengthen

طويل ṭawīl (طوال ṭiwāl) 1. long 2. tall 3. طويل الأمد ṭawīl al-amad long-term 4. طويل النظر ṭawīl an-naẓar long-sighted

طويلاً ṭawīlan for a long time

طيّار ṭayyār (-ūn) pilot

طيّب ṭayyib 1. good 2. fine 3. okay; OK

طيبة ṭība goodness

طير ṭayr collective (طيور ṭuyūr) bird(s)

طيران ṭayarān 1. flight 2. aviation 3.

سلاح الطيران silāḥ aṭ-ṭayarān airforce 4. خطوط الطيران khuṭūṭ aṭ-ṭayarān airline, airways

طين ṭīn 1. mud 2. clay

ظالم ẓālim 1. unjust 2. unfair 3. oppressive

ظاهرة ẓāhira (ظواهر ẓawāhir) phenomenon

ظاهري ẓāhirī apparent

ظرافة ẓarāfa wit

ظرف ẓarf (ظروف ẓurūf) 1. envelope 2. adverb 3. circumstance

ظروف ẓurūf pl circumstances

ظفر ẓufr (أظافر aẓāfir) nail

ظلّ ẓill (ظلال ẓilāl) 1. shade 2. shadow

ظلّ ẓalla (a; ظلّ ẓall) 1. to remain 2. to continue

ظلام ẓalām dark; darkness

ظلم ẓulm 1. wrong 2. injustice

ظلم ẓalama (i; ظلم ẓulm) 1. to treat unfairly 2. to oppress

ظنّ ẓann (ظنون ẓunūn) 1. opinion 2. idea 3. خيّب الظن khayyaba aẓ-ẓann to disappoint

ظنّ ẓanna (u; ظنّ ẓann) 1. to think 2. to consider 3. to suspect

ظهر ẓahr (ظهور ẓuhūr) 1. back 2. حقيبة الظهر ḥaqībat al-ẓahr backpack 3. عن ظهر قلب 'an ẓahr qalb by heart 4. ظهر السفينة ẓahr as-safīna ship's deck

ظهر ẓahara (a; ظهور ẓuhūr) to appear

ظهر ẓuhr 1. noon 2. بعد الظهر ba'd aẓ-ẓuhr afternoon; p.m. 3. قبل الظهر qabl aẓ-ẓuhr a.m.

ظهور ẓuhūr appearance

ع

عائِد 'ā'id (-āt; عوائِد 'awā'id) return

عائِدة 'ā'ida (-āt; عوائِد 'awā'id) profit

عائِقة 'ā'iqa (عوائِق 'awā'iq) obstacle; obstruction

عائِلة 'ā'ila (-āt) 1. family 2. اسم العائلة ism al-'ā'ila surname

عاج 'āj ivory

عاجِز 'ājiz 1. unable 2. helpless 3. impotent 4. invalid 5. عاجز عن الكلام 'ājiz 'an al-kalām speechless

عاجِل 'ājil 1. speedy 2. urgent 3. instant

عاجِلاً 'ājilan 1. speedily 2. urgently 3. instantly 4. عاجلاً أو آجلاً 'ājilan aw ājilan sooner or later

عاد 'āda (u; عودة 'awda) 1. to return (ل li/إلى ilā to) 2. to be due (إلى ilā to) 3. to do again; to resume 4. not again; no more; no longer

عادة 'āda (-āt) 1. custom 2. habit 3. عادةً 'ādatan usually 4. خارق للعادة khāriq li l-'āda; فوق العادة fawq al-'āda extraordinary

عادَلَ 'ādala to equal

عادِل 'ādil just

عادي 'ādī 1. normal 2. غير عادي ghayr 'ādī unusual

عار 'ār 1. disgrace 2. shame

عارٍ 'ārin naked; nude

عارَضَ 'āraḍa 1. to oppose 2. to object to

عارِض 'āriḍ: عارض الأزياء 'āriḍ al-azyā' fashion model

عازِب 'āzib unmarried

عازِف 'āzif (-ūn) 1. player 2. عازف الغيتار 'āzif al-gītār guitarist

عاشَ 'āsha (i; عيش 'aysh) to live

عاشِر 'āshir tenth

عاشِق 'āshiq (-ūn; عشّاق 'ushshāq) lover

عاشِقة 'āshiqa (-āt) 1. lover 2. mistress

عاشورة 'āshūrā' Festival of Ashura (10th Muharram)

عاصٍ 'āṣin disobedient

عاصِف 'āṣif 1. windy 2. stormy

عاصِفة 'āṣifa (عواصف 'awāṣif) storm

عاصِمة 'āṣima (عواصم 'awāṣim) capital

عاطِفة 'āṭifa (عواطف 'awāṭif) emotion

عاطِفي 'āṭifī emotional

عاطِل 'āṭil 1. inactive 2. out of order 3. functionless 4. عاطل عن العمل 'āṭil 'an al-'amal unemployed

عاقَ 'āqa (u; عوق 'awq) to deter

عاقَبَ 'āqaba 1. to punish 2. يعاقب عليه yu'āqab 'alayh punishable

عاقِبة 'āqiba (عواقب 'awāqib) consequence

عاقر ‘āqir barren

عاقل ‘āqil 1. intelligent 2. sensible 3. غير عاقل ghayr ‘āqil unwise

عاكس ‘ākasa to harass

عال ‘āla (u; عول ‘awl; عيالة ‘iyāla) to provide for

عالٍ ‘ālin 1. high 2. بصوت عالٍ bi ṣawtin ‘ālin aloud

عالج ‘ālaja (معالجة mu‘ālaja; علاج ‘ilāj) 1. to handle 2. (med.) to treat 3. عالج صناعياً ‘ālaja ṣinā‘īyan to process

عالم ‘ālam 1. the world 2. كأس العالم ka’s al-‘ālam World Cup 3. عالم المسرح ‘ālam al-masraḥ show business

عالم ‘ālim (علماء ‘ulamā’) 1. scholar 2. scientist 3. عالم إقتصادي ‘ālim iqtiṣādī economist 4. عالم النفس ‘ālim an-nafs psychologist

عالمي ‘ālamī 1. world 2. global 3. رقم قياس عالمي raqm qiyās ‘ālamī world record

عام ‘āma (u; عوم ‘awm) to float

عام ‘ām (أعوام a‘wām) 1. year 2. منذ عام mundhu ‘ām a year ago

عام ‘āmm 1. common 2. public 3. general 4. مدير عام mudīr ‘āmm managing director 5. طريق عام ṭarīq ‘āmm highway 6. مغسلة عامة maghsala ‘āmma launderette, laundrette 7. إستعراض عام isti‘rāḍ ‘āmm spectacle 8. ساحة عامة sāḥa ‘āmma plaza 9. الصحة العامة aṣ-ṣiḥḥa al-‘āmma sanitation 10. صيانة الصحة العامة

صيانة الصحة العامة ṣiyānat aṣ-ṣiḥḥa al-‘āmma sanitation 11. مرافق عام mirfaq ‘āmm (مرافق عامة marāfiq ‘āmma) public utility

عامةً ‘āmmatan in general

عامل ‘āmala 1. to treat 2. to deal with

عامل ‘āmil (عمال ‘ummāl) 1. worker 2. operator 3. labourer 4. (عوامل ‘awāmil) factor; element 5. عامل حر ‘āmil ḥurr freelance, freelancer 6. عامل المناجم ‘āmil al-manājim miner 7. عامل مؤقت ‘āmil mu‘aqqat temporary worker 8. القوة العاملة al-qūwa al-‘āmila workforce 9. and see عمّال

عامّي ‘āmmī 1. colloquial 2. لغة عامّية lugha ‘āmmīya slang

عامود ‘āmūd (عواميد ‘awāmīd) 1. post 2. عامود المرمى ‘āmūd al-marmā goalpost

عانى ‘ānā 1. to suffer (من/ه min from) 2. to undergo 3. to take great pains with

عانق ‘ānaqa to embrace

عاهل ‘āhil (عواهل ‘awāhil) 1. sovereign; monarch 2. ruler

عاون ‘āwana to help

عبادة ‘ibāda 1. worship 2. adoration

عبارة ‘ibāra (-āt) 1. phrase 2. expression 3. عبارة متكررة ‘ibāra mutakarrira refrain

عبثاً ‘abathan in vain

عبد ‘abada (u; عبادة ‘ibāda) 1. to worship 2. to idolize

عبد 'abd (عبيد 'abīd) slave

عبر 'abara (u; عبر 'abr; عبور 'ubūr) to cross

عبّر 'abbara to express

عبر 'abr 1. across 2. through 3. عبر البحار 'abr al-biḥār overseas

عبري 'ibrī Hebrew

عبقري 'abqarī (-ūn) genius

عبقرية 'abqarīya genius

عبودية 'ubūdīya slavery

عبور 'ubūr crossing

عتّال 'attāl (-ūn) porter

عتبة 'ataba (أعتاب a'tāb) threshold

عتيق 'atīq 1. ancient 2. vintage 3. عتيق الطراز 'atīq aṭ-ṭarāz out of date 4. عتيق النمط 'atīq al-namaṭ old-fashioned

عجز 'ajz 1. inability 2. deficiency 3. deficit

عجل 'ajila (a; عجلة 'ajala) to hurry

عجّل 'ajjala to speed up

عجل 'ijl (عجول 'ujūl) 1. calf 2. لحم العجل laḥm al-'ijl veal

عجلة 'ajala 1. haste 2. (-āt) wheel 3. عجلة القيادة 'ajalat al-qiyāda steering wheel

عجوز 'ajūz elderly

عجيب 'ajīb wonderful

عجين 'ajīn dough

عدّ 'adda (u; عد 'add) 1. to count 2. لا يعدّ lā yu'add countless

عدا 'adā (u; عدو adw) to run

عدا 'adā 1. except 2. ما عدا mā 'adā except 3. عدا عليه الزمن 'adā 'alayh az-zaman out of date

عداء 'adā' hostility

عدائي 'adā'ī hostile

عدّاد 'addād meter

عدالة 'adāla justice

عدّة 'udda (عدد 'udad) apparatus

عدّة 'idda 1. several 2. بعد عدّة أيام ba'd 'iddat ayyām in a few days 3. قبل عدّة أيام qabl 'iddat ayyām a few days ago

عدّد 'addada to list

عدد 'adad (أعداد a'dād) 1. number 2. figure 3. كم عدد؟ kam 'adad? how many? 4. عدد السكّان 'adad as-sukkān population 5. عدد كبير 'adad kabīr a great deal 6. فوّقه عدداً fawwaqah 'adadan to outnumber

عدسة 'adasa (-āt) 1. lens 2. عدسة لاصقة 'adasa lāṣiqa contact lens

عدّل 'addala 1. to modify 2. to adjust 3. to regulate

عدل 'adl justice

عدم 'adam 1. lack 2. non- 3. عدم إحترام 'adam iḥtirām disrespect 4. عدم إستقرار 'adam istiqrār instability 5. عدم الصدق 'adam aṣ-ṣidq dishonesty 6. عدم الإستعمال 'adam al-isti'māl disuse 7. الرجاء عدم الإزعاج ar-rajā' 'adam al-iz'āj please do not disturb

عدّن 'addana to mine

عدو 'adw run

عدو (أعدا 'a'dā') 'adūw enemy

عدوان 'udwān aggression

عدواني 'udwānī aggressive

عديد 'adīd many

عديل 'adīl brother-in-law

عذاب (أعذبة 'a'dhiba) 'adhāb suffering

عذّب 'adhdhaba to torture

عذب 'adhb fresh

عذراء (عذارا 'adhārā') 'adhrā virgin

عذر (عذار a'dhār) 'udhr excuse

عرّى 'arrā to strip

عرّاب (-ūn) 'arrāb sponsor

العراق al-'irāq Iraq

عراقي (-ūn) 'irāqī Iraqi

عراك 'irāk fight

عرب 'arab pl Arabs

عربة (-āt) 'araba 1. carriage 2. cart 3. waggon

عربون (عرابين 'arābīn) 'urbūn deposit

عربي 'arabī 1. Arabic 2. Arab

عرس (أعراس a'rās) 'urs wedding

عرس 'irs 1. ابن عرس ibn 'irs بنات عرس banāt 'irs) weasel 2. ابن عرس أبيض ibn 'irs abyaḍ stoat

عرش (أعراش a'rāsh) 'arsh throne (عرش 'urush;)

عرض (عرض 'arḍ) 'araḍa (i;) 1. to show 2. to display 3. to present (ه sth; على 'alā to)

عرض الأزياء 'araḍa al-azyā' to model 4.

عرض 'aruḍa (u) to be wide

عرّض 'arraḍa 1. expose (to ل li) 2. عرّض للخطر 'arraḍa li 'l-khaṭar to endanger

عرض (عروض 'urūḍ) 'arḍ 1. width 2. offer 3. tender 4. display 5. exhibition; show 6. parade 7. خط العرض khaṭṭ al-'arḍ latitude 8. جهاز العرض jihāz al-'arḍ projector 9. عرض مسبق 'arḍ musabbaq preview 10. عرض أول 'arḍ awwal premiere 11. عرض بعد الظهر 'arḍ ba'd aẓ-ẓuhr matinee 12. العرض والطلب al-'arḍ wa 'ṭ-ṭalab supply and demand

عرض (أعراض a'rāḍ) 'araḍ symptom

عرضة 'urḍa :عرضة ل 'urḍa li subject to

عرف (i; معرفة ma'rifa; عرفان 'irfān) 'arafa 1. to know 2. to know how to 3. to recognise

عرّف 'arrafa 1. to introduce 2. to define

عرف 'urf custom

عرق 'ariqa (a; عرق 'araq) to sweat

عرق 'araq sweat

عرق (عروق 'urūq) 'irq 1. vein 2. (-āt) race 3. ethnic group 4. بين العرقات bayn al-'irqāt interracial

عرقل 'arqala 1. to hinder 2. to hold up 3. (spor.) to tackle

عرقلة (-āt) 'arqala (spor.) tackle

عرقي 'irqī 1. racial 2. ethnic 3. (-yūn) racist 4. أقلية عرقية aqallīya 'irqīya ethnic minority 5. التطهير العرقي attaṭhīr al-'irqī ethnic cleansing

عرقية 'irqīya racism

عروس 'arūs bride

عروسة 'arūsa (عرائس 'arā'is) 1. bride 2. doll

عريان 'uryān nude; naked

عريس 'arīs bridegroom

عريض 'arīḍ broad

عريضة 'arīḍa (عرائض 'arā'iḍ) 1. petition 2. قدّم عريضة qaddama 'arīḍa to petition

عزبة 'izba (عزب 'izab) estate

عزّز 'azzaza to strengthen

عزف 'azafa (i; عزف 'azf) (mus.) to play

عزل 'azl 1. isolation 2. insulation

عزل 'azala (i; عزل 'azl/'uzl) 1. to isolate 2. to insulate

عزلة 'uzla privacy

عزم 'azm determination

عزيز 'azīz dear

عزيم 'azīm grand

عسى 'asā 1. perhaps 2. so that (perhaps)

عسر 'usr 1. difficulty 2. عسر الهضم 'usr al-haḍm indigestion

عسكري 'askarī 1. military 2. (عساكر 'asākir) soldier 3. وحدة عسكرية waḥda 'askariya military unit 4. سرّ عسكري sirr 'askarī military secret 5. منشأة عسكرية munsha'a 'askarīya military installation

عسل 'asal 1. honey 2. شهر العسل shahr al-'asal honeymoon

عسير 'asīr tough

عشّ 'ushsh (أعشاش a'shāsh) nest

عشاء 'ashā' (أعشية a'shiya) dinner; supper

عشب 'ushb (أعشاب a'shāb) 1. grass 2. herb 3. lawn 4. قصّ العشب qaṣṣa al-'ushb (u; قصّ qaṣṣ) to mow

عشرة 'ashara ten

عشرون 'ishrūn 1. twenty 2. العشرون al-'ishrūn twentieth

عشوائي 'ashwā'ī 1. indiscriminate 2. random

عشوائياً 'ashwā'īyan at random

عشيقة 'ashīqa (-āt) 1. lover 2. mistress

عشية 'ashīya (-āt) 1. evening 2. عشية عيد الميلاد 'ashīyat 'īd al-mīlād Christmas Eve

عصا 'aṣā f (عصي 'uṣīy) 1. stick 2. cane

عصى 'aṣā (i; عصي 'aṣy; معصية ma'ṣīya; عصيان 'iṣyān) 1. to disobey 2. to rebel 3. to mutiny

عصابة 'iṣāba (-āt) 1. gang 2. عضو عصابة 'uḍw 'iṣāba gangster

عصب 'aṣab (أعصاب a'ṣāb) 1. nerve 2. and see أعصاب

عصبي 'aṣabī nervous

عصبية 'aṣabīya nervousness

عصر 'aṣr (عصور 'uṣūr; أعصار a'ṣār) 1. time 2. period 3. era 4. afternoon

عصر 'aṣara (i; عصر 'aṣr) 1. to press 2. to squeeze

عصيان 'iṣyān 1. disobedience 2. rebellion 3. mutiny

عصير 'aṣīr juice

عصي 'aṣīy (-ūn; ء أعصيا a'ṣiyā') rebel

عضّ 'aḍḍa (a; عضّ 'aḍḍ) to bite

عضال 'uḍāl incurable

عضّة 'aḍḍa 1. bite 2. عضّة حشرة 'aḍḍat ḥashara insect bite

عضلة (-āt) 'aḍala muscle

عضو 'uḍw (ء أعضا a'ḍā') 1. limb 2. organ 3. member 4. عضو بلدية 'uḍw baladīya councillor 5. عضو جديد 'uḍw jadīd recruit 6. عضو عصابة 'uḍw 'iṣāba gangster

عضوية 'uḍwīya membership

عطا ء 'aṭā' 1. gift 2. offer 3. (com.) tender 4. قدّم عطا ء qaddama 'aṭā' to tender

عطر 'aṭir aromatic

عطر 'iṭr (عطور 'uṭūr) perfume; scent

عطري 'iṭrī aromatic

عطس 'aṭasa (i, u; عطس 'aṭs) to sneeze

عطسة 'aṭsa sneeze

عطش 'aṭash thirst

عطشان 'aṭshān (أطشى aṭshā) thirsty

عطّل 'aṭṭala to disrupt

عطلان 'aṭlān out of order

عطلة 'uṭla (-āt; عطل 'uṭal) 1. vacation 2. يوم عطلة yawm 'uṭla day off

عظّم 'aẓẓama to make greater

عظم 'aẓm (أعظام a'ẓām) bone

عظمى 'uẓmā 1. great(er) (f of أعظم) 2. بريطانيا العظمى brīṭāniyā al-'uẓmā Great Britain

عظمي 'aẓmī 1. bone 2. هيكل عظمي haykal 'aẓmī skeleton

عظيم 'aẓīm (ء عظما 'uẓamā') great

عفا 'afā (u; عفو 'afw) (leg.) to pardon

عفريت 'ifrīt (عفاريت 'afārīt) demon

عفن 'afina (a; عفن 'afn) to rot

عفن 'afan rot

عفن 'afin 1. rotten 2. foul 3. septic

عفو 'afw 1. pardon 2. amnesty

عفواً 'afwan 1. excuse me! 2. I beg your pardon? 3. don't mention it!

عفوي 'afwī spontaneous

عقاب 'uqāb (أعقب a'qub) eagle

عقاب 'iqāb 1. punishment 2. penalty

عقار 'aqār (-āt) property

عقارات 'aqārāt pl 1. real estate 2. قرض للعقارات qarḍ li 'l-'aqārāt mortgage

عقاري 'aqārī 1. property 2. سمسار عقاري simsār 'aqārī realtor

عقّب 'aqqaba to track

عقب 'uqb (أعقاب a'qāb) 1. end; consequence 2. في أعقاب fī a'qāb straight after

عقب 'aqib: على عقب 'alā 'aqib straight after

عقد 'aqada (i; عقد 'aqd) 1. to tie 2. عقد إجتماعاً 'aqada ijtimā'an to hold a meeting

عقد **'aqd** (عقود**'uqūd**) 1. contract 2. lease 3. decade

عقد **'iqd** (عقود **'uqūd**) necklace

عقدة **'uqda** (عقد **'uqad**) 1. complex 2. knot

عقل **'aql** (عقول **'uqūl**) 1. mind 2. intelligence 3. reason 4. wit 5. سليم العقل **salīm al-'aql** sane 6. سلامة العقل **salāmat al-'aql** sanity

عقلي **'aqlī** 1. mental 2. intellectual 3. rational 4. مستشفى الأمراض العقلية **mustashfa 'l-amrāḍ al-'aqlīya** mental institution 5. مضطرب عقلياً **muḍṭarib 'aqlīyan** mentally disturbed

عقلية **'aqlīya** mentality

عقّم **'aqqama** to sterilize

عقوبة **'uqūba** (-āt) 1. penalty 2. sanction

عقيد **'aqīd** colonel

عقيدة **'aqīda** (عقائد **'aqā'id**) belief

عقيصة **'aqīṣa** (-āt) curl

عقيم **'aqīm** 1. useless 2. ineffective 3. infertile 4. sterile

عكس **'akasa** (عكس i; **'aks**) to reflect

عكس **'aks** 1. opposite; reverse 2. reflection 3. والعكس **wa 'l-'aks** vice versa 4. بالعكس **bi 'l-'aks** on the contrary 5. على العكس **'alā 'l-'aks** rather; contrary to

علّ **'alla; لعلّ la'alla** 1. perhaps 2. so that

على **'alā** 1. on 2. on top of 3. onto 4. to 5. at 6. against 7. by 8. over 9. in spite of 10. على الراديو **'alā 'r-rādiyō** on the radio 11. على الطاولة **'alā 'ṭ-ṭāwula** on the table 12. على البحر **'alā 'l-baḥr** at sea 13. على الموعد **'alā 'l-maw'id** on time 14. على اليسار **'alā 'l-yasār** on the left 15. على الأقدام **'alā 'l-aqdām** on foot 16. على الأقل **'alā 'l-aqall** at least 17. على العكس **'alā 'l-'aks** rather 18. على الموضة **'alā 'l-mooḍa** fashionable 19. على خلاف **'alā khilāf** unlike 20. على طول **'alā ṭūl** along; straight 21. على كل حال **'alā kull ḥāl** anyway 22. على فكرة **'alā fikra** incidentally 23. على مهل **'alā mahl** leisurely 24. على نحو رديء **'alā naḥw radī'** badly 25. على نحو غير مباشر **'alā naḥw ghayr mubāshir** indirectly 26. على نطاق الوطن كلّه **'alā niṭāq al-waṭan kulluh** nationwide 27. على نحو متساوي **'alā naḥw mutasāwī** even 28. على أن **'alā an** provided that 29. على أن **'alā anna** although 30. علاوتا على ذلك **'ilāwatan 'alā dhālik** furthermore 31. على أية حال **'alā ayyati ḥāl** at any rate 32. على الرغم من **'alā ar-raghm min** despite; while 33. على شرط أن **'alā sharṭ an** on condition that 34. على وشك أن **'alā washk an** on the point of 35. تصبح على خير! **tuṣbiḥ 'alā khayr!** good night! 36. عيلك **'alayk** you owe 37. عليك أن... **'alayka an...** You have to... 38. مغمى عليه **mughmā 'alayh** unconscious 39. عدا عليه الزمن **'adā 'alayh az-zaman** out of date 40. هو على شيء من... **huwa 'alā shay' min...** he has a certain... 41. هو على علم ب... **huwa 'alā 'ilm b...**

huwa 'alā 'ilm bi... he is informed about...

علاج **'ilāj** 1. cure 2. therapy 3. علاج نفساني **'ilāj nafsānī** therapy 4. العلاج الطبيعي **al-'ilāj al-ṭabī'ī** physiotherapy

علاقة **'alāqa (-āt)** 1. relation 2. relationship 3. كان على علاقة حسنة **kāna 'alā 'alāqa hasana** to be on good terms (with مع **ma'a**)

علاقات **'alāqāt** pl: العلاقات الدبلوماسية **'alāqāt ad-diblōmāsīya** diplomatic relations

علاّقة **'allāqa (-āt)** hanger

علاقي **'alāqī** 1. relevant 2. لا علاقي **lā 'alāqī** irrelevant

علامة **'alāma (-āt؛** علائم **'alā'im)** 1. sign 2. mark 3. label 4. علامة إستفهام **'alāmat istifhām** question mark

علانيةً **'alāniyatan** publicly

علاوة **'ilāwa (-āt)** 1. allowance 2. bonus 3. pay rise

علبة **'ulba ('ulab/'ilab** علب) 1. can; tin 2. علبة كارتون **'ulbat kārtūn** carton 3. فتاحة علب/علبة مفتاح **miftāḥ 'ulba/'ilab fattāḥat 'ilab** can-opener

علّة **'illa (-āt؛** علل **'ilal)** 1. defect 2. disease 3. علة في برنامج **'illa fī barnāmij** computer bug

علق **'alaqa (a؛** علق **'alaq)** to trap

علّق **'allaqa** 1. to hang (على **'alā/ب bi** on) 2. to attach (على **'alā/ب bi** to) 3. to comment (على **'alā** on)

علِم **'alima (a؛** علم **'ilm)** 1. to know 2. to learn about/of

علّم **'allama** 1. to teach 2. to educate 3. to instruct 4. to mark

علم **'alam (**أعلام **a'lām)** 1. flag 2. banner

علم **'ilm (**علوم **'ulūm)** 1. knowledge 2. science 3. علم البيئة **'ilm at-bay'a** ecology 4. علم الصحة **'ilm aṣ-ṣiḥḥa** hygiene 5. علم الآثار **'ilm al-āthār** archeology 6. علم الحساب **'ilm al-ḥisāb** arithmetic 7. علم الإحصاء **'ilm al-iḥṣā'** statistics 8. علم الإجتماع **'ilm al-ijtimā'** sociology 9. علم الأحياء **'ilm al-aḥyā'**; علم الحياة **'ilm al-ḥayāh** biology 10. علم الأساطير **'ilm al-asāṭīr** mythology 11. علم الكيمياء **'ilm al-kīmyā'** chemistry 12. علم اللغة **'ilm al-lugha** linguistics 13. علم الإنسان **'ilm al-insān** anthropology 14. علم النفس **'ilm an-nafs** psychology 15. علم الإقتصاد **'ilm al-iqtiṣād** economics

علمي **'ilmī** scientific

علناً **'alanan** openly

علني **'alanī** 1. open 2. مزاد علني **mazād 'alanī** auction

عليا **'ulyā** f 1. المحكمة العليا **al-maḥkama al-'ulyā** high court; supreme court 2. see أعلى

علّية **'ullīya/'illīya:** علّية البيت **'ullīyat al-bayt** attic

عليّق **'ullayq:** توت العليق **tūt al-'ullayq** raspberry

عمّ **'amm (**عموم **'umūm)** 1. uncle 2. إبن عمّ **ibn 'amm** ibn 'amm male cousin 3. عمّ bint 'amma female cousin

عمىً 'aman blindness

عمّة 'amma (-āt) 1. aunt 2. إبن عمّة ibn 'amma cousin 3. بنت عمّة bint 'amma cousin

عمّال 'ummāl pl 1. workers 2. نقابة عمّال niqābat 'ummāl (-āt) trade union; trades union 3. حزب العمّال ḥizb al-'ummāl Labour Party 4. and see عامل

عمّالي 'ummālī 1. workers'... 2. labour

عمد 'amd 1. intent 2. القتل العمد al-qatl al-'amd murder 3. قتل بالعمد qatala bi 'l-'amd to murder 4. قاتل بالعمد qātil bi 'l-'amd murderer 5. قاتلة بالعمد qātila bi 'l-'amd murderess

عمدة 'umda (عمد 'umad) mayor

عمداً 'amdan/'amadan on purpose

عمر 'amara (u/i; عمر 'amr/'umr) 1. to live in; to inhabit 2. to make prosper 3. to fill with life

عمر 'umr (أعمار a'mār) 1. age 2. life 3. كم عمرك؟ kam 'umrak? How old are you? 4. منتصف العمر muntaṣif al-'umr middle-age; middle-aged

عمري 'umarī: حدّ عمري ḥadd 'umarī age limit

عمق 'umq depth

عمل 'amila (a; عمل 'amal) 1. to make; to do 2. to work 3. to function 4. عمل أكثر من اللازم 'amala akthar min al-lāzim to overwork

عمل 'amal (أعمال a'māl) 1. work 2. job 3. trade 4. business 5. action 6. مكان العمل makān al-'amal workplace 7. ورشة عمل (-āt) warshat 'amal workshop 8. صاحب العمل ṣāḥib al-'amal employer 9. عمل احتيالي 'amal iḥtiyālī racket 10. عمل مثير 'amal muthīr stunt 11. جاري العمل فيه jāri al-'amal fīh in process 12. عاطل عن العمل 'āṭil 'an al-'amal out of work 13. سرّح عن العمل sarraḥa 'an al-'amal to lay off from work 14. فصل عن العمل (i; فصل faṣl) faṣala 'an al-'amal to fire from a job 15. فاصل عن العمل fāṣil 'an al-'amal redundant 16. فصل عن العمل faṣl 'an al-'amal redundancy 17. وقف الأمل waqf al-'amal shutdown 18. إضراب عن العمل iḍrāb 'an al-'amal (pol.) strike 19. أضرب عن العمل aḍraba 'an al-'amal (pol.) to strike

عملة 'umla (-āt) 1. currency 2. عملة أجنبية 'umla ajnabīya foreign currency 3. سعر تحويل العملة si'r taḥwīl al-'umla rate of exchange 4. دار سكّ العملة dār sakk al-'umla (fin.) mint

عملاق 'imlāq (عمالقة 'amāliqa) giant

عملي 'amalī 1. practical 2. غير عملي ghayr 'amalī impractical

عملياً 'amalīyan practically

عملية 'amalīya (-āt) 1. job 2. process 3. (med/mil.) operation 4. غرفة العمليات ghurfat al-'amalīyāt operating theatre 5. أجرى عملية جراحية (med.) ajrā 'amalīya jarāḥīya to operate

عمّم **'ammama** to generalize

عمود **'amūd** (أعمدة **a'mida;** عمد **'umud)** 1. column 2. pillar 3. post 4. shaft 5. العمود الفقري **al-'amūd al-faqrī** spine 6. عمود في صحيفة **'amūd fī ṣaḥifa** newspaper column 7. عمود الإضاءة **'amūd al-'iḍā'a** lamp-post

عمودي **'amūdī** 1. vertical 2. خطّ عمودي **khaṭṭ 'amūdī** vertical 3. مدخل عمودي لمنجم **madkhal 'amūdī li manjam** mining shaft 4. طائرة عمودية **ṭā'ira 'umūdīya** helicopter

عمولة **'amūla** (fin.) commission

عموماً **'umūman** generally

عمومي **'umūmī** 1. public 2. مرحاض عمومي **mirḥāḍ 'umūmī** public lavatory

عمي **'umy;** عمياء **'amyā'** see أعمى

عميق **'amiq** deep

عميل **'amīl** (عملاء **'umalā')** 1. representative 2. عميل سري **'amīl sirrī** secret agent

عن **'an** 1. of 2. from 3. away from 4. about; concerning 5. عن ظهر قلب **'an zahr qalb** by heart 6. كتاب عن شيكسبير **kitāb 'an Shakespeare** a book on Shakespeare 7. عن طريق **'an ṭarīq** by way of; via 8. عن طريق الفم **'an ṭarīq al-fam** oral 9. عن قريب **'an qarīb** soon; shortly

عنى **'anā** (i; عني **'any)** 1. to mean (ه **sth;** ب **bi** by) 2. يعني... **ya'nī...** I mean...; that is... 3. and see عني

عنان **'inān** (أعنّة **a'inna)** rein

عناية **'ināya** care; attention

عنبة **'inaba** (collective عنب **'inab;** pl أعناب **a'nāb)** grape

عند **'inda;** عند **'ind** 1. with 2. at 3. by 4. near 5. عند فريد **'ind Fred** at Fred's 6. عند ذلك **'inda dhālik** then 7. عندي قلم **'indī qalam** I have a pen.

عندما **'indamā** when; as; just as

عنصر **'unṣur** (عناصر **'anāṣir)** 1. element 2. ingredient 3. race 4. stock

عنصري **'unṣurī** (-yūn) 1. racial 2. racist

عنصرية **'unṣurīya** racism

عنف **'unf** 1. force 2. بعنف **bi 'unf** by force

عنق **'unq** (أعناق **a'nāq)** 1. neck 2. ربطة العنق **rabṭ al-'unq** (-āt) tie

عنقود **'unqūd** (عناقيد **'anāqīd)** bunch

عنكبوت **'ankabūt** (عناكيب **'anākīb)** spider

عنوان **'unwān** (عناوين **'anāwīn)** 1. address 2. title 3. headline

عني **'uniya** passive 1. to be worried (ب **bi** about) 2. to be interested (ب **bi** in) 3. to take care (ب **bi** of) 4. and see عنى

عنيد **'anīd** stubborn

عنيف **'anīf** violent

عهد **'ahd** (عهود **'uhūd)** 1. period 2. era 3. reign 4. منذ عهد بعيد **mundhu 'ahd ba'īd** long ago

عوى **'awā** (i; عواء **'uwā')** to howl

عوائد **'awā'id** pl proceeds

عود **'ūd** (أعواد **a'wād)** 1. rod 2. lute

عودة **'awda** return

عوّد 'awwada to accustom

عوّض 'awwaḍa repay

عولمة 'awlama globalisation

عوّم 'awwama to launch

عون 'awn 1. help; aid 2. (أعوان a'wān) helper; assistant

عوينات 'uwaynāt pl spectacles; glasses

عيادة 'iyāda (-āt) 1. clinic 2. doctor's surgery

عيان 'iyān: شاهد عيان shāhid 'iyān eyewitness

عيب 'ayb (عيوب 'uyūb) 1. defect 2. fault 3. shame

عيد 'id (أعياد a'yād) 1. festival 2. العيد الصغير al-'id aṣ-ṣaghīr; عيد الفطر 'id al-fiṭr Feast of Breaking the Ramadan Fast (1st Shawwal) 3. العيد الكبير al-'id al-kabīr; عيد الأضحى 'id al-aḍḥā Feast of Immolation (10th Zulhijja) 4. عيد القيامة 'id al-qiyāma Easter 5. عيد الميلاد 'id al-mīlād Christmas

عيّن 'ayyana 1. to appoint 2. to specify

عين 'ayn (عيون 'uyūn; أعين a'yun) 1. eye 2. spring 3. very 4. عينه 'aynah same 5. مقلة العين (مقل muqal) muqlat al-'ayn eyeball 6. محجر العين (محاجر maḥājir) maḥjir al-'ayn eye socket 7. إنسان العين insān al-'ayn pupil 8. إذا أخذنا في عين الإعتبار idhā akhadhnā fī 'ayn al-i'tibār considering

عيّنة 'ayyina (-āt) 1. sample 2. specimen

عيون 'uyūn pl: طبيب العيون ṭabīb al-'uyūn optician

غائب ghā'ib absent

غائم ghā'im cloudy

غاب ghāba (i; غيبة ghayba; غياب ghiyāb) to disappear

غابة ghāba (-āt) 1. wood 2. forest 3. jungle

غادر ghādara 1. to leave; to depart 2. to quit

غار ghār (-āt) cave

غارة ghāra (-āt) 1. raid 2. غارة جوّية ghāra jawwīya air-raid 3. شنّ غارة على shanna ghāra 'alā (u; شنّ shann) to raid

غارق ghāriq: سفينة غارقة safīna ghāriqa shipwreck

غاز ghāz (-āt) 1. gas 2. الغاز المسيّل للدموع al-ghāz al-musayyil li 'd-dumū' tear gas 3. بئر غاز bi'r ghāz gas well

غازٍ ghāzin (غزاة ghuzāh) invader

غازي ghāzī 1. gas; gaseous 2. ماء غازية mā' ghāzīya soda water

غاص ghāṣa (u; غوص ghawṣ) to dive

غاضب ghāḍib angry

غافل ghāfil unaware

غالٍ ghālin expensive

غالب ghālib 1. most 2. predominant 3. (غلبة ghalaba) victor 4. في الغالب fi 'l-ghālib mostly; mainly

غالباً ghāliban mostly; mainly

غالون ghālūn gallon

غامر ghāmara to venture

غامض ghāmiḍ 1. dark 2. obscure 3. vague 4. mysterious

غاية ghāya (-āt) 1. purpose 2. للغاية li 'l-ghāya extremely 3. مسرور للغاية masrūr li 'l-ghāya delighted 4. سارّ للغاية sārr li 'l-ghāya delightful 5. مثير للغاية muthīr li 'l-ghāya sensational

غباء ghabā' stupidity

غبار ghubār (أغبرة aghbira) dust

غبي ghabī stupid

غجري ghajarī (غجر ghajar) Gypsy

غد ghad 1. الغد al-ghad tomorrow 2. قبل الغد qabl al-ghad by tomorrow 3. بعد غد ba'd ghad the day after tomorrow 4. and see غداً

غداً ghadan 1. tomorrow 2. and see غد

غداء ghadā' (أغدية aghdiya) 1. meal 2.

وقت الغداء waqt al-ghadā' lunchtime

غذّى ghadhdhā 1. to nourish 2. to sustain

غذاء ghidhā' (أغذية aghdhiya) 1. diet 2. nourishment 3. food

غذائي ghidhā'ī 1. food 2. موادّ غذائية mawādd ghidhā'īya provisions

غرّ ghirr inexperienced

غراء ghirā' glue

غراب ghurāb (غربان ghirbān) crow

غرام grām (-āt) gramme

غرامة gharāma (-āt) fine

غرب gharb west

غربي gharbī 1. western 2. westerner 3. الجنوب الغربي al-janūb al-gharbī southwest 4. الشمال الغربي ash-shamāl al-gharbī northwest

غرّز gharraza to thrust

غرزة ghurza (غرز ghuraz) stitch

غرس gharasa (i; غرس ghars) 1. to plant 2. to insert 3. to set

غرسون garsōn waiter

غرض gharaḍ (أغراض aghrāḍ) aim

غرفة ghurfa (-āt; غرف ghuraf) 1. room 2. chamber 3. غرفة الجلوس ghurfat al-julūs living-room 4. غرفة النوم ghurfat an-nawm bedroom 5. غرفة الأكل ghurfat al-akl dining-room 6. غرفة الغسيل ghurfat al-ghasīl washroom 7. غرفة العمليات ghurfat al-'amaliyāt operating theatre 8. غرفة الأموات ghurfat al-amwāt mortuary

غرق **ghariqa** (a; غرق gharaq) 1. to sink 2. to drown 3. to be immersed (في fī in)

غرّق **gharraqa** to sink

غرّم **gharrama** to fine

غروب **ghurūb** sunset

غرور **ghurūr** vanity

غروي **ghirawī** slimy

غرّى **gharrā** to glue

غريب **gharīb** (ء غربا ghurabā') 1. strange 2. foreign 3. stranger 4. foreigner 5. جديد وغريب **jadīd wa gharīb** novel 6. غريب الأطوار **gharīb al-aṭwār** peculiar

غرير **gharīr** inexperienced

غريزة **gharīza** (غرائز gharā'iz) instinct

غزا **ghazā** (u; غزو ghazw) to invade

غزل **ghazala** (i; غزل ghazl) to spin

غزو **ghazw** (غزوات ghazawāt) invasion

غزير **ghazīr** abundant

غسّالة **ghassāla** (-āt) washing machine

غسق **ghasaq** dusk

غسل **ghasala** (i; غسل ghasl) to wash

غسيل **ghasīl** 1. washing 2. laundry 3. غرفة الغسيل **ghurfat al-ghasīl** washroom 4. مسحوق الغسيل **masḥūq al-ghasīl** washing powder

غشّ **ghashsha** (u; غشّ ghashsh) to cheat

غشي **ghashiya** (a; غشاوة ghashāwa) 1. to cover 2. *passive* غشي عليه **ghushiya ‘alayh** he fainted

غضبان **ghaḍbān** angry

غضب **ghaḍiba** (a; غضب ghaḍab) to get angry

غضب **ghaḍab** anger

غضون **ghuḍūn** في غضون ذلك: **fī ghuḍūn dhālik** in the meantime

غطّ **ghaṭṭa** (i; غطيط ghaṭīṭ) to snore

غطّى **ghaṭṭā** 1. to cover 2. to obscure

غطاء **ghiṭā'** (أغطية aghṭiya) 1. cover 2. lid 3. فكّ الغطاء **fakka al-ghiṭā'** (u; فكّ fakk) to unwrap

غطّاس **ghaṭṭās** (-ūn) diver

غطرسة **ghaṭrasa** arrogance

غطس **ghaṭasa** (i; غطس ghaṭs) 1. to dive 2. to dip

غطس **ghaṭs** diving

غفر **ghafara** (i; غفر ghafr; مغفرة maghfira) 1. to forgive 2. to pardon

غفوة **ghafwa** (-āt) to nap

غلى **ghalā** (i; غلي ghaly; غليان ghalayān) to boil

غلاء **ghalā'** high price(s)

غلام **ghulām** (غلمان ghilmān) 1. boy 2. youth

غلاّية **ghallāya** (-āt) kettle

غلب **ghalaba** (i; غلب ghalb; غلبة ghalaba) to defeat

غلطة **ghalṭa** (غلطات ghalaṭāt; أغلاط aghlāṭ) 1. mistake; error 2. wrong

غليظ **ghalīẓ** 1. thick 2. غليظ القلب **ghalīẓ al-qalb** nasty

غليون **ghalyūn** (غلايين ghalāyīn) pipe

غمر ghamura (u; غمر ghamr; غمارة ghamāra) 1. to flood 2. to cover 3. to overwhelm (ب bi with)

غمز ghamaza (i; غمز ghamz) to wink

غمّض ghammaḍa obscure

غنّى ghannā 1. to sing 2. to enrich

غناء ghinā' singing

غني ghanī (ء أغنياء aghniyā') rich

غوى ghawā (i; غيّ ghayy) to seduce

غوغاء ghawghā' mob

غوّاصة ghawwāṣa (-āt) submarine

غياب ghiyāb disappearance

غيار ghiyār: قطع غيار qiṭaʻ ghiyār spare parts

غيبوبة ghaybūba 1. coma 2. trance

غيتار gītār 1. guitar 2. عازف الغيتار ʻāzif al-gītār guitarist

غيّر ghayyara to change

غير ghayr 1. not; un-; non- 2. other (than) 3. من غير min ghayr; بغير bi ghayr without 4. غير أنّ ghayr anna however; except that 5. ليس غير laysa ghayr merely 6. من غير أن min ghayr an without 7. من غير شرط min ghayr sharṭ unconditional 8. من غير شك min ghayr shakk surely 9. عدد غير قليل ʻadad ghayr qalīl quite a few 10. على نحو غير مباشر ʻalā naḥw ghayr mubāshir indirectly 11. في غير محله fī ghayr maḥallih out of place

غير إرادي ghayr irādī involuntary

غير أناني ghayr anānī unselfish

غير إنساني ghayr insānī inhumane

غير بارئ ghayr bāri' unskilled

غير ثابت ghayr thābit unstable

غير جدير بالثقة ghayr jadīr bi 'th-thiqa unreliable

غير جذّاب ghayr jadhdhāb unattractive

غير حادّ ghayr ḥādd blunt

غير حاسم ghayr ḥāsim inconclusive

غير حسّاس ghayr ḥassās insensitive

غير خطير ghayr khaṭīr minor

غير راضٍ ghayr rāḍin unsatisfied

غير رسمي ghayr rasmī informal; unofficial

غير سكران ghayr sakrān sober

غير سليم ghayr salīm unsafe

غير شرعي ghayr sharʻī 1. illegal 2. مقيم غير شرعي muqīm ghayr sharʻī illegal alien

غير صادق ghayr ṣādiq dishonest

غير صحي ghayr ṣiḥḥī unhealthy

غير صحيح ghayr ṣaḥīḥ untrue

غير ضروري ghayr ḍurūrī unnecessary

غير طازج ghayr ṭāzij stale

غير طاهر ghayr ṭāhir impure

غير طبيعي ghayr ṭabīʻī unnatural

غير عادي ghayr ʻādī unusual

غير عاقل ghayr ʻāqil unwise

غير عملي ghayr ʻamalī impractical

غير فعّال ghayr faʿʿāl inefficient

غير قادر ghayr qādir incapable (على ʿalā of)

غير قانوني ghayr qānūnī 1. illegal 2. بطريقة غير قانونية bi ṭarīqa ghayr qānūnīya illegally

غير كافٍ ghayr kāfin inadequate

غير كفء ghayr kafʾ inefficient

غير مؤذٍ ghayr muʾdhin harmless

غير مؤلم ghayr muʾlim painless

غير مأمون ghayr maʾmūn unsafe

غير مؤهّل ghayr muʾahhal unfit

غير متأثّر ghayr mutaʾaththar unaffected

غير متخرّج ghayr mutakharrij: طالب غير متخرّج ṭālib ghayr mutakharrij undergraduate

غير متزوّج ghayr mutazawwij unmarried

غير متساوٍ ghayr mutasāwin 1. unequal 2. uneven

غير متّصل بالموضوع ghayr muttaṣil bi ʾl-mawḍūʿ irrelevant

غير متطوّر ghayr mutaṭawwir underdeveloped

غير متعلّق ghayr mutaʿalliq unrelated

غير متعلّم ghayr mutaʿallim uneducated

غير متعمّد ghayr mutaʿammid 1. unintentional 2. القتل غير المتعمد al-qatl ghayr al-mutaʿammid manslaughter

غير متوقّع ghayr mutawwaqqaʿ unexpected

غير مجروح ghayr majrūḥ unhurt

غير محبوب ghayr maḥbūb unpopular

غير محترف ghayr muḥtarif unskilled

غير محترف ghayr muḥtarif: حاوٍ غير محترف ḥāwin ghayr muḥtarif (هواة huwāh) amateur

غير محتمل ghayr muḥtamal unlikely

غير محدّد ghayr muḥaddad: إلى أمد غير محدّد ilā amad ghayr muḥaddad indefinitely

غير محدود ghayr maḥdūd unlimited

غير محمي ghayr maḥmī unprotected

غير مخطّط ghayr mukhaṭṭaṭ unplanned

غير مدفوع ghayr madfūʿ (fin.) outstanding

غير مرئي ghayr marʾī invisible

غير مرافق ghayr murāfaq unaccompanied

غير مربح ghayr murbiḥ unprofitable

غير مرتّب ghayr murattab untidy

غير مرحّب به ghayr muraḥḥab bih unwelcome

غير مريح ghayr murīḥ uncomfortable

غير مزخرف ghayr muzakhrif plain

غير مسؤول ghayr masʾūl irresponsible

غير مستعدّ ghayr mustaʿidd unwilling

غير مستقرّ ghayr mustaqirr 1. unsteady 2. جعل غير مستقرّ jaʿala ghayr mustaqirr (a) to destabilize

غير مسدّد ghayr musaddad unpaid

غير مضبوظ ghayr maḍbūṭ inaccurate

غير معتاد على ghayr muʿtād ʿalā unaccustomed to

غير معقول ghayr maʿqūl unreasonable

غير معلن ghayr muʿlin unsaid

غير مقبول ghayr maqbūl unacceptable (ل li to)

غير مقتنع ghayr muqtanaʿ unconvinced

غير مقصود ghayr maqṣūd unintentional

غير ملائم ghayr mulāʾim inconvenient

غير مناسب ghayr munāsib unsuitable

غير منتظم ghayr muntaẓim irregular

غير منصف ghayr munṣif unfair

غير منفعل ghayr munfaʿil impassive; cool

غير منقطع ghayr munqaṭiʿ 1. unbroken 2. uninterrupted

غير مهذّب ghayr muhadhdhab rough

غير مهمّ ghayr muhimm unimportant

غير موطّد ghayr muwaṭṭad unstable

غير ناضج ghayr nāḍij unripe

غير نافع ghayr nāfiʿ useless

غير نشيط ghayr nashīṭ inactive

غير نضيج ghayr naḍīj rare

غير نقي ghayr naqī impure

غير هامّ ghayr hāmm minor

غير واضح ghayr wāḍiḥ unclear

غير واقعي ghayr wāqiʿī unrealistic

غيرة ghayra jealousy

غيظ ghayẓ rage

غيور ghayūr jealous

غيوم ghuyūm pl 1. clouds 2. ملبّد بالغيوم mulabbad bi ʾl-ghuyūm overcast

ف

ف fa 1. then 2. and; and then 3. so; because 4. so that 5. فإن fa inna for; because 6. فحسب fa ḥasb merely 7. خطوة فخطوة khaṭwa fa khaṭwa step by step

فائدة fāʾida (-āt; فوائد fawāʾid) 1. use 2. benefit 3. profit 4. (fin.) interest 5.

معدّل الفائدة muʿaddal al-fāʾida interest rate 6. ما فائدة ...؟ mā fāʾidat...? What's the use of...? 7. and see فوائد

فائز fāʾiz (-ūn) 1. winner 2. المتسابق الذي يتلو الفائز al-mutasābiq alladhī yatlū al-fāʾiz runner-up

فائض fāʾiḍ surplus

فائق fā'iq 1. superior 2. فائق الجمال fā'iq al-jamāl gorgeous

فات fāta (u; fawt فوت; fawāt فوات) 1. to be over 2. to pass 3. to escape 4. to exceed 5. to fail to

فاتح fātiḥ 1. winner 2. opener 3. light

فاتن fātin attractive

فاتورة fātūra (فواتير fawātīr) invoice

فاجأ fāja'a to surprise

فاحش fāḥish obscene

فاخر fākhara to show off

فاخر fākhir lavish; luxury

فار fāra (u; فور fawr; فوران fawarān) to boil

فأرة fa'ra (collective فأر fa'r; pl فئران fi'rān) mouse

فارس fāris (فرسان fursān) 1. horseman; rider 2. knight

فاز fāza (u; فوز fawz) to win (ب bi a prize; في fī contest/election)

فأس fa's; فؤوس fu'ūs axe

فاسد fāsid 1. spoiled 2. rotten 3. corrupt

فاشل fāshil unsuccessful

فاصل fāṣala 1. to separate 2. to bargain

فاصل fāṣil 1. separating 2. conclusive 3. interval 4. interruption 5. فاصل عن العمل fāṣil 'an al-'amal redundant 6. فاصل إنتصافي fāṣil intiṣāfī (spor.) half-time

فاصلة fāṣila (فواصل fawāṣil) 1. interval 2. comma

فاصوليا fāṣūliyā beans

فاضح fāḍiḥ disgraceful

فاض fāḍa (i; فيض fayḍ; فيضان fayaḍān) 1. to flood 2. to overflow 3. to stream

فاضل fāḍil (-ūn) worthy

فاقد fāqid: فاقد الوعي fāqid al-wa'y senseless

فاقم fāqama to aggravate

فاكس fāks 1. fax 2. بعث فاكس ba'atha fāks (a; بعث ba'th) to fax

فاكهة fākiha (فواكه fawākih) fruit

فإنّ fa inna for; because

فان fānin mortal

فانيلا vanīllā vanilla

فبراير febrāyir February

فتى fatā (فتية fitya; فتيان fityān) 1. youth; teenager 2. young man

فتاة fatāh (فتيات fatayāt) 1. girl; teenager 2. young woman

فتّاحة fattāḥa 1. opener 2. فتّاحة علب fattāḥat 'ilab tin-opener

فتح fataḥa (a; فتح fatḥ) 1. to open 2. to turn on; to switch on 3. to conquer فتح القفل fataḥa 'l-qufl to unlock

فتح fatḥ (فتوحات futūḥāt; فتوح futūḥ) 1. opening 2. turning on; switching on 3. conquest

فتحة futḥa/fatḥa (-āt) 1. opening 2. فتحة الأنف fatḥat al-anf nostril

فترة fatra (فترات fatarāt) 1. period 2. interval; while; spell 3. فترة إستراحة fatrat istirāḥa intermission

فتّش fattasha to inspect

فتّل fattala to twist

فتنة fitna (فتن fitan) 1. attraction 2. strife 3. riot 4. زعيم فتنة za'īm fitna (زعماء zu'amā') ringleader

فجأةً faj'atan 1. suddenly 2. all at once 3. سقط فجأةً saqaṭa faj'atan to slump

فجّر fajjara to blow up

فجر fajr dawn

فجوة fajwa (فجوات fajawāt) gap

فحص faḥaṣa (a; فحص faḥṣ) (med.) 1. to examine 2. to probe

فحص faḥṣ (فحوص fuḥūṣ) (med.) 1. examination 2. probe 3. فحص طبّي faḥṣ ṭibbī check-up

فحم faḥm coal

فخّ fakhkh (فخاخ fikhākh) trap

فخّار fakhkhār 1. pottery 2. صانع الفخّار ṣāni' al-fakhkhār (صنّاع ṣunnā') potter

فخامة fakhāma luxury

فخذ fakhdh (أفخاذ afkhādh) thigh

فخر fakhr pride

فخم fakhm 1. magnificent 2. luxurious

فخور fakhūr proud (ب bi of)

فداء fidā' 1. ransom 2. sacrifice 3. كبش الفدا kabsh al-fidā' scapegoat

فدائي fidā'ī (-yūn) fedayeen

فدرالي federālī federal

فدية fidya (فديات fidāyāt) ransom

فرّ farra (i; فرار firār) 1. to flee (من min from) 2. to escape (من min from)

الفرات al-furāt Euphrates

فرار firār escape

فرّاشة farrāsha butterfly

فراغ farāgh 1. space 2. vacuum 3. وقت الفراغ waqt al-farāgh leisure

فراق firāq 1. separation 2. اجتمع بعد فراق ijtama'a ba'd firāq to reunite

فرامل farāmil brake; brakes

فراولة farāwala strawberry

فرج faraj relief

فرح fariḥa (a; فرح faraḥ) to be happy

فرح faraḥ (أفراح afrāḥ) joy

فرح fariḥ joyful

فرد fard (أفراد afrād) individual; person

فردوس firdaws paradise

فردي fardī individual

فرّش farrasha to brush

فرشة furshāh (فرش furash) 1. brush 2. فرشاة الأسنان furshāt al-asnān toothbrush 3. فرشاة شعر furshāt sha'r hairbrush 4. فرشاة طلاء furshāt ṭilā' paintbrush

فرشة farsha mattress

فرصة furṣa (فرص furaṣ) 1. chance; opportunity 2. انتهز الفرصة intahaza 'l-furṣa to make the most of

فرض faraḍa (i; فرض farḍ) 1. to impose (ه sth; على 'alā on) 2. to determine 3. فرض الضريبة على faraḍa aḍ-ḍarība 'alā to tax

فرض farḍ (فروض furūḍ) duty

فرط farṭ excess

فرع far‘ (فروع furū‘) branch

فرعون fir‘awn (فراعنة farā‘ina) pharaoh

فرعوني fir‘awnī pharaonic

فرّغ farragha 1. to empty 2. to clear 3. to unload 4. فرّغ الحقيبة farragha al-ḥaqība to unpack

فرّق farraqa (تفريق/تفرقة tafrīq/tafriqa) 1. to separate; to divide 2. to discriminate (بين bayn between)

فرق farq (فروق furūq) difference

فرقة firqa (فرق firaq) 1. group 2. squad 3. *(mus.)* band 4. *(mil.)* division

فرقع farqa‘a to pop

فرمل farmala to brake

فرن furn (أفران afrān) 1. oven 2. furnace 3. bakery

فرنسا faransā France

فرنسي faransī (-yūn) 1. French 2. كندي فرنسي kanadī faransī French-Canadian

فروة farwa (فرو farw) fur

فريد farīd 1. unique 2. alone

فريسة farīsa prey

فريق farīq (فرقاء furaqā’) 1. team 2. party 3. faction

فزّاعة fazzā‘a scarecrow

فزع faza‘ (أفزاع afzā‘) 1. fear 2. dismay

فساد fasād 1. decay 2. corruption

فستان fustān (فساتين fasātīn) dress

فسد fasada (u/i; فساد fasād) 1. to go bad 2. to decay 3. to be corrupt

فشل fashal failure

فشل fashila (a; فشل fashal) to fail

فصاعداً faṣā‘idan 1. forth 2. من الآن فصاعداً min al‘ān faṣā‘idan henceforth

فصل faṣala (i; فصل faṣl) 1. to separate (ه sth; عن ‘an from) 2. to sever 3. to disconnect 4. to break up 5. فصل مؤقتاً faṣala mu‘aqqatan *(ed.)* to suspend 6. فصل عن العمل faṣala ‘an al-‘amal to dismiss; to sack (ه so; عن ‘an/ من min from) 7. to make redundant

فصّل faṣṣala 1. to divide 2. to classify 3. to detail

فصل faṣl (فصول fuṣūl) 1. section 2. chapter 3. act 4. season 5. class; year 6. فصل دراسي faṣl dirāsī *(ed.)* term 7. فصل مؤقّت faṣl mu‘aqqat *(ed.)* suspension 8. فصل عن العمل faṣl ‘an al-‘amal dismissal 9. redundancy

فصيح faṣīḥ 1. eloquent 2. fluent

فصيلة faṣīla (فصائل faṣā’il) 1. group 2. squad 3. squadron 4. species 5. فصيلة دم faṣīlat dam blood group

فضاء faḍā’ 1. space 2. الفضاء الخارجي al-faḍā’ al-khārijī outer space 3. رائد الفضاء rā’id al-faḍā’ spaceman 4. سفينة الفضاء safīnat al-faḍā’ spacecraft

فضائي faḍā’ī 1. space 2. (-ūn) astronaut 3. المكّوك الفضائي al-makkūk al-faḍā’ī space shuttle

فضّة fiḍḍa silver

فضل faḍala (u; فضل faḍl) 1. to be best 2. to be left over

فضّل faḍḍala 1. to prefer (ه sth/ه so; على 'alā to) 2. تفضّل! tafaḍḍal! please!

فضل faḍl 1. kindness 2. grace 3. merit 4. surplus 5. فضلاً عن faḍlan 'an aside from 6. من فضلك min faḍlik please

فضّي fiḍḍī silver

فضولي fuḍūlī curious

فضيحة faḍīḥa disgrace

فضح faḍīḥa (فضائح faḍā'iḥ) scandal

فضيلة faḍīla (فضائل faḍā'il) virtue

فطار fiṭār breakfast

فطرة fiṭra 1. nature; character 2. الفطرة الإنسانية al-fiṭrat al-insānīya human nature

فطرة fuṭra (collective فطر fuṭr) 1. mushroom 2. fungus

فطور fuṭūr breakfast

فطيرة faṭīra (فطائر faṭā'ir) pie

فظّ faẓẓ (أفظاظ afẓāẓ) rude

فظاظة faẓāẓa rudeness

فظيع faẓī' 1. terrible 2. shocking

فظيعة faẓī'a (فظائع faẓā'i') outrage

فعّال fa''āl 1. active 2. efficient 3. غير فعّال ghayr fa''āl inefficient

فعّالية fa''ālīya 1. efficiency 2. لا فعّالية lā fa''ālīya inefficiency

فعل fa'ala (a; فعل fa'l/fi'l) 1. to do 2. to make

فعل fi'l (أفعال af'āl) 1. action 2. act 3. verb 4. ردّ فعل radd fi'l; ردود فعل rudūd fi'l reaction

فعلاً fi'lan indeed

فعلي fi'lī 1. actual 2. effective 3. verbal

فقر faqr 1. poverty 2. فقر الدم faqr ad-dam anaemia

فقراء fuqarā' pl 1. الفقراء al-fuqarā' the poor 2. حيّ الفقراء ḥayy al-fuqarā' slum 3. and see فقير

فقرة fiqra (فقرات fiqarāt) 1. paragraph 2. passage

فقري faqrī 1. spinal 2. العمود الفقري al-'amūd al-faqrī spine 3. حيوان فقري ḥayawān fiqrī vertebrate

فقط faqaṭ 1. only 2. تذكرة للذهاب فقط tadhkara li 'dh-dhihāb faqaṭ single ticket 3. ليس فقط... لكن... أيضاً laysa faqaṭ... lākin... ayḍan not only... but also

فقم fuqqam/fuqm collective seal(s)

فقير faqīr (فقراء fuqarā') 1. poor 2. and see فقراء

فكّ fakka (u; فكّ fakk) 1. to loosen 2. to undo 3. to unfold 4. to unscrew 5. (fin.) to change

فك fakk (فكوك fukūk) jaw

فكاهة fukāha humour

فكّة fakka (fin.) change

فكّر fakkara 1. to think (في fī about/of) 2. فكّر في fakkara fī to consider

فكر fikr (أفكار afkār) thought

فكرة fikra (فكر fikar) 1. idea 2. على فكرة 'alā fikra by the way

فكه fakih funny; humorous

فلّاح fallāḥ (-ūn; فلّاحة fallāḥa) 1. farmer 2. peasant

فلان fulān so-and-so

فلسطين filasṭīn Palestine

فلسطيني filasṭīnī Palestinian

فلسفة falsafa (-āt) philosophy

فلسفي falsafī philosophical

فلفل filfil/fulful collective pepper

فلم film (أفلام aflām) 1. film 2. نصّ فلم naṣṣ film film script 3. موسيقى فلم mūsīqā film soundtrack 4. ترجمة فلم tarjamat film subtitles 5. فلم كاريكتوري film kārīkatūrī cartoon 6. أنتج فلماً antaja filman to produce a film

فلّين fallīn; فلّينة fallīna cork

فم fam (أفواه afwāh) 1. mouth 2. عن طريق الفم ‘an ṭarīq al-fam (med.) oral

فنّ fann (فنون funūn) 1. art 2. craft 3. field; specialty 4. فنّ العمارة fann al-‘imāra architecture 5. and see فنون

فناء fanā’ 1. mortality 2. extinction

فنّان fannān (-ūn) artist

فنجان finjān (فناجين fanājīn) 1. cup 2. صحن الفنجان ṣaḥn al-finjān saucer

فندق funduq (فنادق fanādiq) 1. hotel 2. إستقبال الفندق istiqbāl al-funduq hotel reception; hotel lobby 3. مغادرة الفندق mughādarat al-funduq hotel check-out

فنلندا finlandā Finland

فنلندي finlandī (-ūn) 1. Finnish 2. Finn

فنون funūn pl 1. arts 2. معرض فنون ma‘raḍ funūn art gallery 3. الفنون التخطيطية al-funūn at-takhṭīṭīya graphic arts 4. and see فنّ

فنّي fannī 1. artistic 2. technical 3. (-yūn) technician

فهرس fihris (فهارس fahāris) index

فهم fahima (a; فهم fahm) 1. to understand 2. لا يفهم lā yufham incomprehensible

فهم fahm 1. understanding 2. سوء الفهم sū’ al-fahm misunderstanding 3. ساء الفهم sā’a al-fahm to misunderstand

فوائد fawā’id pl 1. خال من الفوائد khālin min al-fawā’id (fin.) interest-free 2. and see فائدة

فوتر fawtara invoice

فوتيه fōtēh (-āt) armchair

فوج fawj (أفواج afwāj) regiment

فوراً fawran immediately

فوّض fawwaḍa to authorize

فوضى fawḍā chaos

فوضوي fawḍawī chaotic

فوّق fawwaqa 1. to aim 2. to restore 3. فوّقه عدداً fawwaqah ‘adadan to outnumber

فوق fawq 1. on 2. on top of 3. over; above 4. up 5. upstairs 6. super- 7. ultra- 8. فوق البشري fawq al-basharī superhuman

فوقاني fawqānī upper

فول fūl collective 1. beans 2. فول سوداني fūl sūdānī peanuts

في fī 1. in 2. into 3. at 4. about; concerning 5. there is/are... 6. per 7. *(maths)* times 8. في البيت fī 'l-bayt at home 9. في الريف fī 'r-rīf in the country 10. في الصباح fī 'ṣ-ṣabāḥ in the morning 11. في الوقت نفسه fī 'l-waqt nafsuh at the same time 12. في آخر لحظة fī ākhir laḥẓa in the nick of time 13. في تلك اللحظة fī tilka 'l-laḥẓa at that point 14. في إثر fī ithr after 15. في حين fī ḥīn while 16. في غضون ذلك fī ghuḍūn dhālik meanwhile 17. في الوقت المناسب fī 'l-waqt al-munāsib in due course 18. في النهاية fī 'n-nihāya in the end 19. في ذلك الوقت fī dhālika 'l-waqt at that time 20. في كلّ ساعة fī kull sāʿa hourly 21. في ما بعد fī mā baʿd afterwards 22. في ما مضى fī mā maḍā since 23. في وقت غير محدّد fī waqt ghayr muḥaddad sometime 24. في الطريق fī 'ṭ-ṭarīq en route 25. في الجوار fī 'l-jiwār about 26. في الخارج fī 'l-khārij outside; abroad 27. في الغالب fī 'l-ghālib mostly 28. في الأغلب fī 'l-aghlab chiefly 29. في المئة fī 'l-miʾa per cent 30. في الواقع fī 'l-wāqiʿ in fact 31. في ما يبدو fī mā yabdū apparently 32. فيما يتعلق ب fīmā yataʿallaqu bi concerning 33. في مكان قريب fī makān qarīb around 34. في هذا الجوار fī hādhā 'l-jiwār hereabouts 35. في وسط من fī wasaṭin min in the midst of 36. في حاله fī ḥālih

في غير محلّه fī ghayr maḥallih out of place 37. private 38. في رأي fī ra'yī in my opinion 39. في السلطة fī 's-sulṭa in power 40. هل لك في...؟ hal lak fī an...? would you like to...?

فيتامين vītāmīn (-āt) vitamin

فيتنام fiyatnām Vietnam

فيتنامي fiyatnāmī Vietnamese

فيديو vīdiyō 1. video 2. لعب الفيديو laʿb al-vīdiyo (ألعاب alʿāb) video game 3. أشرطة شريط الفيديو sharīṭ al-vīdiyo ashriṭa) video tape 4. جهاز الفيديو jihāz al-vīdiyo أجهزة ajhiza) video recorder 5. صوّر\سجّل على الفيديو ṣawwara/sajjala ʿalā al-vīdiyo to video

فيروس vayrūs (-āt) virus

الفيزياء al-fīzyā' physics

فيزيائي fizyā'ī (-ūn) physicist

فيما fī mā 1. whereas 2. في ما بعد fī mā baʿd after; in what follows 3. في ما مضى fī mā maḍā formerly 4. *and see* في

فيضان fayaḍān flood

فيل أفيال afyāl) elephant

فيلّا villā فيلّات villāt) villa

فيلم film *see* فلم

فيليبين fīlībīn Philippines

فيليبيني fīlībīnī (-ūn) Filipino

ق

قائد qā'id (-ūn; قادة qāda; قوّاد quwwād) 1. leader 2. commander 3. pilot

قائم qā'im 1. erect 2. existing

قائمة qā'ima (-āt; قوائم qawā'im) 1. support 2. leg 3. list 4. قائمة الطعام qā'imat aṭ-ṭa'ām menu

قابس qābis 1. plug 2. قابس كهربائي qābis kahrabā'ī electric plug 3. أدخل القابس في المأخذ adkhala al-qābis fi 'l-ma'khadh to plug in 4. أخرج القابس من المأخذ akhraja al-qābis min al-ma'khadh to unplug

قابض qābiḍ clutch

قابل qābala 1. to meet 2. to interview 3. to confront

قابل qābil 1. suitable (ل li to/for) 2. subject (ل li to) 3. receptive (ل li to) 4. -able 5. قابل للإنجراح qābil li 'l-injirāḥ vulnerable 6. قابل للحركة qābil li 'l-ḥaraka mobile; portable

قابلة qābila (-āt) midwife

قابلية qābilīya 1. suitability 2. receptiveness 3. قابلية للإنجراح qābiliya li 'l-injirāḥ vulnerability 4. قابلية للحركة qābilīya li 'l-ḥaraka mobility

قاتل qātala 1. to fight 2. (mil.) to engage

قاتل qātil 1. lethal 2. (-ūn; قتلة qatala) killer 3. قاتل بالعمد qātil bi 'l-'amd

murderer 4. قاتل مسلسل qātil musalsal serial killer

قاحل qāḥil barren

قاد qāda (u; قيادة qiyāda; قود qawd) 1. to drive 2. to lead 3. قاد طائرة qāda ṭā'ira to fly a plane

قادر qādir 1. able; capable (على 'alā of) 2. غير قادر ghayr qādir incapable (على 'alā of)

قادم qādim 1. next; coming 2. قادم جديد qādim jadīd newcomer

قاذفة qādhifa: طائرة قاذفة ṭā'ira qādhifa bomber plane

قارئ qāri' (-ūn; قرّاء qurrā') reader

قارب qārib (قوارب qawārib) 1. boat 2. قارب النجاة qārib an-najāh lifeboat

قارّة qārra (-āt) 1. continent 2. بين القارّات bayn al-qārrāt intercontinental

قارن qārana to compare

قارورة qārūra flask

قارّي qārrī continental

قاس qāsa (i; قياس qiyās) 1. to measure 2. to try on

قاس qāsin 1. severe 2. hard 3. unkind 4. cruel 5. rigorous 6. drastic

قاسم qāsama to share

قاسى qāsā to suffer

قاضٍ **qāḍin** (قضاة quḍāh) 1. judge 2. magistrate

قاطرة **qāṭira** 1. locomotive 2. قاطرة مجرورة **qāṭira majrūra** trailer 3. مخيّم القاطرات **mukhayyam al-qāṭirāt** trailer park

قاطع **qāṭa'a** 1. to interrupt 2. to break (off) with 3. to boycott

قاطع **qāṭi'** 1. cutting 2. definitive 3. قاطع طريق **qāṭi' ṭarīq** bandit 4. قاطع التذاكر **qāṭi' at-tadhākir** ticket collector

قاع **qā'** (أقواع aqwā') (coll.) bottom

قاعة **qā'a** (-āt) hall

قاعدة **qā'ida** (قواعد qawā'id) 1. base 2. قاعدة تمثال **qā'idat timthāl** pedestal

قاعدة **qā'ida** (قواعد qawā'id) 1. rule 2. regulation 3. base

قافلة **qāfila** (قوافل qawāfil) 1. convoy 2. caravan

قافية **qāfiya** (قوافٍ qawāfin) rhyme

قاقم **qāqum** stoat

قال **qāla** (u; قول qawl) 1. to say 2. to tell 3. to state (ب bi sth) (بأن bi an that) 4. قيل وقال **qīl wa qāl** gossip

قالب **qālib** (قوالب qawālib) mould

قام **qāma** (u; قيام qiyām) 1. to stand 2. to get up 3. to depart 4. to be 5. to start 6. قام ب **qāma bi** to undertake; to carry out 7. قام بدورية **qāma bi dawrīya** to patrol

قامر **qāmara** to gamble

قاموس **qāmūs** (قواميس qawāmīs) dictionary

قانع **qāni'** content

قانون **qānūn** (قوانين qawānīn) 1. law 2. regulation 3. مشروع قانون **mashrū' qānūn** (pol.) bill 4. مخالف للقانون **mukhālif li 'l-qānūn** against the law 5. مرّر قانوناً **marrara qānūnan** to pass a law 6. أطاع القانون **aṭā'a al-qānūn** to observe the law 7. انتهك القانون **intahaka al-qānūn** to break the law

قانوني **qānūnī** 1. lawful; legal 2. لا قانوني **lā qānūnī** lawless 3. غير قانوني **ghayr qānūnī** illegal; unlawful 4. بطريقة غير قانونية **bi ṭarīqa ghayr qānūnīya** illegally 5. مسؤول قانونياً **mas'ūl qānūnīyan** liable

القاهرة **al-qāhira** Cairo

قاوم **qāwama** 1. to oppose 2. to resist 3. to combat 4. لا يقاوم **lā yuqāwam** irresistible

قبّة **qubba** (قباب qibāb; قبب qubab) dome

قبر **qabr** (قبور qubūr) 1. grave 2. tomb

قبرص **qubruṣ** Cyprus

قبرصي **qubruṣī** Cypriot

قبض على **qabaḍa 'alā** (i; قبض qabḍ) 1. to hold 2. to grip 3. to arrest

قبضة **qabḍa** (قبضات qabaḍāt) 1. grip 2. handful 3. قبضة اليد **qabḍat al-yad** fist

قبطان **qubṭān** (قباطين qabāṭīn; قباطنة qabāṭina) captain

قبّعة **qubba'a** (-āt) 1. hat 2. cap

قبل **qabila** (a; قبول qubūl) 1. to receive 2. to accept 3. to take

قبّل **qabbala** to kiss

قبل qabl 1. before 2. قبل من qabl min; قبل أن qabl an before... 3. من قبل min qabl previously 4. قبل الظهر qabl aẓ-ẓuhr a.m. 5. قبل الآن qabl al-ān already 6. قبل الغد qabl al-ghad by tomorrow 7. قبل كلّ شيء qabl kull shay' primarily 8. قبل عدّة أيّام qabl ʻiddat ayyām the other day

قبل qibal: من قبل min qibal by

قبلة qubla (قبلات qubulāt) kiss

قبلما qablama before

قبلي qablī tribal

قبو qabw (أقبية aqbiya) cellar

قبيح qabīḥ ugly

قبيل qubayla shortly before

قبيلة qabīla (قبائل qabāʼil) tribe

قتال qitāl 1. fight; fighting 2. combat

قتل qatala (u; قتل qatl) 1. kill 2. قتل بالعمد qatala bi 'l-ʻamd murder

قتل qatl 1. homicide 2. القتل العمد al-qatl al-ʻamd murder

قتل qatl killing

قتيل qatīl (قتلى qatlā) 1. killed person 2. (mil.) casualty

قد qad 1. particle indicating completed action with past tense 2. already 3. may; might 4. قد أرافقك qad urāfiquka I may come with you. 5. قد يكون qad yakūn perhaps

قدّاحة qaddāḥa (-āt) lighter

قدّاس quddās (-āt) (rel.) mass

قدح qadaḥ (أقداح aqdāḥ) mug

قدر qadira ʻalā (a; قدر qadar) 1. to be able to 2. to afford

قدّر qaddara 1. to appreciate 2. to value 3. to estimate 4. to recognise 5. لا يقدّر بالمال lā yuqaddir bi 'l-māl priceless

قدر qadr (أقدار aqdār) 1. amount 2. quantity 3. بقدر الإمكان bi qadr al-imkān; على قدر الإمكان ʻalā qadr al-imkān as much as possible

قدر qadar fate

قدر qadir capable

قدر qidr (قدور qudūr) pot

قدرة qudra (-āt) 1. power 2. ability 3. قدرة حصانية qudra ḥiṣānīya horsepower 4. قدرة على الإحتمال qudra ʻalā 'l-iḥtimāl stamina

قدرما qadramā as much as

القدس al-quds Jerusalem

قدّم qaddama 1. to offer (ه sth; إلى ilā to) 2. to present 3. to submit 4. to deliver 5. to introduce (ه so; ل li to) 6. قدّم طلباً qaddama ṭalaban to apply 7. قدم شكوة qaddama shakwa to lodge a complaint 8. قدّم عريضة qaddama ʻarīḍa to petition 9. قدّم عطاء qaddama ʻaṭāʼ (com.) to tender

قدم qadam usually f أقدام aqdām) 1. foot 2. أصابع القدم (اصبع القدم) aṣābiʻ al-qadam (iṣbaʻ al-qadam) toe 3. أخمص القدم akhmaṣ al-qadam sole 4. على قدميه ʻalā qadamayh on foot 5. كرة القدم kurat al-qadam football

قدّيس qiddīs (-ūn) saint

قديم qadīm (قدماء qudamā') 1. old 2. ancient 3. antique

قذارة qadhāra dirt

قذر qadhir 1. dirty 2. قذر جداً qadhir jiddan squalid

قذف al-qadhf 1. shelling 2. تحت القذف taht al-qadhf under fire

قذف qadhafa (i; قذف qadhf) 1. to eject 2. to shell 3. قذف بالقنابل qadhafa bi 'l-qanābil to bomb

قذفي qadhfī 1. libellous 2. نشر أقوال قذفية nashr aqwāl qadhfiya libel 3. نشر أقوال قذفية nashara aqwāl qadhfiya (u; نشر nashr) to libel

قذيفة qadhīfa (قذائف qadhā'if) (mil.) shell

قرأ qara'a (a; قراءة qirā'a) 1. to read 2. قرأ الشفاه qara'a ash-shifāh to lip-read

قراءة qirā'a 1. reading 2. معرفة القراءة والكتابة ma'rifat al-qirā'a wa 'l-kitāba literacy

القرآن الكريم al-qur'ān al-karīm the Quran

قرابة qurāba 1. relationship 2. مرتبط بصلة القرابة murtabiṭ bi ṣilat al-qarāba related

قرادة qurāda (collective قراد qurād) tick

قرار qarār (-āt) 1. decision 2. (pol.) resolution

قرب qurb 1. nearness 2. vicinity 3. بالقرب من bi 'l-qurb min near (to) 4. قرب الشاطئ qurb al-shāṭi' off the coast

قرّب qarraba to approach

قرحة qarḥa (قرح qiraḥ) sore

قرد qird (قردة qirada; قرود qurūd) 1. monkey 2. ape

قرّر qarrara to decide

قرش qirsh (قروش qurūsh) 1. penny 2. shark

قرص qaraṣa (u; قرص qarṣ) 1. to pinch 2. to sting

قرص qurṣ (أقراص aqrāṣ) 1. disk 2. dial 3. tablet 4. roll

قرض qarḍ (قروض qurūḍ) 1. loan 2. قرض للعقّارات qarḍ li 'l-'aqqārāt mortgage

قرطاسية qirṭāsīya 1. stationery 2. stationer's

قرع qara'a (a; قرع qar') 1. to knock 2. to ring

قرع qar' collective squash

قرّف qarrafa to revolt

قرف qaraf disgust

قرفان qarfān disgusted

قرفص qarfaṣa to crouch

قرمزي qirmizī 1. scarlet 2. purple

قرميد qirmīd collective (pl قراميد qarāmīd) bricks

قرن qarn (قرون qurūn) 1. century 2. horn 3. متعلّق بالقرون الوسطى muta'alliq bi 'l-qurūn al-wusṭā medieval

قروي qarawī (-yūn) 1. villager 2. provincial 3. rural

قريب qarīb 1. near; close (من min to) 2. handy 3. (أقرباء aqribā') relation;

relative 4. في مكان قريب fī makān qarīb around

قريباً qarīban 1. near 2. soon

قريدس quraydis *collective* shrimp

قرية qarya قرىً quran 1. village 2. قرية سياحية qarya siyāḥīya holiday resort

قوس *see* قزح

قزم qazm أقزام aqzām dwarf

قسّى qassā to harden

قساوة qasāwa 1. severity 2. cruelty

قساوسة qasāwisa clergy

قسط qisṭ أقساط aqsāṭ (*pl.*) instalment

قسم على qasama ‘alā (i; قسم qasm) to divide

قسّم qassama to divide

قسم qasam أقسام aqsām (*pl.*) oath

قسم qism أقسام aqsām 1. part 2. section 3. department

قسمة qisma fate

قسوة qaswa 1. severity 2. cruelty 3. بقسوة bi qaswa roughly

قسّيس qissīs (-ūn) priest

قشّ qashsh 1. straw; hay 2. مخزن قشّ makhzan qashsh barn

قشدة qishda cream

قشّر qashshara 1. to peel 2. to shell

قشر qishr tree bark

قشرة qishra 1. peel 2. shell

قصّ qaṣṣa (u; قصّ qaṣṣ) 1. to cut 2. to tell 3. قصّ بمقصّ qaṣṣa bi miqaṣṣ to snip

قصّاب qaṣṣāb (-ūn) butcher

قصّة qiṣṣa قصص qiṣaṣ 1. story 2. قصّة حبّ qiṣṣat ḥubb romance

قصد qaṣada (i; قصد qaṣd) 1. to intend (إلى\ه ilā *sth*) 2. to mean 3. to aim (إلى\ه ilā at)

قصد qaṣd 1. intent; intention 2. purpose

قصداً qaṣdan on purpose

قصدير qaṣdīr tin

قصّر qaṣṣara to shorten

قصر qaṣr قصور quṣūr 1. palace 2. mansion

قصصي qaṣaṣī 1. fiction 2. أدب قصصي adab qaṣaṣī fiction

قصم qaṣim fragile

قصي qaṣī far; far away

قصير qāṣir قصار qiṣār 1. short 2. small 3. minor 4. قصير الأجل qaṣīr al-ajal; قصير الأمد qaṣīr al-amad short-term 5. قصير النظر qaṣīr an-naẓar near-sighted

قضى qaḍā (i; قضاء qaḍā’) 1. to pass time; to spend time 2. to serve 3. to carry out 4. to settle 5. to complete 6. قضى الوقت qaḍā al-waqt to spend time

قضاء qaḍā’ fate

قضائي qaḍā’ī legal; judicial

قضيب qaḍīb قضبان quḍbān 1. bar 2. rod 3. rail

قضية qaḍīya قضايا qaḍāyā 1. question 2. (*leg.*) case

قطّ **qaṭṭ** never; ever

قطّ **qiṭṭ** (قطط qiṭaṭ); قطّة **qiṭṭa** cat

قطار **qiṭār** (-āt; قطرات quṭurāt) 1. train 2. بالقطار **bi-l-qiṭār** by train 3. قطار سريع **qiṭār sarī'** express train

قطاع **qiṭā'** (-āt) 1. section 2. sector 3. قطاع السياحة **qiṭā' as-siyāḥa** travel industry

قطب **quṭb** (أقطاب aqṭāb) 1. pole 2. القطب الشمالي **al-quṭb ash-shamālī** the North Pole 2. القطب الجنوبي **al-quṭb al-janūbī** the South Pole

قطر **quṭr** (أقطار aqṭār) 1. country 2. region

قطر **qaṭr** collective drip(s)

قطع **qaṭa'a** (a; قطع qaṭ') 1. to cut 2. to sever

قطع **qaṭṭa'a** 1. to cut up 2. قطع شرائح **qaṭṭa'a sharā'iḥ** to slice

قطعة **qiṭ'a** (قطع qiṭa') 1. piece 2. lump 3. scrap 4. strip 5. قطعة أرض **qiṭ'at arḍ** plot of land 6. قطعة شكولاته **qiṭ'at shukūlāta** a bar of chocolate 7. قطعة ورقة **qiṭ'at waraqa** slip of paper 8. قطعة نادرة **qiṭ'a nādira** masterpiece

قطف **qaṭafa** (i; قطف qaṭf) to pick

قطن **quṭn** 1. cotton 2. قطن طبي **quṭn ṭibbī** cotton wool

قطيطة **quṭayṭa** kitten

قعد **qa'ada** (u; قعود qu'ūd) to sit

قفّاز **quffāz** (-āt) glove

قفز **qafaza** (i; قفز qafz; قفزان qafazān) to jump; to leap

قفزة **qafza** (قفزات qafazāt) jump; leap

قفص **qafaṣ** (أقفاص aqfāṣ) cage

قفل **qufl** (أقفال aqfāl) 1. lock 2. padlock 3. فتح القفل **fataḥa al-qufl** (a; فتح fatḥ) to unlock

قلى **qalā** (i; قلي qaliy) to fry

قلب **qalaba** (i; قلب qalb) 1. to overturn 2. (pol.) to overthrow

قلّب **qallaba** 1. to upset 2. to topple

قلب **qalb** (قلوب qulūb) 1. heart 2. ظهر قلب **'an ẓahr qalb** by heart 3. نوبة القلب **nawbat al-qalb** heart attack

قلبي **qalbī** 1. heart 2. cardiac

قلّة **qilla** 1. shortage; lack 2. few; a few

قلّد **qallada** to copy; to imitate

قلص **qalaṣa** (i; قلوص qulūṣ) to shrink

قلع **qala'a** (a; قلع qal') 1. to take off 2. to undress

قلعة **qal'a** (قلاع qilā') castle

قلق **qalaq** (أقلاق aqlāq) 1. anxiety 2. worry 3. concern

قلق **qaliq** 1. anxious 2. worried 3. concerned

قلّل **qallala** 1. to lessen 2. to reduce 3. to minimize 4. قلل من أهميّة... **qallala min ahammiyyat...** to underestimate

قلّم **qallama** to clip

قلم **qalam** (أقلام aqlām) 1. pen 2. stripe 3. قلم رصاص **qalam raṣāṣ** pencil 4. سكّين القلم **sikkīn al-qalam** penknife

قليل **qalīl** 1. little 2. few, a few 3. scarce 4. قليل الدهن **qalīl ad-duhn** lean 5.

قليل جداً ba'd qalīl shortly **6.** قليل بعد
qalīl jiddan next to nothing **7.**
عدد غير قليل 'adad ghayr qalīl quite a
few

قليلاً qalīlan **1.** little; a little **2.** slightly
3. for a while **4.** قليلاً ما qalīlan mā
seldom

قمار qimār **1.** gambling **2.** نادٍ للقمار nādin
li 'l-qimār casino

قماش qumāsh/qimāsh (aqmisha أقمشة) **1.**
cloth; material; fabric **2.** لفة قماش
laffat qumāsh roll of cloth

قمامة qumāma **1.** litter; rubbish **2.**
صندوق القمامة ṣundūq al-qumāma dustbin

قمة qimma (qimam قمم) **1.** top **2.** peak **3.**
summit **4.** tip

قمح qamḥ **1.** wheat **2.** corn

قمر qamar (aqmār أقمار) **1.** moon **2.**
satellite **3.** ضوء القمر ḍaw' al-qamar
moonlight **4.** قمر صناعي qamar ṣinā'ī
communications satellite

قمرة qamra (-āt) cabin

قمري qamarī lunar

قمع qama'a (a; قمع qam') to suppress

قميص qamīṣ (qumṣān قمصان) shirt

قناة qanāh (qanāwāt قناوات) **1.** canal **2.**
channel

قناع qinā' (aqni'a أقنعة) mask

قناعة qanā'a satisfaction

قنبلة qunbula (qanābil قنابل) **1.** bomb **2.**
قنبلة يدوية qunbula yadawīya (qanābil قنابل)
grenade

قنصل qunṣul (qanāṣil قناصل) consul

قنصلية qunṣulīya (-āt) consulate

قنطرة qanṭara (qanāṭir قناطر) **1.** arch **2.**
vault

قنفذ qunfudh (qanāfidh قنافذ) hedgehog

قنّع qanna'a to mask

قنّينة qinnīna (qanānin قنانٍ) bottle

قهوة qahwa coffee

قوّى qawwā to strengthen

قوة qūwa (quwan قوى; qūwāt قوات) **1.**
strength **2.** power **3.** قوة عظمى qūwa
'uẓmā superpower **4.** قوة خاصّة qūwa
khāṣṣa task force **5.** القوة العاملة al-qūwa
al-'āmila workforce **6.** القوة البشرية
al-qūwa al-basharīya manpower **7.**
قوة الدفع qūwat al-daf' momentum **8.**
أغلق بقوة aghlaqa bi qūwa to slam **9.**
داس بقوة dāsa bi qūwa (u; دوس daws)
to stamp **10.** شدّ بقوة shadda bi qūwa (u;
شدّ sadd) to tug **11.** لجأ إلى القوة laja'a
ilā 'l-qūwa (a; لجوء lujū') to resort to
force **12.** and see قوات

قوات qūwāt pl **1.** القوات المسلّحة forces **2.**
al-qūwāt al-musallaḥa military; armed
forces **3.** القوات البحرية al-qūwāt al-
baḥrīya navy **4.** and see قوة

قوس qaws (aqwās أقواس) **1.** bow **2.** arch **3.**
قوس قزح qaws quzaḥ rainbow

قوقع qawqa' shell(s)

قوقعة qawqa'a (qawāqi' تراقع) snail

قول qawl (aqwāl أقوال) **1.** speech **2.** talking
3. words **4.** statement

قوم qawm (أقوام aqwām) 1. people 2. folk
3. nation

قوّم qawwama 1. to straighten 2.
لا يقوّم بمال lā yuqawwam bi māl
invaluable

قومي qawmī 1. national 2. (-yūn) nationalist
قومية qawmīya nationalism

قوي qawī (أقوياء aqwiyā') 1. strong 2.
powerful 3. tough

قيء qay' vomit

قيادة qiyāda (-āt) 1. leadership 2.
command 3. driving 4. مقرّ القيادة
maqarr al-qiyāda headquarters 5.
عجلة القيادة 'ajalat al-qiyāda steering
wheel 6. رخصة قيادة السيّارات rukhṣat
qiyādat as-sayyārāt driving licence

قياس qiyās (-āt) 1. measure 2. record

قياسي qiyāsī 1. record 2. رقم قياسي
raqm qiyāsī (أرقام arqām) record 3.
رقم قياسي عالمي raqm qiyāsī 'ālamī
world record 4. حطم رقماً قياسياً

حطّم رقماً قياسياً/kasara raqman qiyāsiyan
kasara raqman qiyāsiyan (i; كسر kasr) to
break a record

قيامة qiyāma 1. rising 2. outbreak 3.
existence 4. departure 5. carrying
out 6. support 7. عيد القيامة 'id al-
qiyāma Easter

قيّد qayyada 1. to bind 2. to restrict

قيد qayd (قيود quyūd) 1. bond 2. chain 3.
restriction 4. registration

قيمة qīma (قيم qiyam) 1. value 2. worth
ذو قيمة dhū qīma worthwhile 3.
لا قيمة له lā qīma lah worthless 4.
قيمة المبيعات qīmat al-mabī'āt (fin.)
turnover 5. ضريبة القيمة المضافة ḍaribat
al-qimat al-muḍāfa value added tax
(VAT)

قيل qīl: قيل وقال qīl wa qāl gossip

قيّم qayyama 1. to value 2. to assess

قيّم qayyim 1. valuable 2. قيّمة qayyima أشياء
ashyā'
qayyima pl valuables

ك

ك ka 1. as 2. like 3. such as 4. in the
capacity of 5. كأنّ ka anna as 5.
كملاذ آخر ka malādh ākhir as a last resort

ك ka m 1. you 2. your

ك ki f 1. you 2. your

كائن kā'in (-āt) 1. being 2. كائن حيّ
ḥayy organism

كابوس kābūs (كوابيس kawābīs) nightmare

كاتالوج **kātālōg** (-āt) catalogue

كاتب **kātib** (-ūn) كتّاب ;كتاب **kuttāb; kataba**)
1. writer 2. clerk 3. الآلة الكاتبة
al-āla al-kātiba typewriter 4.
طابع على الآلة الكاتبة **ṭābiʿ ʿalā 'l-ālati '-l-kātiba** typist 5. طبع على الآلة الكاتبة
ṭabaʿa ʿalā l-ālati 'l-kātiba type (a; ṭabʿ
طبع)

كاتدرائية **kātidrā'īya** cathedral

كاثوليكي **kāthūlīkī** (-yūn) Catholic

كاحل **kāḥil** (كواحل **kawāḥil**) ankle

كاد **kāda** (يكاد **yakādu**) 1. to be about to;
almost 2. hardly

كاد **kād:** بالكاد **bi 'l-kād** barely

كاذب **kādhib** 1. untrue 2. lying

كاراج **gārāzh** (-āt) garage

كارتون **kārtūn;** علبة كارتون **ʿulbat kārtūn** carton

كارثة **kāritha** (ث كوار **kawārith**) disaster

كاريبي **kārībī** Caribbean

كاريكتوري **kārīkatūrī** 1. فلم كاريكتوري
film kārīkatūrī cartoon; animated film
2. رسم كاريكتوري **rasm kārīkatūrī**
cartoon; caricature

كأس **ka's** (ku'ūs كؤوس) 1. glass 2. cup 3.
(spor.) trophy 4. كأس العالم **ka's al-ʿālam**
World Cup

كاسب **kāsib** (-ūn) wage earner

كاف **kāfin** 1. enough 2. غير كاف **ghayr kāfin** insufficient

كافأ **kāfa'a** (ب **bi** with; ل **li** for) 1. to
reward 2. to recompense

كافّة **kāffa** all

كافح **kāfaḥa** to struggle

كامل **kāmil** 1. whole; entire 2. perfect
3. بشكل كامل **bi shakl kāmil** perfectly

كاميرا ;كاميرة **kāmera** (-āt) camera

الكاميرون **al-kāmīrūn** Cameroon

كان **kāna** (يكون **yakūnu**; كون **kawn**) 1. to be
2. أيّاً كان **ayyan kān;** whatever;
whoever 3. حيث كان **ḥayth kān**
whereas 4. لمّا كان **lammā kāna** as
5. قد يكون **qad yakūn** perhaps 6.
مهما يكن **mahmā yakun** whatever;
regardless

كأنّ **ka'anna;** كأن **ka'an** as; as if

كأنّما **ka annamā** as if

كانون الأوّل **kānūn al-awwal** December

كانون الثاني **kānūn ath-thānī** January

كباب **kabāb** kebab

كبح **kabḥ** restraint

كبد **kabd** (أكباد **akbād**) liver

كبر **kabura** (u; kabr أكبر) 1. to grow 2. to
grow up

كبّر **kabbara** to enlarge

كبرى **kubrā** f 1. great; greatest 2.
الجائزة الكبرى **al-jā'iza al-kubrā** jackpot
3. and see أكبر

كبس على **kabasa ʿalā** (i; كبس **kabs**) to
squeeze

كبش **kabsh:** كبش الفداء **kabsh al-fidā'**
scapegoat

كبير **kabīr** 1. big 2. great 3. major 4.
senior 5. old 6. عدد كبير **ʿadad kabīr**

a lot; lots (of) 7. موظّف كبير muwaẓẓaf kabīr senior official

كبيس kabīs 1. pickled 2. سنة كبيسة sana kabīsa leap year

كتاب kitāb (كتب kutub) 1. book 2. كتاب منهجي kitāb manhajī textbook 3. كتاب عن شيكسبير kitāb 'an Shakespeare a book on Shakespeare 4. الكتاب المقدّس al-kitāb al-muqaddas the Bible

كتابة kitāba 1. writing 2. script 3. معرفة القراءة والكتابة ma'rifat al-qirā'a wa 'l-kitāba literacy 4. أعاد الكتابة a'āda 'l-kitāba to rewrite

كتب kataba (u; كتب katb; كتابة kitāba) to write

كتف katf (أكتاف aktāf) shoulder

كتكوت katkūt (كتاكيت katākīt) chick

كتّل kattala 1. to gather up 2. to amass

كتلة kutla (كتل kutal) 1. mass 2. block 3. (pol.) bloc

كتوم katūm discreet

كتيّب kutayyib (-āt) 1. booklet 2. pamphlet 3. brochure 4. prospectus

كثافة kathāfa 1. density 2. concentration

كثرة kathra large number

كثّف kaththafa to concentrate

كثير kathīr (كثار kithār) 1. many 2. much 3. كثير من kathīr min a lot of 4. أكثر بكثير akthar bi kathīr much more 5. بكثير bi kathīr much; vastly 6. كثير التلال kathīr at-tilāl hilly

كثيراً kathīran 1. much; very much 2.

greatly 3. often 4. plenty 5. كثيراً ما kathīran mā (very) often...

كثيف kathīf 1. dense 2. thick

كحّ kaḥḥa (u) to cough

كحّة kuḥḥa cough

كحول kuḥūl 1. alcohol 2. مدمن بالكحول mudmin bi 'l-kuḥūl alcoholic person 3. الإدمان بالكحول al-idmān bi 'l-kuḥūl alcoholism 4. بدون الكحول bi dūn al-kuḥūl alcohol-free

كحولي kuḥūlī alcoholic

كدح kadaḥa (a; كدح kadḥ) to labour

كدّس kaddasa to accumulate

كذا kadhā 1. such 2. وكذا kadhā wa kadhā such and such 3. أليس كذا ؟ laysa kadhā? isn't that right? 4. and see كذلك

كذّاب kadhdhāb (-ūn) liar

كذب kadhaba (i; كذب kidhb) to lie

كذب kidhb lie

كذلك kadhālik 1. too 2. likewise; this way 3. and see كذا

كرامة karāma dignity

كرة kura (-āt; كرى kuran) 1. ball 2. globe 3. sphere 4. لاعب الكرة lā'ib al-kura footballer 5. كرة القدم kurat al-qadam football 6. كرة السلّة kurat as-salla basketball 7. الكرة الأرضية al-kura al-arḍīya the globe

الكرد al-kurd pl the Kurds

كردي kurdī 1. Kurdish 2. Kurd

كرّر karrara (تكرير takrīr; تكرار takrār) 1. to repeat 2. to reduplicate

كرّس **karrasa** to devote

كرسي **kursī** (كراسي **karāsīy**) 1. chair 2. كرسي متحرك **kursī mutaḥarrik** wheelchair

كرش **kirsh** see كروش

كركي **kurkī** (كراكي **karākī**) crane

كرم **karm** (كروم **kurūm**) vineyard

كرم **karam** generosity

كرنب **kurunb** collective cabbage

كره **kariha** (a; كره **kurh**) to hate

كره **kurh** 1. hate; hatred 2. كره الأجانب **kurh al-ajānib** xenophobia

كروش **kurūsh** tripe

كريكت **krīkit** (spor.) cricket

كريم **krīm** cream

كريم **karīm** (كرام **kirām**) 1. generous 2. liberal 3. kind 4. sympathetic

كريه **karīh** 1. unpleasant 2. horrible 3. hateful 4. رائحة كريهة **rā'iḥa karīha** stink 5. مزيل للروائح الكريهة **muzīl li-'r-rawā'iḥ al-karīha** deodorant

كساء **kisā'** (أكسية **aksiya**) garment

كساد **kasād** (ec.) depression

كسب **kasb** 1. earnings 2. gain

كسب **kasaba** (i; كسب **kasb**) 1. to earn 2. to gain

كسر **kasara** (i; كسر **kasr**) 1. to break 2. to fracture 3. كسر رقماً قياسياً **kasara raqman qiyāsīyan** to break a record

كسّر **kassara** to shatter

كسر **kasr** (كسور **kusūr**) 1. break 2. fracture 3. fraction

كسرة **kisra** (-āt; كسر **kisar**) fragment

كسل **kasal** laziness

كسلان **kaslān** (f كسلى **kaslā**; pl كسالى **kasālā**) lazy

كسول **kasūl** idle

كشّاف **kashshāf** (كشّافة **kashshāfa**) 1. explorer 2. (mil.) scout

كشف **kashf** exposure

كشف **kashafa** (i/u; كشف **kashf**) 1. to uncover 2. كشف عن **kashafa 'an** to expose 3. جهاز الكشف عن الألغام **jihāz al-kashf 'an al-alghām** mine detector 4. كشف الحساب **kashf al-ḥisāb** bank statement

كشك **kushk** (أكشاك **akshāk**) 1. kiosk 2. stall 3. كشك التلفون **kushk at-tilifōn** telephone booth 4. كشك الصحف **kushk aṣ-ṣuḥuf** newsstand

كعب **ka'b** (كعاب **ki'āb**) heel

كعك **ka'k** collective cake

كفّ **kaffa** (u; كفّ **kaff**) to stop (عن **'an** doing sth)

كفّ **kaff** (f كفوف **kufūf**) palm

كفى **kafā** (i; كفاية **kifāya**) to be enough for

كفء **kaf'** 1. efficient 2. competent (ل **li** at) 3. adequate 4. غير كفء **ghayr kaf'** inefficient 5. incompetent 6. inadequate

كفاءة **kafā'a** 1. efficiency 2. competence 3. لا كفاءة **lā kafā'a** inefficiency 4. incompetence

كفاح **kifāḥ** struggle

كفاف **kifāf 1.** edge **2.** خط كفافي **khaṭṭ kifāfi** outline

كفاية **kifāya** sufficiency

كل **kull 1.** each **2.** every **3.** either **4.** all **5.** whole **6.** total **7.** كل شيء **kull shay'** everything **8.** كل من **kull min** each of **9.** و... كل من **kull min... wa** both... and **10.** في كل ساعة **fī kull sā'a** hourly **11.** كل يوم **kull yawm** every day **12.** كل ليلة **kull layla** nightly **13.** كل مكان **kull makān** everywhere **14.** كل واحد **kull wāḥid** everyone **15.** لكل واحد **li kull wāḥid** each **16.** في كل مكان **fī kulli makān** throughout **17.** الوقت كله **al-waqt kulluh** all along **18.** بكل سرور **bi kull surūr** gladly **19.** قبل كل شيء **qabl kull shay'** primarily **20.** على كل حال **'alā kull ḥāl** anyway **21.** على نطاق الوطن كله **'alā niṭāq al-waṭan kulluh** nationwide

كلا **kallā** no not at all

كلا **kilā** m **1.** both **2.** كلا الأمرين **kilā al-amrayn** neither

كلاسيكي **klāsikī 1.** classic **2.** classical

كلام **kalām 1.** talk **2.** speech **3.** عاجز عن الكلام **'ājiz 'an al-kalām** speechless

كلب **kalb** (كلاب **kilāb**) dog

كلتا **kiltā** f both

كلس **kils** lime

كلّف **kallafa 1.** to charge (ب\ه ه so; **bi** with) **2.** to cost

كلم **kallama** to speak to

كلمة **kalima** (-āt) **1.** word **2.** speech **3.**

كلمات أغاني **kalimāt aghānī** lyrics **4.** مؤلف كلمات الأغاني **mu'allif kalimāt al-aghānī** lyricist **5.** كلمات متقاطعة **kalimāt mutaqāṭi'a** crossword puzzle

كلما **kullamā** whenever

كلي **kulli** entire

كلياً **kulliyan** entirely

كلية **kulya** (كلاوي **kalāwī**) kidney

كلية **kullīya** (-āt) **1.** college **2.** faculty **3.** school **4.** كلية الطب **kullīyat aṭ-ṭibb** medical school **5.** كلة مسائية **kullīya masā'īya** night school **5.** مدير كلية **mudīr kullīya** (ed.) principal

كلية **kullīyatan** outright

كليل **kalīl** blunt

كم **kam 1.** how many?; how much? **2.** كم عدد ؟ **kam 'adad?** how many? **3.** كم المدة؟ **kam al-mudda** how long? **4.** كم عمرك؟ **kam 'umrak?** How old are you?

كم **kum** mpl **1.** you **2.** your

كمّ **kumm** (أكمام **akmām**) sleeve

كما **kamā 1.** as; just as **2.** as well; equally **3.** كما ينبغي **kamā yanbaghī** properly

كما **kumā** dual **1.** you **2.** your

كمال **kamāl** perfection

كمان **kamān** violin

كمبيوتر **kombyūtar 1.** computer **2.** جهاز كمبيوتر **jihāz kombyūtar** computer terminal **3.** كمبيوتر محمول **kombyūtar maḥmūl**; كمبيوتر نقال **kombyūtar naqqāl** laptop; powerbook **4.**

أشغل جهاز الكمبيوتر ashghala jihāz al-kombyūtar to log in

كمّثرة kummathra (كمّثريات kummathrayāt) pear

كمل kamila (a; كمال kamāl) to complete

كمّل kammala to perfect

كمّية kammīya (-āt) quantity; amount

كومبيوتر kompyūtir see كمبيوتر

كنّ kunna fpl 1. you 2. your

كنّة kanna (كنائن kanā'in) daughter-in-law

كنغرس kongres Congress

كندا kanadā Canada

كندي kanadī (-yūn) 1. Canadian 2. كندي فرنسي kanadī faransī French-Canadian

كنز kanz (كنوز kunūz) treasure

كنزة kinza sweater

كنس kanasa (u; كنس kans) to sweep

كنيسة kanīsa (كنائس kanā'is) 1. church 2. راعي كنيسة rā'ī kanīsa (rel.) minister

كنيسي kanīsī 1. church 2. دائرة إدارية كنيسية dā'ira idārīya kanīsīya parish

كهرباء kahrabā' 1. electricity 2. أعدم بالكهرباء a'dama bi 'l-kahrabā to electrocute

كهربائي kahrabā'ī 1. electric 2. (-yūn) electrician 3. صدمة كهربائية ṣadma kahrabā'īya electric shock 4. مشعل كهربائي mish'al kahrabā'ī flashlight 5. قابس كهربائي qābis kahrabā'ī electric plug 6. مكنسة كهربائية miknasa kahrabā'iya (مكانس makānis) vacuum

cleaner 7. نظف بمكنسة كهربائية naẓẓafa bi miknasa kahrabā'iya to vacuum; to hoover up

كهف kahf (كهوف kuhūf) cave

كهيرب kuhayrib (-āt) electron

كوى kawā (i; كيّ kayy) to iron

كوب kūb (أكواب akwāb) cup

كوبا kūbā Cuba

كوبوي kūbawī Cuban

كوخ kūkh (أكواخ akwākh) 1. hut 2. cabin 3. cottage

كورس kōras chorus

كوري kōrī Korean

كوريا kōrīyā Korea

كوكب kawkab (كواكب kawākib) planet

كومة kawma (أكوام akwām); كوم kawm (-āt) 1. pile 2. stack 3. mound

الكويت al-kuwayt Kuwait

كويتي kuwaytī Kuwaiti

كوميدية kōmīdīya comedy

كوّم kawwama 1. to pile up 2. to stack

كوّن kawwana 1. to create; to form 2. to compose

كون kawn 1. existence 2. الكون al-kawn the universe

كوني kawnī universal

كي kay 1. in order to; so (that); in order that 2. كي لا kay lā so that... not

كيس kīs (أكياس akyās) 1. pouch 2. sack 3. كيس الشاي kīs ash-shay teabag 4. كيس للنوم kīs li 'n-nawm sleeping bag

كيّف **kayyafa** to adapt

كيف **kayf** how

كيفية **kayfīya** 1. manner; mode 2. quality

كيلوغرام **kīlōgrām**; كيلو **kīlō** kilogramme; kilo

كيلومتر **kīlōmitr** 1. kilometre 2. كيلومتر بالساعة **kīlōmitr bi 's-sā'a**

kilometres per hour; k.p.h. 3. مربّع كيلومتر **kīlōmitr murabba'** square kilometre

كيمياء/كيمياء **kīmyā'/kīmīyā'**: علم الكيمياء **'ilm al-kīmyā'** chemistry

كيمياوي; كيميائي **kīmya'ī; kīmīyawī**; كيماوي **kīmāwī** 1. chemical 2. (-yūn) chemist 3. مادّة كيميائية **mādda kīmyā'īya** chemical

ل

ل **la** *intensifying particle*

ل **li** 1. to 2. for 3. in order to; so that 4. للبيع **li 'l-bī'** for sale 5. للإيجار **li 'l-ījār** for hire 6. للنشر **li 'n-nashr** for the record 7. للأسف **li 'l-asaf** unfortunately 8. للغاية **li 'l-ghāya** extremely 9. مخالف للقانون **mukhālif li 'l-qānūn** against the law 10. كتاب لشارلز ديكنس **kitāb li Charles Dickens** a book by Charles Dickens 11. لأجل **li ajli** for 12. لحدّ ما **li haddin mā** quite; to some extent 13. لحسن الحظّ **li husn al-hazz** fortunately 14. لكلّ **likull** per 15. لكلّ واحد **li kull wāhid** each

لا **lā** 1. no 2. not 3. ولا **wa lā** neither 4. لا... ولا **lā... wa lā** neither... nor 5.

بلا **bilā** without 6. لولا **law lā** except for 7. لِمَ لا ؟ **lima lā?** why not? 8. لا بأس! **lā ba's!** no problem!; never mind! 9. لا جهد له **lā juhd lah** effortless 10. لا حدّ له **lā hadd lah** limitless 11. لا أحد **lā ahad** no one; none 12. لا شيء **lā shay'** nothing 13. لا شعبية **lā sha'bīya** unpopularity 14. لا شكّ **lā shakk** undoubtedly 15. لا ريب فيه **lā rayb fīh** doubtlessly 16. بلا حياء **bi lā hayā'** shameless 17. لا أخلاقي **lā akhlāqī** immoral 18. إنعكاس لا إرادي **in'ikās lā irādī** (-āt) reflex 19. لا طعم له **lā ta'm lah** tasteless 20. لا علاقي **lā 'alāqī** irrelevant 21. لا فعّالية **lā fa''ālīya** inefficiency 22. لا قانوني **lā qānūnī** lawless 23. لا قيمة له **lā qīma lah** worthless 24. لا كفاءة **lā kafā'a** incompetence; inefficiency 25. لا مبالاة lā mubālāh indifference 26. لا مبرّر له lā mubarrir lah inexcusable 27. هاوٍ لا محترف hāwin lā muḥtarif amateur 28. بلا معنى bi lā maʿnan meaningless 29. لا مكان lā makān nowhere 30. لا مهرب منه lā mahrab minh unavoidable 31. لا نهائي lā nihāʾī infinite 32. لا نهائية lā nihāʾīya infinity 33. لا نهاية له lā nihāya lah; لا يهمّ lā yantahī endless 34. لا ينتهي yuhimm it doesn't matter 35. لا يتخيّل lā yutakhayyal inconceivable 36. لا يتغيّر lā yataghayyar fixed 37. لا يتلطّخ lā yatalaṭṭakh stainless 38. لا يحصى lā yuḥṣā countless 39. لا يرحم lā yarḥam ruthless 40. لا يزال lā yazāl still 41. لا يصدّق lā yuṣaddaq incredible 42. لا يطاق lā yuṭāq unbearable 43. لا يعتمد عليه lā yuʿtamad ʿalayh unreliable 44. لا يعدّ lā yuʿadd countless 45. لا يفهم lā yufham incomprehensible 46. لا يقاوم lā yuqāwam irresistible 47. لا يقدّر بالمال lā yuqaddar bi ʾl-māl priceless 48. لا يقوّم بمال lā yuqawwam bi māl invaluable 49. لا يمكن التنبّؤ به lā yumkin at-tanabbuʾ bih unpredictable 50. لا يمكن نسيانه lā yumkin nisyānuh memorable 51. لا يمكن إنكاره lā yumkin inkāruh undeniable 52. لا يمكن وصفه lā yumkin waṣfuh indescribable 53. لا مساواة lā musāwāh inequality

لا ءم lāʾama to suit

لاتيني lātīnī Latin

لاجئ lājiʾ (-ūn) refugee

لاحظ lāḥaẓa 1. to notice 2. to observe 3. to note

لاحق lāḥaqa to pursue

لاحق lāḥiq subsequent

لاحقاً lāḥiqan subsequently

لازم lāzim 1. necessary 2. required 3. must 4. أنفق أكثر من اللازم anfaqa akthar min al-lāzim to overspend 5. مكث أكثر من اللازم makatha akthar min al-lāzim (u; مكث makth) to overstay 6. طلب ثمناً أكثر من اللازم ṭalaba thamanan akthar min al-lāzim to overcharge 7. عمل أكثر من اللازم ʿamala akthar min al-lāzim to overwork

لاصق lāṣiq: عدسة لاصقة ʿadasa lāṣiqa contact lens (-āt)

لاطف lāṭafa 1. to stroke 2. to coax

لاعب lāʿib (-ūn) 1. player 2. لاعب الكرة lāʿib al-kura footballer 3. دور اللاعب dawr al-lāʿib move

لافت lāfit: لافت للنظر lāfit li ʾn-naẓar striking

لاق lāqa (i; ليق layq) to fit

لاقى lāqā to experience

لئلّا liʾallā so that not; in order not to

لام lāma (u; لوم lawm) to blame

لامع lāmiʿ 1. shiny 2. brilliant

لأن liʾan in order so; so that

لأنّ liʾanna because

لاوس

لاوس **lāwos** Laos

لبّ **labb** core

لبّى **labbā** 1. to respond to; to accept 2. to oblige

لباس **libās** (ألبسة **albisa**) clothes; clothing

لباقة **labāqa** tact

لبرالي **librālī** liberal

لبس **labisa** (a; لبس **lubs**) 1. to put on 2. to wear

لبق **labiq** tactful

لبن **laban** 1. milk 2. لبن زبادي **laban zabādī** yoghurt

لبنان **lubnān** Lebanon

لبناني **lubnānī** (-ūn) Lebanese

لتر **litr** (-āt) litre

لثات **lithāt** pl gums

لجأ **laja'a** (a; لجوء **lujū'**) 1. to take shelter 2. لجأ إلى القوة **laja'a ilā 'l-qūwa** to resort to force

لجام **lijām** 1. rein(s) 2. bridle 3. حديدة اللجام **ḥadīdat al-lijām** bridle bit

لجنة **lajna** (-āt; لجان **lijān**) 1. committee 2. commission

لجوء **lujū'** (pol.) asylum

لحاف **liḥāf** (ألحفة **alḥifa**؛ لحف **luḥuf**) quilt

لحس **laḥisa** (a; لحسة **laḥsa**) to lick

لحظة **laḥẓa** (لحظات **laḥaẓāt**) 1. second 2. moment 3. glance 4. منذ لحظات **mundhu laḥaẓāt** just now 5. لحظة خاطفة **laḥẓa khāṭifa** flash 6. بعد لحظة **ba'd laḥẓa** in a moment 7. في آخر لحظة **fī āḫir**

laḥẓa in the nick of time 8. في تلك اللحظة **fī tilka 'l-laḥẓa** at that point

لحم **laḥm** (لحوم **luḥūm**) 1. meat 2. flesh 3. لحم بقر **laḥam baqar** beef 4. لحم الضأن **laḥm aḍ-ḍa'n** mutton

لحّن **laḥḥana** (mus.) to compose

لحن **laḥn** (ألحان **alḥān**) melody

لحية **liḥya** beard

لخّص **lakhkhaṣa** to sum up

لدى **ladā** 1. at; by 2. with; in the presence of 3. in the opinion of 4. لدى وصوله **ladā wuṣūlih** on his arrival 5. لدي شعور أن **laday shu'ūr an** I have a hunch that

لدغ **ladagha** (u; لدغ **ladgh**) to sting

لذلك **lidhālik**؛ لذا **lidhā** (and) so; therefore

لذيذ **ladhīdh** 1. tasty; delicious 2. savoury

لزج **lazij** 1. sticky 2. slimy

لزقة **lazqa** plaster; bandaid

لسان **lisān** (ألسنة **alsina**؛ ألسن **alsun**) tongue

لسع **lasa'a** (a; لسع **las'**) to sting

لصّ **liṣṣ** (لصوص **luṣūṣ**) thief

لصق **laṣiqa** (a; لصق **laṣq**) to stick

لصوق **laṣūq** (med.) plaster; bandaid

لطافة **laṭāfa** 1. charm 2. politeness 3. refinement

لطخ **laṭakha** (a; لطخ **laṭkh**) to stain

لطخة **laṭkha** (لطخات **laṭakhāt**) stain; spot

لطف **luṭf 1.** kindness **2.** courtesy

لطم **laṭama (i; لطم laṭm)** to slap

لطمة **laṭma** slap

لطيف **laṭīf (لطفاء luṭafā') 1.** kind **2.** nice; pleasant **3.** gentle **4.** mild **5.** subtle

لعب **la'iba (a; لعب lu'b/li'b/la'ib)** to play

لعب **la'b (ألعاب al'āb) 1.** game **2.** play **3.** لعب الفيديو **la'b al-vīdiyo** video game

لعبة **lu'ba (لعب lu'ab) 1.** toy **2.** doll **3.** game

لعلّ **la'alla** perhaps

لعن **la'ana (a; لعن la'n)** to curse

لعنة **la'na** curse

لعوب **la'ūb** mischievous

لغة **lugha (-āt) 1.** language **2.** اللغة الأمّ **al-lughat al-umm** mother-tongue **3.** لغة الصمّ **lughat al-ṣumm** sign language **4.** لغة عامّية **lugha 'āmmīya** slang **5.** متعدّد اللغات **muta'addid al-lughāt** multilingual

لغز **lughz (ألغاز alghāz) 1.** mystery **2.** puzzle

لغم **laghama (a; لغم laghm)** (mil.) to mine

لغم **laghm (ألغام alghām)** (mil.) **1.** mine **2.** and see ألغام

لغوي **lughawī 1.** linguistic **2.** (-yūn) linguist

لفّ **laffa (u; لف laff) 1.** to fold **2.** to wind **3.** to wrap **4.** لفّة قماش **laffat qumāsh** roll of cloth

لفافة **lifāfa (-āt)** bandage

لفظ **lafaẓa (i; لفظ lafẓ)** to pronounce

لفظ **lafẓ (ألفاظ alfāẓ) 1.** expression **2.** pronunciation

لفظة **lafẓa (لفظات lafaẓāt) 1.** word **2.** saying

لقاء **liqā' 1.** meeting **2.** إلى اللقاء! **ilā 'l-liqā'!** goodbye!; till we meet again!

لقاح **laqāḥ** vaccine

لقب **laqab (ألقاب alqāb)** nickname

لقح **laqqaḥa (ضدَّ ḍidda** against) to vaccinate

لقي **laqiya (a; لقاء liqā')** to meet

لك **la ka m 1.** to/for you **2.** yours

لك **la ki f 1.** to/for you **2.** yours

لكلّ **likull 1.** per **2.** لكلّ واحد **li kull wāḥid** each

لكم **lakama (u; لكم lakm)** to punch

لكم **la kum mpl 1.** to/for you **2.** yours

لكما **la kumā dual** yours

لكمة **lakma (لكمات lakamāt)** punch

لكنّ **la kunna fpl 1.** to/for you **2.** yours

لكن **lākin; لكنّ lākinna 1.** but **2.** ليس فقط... لكن... أيضاً **laysa faqaṭ... lākin... ayḍan** not only... but also

لكي **likay 1.** so; so that; in order to **2.** لكيلا\لكي لا **likay lā** so that not; in order not to

لمّ **lamma (u; لمّ lamm)** to collect

لم **lam 1.** not **2.** ما لم **mā lam** unless **3.** لم يتمّ **lam yatimm** unfinished **4.** لم يهزم **lam yuhzam** undefeated

لم lima; لما limā 1. why 2. لم لا؟ lima lā? why not?

لمّا lamma 1. when 2. لمّا كان lammā kāna as

لماذا limādhā 1. why 2. what for?

لمبة lamba (-āt) 1. lamp 2. light bulb

لمح lamaḥa (a; لمح lamḥ) to glimpse

لمّح lammaḥa 1. imply 2. hint (إلى ilā at)

لمس lamasa (u/i; لمس lams) 1. to touch 2. to feel 3. to handle

لمسة lamsa (-āt) touch

لمع lama'a (a; لمع lam'; لمعان lama'ān) to shine

لمّع lamma'a to polish

لمع lam' shine

لمعان lama'ān shine

لمعة lum'a polish

لمن liman whose

لنا la nā 1. to/for us 2. ours

لن lan not

له lah 1. to/for him 2. his

لها lahā 1. to/for her 2. to/for them 3. hers 4. theirs

لهب lahab flame

لهث lahatha (a; لهث lahth) to pant

لهجة lahja (لهجات lahajāt) 1. dialect 2. accent

لهذا lihādhā 1. (and) so 2. لهذه الدرجة li hādhihi 'd-daraja so

لهم lahum mpl 1. to/for them 2. theirs

لهن lahunna fpl 1. to/for them 2. theirs

لهو lahw fun

لو law 1. if 2. ولو wa law even if 3. حتى لو ḥattā law even if 4. لولا law lā except (for)

لوى lawā (i; لوي luwīy) to twist

لواء liwā' 1. banner 2. province 3. general

لوبيا lūbyā collective beans

لوّث lawwatha to pollute

لوّح lawwaḥa to wave

لوح lawḥ (ألواح alwāḥ) 1. panel 2. sheet 3. لوح خشب lawḥ khashab board

لوحة lawḥa (-āt) 1. painting 2. signboard 3. لوحة زيتية lawḥa zaytīya oil painting 4. لوحة التحويل الهاتفي lawḥat at-taḥwīl al-hātifī telephone switchboard 5. لوحة الإعلانات lawḥat al-i'lānāt noticeboard 6. لوحة المفاتيح lawḥat al-mafātīḥ keyboard

لوز lawz collective almond

لولا lawlā except (for)

لولب lawlab (لوالب lawālib) 1. screw 2. أثبت بلولب athbata bi lawlab to screw

لؤلؤة lu'lu'a (collective لؤلؤ lu'lu') pearl

لوم lawm blame

لون lawn (ألوان alwān) 1. colour 2. kind; sort

لي lī mine

ليبي lībī Libyan

ليبيري lībīrī Liberian

ليت layta if only...

ليزر layzer; إشعاع الليزر ish'ā' al-layzer 1. laser 2. جهاز طباعة الليزر jihāz ṭibā'at al-layzer laser printer

ليس laysa 1. not to be; it is not 2. not 3. ليس للنشر laysa li 'n-nashr off the record 4. ليس غير laysa ghayr; ليس إلا laysa illā merely 5. أيضاً... لكن... ليس فقط laysa faqaṭ... lākin... ayḍan not only... but also 6. ليس للنشر laysa li 'n-nashr off the record 7. أليس كذلك؟ a laysa kadhālik? isn't that so?

ليلة layla; ليل layl (ليال layālin) 1. night 2. هذه الليلة al-layla; هذه الليلة hādhihi 'l-layla tonight 3. ليلة الأمس laylat al-ams last night 4. منتصف الليل muntaṣif al-layl midnight 5. كل ليلة kull layla nightly 6. نوبة الليل nawbat al-layl night shift 7. ليلة رأس السنة laylat ra's as-sana New Year's Eve

ليلاً laylan 1. at night 2. overnight

ليلي laylī 1. night 2. nocturnal 3. ملهى ليلي malhan laylī nightclub

ليمون laymūn collective 1. lemon 2. ليمون حامض laymūn ḥāmiḍ lime

ليّن layyana to soften

ليّن layyin flexible

م

ما mā 1. what 2. not 3. لما limā why 4. ما دام mā dāma while 5. ما إذا mā idhā whether 6. ما إن mā in once 7. بما أنّ bi mā anna since 8. ما لم mā lam unless 9. ما عدا mā 'adā except 10. بما فيه bi mā fīh including; بما في ذلك bi mā fī dhālik including 11. وما إليه wa mā ilayh; وما إلى ذلك wa mā ilā dhālik and the like; etc; et cetera 12. ما يتبع mā yatba' sequel 13. ما الأمر؟ mā al-amr? What's the matter? 14. ما فائدة...؟ mā fā'idat...? What's the use of...? 15. see ماذا

ماء mā' (مياه miyāh) 1. water 2. ماء معدني mā' ma'dinī mineral water 3. ماء غازية mā' ghāzīya soda water 4. تحت سطح الماء taḥt saṭḥ al-mā' underwater 5. see مياه

مائدة mā'ida (-āt) موائد mawā'id) table

مائل mā'il 1. leaning 2. tending to 3. الحروف المائلة al-ḥurūf al-mā'ila pl italics

مؤامرة mu'āmara (-āt) conspiracy

مائي mā'ī 1. aquatic 2. الألعاب المائية al'āb al-mā'īya pl watersports

مئة ؛مية mi'a (-āt) 1. hundred 2. في المئة fi 'l-mi'a؛ بالمئة bi 'l-mi'a per cent 3. مخفّض بخمسين بالمئة mukhaffaḍ bi khamsīn bi 'l-mi'a half-price 4. مئة بالمئة mi'a bi 'l-mi'a absolutely

مات māta (u؛ موت mawt) to die

مؤتمر mu'tamar (-āt) 1. conference 2. congress 3. convention 4. مؤتمر خبراء mu'tamar khubarā' seminar

مؤثّر mu'aththir 1. impressive 2. moving 3. مؤثّر للعقل mu'aththir li 'l-aql mind-altering

مؤخّر mu'akhkhar 1. rear 2. مؤخّر السفينة mu'akhkhar al-safina (mar.) stern

مؤخّراً mu'akhkharan lately

مأخذ ma'khadh (مآخذ ma'ākhidh) 1. power socket 2. أدخل القابس في المأخذ adkhala al-qābis fi 'l-ma'khadh to plug in 3. أخرج القابس من المأخذ akhraja al-qābis min al-ma'khadh to unplug

مؤدّب mu'addab polite

مادّة mādda (مواد mawādd) 1. material 2. subject 3. substance 4. مادّة صلبة mādda ṣulba solid 5. مادّة كيميائية mādda kīmyā'īya chemical 6. مادّة للتجميل mādda li 't-tajmīl cosmetic

مادّي māddī 1. physical 2. concrete

مؤذٍ mu'dhin 1. harmful 2. غير مؤذٍ ghayr mu'dhin harmless

ماذا mādhā 1. what 2. لماذا limādhā what for?; why? 3. ماذا وإلاّ mādhā wa illā otherwise 4. and see ما

مؤرّخ mu'arrikh (-ūn) historian

مارس mārasa 1. to practise 2. to exert

مارس māris March

ماركسي mārksī marxist

مأزق ma'zaq (مآزق ma'āziq) dilemma; impasse

ماس mās diamond

مأساة ma'sā (مآسٍ ma'āsin) tragedy

ماسورة māsūra (-āt؛ مواسير mawāsīr) 1. barrel 2. pipe

مؤسّسة mu'assasa (-āt) 1. establishment 2. institution 3. foundation 4. مؤسّسة خيرية mu'assasa khayrīya charity

مؤسّس mu'assis (-ūn) founder

مؤسف mu'sif regrettable

مأسوي ma'sawī tragic

ماشٍ māshin (مشاة mushāh) pedestrian

مؤشّر mu'ashshir indicator

ماضٍ māḍin 1. past 2. last 3. الماضي al-māḍī the past 4. السنة الماضية al-sanat al-māḍīya last year 5. الحنين إلى الماضي al-ḥanīn ilā 'l-māḍī nostalgia 6. فكّر في الماضي fakkara fi 'l-māḍī to look back; to recall

مؤقّت mu'aqqat 1. temporary 2. provisional 3. مؤقّت عامل 'āmil mu'aqqat temporary worker 4. فصل مؤقّت faṣl mu'aqqat (ed.) suspension 5. فصل مؤقّتاً faṣala mu'aqqatan (a؛ فصل faṣl) (ed.) to suspend

ماكياج mākiyāj make-up

ماكينات mākīnāt pl machinery

ماكينة makina/mākīna (-āt; مكائن makā'in)
machine

مال māla (i; ميل mayl) 1. to lean 2. to feel
inclined (إلى ilā to) 3. to tend (إلى ilā to)

مال māl (أموال amwāl) 1. money 2. finance
3. wealth 4. property 5. وزارة المال
wizārat al-māl treasury 6. لا يقوم بمال
lā yuqawwam bi māl invaluable 7.
لا يقدر بالمال lā yuqaddir bi 'l-māl
priceless 8. إعادة مال i'ādat māl refund
9. أعاد مالاً a'āda mālan to refund

مالح māliḥ 1. salty 2. savoury 3. saline

مؤلف mu'allif (-ūn) 1. author; writer 2.
composer 3. حقّ المؤلف ḥaqq al-mu'allif
copyright 4. مؤلف كلمات الأغاني
mu'allif kalimāt al-aghānī lyricist

مؤلف mu'allaf (-āt) (mus.) composition

مؤلفات mu'allafāt pl 1. writings 2.
publications

مالك mālik (ملاك mullāk) 1. owner 2.
holder 3. possessor

مؤلم mu'lim 1. distressing 2. painful 3.
غير مؤلم ghayr mu'lim painless

مألوف ma'lūf 1. usual 2. custom 3. norm
4. أكبر من المألوف akbar min al-ma'lūf outsize

مالي mālī 1. financial 2. إمكانيات مالية
imkānīyāt mālīya means 3. إعانة مالية
i'āna mālīya subsidy 4. benefit

مالية mālīya finance

مامة māma mum; mamma

مأمون ma'mūn 1. secure 2. safe 3.
غير مأمون ghayr ma'mūn unsafe

مؤن mu'an pl supplies

مؤنث mu'annath feminine

مانع māna'a to mind

مانع māni' 1. preventative 2. مانع الحمل
māni' al-ḥamal contraceptive

مؤونات ma'ūnāt pl supplies

ماهر māhir 1. clever 2. skilful

مؤهل mu'ahhal 1. eligible 2. qualified 3.
غير مؤهل ghayr mu'ahhal ineligible 4.
unqualified

مؤهل mu'ahhil (-āt) qualification

مأوى ma'wā (مآو ma'āwin) shelter

مئة mi'a see منة

ماية māya

مؤيد mu'ayyid (-ūn) supporter

مايو māyū May

مايو māyō swimsuit

مباح mubāḥ kosher

مباحثات mubāḥathāt pl talks; discussions

مبادرة mubādara (-āt) initiative

مباراة mubārāh (مباريات mubārayāt) (spor.)
1. match 2. tournament 3. contest 4.
مباراة نهائية mubārāh nihā'īya final 5.
مشترك في مباراة نهائية mushtarik fī
mubārāh nihā'īya finalist

مباشر mubāshir 1. direct 2. immediate 3.
على نحو غير مباشر 'alā naḥw ghayr
mubāshir indirectly

مباشرةً mubāsharatan 1. directly 2.
immediately 3. live

مبالاة mubālāh 1. consideration 2. لا مبالاة lā mubālāh indifference

مبتدئ mubtadi' (-ūn) beginner

مبتهج mubtahij happy (ب bi at/with)

مبدأ mabda' (مبادئ mabādi') 1. beginning 2. basis 3. من حيث المبدأ min hayth al-mabda' as a matter of principle

مبدئي mabda'ī basic

مبدع mubdi‛ 1. creative 2. ingenious 3. creator

مبرد mibrad (مبارد mabārid) file

مبرر mubarrir 1. justification 2. لا مبرر له lā mubarrir lah inexcusable

مبرمج mubarmij (-ūn) programmer

مبسّط mubassaṭ streamlined

مبشّر mubashshir (-ūn) 1. missionary 2. مبشر بالخير mubashshir bi 'l-khayr promising

مبعوث mab‛ūth envoy

مبكر mubakkir early

مبكّراً mubakkiran early

مبلغ mablagh (مبالغ mabāligh) 1. sum; amount 2. total

مبلول mablūl wet

مبنى mabnan (مبانٍ mabānin) 1. building 2. مبنى المطار mabnā 'l-maṭār airport terminal 3. مبنىً والأراضي التابعة له mabnan wa 'l-arāḍī at-tābi‛a lah premises

مبهج mubhij cheerful

مبيع mabī‛ (-āt) 1. sale 2. قيمة المبيعات qīmat al-mabī‛āt (fin.) turnover

مبين mubīn unmistakable

متى matā 1. when 2. منذ متى mundhu matā since when

متأثر muta'aththar 1. affected 2. غير متأثر ghayr muta'aththar unaffected

متأخّر muta'akhkhir 1. late 2. delayed 3. underdeveloped 4. developing 5. هذه الساعة متأخّرة hādhihi 's-sā‛a muta'akhkhira This clock is slow.

متأسّف muta'assif 1. sorry 2. أنا متأسّف أن ana muta'assif an I'm afraid that...

متأكّد muta'akkid 1. sure 2. هل أنت متأكّد؟ hal anta muta'akkid? Are you positive?

متأهّب muta'ahhib ready

متبادل mutabādal mutual

متبّل mutabbal spicy

متبرّع mutabarri‛ donor

متبقٍ mutabaqqin left over

متتابع mutatābi‛ successive

متتالٍ mutatālin consecutive

متجاوز mutajāwiz past

متجر matjar (متاجر matājir) 1. store 2. business 3. متجر كبير matjar kabīr supermarket

متجعّد mutaja‛‛id rugged

متجهّم mutajahhim grim

متجوّل mutajawwil wanderer

متّحد muttaḥid 1. united 2. المملكة المتّحدة al-mamlaka al-muttaḥida United Kingdom 3. الولايات المتّحدة al-wilāyāt al-muttaḥida United States 4.

الأمم المتّحدة al-umam al-muttaḥida United Nations (UN)

متحدّ mutaḥaddin defiant

متحدّث mutaḥaddith 1. speaker 2. spokesman; spokesperson (باسم bi 'sm for) 3. متحدّث بالتلفون mutaḥaddith bi 't-tilifūn caller

متحدّثة mutaḥadditha 1. spokeswoman; spokesperson (باسم bi 'sm for) 2. *and see* متحدّث

متحرّك mutaḥarrik 1. moving 2. mobile 3. سلم متحرّك sullam mutaḥarrik escalator 4. كرسي متحرّك kursī mutaḥarrik wheelchair 5. دمية متحرّكة (دمى duman) dumya mutaḥarrika puppet

متحضّر mutaḥaḍḍir civilised

متحف matḥaf (متاحف matāḥif) museum

متحفّظ mutaḥaffiẓ reserved

متحمّس mutaḥammis enthusiastic

متخرّج mutakharrij (-ūn) 1. graduate 2. طالب غير متخرّج ṭālib ghayr mutakharrij undergraduate

متخصّص mutakhaṣṣiṣ (-ūn) specialist

متخلّف mutakhallif backward

متديّن mutadayyin religious

متذبذب mutadhabdhib vibrating

متر mitr (أمتار amtār) 1. metre 2. متر مربّع mitr murabbaʿ square metre

مترجم mutarjim (-ūn) 1. translator 2. interpreter

متردّد mutaraddid undecided

مترف mutraf luxurious

مترو metrō; مترو الأنفاق metrō al-anfāq metro; the Underground; subway

متري mitrī 1. metric 2. طنّ متري ṭunn mitrī tonne

متزامن mutazāmin simultaneous

متزحلق mutazaḥliq: متزحلق على الثلج mutazaḥliq ʿalā 'th-thalj (-ūn) skier

متزعزع mutazaʿziʿ shaky

متزلّج mutazallij: متزلّج على الجليد mutazallij ʿalā 'l-jalīd (-ūn) skater

متزوّج mutazawwij 1. married (man) 2. غير متزوّج ghayr mutazawwij unmarried

متزوّجة mutazawwija married (woman)

متسابق mutasābiq (-ūn) 1. competitor 2. contestant 3. المتسابق الذي يتلو الفائز al-mutasābiq alladhī yatlū al-fā'iz runner-up

متسامح mutasāmiḥ tolerant

متساهل mutasāhil lenient

متساوٍ mutasāwin 1. equal 2. even 3. غير متساوٍ ghayr mutasāwin unequal 4. uneven 5. متساوٍ مع mutasāwin maʿa on a par with 6. على نحو متساوي ʿalā naḥw mutasāwī even

متساوق mutasāwiq compatible

متّسع muttasaʿ spacious

متّصل muttaṣil 1. continuous 2. connected 3. adjacent 4. غير متّصل بالموضوع ghayr muttaṣil bi 'l-mawḍūʿ irrelevant 5. متّصل بالإنترنت muttaṣil bi 'l-internet on-line

متسلق mutasalliq (-ūn) 1. climber 2. متسلق الجبال mutasalliq al-jibāl mountaineer

متشائم mutashā'im pessimist

متشابه mutashābih similar

متشرّد mutasharrid 1. homeless 2. (-ūn) tramp

متضارب mutaḍārib incompatible

متضايق mutaḍāyiq uncomfortable

متطرّف mutaṭarrif 1. extreme 2. (-ūn) extremist 3. fanatic 4. (pol.) ultra-

متطلّب mutaṭallib متطلب المهارة mutaṭallib al-mahāra skilled

متطلّب mutaṭallab (-āt) requirement

متطوّر mutaṭawwir 1. developed 2. غير متطوّر ghayr mutaṭawwir underdeveloped

متطوّع mutaṭawwiʿ volunteer

متظاهر mutaẓāhir (-ūn) (pol.) 1. demonstrator 2. protester

متعة mutʿa (متع mutaʿ) pleasure

متعاطف mutaʿāṭif sympathetic

متعاقب mutaʿāqib consecutive

متعدّد mutaʿaddid 1. numerous; multiple 2. متعدّد الـ mutaʿaddid al- multi- 3. متعدّد الأجناس mutaʿaddid al-ajnās multi-racial 4. متعدّد الجنسيات mutaʿaddid al-jinsīyāt multinational 5. متعدّد الأحزاب mutaʿaddid al-aḥzāb multi-party 6. متعدّد الطبقات mutaʿaddid al-ṭabaqāt multistorey 7. متعدّد اللغات mutaʿaddid al-lughāt multilingual

متعذّر mutaʿadhdhir 1. impossible 2. متعذّر إستبداله mutaʿadhdhir istibdāluh irreplaceable 3. متعذّر إصلاحه mutaʿadhdhir iṣlāḥuh irreparable 4. متعذّر إلغاءه mutaʿadhdhir ilghā'ihi irreversible

متعفّن mutaʿaffin rotten

متعلّق mutaʿalliq 1. related (ب bi to) 2. غير متعلّق ghayr mutaʿalliq unrelated 3. متعلّق بالضواحي mutaʿalliq bi 'ḍ-ḍawāḥī suburban 4. متعلّق بالقرون الوسطى mutaʿalliq bi 'l-qurūn al-wusṭā medieval

متعلّم mutaʿallim 1. literate 2. غير متعلّم ghayr mutaʿallim uneducated

متعمّد mutaʿammid 1. deliberate 2. القتل غير المتعمّد al-qatl ghayr al-mutaʿammid manslaughter 3. غير متعمّد ghayr mutaʿammid unintentional

متعمّد mutaʿammad premeditated

متعهّد mutaʿahhid (-ūn) contractor

متعوس matʿūs unhappy

متغطرس mutaghaṭris 1. proud 2. arrogant

متفائل mutafā'il 1. optimistic 2. optimist

متفاوت mutafāwit unequal

متفجّر mutafajjir explosive

متفجّرات mutafajjirāt explosives

متفرّج mutafarrij (-ūn) onlooker

متفهّم mutafahhim understanding

مقاطع mutaqāṭiʿ: كلمات مقاطعة kalimāt mutaqāṭiʿa crossword puzzle

متقاعد mutaqā'id retired

متقدّم mutaqaddim advanced

متقلّب mutaqallib volatile

متكبّر mutakabbir (-ūn) 1. proud 2.
arrogant 3. snob

متكرّر mutakarrir 1. frequent 2.
عبارة متكرّرة 'ibāra mutakarrira refrain

متّكل muttakil reliant (على 'alā on)

متكلّم mutakallim 1. speaker 2. متكلم باسم
mutakallim bi 'sm spokesman for

متلبّس mutalabbis red-handed

متلمّع mutalammi' shiny

متلهّف mutalahhif eager

متمرّد mutamarrid 1. disobedient 2.
rebellious 3. (-ūn) rebel 4. guerrilla

متمرّس mutamarris experienced

متمغّط mutamaghghiṭ elastic

متململ mutamalmil restless

متمهّل mutamahhil leisurely

متميّز mutamayyiz prominent

متن matn 1. back 2. deck 3. على متن 'alā
matn on board

متين matin sturdy

متناوب mutanāwib alternate

متنوّع mutanawwi' 1. various 2.
miscellaneous

متهكّم mutahakkim ironic; ironical

متّهم muttaham accused

متهوّر mutahawwir 1. hasty 2. impulsive
3. inconsiderate 4. rash

متوازٍ mutawāzin parallel

متواصل mutawāṣil uninterrupted

متواضع mutawāḍi' modest; humble

متوالٍ mutawālin successive

متوتّر mutawattir 1. tense 2.
متوتّر الأعصاب mutawattir al-a'ṣāb
nervous

متوحّش mutawaḥḥish savage

متورّم mutawarrim swollen

متوسّط mutawassiṭ 1. middle 2. medium
3. average 4. intermediate 5.
متوسّط الجودة mutawassiṭ al-jūda
mediocre 6. متوسّط الحجم mutawassiṭ
al-ḥajm medium-sized 7.
البحر الأبيض المتوسّط al-baḥr al-abyaḍ
al-mutawassiṭ Mediterranean Sea

متوقّع mutawaqqa' 1. predictable 2.
prospective 3. المستقبل المتوقّع al-
mustaqbal al-mutawaqqa' outlook 4.
(من) المتوقّع أن (min) al-mutawaqqa' an
it is expected that

متوقّف mutawaqqif dependent (على 'alā
on)

متوهّج mutawahhij red-hot

متوقّع mutawwaqqa' 1. expected 2.
غير متوقّع ghayr mutawwaqqa'
unexpected

متيسّر mutayassir available

متين matīn 1. solid 2. tough

مثابرة muthābara persistence

مثابر muthābir persistent

مثال mathāl (أمثال amthāl) 1. pattern 2.

مثال أعلى (مثل عليا muthul 'ulyā) mithāl a'lā ideal

مثّال maththāl (-ūn) sculptor

مثالي mithālī 1. ideal 2. مثالي النزعة mithālī an-naz'a idealist

مثبّت muthabbat set

مثقب mithqab (مثاقب mathāqib) drill

مثقّف muthaqqaf learned

مثل mathala (u; مثول muthūl) to appear

مثّل maththala 1. to perform 2. to act 3. to represent

مثل mithl; mithla 1. as; like 2. such; such as

مثل mithl (أمثال amthāl) 1. similar 2. المقابلة بالمثل al-muqābala bi 'l-mithl retaliation

مثل mathal (أمثال amthāl; أمثلة amthila) 1. example 2. instance 3. proverb 4. saying 5. ضرب مثلاً ل ḍaraba mathalan li to give as an example of

مثلاً mathalan for example; e.g.

مثلّث muthallath (-āt) triangle

مثلي mithlī (-yūn) homosexual; gay

مثلية mithlīya homosexuality

مثمر muthmir 1. fruitful 2. prolific

مثنّى muthannan 1. double 2. dual

مثول muthūl appearance

مثير muthīr 1. exciting 2. stimulating 3. dramatic 4. رواية مثيرة riwāya muthīra thriller 5. عمل مثير 'amal muthīr stunt 6. مثير للشفقة muthīr li 'sh-shafaqa

pathetic 7. مثير للجدل muthīr li 'l-jadal controversial 8. مثير للاشمئزاز muthīr li 'l-ishmi'zāz disgusting 9. مثير للغاية muthīr li 'l-ghāya sensational

مثيل mathīl (مثل muthul) match

مجادلة mujādala (-āt) dispute

مجاذيب majādhīb: مستشفى المجاذيب mustashfā 'l-majādhīb asylum

مجاز majāz metaphor

مجال majāl 1. room 2. area 3. scope 4. field; sphere; domain

مجاناً majjānan free (of charge)

مجاني majjānī free (of charge)

مجاور mujāwir neighbouring

مجتمع mujtama' (-āt) society

مجتهد mujtahid hard-working

مجد majd (أمجاد amjād) glory

المجر al-majar Hungary

مجرىً majran (مجارٍ majārin) 1. course 2. channel 3. مجرى السباق majra 's-sibāq (spor.) course; track

مجراف mijrāf (مجاريف majārīf) shovel

مجرّد mujarrad 1. naked 2. denuded 3. purely

مجرم mujrim (-ūn) criminal

مجروح majrūḥ 1. hurt 2. injured 3. wounded 4. غير مجروح ghayr majrūḥ unhurt 5. uninjured 6. not wounded

مجرور majrūr: قاطرة مجرورة qāṭira majrūra trailer

مجري majarī Hungarian

مجزرة majzara (مجازر majāzir) massacre

مجلس majlis (مجالس majālis) 1. council 2. meeting 3. chamber 3. رئيس المجلس ra'īs al-majlis chairman 4. رئيس مجلس الإدارة ra'īs majlis al-idāra (com.) president 5. مجلس الإدارة majlis al-idāra board of directors 6. مجلس الوزراء majlis al-wuzarā' (pol.) cabinet 7. مجلس الأمن majlis al-amn Security Council 8. مجلس النواب البريطاني majlis an-nawwāb al-brīṭānī lower house; chamber of deputies; House of Commons; House of Representatives 9. مجلس الشيوخ majlis ash-shuyūkh upper house; senate; House of Lords

مجلّة majalla (-āt) 1. magazine 2. journal

مجلّد mujallad (-āt) volume

مجمّد mujammad frozen

مجمّع mujamma': مجمّع تجاري mujamma' tijārī shopping mall

مجموع majmū' 1. total 2. مجموع موظفين majmū' muwaẓẓafīn staff 3. مجموع الإصابات majmū' al-iṣābāt (spor.) score

مجموعة majmū'a (-āt) 1. set 2. pack 3. group 4. bloc 5. bunch 6. collection 7. مجموعة من المقتطفات الأدبية majmū'a min al-muqtaṭafāt al-adabīya anthology 8. مجموعة أتباع majmū'at atbā' following 9. مجموعة الموظفين majmū'at al-muwaẓẓafīn personnel

مجنّد mujannad: مجنّد جديد mujannad jadīd

(-ūn) (mil.) recruit

مجنون majnūn (مجانين majānīn) 1. mad; insane 2. lunatic; maniac

مجهود majhūd effort; hard work

مجهول majhūl 1. unknown 2. unidentified 3. anonymous

مجوّف mujawwaf hollow

محى maḥā (u; محو maḥw) 1. to erase 2. to eradicate

محادثة muḥādatha (-āt) 1. coversation 2. محادثات muḥādathāt discussions

محارب muḥārib (-ūn) warrior

محاسب muḥāsib (-ūn) accountant

محاضر muḥāḍir (-ūn) lecturer

محاضرة muḥāḍara (-āt) 1. talk 2. presentation 3. lecture

محافظ muḥāfiẓ (-ūn) (pol.) 1. conservative 2. حزب المحافظين ḥizb al-muḥāfiẓīn Conservative party

محاكاة muḥākāh: محاكاة سخرية muḥākāh sukhrīya parody

محاكمة muḥākama (محاكم maḥākim) (leg.) trial

محام muḥāmin (محامون muḥāmūn) lawyer

محاولة muḥāwala attempt

محايد muḥāyid neutral

محبّ muḥibb loving

محبط muḥbaṭ frustrated

محبوب maḥbūb 1. loved 2. loved person 3. favourite 4. popular 5. غير محبوب ghayr maḥbūb unpopular

محترس muḥtaris vigilant

محترف muḥtarif 1. skilled 2. professional 3. غير محترف ghayr muḥtarif unskilled 4. هاو لا محترف; حاو غير محترف hāwin lā muḥtarif; hāwin ghayr muḥtarif (هواه huwāh) amateur

محترم muḥtaram 1. honourable 2. proper 3. decent 4. respectable

محتشم muḥtashim decent

محتلّ muḥtall (-ūn) occupier

محتمل muḥtəmal 1. likely; possible 2. غير محتمل ghayr muḥtamal unlikely 3. من المحتمل min al-muḥtamal probably

محتوم maḥtūm inevitable

محتويات muḥtawayāt pl 1. contents 2. ingredients

محجر maḥjir (محاجر maḥājir): محجر العين maḥjir al-ʿayn eye socket

محدّد muḥaddad 1. definite 2. specific 3. إلى أمد غير محدّد ilā amad ghayr muḥaddad indefinitely 4. في وقت غير محدّد fī waqt ghayr muḥaddad sometime

محدود maḥdūd 1. limited 2. غير محدود ghayr maḥdūd unlimited 3. شركة محدودة sharika maḥdūda limited company

محراث miḥrāth (محاريث maḥārīth) plough

محرّر muḥarrir (-ūn) editor

محرّك muḥarrik (-āt) 1. engine; motor 2. بخار المحرّك bukhār al-muḥarrik exhaust

محرّم muḥarram (-āt) taboo

محروم maḥrūm 1. need 2. needy

محزن muḥzin distressing

محصول maḥṣūl (āt; محاصيل maḥāṣīl) 1. crop, crops 2. yield 3. produce

محض maḥḍ sheer

محطّة maḥaṭṭa (-āt) 1. station 2. stop 3. محطة باصات maḥaṭṭat bāṣāt bus station 4. محطة بنزين maḥaṭṭat banzīn petrol station 5. محطة الطاقة maḥaṭṭat aṭ-ṭāqa power plant; power station 6. محطة الإطفاء maḥaṭṭat al-iṭfāʾ fire station

محظوظ maḥẓūẓ lucky

محفظة (-āt; محافظ maḥāfiẓ) 1. wallet 2. purse

محفوف maḥfūf: محفوف بالمخاطر maḥfūf bi 'l-makhāṭir risky

محقّق muḥaqqiq 1. investigator 2. محقق بوليسي muḥaqqiq būlīsī detective 3. محقق خاصّ muḥaqqiq khāṣṣ private detective; private investigator

محقنة miḥqana (محاقن maḥāqin) hypodermic syringe

محكمة maḥkama (محاكم maḥākim) 1. law court 2. tribunal 3. المحكمة العليا al-maḥkama al-ʿulyā high court; supreme court

محلّ maḥall (-āt) 1. place 2. في غير محله fī ghayr maḥallihi out of place 3. حلّ محلّ شخص ḥalla maḥall shakhṣ to relieve

محلّف muḥallif (-ūn) 1. juror 2. هيئة المحلفين hay'at al-muḥallifin jury

محلل muḥallil analyst

محلول maḥlūl 1. loose 2. liquid

محلي maḥallī 1. local 2. native 3. الحكم المحلي al-ḥukm al-maḥallī local government

محمّص muḥammaṣ 1. toasted 2. خبز محمّص khubz muḥammaṣ toast

محمول maḥmūl 1. portable 2. هاتف محمول hātif maḥmūl mobile phone 3. كمبيوتر محمول kombyūtar maḥmūl laptop

محمي maḥmī 1. protected 2. غير محمي ghayr maḥmī unprotected

محنة miḥna (محن miḥan) ordeal

محنّط muḥannaṭ stuffed

محنّك muḥannak sophisticated

محوّل muḥawwil transformer

محيّة maḥayya (-āt) rubber

محيط muḥīṭ (-āt) 1. ocean 2. environment 3. setting 4. surroundings

مخّ mukhkh (مخاخ mikhākh) brain

مخابرات mukhābarāt pl 1. secret service; intelligence 2. وكالة المخابرات المركزية wikālat al-mukhābarāt al-markazīya C.I.A. (Central Intelligence Agency)

مخاطر makhāṭir pl dangers

مخاطرة mukhāṭira (-āt) 1. risk 2. venture 3. محفوف بالمخاطر maḥfūf bi 'l-makhāṭir risky

مخالف mukhālif: مخالف للقانون mukhālif li 'l-qānūn against the law

مخالفة mukhālafa (-āt) 1. offence 2. (spor.) foul

مخبأ mukhabba' in hiding

مخبر mukhbir (-ūn) informer

مخبز makhbaz bakery

مختبر mukhtabar (-āt) laboratory

مخترع mukhtari' inventor

مختصر mukhtaṣar 1. concise 2. طريق مختصرة ṭarīq mukhtaṣira short cut

مختطف mukhtaṭif (-ūn) 1. kidnapper 2. hijacker

مختلف mukhtalif 1. different 2. various

مخجل mukhjil shameful

مخدّر mukhaddir (-āt) 1. drug 2. المخدّرات المؤثرة al-mukhaddirāt al-mu'aththira mind-altering drugs

مخرّب mukharrib (-ūn) 1. vandal 2. subversive

مخرج mukhrij (-ūn) director

مخرج makhraj (مخارج makhārij) exit; way out

مخزٍ mukhzin 1. disgraceful 2. infamous

مخزن makhzan (مخازن makhāzin) 1. store 2. warehouse 3. depot 4. مخزن قشّ makhzan qashsh barn

مخضت makhiḍat (a; مخاض makhāḍ) to be in labour

مخط makhaṭa (u; مخط makhṭ) to blow one's nose

مخطئ mukhṭi' mistaken

مخطط **mukhaṭṭaṭ 1.** planned **2.** striped **3.** غير مخطط **ghayr mukhaṭṭaṭ** unplanned

مخطوبة **makhṭūba** *f* **1.** engaged **2.** fiancée

مخطوط **makhṭūṭ (-āt)** manuscript

مخفض **mukhaffaḍ:** مخفض بخمسين بالمئة **mukhaffaḍ bi khamsīn bi 'l-mi'a** half-price

مخفق **mukhfaq** unsuccessful

مخفي **makhfī** hidden

مخلب **mikhlab** (مخالب **makhālib) 1.** paw **2.** claw

مخلص **mukhliṣ 1.** sincere **2.** loyal

مخمس **mukhammaṣ** pentagon

مخلوق **makhlūq (-āt)** creature

مخيف **mukhīf** formidable

مخيم **mukhayyam (-āt) 1.** camp **2.** مخيم القاطرات **mukhayyam al-qāṭirāt** trailer park

مد **madda (u; مد madd) 1.** to reach **2.** to stretch **3.** to extend

مد **madd 1.** extension **2.** spreading **3.** rise **4.** supply **5.** المد والجزر **al-madd wa 'l-jazr** tide

مدى **madan 1.** range **2.** distance **3.** scale **4.** duration **5.** مدى الحياة **mada 'l-ḥayāh** lifetime **6.** بعيد المدى **ba'īd al-madā** long-range

مدار **madār (-āt)** orbit

مدارس **madāris** *pl* **1.** زيّ المدارس **ziyy al-madāris** school uniform **2.** *and see* مدرسة

مدافع **mudāfi' (-ūn)** defender

مدام **madām** madam

مدان **mudān** guilty

مدة **mudda** (مدد **mudad) 1.** duration **2.** period **3.** term **4.** كم المدة؟ **kam al-mudda** how long?

مدح **madaḥa (a; مدح madḥ)** to praise

مدح **madḥ** praise

مدخن **mudakhkhin (-ūn)** smoker

مدخل **madkhal** (مداخل **madākhil) 1.** entrance **2.** access **3.** foyer; lobby **4.** introduction **5.** مدخل عمودي لمنجم **madkhal 'amūdī li manjam** mining shaft

مدخنة **madkhana** (مداخن **madākhin)** chimney

مدد **maddada 1.** to extend **2.** to prolong

مدد **madad** (أمداد **amdād) 1.** asssistance **2.** resource **3.** المدد! **al-madad!** help!

مدرب **mudarrib (-ūn) 1.** trainer **2.** مدرب رياضي **mudarrib riyāḍī** *(spor.)* coach

مدرج **madraj** (مدارج **madārij)** runway

مدرس **mudarris (-ūn)** teacher; schoolmaster

مدرسة **madrasa** (مدارس **madāris) 1.** school **2.** مدير المدرسة **mudīr al-madrasa** headmaster **3.** مديرة المدرسة **mudīrat al-madrasa** headmistress **4.** مدرسة إبتدائية **madrasa ibtidā'īya** primary school **5.** مدرسة ثانوية **madrasa thānawīya** secondary school

مدرّسة mudarrisa (-āt) teacher; schoolmistress

مدرسي madrasi 1. school; academic 2. تلميذ مدرسي tilmīdh madrasi schoolboy 3. تلميذة مدرسية tilmīdha madrasīya schoolgirl

مدّع mudda'in (مدّعون mudda'ūn) prosecutor

مدفع midfa' (مدافع madāfi') cannon

مدفعية madfa'īya artillery

مدفوع madfū': غير مدفوع ghayr madfū' (fin.) outstanding

مدفوعات madfū'āt pl payments

مدلّع mudalla': طفل مدلّع ṭifl mudalla' a spoiled child

مدلية madalya (-āt) medal

مدمج mudmaj compact

مدمّرة mudammira (-āt) naval destroyer

مدمن mudmin (-ūn) 1. addict 2. مدمن بالكحول mudmin bi 'l-kuḥūl alcoholic

مدني madanī (-ūn) 1. civil 2. civilian 3. urban 4. الحقوق المدنية al-ḥuqūq al-madanīya civil rights

مدنية madanīya civilisation

مدوّر mudawwar round

مدوّنة mudawwana (-āt) record

مدّي maddī tidal

مدير mudīr (مدراء mudarā') 1. director 2. manager 3. boss 4. superior 5. administrator 6. مدير المدرسة mudīr al-

madrasa headmaster 7. مدير كلّية mudīr kullīya (ed.) principal 8. مدير عامّ mudīr 'āmm managing director 9. مدير الأوركسترا mudīr al-orkestrā (mus.) conductor

مدين madīn 1. debtor 2. ... كان مديناً له ب kāna mudīnan lah bi... to owe... to so

مدينة madīna (مدن mudun; مدائن madā'in) 1. town; city 2. مدينة الولادة madīnat al-wilāda hometown 3. مركز المدينة markaz al-madīna city centre 4. وسط المدينة wasaṭ al-madīna inner city 5. مفتاح المدينة miftāḥ al-madīna area code

مديون madyūn debtor

مذبحة madhbaḥa (مذابح madhābiḥ) massacre

مدهش mudhish wonderful

مذعر mudh'ir alarming

مذكّر mudhakkar masculine

مذكّرة mudhakkira (-āt) 1. note 2. reminder 3. memorandum

مذكّرات mudhakkarāt pl memoirs

مذنب mudhnib guilty

مذهّل mudhhil spectacular

مذيع mudhī' 1. announcer 2. مذيع نشرة الأخبار mudhī' nashrat al-akhbār newscaster, newsreader

مرّ marra (u; مرور murūr) 1. to pass; to elapse 2. to pass (ب bi by/through) 3. مرّ على marra 'alā to pay a short visit to

مُرّ murr bitter

مَرْء mar' 1. man 2. المَرْء al-mar' one

مِرْأَب mir'ab (مَرائِب marā'ib) 1. garage 2.
مِرْأَب السَّيّارات mir'ab as-sayyārāt car-park

مَرّات marrāt pl 1. several times 2. see مَرّة

مَرْأَة mar'a woman

مِرْآة mir'āh (مِرآء marā'in; مَرايا marāyā)
mirror

مِراث mirāth legacy

مُراجِع murāji' (-ūn) reviewer

مُراجَعة murāja'a 1. (media) review 2. (ed.)
revision

مُراسِل murāsil (-ūn) 1. reporter 2.
correspondent 3. sender

مُراسَلة murāsala correspondence

مَراسِم marāsim pl ceremony

مُراعٍ murā'in: مُراعي المواعيد murā'ī 'l-mawā'īd punctual

مُراعاة murā'a: مُراعاة المواعيد murā'at al-mawā'īd punctuality

مُرافِق murāfiq (-ūn) 1. escort 2. غير مُرافق
ghayr murāfaq unaccompanied

مُراقِب murāqib (-ūn) 1. observer 2.
controller 3. supervisor 4. watcher 5.
warden

مُراقَبة murāqaba observation

مُراهِق murāhiq (-ūn) teenager; adolescent

مُراهَقة murāhaqa 1. adolescence 2.
سِنّ المراهقة sinn al-murāhaqa teens

مُراهَنة murāhana bet

مَرْؤوس mar'ūs (-ūn) subordinate

مَرْئي mar'ī 1. visible 2. غير مرئي ghayr
mar'ī invisible

مَرْئيّة mar'īya visibility

مُرَبّى murabbā (مُرَبّيات murabbayāt) jam

مُرْبِح murbiḥ 1. profitable 2. غير مربح
ghayr murbiḥ unprofitable

مُرَبّع murabba' (-āt) 1. square 2.
مِتر مربّع mitr murabba' square metre 3.
كيلومِتر مربّع kīlōmitr murabba' square
kilometre

مُرْبِك murbik awkward

مُرَبّية murabbīya; مُرَبّية أطفال
murabbīyat aṭfāl nanny

مَرّة marra (-āt) 1. once 2. time 3. مرّة واحدة
marra wāḥida; ذات مرّة dhāt marra once
4. ضاعف ثلاث مرّات ḍā'afa thulāth
marrāt to triple 5. and see مرّات; مرّة؛
مرّتين

مَرّةً marratan once

مُرتاح mirtāḥ 1. relieved 2. مرتاح البال
mirtāḥ al-bāl unconcerned

مُرَتَّب murattab 1. neat 2. in order 3.
غير مرتّب ghayr murattab untidy

مُرتَبِط murtabiṭ 1. connected 2.
مرتبط بصلة القرابة murtabiṭ bi ṣilat al-qarāba related

مُرتَزِق murtaziq (-ūn; مرتزقة murtaziqa)
mercenary

مُرتَعِش murta'ish shaky

مُرتَفِع murtafi': مرتفع الصوت murtafi' aṣ-
ṣawt loud

مرتفعات murtafa'āt pl 1. heights 2. highlands

مرتكب murtakib (-ūn): مرتكب جرائم حرب murtakib jarā'im ḥarb war criminal

مرّتين marratayn 1. twice 2. *and see* مرّ

مرثون marathōn: سباق المرثون sibāq al-marathōn marathon

مرجّح murajjaḥ favourite

مرجع marja' (مراجع marāji') 1. authority 2. reference

مرجوحة marjūḥa (مراجيح marājīḥ) swing

مرح mariḥ 1. merry 2. hilarious

مرحاض mirḥāḍ (مراحيض marāḥīḍ) 1. toilet 2. مرحاض عمومي mirḥāḍ 'umūmī public lavatory 3. ورق المرحاض waraq al-mirḥāḍ toilet paper

مرحباً marḥaban hello!

مرحّب muraḥḥab 1. مرحّب به muraḥḥab bih welcome 2. غير مرحّب به ghayr muraḥḥab bih unwelcome

مرحلة marḥala (مراحل marāḥil) 1. phase 2. stage 3. (spor.) leg

المرحوم al-marḥūm the late Mr...

مرّر marrara 1. to pass 2. مرّر قانوناً marrara qānūnan to pass a law

مرس maris (أمراس amrās) veteran

مرساة mirsāh (مراس marāsin) anchor

مرسلة mursila (-āt) transmitter

مرسوم marsūm (مراسيم marāsīm) (pol.) act

مرشد murshid (-ūn) 1. guide 2. مرشد سياحي murshid siyāḥī tour guide

مرشّح murashshaḥ (-ūn) candidate

مرض maraḍ (أمراض amrāḍ) 1. illness; sickness 2. disease 3. مرض السكّر maraḍ as-sukkar diabetes 4. مرض تناسلي maraḍ tanāsulī venereal disease 5. مرض الشك maraḍ ash-shakk paranoia 6. مصيب بمرض الشكّ muṣīb bi maraḍ al-shakk paranoid 7. *and see* أمراض

مرض murḍin satisfactory

مرّض marraḍa (med.) to nurse

مرطبات muraṭṭibāt pl refreshments

مرعب mur'ib dreadful

مرعوب mar'ūb frightened

مرغوب marghūb 1. مرغوب فيه marghūb fīh desirable

مرفأ marfa' (مرافئ marāfi') port

مرفق mirfaq (مرافق marāfiq) 1. elbow 2. service 3. مرفق عامّ mirfaq 'āmm (مرافق عامّة marāfiq 'āmma) public utility

مرق maraq 1. gravy 2. stock

مركب markab (مراكب marākib) 1. boat 2. ship 3. craft 4. مركب شراعي markab shirā'ī sailing-ship

مركبة markaba (-āt) vehicle

مركز markaz (مراكز marākiz) 1. centre 2. headquarters 3. central office 4. station 5. status 6. مركز إجتماعي markaz ijtimā'ī position 7. مركز المدينة markaz al-madīna city centre 8. مركز الشرطة markaz ash-shurṭa police station; police precinct 9.

مركز للبحوث markaz li 'l-buḥūth research centre

مركزي markazī central

مركّب murakkab compound

مرمر marmar marble

مرمى marman (مرام marāmin) 1. (mil.) range 2. (spor.) goal 3. عامود المرمى 'āmūd al-marmā goalpost 4. حارس المرمى ḥāris al-marmā goalkeeper

مرّن marrana to rehearse

مرهق murhaq exhausted

مروحة mirwaḥa (مراوح marāwiḥ) 1. fan 2. propeller

مروّج murawwij (-ūn) promoter

مرور murūr 1. passage 2. movement 3. traffic 4. إزدحام المرور izdiḥām al-murūr traffic jam 5. تذكرة المرور tadhkirat al-murūr pass

مروّع murawwi' 1. dreadful 2. shocking

مريب murīb 1. doubtful 2. suspicious

مريح murīḥ 1. comfortable 2. غير مريح ghayr murīḥ uncomfortable

مريض marīḍ 1. ill; sick 2. (مرضى marḍā) patient 3. invalid

مزاج mizāj 1. mood 2. temper 3. مزاج جيّد mizāj jayyid a good mood 4. مزاج سيّئ mizāj sayyi' a bad mood 5. مزاجي أن mizājī an I am in the mood to...

مزاد mazād: مزاد علني mazād 'alanī auction

مزار mazār (-āt) shrine

مزارع muzāri' (-ūn) farmer

مزبلة mazbala (مزابل mazābil) rubbish tip

مزج mazaja (u; مزج mazj) to mix

مزج mazij mixture

مزح mazaḥa (a; مزح mazḥ) joke

مزحاً mazḥan in fun

مزخرف muzakhrif 1. fancy 2. غير مزخرف ghayr muzakhrif plain

مزدحم muzdaḥim 1. crowded 2. packed

مزدهر muzdahir prosperous

مزدوج muzdawij double

مزراب mizrāb (مزاريب mazārib) spout

مزرعة mazra'a (مزارع mazāri') 1. farm 2. field

مزّق mazzaqa to tear up

مزعج muz'ij 1. irritating 2. pest

مزق mazaqa (i; مزق mazq) to rip

مزق mazq rip

مزلاج mizlāj (مزاليج mazālij) bolt

مزلج mizlaj (مزالج mazālij) 1. skate 2. ski

مزلق mazlaq (مزالق mazāliq) slide

مزهرية mazharīya (-āt) vase

مزوّد muzawwid (-ūn) supplier

مزوّر muzawwir phony

مزيد mazīd 1. more 2. increase

مزيل muzīl: مزيل للروائح الكريهة muzīl li 'r-rawā'iḥ al-karīha deodorant

مزيّف muzayyaf 1. fake 2. counterfeit

مساء masā' (أمساء amsā') 1. evening 2. مساء الخير! masā' al-khayr good evening! 3. في المساء fi 'l-masā in the

مساء اليوم masā' al-yawm .4 evening

this evening 5. مساء أمس masā' ams yesterday evening 6. غداً في المساء ghadan fī 'l-masā' tomorrow evening

مساءً masā'an in the evening

مسائي masā'ī 1. night 2. nocturnal 3. كلة مسائية kullīya masā'īya night school

مسّاح massāḥ (-ūn) surveyor

مسابقة musābaqa (-āt) 1. race 2. racing 3. tournament 4. مسابقة معلوماتية musābaqa ma'lūmātīya quiz

مساحة masāḥa (-āt) area; space

مساحقة musāḥaqa lesbianism

مساعد musā'id (-ūn) 1. assistant; helper 2. مساعد على جريمة musā'id 'alā jarīma (leg.) accessory

مساعدة musā'ada aid; assistance; help

مسافة masāfa (-āt) distance

مسافر musāfir (-ūn) 1. traveller 2. passenger

مسألة\مسائل mas'ala (مسائل masā'il) 1. affair 2. matter 3. business

مساندة musānada backing

مساوٍ musāwin equivalent

مساواة musāwah 1. equality 2. لا مساواة lā musāwāh inequality

مسؤول mas'ūl (-ūn) 1. official 2. responsible (عن 'an for) 3. مسؤول عن mas'ūl 'an in charge of 4. غير مسؤول ghayr mas'ūl irresponsible 5. مسؤول قانونياً mas'ūl qānūnīyan liable

مسؤولية mas'ūlīya (-āt) responsibility (عن 'an for)

مسبّب musabbib: مسبّب الصدمة musabbib aṣ-ṣadma traumatic

مسبّق musabbaq: عرض مسبّق 'arḍ musabbaq preview

مستثمر mustathmir (-ūn) investor

مستحسن mustaḥsan advisable

مستحضر mustaḥḍar: مستحضر تجميلي mustaḥḍar tajmīlī; مستحضر طبّي mustaḥḍar ṭibbī cream

مستحيل mustaḥīl impossible

مستخدم mustakhdam used

مستدير mustadīr round

مسترخٍ mustarkhin; مستريح mustarīḥ relaxed

مستشار mustashār (-ūn) 1. adviser 2. consultant 3. counsellor

مستشفى mustashfan (مستشفيات mustashfayāt) 1. hospital 2. infirmary 3. مستشفى الولادة mustashfa 'l-wilāda maternity clinic 4. مستشفى المجاذيب mustashfā 'l-majādhīb; مستشفى الأمراض العقلية mustashfa 'l-amrāḍ al-'aqlīya mental hospital

مستطيل mustaṭīl (-āt) rectangle

مستعار musta'ār: اسم مستعار ism musta'ār alias

مستعدّ musta'idd 1. willing 2. prepared (ل li for) 3. ready (ل li for) 4. غير مستعدّ ghayr musta'idd unwilling

مستعمرة musta'mara (-āt) colony

مستعمل musta'mil (-ūn) user

مستعمل musta'mal 1. used 2. second-hand

مستقبل mustaqbal 1. future 2. المستقبل المتوقّع al-mustaqbal al-mutawaqqa' outlook

مستقبلي mustaqbalī prospective

مستقرّ mustaqirr 1. constant 2. stable 3. steady 4. غير مستقرّ ghayr mustaqirr unsteady 5. جعل غير مستقرّ ja'ala ghayr mustaqirr (a) to destabilize

مستقلّ mustaqill independent

مستقيم mustaqīm 1. straight 2. upright

مستلم mustalim receiver; recipient

مستمرّ mustamirr continuous

مستمع mustami' (-ūn) listener

مستنقع mustanqa' (-āt) marsh; swamp

مستهلك mustahlik (-ūn) consumer

مستودع mustawda' (-āt) 1. warehouse 2. depot 3. reservoir

مستودع mustawdi': مستودع للأكل mustawdi' li 'l-akl pantry

مستوصف mustawṣaf (-āt) 1. clinic 2. dispensary

مستوطن mustawṭin (-ūn) settler

مستوطن mustawṭan (-āt) settlement

مستوقد mustawqad fireplace

مستوٍ mustawin 1. even 2. level

مستوى mustawan 1. level 2. standard 3. دون المستوى dūn al-mustawā unsatisfactory 4. مستوى سطح البحر mustawā saṭḥ al-baḥr sea-level

مسجد masjid (مساجد masājid) mosque

مسجّل musajjil (-āt) 1. cassette recorder; tape recorder 2. مسجّل إصابة musajjil iṣāba scorer

مسح masaḥa (a; مسح masḥ) 1. to survey 2. to wipe 3. to stroke

مسح masḥ survey

مسحاة misḥāh (مساح masāḥin) spade

مسحوق masḥūq 1. powder 2. powdered 3. مسحوق الغسيل masḥūq al-ghasīl washing powder; detergent

مسدّد musaddad: غير مسدّد ghayr musaddad unpaid

مسدّس musaddas (-āt) pistol

مسرح masraḥ (مسارح masāriḥ) 1. stage 2. theatre 3. عالم المسرح 'ālam al-masraḥ show business 4. ضوء المسرح ḍaw' al-masraḥ spotlight

مسرحي masraḥī 1. dramatic 2. stage 3. إستعراض مسرحي isti'rāḍ masraḥī show

مسرحية masraḥīya (-āt) 1. play 2. نصّ مسرحية naṣṣ masraḥīya stage script 3. مسرحية موسيقية masraḥīya mūsīqīya musical

مسرف musrif 1. wasteful 2. extravagant

مسرور masrūr 1. glad 2. مسرور للغاية masrūr li 'l-ghāya delighted

مسّد massada to stroke

مسطرة misṭara (مساطر masāṭir) ruler

مسطّح musaṭṭaḥ flat

مسطول masṭūl intoxicated

مَعْسًى mas'an (مَساع masā'in) effort

مسفوع masfū' sunburnt

مسقط masqaṭ 1. place 2. site 3. مسقط الرأس masqaṭ ar-ra's birthplace

مسك masaka (u/i; مسك mask) 1. to hold 2. مسك ب masaka to seize 3. to catch

مسكّن musakkin (-āt) 1. tranquillizer 2. painkiller

مسكون maskūn 1. inhabited

مسكين miskīn poor

مسلٍّ musallin entertaining

مسلّح musallaḥ (-ūn) 1. armed 2. gunman 3. guerrilla 4. terrorist 5. قوات مسلحة qūwāt musallaḥa armed forces; military

مسلخ maslakh (مسالخ masālikh) slaughterhouse

مسلسل musalsal (-āt) 1. series 2. serial 3. soap opera 4. قاتل مسلسل qātil musalsal serial killer

مسلم muslim (-ūn) Muslim

مسمار mismār (مسامير masāmīr) 1. nail 2. مسمار ملولب mismār mulawlab bolt

مسموح masmūḥ: الحدّ المسموح به للسرعة al-ḥadd al-masmūḥ bih li 's-sur'a speeding

مسهل mushil (-āt); مسهّل musahhil (-āt) laxative

مسوّدة musawwada (-āt) 1. draft 2. وضع مسوّدة waḍa'a musawwada to draft

مسيحي masīḥī (-yūn) Christian

مسيحية masīḥīya Christianity

مسيرة masīra march

مسيطر musayṭir dominant

مسيّل musayyil: الغاز المسيّل للدموع al-ghāz al-musayyil li 'd-dumū' tear gas

مشى mashā (i; مشي mashy) 1. to walk 2. to go

مشابه mushābih similar

مشاة mushāh infantry

مشاجرة mushājara (-āt) quarrel

مشارك mushārik (-ūn) participant

مشاركة mushāraka 1. turn-out 2. participation (في fī in)

مشاعر mashā'ir pl (singular مشعر mash'ar) 1. feelings 2. أثار المشاعر athāra al-mashā'ir to move one's feelings 3. جرح المشاعر jarḥ al-mashā'ir offence 4. أجرح مشاعر غيره ajraḥa mashā'ir ghayrih to offend 5. جارح مشاعر الغير jāriḥ mashā'ir al-ghayr offensive

مشاغب mushāghib (-ūn) rioter

مشاهد mushāhid (-ūn) 1. viewer 2. spectator 3. onlooker

مشؤوم mash'ūm 1. unlucky 2. sinister

مشبك mishbak 1. clip 2. مشبك الورق mishbak al-waraq paper clip

مشبوه mashbūh 1. suspect 2. suspicious

مشتبه mushtabih: مشتبه فيه mushtabih fīh suspect

مشترك mushtarik (-ūn) 1. joint 2. participant 3. subscriber 4.

مشترك في مباراة نهائية mushtarik fī
mubārāh nihā'iya finalist

مشترٍ mushtarin (-yūn) purchaser

مشتريات mushtarayāt pl shopping

مشته mushtahin: 1. مشته لأفراد الجنس الآخر
mushtahin li afrād al-jins al-ākhar heterosexual 2. مشتهي الأفراد الجنس المماثل
mushtahi 'l-afrād al-jins al-mumāthil
homosexual

مشجّ mushajjin pathetic

مشدود mashdūd tight

مشرب mashrab (مشارب mashārib) bar

مشرحة mashraḥa mortuary

مشرّد musharrad (-ūn) vagrant

مشرف mushrif (-ūn) supervisor

مشرق mushriq brilliant

مشروع mashrū‘ (مشاريع mashārī‘) 1. plan
2. scheme 3. project 4. (com.)
business 5. venture 6. enterprise 7.
مشروع قانون mashrū‘ qānūn (pol.) bill

مشط mushṭ (أمشاط amshāṭ) comb

مشعّ mushi‘‘ radiant

مشعر mash‘ar (مشاعر mashā‘ir) feeling

مشعل mash‘al/mish‘al (مشاعل mashā‘il) 1.
torch 2. مشعل كهربائي mish‘al kahrabā'ī
flashlight

مشغّل mushaghghil (-ūn) operator

مشغول mashghūl 1. busy 2. engaged 3.
مشغول جداً mashghūl jiddan hectic

مشقّة mashaqqa (-āt) hardship

مشكلة mushkila (-āt; مشاكل mashākil);

مشكل mushkil (مشاكل mashākil) 1.
trouble 2. problem 3. حلّ مشكلة ḥalla
mushkila to solve a problem

مشكوك mashkūk: مشكوك فيه mashkūk fīh
doubtful

مشمئزّ mushma'izz disgusted

مشمس mushmis sunny

مشمش mishmish collective apricot(s)

مشمّع mushamma‘ (-āt) 1. lino; linoleum
2. معتف مشمّع mi‘ṭaf mushamma‘;
قماش مشمّع qumāsh mushamma‘
mackintosh; raincoat

مشهد mashhad (مشاهد mashāhid) 1. scene
2. sight

مشهّر mashahhar notorious

مشهور mashhūr 1. well-known 2.
famous

مشواة mishwāh barbecue

مشوار mishwār (مشاوير mashāwīr) errand

مشوّق mushawwiq interesting

مشير mushīr (-ūn) 1. adviser 2. field-
marshal

مصّ maṣṣa (a/u; مص maṣṣ) to suck

مصّاص maṣṣāṣ: مصّاص الدماء maṣṣāṣ ad-
dimā' vampire

مصادفة muṣādafa coincidence

مصادفةً muṣādafatan 1. accidentally 2.
سمع مصادفةً sami‘a muṣādafatan (a;
sam‘) to overhear

مصارعة muṣāra‘a wrestling

مصافحة muṣāfaḥa handshake

مصالح maṣāliḥ pl interests

مَصَبّ maṣabb 1. outlet 2. river mouth

مِصْباح miṣbāḥ (مصابيح maṣābīḥ) 1. torch 2. lightbulb 3. مصباح الشارع miṣbāḥ ash-shāriʿ streetlamp; streetlight

مُصَحِّح muṣaḥḥiḥ marker

مَصْدَر maṣdar (مصادر maṣādir) source

مُصَدِّر muṣaddir (-ūn) exporter

مِصْر miṣr/maṣr Egypt

مُصِرّ muṣirr insistent

مَصْرِفي maṣrifī (-yūn) 1. bank 2. banker 3. ورقة مصرفية waraqa maṣrifīya banknote

مَصْروف maṣrūf (مصاريف maṣārīf) expense; expenses

مِصْري miṣrī/maṣrī (-ūn) Egyptian

مِصْعَد miṣʿad (مصاعد maṣāʿid) lift

مُصَغَّر musaghghar 1. miniature 2. دورة تعليمية مصغّرة dawra taʿlīmīya musaghghara seminar

مِصْفاة miṣfāh (مصاف maṣāfin) 1. filter 2. refinery

مَصْلَحة maṣlaḥa (مصالح maṣāliḥ) 1. advantage 2. interest 3. (pol.) department 4. المصلحة الشخصية al-maṣlaḥa ash-shakhṣīya self-interest

مُصْمَت muṣmat solid

مُصَمَّغ muṣammagh: ورقة مصمّغة waraqa muṣammagha sticker

مُصَمِّم muṣammim (-ūn) designer

مَصْنَع maṣnaʿ (مصانع maṣāniʿ) 1. factory 2. plant

مَصْنوع maṣnūʿ 1. made 2. manufactured 3. مصنوع باليد maṣnūʿ bi 'l-yad hand-made 4. مصنوع في البيت maṣnūʿ fī 'l-bayt homemade

مُصَوِّر muṣawwir (-ūn) photographer

مُصيب muṣīb 1. afflicted 2. suffering (from) 3. مصيب بمرض الشكّ muṣīb bi maraḍ al-shakk paranoid

مُصيبة muṣība (مصائب maṣāʾib) disaster

مِصْيَدة maṣyada (مصايد maṣāyid) trap

مَصير maṣir 1. outcome 2. fate

مَضى maḍā (a; مضي muḍīy) 1. to pass 2. to continue (في fī with)

مُضادّ muḍādd 1. anti- 2. مضادّ حيوي muḍādd ḥayawī antibiotics

مُضارَبة muḍāraba (fin.) speculation

مُضارِع muḍāriʿ (grammar) imperfect

مُضاف muḍāf: ضريبة القيمة المضافة ḍarībat al-qimat al-muḍāfa value added tax (VAT)

مُضايَقة muḍāyaqa (-āt) inconvenience

مَضْبوط maḍbūṭ 1. accurate 2. okay; OK 3. غير مضبوط ghayr maḍbūṭ inaccurate

مُضْحِك muḍḥik 1. funny 2. ridiculous

مِضَخّة miḍakhkha (-āt) pump

مُضِرّ muḍirr harmful

مِضْرَب miḍrab (مضارب maḍārib) (spor.) 1. bat 2. مضرب التنس miḍrab al-tanis tennis racket

مُضْطَرِب muḍṭarib 1. disturbed 2. مضطرب عقلياً muḍṭarib ʿaqlīyan mentally disturbed

مضغ **maḍagha** (a/u; مضغ maḍgh) to chew

مضمار **miḍmār** (مضامير maḍāmīr) racecourse; racetrack

مضيف **muḍīf** 1. host 2. steward

مضيفة **maḍyafa** guest house

مضيفة **muḍifa** stewardess

مضيق **maḍīq** (مضايق maḍāyiq) straits

مطار **maṭār** (-āt) 1. airport 2. مبنى المطار mabnā 'l-maṭār airport terminal

مطاردة **muṭārada** 1. hunt 2. manhunt

مطالبة **muṭālaba** (-āt) 1. demand 2. (fin.) claim

مطبخ **maṭbakh** (مطابخ maṭābikh) kitchen

مطبع **maṭba'**; مطبعة **maṭba'a** printer's; press

مطبعي **maṭba'ī** 1. print 2. خطأ مطبعي khaṭa' maṭba'ī (أخطاء akhṭā') misprint

مطر **maṭara** (u; مطر maṭar) to rain

مطر **maṭar** (أمطار amṭār) 1. rain 2. واق ضد المطر wāqin ḍidda 'l-maṭar waterproof

مطر **maṭir** rainy

مطرقة **miṭraqa** (مطارق maṭāriq) hammer

مطاط **maṭṭāṭ** rubber

مطاطي **maṭṭāṭī** 1. rubber 2. ختم مطاطي khatm maṭṭāṭī rubber stamp

مطعم **maṭ'am** (مطاعم maṭā'im) restaurant

مطفأة **miṭfa'a** (مطافئ maṭāfi') extinguisher

مطلب **maṭlab** (مطالب maṭālib) 1. demand 2. request

مطلق **muṭlaq** 1. outright 2. unconditional 3. perfect 4. مطلقاً **muṭlaqan** absolutely

مطمئن **muṭma'inn** 1. unconcerned 2. confident

مطمر **miṭmar** (مطامر maṭāmir) raincoat

مطهر **muṭahhir** antiseptic

مطيع **muṭī'** obedient

مظاهر **maẓāhir** pl looks

مظاهرة **muẓāhara** (-āt) (pol.) demonstration

مظلة **miẓalla** (-āt) 1. parachute 2. أنزل بالمظلة anzala bi 'l-miẓalla to parachute

مظلل **muẓallil** shadowy

مظلم **muẓlim** 1. dark 2. dim

مظلي **miẓallī**: جند المظليين jund al-miẓalliyīn pl paratroops

مظهر **maẓhar** (مظاهر maẓāhir) 1. appearance 2. مظهر جانبي maẓhar jānibī profile

مع **ma'a** 1. with 2. in spite of 3. مع السلامة! ma'a 's-salāma! goodbye! 4. (و)مع هذا؛ (و)مع ذلك (wa) ma'a dhālik; (wa) ma'a hādhā however; yet 5. مع أنّ ma'a anna although

معاً **ma'an** 1. together 2. jointly

معاد **mu'ādin** hostile

معارض **mu'āriḍ** 1. opposing 2. حزب معارض ḥizb mu'āriḍ (pol.) opposition party

معارضة **mu'āraḍa** (pol.) opposition

معاش ma'āsh (-āt) 1. way of life 2. living; livelihood 3. pension

معاصر mu'āsir 1. modern 2. contemporary

معافى mu'āfan: معافى من الضرائب mu'āfan min ad-darā'ib tax-free

معاقبة mu'āqaba punishment

معالج mu'ālij (-ūn) therapist

معالجة mu'ālaja (med.) treatment

معالم ma'ālim: زيارة المعالم ziyārat al-ma'ālim sightseeing

معاملة mu'āmala 1. treatment 2. سوء المعاملة sū' al-mu'āmala mistreatment

معاهدة mu'āhada (-āt) 1. treaty 2. convention 3. معاهدة السلام mu'āhadat as-salām peace treaty

معاير ma'āyīr pl: وحّد المعاير waḥḥada 'l-ma'āyīr to standardize

معبد ma'bad (معابد ma'ābid) 1. temple 2. معبد يهودي ma'bad yahūdī synagogue

معبود ma'būd idol

معتاد mu'tād 1. usual 2. غير معتاد على ghayr mu'tād 'alā unaccustomed to

معتدل mu'tadil moderate

معترف mu'tarif: معترف به mu'tarif bih standard

معتقدات mu'taqadāt pl beliefs

معتم mu'tim dim

معتوه ma'tūh (معاتيه ma'ātīh) idiot

معجب mu'jab (-ūn) fan

معجزة mu'jiza (-āt) 1. miracle 2. sign

معجون ma'jūn (معاجين ma'ājīn) 1. paste 2. معجون الأسنان ma'jūn al-asnān toothpaste

معدٍ mu'din 1. infectious 2. contagious

معدة mi'da (معد mi'ad) stomach

معدّل mu'addal 1. average 2. معدّل الفائدة mu'addal al-fā'ida interest rate

معدن ma'din (معادن ma'ādin) 1. mineral 2. ore 3. metal 4. خليط من معدنين khalīṭ min ma'danayn alloy

معدني ma'dinī 1. mineral 2. ore 3. metal 4. نقد معدني naqd ma'dinī coin 5. ماء معدني mā' ma'dinī mineral water

معدية ma'diya (معاد ma'ādin) ferry

معذّب mu'adhdhib (-ūn) torturer

معرض ma'riḍ (معارض ma'āriḍ) 1. gallery 2. showroom 3. exhibition 4. معرض فنون ma'raḍ funūn art gallery 5. معرض تجاري ma'raḍ tijārī trade fair

معرفة ma'rifa (معارف ma'ārif) 1. knowledge 2. learning 3. acquaintance 4. معرفة القراءة والكتابة ma'rifat al-qirā'a wa 'l-kitāba literacy

معركة ma'raka/ma'ruka (معارك ma'ārik) (mil.) 1. battle 2. action

معروف ma'rūf known; well-known

معزة ma'za (collective معز ma'z) goat

معزول ma'zūl remote

معسكر mu'askar (-āt) camp

معصرة mi'ṣara (معاصر ma'āṣir) press

معصم mi'ṣam (معاصم ma'āṣim) wrist

معطف mi'ṭaf (معاطف ma'āṭif) 1. coat; overcoat 2. معتف مشمّع mi'ṭaf mushamma' mackintosh; raincoat

معظم mu'ẓam 1. majority 2. most

معظم mu'aẓẓam 1. most 2. معظم الأحيان mu'aẓẓam al-aḥyān for the most part

معفاة mu'fāh: معفاة من الرسوم mu'fāh min ar-rusūm duty-free

معقّد mu'aqqad 1. complicated 2. complex 3. intricate

معقول ma'qūl 1. reasonable 2. غير معقول ghayr ma'qūl unreasonable

معكرونة ma'kārūna 1. pasta 2. معكرونة السباغيتي ma'kārūna 's-spaghītī spaghetti 3. معكرونة شعرية صينية ma'karūna shi'rīya ṣīnīya noodles

معلم ma'lam (معالم ma'ālim) 1. landmark 2. sight 3. signpost

معلّم mu'allim (-ūn) 1. teacher 2. instructor

معلّمة mu'allima (-āt) 1. teacher 2. instructor

معلن mu'lin: غير معلن ghayr mu'lin unsaid

معلومات ma'lūmāt pl 1. information 2. data 3. إختبار المعلومات ikhtibār al-ma'lūmāt quiz 4. جدّد المعلومات jaddada al-ma'lūmāt to update

معلوماتي ma'lūmātī 1. information 2. مسابقة معلوماتية musābaqa ma'lūmātīya quiz

معمار mi'mār (-ūn) architect

معنى ma'nan (معان ma'ānin) 1. meaning 2. sense 3. significance 4. concept 5.

ذو معنى dhū ma'nā significant 6. بلا معنى bilā ma'nā meaningless

معنوي ma'nawī 1. semantic 2. moral 3. spiritual

معنويات ma'nawīyāt pl morale

معهد ma'had (معاهد ma'āhid) institute

معونة ma'ūna 1. assistance; aid 2. بطاقة معونة biṭāqa ma'ūna (-āt) voucher

معيار mi'yār (معايير ma'āyīr) standard

معياري mi'yārī standard

معيب ma'īb defective; faulty

معيشة ma'īsha livelihood

معيل mu'īl (-ūn) wager earner

معيّن mu'ayyan 1. specific 2. (-āt) rate

مغادرة mughādara 1. departure 2. مغادرة الفندق mughādarat al-funduq hotel check-out

مغامرة mughāmara (-āt) adventure

مغتصب mughtaṣib (-ūn) rapist

مغذّ mughadhdhin nourishing

مغر mughrin appealing

المغرب al-maghrib 1. Morocco 2. North-West Africa

مغربي maghribī 1. Moroccan 2. North-West African

مغرور maghrūr 1. proud 2. vain

مغسلة maghsala (-āt) 1. laundry 2. مغسلة عامّة maghsala 'āmma launderette, laundrette

مغص maghaṣ stomach ache

مغفرة maghfira 1. forgiveness 2. pardon

مغلق mughlaq closed

مغمى mughmā: مغمى عليه mughmā 'alayh unconscious

مغنٍّ mughannin (مغنيون mughanniyūn) singer

مغير mughīr (-ūn) raider

مفاتيح mafātīḥ pl 1. لوحة المفاتيح lawḥat al-mafātīḥ keyboard 2. see مفتاح

مفاجئ mufāji' 1. surprising 2. sudden

مفاجأة mufāja'a (-āt) surprise

مفاصل mafāṣil: إلتهاب المفاصل iltihāb al-mafāṣil arthritis

مفاقمة mufāqama aggravation

مفاوض mufāwiḍ (-ūn) negotiator

مفاوضات mufāwaḍāt pl negotiations

مفتاح miftāḥ (مفاتيح mafātīḥ) 1. key 2. مفتاح تحويل miftāḥ taḥwīl switch 3. مفتاح ربط miftāḥ rabṭ spanner 4. مفتاح زجاجة miftāḥ zujāja bottle-opener 5. مفتاح علبة miftāḥ 'ulba can-opener 6. مفتاح المدينة miftāḥ al-madīna area code

مفتش mufattish (-ūn) 1. inspector 2. مفتش التذاكر mufattish at-tadhākir ticket inspector

مفترس muftaris fierce

مفترق muftaraq: مفترق الطرق muftaraq al-ṭuruq crossroad, crossroads

مفتوح maftūḥ open

مفر mafarr escape

مفرد mufrad 1. isolated 2. simple 3. (grammar) singular 4. مفردات mufradāt pl vocabulary 5. terminology

مفرط mufriṭ 1. excessive 2. جرعة مفرطة jur'a mufriṭa (-āt) overdose

مفصل mafṣil (مفاصل mafāṣil) joint

مفصّل mufaṣṣal detailed

مفضّل mufaḍḍal 1. preferable 2. (spor.) favourite

مفعم muf'am: مفعم بالأمل muf'am bi 'l-amal hopeful

مفعول maf'ūl 1. done 2. ساري المفعول sārī al-maf'ūl valid

مفقود mafqūd missing

مفكّ mifakk (-āt) screwdriver

مفكّرة mufakkira (-āt) notebook

مفلس muflis 1. bankrupt 2. ruined

مفهوم mafhūm 1. understood 2. understandable 3. (مفاهيم mafāhīm) concept

مفاوضة mufāwaḍa (-āt) negotiation

مفيد mufid 1. useful 2. profitable

مقابل muqābil 1. opposite 2. counter

مقابل muqābila in return for

مقابلة muqābala (-āt) 1. interview 2. in return for 3. المقابلة بالمثل al-muqābala bi 'l-mithl retaliation 4. مقابلة رسمية muqābala rasmīya audience

مقاتل muqātil (-ūn) 1. fighter 2. طائرة مقاتلة ṭā'ira muqātila fighter plane

مقارنة muqārana comparison

مقاس maqās (-āt) 1. size 2. measurement

مقاطعة muqāṭaʿa (-āt) 1. district 2. province 3. county 4. interruption 5. boycott

مقاطعة ويلز muqāṭaʿat waylz Wales

مقالة maqāla (-āt) 1. article 2. paper 3. essay 4. composition

مقامر muqāmir (-ūn) gambler

مقاول muqāwil (-ūn) 1. developer 2. contractor

مقاومة muqāwama resistance

مقبل muqbil next

مقبرة maqbara (مقابر maqābir) cemetery

مقبض miqbaḍ (مقابض maqābiḍ) 1. handle 2. shaft

مقبول maqbūl 1. acceptable (ل li to) 2. غير مقبول ghayr maqbūl unacceptable (ل li to)

مقتحم muqtaḥim (-ūn) intruder

مقترح muqtaraḥ (-āt) proposal

مقتصد muqtaṣid 1. economical 2. sober

مقتطف muqtaṭaf (-āt) 1. excerpt 2. مقتطف فلم muqtaṭaf film film clip 3. مجموعة من المقتطفات الأدبية majmūʿa min al-muqtaṭafāt al-adabīya anthology

مقتل maqtal murder

مقتنع muqtanaʿ 1. satisfied 2. غير مقتنع ghayr muqtanaʿ unsatisfied

مقدار miqdār (مقادير maqādīr) 1. quantity 2. measure

مقدّس muqaddas 1. holy 2. الكتاب المقدّس al-kitāb al-muqaddas the Bible

مقدّم muqaddim (-ūn) presenter

مقدماً muqaddaman in advance

مقدّمة muqaddima introduction

مقدرة maqdira strength

مقرّ maqarr: مقرّ القيادة maqarr al-qiyāda headquarters

مقرض muqriḍ (-ūn) lender

مقرض miqraḍ: ابن مقرض ibn miqraḍ ferret

مقرف muqrif revolting

مقروء maqrūʾ legible

مقصّ miqaṣṣ (مقاصّ maqāṣṣ) scissors

مقصد maqṣid (مقاصد maqāṣid) intention

مقصود maqṣūd 1. intentional 2. غير مقصود ghayr maqṣūd unintentional

مقصور maqṣūr exclusive

مقصورة maqṣūra (-āt) compartment

مقطع maqṭaʿ (مقاطع maqāṭiʿ) 1. part 2. مقطع لفظي maqṭaʿ lafẓī syllable

مقعد maqʿad (مقاعد maqāʿid) seat

مقفول maqfūl locked

مقلاة miqlāh (مقال maqālin) 1. pan 2. frying pan

مقلة muqla (مقل muqal): مقلة العين muqlat al-ʿayn eyeball

مقلّد muqallid imitator

مقلّم muqallam striped

مقلوب maqlūb 1. upside down 2. بالمقلوب bi ʾl-maqlūb inside out

بطاطس مقلية maqlī: مقلي baṭāṭis maqlīya
chips; French fries

مقنع muqni' persuasive

مقهى maqhan (مقاه maqāhin) café

مقولب muqawlab (-āt) stereotype

مقوّى muqawwan: ورق مقوى waraq
muqawwan cardboard

مقياس miqyās (مقاييس maqāyīs) 1. scale
2. measurement 3. standard

مقيم muqīm (-ūn) 1. occupant 2. resident
3. dweller 4. مقيم غير شرعي muqīm
ghayr shar'ī illegal alien

مكافأة mukāfa'a (-āt) 1. recompense 2.
reward

مكالمة mukālama 1. call 2. مكالمة تلفونية
mukālama tilifōniya telephone call

مكان makān (أماكن amākin; أمكنة amkina)
1. place 2. space 3. venue 4.
whereabouts 5. مكان العمل makān al-
'amal workplace 6. مكان الإجتماع
makān al-ijtimā' assembly point 7.
مكان وقوف السيّارات makān wuqūf as-
sayyārāt parking space 8. مكان ما
makān mā somewhere 9. أي مكان ayy
makān anywhere 10. لا مكان lā makān
nowhere 11. كلّ مكان kull makān
everywhere 12. في كلّ مكان fī kulli
makān throughout 13. مكان آخر makān
ākhar elsewhere 14. في مكان قريب fī
makān qarīb around

مكانة makāna 1. status 2. respectability
3. prestige 4. أعلى مكانةً a'lā
makānatan senior

مكبّ mikabb (-āt) spool

مكبّر makabbir 1. amplifier 2. مكبّر الصوت
mukabbir aṣ-ṣawt loudspeaker

مكتئب mukta'ib depressed

مكتب maktab (مكاتب makātib) 1. office
2. study 3. desk 4. مكتب التذاكر
maktab at-tadhākir ticket office 5.
مكتب البريد maktab al-barīd post office

مكتبة maktaba (-āt) 1. bookshop 2.
library

مكتبي maktabī 1. office 2. secretarial

مكتشف muktashif (-ūn) discoverer

مكتف muktafin: مكتف ذاتياً muktafin
dhātīyan self-sufficient

مكتوب maktūb (مكاتيب makātīb) 1.
written 2. letter

مكث makatha (u; مكث makth) 1. to
remain 2. مكث أكثر من اللازم makatha
akthar min al-lāzim to overstay

مكثّف mukaththaf intensive

مكسّرات mukassarāt pl nuts

مكسور maksūr broken

مكعّب muka''ab (-āt) 1. cube 2. cubic

مكّن makkana to enable (من ه\ه so/sth;
min to)

مكّوك makkūk (مكاكيك makākīk) 1.
shuttle 2. المكّوك الفضائي al-makkūk al-
faḍā'ī space shuttle

مكلّف mukallif costly

مكنسة miknasa (-āt; مكانس makānis) 1.
broom 2. cleaner 3. مكنسة كهربائية

miknasa kahrabā'iya vacuum cleaner نظّف بمكنسة كهربائية .4 naẓẓafa bi miknasa kahrabā'iya to vacuum; to hoover up

مكواة mikwāh (مكاوٍ makāwin) iron

مكيدة makīda (مكايد makāyid) 1. scheme 2. دبّر مكيدة dabbara makīda to scheme

مكيّف mukayyif: مهواة مكيّف هواء mihwāh mukayyif hawā' ventilator

ملّ malla (a ملل; malal) to bore

ملأ mala'a (a; ملء mal') to fill

ملء mal' 1. filling 2. ملء جيب mil' jayb pocketful 3. أعاد الملء a'āda al-mal' to refill

ملاءة mulā'a (-āt) sheet

ملائم mulā'im 1. convenient 2. suitable 3. غير ملائم ghayr mulā'im inconvenient 4. unsuitable

ملابس malābis pl 1. clothes; clothing 2. ملابس داخلية malābis dākhilīya underwear 3. ملابس رياضية malābis riyāḍīya sportswear 4. خزانة للملابس khazzāna li 'l-malābis (-āt) wardrobe 5. and see ملبس

ملّاح mallāḥ (-ūn) 1. sailor 2. navigator

ملاحة milāḥa navigation

ملاحظة mulāḥaẓa (-āt) 1. note 2. observation 3. جدير بالملاحظة jadīr bi 'l-mulāḥaẓa noteworthy

ملاحقة mulāḥaqa pursuit

ملاحي milāḥī nautical

ملاذ malādh: كملاذ أخير ka malādh akhīr as a last resort

ملاعب malā'ib pl: ملاعب ترفيه malā'ib tarfīh amusement park

ملّاك mallāk (-ūn) 1. owner; proprietor 2. ملّاك أراضٍ mallāk arāḍin landowner

ملاكم mulākim (-ūn) boxer

ملالمة mulākama 1. boxing 2. ملعب الملاكمة mal'ab al-mulākama boxing ring

ملامح malāmiḥ pl features

ملاية milāya (-āt) sheet

ملايين malāyīn pl 1. millions 2. صاحب ملايين ṣāḥib malāyīn millionaire

ملبّد mulabbad: ملبّد بالغيوم mulabbad bi 'l-ghuyūm overcast

ملبس malbas (ملابس malābis) 1. dress 2. garment 3. and see ملابس

ملبنة malbana (-āt) dairy

ملتقى multaqan (ملتقيات multaqayāt) 1. crossroads 2. junction 3. meeting place

ملتوٍ multawin crooked

ملجأ malja' (ملاجئ malāji') 1. shelter 2. refuge

ملح malḥ salt

ملحّ muliḥḥ urgent

ملحّن mulaḥḥin (-ūn) composer

ملحق mulḥaq (-āt) accessory

ملصق mulṣaq (-āt) poster

ملعب mal'ab (ملاعب malā'ib) (spor.) 1. ground(s) 2. field 3. court 4. pitch 5.

ملعب الجولف mal'ab al-gōlf golf course 6. ملعب الملاكمة mal'ab al-mulākama boxing ring

ملعقة mil'aqa (ملاعق malā'iq) spoon

ملفّ milaff (-āt) 1. file 2. folder 3. computer file

ملفت mulfit: ملفت اهتباه mulfit al-intibāh conspicuous

ملفوف malfūf cabbage

ملقط milqaṭ (ملاقط malāqiṭ) peg

ملك malaka (i/u; ملك mulk) 1. to have 2. to possess 3. to reign

ملك mulk 1. reign 2. rule; power 3. sovreignty 4. ownership

ملك milk (أملاك amlāk) 1. property 2. ملكه milkuh his; his own 3. ملكها milkuhā hers; her own 4. ملكهم milkuhum theirs; their own

ملك malak (ملائكة malā'ika) angel

ملك malik (ملوك mulūk) 1. king 2. monarch

ملكة malika (-āt) queen

ملكي malakī royal

ملكي milkī property

ملكية malakīya monarchy

ملهى malhan (ملاهٍ malāhin) 1. place of entertainment 2. entertainment 3. ملهى ليلي malhan laylī nightclub

ملول malūl bored

ملولب mulawlab: مسمار ملولب mismār mulawlab bolt

ملي malī' 1. full 2. ملي بالأحداث malī' bi 'l-aḥdāth eventful

مليون malyūn (ملايين malāyīn) million

مليونير malyūnēr (-ūn) millionaire

ممّا mimmā than

ممات mumāt obsolete

مماثل mumāthil 1. similar 2. identical 3. comparable

ممارسة mumārasa practice

ممتاز mumtāz 1. excellent 2. exceptional 3. ideal 4. distinguished

ممتع mumti' enjoyable

ممتلك mumtalak (-āt) possession

ممتلكات mumtalakāt pl 1. possessions 2. gear

ممثّل mumaththil (-ūn) 1. actor 2. representative

ممثّلة mumaththila (-āt) 1. actress 2. representative

ممرّ mamarr (-āt) 1. lapse 2. passage 3. corridor

ممرّض mumarriḍ (-ūn) (med.) nurse

ممرّضة mumarriḍa (-āt) (med.) nurse

ممطر mumṭir rainy

ممكن mumkin 1. might; may 2. possible 3. ممكن الوصول أليه mumkin al-wuṣūl ilayhi accessible 4. and see أمكن

مملّ mumill boring

مملكة mamlaka (ممالك mamālik) 1. kingdom 2. المملكة المتّحدة al-mamlaka al-muttaḥida United Kingdom

مملوء **mamlū'** full

ممنوع **mamnū'** 1. forbidden 2. ممنوع التدخين **mamnū' at-tadkhīn** no smoking!

ممنون **mamnūn** grateful

مموّن **mumawwin** (-ūn) supplier

مميت **mumīt** 1. deadly 2. fatal 3. *(med.)* terminal

مميّز **mumayyaz** 1. distinguished 2. distinctive 3. unique

من **man** 1. who 2. whoever; whosoever

من **min** 1. from 2. of 3. in relation to 4. than 5. ago 6. من قبل **min qibal** by 7. قبل من **qabl min** before 8. من غير **min ghayr** without 9. من غير شكّ **min ghayr shakk** surely 10. من غير شرط **min ghayr sharṭ** unconditional 11. من جانب إلى آخر **min jānib ilā ākhar** across 12. من جديد **min jadīd** again 13. من أجل **min ajli** for the sake of 14. من أجلي **min ajlī** for my sake 15. من نفسه **min nafsih** of one's own accord 16. من خلال **min khilāl** through 17. من أين **min ayna** from where? 18. من زمان **min zamān** long ago 19. من الآن فصاعداً **min al'ān faṣā'idan** henceforth 20. من المحتمل **min al-muḥtamal** probably 21. من نوع ما **min naw'in mā** kind of 22. من حيث المبدأ **min ḥayth al-mabda'** as a matter of principle

مناجم **manājim** *pl*: عامل المناجم **'āmil al-manājim** miner

مناخ **munākh/manākh** climate

منار (مناور) **manār (manāwir)** lighthouse

مناسب **munāsib** 1. suitable 2. غير مناسب **ghayr munāsib** unsuitable 3. في الوقت المناسب **fi'l-waqt al-munāsib** in due course

مناسبة **munāsaba** (-āt) 1. occasion 2. connection

مناضل **munāḍil** (-ūn) militant

مناطق **manāṭiq** *pl* 1. المناطق الإستوائية **manāṭiq al-istiwā'iya** tropics 2. *see* منطقة

مناعة **manā'a** immunity

منافس **munāfis** (-ūn) 1. competitor 2. rival

منافسة **munāfasa** competition

منافق **munāfiq** (-ūn) 1. hypocrite 2. hypocritical

مناقشة **munāqasha** (-āt) 1. discussion 2. debate

مناقضة **munāqaḍa** contradiction

مناوبة **munāwaba** (-āt) shift

مناورة **manāwara** (-āt) manoeuvre

مناورات **munāwarāt** *pl (mil.)* manoeuvres

منبّه **munabbih;** منبّهة **munabbiha** (-āt) alarm clock

منبع **manba'** (منابع **manābi'**) 1. spring 2. source

منتبه **muntabih** vigilant

منتج **muntij** 1. producer 2. منتج سينمائي **muntij sīnamā'ī** film producer

منتج **muntaj** (-āt) 1. product 2. منتجات **muntajāt**

muntajāt produce

منتخب muntakhib (-ūn) voter

منتشر muntashir widespread

منتصر muntaṣir 1. victor 2. victorious

منتصف muntaṣif 1. middle 2. mid 3. منتصف الليل muntaṣif al-layl midnight 4. منتصف النهار muntaṣif an-nahār midday 5. منتصف الطريق muntaṣif aṭ-ṭarīq midway 6. منتصف الأسبوع muntaṣif al-usbū' midweek 7. منتصف العمر muntaṣif al-'umr middle-age, middle-aged

منتظر muntaẓar: من المنتظر min al-muntaẓar it is expected that

منتظم muntaẓim 1. regular 2. غير منتظم ghayr muntaẓim irregular

منجم manjam (مناجم manājim) 1. mine 2. مدخل عمودي لمنجم madkhal 'amūdī li manjam mining shaft

منح manaḥa (a; منح manḥ) 1. to provide 2. to award 3. to grant 4. *(mil.)* to decorate

منحة minḥa (منح minaḥ) 1. grant 2. منحة تعليمية minḥa ta'līmīya scholarship

منحاز munḥāzin 1. biased 2. غير منحازٍ ghayr munḥāzin non-aligned

منحدر munḥadar (-āt) slope

منحرف munḥarif pervert

منحنٍ munḥanin curved

منحنى munḥanan (منحنيات munḥanayāt) curve

منحوس manḥūs unlucky

منخفض munkhafiḍ low

منخفض munkhafaḍ: منخفض جوّي munkhafaḍ jawwī turbulence

مندمج mundamij compact

مندوب mandūb 1. delegate 2. representative

منديل mandīl (مناديل manadīl) 1. handkerchief 2. منديل ورقي mandīl waraqī tissue paper

منذ mundhu 1. since 2. ago 3. for 4. منذ لحظة mundhu an since 5. منذ لحظات mundhu laḥẓa; mundhu laḥaẓāt just now 5. منذ عام mundhu 'ām a year ago 6. منذ ذلك الوقت mundhu dhālika 'l-waqt since 7. منذ عهد بعيد mundhu 'ahd ba'īd long ago 8. منذ متى mundhu matā since when

منزعج munza'ij vexed

منزل manzil (منازل manāzil) 1. house 2. flat; apartment 3. dwelling 4. residence 5. ربة منزل rabbat manzil housewife

منزلة manzila 1. status 2. أرفع منزلةً arfa' manzilatan superior

منزلي manzilī 1. domestic 2. واجبات منزلية wājibāt manzilīya *pl* homework

منسجم munsajim compatible

منسوب mansūb 1. related (إلى ilā to) 2. water level

منشأة munsha'a: منشأة عسكرية munsha'a 'askarīya *(mil.)* installation

منشار minshār (مناشير manāshīr) saw

منشفة minshafa (مناشف manāshif) towel

منشقّ munshaqq (-ūn) dissident

منشور manshūr (-āt) 1. leaflet 2. pamphlet 3. publication

منصب manṣib (مناصب manāṣib) 1. post; position 2. طرده من منصبه ṭaradah min manṣibihi to sack someone 3. أعاد ترتيب المناصب a'āda tartīb al-manāṣib *(pol.)* to reshuffle

منصّة minaṣṣa (-āt) platform

منصف munṣif 1. fair 2. غير منصف ghayr munṣif unfair

منضدة minḍada 1. table 2. stand 3. منضدة دكّان minḍadat dukkān shop counter

منطق manṭiq logic

منطقة minṭaqa (مناطق manāṭiq) 1. area 2. zone 3. district 4. territory 5. region

منطقي manṭiqī logical

منظر manẓar (مناظر manāẓir) 1. view 2. scene 3. منظر طبيعي manẓar ṭabī'ī landscape

منظّف munaẓẓif cleaner

منظّم munaẓẓam 1. regular 2. منظم شخصي munaẓẓim shakhṣī personal organizer

منظّمة munaẓẓama (-āt) organization

منظور manẓūr perspective

منع mana'a (a; منع man') 1. to forbid (ه\ه so/sth; عن 'an from) 2. to ban 3. to deter 4. to prevent 5. to stop 6. to exclude 7. منع حرّية الصحافة mana'a ḥurrīyat aṣ-ṣaḥāfa to gag the press

منع man' 1. prohibition 2. prevention 3. منع الحمل man' al-ḥamal contraception 4. وسيلة منع الحمل wasīlat man' al-ḥamal contraceptive

منعش mun'ish refreshing

منعطف min'aṭaf turning

منفرد munfarid 1. single 2. solo

منفرداً munfaridan apart

منفصل munfaṣil 1. separate 2. اكلب اسمك بالحروف المنفصلة. uklub ismak bi 'l-ḥurūf al-munfaṣila. Please print your name.

منفصلاً munfaṣilan separately

منفضة minfaḍa: منفضة سجاير minfaḍat sajāyir ashtray

منفعل munfa'il: غير منفعل ghayr munfa'il cool

منفى manfan exile

منقار minqār (مناقير manāqīr) beak

منقرض munqariḍ extinct

منقطع munqaṭi' 1. interrupted 2. غير منقطع ghayr munqaṭi' uninterrupted

منقّى munaqqan refined

منقول manqūl (-āt) movable

منهاج minhāj (مناهيج manāhīj) 1. programme 2. منهاج الدراسة minhāj ad-dirāsa; منهج التعليم manhaj at-ta'līm curriculum; syllabus

منهجي manhajī: كتاب منهجي kitāb manhajī textbook

منوّم munawwim: حبّة منوّمة ḥabba

munawwima sleeping pill

مني minan 1. sperm 2. semen

منيع mani‘ immune

مهاجر muhājir (-ūn) 1. migrant 2. emigrant 3. immigrant

مهاجم muhājim (-ūn) attacker

مهاجمة muhājama (-āt) attack

مهارة mahāra 1. skill 2. know-how 3. متطلب المهارة mutaṭallib al-mahāra skilled

مهامّ mahāmm 1. مهام المنصب mahāmm al-manṣib official duties 2. see مهمّة

مهبل mahbal (مهابل mahābil) vagina

مهجور mahjūr 1. uninhabited 2. derelict

مهدّئ muhaddi’ (-āt) tranquillizer

مهذّب muhadhdhab 1. civil 2. غير مهذب ghayr muhadhdhab crude

مهرب mahrab (مهارب mahārib) 1. refuge 2. escape 3. لا مهرب منه lā mahrab minh unavoidable

مهرّب muharrib (-ūn) smuggler

مهرّج muharrij (-ūn) 1. comedian 2. clown

مهرجان mihrajān (-āt) 1. festival 2. gala

مهل mahl 1. leisure 2. على مهل ‘alā mahl leisurely

مهلاً mahlan leisurely

مهمّ muhimm 1. important 2. غير مهمّ ghayr muhimm unimportant 3. شخص مهمّ جداً shakhṣ muhimm jiddan V.I.P.

مهما mahmā 1. however 2. مهما يكن

mahmā yakun whatever; regardless

مهمّة muhimma (-āt) 1. important matter 2. see مهمّات

مهمّة mahamma (مهامّ) 1. important matter 2. task 3. mission 4. function 5. assignment 6. مهمّة صعبة mahamma ṣa‘ba enterprise 7. see مهامّ

مهمّات muhimmāt 1. requirements 2. supplies 3. مهمّات حربية muhimmāt ḥarbīya war materiel 4. see مهمّة

مهمل muhmil careless

مهنة mihna (مهن mihan) 1. occupation 2. career 3. profession 4. vocation

مهندس muhandis (-ūn) engineer

مهني mihnī (-yūn) professional

مهواة mihwāh 1. ventilator 2. مهواة مكيف هواء mihwāh mukayyif hawā’

مهيب muhīb solemn

مواجه muwājih opposite

مواجهة muwājaha 1. encounter 2. interview

موادّ mawādd pl 1. materials 2. موادّ بناء mawādd binā’ building materials 3. موادّ خام mawādd khām raw materials 3. موادّ غذائية mawādd ghidhā’īya provisions

موارد mawārid pl resources

موازٍ muwāzin parallel

مواشٍ mawāshin pl 1. cattle 2. livestock

مواصفة muwāṣafa (-āt) specification

مواصلات muwāṣalāt pl communications

مواطن muwāṭin (-ūn) 1. citizen 2. national

مواظب muwāẓib persistent

مواظبة muwāẓaba perseverance

مواعيد mawā'īd pl: 1. جدول مواعيد jadwal mawā'īd timetable 2. مراعي المواعيد murā'ī 'l-mawā'īd punctual 3. مراعاة المواعيد murā'at al-mawā'īd punctuality 4. حدّد مواعيد ḥaddada mawā'īd to schedule 5. see موعد

موافقة muwāfaqa 1. agreement 2. consent 3. approval

مواليد mawālīd pl: 1. نسبة المواليد nisbat al-mawālīd birth rate 2. see مولد

موت mawt death

موتى mawtā pl: الموتى al-mawtā the dead

موثوق mawthūq 1. authentic 2. موثوق به mawthūq bih trustworthy

موج mawj أمواج amwāj) ripple

موجة mawja (-āt) wave

موجز mūjaz 1. concise 2. summary

موجود mawjūd 1. present 2. existing

موضة mōda see موضة

مودم mōdem modem

مورد mawrid (موارد mawārid) resource

موز mawz collective bananas

موزامبيق mōzāmbīq Mozambique

موزّع muwazzi' (-ūn) distributor

موسى mūsā (أمواس amwās; مواس mawāsin) razor

موسقي mūsiqī see موسيقي

موسم mawsim (مواسم mawāsim) 1. season 2. الموسم السياحي al-mawsim as-siyāḥī tourist season

موسمي mawsimī seasonal

موسوعة mawsū'a encyclopaedia

موسيقى mūsiqā 1. music 2. موسيقى فلم mūsiqā film soundtrack

موسيقار mūsiqār musician

موسيقي mūsiqī 1. musical 2. سلم موسيقي sullam mūsiqī scale 3. حفلة موسيقية ḥafla mūsiqīya concert 4. مسرحية موسيقية masraḥiya mūsiqīya musical

موضة mōḍa (-āt) 1. fashion 2. على الموضة 'alā 'l-mōḍa fashionable

موضع mawḍi' (مواضع mawāḍi') 1. place 2. position

موضوع mawḍū' (مواضيع mawāḍī') 1. subject 2. theme 3. غير متصل بالموضوع ghayr muttaṣil bi 'l-mawḍū' irrelevant

موضوعي mawḍū'ī objective

موطّد muwaṭṭad 1. stable 2. غير موطّد ghayr muwaṭṭad unstable

موظّف muwaẓẓaf (-ūn) 1. civil servant 2. official 3. employee 4. موظف حكومي muwaẓẓaf ḥukūmī civil servant 5. مجموعة الموظفين ؛مجموع موظفين majmū' muwaẓẓafīn staff; personnel 6. موظف الإستقبال muwaẓẓaf al-istiqbāl receptionist 7. موظف كبير muwaẓẓaf kabīr senior official 8. موظف صغير muwaẓẓaf ṣaghīr minor official

موعد maw'id (مواعيد mawā'id) 1. date 2.

engagement 3. appointment 4. meeting 5. على الموعد 'alā 'l-maw'id on time 6. موعد أخير maw'id akhīr deadline 7. حدّد موعداً ḥaddada maw'idan to set a time 8. فات موعد إستحقاقه fāt maw'id istiḥqāquh; فات موعد وصوله fāt maw'id wuṣūluh overdue

موقّت muwaqqat see مؤقّت

موقد mawqid (مواقد mawāqid) stove

موقع mawqi' (مواقع mawāqi') 1. position 2. location 3. site 4. situation

موقف mawqif (مواقف mawāqif) 1. position 2. attitude 3. stop 4. موقف سيّارات mawqif sayyārāt car park 5. موقف باص mawqif bāṣ; موقف الأوتوبيس mawqif al-otobīs bus stop

موكب mawkib (مواكب mawākib) procession

موّل mawwala 1. to finance 2. to maintain

ميل mayl (ميول muyūl) tendency

ميل mīl (أميال amyāl) 1. mile 2. ميل في الساعة mīl fī 's-sā'a miles per hour (m.p.h.)

ميلاد mīlād 1. birth 2. عيد الميلاد 'īd al-mīlād birthday 3. شهادة ميلاد shahādat mīlād birth certificate 4. عيد الميلاد 'īd al-mīlād Christmas

ميناء mīnā' f (موانٍ mawānin; موانئ mawāni') 1. harbour 2. port

مايونيز mayūnīz: صلصة المايونيز ṣalṣat al-mayūnīz mayonnaise

ن

نا -nā 1. us 2. our

نائب nā'ib (نوّاب nuwwāb) (pol.) 1. deputy 2. representative 3. نائب برلمان nā'ib barlamān member of parliament; M.P. 3. نائب الرئيس nā'ib ar-ra'īs vice president 5. and see نوّاب

نائم nā'im asleep

ناجٍ nājin (ناجون nājūn) survivor

ناجح nājiḥ successful

ناحية nāḥiya (نواحٍ nawāḥin) 1. side 2. direction 4. viewpoint 5. من ناحية min nāḥiyat with regard to 6. ومن ناحية أخرى wa min nāḥiya ukhrā in addition 7. region 8. من ناحية... ومن ناحية أخرى min nāḥiya... wa min nāḥiya ukhrā on the one hand..., and on the other

ناخب nākhib (-ūn) voter

نادٍ nādin (أندية andiya; نوادٍ nawādin) 1.

نادٍ للقمار nādin li 'l-qimār 2. club casino

نادى nādā to call

نادب nādib (نوادب nawādib) mourner

نادر nādir 1. rare 2. unusual 3. قطعة نادرة qiṭ'a nādira masterpiece

نادراً nādiran 1. rarely 2. نادراً ما nādiran mā hardly

نادل nādil waiter

نادلة nādila waitress

نار nār (نيران nīrān) 1. fire 2. النار an-nār hell 3. ضرّم النار في ḍarrama al-nār fī to set fire to 4. إطلاق النار iṭlāq an-nār shooting 5. أطلق النار على aṭlaqa an-nār 'alā to shoot at 6. وقف إطلاق النار waqf iṭlāq an-nār cease-fire 7. خمدت النار khamadat an-nār The fire has gone out.

ناري nārī 1. fire 2. ألعاب نارية al'āb nārīya pl fireworks 3. سلاح ناري silāḥ nārī (أسلحة نارية asliḥa nārīya) firearm 4. دراجة نارية darrāja nārīya motorcycle

نازع nāzi'(نزاع nizā') to struggle; to fight with

نازعة nāzi'a: نازعة الفلّينة nāzi'at al-fallīna corkscrew

ناس nās people

ناسب nāsaba 1. to suit 2. to correspond with

ناشد nāshada 1. to appeal 2. to plead

ناشر nāshir (-ūn) 1. publisher 2. حقّ الناشر ḥaqq an-nāshir copyright

ناشط nāshiṭ active

ناصح nāṣiḥ (نصّاح nuṣṣāḥ) counsellor

ناضج nāḍij 1. mature 2. ripe 3. غير ناضج ghayr nāḍij unripe

ناضل nāḍala to struggle

ناطحة nāṭiḥa: ناطحة سحاب nāṭiḥat saḥāb (نواطح nawāṭiḥ) skyscraper

ناطق nāṭiq 1. speaker 2. spokesman (باسم bi 'sm/بلسان bi lisān for)

ناعم nā'im 1. soft 2. smooth

ناعناع nā'nā' mint

نافد nāfid: نافد الصبر nāfid aṣ-ṣabr impatient

نافس nāfasa 1. to rival 2. to vie (على 'alā for)

نافع nāfi' 1. useful 2. غير نافع ghayr nāfi' useless

نافورة nāfūra (نوافير nawāfir) fountain

ناقد nāqid (-ūn; نقّاد nuqqād) 1. critic 2. reviewer

ناقش nāqasha 1. to discuss 2. to debate

ناقص nāqiṣ 1. defective 2. imperfect 3. incomplete 4. minus

ناقض nāqaḍa to contradict

ناقل nāqil (-ūn) carrier

ناقلة nāqila: ناقلة النفط nāqilat an-nafṭ tanker

نال nāla (u; نول nawl) to get

نام nāma (ينام yanāmu; نوم nawm) to sleep

نامٍ nāmin growing; developing

ناموس nāmūs collective mosquitoes

نبأ naba·a (ء‫;‬ أنباء anbā') news item; news

نبات nabāt *collective* plants; vegetation

نباتي nabātī 1. vegetable 2. (نباتيون nabātiyūn) vegetarian 3. الزبدة النباتية az-zubda an-nabātīya margarine

نباح nubāḥ bark

نبت nabata (u; نبت nabt) to grow

نبتة nabata (-āt) plant

نبح nabaḥa (a; نبح nabḥ; نباح nubāḥ) to bark

نبذ nabadha (i; نبذ nabdh) to discard to scrap

نبرة nabra (نبرات nabarāt) 1. tone 2. stress

نبض nabḍ (أنباض anbāḍ) pulse

نبل nubl nobility

نبي nabī (أنبياء anbiyā') prophet

نبيذ nabīdh (أنبذة anbidha) wine

نبيل nabīl noble

نتأ nata·a (a; نتوء nutū') to protrude

نتج nataja (i; نتوج nutūj) to result (عن 'an; من min from)

نتن natana (i; نتن natn) to stink

نتن natin rotten

نتيجة natīja (نتائج natā'ij) 1. result 2. score 3. نتيجةً لِ natījatan li as a result of

نثر nathara (u; نثر nathr) to sprinkle

نجا najā (u; نجاء najā'; نجاة najāh) to survive

نجاة najāh 1. rescue 2. سترة النجاة sitrat an-

najāh life jacket 3. قارب النجاة qārib an-najāh lifeboat

نجاح najāḥ success

نجّار najjār (-ūn) carpenter

نجح najaḥa (a; نجاح najāḥ) 1. to succeed (في fī in) 2. to manage 3. to pass an exam

نجم najama (u; نجوم nujūm) to stem (من min from)

نجم najm (نجوم nujūm) 1. star 2. نجم كبير najm kabīr superstar

نجمة najma (-āt) star

نجّى najjā to save

نحّات naḥḥāt (-ūn) sculptor

نحاس naḥās copper

نحب naḥaba (a/i; نحب naḥb; نحيب naḥīb) to wail

نحت naḥata (i/u; نحت naḥt) to carve

نحل naḥl *collective* bees

نحن naḥnu we

نحو naḥw (أنحاء anḥā') 1. direction 2. way 3. grammar 4. similiar to 5. في نحو fī naḥw at about 6. على نحو غير مباشر 'alā naḥw ghayr mubāshir indirectly 7. على نحو متساوي 'alā naḥw mutasāwī even 8. على نحو ردي‪ء‬ 'alā naḥw radī' badly 9. النحو والصرف an-naḥw wa 'ṣ-ṣarf grammar

نحو naḥw; نحوا naḥwa 1. toward; towards 2. to 3. approximately 4. نحو الخارج naḥw al-khārij outwards 5. نحو الشمال naḥw

ash-shamāl northward(s) 6. نحو الجنوب
naḥw al-janūb southwards

نحيف naḥīf thin

نخب nakhb 1. toast *to one's health* 2. شرب نخبه shariba nakhbah (a; شرب shurb) to drink a toast to *so*

نخل nakhl *collective* palm tree(s)

ندب nadb mourning

ندب nadab (أنداب andāb) scar

ندرة nadra (-āt) scarcity

ندم nadam regret

ندم nadima (a; ندم nadam) to regret

ندوة nadwa panel

نرجسة narjasa vanity

نرجسي narjisī vain

نرويج nurwīj Norway

نزاع nizā' (-āt) 1. *(mil.)* conflict 2. بلا نزاع bilā nizā' indisputably

نزع naza'a (i; نزع naz') to remove

نزع naz' 1. removal 2. نزع السلاح naz' as-silāḥ disarmament

نزعة naz'a: مثالي النزعة mithālī an-naz'a idealist

نزف nazafa (i; نزف nazf) to bleed

نزل nazl (نزول nuzūl) motel

نزل nazala (i; نزول nuzūl) 1. to go down 2. to descend 3. to get off 4. نزل من السفينة nazala min as-safīna to disembark

نزل nazila (a; نزلة nazla) to get off

نزهة nuzha (-āt; نزه nuzah) 1. walk 2. outing; trip 3. picnic

نزوة nazwa (نزوات nazawāt) impulse

نزول nuzūl descent

نزولاً nuzūlan downwards

نساء nisā' *pl* 1. women 2. طبيب أمراض النساء ṭabīb amrāḍ an-nisā' gynaecologist 3. طبّ أمراض النساء ṭibb amrāḍ an-nisā' gynaecology 4. *and see* إمرة

نسائي nisā'ī 1. female 2. woman's 3. ثوب نسائي thawb nisā'ī gown; dress

نسب nasab relationship

نسبة nisba (نسب nisab) 1. rate 2. proportion 3. نسبة المواليد nisbat al-mawālīd birth rate 4. بالنسبة إلى\ل bi 'n-nisbati ilā/li regarding

نسبي nisbī relative

نسبياً nisbīyan relatively

نسج nasaja (u/i; نسيج nasīj) to weave

نسخ nasakha (a; نسخ naskh) 1. to copy 2. to reproduce

نسخ naskh reproduction

نسخة nuskha (نسخ nusakh) 1. copy 2. reproduction

نسر nasr (نسور nusūr) 1. vulture 2. eagle

نسف nasafa (i; نسف nasf) to blow up

نسل nasl 1. offspring 2. حدّ النسل ḥadd an-nasl birth control

نسوان niswān; نسوة niswa *pl* 1. women 2. *and see* إمرة ; نساء

نسي nasiya (a; نسيان nisyān; نسي nasy) to forget

نسيان nisyān: لا يمكن نسيانه lā yumkin nisyānah memorable

نسيب nasīb (أنساب ansāb) relation

نسيج nasīj (أنسجة ansija) 1. textile 2. texture 3. tissue 4. web

نشأ nasha'a (u; نشء nash'; نشوء nushū'; نشأة nash'a) 1. to grow 2. to grow up 3. to evolve 4. نشأ عن nasha'a 'an to result from

نشاط nashāṭ 1. energy 2. activity

نشّال nashshāl (-ūn) pickpocket

نشج nashaja (i; نشيج nashīj) to sob

نشر nashara (u; نشر nashr) 1. to spread 2. to publish 3. to saw 4. نشر أقوال قذفية nashara aqwāl qadhfīya to libel

نشر nashr 1. spread 2. publishing 3. للنشر li 'n-nashr for the record 4. ليس للنشر laysa li 'n-nashr off the record 5. نشر أقوال قذفية nashr aqwāl qadhfīya libel

نشرة nashara (نشرات nasharāt) 1. notice 2. publication 3. decree 4. نشرة الأخبار nashrat al-akhbār newscast 5. مذيع نشرة الأخبار mudhī' nashrat al-akhbār newscaster, newsreader 6. نشرة الأخبار الأخيرة nashrat al-akhbār al-akhīra the late news

نشوء nushū' 1. growth 2. evolution

نشوب nushūb outbreak

نشيد nashīd; أنشودة unshūda) nashā'id) anthem

نشيط nashīṭ 1. energetic 2. active 3. غير نشيط ghayr nashīṭ inactive

نص naṣṣ (نصوص nuṣūṣ) 1. text 2. نصّ فلم naṣṣ film film script 3. نصّ مسرحية naṣṣ masraḥīya stage script

نصّاب naṣṣāb (-ūn) crook

نصب naṣb fraud

نصب nuṣub pl.: نصب تذكاري nuṣub tadhkārī memorial; monument

نصح naṣaḥa (a; نصح naṣḥ) to advise

نصر naṣr victory; triumph

نصراني naṣrānī Christian

نصرانية naṣrānīya Christianity

نصّف naṣṣafa to halve

نصف niṣf (أنصاف anṣāf) 1. half 2. semi- 3. نصف ساعة niṣf sā'a half an hour, half-hour 4. ثلاثة ونصف thalatha wa niṣf half past three 5. نصف كرة niṣf kura hemisphere

نصفي niṣfī 1. semi- 2. صداع نصفي ṣudā' niṣfī migraine

نصيب naṣīb (نصب nuṣub; أنصبة anṣiba) 1. share 2. portion 3. quota 4. destiny 5. يا نصيب yā naṣīb lottery

نصيحة naṣīḥa (نصائح nasā'iḥ) advice

نصير naṣīr (نصراء nuṣarā') 1. supporter 2. patron

نضال niḍāl 1. struggle 2. crusade

نضج naḍija (a; نضج naḍj) mature

نطاق niṭāq (نطق nuṭuq) 1. belt 2. ring 3. limit 4. sphere 5. range 6. خارج نطاق الرقابة khārij niṭāq ar-raqāba offshore 7. واسع النطاق wāsi' an-niṭāq large-scale 8. على نطاق الوطن كله 'alā niṭāq al-waṭan kulluh nationwide

نطق **naṭaqa** (u; نطق nuṭq) to utter

نظّارة **naẓẓāra** (-āt) 1. glasses; spectacles 2. sunglasses

نظافة **naẓāfa** cleanness

نظام **niẓām** (أنظمة anẓima; نظم nuẓum) 1. order 2. system 3. regime 4. النظام an-niẓām law and order 5. نظام درجي niẓām darajī scale

نظر **naẓara** (u; نظر naẓar) 1. to look 2. to regard 3. to view 4. نظر في naẓara fī to look into

نظر **naẓar** 1. sight 2. view 3. طويل النظر ṭawīl an-naẓar; بعيد النظر ba'īd an-naẓar long-sighted 4. قصير النظر qaṣīr an-naẓar near-sighted 5. وجهة نظر wajhat naẓar point of view 6. لافت للنظر lāfit li 'n-naẓar striking 7. بالنظر عن bi ṣarf an-naẓar 'an apart from 8. بصرف النظر عن bi ṣarf an-naẓar 'an regardless of 9. أعاد النظر في a'āda al-naẓar fī to reconsider 10. نظراً ل naẓaran li seeing that; since

نظرة **naẓra** (نظرات naẓarāt) 1. look 2. ألقى نظرة على alqā naẓra 'alā to look over

نظرية **naẓariya** (-āt) theory

نظّف **naẓẓafa** 1. to clean 2. to wash 3. نظف بمكنسة كهربائية naẓẓafa bi miknasa kahrabā'iya to vacuum; to hoover up

نظم **naẓm** verse

نظّم **naẓẓama** 1. to arrange 2. to organize 3. to regulate

نظير **naẓīr** (نظراء nuẓurā') 1. match 2. equivalent

نظيف **naẓīf** (نظاف niẓāf) 1. clean 2. neat

نعاس **nu'ās** sleepiness

نعسان **na'sān** sleepy

نعّم **na''ama** to smooth

نعم **na'am** yes

نغم **nagham** (أنغام anghām) (mus.) 1. note 2. tune 3. درجة النغم darajat an-naghm pitch

نفى **nafā** (i; نفي nafy) 1. to reject 2. to exile

نفّاثة **naffātha** نفّاثة: طائرة ṭā'ira naffātha jet plane

نفّاثي **naffāthī** نفّاثية طائرة ṭā'ira naffāthīya jet plane

نفّاج **naffāj** (-ūn) snob

نفاد **nafād** نفاد الصبر nafād aṣ-ṣabr impatience

نفاق **nifāq** hypocrisy

نفاية **nufāya** (-āt) 1. rubbish 2. waste

نفخ **nafakha** (u; نفخ nafkh) to blow

نفد **nafida** (a; نفاد nafād) 1. to run out 2. نفد الوقت nafida al-waqt There is no time left.

نفس **nafs** (أنفس anfus; نفوس nufūs) 1. self 2. soul 3. same 4. نفسي nafsī myself 5. نفسه nafsuh same; himself 6. نفسها nafsuhā same; herself 7. من نفسه min nafsih by himself 8. في الوقت نفسه fī 'l-waqt nafsuh at the same time 9. واثق بالنفس wāthiq bi 'n-nafs confident 10. الثقة بالنفس ath-thiqa bi 'n-nafs confidence; self-confidence 11. إحترام النفس iḥtirām an-nafs self-respect 12. تحكم في النفس taḥakkum fī

نقال **naqqāl** 1. mobile 2. portable 3. التلفون النقال al-tilifūn an-naqqāl; هاتف نقال hātif naqqāl mobile phone 4. كمبيوتر نقال kombyūtar naqqāl powerbook; laptop computer

نقّح **naqqaḥa** to revise

نقد **naqada** (u; نقد naqd) (media) to review

نقد **naqd** 1. criticism 2. (media) review 3. (نقود nuqūd) money 4. cash 5. change 6. نقد معدني naqd maʿdinī coin 7. سحب نقداً saḥaba naqdan (a; سحب saḥb) to withdraw money

نقدي **naqdī** 1. monetary 2. critical

نقر **naqr** (mus.) percussion

نقص **naqaṣa** (u; نقص naqṣ; نقصان nuqṣān) 1. to lack 2. to be short of 3. to decrease

نقص **naqṣ** 1. lack 2. shortage 3. decrease 4. deficiency 5. imperfection

نقض **naqḍ** 1. veto 2. استعمل حقّ النقض istaʿmala haqq an-naqḍ to veto

نقطة **nuqṭa** (نقط nuqaṭ; نقاط niqāṭ) 1. point 2. dot 3. نقطة تفتيش nuqṭat taftīsh checkpoint 4. صفر نقطة ثلاثة ṣifr nuqṭa thalātha zero point three (0.3)

نقل **naqala** (u; نقل naql) 1. to move 2. to transport 3. to transfer 4. to report

نقل **naql** 1. transport 2. transfer 3. شركة نقل sharikat naql (com.) carrier 4. شحينة نقل صغيرة shāḥinat naql ṣaghīra pick-up truck 5. نقل الدم naql ad-dam blood transfusion

نقلاً عن **naqlan ʿan** according to

'n-nafs; ضبط النفس ḍabṭ an-nafs self-control 13. الدفاع عن النفس ad-difāʿ ʿan an-nafs self-defence 14. علم النفس ʿilm an-nafs psychology 15. عالم النفس ʿālim an-nafs psychologist

نفس **nafas** (أنفاس anfās) breath

نفساني **nafsānī** 1. علاج نفساني ʿilāj nafsānī therapy 2. طبيب نفساني ṭabīb nafsānī therapist 3. الصحّة النفسانية aṣ-ṣiḥḥa an-nafsānīya mental health

نفسي **nafsī** 1. psychological 2. طبيب نفسي ṭabīb nafsī psychiatrist 3. طبّ نفسي ṭibb nafsī psychiatry

نفط **nafṭ** 1. oil; petroleum 2. بئر نفط biʾr nafṭ (آبار ābār) oil well 3. حقل نفط ḥaql nafṭ (حقول ḥuqūl) oilfield 4. ناقلة النفط nāqilat an-nafṭ oil tanker

نفطي **nafṭī** oil

نفع **nafʿ** use

نفعة **nafʿa** usefulness

نفع **nafaʿa** (a; نفع nafʿ) to serve

نفّذ **naffadha** to carry out; to execute

نفق **nafaq** (أنفاق anfāq) 1. tunnel 2. subway

نفقة **nafaqa** (-āt) (fin.) maintenance

نفوذ **nufūdh** 1. influence 2. ذو نفوذ dhū nufūdh influential

نقّ **naqqa** (i; نقيق naqīq) to croak

نقّى **naqqā** to refine

نقابة **niqāba** (-āt) 1. syndicate 2. نقابة عمّال niqābat ʿummāl trade union; trades union

نقابي **niqābī** union

نقي naqī (أنقياء anqiyā') 1. pure 2. immaculate 3. غير نقي ghayr naqī impure

نقيب naqīb (نقبا nuqabā') (mil.) captain

نكتة nukta (نكت nukat) joke

نكسة naksa setback

نما namā (u; نمو numūw); نمى namā (i; نماء namā') to grow

نماء namā' growth

النمسا nimsā; النمسا an-nimsā Austria

نمساوي nimsāwī (-ūn) Austrian

نمط namaṭ: عتيق النمط ʿatīq al-namaṭ old-fashioned

نملة namla (collective نمل naml) ant

نموذج namūdhaj (-āt) 1. model 2. pattern 3. specimen 4. نموذج أولي namūdhaj awwalī prototype

نموذجي namūdhajī typical

نموذجياً namūdhajiyan typically

نهائي nihā'ī 1. final 2. لا نهائي lā nihā'ī infinite 4. شبه نهائي shibh nihā'ī semi-final 5. and see نهاية

نهار nahār 1. daytime 2. منتصف النهار muntaṣif an-nahār midday 3. ليل نهار layla nahāra (by) day and night

نهاراً nahāran by day

نهاية nihāya (-āt) 1. end 2. finish 3. term 4. نهاية الأسبوع nihāyat al-usbūʿ weekend 5. في النهاية fi 'n-nihāya in the end; ultimately 6. لا نهاية له lā nihāya lah endless 7. مباراة نهائية mubārāh nihā'iya (spor.) final 8. مشترك في مباراة نهائية mushtarik fī mubārāh nihā'iya

finalist 9. لا نهائية mubārāh nihā'iya finalist 9. نهائية nihā'iya infinity 10. and see نهائي

نهب nahaba (a; نهب nahb) to ravage

نهر nahr (أنهار anhār) 1. river 2. stream

نهض nahaḍa (a; نهوض nuhūḍ) 1. to arise 2. نهض عن السرير nahaḍa ʿan as-sarīr to get out of bed

نهضة nahḍa (-āt) 1. rebirth 2. renaissance

نوى nawā (i; نية nīya; نواة nawāh) to intend

نواب nuwwāb pl 1. مجلس النواب البريطاني majlis an-nawwāb al-brīṭānī House of Commons 2. مجلس النواب الأمريكي majlis al-nawwāb al-amrīkī House of Representatives 3. and see نائب

نوبة nuwab) 1. change 2. instance 3. turn 4. fit 5. نوبة الليل nawbat al-layl night shift 6. نوبة القلب nawbat al-qalb; نوبة قلبية nawba qalbīya heart attack

نور nūr (أنوار anwār) 1. light 2. أضاء النور aḍā'a an-nūr to put the light on

نورز nawraz collective seagulls

نورويجا nūrwījā Norway

نورويجي nūrwījī (-ūn) Norwegian

نوع nawʿ (أنواع anwāʿ) 1. kind; sort; type; variety 2. من نوع ما min nawʿin mā kind of 3. بنوع خاص bi nawʿ khāṣṣ especially

نوعية nawʿīya quality

نوفمبر novembir November

نوم nawm 1. sleep 2. غرفة النوم ghurfat an-nawm bedroom 3. كيس للنوم kīs li 'n-nawm (أكياس akyās) sleeping bag

نوّار nawwār May

نوّر nawwara to illuminate

نوّع nawwa'a to vary

نووي nawawī nuclear

ني- -nī me

نيء nī' raw

نيابة niyāba: نيابةً عن niyābatan 'an; عن بالنيابة bi 'n-niyāba 'an 1. on behalf of 2. deputy; vice 3. acting

النيبال an-nībāl Nepal

نيبالي nībālī Nepali

نية (نوايا nawāyā) nīya 1. intention 2. النية حسن an-nīya husn an-nīya goodwill

نيزك (نيازك nayāzik) nayzak meteor

نيسان nīsān April

النيل an-nīl the Nile

نيو زيلاندا nyū zīlanda New Zealand

نيون niyūn neon

نيّق nayyiq fussy

ه

ه- -hu/-h/-uh him; his; it; its

ها- -hā her; it; its; them; their

هائل hā'il formidable

هاتان hātān these *feminine dual*

هاتف (هواتف hawātif) hātif 1. telephone 2. هاتف نقّال hātif maḥmūl; هاتف محمول hātif naqqāl mobile phone 3. هاتف السيّارة hātif as-sayyāra car phone

هاتفي hātifī 1. telephone; 2. tele- 3. الإتّصالات الهاتفية al-ittiṣālāt al-hātifiya telecommunications 4. لوحة التحويل الهاتفي lawḥat at-taḥwīl al-hātifī telephone switchboard

هاجر hājara 1. to migrate 2. to emigrate

3. to immigrate

هاجم hājama 1. to attack 2. to charge

هادئ hādi' 1. quiet 2. calm 3. steady

هارب hārib (-ūn) fugitive

هازئ hāzi' scornful (من min; ب bi of)

هاشمي hāshimī Hashemite

هؤلاء hā'ulā'i these

هامّ hāmm 1. major 2. central 3. significant 4. crucial 5. شخص هامّ shakhṣ hāmm somebody 6. غير هامّ ghayr hāmm minor 7. حدث هامّ ḥadath hāmm landmark

هامش (هوامش hawāmish) hāmish margin

هامشي hāmishī marginal

حاوٍ غير محترف (هواةٍ huwāh): hāwin حاوٍ
hāwin ghayr muḥtarif; هاوٍ لا محترف
hāwin lā muḥtarif amateur

habba (u; هبّ habb) to blow

hiba (-āt) gift; present هبة

habaṭa (u/i; هبوط hubūṭ) 1. to descend هبط
2. to land 3. (fin.) to slide

hubūṭ 1. descent 2. landing 3. (fin.) هبوط
slide 4. هبوط إقتصادي hubūṭ iqtiṣādī
(ec.) slump

hijā' 1. spelling 2. satire هجاء

hijā'ī satirical هجائي

hajara (u; hajr هجر) 1. to migrate 2. هجر
to abandon

hijra migration هجرة

hajama (u; هجام hujūm) to attack (على هجم
'alā so/sth)

hujūm (-āt) 1. attack 2. charge هجوم

hudba (collective هدب hudb; pl أهداب هدبة
ahdāb) eyelash

haddada to threaten (ه so; ب bi هدّد
with)

hadara (i; هدر hadr; هدير hadīr) to roar هدر

hadaf (أهداف ahdāf) 1. aim 2. object; هدف
objective 3. goal 4. target 5.
sajjala hadafan to score a goal سجّل هدفاً

haddafa to aim هدّف

haddama to demolish هدّم

hudna (-āt) truce هدنة

hudū' 1. quiet 2. calm 3. بهدوءٍ bi هدوء
hudū' quietly

hadīya (هدايا hadāyā) gift; present هدية

hadīr 1. roar 2. boom هدير

hādhā m 1. this 2. such 3. هذا و hādhā هذا
wa; هذا وقد hādhā wa qad furthermore

hādhān these masculine dual هذان

hādhihi f 1. this 2. these 3. هذه الليلة هذه
hādhihi 'l-layla tonight

harra (i; هرير harīr) 1. to growl 2. to purr هرّ

hurā' nonsense هراء

haraba (u; هروب hurūb) to flee هرب

harraba 1. to smuggle 2. to traffic هرّب

harasa (u; هرس hars) to squash هرس

harwala to rush هرول

harwala rush هرولة

hurayra kitten هريرة

hazza (u/i; هزّ hazz) 1. to shake 2. to wag هزّ

hazza (-āt) tremor هزّة

haza'a (a; هزء haz') to make fun (من\ب هزأ
min/bi of)

hazil funny هزل

hazlī comic هزلي

hazama (i; هزم hazm) 1. to defeat 2. هزم
lam yuhzam undefeated لم يهزم

hazīma (هزائم hazā'im) defeat هزيمة

histīrī hysterical هستيري

haḍaba (-āt) hill هضبة

haḍama (i; هضم haḍm) to digest هضم

haḍm 1. digestion 2. عسر الهضم 'usr هضم
al-haḍm indigestion

hafwa (هفوات hafawāt) lapse هفوة

هكتار hiktār (-āt) hectare

هكذا hākadhā 1. so; such 2. this way 3. consequently

هل hal *introduces a question:* هل أنت متأكّد؟ hal anta muta'akkid? Are you positive?; هل لك في أن...؟ hal laka fī an...? would you like to...?

هلاك halāk doom

هلام hulām jelly

هلك halaka (i; هلاك halāk) to perish

هولاندا holanda Netherlands

هلندي holandī (-ūn) 1. Dutch 2. Netherlander

هلوسة halwasa (-āt) hallucination

هَمَّ hamma (u; مهمّة mahamma) 1. to interest 2. to concern 3. to affect 4. هَمَّ ب hamma bi to intend to

هم hamm (هموم humūm) 1. interest 2. concern

هم hum *mpl* they; them; their

هما humā *dual plural* they

همس hamasa (i; همس hams) 1. to whisper 2. to mutter

هنّ hunna *fpl* they; them; their

هنا hunā here

هناك hunāk; هنالك hunālik 1. there 2. there is/are...

هنّأ hanna'a to congratulate (على 'alā/ب bi on)

الهند al-hind 1. India 2. جوزة الهند jawzat al-hind (*collective* جوز الهند jawz al-hind) coconut

هندسة handasa engineering

هندي hindī (-yūn) Indian

هواء hawā' 1. air 2. مهواة مكيّف هواء mihwāh mukayyif hawā' ventilator 3. بالهواء الطلق bi 'l-hawā' aṭ-ṭalq open-air

هوائي hawā'ī 1. aerial 2. antenna 3. تيّار هوائي tayyār hawā'ī draught

هوامّ hawāmm vermin

هواية hawāya (-āt) pastime

هوايات hawāyāt *pl* interests

هو huwa he; it

هوكي hōkī 1. hockey 2. الهوكي على الجليد hōkī 'alā 'l-jalīd ice hockey

هوية huwīya 1. identity 2. أثبت الهوية athbata al-huwīya to identify 3. إثبات الهوية ithbāt al-huwīya identification

هي hiya she; it; they

هيئة hay'a 1. organisation 2. هيئة المحلّفين hay'at al-muḥallifīn jury 3. هيئة الإذاعة البريطانية hay'at al-idhā'a al-brīṭānīya British Broadcasting Corporation (BBC) 4. هيئة الأمم المتّحدة hay'at al-umam al-muttaḥida United Nations

هيبة hayba prestige

هيكل haykal (هياكل hayākil) 1. frame 2. هيكل عظمي haykal 'aẓmī skeleton

هيمنة haymana 1. domination 2. supremacy

هيّج hayyaja to agitate

هيّر hayyir inconsiderate

و

و

و wa 1. and 2. while 3. with 4. by 5. ‏...و ...و‏ wa... wa... both... and... 6. ‏ولا‏ wa lā neither 7. ‏و إلاّ‏ illā wa; ‏وإلا‏ wa illā otherwise; or else 8. ‏والعكس‏ wa 'l-'aks vice versa 9. ‏ومع ذلك‏ wa ma'a dhālik; ‏ورغم ذلك‏ wa raghma dhālik nevertheless 10. ‏وإن‏ wa in even if

وابل wābil shower

واثق wāthiq 1. sure (‏ب‏ bi/‏من‏ min of) 2. confident 3. ‏واثق بالنفس‏ wāthiq bi 'n-nafs self-confident

واجب wājib 1. necessary 2. obligatory 3. (-āt) duty 4. obligation 5. imperative 6. ‏واجبات منزلية‏ wājibāt manzilīya homework

واجه wājaha 1. to face 2. to encounter 3. to confront

واجهة wājiha (-āt) 1. front 2. facade

واحد wāḥid 1. one 2. a/an 3. mono- 4. ‏مرّة واحدة‏ marra wāḥida once 5. ‏كلّ واحد‏ kull wāḥid everyone 6. ‏لكلّ واحد‏ li kull wāḥid each 7. ‏الواحد بعد الآخر‏ al-wāḥid ba'd al-ākhar one after the other 8. ‏شارع واحد الإتجاه‏ shāri' wāḥid al-ittijāh one-way street

واحة wāḥa (-āt) oasis

واد wādin (‏أودية‏ awdiya; ‏وديان‏ widyān) 1. valley 2. gorge 3. wadi

وارد wārid 1. incoming 2. (-āt) import

واسطة wāsiṭa 1. intermediary 2. mediation 3. means 4. ‏بواسطة‏ bi wāsiṭa through; by means of

واسع wāsi' 1. wide 2. extensive 3. vast 4. spacious 5. ‏واسع النطاق‏ wāsi' an-niṭāq large-scale

واصل wāṣala 1. to proceed (‏في\ه‏ fī with) 2. to persist 3. ‏واصل في...‏ wāṣala fī... He kept on...

واضح wāḍiḥ 1. clear 2. obvious 3. ‏غير واضح‏ ghayr wāḍiḥ vague

واظب wāẓaba to persevere (‏على‏ 'alā in)

واعٍ wā'in 1. conscious 2. aware

وافر wāfir plenty; abundant

وافق wāfaqa 1. to agree (‏ه‏ h with; ‏على/في‏ fī/'alā about) 2. to suit 3. ‏وافق على‏ wāfaqa 'alā to approve

واقٍ wāqin 1. resistant ‏ضدّ‏ ḍidd to) 2. protective 3. ‏واق ضدّ المطر‏ wāqin ḍidd al-maṭar waterproof

واقع wāqi' 1. reality 2. ‏في الواقع‏ fī 'l-wāqi' in reality; in fact 3. ‏شابه الواقع‏ shābih al-wāqi' virtual

واقعي wāqi'ī 1. realistic 2. actual 3. realist 4. ‏غير واقعي‏ ghayr wāqi'ī unrealistic

واقف wāqif 1. upright 2. stationary

والد wālid (-ūn) 1. father 2. parent

والدة wālida mother

والدان wālidān *dual* parents

وبا ء wabā' (أوبئة 'awbi'a) epidemic

وبّخ wabbakha to rebuke; to lecture

وتد watad (أوتاد 'awtād) 1. peg 2. stake

وتر watar (أوتار 'awtār) (*mus.*) chord

وتري watrī odd

وثاقة wathāqa 1. firmness 2. reliability 3. وثاقة الصلة wathāqat aṣ-ṣila relevance

وثب wathaba/wathiba (يثب yathibu; وثب wathb) 1. to hop 2. to bounce

وثق wathiqa (يثق yathiqu; ثقة thiqa) to trust (ب bi *so/sth*)

وثّق waththaqa to strengthen

وثن wathan (أوثان 'awthān) idol

وثيق wathīq (وثاق withāq) 1. firm 2. reliable 3. وثيق الصلة wathīq aṣ-ṣila relevant

وثيقة wathīqa (وثائق wathā'iq) document

وجب wajaba (يجب yajibu; وجوب wujūb) to be necessary; must

وجبة wajba (-āt) 1. meal 2. وجبة خفيفة wajba khafīfa snack

وجد wajada (يجد yajidu; وجود wujūd) to find

وجد wujida *passive* (يوجد yūjad; وجود wujūd) 1. to exist 2. to be located

وجع waji'a (يوجع yawja'u; وجع waja') 1. to ache 2. to hurt

وجع waja' (أوجاع 'awjā') 1. ache 2. pain

وجّه wajjaha 1. to send 2. to direct 3. to steer

وجه wajh (وجوه wujūh; أوجه 'awjuh) 1. face 2. front 3. aspect 4. ذو وجهين dhū wajhayn two-faced 5. احمرّ الوجه iḥmarra al-wajh blush

وجهة wijha/wujha/wajha 1. direction 2. intention 3. respect 4. وجهة النظر wijhat an-naẓar point of view 5. outlook

وجود wujūd 1. existence 2. presence

وجيز wajīz brief

وحّد waḥḥada 1. to unite 2. ثانيةً waḥḥada thāniyatan to reunite 3. وحّد المعاير waḥḥada 'l-ma'āyīr to standardize

وحد waḥda 1. alone 2. وحده waḥdah by himself

وحداني waḥdānī solitary

وحدة waḥda (-āt) 1. unity 2. (-āt) unit 3. تركه وحده tarakah waḥdah let alone 4. وحدة عسكرية waḥda 'askariya military unit

وحش waḥsh (وحوش wuḥūsh; وحشان wuḥshān) 1. beast; wild animal 2. monster

وحشي waḥshī 1. wild 2. brutal

وحشية waḥshīya ferocity

وحل waḥl mud

وحلي waḥlī muddy

وحيد waḥīd 1. single 2. sole; unique 3. alone 4. lonely 5. only

وخز wakhaza (يخز yakhizu; وخز wakhz) to prick

ودّ wadda (يودّ yawaddu; ودّ wadd; وداد wadād) 1. to like 2. to love 3. to want (أن an to)

وداع widāʿ farewell; goodbye

ودع wadaʿa (يدع yadaʿu; ودع wadʿ) 1. to let 2. to leave 3. to stop

ودّع waddaʿa to say goodbye to

ودود wadūd; ودّي waddī friendly

ودّية waddīya friendliness

وديعة wadīʿa (ودائع wadāʾiʿ) 1. deposit 2. وديعةً wadīʿatan on trust

وراء warāʾ; warāʾa 1. behind 2. beyond 3. إلى الوراء ilā ʾl-warāʾ backwards 4. تحرّك إلى الوراء taḥarraka ilā ʾl-warāʾ to reverse

وراثي wirāthī genetic

ورث waritha (يرث yarithu; وراثة wirth; wirātha) to inherit

ورد warada (يرد yaridu; ورود wurūd) to arrive (إلى\ه ilā at)

وردة warda (collective ورد ward) rose

ورّط warraṭa to involve

ورشة warsha (-āt): ورشة عمل warshat ʿamal workshop

ورطة warṭa (ورطات waraṭāt) dilemma

ورقة waraqa (collective ورق waraq; pl أوراق awrāq) 1. paper 2. leaf 3. صحيفة من الورق ṣaḥīfa min al-waraq a sheet of paper 4. ورق الحيطان waraq al-ḥīṭān wallpaper 5. ورق المرحاض waraq al-mirḥāḍ toilet paper 6. ورقة مصرفية waraqa maṣrifīya banknote 7. ورقة مصمّغة waraqa muṣammagha sticker 8. ورق مقوّى waraq muqawwan cardboard

ورقي waraqī 1. paper 2. منديل ورقي mandīl waraqī tissue paper 3. طائرة ورقية ṭāʾira waraqīya kite

ورك wark (أوراك awrāk) f hip

ورم waram (أورام awrām) 1. bump 2. (med.) lump

وريث wurathāʾ) heir

وريثة warītha (-āt) heiress

وزارة wizāra (-āt) 1. ministry 2. وزارة المال wizārat al-māl treasury

وزاري wizārī ministerial

وزراء wuzarāʾ pl (pol.) 1. رئيس الوزراء raʾīs al-wuzarāʾ prime minister 2. مجلس الوزراء majlis al-wuzarāʾ cabinet 3. and see وزير

وزّع wazzaʿa 1. to deal 2. to distribute

وزن wazana (يزن yazinu; وزن wazn) 1. to weigh 2. to balance

وزن wazn (أوزان awzān) 1. weight 2. balance

وزير wazīr (وزراء wuzarāʾ) 1. minister; secretary of state 2. وزير بالوكالة wazīr bi ʾl-wikāla acting minister 3. and see وزراء

وسائل **wasā'il** *pl* 1. means 2. إتّصال وسائل **wasā'il ittiṣāl** communications 3. تعدّد وسائل الإعلام **ta'addud wasā'il al-i'lām** multimedia

وساخة **wasākha** dirt

وسادة **wisāda** (-āt; وسائد **wasā'id**) 1. pillow 2. cushion

وساطة **wasāṭa** mediation

وسام **wisām** (أوسمة **awsima**) *(mil.)* decoration

وسّخ **wassakha** to make dirty

وسخ **wasikh** dirty

وسّع **wassa'a** to expand

وسط **wasaṭ; wasaṭa** 1. among 2. in the middle of

وسط **wasaṭ** (أوساط **awsāṭ**) 1. middle 3. average 4. *(fin.)* mean 5. في وسط من **fī wasaṭin min** in the midst of 6. وسط المدينة **wasaṭ al-madīna** inner city 7. *and see* أوساط

وسطى **wusṭā** *f* 1. الطبقة الوسطى **aṭ-ṭabaqa 'l-wusṭā** middle class 2. متعلّق بالقرون الوسطى **muta'alliq bi 'l-qurūn al-wusṭā** medieval 3. *and see* أوسط

وسطي **wasaṭī** 1. middle 2. average 3. *(fin.)* mean

وسكي **wiskī** whisky

وسيط **wasīṭ** (وسطاء **wusaṭā'**) 1. middle 2. average 3. *(fin.)* medium 4. mediator 5. جهاز وسيط **jihāz wasīṭ** modem

وسيلة **wasīla** (وسائل **wasā'il**) 1. means 2. medium 3. device 4. aid

وسيم **wasīm** handsome

وشاح **wishāḥ** (أوشحة **awshiḥa**) scarf

وشّم **washshama** to tattoo

وشك **washk:** على وشك أن ' **alā washk an** on the point of; about to

وشم **washm** (وشام **wishām**) tattoo

وشيع **washī'** hedge

وشيك **washīk** 1. forthcoming 2. imminent

وصّى **waṣṣā** to recommend

وصف **waṣafa** (يصف **yaṣifu;** وصف **waṣf**) to describe

وصف **waṣf** (أوصاف **awṣāf**) 1. description 2. quality; characteristic 3. لا يمكن وصفه **lā yumkin waṣfuh** indescribable

وصفة **waṣfa;** وصفة طبّية **waṣfa ṭibbīya** *(med.)* prescription

وصل **waṣala** (يصل **yasilu;** وصل **waṣl;** صلة **ṣila**) 1. to connect (ب **bi** with) 2. وصول **wuṣūl**) to arrive (إلى\ه **ilā** at)

وصّل **waṣṣala** to give a lift to

وصل **waṣl** (أوصال **awṣāl**) 1. link 2. وصل إستلام **waṣl istilām** receipt

وصول **wuṣūl** 1. arrival 2. access 3. ممكن الوصول أليه **mumkin al-wuṣūl ilayhi** accessible 4. فات موعد وصوله **fāt maw'id wuṣūluh** overdue

وصية **waṣīya** *(leg.)* will

وضّب waḍḍaba to pack

وضّح waḍḍaḥa to clarify

وضع waḍa'a (يضع yaḍa'u; وضع waḍ') 1. to put 2. to set 3. to lay; to lay down 4. to situate 5. وضع إشارة waḍa'a ishāra to tick 6. وضع مسوّدة waḍa'a musawwada to draft

وضع waḍ' (أوضاع awḍā') 1. situation 2. وضع شرعي waḍ' shar'ī (leg.) status

وضعي waḍ'ī positive

وضوح wuḍūḥ 1. clarity 2. بوضوح bi wuḍūḥ clearly

وضيع waḍī' 1. low 2. inferior

وطن waṭan (أوطان awṭān) 1. country 2. homeland 3. الوطن الأصلي al-waṭan al-aṣlī native country 4. وطن الأمّ al-waṭan al-umm mainland 5. على نطاق الوطن كله 'alā niṭāq al-waṭan kulluh nationwide

وطني waṭanī 1. national 2. patriotic 3. (-yūn) nationalist 4. patriot

وظّف waẓẓafa to employ

وظيفة waẓīfa (وظائف waẓā'if) 1. position 2. function

وعى wa'ā (يعي ya'ī; وعي wa'y) to perceive

وعاء wi'ā' (أوعية aw'iya; أواع awā'in) 1. container 2. pot 3. vessel 4. وعاء دموي wi'ā' damawī blood vessel

وعد wa'ada (يعد ya'idu; وعد wa'd) to promise

وعد wa'd (وعود wu'ūd) promise

وعظ wa'aẓa (يعظ ya'iẓu; وعظ wa'ẓ;

عظة 'iẓa) to preach

وعي wa'y 1. attention 2. consciousness 3. sense 4. فاقد الوعي fāqid al-wa'y senseless

وعير wa'īr rugged

وغد waghd (أوغاد awghād) villain

وفى wafā (يفي yafī; وفاء wafā'; وفي wafiy) 1. to keep a promise 2. وفى ديناً wafā daynan to repay

وفاء wafā' 1. fulfilment 2. loyalty 3. وفاء الدين wafā' ad-dayn repayment

وفد wafada (يفد yafidu; وفود wufūd) to come; to arrive (إلى ilā at)

وفد wafd (وفود wufūd) delegation

وفّر waffara 1. to increase 2. to supply 3. to save

وفرة wafra plenty; abundance

وفق wafiqa (يفق yafiqu; وفق wafq) to be right; to be appropriate

وفق wafq 1. sufficient amount 2. agreement 3. وفقاً ل wafqan li according to 4. per

وفي wafī loyal

وفير wafīr: وفير الإنتاج wafīr al-intāj prolific

وقاء wiqā' prevention

وقائع waqā'i' pl: وقائع إجتماع waqā'i' ijtimā' minutes of a meeting

وقائي waqā'ī preventative

وقاحة waqāḥa cheek

وقار waqār gravity

وقّت waqqata to time

وقت waqt (أوقات awqāt) 1. time 2. وقت الفراغ waqt al-farāgh leisure time 3. أيّ وقت ayy waqt anytime 4. في ذلك الوقت fī dhālika 'l-waqt at that time; meanwhile 5. منذ ذلك الوقت mundhu dhālika 'l-waqt since 6. في وقت غير محدّد fī waqt ghayr muḥaddad sometime 7. بين وقت والآخر bayn waqt wa ākhar from time to time 8. الوقت كلّه al-waqt kulluh all along 9. في الوقت نفسه fī 'l-waqt nafsuh at the same time 10. في الوقت المناسب fī 'l-waqt al-munāsib in due course 11. أكثر من أيّ وقت مضى akthar min ayy waqt maḍā more than ever 12. قضى الوقت qaḍā al-waqt (i; قضاء qaḍā') to spend time 13. ضيّع الوقت ḍayya'a al-waqt to waste time 14. نفد الوقت nafida al-waqt There is no time left. 15. *and see* أوقات

وقتذاك waqtadhāk at that time

وقح waqiḥ 1. cheeky 2. insolent

وقع waqa'a (يقع yaqi'u/yaqa'u; وقوع wuqū'; وقع waq') 1. to fall 2. to drop 3. to take place 4. to be situated

وقّع waqqa'a 1. to sign 2. to register

وقعة waq'a (وقعات waqa'āt) fall

وقف waqafa (يقف yaqifu; وقوف wuqūf; وقف waqf) 1. to stop 2. to stand 3. وقف في الطابور waqafa fī 'ṭ-ṭābūr to queue

وقّف waqqafa 1. to halt 2. to intercept

وقف waqf 1. stop 2. halt 3. suspension 4. religious endowment 5. وقف إطلاق النار waqf iṭlāq an-nār cease-fire 6. وقف الأمل waqf al-'amal shutdown

وقفة waqfa (-āt) stance

وقود waqūd 1. fuel 2. زوّد بالوقود zawwada bi 'l-waqūd fuel

وقور waqūr solemn

وقوع wuqū' occurrence; happening

وقوف wuqūf: مكان وقوف السيّارات makān wuqūf as-sayyārāt carpark

وقيعة waqī'a (وقائع waqā'i') occurrence

وكالة wakāla/wikāla (-āt) 1. agency 2. وكالة السفر wikālat as-safar travel agency 3. وكالة الأنباء wikālat al-anbā' press agency; news agency 4. وزير بالوكالة wazīr bi 'l-wikāla acting minister

وكر wakr (أوكار awkār) den

وكيل wakīl (وكلاء wukalā') agent

ولا wa lā neither

ولي walā (يلي yalī; ولاية wilāya) to succeed

ولادة wilāda (*med.*) 1. birth 2. delivery 3. مستشفى الولادة mustashfā 'l-wilāda maternity clinic 4. مدينة الولادة madīnat al-wilāda hometown

ولادي wilādī natal

ولّاعة wallā'a (-āt) lighter

ولاية wilāya (-āt) 1. province 2. *federal* state 3. بين الولايات bayn al-wilāyāt interstate 4. الولايات المتّحدة al-wilāyāt

al-muttaḥida United States of America

ولد walad (أولاد awlād) boy

(ولادة wilāda؛ تلد talidu) ولدت waladat: ولد to give birth to

ولد wulida *passive* to be born

ولّد wallada 1. to deliver a baby 2. to breed 3. to generate

ولط walṭ volt

ولطية walṭīya voltage

ولكن walākin؛ ولكنّ walākinna but

ولو wa law *see* لو

ولي walī (أولياء awliyā') 1. guardian 2. saint

ولي waliya (يلي yalī) 1. to be near 2. كما يلي kamā yalī as follows

وليد wulayd little child

وليمة walīma (ولائم walā'im) feast

ونش winsh (-āt) 1. crane 2. winch

وهم wahm (أوهام awhām) illusion

وهمي wahmī unreal

ويلز muqāṭa'at waylz مقاطعة ويلز؛ ويلز Wales

ويلزي waylzī Welsh

ي

ي ī- my

يا yā 1. oh...! 2. يا له من... yā lah min... what...! 3. يا خسارة! yā khasāra what a pity! 4. يا نصيب yā naṣīb lottery

يائس yā'is desperate

ياباني yābānī (-yūn) Japanese

ياردة yārda (-āt) yard

يأس ya's despair

يئس ya'isa (a/i؛ يأس ya's) to despair

ياقة yāqa collar

يباني yabānī (-yūn) Japanese

يبدو yabdū 1. فيما يبدو fī mā yabdū apparently 2. *and see* بدا

يتيم yatīm (أيتام aytām) 1. orphan 2. دار الأيتام dār al-aytām orphanage

يجب yajibu 1. must; ought 2. يجب أن... yajib an... it is necessary that...

يخت yakht (يخوت yukhūt) yacht

يخنة yakhna stew

يد yad *f* (أياد ayādin) 1. hand 2. قبضة اليد qabḍat al-yad fist 3. شنطة يد shanṭat yad handbag 3. حقيبة اليد ḥaqībat al-yad briefcase 4. مصنوع باليد maṣnū' bi 'l-yad hand-made

يدع yada'u let; allow

يدوي yadawī 1. manual 2. قنبلة يدوية qunbula yadawīya (قنابل qanābil) grenade

يرثى yurthā: يرثى له yurthā lah pitiful

يرحم yarḥam 1. لا يرحم lā yarḥam ruthless 2. and see رحم

يرو yurō (يوروهات yurōhāt) (fin.) euro

يسار yasār 1. left 2. (pol.) the left wing

يساراً yasāran on/to the left

يساري yasārī (pol.) 1. left-wing 2. (-yūn) left-winger

يعتمد yu'tamad 1. لا يعتمد عليه lā yu'tamad 'alayh unreliable 2. and see اعتمد

يعني ya'nī 1. that is; i.e.; that is to say 2. and see عنى

يقظ yaqiẓ 1. awake 2. alert

يقظان yaqẓān awake

يكن yakun 1. يكن mahmā yakun whatever 2. and see كان

يمكن yumkin 1. possible 2. maybe 3. لا يمكن lā yumkin impossible 4. لا يمكن التنبّؤ به lā yumkin at-tanabbu' bih unpredictable 5. لا يمكن إنكاره lā yumkin inkāruh undeniable 6. لا يمكن وصفه lā yumkin waṣfuh indescribable 7. see أمكن

يمن yaman Yemen

يمني yamanī (-yūn) Yemeni

يمين yamīn f (أيمان aymān) 1. right 2. (pol.) the right wing 3. oath

يميني yamīnī (pol.) 1. right-wing 2. (-yūn) right-winger

يناير yanāyir January

ينبغي yanbaghī 1. ought; should 2. to be necessary 3. and see انبغى

ينبوع yanbū' (ينابيع yanābī') spring

يهودي yahūdī (يهود yahūd) 1. Jewish 2. Jew

يوبيل yūbīl jubilee

يوجد yūjad 1. there is/are... 2. to be situated 3. and see وجد

يوغوسلافي yūghūslāvī Yugoslavian

يوغوسلافيا yūghūslāviya Yugoslavia

يوليو yūliyū July

يوم yawm (أيام ayyām) 1. day 2. اليوم al-yawm today 3. ...الوم ... al-yawm today's 4. كل يوم kull yawm every day 5. أي يوم ayy yawm anyday 6. يوماً ما yawman mā someday 7. يوم بعد يوم yawm ba'da yawm every other day 8. يوم عطلة yawm 'uṭla a day off 9. and see أيام

يومئذٍ yawma'idhin; يومذاك yawmadhāk 1. on that day 2. then

يوم الإثنين yawm al-ithnayn Monday

يوم الأحد yawm al-'aḥad Sunday

يوم الأربعاء yawm al-arba'ā' Wednesday

يوم الثلاثاء yawm ath-thalāthā' Tuesday

يوم الجمعة yawm al-jum'a Friday

يوم الخميس yawm al-khamīs Thursday

يوم السبت yawm as-sabt Saturday

يومي yawmī 1. daily 2. صحيفة يومية ṣaḥīfa yawmīya daily newspaper

يومياً yawmīyan daily

يوميات yawmīyāt pl diary; journal

اليونان al-yūnān 1. the Greeks 2. Greece

يوناني yūnānī Greek

يونيو yūniyū June

English-Arabic

إنكليزي - عربي

A

a; an [ə, ei; ən, an] wāḥid واحد; (adāt
tankīr أداة تنكير)

abandon [ə'bandən] v 1. tanāzala
ʿan تنازل عن 2. hajara هجر (u; hajr
هجر)

abbreviation [əbriːviˈeishən] n
ikhtiṣār اختصار

abduct [əbˈdʌkt] v khaṭafa خطف (i;
khaṭf خطف)

ability [əˈbiliti] n qudra قدرة

able [ˈeibəl] adj qādir قادر

about [əˈbaut] 1. prep ʿan عن; bi
shaʾn بشأن 2. adv ḥawālā حوالى;
taqrīban تقريباً 3. fi ʾl-jiwār
في الجوار 4. **I am about to go.**
anā ʿalā washk an adhhab
أنا على وشك أن أذهب

above [əˈbʌv] prep/adv 1. fawqa فوق
2. akthar min أكثر من

abroad [əˈbroːd] adv khārij al-balad
خارج البلد

abrupt [əˈbrʌpt] adj mufājiʾ مفاجئ

absence [ˈabsəns] n ghiyāb غياب

absent [ˈabsənt] adj ghāʾib غائب

absolutely [absəˈluːtli] adv
tamāman تماماً; miʾa bi ʾl-miʾa
مئة بالمئة

absorb [əbˈsoːb] v imtaṣṣa امتص

absurd [əbˈsəːd] adj sakhīf سخيف;
muḍḥik مضحك

abundance [əˈbʌndəns] n wafra وفرة

abundant [əˈbʌndənt] adj wāfir وافر;
ghazīr غزير

abuse [əˈbyuːz] v 1. shatama شتم

(i; shatm شتم) 2. asāʾa istiʿmāl
أساء إستعمال

academic [akəˈdemik] adj akādīmī
أكاديمي

academy [əˈkadəmi] n akādīmīya
أكاديمية (-āt)

accent [ˈaksənt] n lahja لهجة (-āt)

accept [akˈsept] v qabila قبل (a;
qubūl قبول)

access [ˈakses] n 1. madkhal مدخل
2. wuṣūl وصول

accessible [akˈsesibəl] adj
mumkin al-wuṣūl ilayhi
ممكن الوصول اليه

accessory [akˈsesəri] n 1. mulḥaq
ملحق (-āt) 2. (leg.) musāʿid (ʿalā
jarīma) مساعد (على جريمة) (-ūn)

accident [ˈaksidənt] n ḥādith حادث
(ḥawādith حوادث)

accidentally [aksiˈdentli] adv
muṣādafatan مصادفةً; min ghayr
qaṣd من غير قصد

accommodation [əkoməˈdeishən]
n sakan سكن

accompany [əˈkʌmpəni] v rāfaqa
رافق

accomplish [əˈkʌmplish] v anjaza
أنجز

accomplishment [əˈkʌmplish-
mənt] n injāz إنجاز (-āt)

according to [əˈkoːding təu] prep
wafqan li وفقاً ل

account [əˈkaunt] n 1. riwāya رواية
(-āt) 2. (fin.) ḥisāb حساب (-āt) 3. **on
account of** bi sababi بسبب

accountant [ə'kauntənt] *n* muḥāsib محاسب (-ūn)

accumulate [ə'kyu:muleit] *v* 1. kaddasa كدّس; rakama ركم (u; rakm ركم) 2. tarākama تراكم

accurate ['akyərət] *adv* 1. maḍbūṭ مضبوط 2. daqīq دقيق

accusation [akyu:'zeishən] *n* ittihām إتّهام; tuhma تهمة

accuse [ə'kyu:z] *v* ittahama bi اتّهم ب

accused [ə'kyu:zd] *n/adj* muttaham متّهم

accustom [ə'kʌstəm] *v* ʿawwada عوّد

ache [eik] 1. *n* alam ألم (ālām آلام); wajaʿ وجع (awjāʿ أوجاع) 2. *v* ālama ألم; wajiʿa وجع (yawjaʿu يوجع; wajaʿ وجع)

achieve [ə'chi:v] *v* anjaza أنجز

achievement [ə'chi:vmənt] *n* injāz إنجاز (-āt)

acid ['asid] 1. *adj* ḥāmiḍ حامض 2. *n* ḥamḍ حمض (aḥmāḍ أحماض)

acknowledge [ə'knolij] *v* iʿtarafa bi اعترف ب

acknowledgement [ə'knolijmənt] *n* iʿtirāf إعتراف

acquaintance [ə'kweintəns] *n* maʿrifa معرفة (maʿārif معارف)

acquire [ə'kwaiə] *v* iktasaba اكتسب

acquisition [akwi'zishən] *n* iktisāb اكتساب

acquit from [ə'kwit] *v* barra'a min برّأ من

acre ['eikə] *n* akr أكر

across [ə'kros] 1. *prep* ʿabr عبر 2. *adv* min jānib ilā ākhar من جانب إلى آخر

act [akt] 1. *n* ʿamal عمل (aʿmāl أعمال); 2. faṣl فصل (fuṣūl فصول) 3. (pol.) marsūm مرسوم (marāsīm مراسيم) 4. *v* taẓāhara bi تظاهر ب 5. maththala مثّل

action ['akshən] *n* 1. ʿamal عمل (aʿmāl أعمال); fiʿl فعل (afʿāl أفعال) 2. (leg.) daʿwā دعوى (daʿāwā دعاوى) 3. (mil.) maʿraka معركة (maʿārik معارك)

active ['aktiv] *adj* 1. faʿʿāl فعّال 2. nāshiṭ ناشط

activity [ak'tivəti] *n* nashāṭ نشاط

actor ['aktə] *n* mumaththil ممثّل (-ūn)

actress ['aktris] *n* mumaththila ممثّلة (-āt)

actual ['akchuəl] *adj* wāqiʿī واقعي

actually ['akchuli] *adv/conj* fi 'l-wāqiʿ في الواقع

acute [ə'kyu:t] *adj* 1. shadīd شديد 2. ḥādd حاد

adapt [ə'dapt] *v* 1. kayyafa كيّف 2. takayyafa تكيّف

adaptor [ə'daptə] *n* **electric adaptor** taqsīm kahrabā' تقسيم كهرباء

add [ad] *v* 1. aḍāfa أضاف 2. ḍamma ضمّ

addict ['adikt] *n* mudmin مدمن (-ūn)

addiction [ə'dikshən] *n* idmān إدمان

addition [ə'dishən] *n* iḍāfa إضافة

additional [ə'dishənəl] *adj* iḍāfī إضافي

address [ə'dres] 1. *n* ʿunwān عنوان (ʿanāwīn عناوين) 2. *v* khāṭaba خاطب

adequate ['adikwət] *adj* kāfin كاف

adhere to [ə'dhiə] *v* 1. iltaṣaqa bi التصق ب 2. taqayyada bi تقيّد ب

adjective ['ajiktiv] *n* ṣifa صفة (-āt)

adjust [ə'jʌst] v ʿaddala عدّل; ḍabbaṭa ضبط

administer [əd'ministə] v adāra أدار

administration [ədminis'treishən] n idāra إدارة (-āt)

administrator [əd'ministreitə] n mudīr مدير (mudarāʾ مدراء)

admiration [admi'reishən] n iʿjāb إعجاب

admire [əd'maiə] v uʿjiba bi أعجب ب (yuʿjabu bi يعجب ب)

admission [əd'mishən] n 1. dukhūl دخول 2. iʿtirāf إعتراف

admit [əd'mit] v 1. iʿtarafa اعترف 2. samuḥa سمح (u; samḥ سمح)

adolescent [adə'lesənt] n murāhiq مراهق (-ūn)

adopt [ə'dopt] v 1. ittakhadha اتخذ 2. **to adopt (a child)** tabannā تبنّى

adoption [ə'dopshən] n 1. ittikhadh إتّخاذ 2. **adoption (of a child)** tabannin تبنّ

adoration [adə'reishən] n ʿibāda عبادة

adore [ə'do:] v ʿabada عبد (u; ʿibāda عبادة)

adult ['adʌlt; ə'dʌlt] n/adj bāligh بالغ سن الرشد; sinn ar-rushd (-ūn)

adultery [ə'dʌltəri] n zinā زنا

advance [ə'dva:ns] 1. n taqaddum تقدّم 2. (fin.) sulfa سلفة 3. **in advance** muqaddaman مقدّماً 4. v taqaddama تقدّم 5. (fin.) sallafa سلّف

advantage [əd'va:ntij] n maṣlaḥa مصلحة (maṣāliḥ مصالح)

adventure [əd'venchə] n mughāmara مغامرة (-āt)

adverb ['advə:b] n ḥāl حال; ẓarf ظرف

advert ['advə:t] n iʿlān إعلان (-āt)

advertise ['advətaiz] v aʿlana أعلن

advertisement ['advə:tismənt] n iʿlān إعلان (-āt)

advice [ə'dvais] n naṣīḥa نصيحة (naṣāʾiḥ نصائح)

advisable [əd'vaizəbəl] adj mustaḥsan مستحسن

advise [ə'dvaiz] v naṣaḥa نصح (a; naṣḥ نصح)

adviser; advisor [ə'dvaizə] n mushīr مشير

advocate ['advəkeit] 1. n see **lawyer** 2. v dāfaʿa ʿan دافع عن

aerial ['eəriəl] 1. adj jawwī جوي 2. n silk hawāʾī سلك هوائي

aeroplane ['eərəplein] n ṭāʾira طائرة (-āt)

affair [ə'feə] n masʾala مسألة\مسئلة (masāʾil مسائل)

affect [ə'fekt] v aththara fī أثر في

affection [ə'fekshən] n ḥubb حب; ḥanān حنان

afford [ə'fo:d] v qadira ʿalā قدر على (a; qadar قدر)

afraid [ə'freid] adj 1. khāʾif خائف 2. **I'm afraid that...** Ana mutaʾassif an... أنا متأسف أن...

Africa ['afrikə] n afrīqā أفريقا; afrīqīyā أفريقيا; ifrīqīyā أفريقيا

African ['afrikən] n/adj afrīqī أفريقي

after ['a:ftə] 1. prep baʿd بعد 2. fī ithr في إثر 3. adv fī mā baʿd ما بعد 4. **after that** baʿd dhālik بعد ذلك

afternoon [a:ftə'nu:n] n aṣīl أصيل; baʿd aẓ-ẓuhr بعد الظهر

afterwards ['a:ftəwədz] adv fī mā baʿd في ما بعد; baʿd dhālik بعد ذلك

again [ə'gen] adv thāniyatan ثانية; min jadīd من جديد

against [ə'genst] *prep* 1. ḍidd ضد 2.
ʿalā على

age [eij] *n* 1. ʿumr عمر 2. ʿaṣr عصر
(aʿṣār أعصار)

agency ['eijənsi] *n* wakāla وكالة (-āt)

agenda [ə'jendə] *n* barnāmij برنامج

agent ['eijənt] *n* wakīl وكيل
(wukalā' وكلاء)

aggravate ['agrəveit] *v* 1. fāqama
فاقم 2. azʿaja أزعج

aggravation [agrə'veishən] *n*
mufāqama مفاقمة

aggression [ə'greshən] *n* ʿudwān
عدوان

aggressive [ə'gresiv] *adj* ʿudwānī
عدواني

agility [ə'jiləti] *n* rashāqa رشاقة

agitate [ajiteit] *v* 1. athāra أثار 2.
hayyaja هيج; ahāja أهاج

ago [əgəu] *adv* 1. mundhu منذ; min من
2. **a year ago** mundhu ʿām منذ عام
3. **long ago** min zamān من زمان

agree [ə'gri:] *v* wāfaqa وافق; ittafaqa
اتفق

agreement [ə'gri:mənt] *n*
muwāfaqa موافقة; ittifāq إتفاق

agriculture ['agrikʌlchə] *n* zirāʿa
زراعة

ahead [əhed] *adv* ilā 'l-amām
إلى الأمام

aid [eid] 1. *n* musāʿada مساعدة;
maʿūna معونة 2. *v* sāʿada ساعد;
ʿāwana عاون

aide [eid] *n* musāʿid مساعد (-ūn)

AIDS [eidz] *n* aʿrāḍ naqsi
'l-manāʿati 'l-muktasaba
أعراض نقص المناعة المكتسبة

aim [eim] 1. *n* hadaf هدف (ahdāf
أهداف); gharaḍ غرض (aghrāḍ
أغراض) 2. *v* ṣawwaba صوب;

haddafa هدف

air [eə] *n* 1. hawā' هواء; jaww جو
2. **to go on the air** baththa بث (u;
bathth بث)

airconditioner [eəkondishənə] *n*
takyīf hawā'ī تكييف هوائي

airconditioning [eəkon'dishəl
ning] *n* takyīf al-hawā' تكييف الهواء

aircraft [eəkra:ft] *n* (*pl* **aircraft**)
ṭā'ira طائرة (-āt)

airforce [eəfo:s] *n* silāḥ aṭ-ṭayarān
سلاح الطيران

airline; airways [eəlain; eəweiz] *n*
khuṭūṭ aṭ-ṭayarān خطوط الطيران;
khuṭūṭ jawwīya خطوط جوية

airliner [eəlainə] *n* ṭā'ira طائرة (-āt)

airmail ['eəmeil] *n* 1. barīd jawwī
بريد جوي 2. **by airmail** bi 'l-barīd
al-jawwī بالبريد الجوي

airplane ['eəplein] *n* ṭā'ira طائرة (-āt)

airport ['eəpo:t] *n* maṭār مطار (-āt)

air-raid *n* ghāra jawwīya غارة جوية

airways [eəwei] *see* **airline**

alarm [ə'la:m] 1. *n* indhār bi khaṭar
إنذار بخطر 2. dhuʿr ذعر; ruʿb رعب 3.
v arʿaba أرعب; adhʿara أذعر

alarm clock *n* munabbiha منبهة

alarming [əla:ming] *adj* mudhʿir
مذعر

Albania [alkəhol] *n* albāniyā ألبانيا

Albanian [alkəhol] *n/adj* albānī
ألباني (-ūn; al-albān الألبان)

alcohol [alkəhol] *n* kuḥūl كحول

alcohol-free *adj* bi dūn kuḥūl
بدون كحول

alcoholic [alkə'holik] 1. *adj* kuḥūlī
كحولي 2. *n* mudmin bi 'l-kuḥūl
مدمن بالكحول

alcoholism [alkəholizm] *n* al-idmān bi 'l-kuḥūl الإدمان بالكحول

ale [eil] *n* bīra بيرة

alert [ə'lə:t] *adj* yaqiẓ يقظ

alias ['eilyəs] *n* ism mustaʿār
اسم مستعار

alien ['eilyən] *adj/n* 1. ajnabī أجنبي;
gharīb غريب 2. **illegal alien** muqīm
ghayr sharʿī مقيم غير شرعي

align [ə'lain] *v* ṣaffafa صفف

alike [ə'laik] *adj* mutashābih متشابه

alive [əlaiv] *adj* ḥayy حي

all [o:l] *adj/adv* kull كل

allegation [ali'geishən] *n* iddiʿā'
إدّعاء

allege [ə'lej] *v* iddaʿā ادّعى; zaʿama
زعم (u; zaʿm زعم)

allergic [a'ləjik] *adj* ḥassāsī حساسي

allergy ['aləji] *n* ḥassāsīya حساسية

alley [ali] *n* zuqāq زقاق (aziqqa أزقة)

alliance [ə'laiəns] *n* ḥilf حلف (aḥlāf
أحلاف)

allow [əlau] *v* 1. samuḥa سمح (u;
samḥ سمح) 2. yadʿu... يدع...

allowance [ə'lauəns] *n* ʿilāwa علاوة
(-āt)

alloy [a'loi] *n* khalīṭ min maʿdanayn
خليط من معدنين

all right [o:l'rait] ḥasanan حسناً

ally ['alai] *n* ḥalīf حليف (ḥulafā' حلفاء)

almond ['o:lmənd] *n* lawz *collective* لوز

almost [o:lməust] *adv* taqrīban تقريباً

alone [ə'ləun] *adj/adv* waḥīd وحيد

along [əlong] 1. *prep* ʿalā ṭūl على طول;
ṭiwāl طوال 2. *adv* **all along** al-waqt
kulluh الوقت كله

alongside [əlongsaid] *prep/adv* ʿalā
ṭūl على طول; ṭiwāl طوال

aloud [əlaud] *adv* bi sawt ʿāl
بصوت عال

alphabet [alfəbet] *n* alifbā' ألفبا ء

already [o:lredi] *adv* 1. qabl al-ān
قبل الآن 2. fī dhālik al-ḥīn
في ذلك الحين

alright [o:lrait] 1. bikhayr بخير 2.
ṭayyib طيب

also ['o:lsəu] ayḍan أيضاً

alter [o:ltə] *v* 1. ghayyara غير 2.
taghayyara تغير

alteration [oltə'reishən] *n* 1.
taghyīr تغيير 2. taghayyur تغير

alternate ['o:ltəneit] *v* mutanāwib
متناوب

alternative [ol'tə:nətiv] *adj/n* badīl
بديل (budalā' بدلا ء)

although [o:ldhəu] *conj* bi raghm
anna أن; برغم; maʿ anna أن; مع; ʿalā
anna أن على

altitude [altichu:d] *n* irtifāʿ إرتفاع

altogether [o:ltə'gedhə] *adv*
jumlatan جملةً; bi 'l-ijmāl بالإجمال

aluminium, *(US)* **aluminum**
[alyu'minyəm; a'lu:minəm] *n*
alūminiyōm ألومنيوم

always ['o:lweiz] *adv* dā'iman دائماً;
abadan أبداً

am [am] *see* be

a.m. *adv* qabl aẓ-ẓuhr قبل الظهر

amateur [amətyə:] 1. *adj/n* hāwin lā
muḥtarif هاو لا محترف 2. *n* hāwin
ghayr muḥtarif هاو غير محترف
(huwāh هواة)

amaze [əmeiz] *v* adhhala أذهل;
adhasha أدهش

amazement [əmeizmənt] *n* idhhāl
إذهال

amazing [ə'meizing] *adj* mudhish
مدهش

ambassador [am'basədə] *n* safir
سفير (sufarā' سفراء)

ambiguous [ambigyuəs] *adj* ghāmiḍ غامض; multabis ملتبس

ambition [ambishən] *n* ṭamaʿ طمع (aṭmāʿ أطماع)

ambitious [ambishəsh] *adj* ṭamūḥ طموح

ambulance ['ambyuləns] *n* sayyārat isʿāf سيارة أسعاف

America [əmerikə] *n* amrīkā أمريكا

American [ə'merikən] *adj/n* amrīkī أمريكي

amid; amidst [ə'mid; -st] *prep* wasaṭ وسط; bayn بين

ammunition [amyu'nishən] *n* dhakhīra ذخيرة (dhakhā'ir ذخائر)

amnesty [amnəsti] *n* ʿafw عفو

among; amongst [ə'mʌng; ə'mʌngst] *prep* wasaṭ وسط; bayn بين

amount [ə'maunt] *n* kammīya كمية

amplifier ['amplifaiyə] *n* makabbir مكبر

amputate ['ampyuteit] *v* (*med.*) batara بتر (u; batr بتر)

amuse [ə'myu:z] *v* alhā ألهى; sallā سلى

an [an] *see* **a**

anaemia [ə'ni:miə] *n* faqr ad-dam فقر الدم

anaesthetist [ani:s'thetist] *n* bannaja بنج

analyse ['anəlaiz] *v* ḥallala حلل

analysis [ə'naləsis] *n* taḥlīl تحليل

analyst ['anəlist] *n* muḥallil محلل

ancestor ['ansestə] *n* salaf سلف (aslāf أسلاف); jadd جد (ajdād أجداد)

anchor ['angkə] *n* mirsāh مرساة (marāsin مراس)

ancient ['einshənt] *adj* qadīm قديم; ʿatīq عتيق

and [ən; and] *conj* wa و; fa ف

anemia [ə'ni:miə] *see* **anaemia**

anesthetist *see* **anaesthetist**

angel [einjl] *n* malak ملك (malā'ika ملائكة)

anger ['anggə] **1.** *n* ghaḍab غضب **2.** *v* aghḍaba أغضب

angle ['anggəl] *n* zāwiya زاوية (zawāyā زوايا)

angry ['anggri] *adj* zaʿlān زعلان; ghaḍbān غضبان

animal ['animəl] *n* ḥayawān حيوان (-āt)

animate ['animeit] *adj* ḥayy حي

ankle ['angkəl] *n* kāḥil كاحل (kawāḥil كواحل)

annihilate [ə'naiəleit] *v* abāda أباد

anniversary [ani'və:səri] *n* dhikrā ذكرى

announce [ə'nauns] *v* aʿlana أعلن

announcement [ə'naunsmənt] *n* i'lān إعلان

announcer [ə'naunsə] *n* mudhī' مذيع

annoy [ə'noi] *v* azʿaja أزعج; ḍāyaqa ضايق

annoying [ə'noying] *adj* muz'ij مزعج

annual ['anyuəl] *adj* sanawī سنوي

anonymous [ə'noniməs] *adj* majhūl مجهول

another [ə'nʌdhə] *adj* ākhar m آخر; ukhrā f أخرى

answer ['a:nsə] **1.** *n* jawāb جواب (ajwiba أجوبة) **2.** *v* ajāba أجاب

ant [ant] *n* namla نملة; naml *collective* نمل

antenna [an'tenə] *n* hawā'ī هوائي

anthem ['anthəm] *n* nashīd/unshūda نشيد\أنشودة (nashā'id نشائد)

anthology [an'tholoji] n majmūᶜa min al-muqtaṭafāt al-adabīya مجموعة من المقتطفات الأدبية

anthropology [anthro'poloji] n ᶜilm al-insān علم الإنسان

anti- ['anti] muḍādd مضاد

antibiotics [antibai'otiks] pl muḍādd ḥayawī مضاد حيوي

anticipate [an'tisipeit] v tawaqqaᶜa توقع

anticipation [antisi'peishən] n tawaqquᶜ توقع

antidote ['antidəut] n tiryāz ترياز

antique [an'ti:k] 1. adj qadīm قديم; atharī أثري 2. n athar أثر (āthār آثار)

antiseptic [anti'septik] adj/n muṭahhir مطهر

anxiety [ang'zaiəti] n qalaq قلق (aqlāq أقلاق)

anxious ['angkshəs] adj qaliq قلق

any ['eni] adj ayy أي

anybody ['enibodi] ayy shakhṣ أي شخص

anyday [eni'dei] adv ayy yawm أي يوم

anyhow ['enihau] adv ᶜalā kull ḥāl على كل حال

anymore ['enimoə] adv baᶜd al-'ān بعد الآن

anyone ['eniwʌn] see anybody

anything ['enithing] ayy shay' أي شيء

anytime ['enitaim] ayy waqt أي وقت

anyway ['eniwei] adv ᶜalā kull ḥāl على كل حال

anywhere ['eniweə] ayy makān أي مكان

apart [ə'pa:t] adv jāniban جانباً; munfaridan منفرداً

apart from prep bi ṣarf an-naẓar ᶜan بصرف النظر عن

apartment [ə'pa:tmənt] n shaqqa شقة (shiqaq شقق)

apathy ['apəthi] n lā mubālāh لا مبالاة

ape [eip] n qird قرد (qirada قردة; qurūd قرود)

apologize [ə'poləjaiz] v iᶜtadhara اعتذر

apology [ə'polaji] n iᶜtidhār إعتذار

appalling [ə'po:ling] adj murᶜib مرعب; murawwiᶜ مروع

apparatus [apə'reitəs] n ᶜudda عدة (ᶜudad عدد); jihāz (ajhiza أجهزة)

apparent [ə'parənt] adj 1. wāḍiḥ واضح 2. ẓāhirī ظاهري

apparently [ə'parəntli] adv fī mā yabdū فيما يبدو

appeal [ə'pi:l] v 1. nāshada ناشد 2. (leg.) ista'nafa استأنف; ṭaᶜana طعن (u/a; ṭaᶜn طعن)

appealing [ə'pi:ling] adj mughrin مغر

appear [ə'piə] v 1. ẓahara ظهر (a; ẓuhūr ظهور) 2. mathala مثل (u; muthūl مثول) 3. badā بدا (u)

appearance [ə'piərəns] n 1. ẓuhūr ظهور 2. muthūl مثول 3. maẓhar مظهر

append [ə'pend] v alḥaqa ألحق

appetite ['apitait] n 1. shahīya شهية 2. shahwa شهوة (shahawāt شهوات)

applause [ə'plo:z] n taṣfīq تصفيق

apple ['apəl] n tuffāḥa تفاحة (collective tuffāḥ تفاح)

application [apli'keishən] n 1. istiᶜmāl إستعمال 2. ṭalab طلب 3. (comp.) barnāmij برنامج (barāmij برامج)

apply [ə'plai] v 1. waḍaʿa ʿalā وضع على (وضع ;yaḍaʿu يضع; waḍʿ) 2. qaddama ṭalaban قدم طلباً

appoint [əpoint] v ʿayyana عيّن

appointment [ə'pointmənt] n 1. mawʿid موعد (mawāʿid مواعيد) 2. tawḍīf توضيف; taʿyīn تعيين

appreciate [əpri:shieit] v qaddara قدّر

approach [əprəuch] v qarraba قرّب; iqtaraba min اقترب من

approval [ə'pru:vəl] n muwāfaqa موافقة

approve [ə'pru:v] v 1. wāfaqa ʿalā وافق على; 2. ṣaddaqa ʿalā صدق على

approximate [əproksimət] adj taqrībī تقريبي

approximately [əproksimətli] adv taqrīban تقريباً

apricot(s) [eiprikot] n mishmish مشمش collective

April [eiprəl] n abrīl أبريل; nīsān نيسان

aquatic [əkwatik] adj māʾī مائي

Arab ['arəb] n/adj ʿarabī عربي

Arabic ['arəbik] n/adj ʿarabī عربي

arch [a:ch] n qanṭara قنطرة (qanāṭir قناطر); qaws قوس (aqwās أقواس)

archbishop [a:ch'bishop] n raʾīs al-asāqifa رئيس الأساقفة

archeology [a:ki'oləji] n ʿilm al-āthār علم الآثار

architect ['a:kitekt] n miʿmār معمار (-ūn)

architecture ['a:kitekchə] n fann al-ʿimāra فن العمارة

archives ['a:kaivz] pl arshīf أرشيف (-āt)

are [a:] see be

area ['eəriə] n 1. masāḥa مساحة 2. minṭaqa منطقة 3. majāl مجال

area code n miftāḥ al-madīna مفتاح المدينة

arena [ə'ri:nə] n maydān ميدان (mayādīn ميادين)

argue ['a:gyu:] v jādala جادل

argument ['a:gyumənt] n 1. mujādala مجادلة 2. ḥujja حجة (ḥujaj حجج)

arise [əraiz] v (arose, arisen) 1. nahaḍa نهض (a; nuhūḍ نهوض) 2. irtafaʿa ارتفع

arithmetic [ə'rithmətik] n ʿilm al-ḥisāb علم الحساب

ark [a:k] n safīnat nūḥ سفينة نوح

arm [a:m] 1. n dhirāʿ ذراع m/f (adhruʿ أذرع; dhurʿān ذرعان) 2. v sallaḥa سلح 3. see arms

armchair ['a:mcheə] n fōtēh فوتيه (-āt)

armed [a:md] adj musallaḥ مسلح

armed forces pl qūwāt musallaḥa قوات مسلحة

arms [a:mz] pl asliḥa أسلحة

army ['a:mi] n jaysh جيش (juyūsh جيوس)

aromatic [arəu'matik] adj ʿaṭir عطر; ʿiṭrī عطري

around [ə'raund] adv/prep 1. ḥawl حول 2. fī makān qarīb في مكان قريب

arouse [ə'rauz] v 1. awqaẓa أوقظ 2. athāra أثار

arrange [ə'reinj] v rattaba رتب; naẓẓama نظم

arrangement [ə'reinjmənt] n tartīb ترتيب

arrest [ərest] 1. n iʿtiqāl إعتقال 2. v iʿtaqala إعتقل

arrival [ə'raivəl] n wuṣūl وصول

arrive [ə'raiv] v waṣala وصل (yaṣilu يصل; wuṣūl وصول)

arrogance ['arəgəns] n takabbur تكبر; ghaṭrasa غطرسة

arrogant ['arəgənt] adj mutakabbir متكبر; mutaghaṭris متغطرس

arrow ['arəu] n sahm سهم (sihām سهام; ashum أسهم)

art [a:t] n fann فن (funūn فنون)

artery ['a:tiəri] n shiryān شريان (sharāyīn شرايين)

art gallery n maʿraḍ funūn معرض فنون

arthritis [a:th'raitəs] n iltihāb al-mafāṣil التهاب المفاصل

article ['a:tikəl] n 1. adāh أداة (adawāt أدوات) 2. shay' شيء (ashyā' أشياء) 3. (leg.) band بند (bunūd بنود) 4. newspaper article maqāla مقالة (-āt)

artificial [a:ti'fishəl] adj iṣṭināʿī إصطناعي

artillery [a:'tiləri] n madfaʿīya مدفعية

artist ['a:tist] n fannān فنان (-ūn)

artistic [a:'tistik] adj fannī فني

as [əz; az] 1. ka كـ 2. ʿindamā عندما 3. lammā kān لما كان 4. mithl مثل 5. kamā كما 6. ka'anna كأن 7. as well ayḍan أيضاً

ashamed [ə'sheimd] adj khajil خجل; khajlān خجلان

ashtray ['ashtrei] n minfaḍat sajāyir منفضة سجاير

Asia ['eizhə] n āsiyā آسيا

Asian ['eizhən] adj/n āsiyawī آسيوي

aside [ə'said] adv jāniban جانباً

aside from prep bi jānib بجانب

ask [a:sk] v 1. sa'ala سأل (a; su'āl سؤال) 2. daʿā دعا (u; duʿā' دعاء)

ask for v ṭalaba طلب (u; ṭalab طلب)

asleep [ə'sli:p] adj nā'im نائم

aspect ['aspekt] n wajh وجه (wujūh وجوه)

aspirin ['asprin] n asparīn أسبرين

assassin [ə'sasin] n qātil قاتل (-ūn; qatala قتلة)

assassination [əsasi'neishən] n ightiyāl إغتيال (-āt)

assault [ə'so:lt] 1. n hujūm هجوم; iʿtidā' إعتداء 2. v hājama هاجم; iʿtadā ʿalā اعتدى على

assemble [ə'sembəl] v 1. ijtamaʿa اجتمع 2. rakkaba ركب

assert [ə'sə:t] v akkada أكد

assess [ə'ses] v qayyama قيم

assignment [ə'sainmənt] n muhimma مهمة (-āt)

assist [ə'sist] v sāʿada ساعد

assistance [ə'sistəns] n musāʿada مساعدة

assistant [ə'sistənt] n musāʿid مساعد (-ūn)

associate [ə'səushieit] v zāmala زامل

association [əsəusi'eishən] n jamʿīya جمعية (-āt)

assume [ə'syu:m] v iftaraḍa افترض

assure [ə'sho:] v akkada أكد

asthma ['asmə] n rabw ربو

astonish [ə'stonish] v adhasha أدهش; adhhala أذهل

astray [ə'strei] adv ḍāll ضال

astronaut ['astrəno:t] n faḍā'ī فضائي (-ūn)

as well as bi 'l-iḍāfati ilā بالإضافة إلى

asylum [ə'sailəm] n 1. mustashfā 'l-majādhīb مستشفى المجاذيب 2. (pol.) lujū' لجوء

at [ət; at] *prep* 1. at home fi 'l-bayt في البيت 2. at Fred's ʿind Fred عند فريد 3. at three o'clock as-sāʿat ath-thālitha الساعة الثالثة

ate [eit] *see* eat

athlete ['athliːt] *n* riyāḍī رياضي (-ūn)

athletic ['athletik] *adj* riyāḍī رياضي

athletics [ath'letiks] *pl* alʿāb riyāḍīya ألعاب رياضية

atlas ['atləs] *n* aṭlas أطلس

at last *adv* akhīran أخيراً

at least *adv* ʿalā 'l-aqall على الأقل

atmosphere ['atməsfiə] *n* jaww جو

at once *adv* ḥālan حالاً; fawran فوراً

attach [ə'tach] *v* taʿallaqa bi تعلق

attack [ə'tak] 1. *n* muhājama مهاجمة 2. heart attack nawbat ul-qalb نوبة القلب 3. *v* hājama هاجم

attacker [ə'takə] *n* muhājim مهاجم (-ūn)

attain [ə'tein] *v* aḥraza أحرز

attempt [ə'tempt] 1. *n* muḥāwala محاولة 2. *v* ḥāwala حاول

attend [ə'tend] *v* ḥaḍara حضر (u; ḥuḍūr حضور)

attendance [ə'tendəns] *n* ḥuḍūr حضور

attention [ə'tenshən] *n* 1. intibāh إنتباه 2. ʿināya عناية; ihtimām إهتمام

attic [atik] *n* ʿullīya علية; ʿullīyat al-bayt علية البيت

attitude ['atichuːd] *n* mawqif موقف (mawāqif مواقف)

attorney [ə'təːni] *n* muḥāmin محام (muḥāmūn محامون)

attract [ə'trakt] *v* jadhdhaba جذب; alfata ألفت

attraction [ə'trakchən] *n* jadhb جذب; fitna فتنة

attractive [ə'traktiv] *adj* jadhdhāb جذاب; fātin فاتن

auction ['oːkshən] *n* mazād ʿalanī مزاد علني

aubergine(s) ['əubəzhiːn] *n* bādhinjān باذنجان *collective*

audience [oːdiəns] *n* 1. jumhūr جمهور 2. muqābila rasmīya مقابلة رسمية

August ['oːgəst] *n* aghusṭus أغسطس; āb آب

aunt [aːnt· ant] *n* ʿamma عمة; khāla خالة

Australia [os'treilyə] *n* usturāliyā أستراليا

Australian [os'treilyən] *adj/n* usturālī أسترالي (-ūn)

Austria [ostriyə] *n* an-nimsā النمسا

Austrian ['ostriyən] *adj/n* nimsāwī نمساوي (-ūn)

authentic [oː'thentik] *adj* ḥaqīqī حقيقي; mawthūq موثوق

author [oːthə] *n* muʾallif مؤلف (-ūn)

authorities [oːthorətiːz] *pl* sulaṭāt سلطات

authority [oːthorəti] *n* 1. sulṭa سلطة 2. marjaʿ مرجع

authorize [oːthəraiz] *v* fawwaḍa فوض

autobiography [oːtəbai'ogrəfi] *n* sīra dhātīya سيرة ذاتية

automatic [oːtə'matik] *adj* otomatikī أوتوماتيكي

automobile ['oːtəməbiːl] *n* sayyāra سيارة (-āt)

autonomy [oː'tonəmi] *n* al-ḥukm adh-dhātī الحكم الذاتي

autumn ['oːtəm] *n* al-kharīf الخريف

availability [əveilə'biliti] *n* tayassur تيسّر

available [ə'veiləbəl] *adj* mutayassir متيسّر

avenue ['avənyu:] *n* jādda جادة (-āt)

average ['avrij] *adj* 1. mu'addal معدل 2. **on average** bi mu'addal بمعدل

aviation [eivi'eishən] *n* ṭayarān طيران

avoid [ə'void] *v* tajannaba تجنب

await [ə'weit] *v* intaṭara انتظر

awake [ə'weik] *adj* **to be awake** yaqiẓ يقظ; yaqẓān يقظان

award [ə'wo:d] *n* manaḥa منح (a;

aware [ə'weə] *adj* wā'in واعٍ منح)

away [ə'wei] *adv/adj* 1. ghā'ib غائب 2. **Go away!** idhhab 'annī! اذهب عني! 3. **far away** ba'īd بعيد

awe [o:] *n* raw' روع; khashya خشية

awful ['o:fəl] *adj* 1. mur'ib مرعب 2. shanī' شنيع 3. *see* **awfully**

awfully ['o:fli] *adv* jiddan جداً

awkward ['o:kwəd] *adj* 1. akhraq حرج 2. murbik مربك; ḥarij أخرق

axe [aks] *n* fa's فأس; fu'ūs فؤوس

B

baby ['beibi] *n* ṭifl طفل (aṭfāl أطفال)

bachelor ['bachələ] *n* a'zab أعزب

back [bak] 1. *n* ẓahar ظهر 2. *v* sānada ساند; ayyada أيد 3. **to come back** raja'a رجع (i; rujū' رجوع) 3. **He gave me the book back.** raddanī al-kitāb. ردني الكتاب.

backache *n* alam ẓahar ألم ظهر

background *n* khalfiya خلفية

backing ['baking] *n* musānada مساندة

backside ['baksaid] *n* ist است

back up *v* 1. sānada ساند; ayyada أيد 2. *(comp.)* ḥafiẓa حفظ (a; ḥifẓ حفظ)

backward ['bakwəd] *adj* mutakhallif متخلف

backwards ['bakwədz] *adv* ilā 'l-warā' إلى الوراء

backyard [bak'ya:d] *n* (US) ḥadīqa حديقة (ḥadā'iq حدائق)

bacon ['beikən] *n* sharā'iḥ laḥm al-khinzīr شرائح لحم الخنزير

bacteria [bak'tiəriə] *pl* baktīrīya بكتيريا; jarāthīm جراثيم

bacterial [bak'tiəriəl] *adj* baktīrī بكتيري

bad [bad] *adj* sayyi' سيء; radī' ردي،

badly ['badli] *adv* 'alā naḥw radī' على نحو ردي،

bag [bag] *n* ḥaqība حقيبة (ḥaqā'ib حقائب); shanṭa شنطة (shanaṭ شنط)

baggage ['bagij] *n* ḥaqā'ib *[pl]* حقائب

bait [beit] *n* ṭuʿam طعم

bake [beik] *v* khabaza خبز (i; khabz خبز)

baker ['beikə] *n* khabbāz خباز (-ūn)

bakery ['beikəri] *n* makhbaz مخبز; furn فرن (afrān أفران)

balance ['baləns] **1.** *n* tawāzun توازن; ittizān إتزان **2.** mīzān ميزان **3.** (fin.) raṣīd رصيد **4.** *v* wazana وزن (yazinu يزن; wazn وزن)

balcony ['balkəni] *n* bālkōn بالكون (-āt)

bald [bold] *adj* aṣlaʿ أصلع

ball [bol] *n* kura كرة (-āt)

ballet ['balei] *n* bālēh باليه

balloon [bə'lu:n] *n* bālūn بالون

ballot ['balət] *n* iqtirāʿ إقتراع; taṣwīt تصويت

ballpoint ['bo:lpoint] *n* qalam قلم (aqlām أقلام)

ban [ban] **1.** *n* taḥrīm تحريم; manʿ منع **2.** *v* ḥarrama حرم; manaʿa منع

banana(s) [bə'na:nə] *n* mawz موز *collective*

band [band] *n* **1.** sharīṭ شريط (ashriṭa أشرطة) **2.** ʿiṣāba عصابة (-āt) **3.** (mus.) firqa فرقة (firaq فرق)

bandage ['bandij] *n* lifāfa ṭibbīya لفافة طبية (-āt)

bandaid ['bandeid] *n* lazqa لزقة; laṣūq لصوق

bandit ['bandit] *n* qāṭiʿ ṭarīq قاطع طريق

bang [bang] **1.** *n* ḍarba ضربة **2.** *v* ḍaraba ضرب (i; ḍarb ضرب)

banish ['banish] *v* anfā أنفى

bank [bangk] *n* **1.** bank بنك (bunūk بنوك) **2.** river bank ḍaffa ضفة (ḍifāf ضفاف) **3.** World Bank al-bank ad-dawalī البنك الدولي

banker ['bankə] *n* maṣrifī مصرفي (-yūn); ṣarrāf صراف (-ūn)

banknote, (US) **bankbill** ['bang-knəut; -bil] *n* waraqa maṣrifīya ورقة مصرفية

bankrupt ['bangkrʌpt] *adj* muflis مفلس

bar [ba:] *n* **1.** bār بار (-āt); mashrab مشرب; ḥāna حانة (mashārib مشارب); (-āt) **2.** qaḍīb قضيب (quḍbān قضبان) **3.** **a bar of chocolate** qiṭʿat shukūlāta قطعة شكولاته

barbecue ['ba:bikyu:] *n* mishwāh مشواة

barbed wire [ba:bd'waiə] *n* aslāk shā'ika أسلاك شائكة

barber ['ba:bə] *n* ḥallāq حلاق (-ūn)

bare [beə] **1.** *adj* ʿārin عار; khālin خال **2.** *v* jarrada جرد; ʿarrā عرى

barely ['beəli] *adv* bi 'l-kād بالكاد

bargain ['ba:gin] **1.** *n* ṣafqa rābiḥa صفقة رابحة **2.** *v* fāṣala فاصل

bark [ba:k] **1.** *n* nubāḥ نباح **2.** **tree bark** qishr قشر **3.** *v* nabaḥa نبح (a; nabḥ نبح; nubāḥ نباح)

barn [ba:n] *n* makhzan qashsh مخزن قش

barrel ['barəl] *n* **1.** barmīl برميل (barāmīl براميل) **2.** māsūra ماسورة (-āt)

barren ['barən] *adj* **1.** ʿāqir عاقر **2.** qāḥil قاحل

barrier ['bariə] *n* ḥājiz حاجز (ḥawājiz حواجز)

barrister ['baristə] *n* muḥāmin محام (muḥāmūn محامون)

bartender ['ba:təndə] *n* ʿāmil fī ḥāna عامل في حانة

base [beis] **1.** *n* asās أساس **2.** (mil.) qāʿida قاعدة (qawā'id قواعد) **3.** *v* assasa أسس

basement ['beismənt] *n* qabw قبو (aqbiya أقبية)

basic ['beisik] *adj* asāsī أساسي

basis ['beisis] *n* asās أساس (usus أسس)

basket ['ba:skit] *n* salla سلة (silāl سلال)

basketball ['ba:skitbo:l] *n* kurat as-salla كرة السلة

bat [bat] *n* 1. khuffāsh خفاش (khafāfīsh خفافيس) 2. (*spor.*) miḍrab مضرب (maḍārib مضارب)

bath [ba:th] *n* ḥammām حمام (-āt)

bathe [beidh] *v* istaḥamma استحم

bathroom ['ba:thru:m] *n* ḥammām حمام (-āt)

battery ['batəri] *n* baṭṭārīya بطرية (-āt)

battle ['batəl] 1. *n* maʿrika معركة (maʿārik معارك) 2. *v* qātala قاتل

bay [bei] *n* khalīj خليج (khuluj خلج)

bazaar [bə'za:] *n* sūq سوق *f/m* (aswāq أسواق)

B.B.C. [bi:bi:'si:] *n* hayʾat al-idhāʿa al-brīṭānīya هيئة الإذاعة البريطانية

be [bi:] *v* kāna كان (yakūnu يكون; kawn كون)

beach [bi:ch; -z] *n* shāṭiʾ شاطئ (shawāṭiʾ شواطئ)

bead(s) [bi:d] *n* kharaz *collective* خرز

beak [bi:k] *n* minqār منقار (manāqīr مناقير)

beans [bi:nz] *pl* fāṣūliyā فاصوليا; lūbyā لوبيا; fūl فول

bear [beə] 1. *n* dubb دب (adbāb أدباب) 2. *v* (**bore, borne**) ḥamala حمل (i; ḥaml حمل) 3. taḥammala تحمل 4. **to bear a child** waladat ولدت (talidu تلد; wilāda ولادة)

beard [biəd] *n* liḥya لحية

beast [bi:st] *n* waḥsh وحش (wuḥūsh وحوش); wuḥshān وحشان

beat [bi:t] *v* (**beat, beaten**) 1. ḍaraba ضرب (i; ḍarb ضرب) 2. khafaq خفق (i/u; khafq خفق) 3. **to beat (an opponent)** taghallaba taghallaba على 4. **to beat a record** ḥaṭṭama raqman qiyāsīyan حطم رقماً قياسياً

beautiful ['byu:tifəl] *adj* jamīl جميل

beauty ['byu:ti] *n* jamāl جمال

became [bi'keim] *see* **become**

because [bi'koz] *conj* liʾanna لأن; bi sabab بسبب

because of *prep* bi sabab بسبب

become [bi'kʌm] *v* (**became, become**) aṣbaḥa أصبح

bed [bed] *n* sarīr سرير (surur سرر)

bedroom ['bedru:m] *n* ghurfat an-nawm غرفة النوم

bee [bi:] *n* naḥl *collective* نحل

beef [bi:f] *n* laḥam baqar لحم بقر

beer [biə] *n* bīra بيرة

before [bi'fo:] 1. *prep* qabl قبل; min من 2. amām أمام 3. *conj* qabl min قبل من 4. *adv* qabl min قبل من

beg [beg] *v* 1. rajā رجا (yarjū يرجو; rajāʾ رجاء) 2. shaḥata شحت (a; shaḥt شحت)

began [bi'gan] *see* **begin**

begin [bi'gin] *v* (**began, begun**) badaʾa بدأ (a; badʾ بدء); ibtadaʾa ابتدأ

beginner [bi'ginə] *n* mubtadiʾ مبتدئ (-ūn)

beginning [bi'gining] *n* bidāya بداية (-āt)

begun [bi'gʌn] *see* **begin**

behalf [bi'ha:f] *n* **on behalf of** bi ʾn-niyāba ʿan بالنيابة عن

behave [bi'heiv] v salaka سلك (u; salk سلك; sulūk سلوك); taṣarrafa تصرف

behaviour, *(US)* **behavior** [bi'heivyə] n sulūk سلوك

behind [bi'haind] prep/adv khalf خلف; warā' وراء

being ['bi:ing] n 1. kā'in كائن 2. **human being** insān إنسان

belief [bi'li:f] n 1. ʿaqīda عقيدة (ʿaqā'id عقائد) 2. *(rel.)* īmān إيمان

believe [bi'li:v] v āmana bi أمن ب; iʿtaqada اعتقد

bell [bel] n jaras جرس (ajrās أجراس)

belong [bi'long] v intamā انتمى (to ilā إلى)

belongings [bi'longingz] pl amtiʿa أمتعة; mumtalakāt ممتلكات

below [bi'ləu] 1. adv taḥt تحت 2. aqall min أقل من 3. prep taḥta تحت

belt [belt] n ḥizām حزام (-āt); aḥzima أحزمة

bend [bend] 1. n ḥinw حنو (aḥnā' أحناء) 2. v (bent) inhanā انحنى

beneath [bi'ni:th] prep taḥt تحت

benefit ['benifit] 1. n nafʿ نفع; fā'ida فائدة 2. iʿāna mālīya إعانة مالية 3. v afāda أفاد 4. istafāda استفاد

bent [bent] see **bend**

beside [bi'said] prep bi jānib بجانب

besides [bi'saidz] 1. prep ʿadā عدا 2. adv bi 'l-iḍāfati ilā بالإضافة إلى

best [best] adj aḥsan أحسن; afḍal أفضل

bet [bet] 1. n rihān رهان; murāhana مراهنة 2. v (bet) rāhana راهن

betray [bi'trei] v khāna خان (u; khiyāna خيانة); khadaʿa خدع (a; khadʿ خدع)

better ['betə] adj 1. aḥsan أحسن 2. **to get better** taḥassana تحسن

between [bi'twi:n] prep bayna بين

beware [bi'weə] v iḥtarasa احترس; ḥadhara حذر

beyond [bi'yond] 1. prep warā' وراء 2. adv ilā mā baʿd إلى ما بعد

bias ['baiyəs] n inḥiyāz إنحياز

Bible ['baibəl] n al-kitāb al-muqaddas الكتاب المقدس

bicycle ['baisikəl] n darrāja دراجة (-āt); bāysikil بايسكل

bid [bid] v (bid) aʿṭā saʿran أعطى سعراً

big [big] adj kabīr كبير

bike [baik] n darrāja دراجة (-āt); bāysikil بايسكل

bill [bil] n 1. ḥisāb حساب 2. *(pol.)* mashrūʿ qānūn مشروع قانون

bind [baind] v (bound) rabaṭa ربط (u/i; rabṭ ربط); qayyada قيد

biology [bai'oləji] n biyūlūjīya بيولوجية; ʿilm al-aḥyā' علم الأحياء

bird [bə:d] n ṭayr طير (ṭuyūr طيور)

birth [bə:th] n 1. wilāda ولادة; mīlād ميلاد 2. **to give birth to** waladat ولدت (talidu تلد; wilāda ولادة)

birth certificate n shahādat mīlād شهادة ميلاد

birth control n ḥadd an-nasl حد النسل

birthday ['bə:thdei] n ʿīd al-mīlād عيد الميلاد

birthplace ['bə:thpleis] n masqaṭ ar-ra's مسقط الرأس

biscuit ['biskit] n biskit بسكت; baskawīt بسكويت

bishop ['bishəp] n usquf أسقف (asāqifa أساقفة)

bit [bit] n 1. qalīl قليل 2. fatra qaṣīra فترة قصيرة 3. **bridle bit** ḥadīdat al-lijām حديدة اللجام 4. see **bite**

bite [bait] **1.** *n* ʿaḍḍa عضة **2. insect bite** ʿaḍḍat ḥashara عضة حشرة **3.** *v* (**bit, bitten**) ʿaḍḍa عض (a; ʿaḍḍ عض)

bitter ['bitə] *adj* murr مر

black [blak] *adj* aswad *m* أسود

blackmail ['blakmeil] *v* ibtazza ابتزّ

black market *n* as-sūq as-sūdā' السوق السوداء

blade [bleid] *n* safra شفرة (shafarāt شفرات)

blame [bleim] **1.** *n* lawm لوم **2.** *v* lāma لام (u; lawm لوم)

blank [blank] *adj* khālin خال

blanket ['blangkit] *n* baṭṭānīya بطانية (-āt)

blast [bla:st] **1.** *n* **bomb blast** infijār إنفجار (-āt) **2.** *v* nasafa (i; nasf نسف)

blaze [bleiz] **1.** *n* ḥarīq حريق **2.** *v* talahhaba تلهب; tawahhaja توهج

bleed [bli:d] *v* (**bled**) nazafa نزف (i; nazf نزف)

bless [bles] *v* bāraka بارك

blew [blu:] *see* **blow**

blind [blaind] **1.** *adj* aʿmā أعمى **2.** *n* sitārat al-nāfidha ستارة النافذة

blindness ['blaindnis] *n* ʿaman عمى

bloc [blok] *n* (*pol.*) kutla كتلة (kutal كتل)

block [blok] **1.** *n* kutla كتلة (kutal كتل) **2.** *v* sadda سد (u; sadd سد)

blond; blonde [blond] *adj* ashqar أشقر

blood [blʌd] *n* dam دم (dimā' دماء)

blood group *n* faṣīlat dam فصيلة دم

blood test *n* taḥalīl ad-dam تحليل الدم

blouse [blauz] *n* blūz بلوز; blūza بلوزة (-āt)

blow [bləu] **1.** *n* ḍarba ضربة (-āt) **2.** *v* (**blew, blown**) nafakha نفخ (u; nafkh نفخ) **3.** habba هب (u; habb هب)

blow up *v* fajjara فجّر; nasafa نسف (i; nasf نسف)

blue [blu:] *adj* azraq أزرق

blunt [blʌnt] *adj* kalīl كليل; ghayr ḥādd غير حاد

blush [blʌsh] *v* iḥmarra al-wajh احمرّ الوجه

board [bo:d] *n* lawḥ khashab لوح خشب

boast [bəust] **1.** *n* iftikhār إفتخار **2.** *v* iftakhara افتخر (**about** bi ب)

boat [bəut] *n* markab مركب (marākib مراكب); safīna سفن (sufun سفن; safā'in سفائن)

body [bodi] *n* jism جسم (ajsām أجسام)

bodyguard ['bodiga:d] *n* ḥaras حرس

boil [boil] **1.** *n* (*med.*) ḥabba حبة (ḥubūb حبوب) **2.** *v* ghalā غلى (i; ghaly غلي; ghalayān غليان); fāra فار (u; fawr فور; fawarān فوران)

bold [bəuld] *adj* jarī' جريء; jasūr جسور

bolt [bəult] *n* **1.** mismār mulawlab مسمار ملولب **2.** mizlāj مزلاج (mazālij مزالج)

bomb [bom] **1.** *n* qunbula قنبلة (qanābil قنابل) **2.** *v* qadhafa bi 'l-qanābil قذف بالقنابل (i; qadhf قذف)

bomber ['bomə] *n* **1.** (plane) ṭā'ira qādhifa طائرة قاذفة **2. suicide bomber** mufajjir intiḥārī مفجّر إنتحاري

bond [bond] *n* **1.** qayd قيد (quyūd قيود); rābiṭa رابطة (rawābiṭ روابط) **2.** (*fin.*) sanad سند (-āt)

bone [bəun] *n* عظم ʿaẓm عِظام ʿiẓām
(أعظم; aʿẓum)

bonfire ['bonfaiə] *n* حريق ḥarīq

bonus ['bəunəs] *n* علاوة ʿilāwa

book [buk] **1.** *n* كتاب kitāb (كتب kutub) **2.** *v* حجز ḥajaza (حجز u/i; ḥajz)

booklet ['buklət] *n* كتيّب kuttayib (-āt)

bookshop; bookstore ['bukshop, 'buksto:] *n* مكتبة maktaba (-āt)

boom [bu:m] *n* **1.** هدير hadīr **2.** *(ec.)* إزدهار إقتصادي izdihār iqtiṣādī

boost [bu:st] *v* زاد zāda (i; ziyāda زيادة)

boot [bu:t] *n* **1.** جزمة jazma (-āt; jizam جزم) **2. car boot** صندوق سيارة ṣandūq sayyāra

border ['bo:də] *n* **1.** حافة ḥāfa (-āt; ḥawāfin حواف) **2.** حد ḥadd (ḥudūd حدود) **3.** جاور jāwara

bore [bo:] *v* **1.** ثقب thaqaba (u; thaqb ثقب) **2.** مل malla (a; malal ملل)

bored [bo:d] *adj* ملول malūl

boring ['bo:ring] *adj* ممل mumill

born [bo:n] *adj* **to be born** tawallada تولد

borrow ['borəu] *v* استعار istaʿāra

boss [bos] *n* رئيس raʾīs (ru'asā' رؤساء; mudīr مدير (mudarā' مدراء)

both [bəuth] *adj* **1.** كلا kilā *m*; كلتا kiltā *f* كلتا kiltā **2. both... and...** kullun min... wa... كل من... و....

bother ['bodhə] *v* **1.** أزعج azʿaja; ضايق ḍāyaqa **2.** *see* **bothered**

bothered ['bodhəd] *adj* **I couldn't be bothered to visit them.** lam ahtammu bi ziyārathum. لم أهتمّ بزيارتهم.

bottle ['botəl] *n* زجاجة zujāja (-āt); قنينة qinnīna (qanānin قنان)

bottle-opener ['botələupnə] *n*

مفتاح زجاجة miftāḥ zujāja

bottom ['botəm] **1.** *adj/n* أدنى adnā; أسفل asfal **2.** *n (col.)* قاع qāʿ (aqwāʿ أقواع)

bought [bo:t] *see* **buy**

bounce [bauns] *v* وثب wathaba (yathibu يثب; wathb وثب)

boundary ['baundri] *n* حد ḥadd (ḥudūd حدود)

bow [bəu] *n* قوس qaws (aqwās أقواس)

bow [bau] *v* انحنى inḥanā

bowl [bəul] *n* زبدية zabdīya (zabādīy زبادي)

box [boks] **1.** *n* صندوق ṣandūq (ṣanādīq صناديق) **2.** *v (spor.)* تلاكم talākama

boxer ['boksə] *n (spor.)* ملاكم mulākim (-ūn)

boxing ['boksing] *n (spor.)* ملاكمة mulākama

box office *n* شباك التذاكر shubbāk at-tadhākir

boy [boi] *n* ولد walad (awlād أولاد); صبي ṣabī (ṣibyān/ṣubyān صبيان); غلام ghulām (ghilmān غلمان)

boycott ['boikot] **1.** *n* مقاطعة muqāṭaʿa **2.** *v* قاطع qāṭaʿa

boyfriend ['boifrend] *n* صديق ṣadīq (aṣdiqā' أصدقاء); رفيق rafīq (rufaqā' رفقاء)

bra [bra:] *n* صديرية ṣudayrīya

bracelet ['breislit] *n* سوار/سوار siwār/suwār (asāwīr أساوير; aswira أسورة) سوار

brain [brein] *n* مخ mukhkh (mikhākh مخاخ)

brake; brakes [breik; breiks] **1.** *n* فرامل farāmil **2.** *v* فرمل farmala

branch [bra:nch] *n* فرع farʿ (furūʿ فروع)

brand new *adj* جديد تماماً jadīd tamāman

brassiere [bra'siə] *n* ṣudayrīya صديرية

brave [breiv] *adj* shajjāʿ شجاع

breach [bri:ch] *v* kharaqa خرق (i/u; kharq خرق)

bread [bred] *n* khubz خبز

breadth [bredth] *n* ʿarḍ عرض

break [breik] 1. *n* istirāḥa استراحة (-āt) 2. *v* (broke, broken) kasara كسر (i; kasr كسر)

breakdown ['breikdaun] *n* 1. taʿaṭṭul تعطل 2. inhiyār إنهيار

breakfast ['brekfəst] *n* fiṭār فطار; fuṭūr فطور

break up *v* 1. taḥaṭṭama تحطم 2. faṣala فصل (i; faṣl فصل)

breast [brest] *n* 1. thady ثدي (athdāʾ أثداء) 2. ṣadr صدر (ṣudūr صدور)

breasts [brests] *pl* athdāʾ أثداء

breath [breth] *n* nafas نفس (anfās أنفاس)

breathe [bri:dh] *v* tanaffasa تنفس

breed [bri:d] *v* (bred) wallada ولد; istawlada استولد

bribe [braib] 1. *n* rashwa/rishwa/rushwa رشوة (rishan/rushan رشا\رشى; rashāwī رشاوي) 2. *v* irtashā ارتشى

bribery ['braibəri] *n* irtishāʾ إرتشاء

brick(s) [brik] *n* qirmīd *collective* قرميد (qarāmīd قراميد)

bride [braid] *n* ʿarūs عروس; ʿarūsa عروسة (ʿarāʾis عرائس)

bridegroom ['braidgru:m] *n* ʿarīs عريس

bridge [brij] *n* jisr جسر (jusūr جسور)

brief [bri:f] *adj* wajīz وجيز; qaṣīr قصير

briefcase ['bri:fkeis] *n* ḥaqībat al-yad حقيبة اليد

briefly ['bri:fli] *adv* bi 'l-ījāz بالإيجاز

bright [brait] *adj* 1. sāṭiʿ ساطع; mushriq مشرق 2. dhakī ذكي

brighten ['braitən] *v* ashraqa أشرق

brightness ['braitnis] *n* saṭʿ سطع

brilliant ['briliənt] *adj* lāmiʿ لامع; mushriq مشرق

bring [bring] *v* jalaba جلب (i/u; jalb جلب)

bring about *v* aḥdatha أحدث; sabbaba سبب

bring up *v* rabbā ربى; dhakara ذكر (u; dhikr ذكر)

brink [bringk] *n* ḥāffa حافة (-āt)

Britain ['britən] *n* brīṭāniyā بريطانيا

British ['british] *adj* brīṭānī بريطاني

Briton ['briton] *n* brīṭānī بريطاني

broad [bro:d] *adj* ʿarīḍ عريض

broadcast ['bro:dka:st] *n* 1. idhāʿa إذاعة 2. *v* (broadcast) adhāʿa أذاع

brochure ['brəushə] *n* kutayyib كتيّب (-āt)

broke; broken [brəuk; 'brəukən] 1. maksūr مكسور 2. *see* **break**

brother ['brʌdhə] *n* akh أخ (ikhwa إخوة; ikhwān إخوان)

brother-in-law ['brʌdhərin'lo:] *n* ʿadīl عديل

brought [bro:t] *see* **bring**

brow [brau] *n* ḥājib حاجب (hawājib حواجب)

brown [braun] *adj* bunnī بني

brush [brʌsh] 1. *n* fursha فرشة (furash فرش) 2. *v* farrasha فرش

brutal ['bru:təl] *adj* waḥshī وحشي

bubble ['bʌbəl] *n* baqbaqa بقبقة

bucket ['bʌkit] *n* dalw دلو *usually f* (adlāʾ أدلاء)

bud [bʌd] *n* burʿūm برعوم (barāʿīm براعيم)

budget ['bʌjit] n mīzānīya ميزانية

buffet ['bufei] n būfēh بوفيه

bug [bʌg] 1. n ḥashara حشرة (-āt) 2. **electronic bug** ālat taṣannut آلة تصنت 3. **computer bug** ʿilla fī barnāmij علة في برنامج 4. v ḍāyaqa ضايق 5. (elect.) taṣannata تصنت

build [bild] v (**built**) banā بنى (i; binā' بناء; bunyān بنيان)

builder ['bildə] n bannā' بناء (-ūn)

building ['bilding] n bināya بناية (-āt); mabnā مبنى (mabānin مبان)

built [bilt] see **build**

bulb [bʌlb] n **light bulb** lamba لمبة (-āt)

bulk [bʌlk] 1. adj bi 'l-jumla بالجملة 2. n ḥajm حجم

bull [bul] n thawr ثور (thīrān ثيران)

bullet ['bulit] n raṣāṣa رصاصة (raṣāṣ رصاص collective)

bump [bʌmp] 1. n waram ورم (awrām أورام) 2. ḍarba ضربة (-āt) 3. v ḍaraba ضرب (i; ḍarb ضرب)

bunch [bʌnch] n 1. ʿunqūd عنقود (ʿanāqīd عناقيد) 2. majmūʿa مجموعة (-āt)

burden ['bə:dən] n athqala أثقل

bureau ['byu:rəu] n maktab مكتب (makātib مكاتب); dā'ira rasmīya دائرة رسمية

bureaucracy [byuə'rokrasi] n bīrūqrāṭīya بيروقراطية

bureaucrat ['byuərəkrat] n bīrūqrāṭī بيروقراطي

bureaucratic [byuərə'kratik] adj bīrūqrāṭī بيروقراطي

bureau de change ['byu:rəu də 'sho:nj] n ṣarrāf صراف

burger ['bə:gə] n burghar برغر

burglary ['bə:gləri] n saṭw سطو

burial ['beriəl] n dafn دفن

burn [bə:n] 1. n ḥarq حرق; iḥrāq إحراق 2. v (**burnt**) iḥtaraqa أحترق; ishtaʿala اشتعل 3. ḥarraqa حرق

burst [bə:st] v (**burst**) infajara انفجر

bury ['beri] v dafana دفن (i; dafn دفن)

bus [bʌs] n bāṣ باص (-āt); otobīs أوتوبيس (-āt)

bush [bush] n shujayra شجيرة (-āt)

business ['biznis] n 1. ʿamal عمل; mihna مهنة 2. aʿmāl أعمال 3. (com.) mashrūʿ مشروع 4. tijāra تجارة 5. mas'ala مسألة (masā'il مسائل)

businessman ['biznismən] n rajul aʿmāl رجل أعمال

businesswoman ['bizniswumən] n sitt aʿmāl ست أعمال

bus station n maḥaṭṭat bāṣāt محطة باصات

bus stop n mawqif bāṣ موقف باص

bust [bʌst] n ṣadr صدر

busy ['bizi] adj mashghūl مشغول

but [bʌt] conj lākin لكن; walākin ولكن

butcher ['buchə] n qaṣṣāb قصاب (-ūn); jazzār جزار (-ūn)

butter ['bʌtə] n zubda زيدة

butterfly ['bʌtəflai] n farrāsha فراشة

button ['bʌtən] n zirr زر (azrār أزرار; zurūr زرور)

buy [bai] v ishtarā اشترى

buyer ['baiyə] n shārin شار

buzzer ['bʌzə] n ṭannān طنان

by [bai] prep 1. **by the house** janb al-bayt جنب البيت 2. **by train** bi 'l-qiṭār بالقطار 3. **by day** nahāran نهاراً 4. **by tomorrow** qabl al-ghad قبل الغد 5. **a book by Charles Dickens** kitāb li Charles Dickens كتاب لشارلز ديكنس

C

cab [kab] *n* تاكسي tāksī (-āt)

cabaret [kabərei] *n* إستعراض istiʿrāḍ

cabbage(s) ['kabij] *n* malfūf ملفوف; kurunb *collective* كرنب

cabin [kabin] *n* **1.** qamra قمرة (-āt) **2.** kūkh كوخ (akwākh أكواخ)

cabinet [kabinit] *n* **1.** dūlāb دولاب (dawālīb دواليب) **2.** (pol.) majlis al-wuzarā' مجلس الوزراء

cable ['keibəl] *n* silk سلك (aslāk أسلاك)

cable television *n* al-qanawāt al-faḍā'īya القنوات الفضائية

café ['kafei] *n* maqhan مقهى (maqāhin مقاه)

cage [keij] *n* qafaṣ قفص (aqfāṣ أقفاص)

cake(s) [keik] *n* kaʿk *collective* كعك

calculate ['kalkyuleit] *v* ḥasaba حسب (u; ḥasb حسب;ḥisāb حساب; ḥisbān/ḥusbān حسبان)

calculation [kalkyu'leishən] *n* ḥusbān حسبان; ḥisāb حساب

calculator ['kalkyuleitə] *n* ḥāsib حاسب

calendar ['kalində] *n* taqwīm تقويم

calf [ca:f] *n* (*pl* calves) **1.** ʿijl عجل (ʿujūl عجول) **2.** of leg baṭṭat as-sāq بطة الساق

call [ko:l] *v* **1.** nādā نادى **2.** sammā سمى **3.** see called, telephone call

called [ko:ld] *adj* I am called Fred. ismī Fred. إسمي فريد.

caller ['ko:lə] *n* mutaḥaddith bi 't-tilifūn متحدث بالتلفون

calm [ka:m] **1.** adj hādi' هادئ **2.** n hudū' هدوء

calves [ka:vz] *see* calf

came [keim] *see* come

camel ['kaml] *n* jamal جمل (jimāl جمال;ajmāl أجمال); baʿīr بعير (abʿira أبعرة;buʿrān بعران)

camera ['kamərə] *n* kāmera كاميرة (-āt); ālat taṣwīr آلة تصوير

camp [kamp] **1.** n mukhayyam مخيم (-āt); muʿaskar معسكر (-āt) **2.** v khayyama خيم

campaign [kam'pein] **1.** n ḥamla حملة **2.** v ishtaraka fī ḥamla اشترك في حملة

campus ['kampəs] *n* ḥaram jāmiʿī حرم جامعي; madīna jāmiʿī مدينة جامعي

can [kan; kən] **1.** n ʿulba علبة (ʿulab علب) **2.** v (could) istaṭāʿa استطاع **3.** qadira ʿalā قدر على (a; qadar قدر)

Canada ['kaneidə] *n* kanadā كندا

Canadian [kə'neidiən] *adj/n* kanadī كندي (-yūn)

canal [kə'nal] *n* qanāh قناة (qanāwāt قناوات)

cancel ['kansəl] *v* (cancelled) alghā ألغى

cancellation [kansə'leishən] *n* ilghā' إلغاء

cancer [kansə] *n* (med.) saraṭān سرطان

candidate ['kandidət] *n* murashshaḥ مرشح (-ūn)

candle ['kandəl] *n* شمعة sham⁽a (شمع collective ⁽sham)

candy ['kandi] *n* حلوى ḥalwā (حلاوى ḥalāwā)

cane [kein] *n* عصا ⁽aṣā

cannon ['kanən] *n* مدفع midfa⁽ (مدافع madāfi⁽)

can-opener ['kanəupnə] *n* مفتاح علبة miftāḥ ⁽ulba

cap [kap] *n* قبعة qubba⁽a (-āt)

capable ['keipəbəl] *adj* قدر qadir; كفء ʾkaf

capacity [kə'pasəti] *n* سعة si⁽a

cape [keip] *n* **1.** رداء ridā' (ardiya أردية) **2.** *(geographical)* رأس ra's

capital ['kapitəl] *n* **1.** عاصمة ⁽āṣima (عواصم ⁽awāṣim) **2.** *(fin.)* رأسمال ra'smāl

capitalism ['kapitəlizm] *n* رأسمالية ra'smālīya

capitalist ['kapitəlizm] *n* رأسمالي ra'smālī

captain ['kaptin] *n* **1.** قبطان qubṭān (قباطين ;قبابطة qabāṭin; qabāṭina) **2.** *(mil.)* نقيب naqīb (نقباء nuqabā') **3.** *(spor.)* رئيس ra'īs (رؤساء ru'asā')

captive ['kaptiv] *n* أسير asīr (أسرى asrā)

capture ['kapchə] *v* أسر asara (i; أسر asr); استولى على istawlā ⁽alā

car [ka:] *n* سيارة sayyāra (-āt)

caravan ['karəvan] *n* قافلة qāfila (قوافل qawāfil)

card [ka:d] *n* بطاقة biṭāqa (-āt)

cardboard ['ka:dbo:d] *n* ورق مقوى waraq muqawwan

care [keə] *n* **1.** إهتمام ihtimām; عناية ⁽ināya **2. to take care of** اعتنى ب i⁽tanā bi

career [kə'riə] *n* مهنة mihna (مهن mihan)

careful ['keəfəl] *adj* حذر ḥadhir

careless ['keəlis] *adj* مهمل muhmil

cargo ['ka:gəu] *n* حمولة ḥumūla

carnival ['ka:nivəl] *n* إحتفال شعبي iḥtifāl sha⁽bī

car park ['ka:pa:k] *n* موقف سيارات mawqif sayyārāt

carpenter ['ka:pintə] *n* نجار najjār (-ūn)

carpet ['ka:pit] *n* سجادة sajjāda (سجاجيد sajājīd); بساط bisāṭ (-āt)

carriage ['karij] *n* عربة ⁽araba; حافلة ḥāfila

carrier ['kariə] *n* **1.** ناقل nāqil (-ūn) **2.** *(com.)* شركة نقل sharikat naql

carrot ['karət] *n* جزرة jazra (جزر jazar collective)

carry ['kari] *v* حمل ḥamala (i; حمل ḥaml)

carry on *v* استمر istamarra

carry out *v* نفذ naffadha

cart [ka:t] *n* عربة ⁽araba

carton ['ka:tən] *n* علبة كارتون ⁽ulbat kārtūn

cartoon [ka:'tu:n] *n* **1.** رسم كاريكاتوري rasm kārīkatūrī **2. film** فلم كاريكاتوري film kārīkatūrī

carve [ka:v] *v* نحت naḥata (i/u; نحت naḥt)

case [keis] *n* **1.** حالة ḥāla **2.** صندوق ṣundūq (صناديق ṣanādīq) **3.** *(leg.)* قضية qaḍīya **4. in any case** على كل حال ⁽alā kull ḥāl

cash [kash] **1.** *n* نقد naqd **2.** *v* صرف ṣarrafa

cashier [ka'shi:ə] *n* أمين الصندوق amīn aṣ-ṣandūq

casino [kə'si:nəu] *n* نادٍ للقمار nādin li 'l-qimār

cassette [kə'set] *n* shariṭ شريط
(sharā'iṭ شرائط; ashriṭa أشرطة)

cassette recorder *n* musajjil
مسجل (-āt)

cast [ka:st] *v* **1.** alqā ألقى **2.**
ikhtāra mumaththilan li dawr
اختار ممثلاً لدور

castle ['ka:səl] *n* qalʿa قلعة (qilāʿ
قلاع)

cat [kat] *n* qiṭṭ قط (qiṭaṭ قطط)

catalogue ['katəlog] *n* kātālōg
كاتالوج (-āt)

catastrophe [kə'tastrəfi] *n* kāritha
كارثة (kawārith كوارث)

catch [kach] *v* (**caught**) **1.** masaka
bi مسك ب (u/i; mask مسك) **2. He
caught a cold.** uṣība bi bard.
أصيب ببرد

category ['katəgri] *n* ṣanf صنف
(aṣnāf أصناف)

cathedral [kə'thi:drəl] *n*
kātidrā'īya كاتدرائية

Catholic ['kathəlik] *adj/n* kāthūlīkī
كاثوليكي

cattle [katl] *pl* mawāshin مواش

caught [ko:t] *see* **catch**

cause [ko:z] **1.** *n* sabab سبب (asbāb
أسباب) **2.** *v* sabbaba سبب

caution ['ko:shən] *n* ḥadhar حذر

cautious ['ko:shəs] *adj* ḥadhir حذر

cave [keiv] *n* kahf كهف (kuhūf
كهوف); ghār غار (-āt)

c.d. [si:'di:] *see* **compact disc**

cease [si:s] *v* tawaqqafa توقف;
intahā انتهى

cease-fire [si:s'faiə] *n* waqf iṭlāq
an-nār وقف إطلاق النار

ceiling ['si:ling] *n* saqf سقف (suqūf
سقوف; asquf أسقف)

celebrate ['selibreit] *v* iḥtafala
احتفل

celebration [seli'breishən] *n* iḥtifāl
إحتفال

celebrity [si'lebrəti] *n* shakhṣ
mashhūr شخص مشهور

cell [sel] *n* **1.** zinzāna زنزانة (-āt) **2.**
khalīya خلية (khalāyā خلايا)

cellar ['selə] *n* qabw قبو (aqbiya
أقبية)

cement [si'ment] *n* ismant إسمنت

cemetery ['semətri] *n* maqbara
مقبرة (maqābir مقابر)

censorship ['sensəship] *n* raqāba
رقابة

census ['sensəs] *n* iḥṣā' as-sukkān
إحصاء السكان (-āt)

cent [sent] *n* **1.** sant سنت **2. per
cent** fi 'l-mi'a في المئة; bi 'l-mi'a
بالمئة

centimetre, *(US)* **centimeter**
['sentimi:tə] *n* santimitr سنتمتر (-āt)

central ['sentrəl] *adj* **1.** markazī
مركزي **2.** hāmm هام

centre, *(US)* **center** ['sentə] *n*
markaz مركز (marākiz مراكز)

century ['senchəri] *n* qarn قرن
(qurūn قرون)

ceramic [sə'ramik] *adj* khazafī
خزفي

ceremony ['seriməni] *n* iḥtifāl
إحتفال; marāsim مراسم

certain ['sə:tən] *adj* **1.** akīd أكيد **2.**
muʿayyan معيّن

certainly ['sə:tnli] *adv* ṭabʿan طبعاً;
bi 't-ta'kīd بالتأكيد

certificate [sə'tifikət] *n* shahāda
شهادة (-āt)

chain [chein] *n* silsila سلسلة (salāsil
سلاسل)

chair [cheə] *n* kursī كرسي (karāsīy كراسي)

chairman [cheəmən] *n* ra'īs al-majlis رئيس المجلس

chalk [cho:k] *n* ṭabāshīr طباشير

challenge [chalinj] 1. *n* taḥaddin تحدّ (taḥaddiyāt تحديات) 2. *v* taḥaddā تحدى

chamber ['cheimbə] 1. *n* ghurfa غرفة (ghuraf غرف) 2. *(pol.)* majlis مجلس (majālis مجالس)

champagne [sham'pein] shām-bānya شامبانية

champion ['champiən] *n* baṭal بطل (abṭāl أبطال)

championship ['championship] *n* buṭūla بطولة (-āt)

chance [cha:ns] *n* 1. ḥaẓẓ حظّ 2. ṣudfa صدفة 3. furṣa فرصة (furaṣ فرص) 4. **by chance** bi 'ṣ-ṣudfa بالصدفة

chancellor ['cha:nsələ] *n* 1. ra'īs رئيس 2. *(acad.)* ra'īs al-jāmiʿa رئيس الجامعة

change [cheinj] 1. *n* taghyīr تغيير; taghayyur تغيّر 2. *(fin.)* fakka فكة 3. *v* baddala بدّل; ghayyara غير 4. *(fin.)* ṣarrafa صرف; fakka فك (u)

channel ['chanəl] *n* qanāh قناة (qanāwāt قنوات)

chaos ['keios] *n* fawḍā فوضى

chapter ['chaptə] *n* faṣl فصل (fuṣūl فصول)

character ['kariktə] *n* 1. shakhṣīya شخصية (-āt) 2. khuluq خلق (akhlāq أخلاق)

charge [cha:j] 1. *n (com.)* thaman ثمن 2. *(elect.)* shaḥna شحنة 3. *(leg.)* ittihām اتهام (-āt) 4. *(mil.)* hujūm هجوم (-āt) 5. **free of charge**

majānan مجاناً 6. **in charge of** mas'ūl ʿan مسؤول عن 7. *v (com.)* taqāḍā thamanan تقاضى ثمناً 8. *(leg.)* ittahama اتهم 9. *(mil.)* hājama هاجم

charity ['charəti] *n* 1. mu'assasa khayrīya مؤسسة خيرية 2. iḥsān إحسان; ṣadaqa صدقة

charm [cha:m] *n* jādhibīya جاذبية

chart [cha:t] *n* 1. kharīṭa خريطة (kharā'iṭ خرائط) 2. jadwal جدول (jadāwil جداول)

charter ['cha:tə] 1. *n* mīthāq ميثاق (mawāthīq مواثيق) 2. *v* ista'jara استأجر

chase [cheis] *v* ṭārada طارد

chat [chat] *v* taḥaddatha تحدث

chauffeur [shəu'fə] *n* sā'iq سائق (-ūn)

cheap [chi:p] *adj* rakhīṣ رخيص

cheat [chi:t] *v* 1. khadaʿa خدع (a) 2. *(acad./spor.)* ghashsha غش (u; ghashsh غش)

check [chek] 1. *n (US)* ḥisāb حساب 2. *v* ta'akkada تأكد 3. rājaʿa راجع 4. *see* **cheque**

check-in ['chekin] *n* tasjīl تسجيل

check-out ['chekaut] *n* mughā-darat al-funduq مغادرة الفندق

checkpoint ['chekpoint] *n* nuqṭat taftīsh نقطة تفتيش

check-up ['chekʌp] *n (med.)* faḥs ṭibbī فحص طبي

cheek [chi:k] *n* 1. khadd خد (khudūd خدود) 2. waqāḥa وقاحة

cheeky ['chi:ki] *adj* waqiḥ وقح

cheerful ['chiəfəl] *adj* mubhij مبهج

cheers! 1. bi ṣiḥḥatika! بصحتك! 2. *(UK)* shukran! شكراً!

cheese [chi:z] n jubn جبن; jubna جبنة

chef [shef] n ṭabbākh طباخ (-ūn)

chemical ['kemikəl] 1. adj kīmyā'ī كيميائي 2. n mādda kīmyā'īya مادة كيميائية

chemist ['kemist] n 1. kīmyā'ī كيميائي 2. (UK) ṣaydalī صيدلي

chemistry ['kemistri] n ʿilm al-kīmyā علم الكيمياء

chemist's ['kemists] n ṣaydalīya صيدلية

cheque [chek] 1. bank cheque shīk شيك (-at) 2. see check

cheque book n daftar shīkāt دفتر شيكات

chess [ches] n shaṭranj شطرنج

chest [chest] n 1. ṣadr صدر 2. sandūq صندوق (ṣanādīq صناديق)

chew [chu:] v maḍagha مضغ (a/u; maḍgh مضغ)

chick [chik] n katkūt كتكوت (katākīt كتاكيت)

chicken ['chikin] n dajāja دجاجة (dajāj collective جبن)

chickpeas ['chikpi:z] pl ḥummuṣ حمص

chief [chi:f] 1. adj ra'īsī رئيسي 2. n ra'īs رئيس (ru'asā رؤساء)

chiefly ['chi:fli] adv fi 'l-aghlab في الأغلب

child [chaild] n (pl children) ṭifl طفل (aṭfāl أطفال)

childbirth ['chaildbə:th] n wilāda ولادة

childhood ['chaildhud] n ṭufūla طفولة

children ['childrən] see child

chilly ['chili] adj bārid بارد

chimney ['chimni] n (pl chimneys) madkhana مدخنة (madākhin مداخن)

chin [chin] n dhaqan ذقن (adhqān أذقان); dhuqūn ذقون)

chip [chip] n 1. shaẓīya شظية (shaẓāyā شظايا) 2. **chips** baṭāṭis maqlīya بطاطس مقلية 3. **microchips** ar-raqā'iq الرقائق

chocolate ['choklət] n shikolāta شيكولاته

choice [chois] n ikhtiyār إختيار; khiyār خيار (-āt)

choir ['kwaiə] n jawqa جوقة (ajwāq أجواق)

choke [chəuk] v ikhtanaqa اختنق

choose [chu:z] v (chose, chosen) ikhtāra اختار

chop [chop] 1. n ḍilʿ ضلع (ḍulūʿ ضلوع; aḍlāʿ أضلاع) 2. v (chopped) qaṭaʿa قطع (a; qaṭʿ قطع)

chord [ko:d] n (mus.) watar وتر (awtār أوتار)

chorus ['ko:rəs] n kōras كورس

chose; chosen [chəuz; 'chəuzən] see choose

Christian ['krischən] n/adj masīḥī مسيحي; naṣrānī نصراني (-yūn)

Christianity [kristi'anəti] n masīḥīya مسيحية; naṣrānīya نصرانية

Christmas ['kristiməs] n ʿīd al-mīlād عيد الميلاد

Christmas Eve n ʿashīyat ʿīd al-mīlād عشية عيد الميلاد

church [chə:ch] n kanīsa كنيسة (kanā'is كنائس)

cigarette [sigəret] n sigāra سجارة (sagā'ir سجائر)

cinema ['sinəmə] n sīnamā سينما (sīnamāhāt سينماهات)

circle ['sə:kəl] n dā'ira دائرة (dawā'ir دوائر)

circuit ['sə:kit] *n* dā'ira دائرة (dawā'ir دوائر)

circular ['sə:kyulə] *adj* dā'irī دائري

circulation [sə:kyu'leishən] *n* dawarān دوران

circumstances [sə:kəm'stansiz] *pl* ẓurūf ظروف

circus ['sə:kəs] *n* sirk سرك

citizen ['sitizən] *n* muwāṭin مواطن (-ūn)

citizenship ['sitizənship] *n* jinsīya جنسية (-āt)

city ['siti] *n* **1.** madīna مدينة (mudun مدن; madā'in مدائن) **2. inner city** wasaṭ al-madīna وسط المدينة **3. city centre** markaz al-madīna مركز المدينة

civil *adj* **1.** madanī مدني **2.** muhadhdhab مهذب

civilian [si'viliən] *adj/n* madanī مدني (-ūn)

civilisation [sivəlai'zeishən] *n* ḥaḍāra حضارة (-āt)

civilised ['sivəlaizd] *adj* mutaḥaddir متحضر; mutamaddin متمدن

civil rights *pl* al-ḥuqūq al-madanīya الحقوق المدنية

civil servant *n* muwaẓẓaf (ḥukūmī) موظف (حكومي) (-ūn)

civil service *n* al-idāra al-ḥukūmīya الإدارة الحكومية

civil war *n* ḥarb ahlīya *f* حرب أهلية

claim [kleim] **1.** *n* iddiʿāʾ إدعاء **2.** *(fin.)* muṭālaba مطالبة **3.** *v* iddaʿā ادعى **4.** *(fin.)* ṭālaba طالب

clap [klap] *v* (**clapped**) ṣaffaqa صفق

clarify ['klarifai] *v* waḍḍaḥa وضح

clash [klash] *v* **1.** iṣṭadama اصطدم **2.** tanāqaḍa maʿa تناقض مع

class [kla:s] *v* **1.** daraja درجة (-āt) **2.**

(ed.) dars درس (durūs دروس) **3.** ṣaff صف (ṣufūf صفوف) **4. social class** ṭabaqa طبقة (-āt)

classic ['klasik] *adj* klāsikī كلاسيكي

classical ['klasikəl] *adj* kilāsikī كلاسيكي

classify ['klasifai] *v* ṣannafa صنف

classmate ['kla:smeit] *n* zamīl fi ṣ-ṣaff زميل في الصف

classroom ['kla:srum] *n* ḥujrat ad-dirāsa حجرة الدراسة

claw [klo:] *n* mikhlab مخلب (makhālib مخالب)

clay [klei] *n* ṭīn طين

clean [kli:n] **1.** *adj* naẓīf نظيف **2.** *v* naẓẓafa نظف

cleaner ['kli:nə] *n* munaẓẓif منظف

cleansing ['klenzing] *n* **ethnic cleansing** taṭhīr ʿirqī تطهير عرقي

clear [kliə] **1.** *adj* wāḍiḥ واضح; ṣāfin صاف **2.** *v* farragha فرغ **3.** *(leg.)* barra'a برأ

clearly ['kliəli] *adv* bi wuḍūḥ بوضوح

clergy ['klə:ji] *n* qasāwisa قساوسة

clerk [kla:k] *n* kātib كاتب (kuttāb كتاب)

clever ['klevə] *adj* dhakī ذكي; māhir ماهر

click [klik] *n* ṭaqṭaqa طقطقة

client ['klaiənt] *n* zabūn زبان (zabā'in زبائن)

cliff [klif] *n* jurf جرف (jurūf جروف; ajrāf أجراف)

climate ['klaimit] *n* munākh/manākh مناخ

climax ['klaimaks] *n* dhurwa/dhirwa (dhuran ذرى) ذروة

climb [klaim] *v* **1.** tasallaqa تسلق **2.** irtafaʿa ارتفع

climber ['klaimə] *n* mutasalliq متسلق (-ūn)

climbing ['klaiming] *n* tasalluq تسلق

cling [kling] *v* (**clung**) tamassaka bi تمسّك ب

clinic ['klinik] *n* 1. ʿiyāda عيادة; mustawṣaf مستوصف 2. **maternity clinic** mustawṣaf al-wilāda مستوصف الولادة

clip [klip] 1. *n* **film clip** muqtaṭaf film مقتطف فلم 2. **paper clip** mishbak al-waraq مشبك الورق 3. *v* qallama قلم

clock [klok] *n* 1. sāʿa ساعة (-āt) 2. **alarm clock** munabbih منبه (-āt)

close [kləus] *adj* qarīb قريب

close [kləuz] *v* aghlaqa أغلق

closed [kləuzd] *adj* mughlaq مغلق

closet ['klozit] *n* khizāna خزانة (khazā'in خزائن)

cloth [kloth] *n* qimāsh قماش

clothe [kləudh] *v* labisa لبس (a; lubs لبس)

clothes; clothing [kləudhz; 'kləudhing] *pl* malābis ملابس

cloud [klaud] *n* saḥāba سحابة (suḥub سحب; saḥā'ib سحائب)

cloudy ['klaudi] *n* ghā'im غائم

clown [klaun] *n* muharrij مهرج (-ūn)

club [klʌb] *n* nādin ناد (andiya أندية; nawādin نواد)

clue [klu:] *n* dalīl دليل (adilla أدلة)

clung [klʌng] *see* **cling**

clutch [klʌch] 1. *n* **car clutch** al-qābiḍ القابض 2. *v* qabaḍa ʿalā قبض على (i; qabḍ قبض)

coach [kəuch] 1. *n* ḥāfila حافلة; otobīs أوتوبيس 2. (*spor.*) mudarrib riyāḍī مدرب رياضي 3. *v* darraba درب

coal [kəul] *n* faḥm فحم

coalition [kəuə'lishən] *n* i'tilāf إئتلاف

coast [kəust] *n* sāḥil ساحل (sawāḥil سواحل)

coastal ['kəustəl] *adj* sāḥilī ساحلي

coat [kəut] *n* mi'ṭaf معطف (ma'āṭif معاطف)

coax [kəuks] *v* lāṭafa لاطف

cock; cockerel [kok; 'kokrəl] *n* dīk ديك (duyūk ديوك)

cockroach ['kokrəuch] *n* ṣurṣūr صرصور (ṣarāṣīr صراصير)

coconut(s) ['kəukənʌt] *n* jawz al-hind جوز الهند *collective* (-āt)

code [kəud] *n* shifra شفرة

coffee ['kofi] *n* qahwa قهوة

coffin ['kofin] *n* tābūt تابوت (tawābīt توابيت)

coil [koil] *v* iltaffa التف

coin [koin] *n* naqd ma'dinī نقد معدني

coincidence [kəu'insidəns] *n* ṣudfa صدفة (ṣudaf صدف); muṣādafa مصادفة

cold [kəuld] 1. *adj* bārid بارد 2. *n* bard برد 3. (*med.*) zukām زكام; bard برد

collaborate [kə'labəreit] *v* ta'āwana تعاون (**with** ma'a مع)

collapse [kə'laps] 1. *n* inhiyār إنهيار 2. *v* inhāra انهار

collar ['kolə] *n* yāqa ياقة

colleague ['koli:g] *n* zamīl زميل (zumalā' زملاء)

collect [kə'lekt] *v* 1. jama'a جمع (a; jam' جمع); lamma لم (u; lamm لم) 2. ijtama'a اجتمع (لم)

collection [kə'lekshən] *n* majmū'a مجموعة (-āt)

college ['kolij] *n* kullīya كلية (-āt)

collide [kə'laid] *v* taṣādama تصادم

collision [kə'liẓhən] *n* taṣādum تصادم

colloquial [kə'ləukwiəl] *adj* ʿāmmī عامي; dārij دارج

colonel ['kə:nəl] *n* ʿaqīd عقيد (ʿuqadāʾ عقداء)

colony ['koləni] *n* mustʿmara مستعمرة (-āt)

colour, *(US)* **color** ['kʌlə] *n* lawn لون (alwān ألوان)

column ['koləm] *n* **1.** ʿamūd عمود (aʿmida أعمدة; ʿumud عمد) **2.** **newspaper column** ʿamūd ṣaḥīfa عمود صحيفة

coma ['kəumə] *n* ghaybūba غيبوبة

comb [kəum] *n* mushṭ مشط (amshāṭ أمشاط)

combat ['kombat] **1.** *n* qitāl قتال **2.** *v* qāwama قاوم

combination [kombi'neishən] *n* ittiḥād إتحاد; tarkīb تركيب

combine [kəm'bain] *v* waḥḥada وحد

come [kʌm] *v* (**came, come**) jāʾa جاء (i; majīʾ مجيء)

come back *v* rajaʿa رجع (i; rujūʿ رجوع)

comedian [kə'mi:diən] *n* muharrij مهرج (-ūn)

come in *v* dakhala دخل (u; dukhūl دخول)

comedy ['komi:di] *n* kōmīdīya كوميديا

come out *v* kharaja خرج (u; khurūj خروج)

comfort ['kʌmfət] *n* rāḥa راحة; rafāhīya رفاهية; tarfīh ترفيه

comfortable ['kʌmftəbəl] *adj* murīḥ مريح

comic ['komik] *adj* hazlī هزلي

coming ['kʌming] *adj* qādim قادم

command [kə'ma:nd] **1.** *n* amr أمر (awāmir أوامر) **2.** qiyāda قيادة **3.** *v* amara أمر (u; amr أمر)

commander [kə'ma:ndə] *n* qāʾid قائد (-ūn)

comment ['koment] *v* ʿallaqa علق

commerce ['komə:s] *n* tijāra تجارة

commercial [kə'mə:shəl] *adj* tijārī تجاري

commission [kə'mishən] *n* **1.** lajna لجنة (-āt; lijān لجان) **2.** *(fin.)* ʿamūla عمولة

commit [kə'mit] *v* (**committed**) **1.** irtakaba ارتكب **2.** taʿahhada bi تعهد ب

commitment [kə'mitmənt] *n* taʿahhud تعهد

committee [kə'miti:] *n* lajna لجنة (-āt; lijān لجان)

common ['komən] *adj* iʿtiyādī إعتيادي; ʿāmm عام

commonplace ['komənpleis] *adj* iʿtiyādī إعتيادي

communicate [kə'myu:nikeit] *v* ittaṣala اتصل

communication [kəmyu:ni'keishən] *n* ittiṣāl إتصال

communications [kəmyu:ni'keishənz] *pl* wasāʾil ittiṣāl وسائل إتصال

community [kə'myu:niti] *n* **1.** jumhūr جمهور **2.** jālīya جالية (-āt)

compact ['kompakt] *adj* mudmaj مندمج; mundamij مدمج

compact disc *n* sī-dī سي دي (sī-dīhāt سي ديهات)

companion [kəm'paniən] *n* rafīq رفيق (rufaqāʾ رفقاء; rifāq رفاق)

company ['kʌmpəni] *n* *(com.)* sharika شركة (-āt)

comparatively [kəm'parətivli] *adv*
nisbīyan نسبياً

compare [kəm'peə] *v* qārana قارن

comparison [kəm'parisn] *n*
muqārana مقارنة

compartment [kəm'pa:tmənt] *n*
maqṣūra مقصورة (-āt)

compatible [kəm'patəbəl] *adj*
mutasāwiq متساوق; munsajim
منسجم

compel [kəm'pel] *v* ajbara أجبر

compensation [kompən'seishən]
n taʿwīḍ تعويض

compete [kəm'pi:t] *v* tanāfasa maʿa
تنافس مع

competent ['kompitənt] *adj* kafʾ
كفء (at li ل)

competition [kompe'tishən] *n*
munāfasa منافسة

competitor [kom'petitə] *n* munāfis
منافس (-ūn)

complain [kəm'plein] *v* shakā شكا
(u; shakwā شكوى) shikāya شكاية)

complaint [kəm'pleint] *n* shakwā
شكوى (shakāwā شكاوى)

complete [kəm'pli:t] **1.** *adj* tāmm
تام; kāmil كامل **2.** *v* kamila كمل
(a; kamāl كمال); tamma تم (i);
atamma أتم

completely [kəm'pli:tli] *adv*
tamāman تماماً

complex ['kompleks] **1.** *adj*
muʿaqqad معقد **2.** *n* ʿuqda عقدة
(ʿuqad عقد)

complicated ['komplikeitid] *adj*
muʿaqqad معقد

compose [kəm'pəuz] *v* **1.** kawwana
كون; rakkaba ركب **2.** *(mus.)* laḥḥana
لحن; allafa ألف

composer [kəm'pəuzə] *n* mulaḥḥin

ملحن; mu'allif مؤلف (-ūn)

composition [kompə'zishən] *n* **1.**
takwīn تكوين; tarkīb تركيب **2.** *(mus.)*
mu'allaf مؤلف **3.** *(acad.)* maqāla
مقالة (-āt)

compound ['kompaund] *n*
murakkab مركب (-āt)

comprehension [kompri'hen-
shən] *n* fahm فهم; idrāk إدراك

compress [kəm'pres] *v* ḍaghaṭa
ضغط (a; ḍaghṭ ضغط)

compulsory [kəm'pʌlsəri] *adj*
ijbārī إجباري

computer [kəm'pyu:tə] *n* kompyūtir
كومبيوتر; āla ḥāsiba آلة حاسبة

conceal [kənsi:l] *v* akhfā أخفى

conceive [kən'si:v] *v* **1.** taṣawwara
تصور; takhayyala تخيل **2.** ḥamala
حمل (i; ḥaml حمل); ḥabila حبل (i;
ḥabal حبل)

concentrate ['konsəntreit] *v* **1.**
rakkaza ركز **2.** kaththafa كثف

concentration [konsən'treishən] *n*
1. tarkīz تركيز **2.** kathāfa كثافة

concept ['konsept] *n* fikra فكرة
(fikar فكر); mafhūm مفهوم
(mafāhīm مفاهيم)

concern [kən'sə:n] **1.** *n* qalaq قلق;
hamm هم (humūm هموم) **2.** *(com.)*
3. mashrūʿ مشروع (mashārīʿ مشاريع).
v aqlaqa أقلق **4.** taʿallaqa bi تعلق ب

concerned [kən'sə:nd] *adj* qaliq
قلق

concerned with; concerning
[kən'sə:ning] *prep* fīmā yataʿallaq
bi فيما يتعلق ب

concert ['konsət] *n* ḥafla mūsīqīya
حفلة موسيقية

concise [kən'sais] *adj* mūjaz موجز;
mukhtaṣar مختصر

conclude [kən'klu:d] v anhā أنهى;
akhtama أختم

conclusion [kən'klu:shən] n 1.
khitām ختام 2. istintāj إستنتاج

concrete ['konkri:t] 1. adj māddī
مادي 2. ismantī إسمنتي 3. n ismant
إسمنت

condemn [kən'dem] v adāna أدان

condition [kən'dishən] n 1. ḥāl
حال (aḥwāl أحوال); ḥāla حالة (-āt)
2. (leg.) sharṭ شرط (shurūṭ شروط)
3. **on condition that** ʿalā sharṭ an
على شرط أن

condom ['kondəm] n al-wāqī adh-
dhakarī الواقي الذكري

conduct [kən'dʌkt] v 1. taṣarrafa
تصرف 2. (mus.) adāra (orkestrā)
أدار (أوركسترا)

conductor [kən'dʌktə] n 1. qāṭiʿ at-
tadhākir قاطع التذاكر 2. (mus.) mudīr
al-orkestrā مدير الأوركسترا

conference ['konfərəns] n 1.
mu'tamar مؤتمر 2. **press conference**
muʿtamar ṣuhufī معتمر صحفي

confession [kən'feshən] n iʿtirāf
إعتراف

confidence ['konfidəns] n thiqa bi
'n-nafs ثقة بالنفس

confident ['konfidənt] adj wāthiq
bi 'n-nafs واثق بالنفس

confidential [konfi'dənshəl] adj
sirrī سري

confine [kən'fain] v ḥabasa حبس
(i; ḥabs حبس)

confirm [kən'fə:m] v akkada أكد

confirmation [konfə'meishən] n
ta'kīd تأكيد

conflict ['konflikt] n 1. taḍārub
تضارب 2. (mil.) nizāʿ تعارض
(-āt); ṣirāʿ صراع (-āt)

conform [kən'fo:m] v tawāfaqa
maʿa توافق مع

confront [kən'frʌnt] v wājaha واجه

confrontation [konfrʌn'teishən] n
muwājaha مواجهة

confuse [kən'fyu:z] v arbaka أربك

confused [kən'fyu:zd] adj **to be**
confused irtabaka ارتبك

confusing [kən'fyu:zing] adj
murbik مربك

confusion [kən'fyu:zhən] n irtibāk
إرتباك

congratulate [kən'grachuleit] v
hanna'a هنأ (**on** ʿalā على/bi ب)

congratulations [kəngrachu'lei-
shənz] pl tahāni' تهاني

congress ['konggres] n 1. ijtimāʿ
إجتماع; mu'tamar مؤتمر 2. (US)
Congress kongres كنغرس

connect [kə'nekt] v rabaṭa ربط
(u/i; rabṭ ربط)

connection [kə'nekshən] n 1.
irtibāṭ إرتباط 2. **in connection**
with fīmā yataʿallaqu bi
فيما يتعلق ب

conquer ['kongkə] v ghalaba غلب
(i; ghalb غلب; ghalaba غلبة)

conquest ['kongkwest] n fatḥ فتح
(futūḥ فتوح)

conscience ['konshəns] n ḍamīr
ضمير

conscious ['konshəs] adj wāʿin واع

consecutive [kən'sekyutiv] adj
mutatālin متتال; mutaʿāqib متعاقب

consent [kən'sent] n muwāfaqa
موافقة

consequence ['konsikwens] n 1.
natīja نتيجة (natā'ij نتائج); ʿāqiba
عاقبة (ʿawāqib عواقب) 2. **in**
consequence of natīja li نتيجة ل

consequently [konsi'kwentli] *conj* بِناءً على ذلك ;binā'an ʿalā dhālik هكذا hākadhā

conservation [konsə'veishən] *n* صِيانة ;şiyāna حِفظ hifz

conservative [kən'sə:vətiv] *(pol.)* *adj/n* محافِظ muḥāfiz (-ūn)

consider [kən'sidə] *v* اعتبر ;iʿtabara فكّر في fakkara fī

considerable [kən'sidrəbəl] *adj* جدير بالإعتبار jadīr bi 'l-iʿtibār

consideration [kənsidə'reishən] *n* اِعتبار iʿtibār

considering [kən'sidəring] *prep* إذا أخذنا في عين الإعتبار idhā akhadhnā fī ʿayn al-iʿtibār

consist [kən'sist] *v* takawwana تكوّن (of min من)

consonant ['konsənənt] *n* حرف ساكن ḥārf sākin

conspicuous [kən'spikyuəs] *adj* ملفت الإنتباه mulfit al-intibāh

conspiracy [kən'spirəsi] *n* مؤامرة mu'āmara (-āt)

constable ['kʌnstəbəl] *n* شرطي shurṭī (-yūn)

constant ['konstənt] *adj* mustaqirr ثابت ;mustaqirr مستقر

constitution [konsti'tyu:shən] *n* 1. takwīn تكوين 2. *(pol.)* دستور dustūr

constitutional [konsti'tyu:shənəl] *adj* دستوري dustūrī

construct [kən'strʌkt] *v* بنى banā (i; binā' بناء; bunyān بنيان)

construction [kən'strʌkshən] *n* بنيان bunyān ;بناء binā'

constructive [kən'strʌktiv] *adj* بناء bannā'

consul ['konsyul] *n* قنصل qunṣul (قناصل qanāşil)

consulate ['konsyulət] *n* قنصلية qunşulīya (-āt)

consult [kən'sʌlt] *v* استشار istashāra

consultant [konsʌltənt] *n* مستشار mustashār (-ūn); خبير khabīr (khubarā' خبراء)

consultation [konsəl'teishən] *n* استشارة istishāra; تشاور tashāwur

consume [kən'syu:m] *v* 1. akala أكل (u; akl أكل) 2. *(ec.)* istahlaka استهلك

consumer [kən'syu:mə] *n* mustahlik مستهلك (-ūn)

consumption [kən'sʌmpshən] *n* istihlāk إستهلاك

contact [kontakt] *n* 1. ittişāl إتصال 2. iḥtikāk إحتكاك

contact lens *n* ʿadasa lāşiqa عدسة لاصقة (-āt)

contagious [kən'teijəs] *adj* muʿdin معدٍ

contain [kən'tein] *v* iḥtawā احتوى

container [kən'teinə] *n* 1. إناء inā' (آنية āniya); وعاء wiʿā' (أوعية awʿiya) 2. **freight container** şundūq ash-shaḥn صندوق الشحن

contemplate ['kontempleit] *v* ta'ammala تأمل

contemporary [kən'tempərери] *adj* muʿāşir معاصر

contempt [kən'tempt] *n* iḥtiqār إحتقار

content [kən'tent] *adj* rāḍin راضٍ; qāniʿ قانع

contents ['kontents] *pl* muḥtawayāt محتويات

contest ['kontest] *n* mubārāh مباراة (mubārayāt مباريات)

continent ['kontinənt] *n* 1. qārra قارة (-āt) 2. **the Continent** *(UK)* urubba أريا

continental [konti'nentəl] *adj* **1.** قاري qārī **2.** *(UK)* urubbī أربي

continually [kən'tinyuəl] *adv* bi istimrār بإستمرار

continue [kən'tinyu:] *v* istamarra استمر

continuous [kən'tinyuəs] *adj* mustamirr مستمر

contraception [kontrə'sepchən] *n* manʿ al-ḥamal منع الحمل

contraceptive [kontrə'septiv] **1.** *adj* māniʿ al-ḥamal مانع الحمل **2.** *n* wasīlat manʿ al-ḥamal وسيلة منع الحمل

contract ['kontrakt] *n* ʿaqd عقد (ʿuqūd عقود)

contractor [kə'ntraktə] *n* muqāwil مقاول (-ūn); mutaʿahhid متعهد (-ūn)

contradict [kontrə'dikt] *v* nāqaḍa ناقض

contradiction [kontrə'dikshən] *n* munāqaḍa مناقضة

contrary ['kontrəri] *n* **on the contrary** bi 'l-ʿaks بالعكس

contrast ['kontra:st] *n* taghāyur تغاير

contribute [kən'tribyu:t] *v* tabarraʿa تبرع

contribution [kontri'byu:shən] *n* tabarruʿ تبرع (-āt)

control [kən'trəul] **1.** *n* sayṭara سيطرة; taḥakkum تحكم **2. remote control** rīmōt kontrōl ريموت كونترول **3. self-control** ḍabṭ an-nafs ضبط النفس **4.** *v* sayṭara سيطر

controller [kən'trəulə] *n* murāqib مراقب (-ūn)

controversial [kontrə'və:shəl] *adj* muthīr li 'l-jadal مثير للجدل

convenient [kən'vi:niənt] *adj* munāsib مناسب; mulā'im ملائم

convention [kən'venshən] *n* **1.** mu'tamar مؤتمر (-āt) **2.** muʿāhada معاهدة (-āt); ittifāqīya إتفاقية (-āt)

conventional [kən'venshənəl] *adj* taqlīdī تقليدي

conversation [kon'vəseishən] *n* ḥadīth حديث; muḥādatha محادثة

conversion [kən'və:shən] *n* (*fin.*) taḥwīl تحويل; taḥawwul تحوّل

convert [kon'və:t] *v* (*fin.*) ḥawwala حوّل; taḥawwala تحول

convey [kən'vei] *v* naqala نقل (u; naql نقل)

convict ['konvikt] *n* sajīn سجين (sujanā' سجناء)

convict [kən'vikt] *v* adāna أدان

convince [kən'vins] *v* aqnaʿa أقنع

convoy ['konvoi] *n* qāfila قافلة (qawāfil قوافل)

cook [kuk] **1.** *n* ṭabbākh طباخ (-ūn) **2.** *v* ṭabakha طبخ (u/a; ṭabkh طبخ)

cooker ['kukə] *n* jihāz li 'ṭ-ṭabkh جهاز للطبخ

cool [ku:l] **1.** *adj* bārid بارد **2.** ghayr munfaʿil غير منفعل **3.** *v* barrada برد

cooperate [kəu'opəreit] *v* taʿāwana تعاون

cooperation [kəuopə'reishən] *n* taʿāwun تعاون

cop [kop] *n* (*sl.*) shurṭī شرطي

cope [kəup] *v* **to cope with** taḥammala تحمل

copier ['kopiə] *see* photocopier

copper ['kopə] *n* **1.** naḥās نحاس **2.** (*sl.*) shurṭī شرطي (-yūn)

copy ['kopi] **1.** *n* nuskha نسخة (nusakh نسخ) **2.** *v* nasakha نسخ (a; naskh نسخ) **3.** qallada قلد

copyright ['kopirait] *n* ḥaqq al-mu'allif حق المؤلف; ḥaqq an-nāshir حق الناشر

cord [ko:d] *n* ḥabl حبل (ḥibāl حبال)

core [ko:] *n* labb لب; jawhar جوهر

cork [ko:k] *n* fallīn فلين; fallīna فلينة

corkscrew ['ko:kskru:] *n* nāziʿat al-fallīna نازعة الفلينة

corn [ko:n] *n* qamḥ قمح; dhurra ذرة

corner ['ko:nə] *n* zāwiya زاوية (zawāyā زوايا)

corporation [ko:pə'reishən] *n* sharika شركة (-āt)

corpse [ko:ps] *n* juththa جثة (juthath جثث)

correct [kə'rekt] 1. *adj* ṣaḥīḥ صحيح; maḍbūṭ مضبوط 2. *v* ṣaḥḥaḥa صحح

correction [kə'rekshən] *n* taṣḥīḥ تصحيح

correspondence [koris'pondəns] *n* murāsala مراسلة

correspondent [koris'pondənt] *n* murāsil مراسل (-ūn)

corridor ['korido:] *n* mamarr ممر (-āt)

corrupt [kə'rʌpt] *adj* fāsid فاسد

corruption [kə'rʌpshən] *n* fasād فساد

cosmetic [koz'metik] 1. *adj* tajmīlī تجميلي 2. *n* mādda li 't-tajmīl مادة للتجميل

cost [kost] *n* 1. thaman ثمن; taklīf تكليف 2. *v* kallafa كلف

costly ['kostli] *adj* mukallif مكلف; ghālin غال

costume ['kostyu:m] *n* ziyy زي (azyā' أزياء)

cottage ['kotij] *n* kūkh كوخ (akwākh أكواخ)

cotton ['kotən] *n* quṭn قطن

cotton wool *n* quṭn ṭibbī قطن طبي

couch [kauch] *n* arīka أريكة (arā'ik أرائك)

cough [kof] 1. *n* kuḥḥa كحة; suʿāl سعال 2. *v* kaḥḥa كح (u);saʿala سعل (u; suʿla سعلة; suʿāl سعال)

could [kəd; kud] *see* **can**

council ['kaunsəl] *n* 1. majlis مجلس (majālis مجالس) 2. baladīya بلدية (-āt)

councillor ['kaunsələ] *n* ʿuḍw baladīya عضو بلدية (aʿḍā' أعضاء)

counsellor ['kaunsələ] *n* nāṣiḥ ناصح (nuṣṣāḥ نصاح); mustashār مستشار (-ūn)

count [kaunt] *v* ʿadda عد (u; ʿadd عد)

counter ['kauntə] 1. *n* minḍadat dukkān منضدة دكان 2. *v* ʿāraḍa عارض

counterfeit ['kauntəfit] *adj* zā'if زائف; muzayyaf مزيف

countless ['kauntlis] *adj* lā yuʿadd لا يعد; lā yuḥṣā لا يحصى

country ['kʌntri] *n* 1. balad بلد (bilād بلاد; buldān بلدان); waṭan وطن 2. rīf ريف (awṭān أوطان)

countryside ['kʌntrisaid] *n* ar-rīf الريف

county ['kaunti] *n* muqāṭaʿa مقاطعة (-āt); iqlīm إقليم (aqālīm أقاليم)

coup; coup d'état [ku:; ku:dei'ta:] *n* inqilāb إنقلاب

couple ['kʌpəl] *n* 1. ithnān إثنان 2. zawjān زوجان

courage ['kʌrij] *n* shajāʿa شجاعة

courier ['kuriyə] *n* sāʿin ساع (sāʿūn ساعون)

course [ko:s] *n* 1. sīr سير; majran مجرى 2. *(ed.)* dawra taʿlīmiya

دورة تعليمية .3 (āt-) **3. (spor.)** majra
's-sibāq مجرى السباق **4. in due
course** fi'l-waqt al-munāsib
في الوقت المناسب; lāḥiqan لاحقاً
5. of course! ṭabʿan طبعاً **6. in
the course of** khilāl خلال; ithnā'
إثناء **7. see racecourse**

court [koːt] n **1. (spor.)** malʿab ملعب
(malāʿib ملاعب) **2. (leg.)** maḥkama
محكمة (maḥākim محاكم) **3. high
court, supreme court** al-
maḥkama al-ʿulyā المحكمة العليا

courtesy ['kəːtəsi] n luṭf لطف; adab
أدب

cousin ['kʌsin] n ibn ʿamm/bint
ʿamm إبن عم\بنت عم; ibn ʿamma/
bint ʿamma إبن عمة\بنت عمة; ibn
khāl /bint khāl إبن خال\بنت خال; ibn
khāla/bint khāla إبن خالة\بنت خالة

cover ['kʌvə] **1.** n ghiṭā' غطاء
(aghṭiyā' أغطية) **2.** v ghaṭṭā غطى

cow [kau] n baqara بقرة (baqar
بقر *collective*)

coward ['kauəd] n jabān جبان
(jubanā' جبناء)

cowboy ['kauboi] n rāʿi 'l-baqar
راعي البقر

crab [krab] n saraṭān al-baḥr
سرطان البحر

crack [krak] v sharkh شرخ (ashrākh
أشراخ); shaqq شق (shuqūq شقوق)

craft [kraːft] n (pl **craft**) **1.** ḥirfa حرفة
(ḥiraf حرف) **2.** mirkab مركب
(marākib مراكب); safina سفينة
(sufun سفن) **3. see aircraft**

craftsman ['kraːftsmən] n ṣāḥib al-
ḥirfa صاحب الحرفة

crane [krein] n **1.** rāfiʿa رافعة
(rawāfiʿ روافع); winsh ونش (āt-)
2. kurkī كركي (karākī كراكي)

crash [krash] **1.** n iṣṭidām إصطدام **2.**

(ec.) inhiyār إنهيار **3.** v iṣṭadama
اصطدم

crawl [kroːl] v zaḥafa زحف (a; zaḥf
زحف)

crazy ['kreizi] adj majnūn مجنون

cream [kriːm] n **1.** qishda قشدة
2. krīm كريم; mustaḥḍar ṭibbī
مستحضر طبي; mustaḥḍar tajmīlī
مستحضر تجميلي

create [kriː'eit] v **1.** khalaqa خلق (u;
khalq خلق); **2.** abdaʿa أبدع

creation [kriː'eishən] n **1.** khalq خلق
2. ibdāʿ إبداع

creative [kriː'eitiv] adj mubdiʿ مبدع

creator [kriː'eitə] n khāliq خالق;
mubdiʿ مبدع

creature ['kriːchə] n makhlūq
مخلوق (āt-)

credible ['kredibəl] adj maʿqūl
معقول

credit [kredit] n **(fin.)** iʿtimād إعتماد

credit card n biṭāqat iʿtimād
بطاقة إعتماد

creditor ['kreditə] n dā'in دائن

crest [krest] n crest of a mountain
qimma قمة (qimam قمم)

crew [kruː] n ṭāqim طاقم

cricket ['krikit] n **1.** judjud جدجد
(jadājid جداجد) **2. (spor.)** krīkit
كريكت

crime [kraim] n **1.** jarīma جريمة
(jarā'im جرائم) **2. to commit a
crime** irtakaba jarīma ارتكب جريمة

criminal ['kriminəl] **1.** adj ijrāmī
إجرامي **2.** n mujrim مجرم (ūn-)

cripple ['kripl] v ashalla أشل

crisis ['kraisis] n (pl **crises**) azma
أزمة (azamāt أزمات)

critic ['kritik] n nāqid ناقد (ūn-);
nuqqād (نقاد)

critical ['kritikəl] adj 1. naqdī نقدي;
intiqādī إنتقادي 2. (med.) khaṭir
خطر; khaṭīr خطير

criticize ['kritisaiz] v intaqada إنتقد

croak [krəuk] v naqqa نق (i; naqīq
نقيق)

crockery ['krokəri] n āniyat aṭ-
ṭaʿām آنية الطعام

crook [kruk] n naṣṣāb نصّاب (-ūn)

crooked ['krukid] adj multawin ملتو

crop; crops [krop; -s] n, pl maḥṣūl
(محاصيل; maḥāṣīl) محصول

cross [kros] 1. adj ghāḍib غاضب 2. n
ṣalīb صليب (ṣulbān صلبان) 3. v
ʿabara عبر (u; ʿabr عبر; ʿubūr عبور)

crossing ['krosing] n ʿubūr عبور

cross out v shaṭaba شطب (u; shaṭb
شطب)

crossroad; crossroads ['kros-
rəud; -z] n, pl muftaraq al-ṭuruq
مفترق الطرق

crossword puzzle ['kroswə:d] n
kalimāt mutaqāṭiʿa كلمات متقاطعة

crouch [krauch] v qarfaṣa قرفص

crow [kreu] 1. n ghurāb غراب
(ghirbān غربان) 2. v ṣāḥa صاح
(i; ṣayḥ صيح; ṣiyāḥ صياح)

crowd [kraud] n ḥashd حشد (ḥushūd
حشود)

crowded ['kraudid] adj muzdaḥim
مزدحم

crown [kraun] n tāj تاج (tījān تيجان)

crucial ['kru:shəl] adj hāmm هام;
ḥāsim حاسم

crude [kru:d] adj 1. khashin خشن;
ghayr muhadhdhab غير مهذب 2.
khām خام

cruel ['kruəl] adj qāsin قاس

cruelty ['kruəlti] n qaswa قسوة;
qasāwa قساوة

cruise [kru:z] n riḥla baḥrīya
رحلة بحرية

cruiser ['kru:zə] n ṭarrād طراد;
ṭarrāda طرّادة

crusade [kru:'seid] n 1. ḥarb
ṣalībīya f حرب صليبية 2. niḍāl نضال;
kifāḥ كفاح 3. ḥamla حملة

crush [krʌsh] v saḥaqa سحق (a; saḥq
سحق)

cry [krai] 1. n ṣarkha صرخة (-āt) 2. v
bakā بكى (i; bukā’ بكاء) 3. ṣarakha
صرخ (u; ṣurākh صراخ; ṣarīkh صريخ)

cube [kyu:b] n mukaʿʿab مكعب (-āt)

cucumber(s) ['kyukʌmbə] n
khiyār collective خيار

cuisine [kwi'zi:n] n ṭabkh طبخ;
uslūb aṭ-ṭabkh أسلوب الطبخ

cult [kʌlt] n ṭā’ifa طائفة (ṭawā’if
طوائف)

cultivation [kʌlti'veishən] n zirāʿa
زراعة

cultural ['kʌlchərəl] adj thaqāfī
ثقافي

culture ['kʌlchə] n thaqāfa ثقافة (-āt)

cup [kʌp] n 1. kūb كوب (akwāb
أكواب); finjān فنجان (fanājīn
فناجين) 2. (spor.) ka’s كأس; ku’ūs
كؤوس

cupboard ['kʌbəd] n dūlāb دولاب
(dawālīb دواليب);khizāna خزانة
(khazā’in خزائن)

curb [kə:b] v ḥāfat ar-raṣīf
حافة الرصيف

cure [kyuə] (med.) 1. n shifā’ شفاء;
ʿilāj علاج; dawā’ دواء 2. v shafā شفى
(i; shifā’ شفاء)

curiosity [kyuəri'osəti] n 1. ḥubb
al-istiṭlāʿ حب الإستطلاع 2. tuḥfa تحفة

curious ['kyuəriəs] adj 1. fuḍūlī
فضولي 2. gharīb غريب

curl [kə:l] *n* ﻋﻘﻴﺼﺔ ʿaqīṣa (-āt)

currency ['kʌrənsi] *n* **1.** ﻋﻤﻠﺔ ʿumla (-āt) **2. foreign currency** ʿumla ajnabīya ﺃﺟﻨﺒﻴﺔ ﻋﻤﻠﺔ

current ['kʌrənt] **1.** *adj* ﺣﺎﻟﻲ ḥālī; rāhin ﺭﺍﻫﻦ **2.** *n* tayyār ﺗﻴﺎﺭ

curriculum [kə'rikyuləm] *n* minhāj ad-dirāsa ﻣﻨﻬﺎﺝ ﺍﻟﺪﺭﺍﺳﺔ

curse [kə:s] *n* **1.** ﻟﻌﻨﺔ laʿna **2.** balā' ﺑﻼء

curtain ['kə:tən] *n* sitāra ﺳﺘﺎﺭﺓ (satā'ir ﺳﺘﺎﺋﺮ)

curve [kə:v] **1.** *n* munḥanan ﻣﻨﺤﻨﻰ (munḥanayāt ﻣﻨﺤﻨﻴﺎﺕ) **2.** *v* inḥanā ﺍﻧﺤﻨﻰ

curved [kə:vd] *adj* munḥanin ﻣﻨﺤﻦ

cushion ['kushən] *n* wisāda ﻭﺳﺎﺩﺓ

custom ['kʌstəm] *n* ʿāda ﻋﺎﺩﺓ (-āt)

customer ['kʌstəmə] *n* zabūn ﺯﺑﻮﻥ (zabā'in ﺯﺑﺎﺋﻦ)

customs ['kʌstəmz] *pl* gumruk ﺟﻤﺮﻙ (gamārik ﺟﻤﺎﺭﻙ)

cut [kʌt] **1.** *n* jurḥ ﺟﺮﺡ **2.** *(ec.)* ḥadhafa ﺣﺬﻑ (i; ḥadhf ﺣﺬﻑ) **3.** *v* (cut) qaṭaʿa ﻗﻄﻊ (a; qatʿ ﻗﻄﻊ)

cutlery ['kʌtləri] *n* adawāt al-mā'ida ﺃﺩﻭﺍﺕ ﺍﻟﻤﺎﺋﺪﺓ

cut off *v* qaṭaʿa ﻗﻄﻊ (a; qatʿ ﻗﻄﻊ)

cycle ['saikəl] **1.** *n* dawra ﺩﻭﺭﺓ (-āt) **2.** *v* rakiba 'd-darrāja ﺭﻛﺐ ﺍﻟﺪﺭﺍﺟﺔ (a; rukūb)

cylinder ['silində] *n* usṭawāna ﺃﺳﻄﻮﺍﻧﺔ (-āt)

D

dad; daddy [dad; 'dadi] *n* bābā ﺑﺎﺑﺎ (bābawāt ﺑﺎﺑﻮﺍﺕ)

daft [daft] *adj* sakhīf ﺳﺨﻴﻒ

dagger ['dagə] *n* khanjar ﺧﻨﺠﺮ (khanājir ﺧﻨﺎﺟﺮ)

daily ['deili] **1.** *n* ṣaḥīfa yawmīya ﺻﺤﻴﻔﺔ ﻳﻮﻣﻴﺔ **2.** *adj* yawmī ﻳﻮﻣﻲ **3.** *adv* yawmīyan ﻳﻮﻣﻴﺎً

dairy ['deəri] *n* malbana ﻣﻠﺒﻨﺔ (-āt)

dam [dam] *n* sadd ﺳﺪ (sudūd ﺳﺪﻭﺩ)

damage ['damij] **1.** *n* ḍarar ﺿﺮﺭ; adhan ﺃﺫﻯ **2.** *v* ḍarra ﺿﺮ (u; ḍarr ﺿﺮ) **3.** *see* **damages**

damages ['damijiz] *pl (leg.)* taʿwīḍ ﺗﻌﻮﻳﺾ

damn [dam] *v* laʿana ﻟﻌﻦ (a; laʿn ﻟﻌﻦ)

damp [damp] **1.** *adj* raṭb ﺭﻃﺐ **2.** *n* ruṭūba ﺭﻃﻮﺑﺔ

dance [da:ns] **1.** *n* raqṣ ﺭﻗﺺ **2.** *v* raqaṣa ﺭﻗﺺ (u; raqṣ ﺭﻗﺺ)

dancer ['da:nsə] *n* rāqiṣ ﺭﺍﻗﺺ (-ūn)

dancing ['da:nsing] *n* raqṣ ﺭﻗﺺ

Dane [dein] *n* danmārkī ﺩﻧﻤﺎﺭﻛﻲ (-yūn)

danger ['deinjə] *n* khaṭar ﺧﻄﺮ

dangerous ['deinjərəs] *adj* khaṭīr خطير

Danish ['deinish] *adj* danmārkī دنماركي

dare [deə] *v* 1. jaru'a جرؤ (u; jur'a جرؤ; jarā'a جراءة) 2. taḥaddā تحدّى

dark [da:k] 1. *adj (colour)* ghāmiḍ غامض 2. *(night)* muẓlim مظلم 3. *n* ẓalām ظلام

darken ['da:kən] *v* aẓlama أظلم

darkness ['da:knis] *n* ẓalām ظلام

darling ['da:ling] *adj/n* ḥabīb حبيب (aḥibbā' أحباء; aḥbāb أحباب)

dash [dash] *v* istaʿjala استعجل

data ['deitə] *n* maʿlūmāt معلومات *pl*

database ['deitəbeis] *n* qāʿidat qāʿidat bayānāt قاعدة بيانات

date [deit] *n* 1. tārīkh تاريخ (tawārīkh تواريخ) 2. mawʿid موعد (mawāʿid مواعد) 3. tamr تمر *collective*; balaḥ بلح *collective*

daughter ['do:tə] *n* ibna ابنة (banāt بنات); bint بنت (banāt بنات)

daughter-in-law ['do:tərinlo:] *n* kanna كنة (kanā'in كنائن); zawjat al-ibn زوجة الإبن

dawn [do:n] 1. *n* fajr فجر 2. *v* bazagha بزغ (u; bazūgh بزوغ)

day [dei] *n* yawm يوم (ayyām أيام)

day after tomorrow *n/adv* baʿd ghad بعد غد

day before yesterday *n/adv* ams al-awwal أمس الأول

daytime ['deitaim] *n* nahār نهار

dead [ded] *adj* 1. mayyit ميت (amwāt أموات; mawtā موتى) 2. the dead al-amwāt الأموات; al-mawtā الموتى

deadline ['dedlain] *n* mawʿid akhīr موعد أخير

deadly ['dedli] *adj* mumīt مميت

deaf [def] *adj* aṣamm أصم; aṭrash أطرش

deaf-mute *n* aṣamm abkam أبكم أصم

deal [di:l] 1. *n* ṣafqa صفقة (ṣafaqāt صفقات) 2. **a great deal** kathīr كثير 3. *v* wazzaʿa وزع 4. taʿāmala تعامل (with maʿa مع) 5. *(com.)* bāʿa باع (i; bayʿ بيع; mabīʿ مبيع)

dealer ['di:lə] *n (com.)* bā'iʿ بائع (-ūn)

dear [diə] *adj* 1. ʿazīz عزيز 2. ghālin غال

death [deth] *n* mawt موت

debate [di'beit] 1. *n* munāqasha مناقشة (-āt) 2. *v* nāqasha ناقش

debit ['debit] 1. *n* dayn دين (duyūn ديون) 2. *v* sajjala fī ḥisāb madīn سجل في حساب مدين

debt [det] *n* dayn دين (duyūn ديون)

debtor ['detə] *n* madīn مدين; madyūn مديون

decade ['dekeid] *n* ʿaqd عقد (ʿuqūd عقود)

decay [di'kei] *v* 1. fasada فسد (u/i; fasād فساد) 2. taʿaffana تعفن

deceive [di'si:v] *v* khadaʿa خدع (a; khudʿa خدعة)

December [di'sembə] *n* disimbir ديسمبر; kānūn al-awwal كانون الأول

decency ['di:sənsi] *n* iḥtishām إحتشام; adab أدب

decent ['di:sənt] *adj* muḥtashim محتشم; muḥtaram محترم

deception [di'sepshən] *n* khudʿa خدعة (khudaʿ خدع)

decide [di'said] *v* qarrara قرّر

decision [di'sizhən] *n* qarār قرار (-āt)

deck [dek] *n* ship's deck ẓahr as-safīna ظهر السفينة

declare [di'kleə] *n* 1. aʿlana أعلن; ṣarraḥa bi صرح ب 2. to declare war aʿlana al-ḥarb أعلن الحرب

decline [di'klain] 1. *n* inḥidār إنحدار 2. *v* inḥadara انحدر

decorate ['dekəreit] *v* 1. zakhrafa زخرف 2. (*mil.*) manaḥa منح (a; manḥ منح)

decoration [dekə'reishən] *n* 1. zakhrafa زخرفة (-āt) 2. (*mil.*) wisām وسام (awsima أوسمة)

decorator [dekə'reitə] *n* muhandis ad-dēkōr مهندس الديكور

decrease [di'kri:s] 1. *n* naqṣ نقص 2. *v* naqaṣa نقص (u; naqṣ نقص; nuqṣān نقصان)

dedicate ['dedikeit] *v* ahdā أهدى

dedication [dedi'keishən] *n* ihdā' إهداء

deduction [di'dʌkshən] *n* 1. ḥasm حسم 2. istintāj إستنتاج

deed [di:d] *n* ʿamal عمل (aʿmāl أعمال)

deem [di:m] *v* ḥasaba حسب (u; ḥasb حسب; ḥisāb حساب); iʿtabara اعتبر

deep [di:p] *adj* ʿamīq عميق

deep-sea *adj* aʿmāq al-baḥr أعماق البحر

deer [diə] *n* ayyil أيل (ayā'il أيائل)

defeat [di'fi:t] 1. *n* hazīma هزيمة (hazā'im هزائم) 2. *v* hazama هزم (i; hazm هزم)

defect [di'fekt] *v* khalal خلل (khilāl خلال); ʿilla علة (āt; ʿilal علل); ʿayb عيب (ʿuyūb عيوب)

defective [di'fektiv] *adj* 1. nāqiṣ ناقص 2. maʿīb معيب

defence, (*US*) **defense** [di'fens] *n*

1. difāʿ دفاع; ḥimāya حماية 2. self-defence ad-difāʿ ʿan an-nafs الدفاع عن النفس

defend [di'fend] *v* dāfaʿa ʿan دافع عن

defender [di'fendə] *n* mudāfiʿ مدافع (-ūn)

defense [di'fens] see defence

defiant [di'faiənt] *adj* mutaḥaddin متحد

deficiency [di'fishnsi] *n* naqṣ نقص; ʿajz عجز

deficit ['defisit] *n* 1. ʿajz عجز 2. trade deficit naqṣ tijārī نقص تجاري

define [di'fain] *v* 1. ḥaddada حدّد 2. ʿarrafa عرّف

definite ['definət] *adj* 1. muḥaddad محدّد 2. akīd أكيد

definitely ['definətli] *adv* bi 't-ta'kīd بالتأكيد

defy [di'fai] *v* taḥaddā تحدّى

degree [di'gri:] *n* 1. daraja درجة (-āt) 2. to a degree ilā ḥaddin mā إلى حد ما 3. shahāda jāmiʿīya شهادة جامعية

delay [di'lei] 1. *n* ta'khīr تأخير 2. *v* akhkhara أخّر; ajjala أجل

delayed [di'leid] *adj* muta'akhkhir متأخر

delegation [delə'geishən] *n* wafd وفد (wufūd وفود)

delete [di'li:t] *v* shaṭaba شطب (u; shaṭb شطب); ḥadhafa حذف (i; ḥadhf حذف)

deliberate [di'libərət] *adj* mutaʿammid متعمد

deliberately [di'libərətli] *adv* bi taʿammud بتعمد

delicate ['delikət] *adj* raqīq رقيق

delicious [di'lishəs] *adj* ladhīdh لذيذ

delight [di'lait] *n* surūr سرور; bahja بهجة

delighted [di'laitid] *adj* masrūr li 'l-ghāya مسرور للغاية

delightful [di'laitfəl] *adj* sārr li 'l-ghāya سار للغاية

deliver [di'livə] *v* 1. sallama سلّم 2. anqadha أنقذ 3. to deliver a baby wallada ولّد 4. to deliver a speech alqā khiṭāban ألقى خطاباً

delivery [di'livəri] *n* 1. taslīm تسليم 2. *(med.)* wilāda ولادة

deluxe [di'lʌks] *adj* fākhir فاخر

demand [di'ma:nd] 1. *n* muṭālaba مطالبة 2. *v* ṭālaba طالب (-āt)

democracy [di'mokrəsi] *n* dīmuqrāṭīya ديمقراطية

democrat ['deməkrat] *n* dimuqrāṭī ديمقراطي

democratic [demə'kratik] *adj* dimuqrāṭī ديمقراطي

demolish [di'moliʃ] *v* dammara دمّر; haddama هدّم

demolition [demə'liʃən] *n* tadmīr تدمير

demon ['di:mən] *n* ʿifrīt عفريت (ʿafārīt عفاريت)

demonstrate ['demənstreit] *v* 1. athbata أثبت; barhana برهن 2. *(pol.)* tazāhara تظاهر

demonstration [demən'streiʃən] *n* 1. barhana برهنة 2. *(pol.)* muẓāhara مظاهرة

demonstrator ['demənstreitə] *n* *(pol.)* mutaẓāhir متظاهر (-ūn)

den [den] *n* wakr وكر (awkār أوكار)

denial [di'nayəl] *n* 1. rafḍ رفض 2. inkār إنكار

Denmark ['denma:k] *n* ad-danmārk الدنمارك

denounce [di'nauns] *v* 1. ittahama اتهم 2 shajjaba شجّب

dense [dens] *adj* kathīf كثيف

density ['densiti] *n* kathāfa كثافة

dental ['dentəl] *adj* sinnī سنّي; asnānī أسناني

dentist ['dentist] *n* ṭabīb al-asnān طبيب الأسنان

deny [di'nai] *v* 1. ankara أنكر 2. rafaḍa رفض (i/u; rafḍ رفض)

deodorant [di'əudərənt] *n* muzīl li 'r-rawā'iḥ al-karīha مزيل للروائح الكريهة

depart [di'pa:t] *v* rahala رحل (a; rahīl رحيل); ghādara غادر

department [di'pa:tmənt] *n* 1. qism قسم (aqsām أقسام); shuʿba شعبة (shuʿab شعب) 2. *(acad.)* qism قسم (aqsām أقسام) 3. *(pol.)* maṣlaha مصلحة (maṣāliḥ مصالح)

department store *n* matjar tanwīʿ kabīr متجر تنويع كبير

departure [di'pa:chə] *n* rahīl رحيل

depend [di'pend] *v* iʿtamada اعتمد (on ʿalā على)

dependant [di'pendənt] *n* tābiʿ تابع (tabaʿa تبعة; tubbāʿ تبّاع)

dependent [di'pendənt] *adj* mutawaqqif متوقّف (on ʿalā على)

deport [di'po:t] *v* rahhala رحّل; abʿada أبعد

deportation [di:po:'teiʃən] *n* tarhīl ترحيل; ibʿād إبعاد

depose [di'pəuz] *v* khalaʿa ʿan al-ḥukm خلع عن الحكم (a; khalʿ خلع)

deposit [di'pozit] 1. *n* ʿurbūn عربون (ʿarābīn عرابين) 2. wadīʿa وديعة (wadā'iʿ ودائع) 3. *v* awdaʿa أودع; istawdaʿa استودع

depot ['di:pəu] *n* mustawdaʿ مستودع (-āt); makhzan مخزن (makhāzin مخازن)

depressed [di'prest] *adj* mukta'ib
مكتئب

depression [di'preshən] *n* **1.** *(med.)* ikti'āb إكتئاب. **2.** *(ec.)* kasād كساد

deprive [di'praiv] *v* ḥarama حرم (i; ḥirm حرم; ḥirmān حرمان) **(of** min من)

depth [depth] *n* ʿumq عمق

deputy ['depyuti] *n* nā'ib نائب (nuwwāb نواب)

derelict ['derəlikt] *adj* mahjūr مهجور

derive [di'raiv] *v* ansha'a أنشأ **(from** ʿan عن)

descend [di'send] *v* habaṭa هبط (u/i; hubūṭ هبوط); nazala نزل (i; nuzūl نزول)

descendant [di'sendənt] *n* salīl سليل (salā'il سلائل)

descent [di'sent] *n* **1.** hubūṭ هبوط; nuzūl نزول **2.** sulāla سلالة

describe [di'skraib] *v* waṣafa وصف (yaṣifu يصف; waṣf وصف)

description [di'skripshən] *n* waṣf وصف

desert ['dezət] *n* ṣaḥrā' صحراء (ṣaḥārin صحار; ṣaḥārā صحارى; ṣaḥrawāt صحروات)

deserve [di'zəːv] *v* istaḥaqqa استحق; ista'halla استأهل

design [di'zain] **1.** *n* taṣmīm تصميم **2.** *v* ṣammama صمّم

designer [di'zainə] *n* muṣammim مصمّم (-ūn)

desirable [di'zaiərəbəl] *adj* marghūb fīh مرغوب فيه

desire [di'zaiə] **1.** *n* raghba رغبة (raghabāt رغبات) **2.** *v* raghiba fī رغب في (a; raghba رغبة)

desk [desk] *n* maktab مكتب (makātib مكاتب)

desktop ['desktop] *n* saṭḥ al-maktab سطح المكتب

despair [di'speə] **1.** *n* ya's يأس **2.** *v* ya'isa يئس (a/i; ya's يأس)

despatch [di'spach] *see* dispatch

desperate ['despərət] *adj* yā'is يائس

despise [di'spaiz] *v* iḥtaqara احتقر

despite [di'spait] *prep* bi 'r-raghm بالرغم; ʿalā ar-raghm min على الرغم من

dessert [di'zəːt] *n* ḥalwayāt حلويات

destabilize [diː'steibilaiz] *v* jaʿala ghayr mustaqirr (a) جعل غير مستقر

destination [desti'neishən] *n* ṭīya طية

destiny ['destini] *n* qadar قدر; naṣīb نصيب; qisma قسمة

destroy [di'stroi] *v* dammara دمّر; ahlaka أهلك

destroyer [di'stroiə] *n* **naval destroyer** mudammira مدمّرة (-āt)

destruction [di'strʌkshən] *n* damār دمار; tadmīr تدمير

detail ['diːteil] *n* **1.** tafṣīl تفصيل (tafāṣīl تفاصيل) **2. in detail** bi tafṣīl بتفصيل

detailed ['diːteild] *adj* mufaṣṣal مفصّل

detect [di'tekt] *v* iktashafa اكتشف

detective [di'tektiv] *n* muḥaqqiq būlīsī محقق بوليسي

detention [di'tenshən] *n* iḥtijāz إحتجاز

deter [di'təː] *v* manaʿa منع (a; manʿ منع); ʿāqa عاق (u; ʿawq عوق)

deteriorate [di'tiəriəreit] *v* tadahwara تدهور

determination [ditəːmi'neishən] *n* ʿazm عزم; taṣmīm تصميم

determine [di'tə:min] v 1. ḥaddada حدَّد 2. qarrara قرَّر

detest [di'test] v abghaḍa أبغض

detour ['di:tuə] n taḥwīla fī khaṭṭ as-sayra تحويلة في خط السيرة

develop [di'veləp] v 1. ṭawwara طوَّر 2. taṭawwara تطوَّر

developer [di'veləpə] n muqāwil مقاول (-ūn)

development [di'veləpmənt] n 1. taṭwīr تطوير; taṭawwur تطوُّر 2. tanmiya تنمية

device [di'vais] n adāh أداة (adawāt أدوات); jihāz جهاز (ajhiza أجهزة)

devil ['devəl] n shayṭān شيطان (shayāṭīn شياطين)

devise [di'vaiz] v ikhtaraʿa اخترع; ibtakara ابتكر

devote [di'vout] v karrasa كرَّس

devotion [di'vəushən] n ikhlāṣ إخلاص

devour [di'vauə] v ibtalaʿa ابتلع; iftarasa افترس

diabetes [daiə'bi:ti:z] n maraḍ as-sukkar مرض السكر

diagnose ['daiəg'nəuz] v shakhkhaṣa شخَّص

diagnosis [daiəg'nəusis] n (pl diagnoses) tashkhīṣ تشخيص

diagram ['daiəgram] n rasm bayānī رسم بياني

dial [daiəl] (tel.) 1. n qurṣ قرص (aqrāṣ أقراص) 2. v talfana تلفن

dialect ['daiəlekt] n lahja لهجة (lahajāt اللهجات)

dialogue ['daiəlog] n ḥiwār حوار

diamond ['daiəmənd] n almās ألماس; mās ماس

diaper ['daiəpə] n ḥifāẓ aṭ-ṭifl حفاظ الطفل

diary ['daiəri] n yawmīyāt يوميات

dice [dais] n (pl dice) zuhr زهر

dictate [di'kteit] v amlā أملى

dictation [di'kteishən] n imlāʾ إملاء

dictator [di'kteitə] n diktātūr دكتاتور

dictatorship [di'kteitəship] n diktātūrīya دكتاتورية

dictionary ['dikshenri] n qāmūs قاموس (qawāmīs قواميس)

did [did] see do

die [dai] v māta مات (u; mawt موت)

diesel ['di:zəl] n dīzal ديزل

diet [daiət] n 1. ghidhāʾ غذاء 2. ḥimya حمية

differ ['difə] v ikhtalafa اختلف

difference ['difrəns] n 1. ikhtilāf إختلاف 2. farq فرق (furūq فروق)

different ['difrənt] adj mukhtalif مختلف

difficult ['difikəlt] adj ṣaʿb صعب

difficulty ['difikəlti] n ṣuʿūba صعوبة

dig [dig] v (dug) ḥafara حفر (i; ḥafr حفر)

digest [di'jest; 'daijest] v haḍama هضم (i; haḍm هضم)

digestion [di'jeschən; dai'jeschən] n haḍm هضم

digit ['dijit] n 1. iṣbaʿ إصبع (aṣābiʿ أصابع) 2. raqm رقم (arqām أرقام)

digital ['dijitəl] adj raqmī رقمي

dignity ['dignəti] n karāma كرامة

dike [daik] n sadd سد (sudūd سدود)

dilemma [di'lemə; dai'lemə] n maʾzaq مأزق (maʾāziq مآزق); warṭa ورطة (waraṭāt ورطات)

dilute [dai'lyu:t] v shaʿshaʿa شعشع

dim [dim] *adj* muˤtim معتم; muẓlim مظلم

dimension [di'menshən] *n* buˤd بعد (abˤād أبعاد); ḥajm حجم (aḥjām أحجام)

diminish [di'minish] *v* qallala قلّل

diminutive [di'minyutiv] *adj* ṣaghīr صغير

dine [dain] *v* taˤashshā تعشّى

dining room ['dainingrum] *n* ḥujrat aṭ-ṭaˤām حجرة الطعام

dinner ['dinə] *n* ˤashā' عشاء (aˤshiya أعشية)

dinosaur ['dainəso] *n* dīnāṣūr ديناصور

dip [dip] *v* ghaṭasa غطس (i; ghaṭs غطس)

diploma [di'pləumə] *n* diblōm/diblōma دبلوم\دبلومة (-āt); shahāda شهادة (-āt)

diplomat ['dipləmat] *n* diblōmāsī دبلوماسي (-yūn)

diplomatic [diplə'matik] *adj* diblōmāsī دبلوماسي

direct [di'rekt; dai'rekt] **1.** *adj* mubāshir مباشر **2.** ṣarīḥ صريح **3.** *v* wajjaha وجّه; arshada أرشد; adāra أدار **4. to direct a film** akhraja أخرج

direction [di'rekshən; dai'rekshən] *n* **1.** ittijāh إتجاه **2.** tawjīh توجيه **3.** **film direction** إخراج

directions [di'rekshənz; dai'rek-shənz] *pl* irshādāt إرشادات

directly [di'rektli; dai'rektli] *adv* **1.** mubāsharatan مباشرةً **2.** ḥālan حالاً

director [di'rektə; dai'rektə] *n* **1.** mudīr مدير (mudurā' مدراء) **2. film director** mukhrij مخرج (-ūn) **3. managing director** mudīr ˤāmm مدير عام **4. board of directors** majlis al-idāra مجلس الإدارة

directory [di'rektəri; dai'rektəri] *n* dalīl دليل (dalā'il دلائل)

dirt [dəːt] *n* **1.** turāb تراب **2.** wasākha وساخة; qadhāra قذارة

dirty ['dəːti] **1.** *n* qadhir قذر; wasikh وسخ **2.** *v* wassakha وسخ

disability [disə'biləti] *n* ˤajz عجز

disabled [dis'eibəld] *adj* **1.** muˤāq معاق; ˤājiz عاجز **2. the disabled** *pl* al-muˤāqūn المعاقون; al-ˤājizūn العاجزون

disadvantage [disəd'vaːntij] *n* ḍarar ضرر (aḍrār أضرار)

disagree [disə'griː] *v* khālafa خالف; ikhtalafa fi 'r-ra'y اختلف في الرأي

disagreement [disə'griːmənt] *n* khilāf خلاف; ikhtilāf fi'l-ra'y إختلاف في الرأي

disappear [disə'piə] *v* ikhtafā اختفى; ghāba غاب (i; ghayba غيبة; ghiyāb غياب)

disappearance [disə'piərəns] *n* ikhtifā' إختفاء; ghiyāb غياب

disappoint [disə'point] *v* khayyaba al-amal خيّب الأمل; khayyaba aẓ-ẓann خيّب الظن

disappointed [disə'pointid] *adj* khā'ib al-'amal خائب الأمل

disappointment [disə'pointmənt] *n* khaybat al-'amal خيبة الأمل

disapproval [disə'pruːvəl] *n* istinkār إستنكار

disarmament [dis'aːməmənt] *n* nazˤ as-silāḥ نزع السلاح

disaster [diz'aːstə] *n* kāritha كارثة (kawārith كوارث); muṣība مصيبة (maṣā'ib مصائب)

disbelief [disbi'liːf] *n* inkār إنكار

disc [disk] *n* qurṣ قرص (aqrāṣ أقراص)

discard [dis'kaːd] *v* nabadha نبذ (i; nabdh نبذ)

discipline ['disiplin] 1. *n* indibāṭ انضباط .2 *v* addaba أدب

disco ['diskəu] *n* diskō دسكو

disconnect [diskə'nekt] *v* faṣala فصل (i; faṣl فصل)

discount ['diskaunt] *n* ḥasm حسم; khaṣm خصم

discover [dis'kʌvə] *v* iktashafa اكتشف

discoverer [dis'kʌvərə] *n* muktashif مكتشف (-ūn)

discovery [dis'kʌvəri] *n* iktishāf إكتشاف

discreet [dis'kri:t] *adj* katūm كتوم; ḥadhir حذر

discriminate [dis'krimineit] *v* mayyaza ميز

discrimination [dis'krimineishən] *n* tamyīz تمييز

discuss [dis'kʌs] *v* nāqasha ناقش

discussion [dis'kʌshən] *n* munāqasha مناقشة (-āt)

disease [di'zi:z] *n* maraḍ مرض (amrāḍ أمراض)

disembark [disim'ba:k] *v* nazala min as-safīna نزل من السفينة (i; nuzūl نزول)

disgrace [dis'greis] *n* faḍīḥa فضيحة; ʿār عار

disgraceful [dis'greisfəl] *adj* fāḍiḥ فاضح; mukhzin مخز

disguise [dis'gaiz] *n* tanakkur تنكر

disgust [dis'gʌst] *n* ishmiʾzāz إشمئزاز; qaraf قرف

disgusted [dis'gʌstid] *adj* mushmaʾizz مشمئز; qarfān قرفان

disgusting [dis'gʌsting] *adj* muthīr li ʾl-ishmiʾzāz مثير للإشمئزاز; muqrif مقرف

dish [dish] *n* ṣahn صحن (ṣuḥūn صحون); ṭabaq طبق (aṭbāq أطباق)

dishonest [dis'onist] *adj* ghayr ṣādiq غير صادق

dishonesty [dis'onisti] *n* ʿadm aṣ-ṣidq عدم الصدق

disk [disk] *n* qurṣ قرص (aqrāṣ أقراص)

dislike [dis'laik] *v* raghiba ʿan رغب عن (a; raghba رغبة; raghab رغب)

dismay [dis'mei] *n* fazaʿ فزع

dismiss [dis'mis] *v* amara bi-l-inṣirāf أمر بالإنصراف

dismissal [dis'misəl] *n* inṣirāf إنصراف

disobedience [disə'bi:diəns] *n* tamarrud تمرد; ʿiṣyān عصيان

disobedient [disə'bi:diənt] *adj* mutamarrid متمرد; ʿāṣin عاص

disobey [disə'bei] *v* tamarrada تمرد; ʿaṣā عصى (i; ʿaṣy عصي; maʿṣīya معصية; ʿiṣyān عصيان)

dispatch; despatch [dis'pach] *v* arsala أرسل

dispensary [dis'pensəri] *n* mustawṣaf مستوصف (-āt)

display [dis'plei] 1. *n* ʿarḍ عرض .2 *v* ʿaraḍa عرض (i; ʿarḍ عرض)

displease [dis'pli:z] *v* athāra al-istiyāʾ أثار الإستياء

disposal [dis'pəuzəl] *n* 1. **waste disposal** takhalluṣ min al-qumāma تخلص من القمامة 2. **bomb disposal** ibṭāl mafʿūl al-qanābil إبطال مفعول القنابل 3. *and see* **mine**

dispose [dis'pəuz] *v* takhallaṣa تخلص (of min من)

dispute [dis'pyu:t; 'dispyu:t] *n* jidāl جدال; mujādala مجادلة (-āt)

disqualify [dis'kwolifai] *v* ḥarrama min al-ahlīya حرم من الأهلية

disregard [disri'ga:d] *v* aghfala أغفل; ahmala أهمل

disrespect [disris'pekt] *n* ʿadm iḥtirām عدم إحترام

disrupt [dis'rʌpt] *v* ʿaṭṭala عطل

disruption [dis'rʌpchən] *n* taʿṭīl تعطيل

dissatisfaction [disatis'fakshən] *n* istiyāʾ إستياء

dissent [di'sent] *n* inshiqāq إنشقاق

dissertation [disə'teishən] *n* uṭrūḥa أطروحة (-āt)

dissident ['disidənt] *n* munshaqq منشقّ (-ūn)

dissolve [di'zolv] *v* 1. adhāba أذاب; dhawwaba ذوّب 2. *(pol.)* aḥalla أحلّ

distance ['distəns] *n* masāfa مسافة (-āt)

distant ['distənt] *adj* baʿīd بعيد

distinct [dis'tingkt] *adj* bayyin بيّن

distinction [dis'tingkshən] *n* tafawwuq تفوّق; imtiyāz إمتياز

distinctive [dis'tingktiv] *adj* mumayyaz مميّز

distinguish [dis'tinggwish] *v* mayyaza ميّز

distinguished [dis'tinggwisht] *adj* mumayyaz مميّز; mumtāz ممتاز

distort [dis'to:t] *v* shawwaha شوّه

distract [dis'trakt] *v* ṣarafa صرف (i; ṣarf صرف; **from** ʿan عن)

distraction [dis'trakshən] *n* ṣarf al-intibāh صرف الإنتباه

distressing [dis'tresing] *adj* mu'lim مؤلم; muḥzin محزن

distribute ['distribyu:t] *v* wazzaʿa وزع

distribution [distri'byu:shən] *n* tawzīʿ توزيع

distributor [distri'byutə] *n* muwazziʿ موزّع (-ūn)

district ['distrikt] *n* minṭaqa منطقة (manāṭiq مناطق); muqāṭaʿa مقاطعة (-āt)

distrust [dis'trʌst] *n* irtiyāb إرتياب

disturb [dis'tə:b] *v* 1. aqlaqa أقلق 2. azʿaja أزعج

disturbance [dis'tə:bəns] *n* iḍṭirāb إضطراب

disturbed [dis'tə:bd] *adj* 1. muḍṭarib مضطرب 2. **mentally disturbed** muḍṭarib ʿaqlīyan مضطرب عقلياً

disuse [dis'yu:s] *n* ʿadm al-istiʿmāl عدم الإستعمال

ditch [dish] *n* khandaq خندق (khanādiq خنادق)

dive [daiv] *v* 1. ghaṭasa غطس (i; ghaṭs غطس); ghāṣa غاص (u; ghawṣ غوص) 2. inqaḍḍa انقض

diver ['daivə] *n* ghaṭṭās غطاس (-ūn)

diverse [dai'və:s] *adj* mutanawwiʿ متنوع

diversion [dai'və:shən] *n* 1. lahw لهو; tasliya تسلية 2. taḥwīl تحويل

diversity [dai'və:səti] *n* tanawwuʿ تنوّع

divert [dai'və:t] *v* ḥawwala حوّل

divide [di'vaid] *v* qassama قسّم

divine [di'vain] *adj* ilāhī إلهي

diving ['daiving] *n* ghaṭs غطس

division [di'vizhən] *n* 1. taqsīm تقسيم; inqisām إنقسام 2. *(mil.)* firqa فرقة

divorce [di'vo:s] 1. *n* ṭalāq طلاق 2. *v* ṭallaqa طلّق (**from** min من)

dizzy ['dizi] *adj* dā'ikh دائخ

do [du:] *v* (**did, done**) faʿala فعل (a; faʿl فعل)

dock; docks [dok; doks] *n* ḥawḍ as-sufun حوض السفن

doctor ['dɒktə] *n* **1.** *(med.)* ṭabīb طبيب (aṭibbā' أطباء) **2.** *(acad.)* duktūr دكتور (dakātira دكاترة)

document ['dɒkyumənt] *n* wathīqa وثيقة (wathā'iq وثائق)

dodge [dɒj] *v* rāwagha راوغ

dog [dɒg] *n* kalb كلب (kilāb كلاب)

doll [dɒl] *n* ʿarūsa عروسة (ʿarā'is عرائس)

dollar ['dɒlə] *n* dōlār دولار (-āt)

dolphin ['dɒlfin] *n* dulfīn دلفين (dalāfīn دلافين)

dome [dəum] *n* qubba قبة (qibāb قباب; qubab قبب)

domestic [də'mestik] **1.** *adj* manzilī منزلي **2.** alīf أليف **3.** *n* khaddām خدام (-ūn)

domicile ['dɒmisail] *n* manzil منزل

dominant ['dɒminənt] *adj* musayṭir مسيطر

dominate ['dɒmineit] *v* sayṭara ʿalā سيطر على

domination [dɒmi'neishən] *n* sayṭara سيطرة; haymana هيمنة

donation [dəu'neishən] *n* tabarruʿ تبرع (-āt)

done [dʌn] *see* do

donkey ['dɒngki] *n (pl* **donkeys)** ḥimār حمار (ḥamīr حمير)

donor ['dəunə] *n* mutabarriʿ متبرع

doom [du:m] *n* halāk هلاك

door [dɔ:] *n* bāb باب (abwāb أبواب; bībān بيبان)

doorway ['dɔ:wei] *n* madkhal مدخل

dose [dəus] *n* jurʿa/jarʿa جرعة (-āt; juraʿ جرع)

dot [dɒt] *n* nuqṭa نقطة (nuqaṭ نقط; niqāṭ نقاط)

double ['dʌbəl] **1.** *adj* muzdawij مزدوج **2.** *v* ḍāʿafa ضاعف; taḍāʿafa تضاعف

doubt [daut] **1.** *n* shakk شك (shukūk شكوك); rayb ريب **2. without doubt** bilā shakk بلا شك; bilā rayb بلا ريب **3.** *v* shakka شك (u; shakk شك)

doubtful ['dautfəl] *adj* murīb مريب; mashkūk fīh مشكوك فيه

doubtless ['dautlis] *adv* lā rayb fīh لا ريب فيه

dough [dəu] *n* ʿajīn عجين

down [daun] *adv* taḥt تحت; ilā 'l-asfal إلى الأسفل

downhill [daun'hil] *adv* ilā asfal إلى أسفل

download [daun'ləud] *v* ḥammala حمل

downstairs ['daunsteəz] *adv* aṭ-ṭābiq al-asfal الطابق الأسفل

downward; downwards ['daun-wəd; -z] *adv* nuzūlā نزولا

dozen ['dʌzən] *n* dazzīna دزينة; ithnā ʿashar إثنا عشر

draft [dra:ft] **1.** *n* musawwada مسودة (-āt) **2.** *v* waḍaʿa musawwada وضع مسودة **3.** *see* **draught**

drag [drag] *v* jarra جر (u; jarr جر); jarjara جرجر

dragon ['dragən] *n* tinnīn تنين (tanānīn تنانين)

drain [drein] **1.** *n* bālūʿa بالوعة (bawālīʿ بواليع) **2.** *v* ṣarrafa صرف

drama ['dra:mə] *n* drāmā دراما

dramatic [drə'matik] *adj* **1.** masraḥī مسرحي; drāmī درامي **2.** muthīr مثير

drank [drangk] *see* **drink**

drastic ['drastik] *adj* qāsin قاس; ṣārim صارم

draught [dra:ft] *n* **1.** tayyār hawā'ī تيار هوائي **2.** *see* **draft**

draw [dro:] 1. *n (spor.)* ta'ādul تعادل 2. *v* (**drew, drawn**) jarra جرّ (u; jarr جرّ) 3. *(spor.)* ta'ādala تعادل 4. **to draw a picture** rasama رسم (u; rasm رسم)

drawback ['dro:bak] *n* shā'iba شائبة (shawā'ib شوائب)

drawer [dro:] *n* durj درج (adrāj أدراج)

drawing ['dro:ing] *n* rasm رسم (rusūm رسوم; rusūmāt رسومات)

drawn [dro:n] *see* draw

dreadful ['dredfəl] *adj* 1. mur'ib مرعب; murawwi' مروع 2. baghīḍ بغيض

dream [dri:m] 1. *n* ḥulm حلم (aḥlām أحلام) 2. *v* (**dreamed/dreamt**) ḥalama حلم (u; ḥulm حلم)

dress [dres] 1. *n* fustān فستان (fasātīn فساتين) 2. malbas ملبس (malābis ملابس); ziyy زي (azyā' أزياء)

drill [dril] 1. *n* mithqab مثقب (mathāqib مثاقب) 2. *v* thaqaba ثقب (u; thaqb ثقب)

drink [dringk] 1. *n* sharāb شراب (ashriba أشربة) 2. *v* (**drank, drunk**) shariba شرب (a; shurb شرب)

drip [drip] 1. *n* qaṭr قطر *(collective)* 2. *v* taqaṭṭara تقطر

drive [draiv] *v* (**drove, driven**) qāda قاد (u; qiyāda قيادة); sāqa ساق (u; siyāqa سياقة)

driver ['draivə] *n* sā'iq سائق (-ūn)

driver's licence *n* rukhṣa qiyādat as-siyārāt رخصة قيادة السيارات

driving ['draiving] *n* siyāqa سياقة

drop [drop] *v* (**dropped**) 1.waqa'a وقع (yaqi'u يقع; wuqū' وقوع); saqaṭa سقط (u; suqūṭ سقوط) 2. awqa'a أوقع; asqaṭa أسقط

drove [drəuv] *see* drive

drown [draun] *v* ghariqa غرق (a; gharaq غرق)

drug [drʌg] *n* mukhaddir مخدّر (-āt)

drugstore ['drʌgsto:] *n (US)* ṣaydalīya صيدلية

drum [drʌm] *n* 1. ṭabla طبلة 2. **oil drum** barmīl برميل (barāmīl براميل)

drummer ['drʌmə] *n* ṭabbāl طبال (-ūn)

drunk [drʌngk] *adj* 1. sakrān سكران 2. *see* drink

dry [drai] 1. *adj* jāff جاف 2. *v* jaffafa جفف

dubious ['dyu:biəs] *adj* mashkūk fīh مشكوك فيه

duck(s) [dʌk] *n* baṭṭ *collective* بط

due [dyu:] 1. *n* ḥaqq حق (ḥuqūq حقوق) 2. *prep* **due to** bisabab بسبب

dug [dʌg] *see* dig

dull [dʌl] *adj* 1. bāhit باهت 2. mumill ممل

dumb [dʌmb] *adj* 1. abkam أبكم; akhras أخرس 2. *(sl.)* balīd بليد

dummy ['dʌmi] *n* 1. dumya دمية (duman دمى) 2. *(sl.)* balīd بليد

dump [dʌmp] 1. *n* **rubbish dump** mazbala مزبلة (mazābil مزابل) 2. *v* takhallaṣa min تخلص من

dung [dʌng] *n* rawth روث

duo ['dyu:əu] *n* thunā'īya ثنائية

duplicate ['dyu:plikeit] 1. *n* nuskha نسخة (nusakh نسخ) 2. *v* nasakha نسخ (a; naskh نسخ)

duration [dyu'reishən] *n* mudda مدة; amad أمد

during ['dyuəring] *prep* خلال khilāl;
أثناء 'ithnā

dusk [dʌsk] *n* غسق ghasaq

dust [dʌst] *n* غبار ghubār (aghbira
(أغبرة

dustbin ['dʌstbin] *n* ṣundūq al-
qumāma صندوق القمامة

Dutch [dʌch] *adj* هلندي holandī

duty ['dyuːti] *n* **1.** واجب wājib **2.**
customs duty rasm رسم (rusūm
(رسوم

duty-free *adj* muʿfāh min ar-rusūm
معفاة من الرسوم

dwarf [dwoːf] *n* (**dwarves** [dwoːvz])
qazm قزم (aqzām أقزام)

dwell [dwel] *v* aqāma أقام

dweller ['dwelə] *n* muqīm مقيم (-ūn)

dwelling ['dweling] *n* manzil منزل
(manāzil منازل)

dye [dai] **1.** *n* ṣibgh صبغ (aṣbāgh
أصباغ) **2.** *v* ṣabagha صبغ (a/i/u;
ṣabgh/ṣibagh صبغ)

dying ['daːying] *see* die

dyke [daik] *n* sadd سد (sudūd سدود)

dynamic [dai'namik] *adj* dīnāmīkī
ديناميكي

each ['iːch] **1.** *adj* kull كل **2.** *adv* li
kull wāḥid لكل واحد

each other *n/adv* baʿḍan بعضاً;
baʿḍahum/baʿḍakum/baʿḍanā
بعضهم\بعضكم\بعضنا; al-baʿḍ البعض

eager ['iːgə] *adj* mutalahhif متلهف;
tawwāq طواق (**for** ilā إلى)

eagerly ['iːgəli] *adv* bi talahhuf
بتلهف

eagle ['iːgəl] *n* nasr نسر (nusūr
نسور); ʿuqāb عقاب (aʿqub أعقب)

ear ['iːə] *n* udhun أذن (ādhān آذان)

early ['əːli] **1.** *adj* mubakkir مبكر **2.**
adv mubakkiran مبكراً

earn ['əːn] *v* kasaba كسب (i; kasb
(كسب

earnings ['əːningz] *pl* kasb كسب

earphones ['iːəfəunz] *pl* sammāʿa
سماعة (-āt)

earrings ['iːəring] *n* ḥalaq حلق

earth ['əːth] *n* **1.** turāb تراب **2. the
earth** al-arḍ الأرض

earthquake ['əːthkweik] *n* zilzāl
زلزال (zalāzil زلازل)

ease ['iːz] *n* rāḥa راحة

easily ['iːzili] *adv* bi-suhūla بسهولة

easiness ['iːzinis] *n* suhūla سهولة

east ['iːst] **1.** *adj* sharqī شرقي **2.** *adv*
sharqan شرقاً **3.** *n* sharq شرق

Easter ['iːstə] *n* ʿīd al-qiyāma
عيد القيامة

eastern ['iːstən] *adj* sharqī شرقي

easterner ['iːstənə] *n* sharqī شرقي
(-yūn)

eastwards ['iːstwədz] *adv* sharqan
شرقاً

easy ['iːzi] *adj* sahl سهل

eat [iːt] *v* (ate, eaten) akala أكل (u;
akl أكل)

echo ['ekəu] *n* ṣadā صدى (aṣdā'
أصداء)

ecological ['iːkəlojikəl] *adj* bay'ī
بيئي

ecology ['ikoloji] *n* 'ilm at-bay'a
علم البيئة

economic [iːkə'nomik; ekə'nomik]
adj iqtiṣādī إقتصادي

economical [iːkə'nomikəl; ekə'no-
mikəl] *adj* iqtiṣādī إقتصادي;
muqtaṣid مقتصد

economist [i'konəmist] *n* 'ālim
iqtiṣādī عالم إقتصادي

economy ['ikonəmi] *n* 1. iqtiṣād
إقتصاد 2. tawfīr توفير

edge [ej] *n* 1. ḥadd حد (ḥudūd حدود)
2. ḥāffa حافة (-āt)

edible ['edibəl] *adj* ṣāliḥ li 'l-akl
صالح للأكل

edit ['edit] *v* ḥarrara حرر

edition [i'dishən] *n* ṭab'a طبعة
(-āt)

editor ['editə] *n* 1. muḥarrir محرر
2. newspaper editor ra'īs al-taḥrīr
رئيس التحرير

editorial [edi'toːriəl] 1. *adj* taḥrīrī
تحريري 2. *n* iftitāḥīya إفتتاحية

educate ['ejukeit] *v* 'allama علم;
rabbā ربى

education [eju'keishən] *n* at-ta'līm
التعليم; at-tarbīya التربية

educational [eju'keishənəl] *adj*
ta'līmī تعليمي; tarbawī تربوي

effect [i'fekt] *n* 1. natīja نتيجة
(natā'ij نتائج) 2. in effect fī 'l-

wāqi' في الواقع 3. **to take effect**
sarā سرى (i; sarayān سريان) (**on** 'alā
على)

effective ['ifektiv] *adj* fa''āl
فعال

efficiency ['ifishənsi] *n* kafā'a
كفاءة; fa''ālīya فعالية

efficient ['ifishənt] *adj* kuf' كفء;
fa''āl فعال

effort ['efət] *n* juhd جهد (juhūd
جهود)

effortless ['efətlis] *adj* lā juhd lah
لا جهد له

e.g. (= for example) mathalan
مثلاً

egg [eg] *n* bayḍa بيضة (bayḍ
collective بيض)

eggplant ['egplant] *n* bādhinjāna
باذنجانة (bādhinjān *collective*
باذنجان; *pl* -āt)

egotistical [egəu'tistikəl] *adj* anānī
أناني

eight [eit] *n/adj* thamāniya ثمانية

eighteen [ei'tiːn] *n/adj* thamaniyata
'ashar ثمانية عشر

eighteenth [ei'tiːnth] *adj* thāmin
'ashar ثامن عشر

eighth ['eitth] *adj* 1. thāmin ثامن 2.
one eighth thumn ثمن

eightieth ['eitiəth] *adj* ath-
thamanūn الثمنون

eighty ['eiti] *n/adj* thamānūn
ثمانون

either ['aidhə; 'iːdhə] 1. *adj* kull min
كل من; ayy min أي من 2. *adv* ayḍan
أيضاً 3. *conj* immā إمّا 4. **either... or**
immā... aw إمّا... أو

eject [i'jekt] *v* qadhafa قذف
(i; qadhf قذف); ṭarada طرد (u; ṭard
طرد)

elaborate [i'labəreit] *adj* mufaṣṣal مفصل

elapse [i'laps] *v* inqaḍā انقضى

elastic [i'lastik] *adj* mutamaghghiṭ متمغط

elbow ['elbəu] *n* mirfaq مرفق (marāfiq مرافق)

elder ['eldə] 1. *adj* akbar أكبر 2. *n* shaykh شيخ (shuyūkh شيوخ)

elderly ['eldəli] *adj* ʿajūz عجوز

eldest ['eldist] *adj* al-akbar الأكبر

elect [i'lekt] *v* intakhaba انتخب

election [i'lekshən] *n* intikhāb انتخاب

elections [i'lekshənz] *pl* intikhābāt انتخابات

elector [i'lektə] *n* nākhib ناخب

electoral [i'lektərəl] *adj* intikhābī انتخابي

electric [i'lektrik] *adj* kahrabāʾī كهربائي

electrician [ilek'trishən] *n* kahrabāʾī كهربائي (-yūn)

electricity [ilek'trisəti] *n* kahrabāʾ كهرباء

electrocute [i'lektrəkju:t] *v* aʿdama bi ʾl-kahrabāʾ أعدم بالكهرباء

electronic [ilek'tronik] *adj* alaktrūnī ألكتروني

electronics [ilek'troniks] *n* al-alaktrūnīyāt الألكترونيات

elegance ['eligəns] *n* anāqa أناقة

elegant ['eligəns] *adj* anīq أنيق

element ['elimənt] *n* ʿunṣur عنصر (ʿanāṣir عناصر)

elementary ['elimentri] *adj* 1. awwalī أولي; ibtidāʾī إبتدائي 2. basīṭ بسيط

elementary school *n* madrasa ibtidāʾīya مدرسة إبتدائية

elephant ['elifənt] *n* fīl فيل (afyāl أفيال)

elevator ['eliveitə] *n* miṣʿad مصعد (maṣāʿid مصاعد)

eleven 'i'levən] *n/adj* aḥad ʿashar أحد عشر

eleventh [i'levənth] *adj* ḥādī ʿashar حادي عشر

eligible ['elijəbəl] *adj* muʾahhal مؤهل

eliminate [i'limineit] *v* azāla أزال

elimination [ilimi'neishən] *n* izāla إزالة

eloquent ['eləkwənt] *adj* faṣīḥ فصيح; balīgh بليغ

else [els] 1. *adj* ākhar آخر 2. *conj* or else wa illā وإلا

elsewhere ['elsweə] *adv* makān ākhar مكان آخر

e-mail ['i:meil] *n* barīd alaktrūnī بريد ألكتروني

embargo [im'ba:gəu] *n* ḥiṣār حصار

embark [im'ba:k] *v* rakiba ركب (a; rukūb ركوب)

embark upon *v* bāshara باشر

embarrass [im'barəs] *v* arbaka أربك; khajjala خجل

embarrassed [im'barist] *adj* khajlān خجلان

embarrassing [im'barəsing] *adj* murbik مربك

embarrassment [im'barəsmənt] *n* irtibāk إرتباك

embassy ['embəsi] *n* sifāra سفارة (-āt)

embrace [im'breis] *v* ʿānaqa عانق

emerge [i'mə:jd] v ẓahara ظهر
a; ẓuhūr (ظهور)

emergency [i'mə:jənsi] n ṭāri'a
طارئة (ṭawāri' طوارئ)

emigrant ['emigrənt] n muhājir
مهاجر (-ūn)

emigrate ['emigreit] v hājara هاجر

emigration ['emigreishən] n hijra
هجرة

emotion [i'məushən] n ʿāṭifa عاطفة
(ʿawāṭif عواطف)

emotional [i'məushənl] adj ʿāṭifī
عاطفي

emperor ['empərə] n imbarāṭūr
إمبراطور

emphasis ['emfəsis] n ta'kīd
تأكيد

emphasize ['emfəsaiz] v akkada
أكّد

empire ['empaiə] n imbarāṭūrīya
إمبراطورية

employ [im'ploi] v 1. waẓẓafa وظّف
2. istaʿmala استعمل

employee ['emploi:] n muwaẓẓaf
موظف (-ūn)

employer [im'ploiə] n ṣāḥib al-
ʿamal صاحب العمل

employment [im'ploimənt] n
khidma خدمة; tawẓīf توظيف

empty ['empti] 1. adj khālin خال 2. v
farragha فرّغ

enable [in'eibəl] v makkana مكّن

enchanting [in'cha:nting] adj sāḥir
ساحر; fātin فاتن

enclose [in'kləuz] v ṭawwaqa طوّق

encounter [in'kauntə] v 1. ṣādafa
صادف 2. wājaha واجه

encourage [in'kʌrij] v shajjaʿa
شجّع

encouragement [in'kʌrijmənt] n
tashjīʿ تشجيع

encyclopaedia [insaiklə'pi:diə] n
mawsūʿa موسوعة

end ['end] 1. n nihāya نهاية (-āt)
2. **in the end** fi 'n-nihāya في النهاية
3. v anhā أنهى

endanger [in'deinjə] v ʿarraḍa li-'l-
khaṭar عرّض للخطر

ending ['ending] n nihāya نهاية (-āt)

endless ['endlis] adj lā nihāyata lah
لا نهاية له

endurance [in'juərəns] n
taḥammul تحمّل; ṣabr صبر

enemy ['enəmi] n ʿaduw عدو (aʿdā'
أعداء)

energetic ['enəjetik] adj nashīṭ
نشيط

energy ['enəji] n 1. nashāṭ نشاط 2.
ṭāqa طاقة

engage [in'geij] v 1. waẓẓafa وظّف
2. shaghala شغل (a) 3. (mil.) qātala
قاتل

engaged [in'geijd] adj 1. mashghūl
مشغول 2. makhṭūb مخطوب 3. **to get
engaged** takhaṭṭaba تخطّب

engagement [in'geijmənt] n 1.
mawʿid موعد (mawāʿid مواعد) 2.
khiṭba خطبة

engine ['enjin] n 1. muḥarrik محرك
2. see **locomotive**

engineer ['enjiniə] n muhandis
مهندس (-ūn)

engineering ['enjiniəring] n
handasa هندسة

England ['ingglənd] n ingiltərā
إنكلترا

English ['ingglish] 1. adj inglīzī
إنكليزي 2. n inglīzī إنكليزي 3. **the
English** al-inglīz الإنكليز

Englishman ['ingglishmən] n
inglīzī إنكليزي

Englishwoman ['ingglish,wəmən]
n inglīzīya إنكليزية

enjoy [in'joi] v tamattaʿa bi تمتع ب

enjoyable [in'joiəbəl] adj mumtiʿ
ممتع

enjoyment [in'joimənt] n mutʿa
(متع muta'c) متعة

enlarge [in'la:j] v kabbara كبر

enormous [i'no:məs] adj ḍakhm
ضخم

enough [inʌf] 1. adj kāfin كاف 2. adv
bi miqdār kāfin بمقدار كاف

enquire [in'kwaiə] v istaʿlama
استعلم

enrich [in'rich] v ghannā غنى

enrol [in'rəul] v tasajjala تسجل

en route [on'ru:t] adv fi 'ṭ-ṭarīq
في الطريق

ensure [i'nsho:] v ḍamina ضمن (a;
ḍamān ضمان)

enter ['entə] v dakhala دخل (u;
dukhūl دخول)

enterprise ['entəpraiz] n 1. iqdām
إقدام; jur'a جرأة 2. (com.) mashrūʿ
مشروع (mashārīʿ مشاريع)

entertain [entə'tein] v 1. sallā سلى
2. istaḍāfa استضاف

entertainment [entə'teinmənt] n
tasliya تسلية

entertaining [entə'teining] adj
musallin مسلّ

enthusiasm [in'thyu:ziazm] n
ḥamās حماس

enthusiastic [in'thyu:ziastik] adj
mutaḥammis متحمس

entire [in'taiə] adj tāmm تام; kāmil
كامل; kulli كلي

entirely [in'taiəli] adv tamāman
تماماً; kulliyan كلياً

entrance ['entrəns] n madkhal
مدخل (madākhil مداخل)

entry ['entri] n 1. dukhūl دخول 2.
(fin.) tadwīn تدوين

envelope ['envələup] n ẓarf ظرف
(ẓurūf ظروف)

environment [in'vaiərənmənt] n
1. bay'a بيئة 2. muḥīṭ محيط

environmental [invaiərən'mentəl]
adj bay'ī بيئي

envious ['enviəs] adj ḥasūd حسود;
ḥāsid حاسد

envy ['envi] 1. n ḥasad حسد 2. v
ḥasada حسد (u; ḥasad حسد)

epidemic [epi'demik] n wabā' وباء
(awbi'a أوبئة)

episode ['episəud] n 1. ḥādith حادث
(ḥawādith حوادث) 2. ḥalaqa حلقة
(-āt)

equal ['i:kwəl] 1. adj mutasāwin
متساو; 2. v sāwā ساوى; ʿādala
عادل

equality [i'kwoləti] n musāwāh
مساواة

equator [i'kweitə] n khaṭṭ al-istiwā'
خط الإستواء

equip [i'kwip] v jahhaza جهز

equipment [i'kwipmənt] n ajhiza
أجهزة

equivalent [i'kwivələnt] 1. adj
musāwin مساو 2. n naẓīr نظير
(nuẓurā' نظراء)

era ['iərə] n ʿaṣr عصر (ʿuṣūr عصور);
ʿahd عهد (ʿuhūd عهود)

eradicate [i'radikeit] v maḥā محى
(u; maḥw محو)

erase [i'reiz] v maḥā محى (u; maḥw
محو)

erect [i'rekt] 1. *adj* qā'im قائم 2. *v* aqāma أقام

erosion [i'rəuzhən] *n* taʿriya تعرية

errand ['erənd] *n* mishwār مشوار (mashāwīr مشاوير)

error ['erə] *n* ghalṭa غلطة (ghalaṭāt غلطات)

erupt [i'rʌpt] *v* infajara انفجر

eruption [i'rʌpshən] *n* infijār إنفجار

escalator ['eskəleitə] *n* sullam mutaḥarrik سلم متحرك

escape [i'skeip] 1. *n* firār فرار; mafarr مفر 2. *v* farra فر (i) (from min من)

escort ['eskɔ:t] 1. *n* murāfiq مرافق (-ūn) 2. *v* rāfaqa رافق

especially ['ispeshəli] *adv* khuṣūṣan خصوصاً; khāṣṣatan خاصة

essay ['esei] *n* maqāla مقالة (-āt)

essence ['esns] *n* jawhar جوهر (jawāhir جواهر)

essential ['isenshəl] *adj* 1. asāsī أساسي 2. jawharī جوهري

establish ['istablish] *v* assasa أسس

establishment ['istablishmənt] *n* 1. mu'assasa مؤسسة (-āt) 2. ta'sīs تأسيس

estate ['isteit] *n* 1. ʿizba عزبة (ʿizab عزب) 2. real estate ʿaqārāt عقارات 3. (UK) housing estate tajammuʿ sakanī تجمع سكني

estimate ['estimət] 1. *n* taqdīr تقدير 2. *v* qaddara قدر

etc. (= et cetera) ['etsetərə] ilā ākhirihi إلى آخره

eternal ['itə:nl] *adj* khālid خالد

eternity ['itə:nəti] *n* khulūd خلود

ethical ['ethikəl] *adj* akhlāqī أخلاقي

ethnic ['ethnik] *adj* ʿirqī عرقي

euro ['yuərəp] *n* 1. ūrūbī أوروبي 2. (fin.) yurō يورو (yurōhāt يوروهات)

Europe ['yuərəp] *n* ūrūbā أوروبا

European ['yuərəpi:ən] 1. *adj* ūrūbī أوروبي 2. *n* ūrūbī أوروبي (-yūn)

European Union (EU) *n* al-ittiḥād al-ūrūbī الإتحاد الأوروبي

evacuate [i'vakyueit] *v* ajlā أجلى

evade [i'veid] *v* taharraba تهرب

evaluate [i'valyueit] *v* qaddara قدر

eve ['i:v] *n* ʿashīya عشية (-āt)

even ['i:vən] 1. *adj* mustawin مستو 2. (maths) shafʿī شفعي 3. *adv* ḥattā حتى

even if *conj* ḥattā law حتى لو

evening ['i:vəning] *n* 1. masā' مساء (amsā' أمساء) 2. good evening! masā' al-khayr! مساء الخير

event [i'vent] *n* ḥadath حدث (aḥdāth أحداث); ḥāditha حادثة (ḥawādith حوادث)

eventful [i'ventfəl] *adj* malī' bi 'l-'aḥdāth مليء بالأحداث

even though *conj* raghma an رغم أن

eventually [i'venchuəli] *adv* akhīran أخيراً

ever ['evə] *adv* abadan أبداً; dā'iman دائماً

ever since *conj* mundhu منذ

everlasting ['evəla:sting] *adj* abadī أبدي; dā'im دائم

evermore ['evəmɔ:] *adv* ilā 'l-abad إلى الأبد

every ['evri] *adj* kull كل

everybody ['evribodi] al-jamīʿ الجميع

every day *adv* kull yawm كل يوم; yawmīyan يومياً

everyone ['evriwʌn] kull wāḥid
كل واحد

everything ['evrithing] kull shay'
كل شيء

everywhere ['evriweə] adv kull
makān كل مكان

evidence ['evidəns] n dalīl دليل
(adilla أدلة)

evident ['evidənt] adj wāḍiḥ واضح;
jalī جلي

evidently ['evidəntli] adv jalīyan
جلياً

evil ['i:vl] 1. adj sharīr شرير 2. n sharr
شر (ashrār أشرار)

evolution ['i:vəlu:shən] n nushū'
نشوء

evolve ['ivolv] v taṭawwara تطور;
nasha'a نشأ (u; nushū' نشوء;
nash'a نشأة)

exact [ig'zakt] adj maḍbūṭ مضبوط

exactly [ig'zaktli] adv bi-'l-ḍabṭ
بالضبط

exaggerate [ig'zajəreit] v bālagha
بالغ

exam [ig'zam] see examination

examination [ig'zamineishən] n 1.
(ed.) imtiḥān إمتحان (-āt) 2. (med.)
faḥṣ فحص (fuḥūṣ فحوص)

examine [ig'zamin] v 1. (ed.)
imtaḥana امتحن 2. (med.) faḥaṣa
فحص (a; faḥṣ فحص)

example [ig'za:mpl] n 1. mathal مثل
(amthāl أمثال) 2. for example
mathalan مثلاً

exceed [ik'si:d] v tajāwaza تجاوز

exceedingly [ik'si:dingli] adv
jiddan جداً

excel [ik'sel] v tafawwaqa تفوق

excellence ['eksələns] n tafawwuq
تفوق

excellent ['eksələnt] adj mumtāz
ممتاز

except [ik'sept] 1. prep mā ʿadā
ما عدا; illā إلا 2. conj lawlā لولا

except for prep law lā لولا

exception [ik'sepshən] n 1.
istithnā' إستثناء 2. without
exception dūn istithnā' دون إستثناء

exceptional [ik'sepshənl] adj 1.
istithnā'ī إستثنائي; mumtāz ممتاز

excess [ik'ses] adj/n farṭ فرط

excessive [ik'sesiv] adj mufriṭ
مفرط

exchange [ik'scheinj] 1. n istibdāl
إستبدال 2. foreign exchange ʿumla
ajnabīya عملة أجنبية (-āt) 3. stock
exchange būrṣa بورصة (-āt) 4.
telephone exchange santrāl سنترال
5. v tabādala تبادل

excite [ik'sait] v athāra أثار

excitement [ik'saitmənt] n ithāra
إثارة

exciting [ik'saiting] adj muthīr مثير

exclude [ik'sklu:d] v manaʿa منع
(a; manʿ منع) (from min من)

exclusive [ik'sklu:siv] adj 1.
maqṣūr مقصور 2. khāṣṣ خاص

excursion [ik'skə:zhən] n riḥla رحلة
(-āt)

excuse [ik'skyu:s] n ʿudhr عذر
(aʿdhār أعذار)

excuse me! ʿafwan! عفواً!

execute ['eksikyu:t] v 1. naffadha
نفذ 2. (leg.) aʿdama أعدم

execution ['eksikyu:shən] n 1.
tanfīdh تنفيذ 2. (leg.) iʿdām إعدام

executive [ig'zekyutiv] 1. adj
tanfīdhī تنفيذي 2. n chief executive
officer (CEO) ra'īs sharika
رئيس شركة

exercise ['eksəsaiz] **1.** *n* tamrīn تمرين **2.** (*mil.*) manāwara مناورة (-āt) **3.** *v* tamarrana تمرن

exhale ['eksheil] *v* zafara زفر (i; zafīr زفير)

exhaust [ig'zo:st] **1.** *n* bukhār al-muḥarrik بخار المحرك **2.** *v* arhaqa أرهق **3.** istafada استنفد

exhausted [ig'zo:stid] *adj* murhaq مرهق

exhaustion [ig'zo:schən] *n* irhāq إرهاق

exhibit [ig'zibit] *v* ʿaraḍa عرض (i; ʿarḍ عرض)

exhibition ['eksibishən] *n* maʿriḍ معرض (maʿāriḍ معارض)

exile ['eksail] **1.** *n* manfan منفًى **2.** *v* abʿada أبعد; nafā نفى (i; nafy نفي)

exist [ig'zist] *v* wujida وجد (yūjad يوجد; wujūd وجود)

existence [ig'zistəns] *n* wujūd وجود

existing [ig'zisting] *adj* **1.** ḥālī حالي **2.** mawjūd موجود

exit ['eksit; egzit] **1.** *n* makhraj مخرج (makhārij مخارج) **2.** *v* kharaja خرج (u; khurūj خروج)

expand [ik'spand] *v* **1.** wassaʿa وسع **2.** ittasaʿa اتسع

expansion [ik'spanshən] *n* **1.** tawsīʿ توسيع **2.** ittisāʿ إتساع

expect [ik'spekt] *v* **1.** tawaqqaʿa توقع **2.** *see* expecting

expectation [ekspek'teishən] *n* tawaqquʿ توقع

expedition [ekspi'dishən] *n* baʿtha بعثة (baʿathāt بعثات)

expel [ik'spel] *v* ṭarada طرد (u; ṭard طرد) (**from** min من)

expense; expenses [ik'spens; -iz] *n* maṣrūf مصروف (maṣārīf مصاريف)

expensive [ik'spensiv] *adj* ghālin غال

experience [ik'spiəriəns] **1.** *n* khibra خبرة **2.** tajruba تجربة **3.** *v* lāqā لاقى

experienced [ik'spiəriənst] *adj* **1.** dhū khibra ذو خبرة **2.** mutamarris متمرس

experiment [ik'sperimənt] *n* ikhtibār إختبار

experimental [ik'sperimentl] *adj* ikhtibārī إختباري

expert ['ekspə:t] *n* khabīr خبير (khubarā' خبراء)

expertise ['ekspə:ti:z] *n* khibra خبرة

expire [ik'spaiə] *v* **1.** inqaḍā انقضى **2.** māta مات (u; mawt موت)

explain [ik'splein] *v* sharaḥa شرح (a; sharḥ شرح)

explanation ['ekspləneishən] *n* sharḥ شرح

explicit [ik'splisit] *adj* wāḍiḥ واضح

explode [ik'spləud] *v* **1.** fajjara فجر **2.** infajara انفجر

exploit [ik'sploit] *v* istaghalla استغل

exploitation [eksploi'teishən] *n* istighlāl إستغلال

exploration [eksplə'reishən] *n* istikshāf إستكشاف

explore [ik'splo:] *v* istakshafa استكشف

explorer [ik'splo:rə] *n* kashshāf (kashshāfa كشافة) كشاف

explosion [ik'spləuzhən] *n* infijār إنفجار

explosive [ik'spləusiv] *adj* mutafajjir متفجر

explosives [ik'spləusivz] *pl* متفجرات mutafajjirāt

export [ik'spo:t] **1.** *n* صادر ṣādir (-āt); تصدير taṣdīr (-āt) **2.** *v* أصدر aṣdara

exporter [ik'spo:tə] *n* مصدر muṣaddir

exports ['ekspo:ts] *pl* صادرات ṣādirāt تصديرات ;taṣdīrāt

expose [ik'spəuz] *v* عرض ʿarraḍa (to لـ li); كشف عن kashafa ʿan (u; kashf كشف)

exposure [ik'spəuzhə] *n* كشف kashf

express [ik'spres] **1.** *adj* سريع sarīʿ **2.** *n* قطار سريع qiṭār sarīʿ **3.** *v* عبر ʿabbara

expression [ik'spreshən] *n* **1.** تعبير taʿbīr **2.** عبارة ʿibāra (-āt)

expressly [ik'spresli] *adv* بوضوح bi wuḍūḥ خصيصاً ;khiṣṣīṣan

exquisite ['ekskwizit; iks'kwizit] *adj* رائع rāʾiʿ

extend [ik'stend] *v* **1.** مد madda (u; مد madd) **2.** مدد maddada

extension [ik'stenshən] *n* **1.** تمديد tamdīd **2.** (*tel.*) **extension number** رقم داخلي raqm dākhilī

extensive [ik'stensiv] *adj* واسع wāsiʿ

extent [ik'stent] *n* **1.** حد ḥadd **2. to a certain extent** إلى حد ما ilā ḥaddin mā

exterior [ik'stiəriə] *adj* خارجي khārijī

exterminate [ik'stə:mineit] *v* أباد abāda

external [ik'stə:nl] *adj* خارجي khārijī

extinct [ik'stingkt] **1.** *adj* منقرض munqariḍ **2. to become extinct** انقرض inqaraḍa

extinguish [ik'stinggwish] *v* أطفأ aṭfaʾa

extinguisher [ik'stinggwishə] *n* مطفأة miṭfaʾa (مطافئ maṭāfiʾ)

extra ['ekstrə] *adj* إضافي iḍāfī; زائد zāʾid

extraordinary [ik'stro:dənri] *adj* **1.** خارق للعادة khāriq li ʾl-ʿāda **2.** رائع rāʾiʿ

extravagant [ik'stravəgənt] *adj* مسرف musrif

extreme [ik'stri:m] *adj* **1.** متطرف mutaṭarrif **2.** أقصى aqṣā

extremely [ik'stri:mli] *adv* جداً jiddan للغاية ;li ʾl-ghāya

extremist [ik'stri:mist] *n* متطرف mutaṭarrif (-ūn)

eye ['ai] *n* عين ʿayn (عيون ʿuyūn; أعين aʿyun)

eyeball ['aibol] *n* مقلة العين muqlat al-ʿayn (مقل muqal)

eyebrow ['aibrau] *n* حاجب ḥājib (حواجب ḥawājib)

eyeglasses ['aigla:siz] *pl* (*US*) عوينات ʿuwaynāt; نظارة naẓẓāra

eyelash ['ailash] *n* هدبة hudba (hudb هدب; أهداب ahdāb)

eyelid ['ailid] *n* جفن jafn (أجفان ajfān)

eyesight ['aisait] *n* بصر baṣar

eyewitness ['aiwitnis] *n* شاهد عيان shāhid ʿiyān

fabric ['fabrik] *n* قماش qumāsh
(أقمشة aqmisha)

fabricate ['fabrikeit] *v* **1.** صنع ṣanaʿa
(صنع sanʿ; صنع) **2.** ikhtaraʿa
اخترع

fabulous ['fabyuləs] *adj* **1.** khurāfī
خرافي **2.** hāʾil هائل

facade ['fəsaːd] *n* واجهة wājiha (-āt)

face ['feis] **1.** *n* وجه wajh (وجوه wujūh)
2. *v* wājaha واجه (وجوه)

facility ['fəsilәti] *n* **1.** سهولة suhūla
2. facilities tas-hīlāt تسهيلات

fact ['fakt] *n* **1.** حقيقة ḥaqīqa
(حقائق ḥaqāʾiq) **2. in fact** fī 'l-
wāqiʿ في الواقع

faction ['fakshən] *n* زمرة zumra
(زمر zumar)

factor ['faktə] *n* عامل ʿāmil (عوامل ʿawāmil)

factory ['faktəri] *n* مصنع maṣnaʿ
(مصانع maṣāniʿ)

faculty ['fakəlti] *n* **1.** قدرة qudra (-āt)
2. (*acad.*) kullīya كلية (-āt)

fade [feid] *v* بهت bahita (a; baht بهت)

fail [feil] *v* **1.** فشل fashila (a; fashal
فشل) **2.** akhfaqa أخفق **3. to fail
an exam** saqaṭa fī imtiḥān
سقط في إمتحان (u) **4. without fail**
ḥatman حتماً

failure ['feilyə] *n* fashal فشل; ikhfāq
إخفاق

faint ['feint] **1.** *adj* bāhit باهت **2.** *v*
ughmiya ʿalayh أغمي عليه

fair ['feə] **1.** *adj* munṣif منصف **2.**
n **trade fair** maʿraḍ tijārī معرض تجاري **3. funfair** madīnat
malāhī مدينة ملاهي

fairly ['feəli] *adv* **1.** ilā ḥaddin mā
إلى حد ما **2.** bi inṣāf بإنصاف

faith [feith] *n* īmān إيمان

faithful ['feithfəl] *adj* wafī وفي

fake [feik] **1.** *adj* muzayyaf مزيف **2.** *n*
zayf زيف (زيوف zuyūf)

fall [foːl] **1.** *n* waqʿa وقعة (waqaʿāt
وقعات) **2.** (*US*) kharīf خريف **3.** *v*
(**fell, fallen**) waqaʿa وقع (yaqaʿu
يقع; wuqūʿ وقوع) **4. to fall asleep**
nāma نام (a; nawm نوم)

false [foːls] *adj* zāʾif زائف

fame [feim] *n* shuhra شهرة

familiar [fə'miliə] *adj* ʿalā ʿilm
(with bi ب) على علم

family ['faməli] *n* usra أسرة (usar
أسر); ʿāʾila عائلة (-āt)

famous ['feiməs] *adj* mashhūr
مشهور

fan [fan] *n* **1.** mirwaḥa مروحة
(marāwiḥ مراوح) **2.** muʿjab معجب
(-ūn)

fanatic [fə'natik] *n* mutaṭarrif
متطرف (-ūn)

fancy ['fansi] **1.** *adj* muzakhrif
مزخرف **2.** *v* raghiba fī رغب في
(a; raghba رغبة)

fantastic [fan'tastik] *adj* rāʾiʿ رائع

fantasy ['fantəsi] *n* **1.** khayāl خيال
2. ikhtirāʿ إختراع

far [faː] **1.** *adj* baʿīd بعيد **2.** *adv*
baʿīdan بعيداً (**from** ʿan عن)

fare [feə] n 1. ujrat as-safar أجرة السفر
2. ṭaᶜām طعام

farewell ['feəwel] n widāᶜ وداع

farm [fa:m] 1. n mazraᶜa مزرعة
(mazāriᶜ مزارع) 2. v zaraᶜa زرع (a;
zarᶜ زرع)

farmer ['fa:mə] n muzāriᶜ مزارع
(-ūn)

farming ['fa:ming] n zirāᶜa زراعة

far-sighted adj baᶜīd an-naẓar
بعيد النظر

farther ['fa:dhə] adj abᶜad أبعد

fascinate ['fasineit] v aftana أفتن

fashion ['faʃən] n mōḍa موضة (-āt)

fashionable ['faʃənəbəl] adj ᶜalā 'l-
mōḍa على الموضة

fast ['fa:st] 1. adj sarīᶜ سريع 2. adv
bi surᶜa بسرعة 3. n ṣiyām صيام 4. v
ṣāma صام (u; ṣiyām صيام)

fasten ['fa:sən] v thabbata ثبت

fastener ['fa:snə] n zip fastener see
zip

fat ['fat] 1. adj samīn سمين 2. n duhn
دهن (duhūn دهون)

fatal ['feitəl] adj mumīt مميت

fate ['feit] n 1. qadar قدر; qaḍā' قضاء
2. maṣīr مصير

father ['fa:dhə] n ab أب (ābā' آباء);
wālid والد (-ūn)

father-in-law ['fadhərinlo:] n ḥam
حم (aḥmā' أحماء)

fatigue [fəti:g] n taᶜab تعب

faucet ['fo:set] n (US) ḥanafīya حنفية

fault [fo:lt] n 1. dhanb ذنب (dhunūb
ذنوب) 2. ᶜayb عيب (ᶜuyūb عيوب)

faulty ['fo:lti] adj maᶜīb معيب

favour ['feivə] 1. n khidma خدمة 2. v
rajjaḥa رجح

favourite ['feivərit] 1. adj murajjaḥ

مرجح 2. n maḥbūb محبوب 3. (spor.)
mufaḍḍal مفضل

fax ['faks] 1. n fāks فاكس 2. v baᶜatha
fāks بعث فاكس (a; baᶜth بعث)

fear ['fiə] 1. n khawf خوف 2. v khāfa
خاف (a; khawf خوف)

fearless ['fiəlis] adj shujāᶜ شجاع

feasible ['fi:zəbəl] adj maᶜqūl
معقول; ᶜamalī عملي

feast ['fi:st] n walīma وليمة
(walā'im ولائم)

feat [fi:t] n ᶜamal عمل (aᶜmāl أعمال)

feather ['fedhə] n rīsha ريشة (rīsh
ريش)

features ['fi:chə] n malāmiḥ ملامح

February ['februəri] n febrāyir
فبراير; shubāṭ شباط

fed ['fedərəl] see feed; fed up

federal ['fedərəl] adj federālī فدرالي;
ittiḥādī إتحادي

federation [fedə'reishən] n ittiḥād
إتحاد

fed up ['fedərəl] 1. adj zahqān زهقان
2. v to be fed up zahaqa زهق (a;
zahq زهق)

fee [fi:] n 1. ajr أجر (ujūr أجور) 2. (ed.)
rasm رسم (rusūm رسوم)

feeble ['fi:bəl] adj ḍaᶜīf ضعيف

feed [fi:d] v (fed) aṭᶜama أطعم

feel [fi:l] v (felt) 1. lamasa لمس (u/i;
lams لمس); ḥassa حس (u; ḥass حس)
2. shaᶜara شعر (u; shuᶜūr شعور) 3. to
feel like raghiba fī رغب في (a;
raghba رغبة)

feeling ['fi:ling] n 1. shuᶜūr شعور;
ḥiss حس 2. mashᶜar مشعر (mashāᶜir
مشاعر); iḥsās إحساس (-āt)

feet ['fi:t] see foot

fell ['fel] see fall

fellow ['feləu] 1. *adj* fellow worker zamīl زميل. 2. *n* rajul رجل (rijāl رجال)

felony ['feloni] *n* jināya جناية (-āt)

felt ['felt] *see* **feel**

female ['fi:meil] 1. *adj* unthawī أنثوي 2. *n* unthā أنثى

feminine ['femənin] *adj* mu'annath مؤنث

feminism ['feminizəm] *n* naẓarīyat al-musāwāh bayn al-jinsayn نظرية المساواة بين الجنسين

femininist ['feminist] *n* naṣīr naẓa-rīyat al-musāwāh bayn al-jinsayn نصير نظرية المساواة بين الجنسين

fence ['fens] *n* siyāj سياج (-āt)

ferocity [fə'rosəti] *n* waḥshīya وحشية

ferret ['ferət] *n* ibn miqraḍ ابن مقرض

ferry ['feri] *n* maʿdiya معدية (maʿādin معاد)

fertile ['fə:tail] *adj* khaṣīb خصيب

fertility ['fətiləti] *n* khiṣb خصب

fertilize ['fə:təlaiz] *v* khaṣṣaba خصب

festival ['festəvl] *n* 1. mihrajān مهرجان (أعياد) 2. (*rel.*) ʿīd عيد (aʿyād أعياد)

festive ['festiv] *adj* bahīj بهيج

festivity ['festivəti] *n* ʿīd عيد (aʿyād أعياد)

fetch [fech] *v* jalaba جلب (i/u; jalb جلب)

feud [fyu:d] *n* khuṣūma خصومة

fever ['fi:və] *n* ḥummā حمى (ḥummayāt حميات)

few; a few [fyu:] 1. *adj* qalīl قليل 2. *n* qilla قلة 3. quite a few ʿadad ghayr qalīl عدد غير قليل 4. in a few days baʿd ʿiddat ayyām بعد عدة أيام

fiancé ['fiyonsei] *n* khāṭib خاطب

fiancée [fi'yonsei] *n* makhṭūb مخطوب

fiasco [fi'yaskəu] *n* ikhfāq إخفاق

fibre ['faibə] *n* khayṭ خيط (khuyūṭ خيوط)

fiction ['fikshən] *n* 1. adab qaṣaṣī أدب قصصي 2. takhayyul تخيل

field ['fi:ld] *n* 1. ḥaql حقل (ḥuqūl حقول) 2. (*spor.*) malʿab ملعب (malāʿib ملاعب)

fierce [fiəs] *adj* muftaris مفترس

fifteen [fif'ti:n] *n/adj* khamsata ʿashar خمسة عشر

fifteenth [fif'ti:nth] *adj* khāmis ʿashar خامس عشر

fifth [fifth] *adj* khāmis خامس

fiftieth ['fiftiəth] *adj* al-khamsūn الخمسون

fifty ['fifti] *n/adj* khamsūn خمسون

fig ['fig] *n* tīna تينة (tīn collective تين)

fight ['fait] 1. *n* ʿirāk عراك 2. *v* (fought) qātala قاتل

fighter ["faitə] *n* muqātil مقاتل (-ūn)

fighting ['faiting] *n* qitāl قتال

figure ['figə] *n* 1. shakl شكل (ashkāl أشكال) 2. ʿadad عدد (aʿdād أعداد)

file [fail] *n* 1. milaff ملف (-āt) 2. mibrad مبرد (mabārid مبارد) 3. computer file milaff ملف

fill [fil] *v* mala'a ملأ (a; mal' ملء)

film [film] 1. *adj* sīnamā'ī سينمائي 2. *n* film فلم (aflām أفلام) 3. *v* ṣawwara صور

filter ['filtə] 1. *n* miṣfāh مصفاة (maṣāfin مصاف) 2. *v* ṣaffā صفى

filthy ['filthi] *adj* qadhir قذر

final ['fainəl] 1. *adj* akhīr أخير; nihā'ī نهائي 2. ḥāsim حاسم 3. *n* (*spor.*) mubārāh nihā'īya مباراة نهائية

finalist ['fainəlist] *n* mushtarik fī mubārāh nihā'iya مشترك في مباراة نهائية

finally ['fainəli] *adv* akhīran أخيراً

finance ['fainans; finans] **1.** *n* mālīya مالية **2.** *v* mawwala مول

financial ['fainanshəl] *adj* mālī مالي

find ['faind] *v* (**found**) wajada وجد (yajidu يجد; wujūd وجود)

find out *v* iktashafa اكتشف

fine ['fain] **1.** *adj* raqīq رقيق **2.** ṭayyib طيب **3.** *n* gharāma غرامة (-āt) **4.** *v* gharrama غرم **5.** *adv* jayyidan جيداً

finger ['finggə] *n* iṣbaᶜ إصبع (aṣābiᶜ أصابع)

finish ['finish] **1.** *n* nihāya نهاية (-āt) **2.** *v* intahā انتهى

Finland ['finlənd] *n* finlandā فنلندا

Finn ['fin] *n* finlandī فنلندي

Finnish ['finnish] *adj* finlandī فنلندي

fire ['faiə] **1.** *n* nār نار (nīrān نيران); ḥarīq حريق (ḥarā'iq حرائق) **2.** *v* **to fire (a weapon)** aṭlaqa أطلق **3. to fire from a job** faṣala ᶜan al-ᶜamal فصل عن العمل (i; faṣl فصل)

fire alarm *n* jaras al-indhār bi 'l-ḥarīq جرس الإنذار بالحريق

firearm ['faiəra:m] *n* silāḥ nārī سلاح ناري (asliḥa nārīya أسلحة نارية)

fire brigade *n* iṭfā'īya إطفائية

fire department *n* (US) iṭfā'īya إطفائية

fire engine *n* siyārat al-iṭfā' سيارة الإطفاء

fire escape; fire exit *n* sullam al-ḥarīq سلم الحريق

firefighter ['faiəfaitə] *n* iṭfā'ī إطفائي

fireman ['faiəmən] *n* iṭfā'ī إطفائي

fireplace ['faiəpleis] *n* mustawqad مستوقد

fire station *n* maḥaṭṭat al-iṭfā' محطة الإطفاء

firewood ['faiwud] *n* ḥaṭab حطب

fireworks ['faiəwə:ks] *pl* alᶜāb nārīya ألعاب نارية

firm ['fə:m] **1.** *adj* thābit ثابت **2.** *n* sharika شركة (-āt)

first ['fə:st] **1.** *adj* awwal أول **2.** *adv* awwalan أولاً **3. at first** awwalan أولاً

first aid *n* al-isᶜāf al-awwalī الإسعاف الأولي

first-class 1. *adj* mumtāz ممتاز **2.** *n* ad-daraja al-ūlā الدرجة الأولى

firstly ['fə:stli] *adv* awwalan أولاً

first name *n* ism اسم (asmā' أسماء); ism awwal اسم أول

fish ['fish] **1.** *n* samaka سمكة (*collective* samak سمك; *pl* asmāk أسماك) **2.** *v* iṣṭāda as-samak اصطاد السمك

fisherman ['fishəmən] *n* ṣayyād as-samak صياد السمك (-ūn)

fishing ['fishing] *n* iṣṭiyād as-samak إصطياد السمك

fist ['fist] *n* qabḍat al-yad قبضة اليد

fit ['fit] **1.** *adj* salīm سليم **2.** *v* lāqa لاق (i; layq ليق)

five ['faiv] khamsa خمسة

fix ['fiks] *v* **1.** thabbata ثبت **2.** ṣallaḥa صلح

flag [flag] *n* ᶜalam علم (aᶜlām أعلام)

flame [fleim] *n* lahab لهب

flap [flap] *v* akhfaqa أخفق

flash [flash] **1.** *n* barīq بريق **2.** laḥẓa khāṭifa لحظة خاطفة **3.** *v* baraqa برق (u; barq برق)

flashlight ['flashlait] n mish'al
kahrabā'ī مشعل كهربائي

flask [fla:sk] n qārūra قارورة (āt-)

flat [flat] 1. adj satīḥ سطيح; musaṭṭaḥ
مسطح 2. n shaqqa شقة (shiqaq
شقق)

flavour, (US) **flavor** ['fleivə] n ṭa'm
طعم (ṭu'ūm طعوم)

flaw [flo:] n 'ayb عيب ('uyūb عيوب)

flea [fli:] n burghūth برغوث
(baraghīth براغيث)

flee [fli:] v (**fled**) haraba هرب (u;
hurūb هروب); farra فر (i; firār فرار)

fleet [fli:t] n usṭūl أسطول (asāṭīl
أساطيل)

flesh [flesh] n laḥm لحم

flew [flu:] see **fly**

flexible ['fleksəbəl] adj layyin لين

flight [flait] n 1. ṭayarān طيران 2.
riḥla (bi ṭ-ṭā'ira) رحلة (بالطائرة)

flip [flip] v qalaba قلب (i; qalb قلب)

float [fləut] v 'āma عام (u; 'awm عوم)

flock [flok] n sirb سرب (asrāb أسراب)

flood [flʌd] 1. n ṭūfān طوفان; fayaḍān
فيضان 2. v fāḍa فاض (i; fayaḍān
فيضان)

floor [flo:] n 1. arḍ أرض 2. ṭābiq طابق
(ṭawābiq طوابق)

florist ['florist] n bā'i' al-zuhūr
بائع الزهور

flour [flauə] n daqīq دقيق

flourish ['flʌrish] v izdahara ازدهر

flow [fləu] 1. n sayalān سيلان 2. v sāla
سال (i; sayalān سيلان)

flower ['flauə] n zahra زهرة (zuhūr
زهور)

flown [fləun] see **fly**

flu (= **influenza**) [flu:] n influwanza
إنفلونزا

fluctuate ['flʌkchueit] v taqallaba
تقلب; tadhabdhaba تذبذب

fluent ['flu:ənt] adj 1. faṣīḥ فصيح 2.
salis سلس

fluid ['flu:id] 1. adj sā'il سائل 2. n
sā'il سائل (sawā'il سوائل)

fly [flai] 1. n (**flies**) dhubāba ذبابة
(dhubāb ذباب; dhibbān ذبان) 2. v
(**flew, flown**) ṭāra طار (i; ṭayarān
طيران) 3. **to fly a plane** qāda ṭā'ira
قاد طائرة (u; qawd قود)

focus ['fəukəs] v 1. 'addala عدل 2.
rakkaza ركز

fog [fog] n ḍabāb ضباب

fold [fəuld] v laffa لف (u; laff لف)

folder ['fəuldər] n milaff ملف (āt-)

folk [fəuk] 1. adj sha'bī شعبي 2. n nās
ناس 3. qawm قوم

follow ['fɒləu] v 1. ittaba'a اتبع 2.
salaka سلك (u; sulūk سلوك)

follower ['fɒləuə] n tābi' تابع (atbā'
أتباع)

following ['fɒləuing] 1. adj tālin تال
2. n majmū'at atbā' مجموعة أتباع

fond [fond] adj **to be fond of**
ughrima bi أغرم ب

food [fu:d] n ṭa'ām طعام

fool [fu:l] 1. n aḥmaq أحمق (ḥumq
حمق) 2. v khāda'a خادع

foolish ['fu:lish] adj aḥmaq أحمق;
ghabī غبي

foot [fut] n (**feet**) 1. qadam usually f.
قدم (aqdām أقدام) 2. **on foot** 'alā
qadamayh على قدميه

football ['futbo:l] n kurat al-qadam
كرة القدم

footballer ['futbo:lə] n lā'ib al-kura
لاعب الكرة

for [fə; fo:] prep 1. li ل 2. li ajli لأجل 3.
ilā إلى

forbid [fə'bid] v (forbade, forbidden) mana‘a منع (a; man‘ منع)

forbidden [fə'bidən] adj mamnū‘ ممنوع

force [fo:s] 1. n qūwa قوة (-āt) 2. ‘unf عنف 3. **military forces** qūwāt قوات 4. v ajbara أجبر

forceful ['fo:sfəl] adj qawī قوي

fore [fo:] n 1. muqaddima مقدمة 2. **to come to the fore** baraza برز (u)

forecast ['fo:ka:st] 1. n tanabbu’ تنبؤ 2. v tanabba’a تنبأ

forehead ['forid; 'fo:hed] n jabīn جبين (ajbina أجبنة)

foreign ['forən] adj ajnabī أجنبي

foreigner ['forənə] n ajnabī أجنبي (ajānib أجانب)

foreign exchange n ‘umla ajnabīya عملة أجنبية (-āt)

foreign minister n wazīr al-khārijīya وزير الخارجية (wuzarā’ وزراء)

foremost ['fo:məust] 1. adj ra’īsī رئيسي 2. adv awwalan أولاً

foresee [fo:'si:] v tanabba’a تنبأ

foresight ['fo:sait] n baṣīra بصيرة

forest ['forist] n ghāba غابة (-āt)

forever [fə'revə] adv ilā ’l-abad إلى الأبد

for example see e.g.

forgave [fə'geiv] see forgive

forgery ['fo:jəri] n tazwīr تزوير

forget [fə'get] v (forgot, forgotten) nasiya نسي (a; nisyān نسيان)

forgive [fə'giv] v (forgave, forgiven) ghafara غفر (i; maghfira مغفرة)

forgiveness [fə'givnis] n maghfira مغفرة

forgot; forgotten [fə'got; fə'gotən] see forget

fork [fo:k] n shawka شوكة (collective shawk شوك)

form [fo:m] 1. n shakl شكل (ashkāl أشكال) 2. istimāra إستمارة (-āt) 3. (ed.) ṣaff صف (ṣufūf صفوف) 4. v shakkala شكل 5. kawwana كون

formal ['fo:məl] adj rasmī رسمي

formality [fo:'məliti] n rasmīya رسمية (-āt)

formally ['fo:məli] adv rasmīyan رسمياً

formation [fo:'meishən] n tashkīl تشكيل

former ['fo:mə] adj sābiq سابق

formerly ['fo:məli] adv sābiqan سابقاً

formidable [fo:'midəbəl] adj mur‘ib مرعب; mukhīf مخيف

formula ['fo:myulə] n ṣīgha صيغة (ṣiyagh صيغ)

fort [fo:t] n ḥiṣn حصن (ḥuṣūn حصون)

forth [fo:th] adv faṣā‘idan فصاعداً

forthcoming [fo:th'kʌming] adj ātin آت; washīk وشيك

fortnight ['fo:tnait] n usbū‘ān أسبوعان

fortress ['fo:tris] see fort

fortunate ['fo:chənət] adj maḥẓūẓ محظوظ

fortunately ['fo:chənətli] adv li ḥusn al-ḥaẓẓ لحسن الحظ

fortune ['fo:chu:n] n 1. ḥaẓẓ حظ 2. tharwa ثروة

forty ['fo:ti] n/adj arba‘ūn أربعون

forward ['fo:wəd] 1. adv amāmī أمامي 2. v arsala أرسل

fought [fo:t] see fight

foul [faul] 1. *adj* ʿafin عفن 2. *n (spor.)* mukhālafa مخالفة

found [faund] 1. *v* assasa أسس 2. *see* **find**

foundation [faun'deishən] *n* 1. asās أساس (asas أسس) 2. mu'assasa مؤسسة (-āt)

founder ['faundə] *n* mu'assis مؤسس (-ūn)

fountain ['fauntin] *n* nāfūra نافورة (nawāfīr نوافير)

four [fo:] *n/adj* arbaʿa أربعة

fourteen [fo:'ti:n] *n/adj* arbaʿata ʿashar أربعة عشر

fourteenth [fo:'ti:nth] *adj* rābiʿ ʿashar رابع عشر

fourth [fo:th] 1. *adj* rābiʿ رابع 2. *n* rubʿ ربع

fox [foks] *n* thaʿlab ثعلب (thaʿālib ثعالب)

fraction ['frakshən] *n* kasr كسر (kusūr كسور)

fracture ['frakchə] 1. *n* kasr كسر (kusūr كسور) 2. *v* kasara كسر (i; kasr كسر)

fragile ['frajail] *adj* qaṣim قصم

fragment ['fragmənt] *n* kisra كسرة (-āt; kisar كسر)

fragrance ['freigrəns] *n* shadhan شذأ

frame [freim] *n* 1. haykal هيكل (hayākil هياكل) 3. picture frame iṭār إطار (-āt)

framework ['freimwə:k] *n* iṭār إطار (-āt)

France [fra:ns] *n* faransā فرنسا

franchise ['franchaiz] *n* 1. ḥaqq al-taṣwīt حق التصويت 2. imtiyāz إمتياز

frankly ['frangkli] *adv* ṣarāḥatan صراحةً

fraud [fro:d] *n* naṣb نصب; iḥtiyāl إحتيال

freak [fri:k] *n* gharīb غريب (ghurabā' غرباء)

free [fri:] 1. *adj* ḥurr حر 2. majjānī مجاني 3. *v* (freed) ḥarrara حرر; aṭlaqa أطلق

freedom ['fri:dəm] *n* ḥurrīya حرية (-āt)

freedom of speech *n* ḥurrīyat at-taʿbīr حرية التعبير

freedom of the press *n* ḥurrīyat aṣ-ṣaḥāfa حرية الصحافة

freelance; freelancer ['fri:la:ns; -ə] *n* ʿāmil ḥurr عامل حر

free of charge *adj* majjānan مجاناً

freeze [fri:z] *v* (froze, frozen) jalada جلد (i; jald جلد); jallada جلد

freezer ['fri:zə] *n* thallāja ثلاجة

freight [freit] *n* shaḥn شحن

freighter ['freitə] *n* safīnat shaḥn سفينة شحن

French [french] 1. *adj* faransī فرنسي 2. *n* faransī فرنسي (-yūn) 3. the French *pl* al-faransīyūn الفرنسيون

French-Canadian *adj* kanadī faransī كندي فرنسي

Frenchman ['frenchmən] *n* faransī فرنسي

Frenchwoman ['frenchwumən] *n* faransīya فرنسية

frequency ['fri:kwənsi] *n* taraddud تردد

frequent ['frikwənt] *adj* mutakarrir متكرر

frequently ['fri:kwəntli] *adv* takrāran تكراراً

fresh [fresh] *adj* 1. ṭāzaj طازج 2. ʿadhb عذب

Friday ['fraidei] *n* al-jum'a الجمعة

fridge [frij] *n* thallāja ثلاجة (-āt)

fried [fraid] *see* **fry**

friend [frend] *n* ṣadīq صديق (aṣdiqā' أصدقاء)

friendliness ['frendlinis] *n* waddīya ودّية

friendly ['frendli] *adj* wadūd ودود; waddī ودّي

friendship ['frendship] *n* ṣadāqa صداقة

fright [frait] *n* ru'b رعب

frighten ['fraitən] *v* ar'aba أرعب; akhāfa أخاف

frightened ['fraitənd] *adj* mar'ūb مرعوب; khā'if خائف

fringe [frinj] *n* ḥāfa حافة (-āt)

fro [frəu] *adv* **to and fro** jay'atan wa dhihāban جيئةً وذهاباً

frog [frog] *n* ḍafda' ضفدع (ḍafādi' ضفادع)

from [from] *prep* 1. min من 2. 'an عن 3. mundhu منذ 4. **from London** min landan من لندن

front [frʌnt] *n* 1. wajh وجه 2. **in front** amām أمام 3. **war front** jabha جبهة (jabahāt جبهات)

frontier ['frʌntiə] *n* ḥadd حد (ḥudūd حدود)

froze [frəuz] *see* **freeze**

frozen ['frəuzən] *adj* 1. mujammad مجمد 2. *see* **freeze**

fruit [fru:t] *n* fākiha فاكهة (fawākih فواكه)

fruitful ['fru:tfəl] *adj* muthmir مثمر

fruitless ['fru:tlis] *adj* fāshil فاشل

frustrate [frʌs'treit] *v* aḥbaṭa أحبط

frustrated [frʌs'treitid] *adj* muḥbaṭ محبط

frustration [frʌs'treishən] *n* iḥbāṭ إحباط

fry [frai] *v* (**fried**) qalā قلى (i; qaliy قلي)

ft. *see* **foot**

fuel ['fyu:əl] 1. *n* wuqūd وقود 2. *v* zawwada bi 'l-wuqūd زود بالوقود

fugitive ['fyu:jətiv] *n* hārib هارب (-ūn)

fulfil, *(US)* **fulfill** [ful'fil] *v* wafā وفى (yafī يفي; wafā' وفاء)

fulfilment, *(US)* **fulfillment** [ful'filmənt] *n* 1. wafā' وفاء 2. taḥqīq al-ahdāf تحقيق الأهداف

full [ful] *adj* malī' مليء; mamlū' مملوء; tāmm تام

full-time *adj* **full-time job** 'amal dā'im عمل دائم

fully ['fuli] *adv* tamāman تماماً

fun [fʌn] *n* 1. lahw لهو 2. **in fun** mazḥan مزحاً 3. **to make fun of** tahazza'a min تهزأ من

function ['fʌnkshən] 1. *n* waẓīfa وظيفة (waẓā'if وظائف) 2. *v* 'amila عمل (a; 'amal عمل)

fund [fʌnd] 1. *n* i'timād mālī إعتماد مالي 2. *v* mawwala مول

fundamental [fʌndə'mentəl] *adj* aṣlī أصلي; asāsī أساسي

fundamentalist [fʌndə'mentəlist] *adj* uṣūlī أصولي

fundamentalism [fʌndə'mentəlizəm] *n* uṣūlīya أصولية

funding ['fʌnding] *n* tamwīl تمويل

funds [fʌndz] *pl* amwāl أموال

funeral ['fyu:nərəl] *n* janāza جنازة (-āt)

fungus ['fʌnggəs] *n* fuṭra فطرة (fuṭr فطر)

funny ['fʌni] *adj* **1.** muḍhik مضحك **2.** hazil هزل **3.** gharīb غريب

fur [fə:] *n* farwa فروة (farw فرو)

furious ['fyuəriəs] *adj* ghaḍbān غضبان

furnace ['fə:nis] *n* attūun أتون (atātīn أتاتين)

furnish ['fə:nish] *v* jahhaza جهز

furniture ['fə:nichə] *n* athāth أثاث

further ['fə:dhə] **1.** *adj* abʿad أبعد **2.** *v* ayyada أيد; sānada ساند

furthermore [fə:dhə'mo:] *adv* ʿilāwatan ilā dhālik علاوة إلى ذلك

fury ['fyuəri] *n* ghaḍab غضب

fussy ['fʌsi] *adj* nayyiq نيق

futile ['fyu:tail] *adj* bilā jadwā بلا جدوى

future ['fyu:chə] **1.** *n* mustaqbal مستقبل **2.** *adj* ātin آت

G

gadget ['gajit] *n* adāh ṣaghīra أداة صغيرة (adawāt أدوات)

gag [gag] *v* to gag the press manaʾa ḥurrīyat aṣ-ṣaḥāfa منع حرية الصحافة (manʿ منع; a)

gain [gein] **1.** *n* kasb كسب; ribḥ ربح **2.** *v* kasab كسب (kasb; a)

gala ['ga:lə] *n* mihrajān مهرجان (-āt)

gallery ['galəri] *n* maʿraḍ معرض (maʿāriḍ معارض)

gallon ['galən] *n* gālūn غالون

gamble ['gambəl] *v* qāmara قامر

gambler ['gamblə] *n* muqāmir مقامر (-ūn)

gambling ['gambling] *n* qimār قمار

game [geim] *n* laʿb لعب (alʿāb ألعاب)

gang [gang] *n* ʿiṣāba عصابة (-āt)

gangster ['gangstə] *n* ʿuḍw ʿiṣāba عضو عصابة; mujrim مجرم (-ūn)

gap [gap] *n* fajwa فجوة (fajawāt فجوات)

garage ['gara:zh; 'garij] *n* **1.** gārāzh كاراج (-āt) **2.** mirʾab مرأب (marāʾib مرائب)

garbage ['ga:bij] *n* nufāyāt نفايات

garden ['ga:dən] *n* ḥadīqa حديقة (ḥadāʾiq حدائق)

gardener ['ga:dnə] *n* bustānī بستاني

gardening ['ga:dning] *n* al-iʿtināʾ bi-l-ḥadāʾiq الإعتناء بالحدائق

garlic ['ga:lik] *n* thūm ثوم

garment ['ga:mənt] *n* kisāʾ كساء (aksiya أكسية)

garrison ['garisən] *n* **1.** qūwāt ʿaskarīya قوات عسكرية **2.** thukna ثكنة (-āt)

gas [gas] *n* **1.** ghāz غاز **2.** *(US)* banzīn بنزين

gasoline ['gasəli:n] *n* banzin بنزين

gas station n (US) maḥaṭṭat banzīn محطة بنزين

gas tank n khazzān al-banzin خزان البنزين

gate [geit] n bāb باب (abwāb أبواب)

gather ['gadhə] v 1. jama'a جمع (a; jam' جمع) 2. i'taqada اعتقد

gathering ['gadhəring] n jam' جمع

gave [geiv] see give

gay [gei] 1. adj mithlī مثلي 2. mariḥ مرح 3. n mithlī مثلي (-yūn)

gaze [geiz] v ḥaddaqa حدق (at fī في)

gazette [gə'zet] n jarīda جريدة (jarā'id جرائد)

gear [giə] n 1. tirs ترس (turūs تروس) 2. jihāz جهاز 3. amwāl أموال; mumtalakāt ممتلكات

geese [gi:s] see goose

gel [jel] n jel جيل; mādda hulāmīya مادة هلامية

gem [jem] n jawhara جوهرة (jawāhir جواهر)

gender ['jendə] n jins جنس (ajnās أجناس)

general ['jenrəl] 1. adj 'āmm عام 2. n liwā' لواء 3. in general 'umūman عموماً

general election n intikhābāt إنتخابات

generalize ['jenrəlaiz] v 'ammama عمم

generally ['jenrəli] adv 'umūman عموماً

generate ['jenreit] v wallada ولد

generation ['jenəreishən] n jīl جيل (ajyāl أجيال)

generator ['jenəreitə] n muwallid مولد

generosity ['dyenərosəti] n karam كرم

generous ['jenərəs] adj karīm كريم

genetic [ji'netik] adj wirāthī وراثي

genitals ['jenitəlz] pl a'ḍā' at-tanāsul أعضاء التناسل

genitive ['jenitiv] n al-jarr الجر

genius ['ji:niəs] n 1. 'abqarīya عبقرية 2. 'abqarī عبقري (-yūn)

genocide ['jenəsaid] n ibāda إبادة

gentle ['jentəl] adj laṭīf لطيف

gentleman ['jentəlmən] n (gentlemen) sayyid سيد (sāda سادة)

genuine ['jenyuwin] adj ḥaqīqī حقيقي

geography [ji'yogrəfi] n zhugh-rāfiya جغرافيا

geology [ji'oləji] n zhiyolōzhiya جيولوجيا

germ [jə:m] n jurthūm جرثوم; (jarāthīm جراثيم) jurthūma جرثومة

German ['jə:mən] 1. adj almānī ألماني 2. n almānī ألماني

Germany ['jə:məni] n almānya ألمانيا

gesture ['jeschə] n ishārat yad يد إشارة; īmā'a إيماءة

get [get] v (got, gotten) 1. ḥaṣala 'alā حصل على (u; ḥuṣūl حصول); nāla نال (u; nawl نول) 2. aṣbḥa أصبح 3. **to get hurt** juriḥa جرح 4. **to get better** taḥassana تحسن 5. **They got to London.** waṣalū ilā landan. وصلوا إلى لندن.

get away v aflata أفلت (**from** min من)

get back v istaradda استرد

get off v nazila نزل (i; nuzūl نزول)

get on v 1. rakiba ركب (a; rukūb ركوب) 2. sāyara ساير

get out v kharaja خرج (u) (of min
من)

get ready v istaʿadda استعد

get to v waṣala وصل (yasilu يصل;
wuṣūl وصول)

get up v nahaḍa ʿan as-sarīr
نهض عن السرير (a; nuhūḍ نهوض)

ghastly ['gɑːstli] adj muqrif مقرف

ghost ['gəust] n shabaḥ شبح (ashbāḥ
أشباح)

giant ['jaiənt] 1. adj ḍakhm ضخم
2. n ʿimlāq عملاق (ʿamāliqa عمالقة)

gift [gift] n hiba هبة (-āt); hadīya هدية
(hadāyā هدايا)

gig [gig] n (mus.) ḥafla mūsiqīya
حفلة موسيقية

gigantic ['jaigantik] adj ʿimlāq
عملاق

giggle ['gigəl] n ḍaḥika ضحك (a;
ḍaḥk ضحك)

Gipsy ['jipsi] see **Gypsy**

girl [gəːl] n bint بنت (banāt بنات)

girlfriend ['gəːlfrend] n ṣadīqa
صديقة (-āt)

give [giv] v (**gave**, **given**) aʿṭā
أعطى

give back v aʿāda أعاد

give birth to v waladat ولدت
(talidu تلد; wilāda ولادة)

give in v 1. qaddama قدم 2.
istaslama استسلم

give up v taraka ترك (u; tark ترك)

glad [glad] adj masrūr مسرور

gladly ['gladli] adv bi kull surūr
بكل سرور

glance at [glɑːns] v almaḥa ilā
ألمح إلى

glass [glɑːs] n 1. zujāj زجاج 2.
drinking glass kaʾs كأس (kuʾūs
كؤوس)

glasses ['glɑːsiz] see **eyeglasses**

gleam [gliːm] v lamaʿa لمع (a; lamʿ
لمع)

glimpse [glimps] v lamaḥa لمح
(a; lamḥ لمح)

glitter ['glitə] v talaʾlaʾa تلألأ

global ['gləubəl] adj ʿālamī عالمي

globalisation [gləubəlaiˈzeishən] n
ʿawlama عولمة

globe [gləub] n 1. kura كرة (-āt;
kuran كرى) 2. **the globe** al-kura al-
arḍīya الكرة الأرضية

glorious ['gloːriəs] adj rāʾiʿ رائع

glory ['gloːri] n majd مجد (amjād
أمجاد)

glove [glʌv] n quffāz قفاز (-āt)

glow [gləu] v tawahhaja توهج

glue [gluː] 1. n ghirāʾ غراء 2. v gharrā
غرى

go [gəu] v (**went**, **gone**) dhahaba ذهب
(a; dhihāb ذهاب)

go ahead v inṭalaqa انطلق

goal [gəul] n 1. hadaf هدف (ahdāf
أهداف) 2. (spor.) hadaf هدف (ahdāf
أهداف); marman مرمى (marāmin
مرام) 3. **to score a goal** sajjala
hadafan سجل هدفاً 4. see **goalpost**

goalkeeper ['gəulkiːpə] n ḥāris al-
marmā حارس المرمى

goalpost ['gəulpəust] n ʿamūd al-
marmā عامود المرمى

goat [gəut] n maʿza معزة (collective
maʿz معز)

go away v inṣarafa انصرف

go back v rajaʿa رجع (a/i; rujūʿ رجوع)

go bad v fasada فسد (u/i; fasād
فساد)

god [god] n 1. ilāh إله (āliha آلهة) 2.
God allāh الله

goddess ['godis] n ilāha إلهة

go down v nazala نزل (i; nuzūl (نزول

go in v dakhala دخل (u; dukhūl (دخول

gold [gəuld] 1. adj dhahabī ذهبي 2. n dhahab ذهب

golden ['gəuldən] adj dhahabī ذهبي

golf [golf] n gōlf جولف

golf course n malʿab al-gōlf ملعب الجولف

gone [gon] see go

good [gud] 1. adj jayyid جيد; ṭayyib طيب; ḥasan حسن 2. n khayr خير (akhyār أخيار) 3. **for good** ilā 'l-abad إلى الأبد 4. see goods

goodbye [gud'bai] n 1. al-widāʿ الوداع 2. **goodbye!** maʿ as-salāma! مع السلامة!

good-looking adj jadhdhāb جذاب

goodness ['gudnis] n ṭība طيبة; jūda جودة

goods [gudz] n baḍā'iʿ بضائع

good-tempered adj damith al-akhlāq دمث الأخلاق

goodwill [gud'wil] n ḥusn an-nīya حسن النية

go on v istamarra استمر

goose [gu:s] n (geese) iwazza إوزة (collective iwazz إوز)

go out v 1. kharaja خرج (u; khurūj خروج) 2. māta مات (u; mawt موت)

go over v rāja'a راجع

gorge [go:j] n ʿaqīq عقيق (a'iqqa أعقة); wādin واد (awdiya أودية)

gorgeous ['go:jəs] adj fā'iq al-jamāl فائق الجمال

gossip ['gosip] n qīl wa qāl قيل وقال

got [got] see get

go through v ijtāza اجتاز

go up v ṣa'ida صعد (a; ṣu'ūd (صعود

govern ['gʌvən] v ḥakama حكم (u; ḥukm (حكم

government ['gʌvənmənt] n 1. ḥukūma حكومة (-āt) 2. ḥukm حكم

governor ['gʌvənə] n ḥākim حاكم (ḥukkām حكام)

go with v rāfaqa رافق

gown [gaun] n thawb (nisā'ī) (ثياب (tiyāb) ثوب (نسائي)

grab [grab] v (**grabbed**) masaka مسك (i; mask مسك)

graceful ['greisfəl] adj rashīq رشيق

grade [greid] n 1. daraja درجة (-āt) 2. (ed.) ṣaff صف (ṣufūf صفوف)

gradual ['grajuəl] adj tadrījī تدريجي

gradually ['grajuli] adv tadrījīyan تدريجياً

graduate ['grajuət] n mutakharrij متخرج (-ūn)

graffiti [grə'fi:ti] n al-kitāba ʿalā 'l-ḥawā'iṭ الكتابة على الحوائط

grain [grein] n ḥabba حبة (collective ḥabb حب; pl ḥubūb حبوب)

gram (US) [gram] see gram

grammar ['gramə] n an-naḥw wa 'ṣ-ṣarf النحو والصرف

gramme [gram] n grām غرام (-āt)

grand [grand] adj ʿaẓīm عظيم

grandchild ['granchaild] n ḥafīd حفيد (aḥfād أحفاد)

granddaughter ['grando:tə] n ḥafīda حفيدة (-āt)

grandfather ['granfa:dhə] n jadd جد (ajdād أجداد)

grandmother ['grandmʌdhə] n jadda جدة (-āt)

grandson ['grandsʌn] n ḥafīd حفيد (aḥfād أحفاد)

granite ['granɪt] *n* ṣawwān صوان

grant [graːnt] **1.** *n* minḥa منحة
(minaḥ منح) **2.** *v* manaḥa منح (a;
manḥ منح)

grape [greɪp] *n* ʿinaba عنبة (*collective*
ʿinab عنب; *pl* aʿnāb أعناب)

grapefruit ['greɪpfruːt] *n* graypfrūt
جريب فروت

graph [graːf] *n* rasm رسم (rusūm
رسوم)

graphic ['grafɪk] *adj* **1.** takhṭīṭī
تخطيطي **2.** bayānī بياني

graphic arts *pl* al-funūn at-
takhṭīṭīya الفنون التخطيطية

graphic designer *n* muṣammim
takhṭīṭī مصمم تخطيطي (-yūn)

grasp [graːsp] *v* **1.** qabaḍa ʿalā
قبض على (i; qabḍ قبض) **2.** fahima
فهم (a; fahm فهم)

grass [graːs] *n* ḥashīsh حشيش
(ḥashāʾish حشائش); ʿushb عشب
(aʿshāb أعشاب)

grateful ['greɪtfəl] *adj* shākir شاكر;
mamnūn ممنون

gratitude ['gratɪtyuːd] *n* shukr شكر;
imtinān إمتنان

grave [greɪv] **1.** *adj* khaṭīr خطير **2.** *n*
qabr قبر (qubūr قبور)

graveyard ['greɪvyaːd] *n* maqbara
مقبرة (maqābir مقابر)

gravity ['gravɪti] *n* **1.** jādhibīyat
ath-thiql جاذبية الثقل **2.** waqār وقار

gravy ['greɪvi] *n* maraq مرق

gray [greɪ] *see* **grey**

grease [griːs] *n* shaḥm شحم
(shuḥūm شحوم)

great [greɪt] *adj* **1.** ʿaẓīm عظيم **2.** a
great deal kathīr كثير

Great Britain ['greɪt'brɪtən] *n*
brīṭāniyā al-ʿuẓmā بريطانيا العظمى

greatly ['greɪtli] *adv* kathīran كثيراً

greed [griːd] *n* ṭamaʿ طمع (aṭmāʿ
أطماع)

greedy ['griːdi] *adj* ṭammāʿ طماع

green [griːn] *adj* **1.** akhḍar أخضر **2.**
sādhij ساذج **3.** (*pol.*) akhḍar أخضر

greenhouse ['griːnhaus] *n* bayt
zujājī بيت زجاجي

greens [griːnz] *pl* khaḍrawāt
خضروات

greet [griːt] *v* ḥayyā حيا

greeting ['griːtɪng] *n* taḥīya تحية
(taḥayyāt تحيات)

grenade [grəˈneɪd] *n* qunbula
yadawīya قنبلة يدوية (qanābil قنابل)

grew [gruː] *see* **grow**

grey [greɪ] *adj* ramādī رمادي

grid [grɪd] *n* shabaka شبكة (-āt)

grief [griːf] *n* asan أسىً

grieve [griːv] *v* asiya أسي (u; asan
أسىً)

grievous ['griːvəs] *adj* khaṭīr خطير

grill [grɪl] *v* shawā شوى (i; shayy شي)

grim [grɪm] *adj* mutajahhim متجهم

grin [grɪn] *v* ibtasama ابتسم

grind [graɪnd] *v* (**ground**) ṭaḥana
طحن (a; ṭaḥn طحن)

grip [grɪp] **1.** *n* qabḍa قبضة (qabaḍāt
قبضات) **2.** *v* qabaḍa ʿalā قبض على (i;
qabḍ قبض)

groan [grəun] *v* taʾawwaha تأوه

grocer ['grəusə] *n* baqqāl بقال (-ūn)

groceries ['grəusəriːz] *pl* baḍāʾiʿ
baqqālīya بضائع بقالية

groom [gruːm] *n* **1.** sāʾis سائس
(sāsa ساسة) **2.** *see* **bridegroom**

groove [gruːv] *n* ukhdūd أخدود
(akhādīd أخاديد)

ground [graund] *n* **1.** arḍ أرض; saṭḥ

al-arḍ سطح الأرض 2. (spor.) malʿab ملعب (malāʿib ملاعب) 3. see grind, grounds

grounds [graundz] pl 1. (leg.) asbāb أسباب 2. see ground

group [gruːp] 1. n jamāʿa جماعة (-āt) 2. v jamaʿa جمع (a; jamʿ جمع) 3. ṣannafa صنف

grow [grəu] v (grew, grown) 1. kabura كبر (u; kabr كبر); nashaʾa (u; nashʾ نشء; nushūʾ نشوء; nashʾa نشأة) 2. nabata نبت (u; nabt نبت) 3. namā نمى (i; namy نمي)

grower ['grəuə] n zāriʿ زارع (-ūn)

growl [graul] v harra هر (i; harīr هرير)

grown-up ['grəunʌp] 1. adj rāshid راشد; bāligh بالغ 2. n rāshid راشد (-ūn); bāligh بالغ (-ūn)

growth [grəuth] n namāʾ نماء; nushūʾ نشوء

grow up v kabura كبر (u; kabr كبر); nashaʾa (u; nashʾ نشء; nushūʾ نشوء; nashʾa نشأة)

guarantee [garənˈtiː] 1. n ḍamān ضمان (-āt) 2. v ḍamina ضمن (a; ḍamān ضمان)

guard [gaːd] 1. n ḥāris حارس (ḥurrās حراس) 2. v ḥarasa حرس (u; ḥirāsa حراسة)

guardian ['gaːdiən] n walī ولي (awliyāʾ أولياء)

guerilla; guerrilla ['gərilə] n mutamarrid متمرد (-ūn); musallaḥ مسلح (-ūn)

guess [ges] 1. n takhmīn تخمين 2. v khammana خمن

guest [gest] n ḍayf ضيف (ḍuyūf ضيوف)

guest house n maḍyafa مضيفة

guidance ['gaidəns] n irshād إرشاد

guide [gaid] 1. n murshid مرشد 2. v arshada أرشد

guidebook ['gaidbuk] n dalīl دليل

guilt [gilt] n ithm إثم

guilty ['gilti] adj 1. mudhnib مذنب 2. mudān مدان

guitar [giˈtaː] n gītār غيتار

guitarist [giˈtaːrist] n ʿāzif al-gītār عازف الغيتار

gulf [gʌlf] n khalīj خليج (khuluj خلج)

gums [gʌmz] pl lithāt لثات

gun [gʌn] n musaddas مسدس (-āt)

gunman ['gʌnmən] n musallaḥ مسلح (-ūn)

guts [gʌts] pl 1. aḥshāʾ أحشاء 2. shujāʿa شجاعة

guy [gai] n rajul رجل (rijāl رجال)

gym; gymnasium ['jim; jimˈneiziəm] n zhimnāziyūm جمنازيوم; ḥujra li ʾt-tamrīnāt ar-riyāḍīya حجرة للتمرينات الرياضية

gymnast ['jimnast] n zhimnāzī جمنازي

gymnastics [jimˈnastiks] n riyāḍat azh-zhimnāziya رياضة الجمنازية

gynaecologist [gainəˈkolojist] n ṭabīb amrāḍ an-nisāʾ طبيب أمراض النساء

gynaecology [gainəˈkoloji] n ṭibb amrāḍ an-nisāʾ طب أمراض النساء

Gypsy ['jipsi] 1. adj ghajarī غجري 2. n ghajarī غجري (ghajar غجر)

H

habit ['habit] *n* ᶜāda عادة (-āt)

had [had] *see* have

hack [hak] *v (comp.)* istaraqa al-maᶜlūmāt استرق المعلومات

hacker ['hakə] *n (comp.)* qurṣān al-kombyūtar قرصان الكمبيوتر (qarāṣin al-kombyūtar قراصن الكمبيوتر)

hair [heə] *n* 1. shaᶜr شعر 2. a hair shaᶜra شعرة (shaᶜr شعر; ashᶜār أشعار)

hairbrush ['heəbrʌsh] *n* furshāt shaᶜr فرشاة شعر

hair-cut ['heəkʌt] *n* qass shaᶜr شعر قص

hairdresser ['heədresə] *n* ḥallāq حلاق (-ūn)

hairdryer ['heədraiə] *n* āla li tanshīf ash-shaᶜr آلة لتنشيف الشعر

hairstyle ['heəstail] *n* tasrīḥa تسريحة

hairy ['heəri] *adj* shaᶜrī شعري; shaᶜrānī شعراني

half ['ha:f; ha:vz] *n (pl halves)* 1. niṣf نصف (anṣāf) 2. half past three thalatha wa niṣf ثلاثة ونصف

half an hour; half-hour *n* niṣf sāᶜa نصف ساعة

half-price *n* mukhaffaḍ bi khamsīn bi 'l-mi'a مخفض بخمسين بالمئة

half-time *n (spor.)* fāṣil intiṣāfī فاصل إنتصافي

hall ['ho:l] *n* qāᶜa قاعة (-āt)

hallo ['hələu] *see* hello

hallucination [həlu:sineishən] *n* halwasa هلوسة (-āt)

hallway ['holwei] *n* madkhal مدخل

halt [ho:lt] *v* waqafa وقف (yaqifu يقف; wuqūf وقوف)

halve [ha:v] *v* naṣṣafa نصف

halves [ha:vz] *see* half

ham [ham] *n* fakhdh al-khinzīr فخذ الخنزير

hammer ['hamə] 1. *n* miṭraqa مطرقة (maṭāriq مطارق) 2. *v* ṭarraqa طرق

hand [hand] 1. *n* yad يد *f* (ayādin أياد) 2. on the one hand... on the other min jiha... wa min jiha ukhrā من جهة... ومن جهة أخرى 3. *v* sallama سلم

handbag ['handbag] *n* shanṭat yad شنطة يد (shunaṭ شنط)

handbook ['handbuk] *n* dalīl دليل (dalā'il دلائل)

handcuffs ['handkʌfs] *pl* aghlāl أغلال

handful ['handful] *n* qabḍa قبضة (-āt)

handicap ['handikap] *n* iᶜāqa إعاقة (-āt)

handkerchief ['hangkəchif] *n* mandīl منديل (manadīl مناديل)

handle ['handəl] 1. *n* miqbaḍ مقبض (maqābiḍ مقابض) 2. *v* lamasa لمس (u/i; lamasa لمس) 3. adāra أدار

hand-made *adj* maṣnūᶜ bi 'l-yad مصنوع باليد

handshake ['handsheik] *n* muṣāfaḥa مصافحة

handsome ['hansəm] *adj* wasīm وسيم

handy ['handi] *adj* 1. mufīd مفيد 2. qarīb قريب

hang [hang] v (hung/hanged) 1. ʿallaqa علّق 2. shanaqa شنق (u; shanq شنق) 3. **to get the hang of** fahima uslūb aw maʿna shayʾ فهم أسلوب أو معنى شيء

hangar [ˈhangə] n ḥaẓīrat aṭ-ṭāʾirāt حظيرة الطائرات

hanger [ˈhangə] n ʿallāqa علّاقة (-āt)

hangman [ˈhangmən] n jallād جلّاد (-ūn)

hang on v 1. istamarra استمرّ 2. intaẓara انتظر

hang-over [ˈhangˈəuvə] n āthār sharāb al-khamr آثار شراب الخمر

hang up the phone v waḍaʿa as-sammāʿa (yaḍaʿu) وضع السماعة (يضع؛ وضع)

happen [ˈhapən] v ḥadatha حدث (u; ḥudūth حدوث)

happiness [ˈhapinəs] n saʿāda سعادة

happy [ˈhapi] adj saʿīd سعيد

harass [ˈharəs] v ʿākasa عاكس

harbour, (US) **harbor** [ˈhaːbə] n mīnāʾ ميناء (mawānin موان)

hard [ˈhaːd] 1. adj ṣaʿb صعب 2. ṣulb صلب 3. qāsin قاس

harden [ˈhaːdən] v qassā قسّى

hard disk n qurṣ ṣulb قرص صلب

hardly [ˈhaːdli] adv 1. nādiran mā نادراً ما 2. bi ʾl-kād بالكاد

hardship [ˈhaːdship] n mashaqqa مشقّة (-āt)

hardware [ˈhaːdweə] n (comp.) ajhizat al-kompyūtir أجهزة الكومبيوتر

harm [ˈhaːm] 1. n adhan أذىً; ḍarar ضرر 2. v adhhā; ḍarrara أذى؛ ضرّر

harmful [ˈhaːmfəl] adj muʾdhin مؤذٍ; muḍirr مضر

harmless [ˈhaːmlis] adj ghayr muʾdhin غير مؤذٍ

harmony [ˈhaːməni] n īqāʿ إيقاع

harsh [ˈhaːsh] adj qāsin قاس

harvest [ˈhaːvist] 1. n ḥaṣād حصاد 2. v ḥaṣada حصد (i; ḥaṣād حصاد)

has see **have**

hassle [ˈhasəl] n ʿākasa عاكس

haste [ˈheist] n ʿajala عجلة

hasten [ˈheisən] v ʿajjala عجّل; istaʿjala استعجل

hasty [ˈheisti] adj mutahawwir متهوّر

hat [hat] n qubbaʿa قبعة (-āt)

hate [heit] 1. n kurh كره 2. v kariha كره (a; kurh كره)

hateful [ˈheitfəl] adj karīh كريه

hatred [ˈheitrid] n kurh كره

haunted [ˈhɔːntid] adj **a haunted house** bayt maskūn بيت مسكون

have [hav] v (**had**) 1. malaka ملك (i; mulk ملك) 2. **to have to** iḍṭarra اضطرّ

hay [hei] n qashsh قش

hazard [ˈhazəd] n khaṭar خطر (akhṭār أخطار)

hazardous [ˈhazədəs] adj khaṭir خطر

he [hiː] pronoun huwa هو

head [hed] 1. adj raʾsī رأسي 2. n raʾs رأس (ruʾūs رؤوس) 3. raʾīs رئيس (ruʾasāʾ رؤساء) 4. v taraʾʾasa ترأّس (-āt)

headache [ˈhedeik] n ṣudāʿ صداع

head for v ittajaha ilā اتجه إلى

headline [ˈhedlain] n ʿunwān عنوان (ʿanāwīn عناوين)

headmaster [hedˈmaːstə] n mudīr al-madrasa مدير المدرسة

headmistress [hedˈmistris] n mudīrat al-madrasa مديرة المدرسة

headphones [ˈhedfəunz] pl sammāʿa سماعة (-āt)

headquarters ['hedkwo:təz] *n* markaz مركز (marākiz مراكز); maqarr al-qiyāda مقر القيادة

heal [hi:l] *v* shafā شفى (i; shifā' شفاء)

health [helth] *n* ṣiḥḥa صحة

healthcare ['helthkeə] *n* ta'mīn ṣiḥīi تأمين صحي

healthy ['helthi] *adj* salīm سليم

heap [hi:p] *n* kawma كومة (-āt)

hear ['hiə] *v* (**heard**) samiʿa سمع (a; samʿ سمع)

hearing ['hiəring] *n* 1. samʿ سمع 2. *(leg.)* jalsa جلسة (-āt)

heart [ha:t] *n* 1. qalb قلب (qulūb قلوب) 2. **by heart** ʿan ẓahr qalb عن ظهر قلب

heart attack *n* nawba qalbīya نوبة قلبية (nuwab)

heat [hi:t] 1. *n* ḥarāra حرارة 2. *v* sakhkhana سخن

heater ['hi:tə] *n* daffāya دفاية

heating ['hi:ting] *n* tadfi'a تدفئة

heaven ['hevən] *n* 1. samā' سماء (asmā' أسماء) 2. janna جنة

heavenly ['hevnli] *adj* samāwī سماوي

heaviness ['hevinis] *n* thuql ثقل

heavy ['hevi] *adj* thaqīl ثقيل

Hebrew ['hi:bru:] *n* ʿibrī عبري

hectare ['hekteə] *n* hiktār هكتار (-āt)

hectic ['hektik] *adj* mashghūl jiddan مشغول جداً

hedge [hej] *n* washiʿ وشيع (awshiʿa أوشعة)

hedgehog ['hejhog] *n* qunfudh قنفذ (qanāfidh قنافذ)

heed [hi:d] *v* intabaha ilā انتبه إلى

heel [hi:l] *n* kaʿb كعب (kiʿāb كعاب)

height [hait] *n* 1. irtifāʿ إرتفاع 2. ṭūl طول

heir [eə] *n* warīth وريث (wurathaʾ ورثاء)

heiress [eə'res] *n* warītha وريثة (-āt)

helicopter ['helikoptə] *n* ṭāʾira ʿamūdīya طائرة عمودية

hell [hel] *n* an-nār النار; jahannam جهنم; jaḥīm جحيم

hello! ['hələu] ahlan! أهلاً!; marḥaban مرحباً

helmet ['helmit] *n* khūdha خوذة (-āt)

help [help] 1. *n* ʿawn عون; musāʿada مساعدة 2. *v* sāʿada ساعد 3. **help!** al-madad! المدد!

helper ['helpə] *n* musāʿid مساعد (-ūn)

helpful ['helpfəl] *adj* mufīd مفيد; nāfiʿ نافع

helpless ['helplis] *adj* ʿājiz عاجز

hemisphere ['hemisfiə] *n* niṣf kura نصف كرة

hen [hen] *n* dajāja دجاجة (dajāj دجاج)

hence [hens] *adv* idhan إذاً

henceforth ['hensfo:th] *adv* min al'ān faṣāʿidan من الآن فصاعداً

her ['hə:] hā ها

herb ['hə:b] *n* ʿushb عشب (aʿshāb أعشاب)

herd ['hə:d] *n* sirb سرب (asrāb أسراب)

here ['hiə] *adv* hunā هنا

hereabouts ['hiərəbautz] *adv* fī hādha 'l-jiwār في هذا الجوار

heritage ['herətij] *n* turāth تراث

hero ['hiərəu] *n* (*pl* **heroes**) baṭal بطل (abṭāl أبطال)

heroine ['herəuin] *n* baṭala بطلة

hers [hə:z] milkuhā ملكها

herself [hə:'self] nafsuhā نفسها

hesitate ['heziteit] v taraddada تردد

hesitation [hezi'teishən] n taraddud تردد

heterosexual [hetərəu'sekshuwəl] n mushtahin li afrād al-jins al-ākhar مشتهٍ لأفراد الجنس الآخر

hidden ['hidən] adj makhfī مخفي

hide [haid] v akhfā أخفى; ikhtafā اختفى

hideous ['hidiəs] adj bashiʿ بشع; shanīʿ شنيع

hiding ['haiding] n in hiding mukhabba' مخبأ

high [hai] 1. adj ʿālin عالٍ 2. (sl.) to get high intashā انتشى

highlands ['hailəndz] pl murtafaʿāt مرتفعات

highlight ['hailait] 1. n dhirwa ذروة (dhuran ذرىً) 2. v akkada أكد

highly ['haili] adv jiddan جداً

high school ['haisku:l] n al-madrasa ath-thānawīya المدرسة الثانوية

highway ['haiwei] n ṭarīq ʿāmm طريق عام

hijack ['haijak] v ikhtaṭafa اختطف

hijacker ['haijəkə] n khāṭif خاطف (-ūn); mukhtaṭif مختطف (-ūn)

hijacking ['haijaking] n ikhtiṭāf اختطاف

hike [haik] v nuzha ʿalā 'l-qadamayn fi r-rīf نزهة على القدمين في الريف

hilarious ['hileəriəs] adj mariḥ مرح

hill [hil] n tall تل (tilāl تلال); haḍaba هضبة (-āt)

hilly ['hili] adj kathīr at-tilāl كثير التلال

him [him] -hu/-uh/-h ه

himself [him'self] nafsuh نفسه

hind [haind] adj khalfī خلفي

hinder ['hində] v ʿarqala عرقل

hint [hint] 1. n talmīḥ تلميح 2. v lammaḥa لمح (at ilā إلى)

hip [hip] n wark f ورك (awrāk أوراك)

hire ['haiə] 1. n for hire li 'l-ījār للإيجار 2. v ajjara أجر 3. to hire out ista'jara استأجر

his [hiz] 1. -hu/-uh/-h ه 2. milkuh ملكه

historian [hi'sto:riən] n mu'arrikh مؤرخ (-ūn)

historical [hi'storikəl] adj tārīkhī تاريخي

history ['histri] n tārīkh تاريخ

hit [hit] v (**hit**) ḍaraba ضرب (i; ḍarb ضرب)

hitch [hich] n iʿāqa إعاقة

hitchhike ['hichhaik] v ṭalaba tawṣīla majārīya طلب توصيلة مجارية (a; ṭalab طلب)

hoax [həuks] n khudʿa خدعة (-āt)

hog [hog] n khinzīr خنزير (khanāzīr خنازير)

hold [həuld] v (**held**) 1. masak مسك (i; mask مسك) 2. to hold a meeting ʿaqada ijtimāʿan عقد إجتماعاً (i; ʿaqd عقد) 3. to hold elections ajrā intikhābāt أجرى إنتخابات

holder ['həuldə] n 1. mālik مالك 2. adāh li ḥaml shay' أداة لحمل شيء

hold up v 1. to hold up (a journey) ʿarqala عرقل 2. to hold up (a bank) saraqa سرق (i; saraqa/sariqa سرقة)

hole [həul] n thuqb ثقب (thuqab ثقب)

holiday ['holədei] n ijāza إجازة (-āt)

hollow ['holəu] adj mujawwaf مجوف

holy ['həuli] *adj* muqaddas مقدس

home [həum] *n* bayt بيت (buyūt بيوت)

homeland ['həumlənd] *n* waṭan وطن (awṭān أوطان)

homeless ['həumlis] *n* mutasharrid متشرد

homemade ['həumeid] *adj* maṣnūʿ fi 'l-bayt مصنوع في البيت

hometown ['həumtaun] *n* madīnat al-wilāda مدينة الولادة

homework ['həumwəːk] *n* wājibāt manzilīya واجبات منزلية

homicide ['homisaid] *n* qatl قتل

homosexual [həumə'sekshuəl] 1. *adj* mithlī مثلي 2. *n* mushtahin li afrād al-jins al-mumāthil مشته للأفراد الجنس المماثل

homosexuality [həuməsekshu'aliti] *n* mithlīya مثلية; ishtihāʾ afrād al-jins al-mumāthil إشتهاء أفراد الجنس المماثل

honest ['onist] *adj* ṣādiq صادق

honestly ['onistli] *adv* ḥaqqan حقاً

honesty ['onəsti] *n* ṣidq صدق

honey ['hʌni] *n* ʿasal عسل

honeymoon ['hʌnimuːn] *n* shahr al-ʿasal شهر العسل

honk [hongk] *v* zammara زمر

honour, (US) **honor** ['onə] 1. *n* sharaf شرف 2. *v* sharrafa شرف

honourable, (US) **honorable** ['onrəbəl] *adj* 1. muḥtaram محترم 2. sharīf شريف

hook [huk] *n* kullāb كلاب (kalālīb كلاليب)

hooligan ['huːligən] *n* mukharrib مخرب (-ūn)

hop [hop] *v* wathiba وثب (yathibu يثب; wathb وثب)

hope [həup] 1. *n* amal أمل (āmāl آمال) 2. *v* amala أمل (a; amal أمل) 3. **to hope for** tamannā تمنى

hopeful ['həupfəl] *adj* mufʿam bi 'l-amal مفعم بالأمل; mutafāʾil متفائل

hopeless ['həuplis] *adj* yāʾis يائس

horde [hoːd] *n* ḥashd حشد (ḥushūd حشود)

horizon [hə'raizən] *n* ufuq أفق (āfāq آفاق)

horizontal [hori'zontəl] *adj* ufuqī أفقي

horn [hoːn] *n* qarn قرن (qurūn قرون)

horrible ['horəbəl] *adj* karīh كريه

horrid ['horid] *adj* karīh كريه

horrify ['horifai] *v* arhaba أرهب

horror ['horə] *n* ruʿb رعب

horse [hoːs] *n* ḥiṣān حصان (aḥṣina أحصنة)

horseback ['hoːsbak] *n/adj* **on horseback** rākib al-ḥiṣān راكب الحصان

horseman ['hoːsmən] *n* fāris فارس (fursān فرسان)

horsepower ['hoːspawə] *n* qudra ḥiṣānīya قدرة حصانية

horse racing *n* sibāq al-khayl سباق الخيل

hose [həuz] *n* khurṭūm خرطوم (kharāṭīm خراطيم)

hospital ['hospitəl] *n* mustashfan مستشفى (mustashfayāt مستشفيات)

hospitality [hospi'taləti] *n* ḥusn aḍ-ḍiyāfa حسن الضيافة

host [həust] *n* muḍīf مضيف

hostage ['hostij] *n* rahīna رهينة (rahāʾin رهائن)

hostel ['hostəl] *n* bayt ash-shabāb بيت الشباب

hostile ['hostail] *adj* muʿādin معاد; عدائي ʿadāʾī

hostility [ho'stiləti] *n* ʿadāʾ عداء

hot [hot] *adj* ḥārr حار; sākhin ساخن

hotel [həu'tel] *n* funduq فندق (fanādiq فنادق)

hour ['auə] *n* sāʿa ساعة (-āt)

hourly ['auəli] *n* fī kull sāʿa في كل ساعة

house [haus] *n* manzil منزل (manāzil منازل)

household ['haushəuld] *n* ahl al-bayt أهل البيت

House of Commons *n (UK)* majlis an-nawwāb al-brīṭānī مجلس النواب البريطاني

House of Lords *n (UK)* majlis ash-shuyūkh al-brīṭānī مجلس الشيوخ البريطاني

House of Representatives *n (US)* majlis al-nawwāb al-amrīkī مجلس النواب الأمريكي

housewife ['hauswaif] *n* rabbat manzil ربة منزل

housing ['hauzing] *n* iskān إسكان

how [hau] kayfa كيف

however [hau'evə] *conj* **1.** mahmā مهما. **2.** walākin ولكن; wa maʿa dhālik ومع ذلك

howl [haul] *v* ʿawā عوى (i; ʿuwāʾ عواء)

how long? *time* mā muddat? ما مدة؟

how many?; how much? kam كم

how old? How old are you? kam ʿumrak? كم عمرك؟

hug [hʌg] *v* ḥaḍana حضن (u; ḥaḍn حضن; ḥaḍāna حضانة)

huge [hyu:j] *adj* ḍakhm ضخم

human ['hyu:mən] **1.** *adj* insānī إنساني. **2.** *n* insān إنسان

human being *n* insān إنسان

humane [hyu'mein] *adj* insānī إنساني; shafūq شفوق

humanitarian [hyu:mani'teəriən] *adj* insānī إنساني

humanity [hyu:'manəti] *n* insānīya إنسانية

human resources *pl* al-mawārid al-basharīya الموارد البشرية

human rights *pl* ḥuqūq al-insān حقوق الإنسان

humble ['hʌmbəl] *adj* mutawāḍiʿ متواضع

humid ['hyu:mid] *adj* raṭib رطب

humiliate [hyu:'miliyeit] *v* adhalla أذل

humiliation [hyu:mili'yeishən] *n* dhull ذل

humility [hyu:'miləti] *n* tawāḍuʿ تواضع

humorous ['hyu:mərəs] *adj* fakih فكه

humour, (US) humor ['hyu:mə] *n* fukāha فكاهة

hunch [hʌnch] *n* I have a hunch that... ladayy shuʿūr bi an... لدي شعور بأن...

hundred ['hʌndrəd] *n/adj* miʾa مئة (-āt)

hundredth ['hʌndrədth] *adj* miʾa مئة

hundredweight ['hʌndrədweit] *n* miʾat raṭl inglīzī مئة رطل إنكليزي

hung [hʌng] *see* hang

hunger ['hʌngə] *n* jūʿ جوع

hungry ['hʌngri] *adj* jawʿān جوعان (jiyāʿ جياع)

hunt [hʌnt] **1.** *n* muṭārada مطاردة. **2.** *v* iṣṭāda اصطاد

hunter ['hʌntə] *n* ṣayyād صياد (-ūn)

hunting ['hʌnting] *n* ṣayd صيد

hurricane ['hʌrikən] *n* i'ṣār إعصار (aʿāṣīr أعاصير)

hurry ['hʌri] 1. *n* ʿajala عجلة 2. *v* ʿajila عجل (a; ʿajala عجلة) 3. to hurry up istaʿjala استعجل

hurt [həːt] 1. *n* adhan أذىً; jurḥ جرح 2. *v* jaraḥa جرح (a; jarḥ جرح)

husband ['hʌzbənd] *n* zawj زوج (azwāj أزواج)

hut [hʌt] *n* kūkh كوخ (akwākh أكواخ)

hygiene ['haijiːn] *n* ʿilm aṣ-ṣiḥḥa علم الصحة

hygienic [hai'jiːnik] *adj* ṣiḥḥī صحي

hymn [him] *n (rel.)* ughniya dīnīya أغنية دينية

hypocrisy [hi'pokrəsi] *n* nifāq نفاق

hypocrite ['hipəkrit] *n* munāfiq منافق (-ūn)

hypocritical [hipə'kritikəl] *adj* munāfiq منافق

hypodermic syringe *n* miḥqana محقنة (maḥāqin محاقن)

hysterical [hi'sterikəl] *adj* histīrī هستيري

I [ai] *pronoun* ana أنا

ice [ais] *n* jalīd جليد

ice cream ['aiskriːm] *n* bōẕa بوظة; jalātī جلاتي

ice hockey *n* al-hōkī ʿalā 'l-jalīd الهوكي على الجليد

icy ['aisi] *adj* thalij ثلج

ID card [ai'diː kaːd] *n* biṭāqa shakhṣīya بطاقة شخصية

idea [ai'diə] *n* fikra فكرة (fikar فكر)

ideal [ai'diəl] 1. *adj* mithālī مثالي 2. mumtāz ممتاز 3. *n* mithāl aʿlā أعلى (muthul ʿulyā مثل عليا) مثال

idealist [ai'diyəlist] *n* mithālī an-nazʿa مثالي النزعة

identical [ai'dentikəl] *adj* dhātuh ذاته; mumāthil مماثل

identification [aidentifi'keishən] 1. *n* ithbāt al-huwīya إثبات الهوية 2. *see* **ID card**

identify [ai'dentifai] *v* athbata al-huwīya أثبت الهوية

identity [ai'dentəti] *n* huwīya هوية

identity card *n* biṭāqa shakhṣīya بطاقة شخصية

idiot ['idiət] *n* ahbal أهبل (hubl هبل); maʿtūh معتوه (maʿātīh معاتيه)

idle ['aidəl] *adj* kasūl كسول

idol ['aidəl] *n* maʿbūd معبود; wathan وثن (awthān أوثان); ṣanam صنم (aṣnām أصنام)

idolize ['aidəlaiz] *v* ʿabada عبد (u; ʿibāda عبادة)

i.e. (id est = that is) yaʿnī يعني

if [if] *conj* **1.** idhā إذا; in إن **2.** law لو

ignite [ig'nait] *v* ashʿala أشعل

ignition [ig'nishən] *n* ishʿāl إشعال

ignorance ['ignərəns] *n* jahl جهل

ignorant ['ignərənt] *adj* jāhil جاهل
(jahala جهلة; juhalā' جهلاء)

ignore [ig'noː] *v* tajāhala تجاهل

ill [il] *adj* marīḍ مريض

illegal [i'liːgəl] *adj* ghayr qānūnī
غير قانوني; ghayr sharʿī غير شرعي

illegally [i'liːgəli] *adv* bi ṭarīqa ghayr
qānūnīya بطريقة غير قانونية

illiteracy [i'litərəsi] *n* al-ummīya
الأمية

illness ['ilnis] *n* maraḍ مرض (amrāḍ
أمراض)

illuminate [i'luːmineit] *v* aḍā'a
أضاء; nawwara نور

illumination [iluːmi'neishən] *n*
iḍā'a إضاءة; tanwīr تنوير

illusion [i'luːzhən] *n* wahm وهم
(awhām أوهام)

illustrate ['iləstreit] *v* **1.** zawwada
bi rusūm زود برسوم **2.** awḍaḥa أوضح

illustration [ilə'streishən] *n* **1.** rasm
رسم (rusūm رسوم) **2.** īḍāḥ إيضاح

illustrator ['iləstreitə] *n* rassām
رسام (-ūn)

image ['imij] *n* ṣūra صورة (ṣuwar صور)

imaginary [i'majineri] *adj* khayālī
خيالي

imagination [imaji'neishən] *n*
khayāl خيال

imagine [i'majin] *v* takhayyala تخيل

imam [i'maːm] *n* imām إمام (a'imma
أئمة)

imitate ['imiteit] *v* qallada قلد

imitation [imi'teishən] **1.** *adj* zā'if
زائف **2.** *n* taqlīd تقليد

imitator ['imiteitə] *n* muqallid مقلد

immaculate [i'makyulət] *adj* naqī
نقي (anqiyā' أنقياء)

immediate [i'miːdiət] *adj* mubāshir
مباشر

immediately [i'miːdiətli] *adv* ḥālan
حالاً; mubāsharatan مباشرةً

immense [i'mens] *adj* ḍakhm ضخم

immigrant ['imigrənt] *n* muhājir
مهاجر (-ūn)

immigrate ['imigreit] *v* hājara هاجر

immigration [imi'greishən] *n* hijra
هجرة

imminent ['iminənt] *adj* washīk
وشيك

immoral [i'morəl] *adj* lā akhlāqī
لا أخلاقي

immortal [i'moːtəl] *adj* khālid خالد

immune [i'myuːn] *adj* manīʿ منيع

immunity [i'myuːnəti] *n* manāʿa
مناعة

immunize ['imyunaiz] *v* ṭaʿʿama طعّم

immunization [imyunai'zeishən] *n*
taṭʿīm تطعيم

impact ['impakt] *n* **1.** taṣādum تصادم
2. ta'thīr تأثير

impatience [im'peishəns] *n* nafād
aṣ-ṣabr نفاد الصبر

impatient [im'peishənt] *adj* nāfid
aṣ-ṣabr نافد الصبر

imperative [im'perətiv] **1.** *adj*
wājib واجب **2.** *n* wājib واجب **3.**
muliḥḥ ملح

imperfect [im'pəːfikt] **1.** *adj* nāqiṣ
ناقص **2.** *n (grammar)* muḍāriʿ مضارع

imperfection [impə'fekshən] *n*
naqṣ نقص; ʿayb عيب

imperial [im'piəriyəl] *adj* imbaraṭūrī
إمبراطوري; imbiriyālī إمبريالي

impersonator [im'pə:səneitə] *n* muqallid مقلد; muqallid shakhṣīyāt ghayrih مقلد شخصيات غيره

impertinent [im'pə:tinənt] *adj* waqiḥ وقح

impetus ['impitəs] *n* dāfiʿ دافع (dawāfiʿ دوافع)

implement ['implimənt] 1. *n* adāh أداة (adawāt أدوات) 2. *v* ṭabbaqa طبق

implicate ['implikeit] *v* warraṭa ورط

implication [impli'keishən] *n* talmīḥ تلميح

imply [im'plai] *v* 1. taḍammana تضمن 2. lammaḥa لمح

impolite [impə'lait] *adj* faẓẓ فظ (afẓāẓ أفظاظ)

import [im'po:t] 1. *n* istīrād إستيراد (-āt); wārid وارد (-āt) 2. *v* istawrada استورد

importance [im'po:təns] *n* ahammīya أهمية

important [im'po:tənt] *adj* muhimm مهم

impose [im'pəuz] *v* faraḍa فرض (i; farḍ فرض)

impossibility [imposə'biləti] *n* istaḥāla إستحالة

impossible [im'posəbəl] *adj* mustaḥīl مستحيل

impotent ['impətənt] *adj* ʿājiz عاجز

impractical [im'povərish] *v* ghayr ʿamalī غير عملي

impress [im'pres] *v* aththara أثر; akkada أكد

impression [im'preshən] *n* intibāʿ إنطباع

impressive [im'presiv] *adj* mu'aththir مؤثر

imprison [im'prizən] *v* ḥabasa حبس (i; ḥabs حبس)

improbable [im'probəbəl] *adj* ghayr muḥtamal غير محتمل

improve [im'pru:v] *v* ḥassana حسن; taḥassana تحسن

improvement [im'pru:vmənt] *n* taḥsīn تحسين; taḥassun تحسن

impulse ['impʌls] *n* nazwa نزوة (nazawāt نزوات)

impulsive [im'pʌlsiv] *adj* mutahawwir متهور

impure [im'pyuə] *adj* ghayr naqī غير نقي; ghayr ṭāhir غير طاهر

in [in] *prep* 1. fī في 2. bi ب 3. in the country fi 'r-rīf في الريف 4. in English bi 'l-inglīzī بالإنكليزي 5. in my opinion fī ra'yī في رأيي 6. in the morning fi 'ṣ-ṣabāḥ في الصباح 7. in a week baʿd usbūʿ بعد أسبوع 8. *see* into

inability [inə'biləti] *n* ʿajz عجز

inaccurate [in'akyərət] *adj* ghayr maḍbūṭ غير مضبوط

inactive [in'aktiv] *adj* ghayr nashīṭ غير نشيط

inadequate [in'adikwət] *adj* 1. ghayr kaf' غير كفء 2. ghayr kāfin غير كاف

inappropriate [inə'prəupriyət] *adj* ghayr mulā'im غير ملائم

incapable [in'keipəbəl] *adj* ghayr qādir غير قادر (of ʿalā على)

incentive [in'sentiv] *n* bāʿith باعث (bawāʿith بواعث)

incessantly [in'səsntli] *adv* dawāman wa istimrāran دواماً وإستمراراً

inch [inch] *n* būṣa بوصة (-āt)

incident ['insidənt] *n* ḥādith حادث (ḥawādith حوادث)

incidentally [insi'dentli] *adv* ʿalā fikra على فكرة

incite [in'sait] v ḥarraḍa حرّض

inclination [ingkli'neishən] n mayl ميل (muyūl ميول)

incline [in'klain] 1. n inḥidār إنحدار 2. v see **inclined**

inclined [in'klaind] adj to feel inclined māl مال (i) (to ilā إلى)

include [in'klu:d] v taḍammana تضمّن

including [in'klu:ding] prep bi mā fī بما في

inclusion [in'klu:zhən] n taḍmīn تضمين; taḍammun تضمّن

income ['ingkʌm] n dakhl دخل; īrād إيراد (-āt)

incoming ['inkʌming] adj 1. wārid وارد 2. jadīd جديد

incompatible [ingkəm'patəbəl] adj mutaḍārib متضارب

incompetence [in'kompitəns] n lā kafā'a لا كفاءة

incompetent [in'kompitənt] adj ghayr kaf' غير كفء

incomplete [ingkəm'pli:t] adj nāqiṣ ناقص

incomprehensible [inkompri-'hensəbəl] adj lā yufham لا يفهم

inconceivable [ingkən'si:vəbəl] adj lā yutakhayyal لا يتخيّل

inconclusive [ingkən'klu:siv] adj ghayr ḥāsim غير حاسم

inconsiderate [ingkən'sidərət] adj hayyir هيّر; mutahawwir متهوّر

inconvenience [ingkən'vi:niəns] n muḍāyaqa مضايقة (-āt)

inconvenient [ingkən'vi:niənt] adj ghayr mulā'im غير ملائم

incorporate [in'ko:pəreit] v admaja أدمج

incorrect [ing'kərekt] adj khāṭi' خاطئ

increase [in'kri:s] 1. n ziyāda زيادة; izdiyād إزدياد 2. v zāda زاد (i; ziyāda زيادة); izdāda ازداد

incredible [in'kredibəl] adj lā yuṣaddaq لا يصدّق

incriminate [in'krimineit] v jarrama جرّم

incur [in'kə:] v taʿarraḍa li تعرّض ل

incurable [in'kyuərəbəl] adj ʿuḍāl عضال

indecision [indi'sizhən] n taraddud تردّد

indeed [in'di:d] adv 1. haqqan حقّاً 2. fiʿlan فعلاً

indefinitely [in'definətli] adv ilā amad gayr muḥaddad إلى أمد غير محدد

independence [indi'pendəns] n istiqlāl إستقلال

independent [indi'pendənt] adj mustaqill مستقل

indescribable [indis'kraibəbəl] adj lā yumkin waṣfuh لا يمكن وصفه

index ['indeks] n fihris فهرس (fahāris فهارس)

indicate ['indikeit] v 1. ashāra ilā أشار إلى 2. bayyana بيّن

indication [indi'keishən] n ishāra إشارة (-āt); dalīl دليل (adilla أدلة)

indicator [indi'keitə] n mu'ashshir مؤشر

indifference [in'difrəns] n lā mubālāh لا مبالاة

indigenous [in'dijinəs] adj baladī بلدي

indigestion [indi'jeschən] n ʿusr al-haḍm عسر الهضم

indignation [indig'neishən] n sukht سخط

indirectly [indai'rektli] *adv* ʿalā naḥw ghayr mubāshir على نحو غير مباشر

indiscreet [indis'kri:t] *adj* ghayr katūm غير كتوم

indiscriminate [indis'kriminət] *adj* ʿashwāʾī عشوائي

indispensable [indis'pensəbəl] *adj* ḍurūrī ضروري

individual [indi'vijuəl] **1.** *adj* fardī فردي (afrād أفراد) 2. *n* fard فرد

indoor ['indo:] *adj* dākhilī داخلي

indoors [in'do:z] *adv* fi 'l-bayt في البيت

indulge [in'dʌlj] *v* dallala دلل

industrial [in'dʌstriəl] *adj* ṣanāʿī صناعي

industrialized [in'dʌstriəlaizd] *adj* ṣanāʿī صناعي

industry ['indəstri] *n* ṣanāʿa صناعة (-āt)

ineffective [ini'fektiv] *adj* **1.** ʿaqīm عقيم 2. ghayr kaf ء غير كفء

inefficiency [ini'fishənsi] *n* lā faʿʿālīya لا فعالية; lā kafāʾa لا كفاءة

inefficient [ini'fishənt] *adj* ghayr faʿʿāl غير فعال; gayr kaf ء غير كفء

ineligible [in'elijibəl] *adj* ghayr muʾahhal غير مؤهل

inequality [ini'kwoləti] *n* lā musāwāh لا مساواة

inevitable [in'evitəbəl] *adj* maḥtūm محتوم

inexcusable [inik'skyu:zəbəl] *adj* lā mubarrir lah لا مبرر له

inexpensive [inik'spensiv] *adj* rakhīṣ رخيص

inexperience [iniks'piəriəns] *n* qillat at-tajriba قلة التجربة; qillat al-khibra قلة خبرة

inexperienced [iniks'piəriənst] *adj* ghirr غر; gharīr غرير

infamous ['infəməs] *adj* mukhzin مخز

infancy ['infənsi] *n* ṭufūla طفولة

infant ['infənt] *n* ṭifl طفل (aṭfāl أطفال)

infantry ['infəntri] *n* mushāh pl مشاة

infect [in'fekt] *v* aʿdā أعدى

infection [in'fekshən] *n* iʿdāʾ إعداء

infectious [in'fekshəs] *adj* muʿdin معد

inferior [in'fiəriə] *adj* waḍīʿ وضيع

infertile [in'fə:tail] *adj* ʿaqīm عقيم

infinite ['infinət] *adj* lā nihāʾī لا نهائي

infinity [in'finəti] *n* lā nihāʾīya لا نهائية

infirmary [in'fə:məri] *n* mustashfan مستشفى (mustashfayāt مستشفيات)

inflammable [in'flaməbəl] *adj* (burnable) sarīʿ al-iltihāb سريع الإلتهاب

inflammation [inflə'meishən] *n* iltihāb إلتهاب

inflation [in'fleishən] *n* (ec.) taḍakhkhum تضخم

inflict [in'flikt] *v* to be inflicted by uṣība bi أصيب بـ

influence ['influəns] **1.** *n* nufūdh نفوذ 2. *v* aththara أثر

influential [influ'enshəl] *adj* dhū nufūdh ذو نفوذ

influenza [influ'enzə] *n* al-influwanza الإنفلونزا

inform [in'fo:m] *v* aʿlama أعلم; akhbara أخبر

informal [in'fo:məl] *adj* ghayr rasmī غير رسمي

information [infə'meishən] *n* maʿlūmāt معلومات

informer [in'fo:mə] n mukhbir مخبر (-ūn)

infrastructure ['infrəstrʌkchə] n al-bunya at-taḥtīya البنية التحتية

infrequently [in'fri:kwəntli] adv nādiran نادراً

ingenious [in'ji:niəs] adj mubdiʿ مبدع

ingredient [in'gri:diənt] n ʿunṣur عنصر ('anāṣir عناصر)

ingredients [in'gri:diənts] pl muḥtawayāt محتويات

inhabit [in'habit] v sakana سكن (u; sukūn سكون)

inhabitant [in'habitənt] n sākin ساكن (sukkān سكان)

inhabited [in'habitid] adj maskūn مسكون

inhale [in'heil] v shahiqa شهق (a; shahīq شهيق)

inherit [in'herit] v waritha ورث (yarithu يرث; wirth ورث; wirātha وراثة)

inhumane [in'hyu:mein] adj ghayr insānī غير إنساني

initial [i'nishəl] 1. adj ibtidāʾī إبتدائي 2. v waqqaʿa وقع

initiative [i'nishətiv] n mubādara مبادرة (-āt)

inject [in'jekt] v ḥaqana حقن (i; ḥaqn حقن)

injection [in'jekshən] n ḥuqna حقنة (ḥuqan حقن)

injure ['injə] v jaraḥa جرح (a; jarḥ جرح)

injury ['injəri] n jurḥ جرح (jurūḥ جروح)

injustice [in'jʌstis] n ẓulm ظلم

ink [ingk] n ḥibr حبر

inn [in] n khān خان (-āt)

inner ['inə] adj dākhilī داخلي

inner city n wasaṭ al-madīna وسط المدينة

innocence ['inəsəns] n barāʾa براءة

innocent ['inəsənt] adj barīʾ بريء

input ['input] 1. n maʿlūmāt pl معلومات 2. v (input/inputted) (comp.) adkhala bayānāt أدخل بيانات

inquire [in'kwaiə] v istaʿlama استعلم (about ʿan عن)

inquiry [in'kwaiəri] n istiʿlām إستعلام

inquisitive [in'kwizətiv] adj fuḍūlī فضولي

insane [in'sein] adj majnūn مجنون

insanity [in'sanəti] n junūn جنون

insect ['insekt] n ḥashara حشرة (-āt)

insecure [insi'kyuə] adj 1. ghayr āmin غير آمن 2. ghayr wāthiq bi 'n-nafs غير واثق بالنفس

insensitive [in'sensitiv] adj ghayr ḥassās غير حساس

insert [in'sə:t] v adkhala أدخل

inside [in'said] 1. adj dākhilī داخلي 2. n dākhil داخل 3. prep dakhila داخل 4. adv dakhilan داخلاً

inside-out adj bi 'l-maqlūb بالمقلوب

insignificant [insig'nifikənt] adj tāfih تافه

insist [in'sist] v aṣarra أصر (on ʿalā على)

insistent [in'sistənt] adj muṣirr مصر

insolent ['insələnt] adj waqiḥ وقح

insomnia [in'somniə] n suhād سهاد; araq أرق

inspect [in'spekt] v fattasha فتش

inspection [in'spekshən] n taftīsh تفتيش

inspector [in'spektə] *n* **1.** mufattish مفتش (-ūn) **2. police inspector** ḍābiṭ sharṭī ضابط شرطي

inspiration [inspə'reishən] *n* ilhām إلهام

inspire [in'spaiə] *v* alhama ألهم

instability [instə'biliti] *n* ʿadm istiqrār عدم إستقرار

install [in'sto:l] *v* rakkaba ركب

installation [instə'leishən] *n* **1.** tarkīb تركيب **2.** *(mil.)* munsha'a ʿaskarīya منشأة عسكرية

instalment, *(US)* **installment** [in'sto:lmənt] *n* **1.** ḥalaqa حلقة (-āt) **2.** qisṭ قسط (aqsāṭ أقساط)

instance ['instəns] *n* **1.** mathal مثل (amthāl أمثال) **2. for instance** mathalan مثلاً

instant ['instənt] **1.** *adj* ʿājil عاجل **2.** *n* laḥẓa لحظة (laḥaẓāt لحظات)

instantly ['instəntli] *adv* ʿājilan عاجلاً; ḥālan حالاً

instead [in'sted] **1.** *adv* badalan بدلاً **2. instead of** *prep/conj* badalan min بدلاً من

instinct ['instingkt] *n* gharīza غريزة (gharā'iz غرائز)

institute ['instityu:t] *n* maʿhad معهد (maʿāhid معاهد)

institution [insti'tyu:shən] *n* **1.** mu'assasa مؤسسة **2. mental institution** mustashfa 'l-amrāḍ al-ʿaqlīya مستشفى الأمراض العقلية

instruct [in'strʌkt] *v* **1.** ʿallama علم **2.** amara أمر (u; amr أمر)

instruction [in'strʌkshən] *n* **1.** taʿlīm تعليم (-āt) **2.** amr أمر (awāmir أوامر)

instructions [in'strʌkshənz] *pl* taʿlīmāt تعليمات

instructor [in'strʌktə] *n* muʿallim معلم (-ūn)

instrument ['instrumənt] *n* **1.** adāh أداة (adawāt أدوات) **2.** āla آلة (ālāt آلات)

insufficient [insə'fishənt] *adj* ghayr kāfin غير كاف

insulate ['insyuleit] *v* ʿazala عزل (i; ʿazl عزل)

insult ['insʌlt] *n* ihāna إهانة

insult [in'sʌlt] *v* ahāna أهان

insurance [in'sho:rəns] *n* ta'mīn تأمين

insure [in'sho:] *v* ammana أمن

intact [in'takt] *adj* salīm سليم

integrate ['intigreit] *v* damaja دمج (u; dumūj دموج); admaja أدمج

integration [inti'greishən] *n* damj دمج; idmāj إدماج

intellect ['intəlekt] *n* ʿaql عقل (ʿuqūl عقول)

intellectual [inti'lekchuəl] *adj* ʿaqlī عقلي

intelligence [in'telijəns] *n* **1.** ʿaql عقل **2.** *(mil.)* istikhbārāt إستخبارات

intelligent [in'telijənt] *adj* ʿāqil عاقل

intelligible [in'telijəbəl] *adj* mafhūm مفهوم

intend [in'tend] *v* qaṣada قصد (i; qaṣd قصد)

intense [in'tens] *adj* shadīd شديد

intensity [in'tensəti] *n* shidda شدة

intensive [in'tensiv] *adj* mukaththaf مكثف

intent; intention [in'tent; in'tenshən] *n* qaṣd قصد; nīya نية (nawāyā نوايا)

intentional [in'tenshənəl] *adj* maqṣūd مقصود

intentionally [in'tenshənəli] *adv* قصداً qaṣdan

intercept ['intəsept] *v* waqqafa وقف; i'taraḍa sabīl اعترض سبيل

interchange ['intəcheinj] *n* taqāṭuʿ تقاطع

intercontinental [intəkonti'nen-təl] *adj* bayn al-qārrāt بين القارات

intercourse ['intəko:s] *n* **1.** muʿāmala معاملة **2.** sexual intercourse jimāʿ جماع

interest ['intrəst] **1.** *n* ihtimām إهتمام **2.** maṣlaḥa (maṣāliḥ مصالح) مصلحة **3.** *(fin.)* fā'ida (fawā'id فوائد) فائدة **4.** *v* hamma هم (u; mahamma مهمة) **5.** *see* **interests**

interest-free *adj (fin.)* khālin min al-fawā'id خال من الفوائد

interesting ['intresting] *adj* mushawwiq مشوق

interests ['intərests] *pl* **1.** maṣāliḥ مصالح **2.** hawāyāt هوايات

interface ['intəfeis] *n* ittiṣāl إتصال (-āt)

interfere ['intəfiə] *v* tadakhkhala تدخل

interference [intə'fiərəns] *n* tadakhkhul تدخل

interior [in'tiəriə] **1.** *adj* dākhilī داخلي **2.** *n* dākhil داخل

intermediate [intə'mi:diət] *adj* mutawassiṭ متوسط

intermission [intə'mishən] *n* fatrat istirāḥa فترة إستراحة

internal [in'tə:nəl] *adj* dākhilī داخلي

international [intə'nashənəl] *adj* duwalī دولي

internet ['intənet] *n* internet إنترنيت

interpret [in'tə:prit] *v* tarjama ترجم

interpretation [intə:pri'teishən] *n* **1.** tarjama ترجمة (-āt) **2.** tafsīr تفسير (tafāsīr تفاسير)

interpreter [in'tə:pritə] *n* mutarjim مترجم

interracial [intə'reishəl] *adj* bayn al-ʿirqāt بين العرقات

interrogate [in'terəgeit] *v* istajwaba استجوب

interrogation [interə'geishən] *n* istijwāb إستجواب

interrupt [intə'rʌpt] *v* qāṭaʿa قاطع

interruption [intə'rʌpshən] *n* muqāṭaʿa مقاطعة (-āt)

interstate ['intəsteit] *adj* bayn al-wilāyāt بين الولايات

interval ['intəvəl] *n* fāṣil فاصل

intervention [intə'venshən] *n* tadakhkhul تدخل

interview ['intəvyu:] **1.** *n* muqābala مقابلة (-āt) **2.** *v* qābala قابل

interviewee [intəvyu'wi] *n* ḍayf al-muqābala ضيف المقابلة

interviewer ['intəvyuə] *n* man yujrī al-muqābala من يجري المقابلة

intimacy ['intiməsi] *n* ulfa ألفة

intimidation [intimi'deishən] *n* takhwīf تخويف

into ['intu] *prep* fī في; ilā إلى

intolerance [in'tolərəns] *n* taʿaṣṣub تعصب

intoxicated [in'toksikeitid] *adj* sakrān سكران

intricate ['intrikət] *adj* muʿaqqad معقد

intrigue [in'tri:g] *v* **1.** athāra 'l-ihtimām أثار الإهتمام **2.** ta'āmara تآمر

introduce [intrə'dyu:s] *v* **1.** ʿarrafa عرف **2.** adkhala أدخل

introduction [intrə'dʌkshən] *n* **1.** muqaddima مقدمة **2.** taʿrīf تعريف

intruder [in'tru:də] *n* **1.** ṭufaylī
طفيلي **2.** muqtaḥim مقتحم

intrusion [in'tru:zhən] *n* **1.** taṭafful
تطفل **2.** iqtiḥām إقتحام

intrusive [in'tru:siv] *adj* **1.** taṭaffulī
تطفلي **2.** iqtiḥāmī إقتحامي

invade [in'veid] *v* ghazā غزا (u;
ghazw غزو)

invader [in'veidə] *n* ghāzin غازٍ
(ghuzāh غزاة)

invalid [in'valid] *adj* bāṭil باطل

invalid ['invəlid] *n* marīḍ مريض; ʿājiz
عاجز

invaluable [in'valyuəbəl] *adj* lā
yuqaddar bi māl لا يقدّر بمال

invasion [in'veizhən] *n* ghazw غزو
(ghazawāt غزوات)

invent [in'vent] *v* ikhtaraʿa اخترع

invention [in'venshən] *n* ikhtirāʿ
إختراع

inventor [in'ventə] *n* mukhtariʿ
مخترع

invest [in'vest] *v* istathmara استثمر

investigate [in'vestigeit] *v*
ḥaqqaqa حقق

investigation [investi'geishən] *n*
taḥqīq تحقيق

investigator [in'vestigeitə] *n* **1.**
muḥaqqiq محقق **2.** private
investigator muḥaqqiq khāṣṣ
محقق خاص

investment [in'vestmənt] *n*
istithmār إستثمار

investor [in'vestə] *n* mustathmir
مستثمر (-ūn)

invisible [in'vizibəl] *adj* khafī خفي;
ghayr marʾī غير مرئي

invitation [invi'teishən] *n* daʿwā دعوى

invite [in'vait] *v* daʿā دعا (u; duʿāʾ
دعاء)

invoice ['invois] **1.** *n* fātūra فاتورة
(fawātīr فواتير) **2.** *v* fawtara
فوتر

involuntary [in'voləntri] *adj* ghayr
irādī غير إرادي

involve [in'volv] *v* **1.** taḍammana
تضمن **2.** warraṭa ورط

involvement [in'volvmənt] *n*
tawarruṭ تورط

Ireland ['aiələnd] *n* āyrlandā آيرلندا

Irish ['aiərish] **1.** *adj* āyrlandī
آيرلندي **2.** *pl* āyrlandīyūn
آيرلنديون

Irishman ['aiərishmən] *n* āyrlandī
آيرلندي (-yūn)

Irishwoman ['aiərishwumən] *n*
āyrlandīya آيرلندية (-āt)

iron ['aiən] **1.** *n* ḥadīd حديد **2.**
mikwāh مكواة (makāwin مكاو) **3.** *v*
kawā كوى (i; kayy كي)

ironic; ironical ['aironik; -əl] *adj*
mutahakkim متهكم; sukhrī سخري

irony ['aiərəni] *n* tahakkum تهكم;
sukhrīya سخرية

irregular [i'regyulə] *adj* ghayr
muntaẓim غير منتظم

irrelevant [i'reləvənt] *adj* lā ʿalāqī
لا علاقي; ghayr muttaṣil bi 'l-
mawḍūʿ غير متصل بالموضوع

irreparable [i'repərəbəl] *adj*
mutaʿadhdhir iṣlāḥuh متعذر إصلاحه

irreplaceable [iri'pleisəbəl]
adj mutaʿadhdhir istibdāluh
متعذر إستبداله

irresistible [iri'zistəbəl] *adj* lā
yuqāwam لا يقاوم

irrespective of [iri'spektiv] *prep*
bi ṣarf an-naẓar ʿan بصرف النظر عن

irresponsible [iri'sponsəbəl] *adj*
ghayr masʾūl غير مسؤول

irreversible [iri'vəːsəbəl] *adj*
mutaʿadhdhir ilghāʾuh متعذر إلغاءه

irrigate ['irigeit] *v* rawwā روى

irrigation [iri'geishən] *n* riyy/rayy ري

irritate ['iriteit] *v* azʿaja أزعج

irritating ['iriteiting] *adj* muzʿij مزعج

irritation [iri'teishən] *n* izʿāj أزعاج

is [iz] *see* be

Islam ['izla:m] *n* al-islām الإسلام

Islamic ['izlamik] *adj* islāmī إسلامي

island ['ailənd] *n* jazīra جزيرة (juzur جزر)

isolate ['aisəleit] *v* ʿazala عزل (i; ʿuzl عزل)

isolated ['aisəleitid] *adj* maʿzūl معزول

isolation [aisə'leishən] *n* ʿazl عزل

issue ['ishu:] *v* aṣdara أصدر

it [it] *pronoun* huwa هو; hiya هي

Italian [i'taliyən] 1. *adj* īṭālī إيطالي 2. *n* īṭālī إيطالي (-yūn)

italics [i'taliks] *pl* al-ḥurūf al-māʾila الحروف المائلة

Italy ['itəli] *n* īṭāliyā إيطاليا

itch [ich] *v* aḥakka أحك

item ['aitəm] *n* 1. shay' شيء (ashyā' أشياء) 2. **news item** khabar خبر (akhbār أخبار)

itinerary [ai'tinərəri] *n* khaṭṭ ar-riḥla خط الرحلة

its [its] -hu/-uh/-h ه; -hā ها

itself [it'self] nafsuh نفسه; nafsuhā نفسها

ivory ['aivəri] *n* ʿāj عاج

J

jacket ['jakit] *n* jāketa جاكتة (-āt); sutra سترة (-āt)

jackpot ['jakpot] *n* al-jā'iza al-kubrā الجائزة الكبرى

jail [jeil] 1. *n* sijn سجن (sujūn سجون) 2. *v* sajana سجن (u; sajn سجن)

jailer ['jeilə] *n* sajjān سجان (-ūn)

jam [jam] 1. *n* (UK) murabbā مربى (murabbayāt مربيات) 2. **traffic jam** izdiḥām al-murūr إزدحام المرور 3. *v* ʿalaqa علق (jammed) (a; ʿalaq علق)

January ['janyuəri] *n* yanāyir يناير; kānūn ath-thānī كانون الثاني

Japan [jə'pan] *n* al-yabān اليبان

Japanese [jəpa'ni:z] 1. *adj* yabānī يباني 2. *n* yabānī يباني (-yūn)

jar [ja:] *n* barṭamān برطمان (-āt)

jaw [jo:] *n* fakk فك (fukūk فكوك)

jazz [jaz] *n* al-jāz الجاز

jealous ['jeləs] *adj* ghayūr غيور

jealousy ['jeləsi] *n* ghayra غيرة

jeans [ji:nz] *pl* banṭalōn al-jīnz بنطلون الجينز

jeep [ji:p] *n* sayārat jīp سيارة جيب

jelly ['jeli] *n* hulām هلام

jeopardize ['jepədaiz] *v* ʿarraḍa li 'l-khaṭar عرض للخطر

jersey ['jəːzi] *n* jirsīya جرسية (āt-)

jet plane ['jetplein] *n* ṭā'ira naffāthīya طائرة نفاثية

Jew [juː] *n* yahūdī يهودي (yahūd يهود)

jewel ['juːəl] *n* jawhara جوهرة (jawāhir جواهر)

jeweller, (US) **jeweler** ['juːələ] *n* jawharī جوهري (yūn-)

jewellery, (US) **jewelry** ['juːəlri] *n* jawāhir جواهر

Jewish ['juːish] *adj* yahūdī يهودي

job [job] *n* shughl شغل (ashghāl أشغال)

jockey ['joki] *n* rākib al-khayl راكب الخيل (rukkāb رکاب; rukbān ركبان)

jog [jog] *v* rakaḍa ركض (u; rakḍ ركض)

jogging ['joging] *n* rakḍ ركض

join [join] *v* iltaḥaqa bi التحق ب

joint [joint] 1. *adj* mushtarik مشترك 2. *n* mafṣil مفصل (mafāṣil مفاصل)

jointly ['jointli] *adv* ma'an معاً

joke [jəuk] 1. *n* nukta نكتة (nukat نكت) 2. *v* mazaḥa مزح (a; mazḥ مزح)

jolly ['joli] *adj* mariḥ مرح

journal ['jəːnəl] *n* 1. majalla مجلة (āt-) 2. yawmīyāt يوميات

journalism ['jəːnəlizəm] *n* aṣ-ṣaḥāfa الصحافة

journalist ['jəːnəlist] *n* ṣaḥafī صحفي (yūn-)

journey ['jəːni] *n* 1. safar سفر (asfār أسفار); riḥla رحلة (āt-) 2. *v* sāfara سافر

joy [joi] *n* faraḥ فرح (afrāḥ أفراح)

joyful ['joifəl] *adj* fariḥ فرح; mubtahij مبتهج

jubilee ['juːbili] *n* yūbīl يوبيل

judge [jʌj] 1. *n* qāḍin قاض (quḍāh قضاة) 2. *v* ḥakama 'alā حكم على (u; ḥukm حكم)

judgement; judgment ['jʌjmənt] *n* ḥukm حكم (aḥkām أحكام)

judicial [juː'dishəl] *adj* qaḍā'ī قضائي

jug [jʌg] *n* ibrīq إبريق (abārīq أباريق)

juice [juːs] *n* 'aṣīr عصير

July [juː'lai] *n* yūliyū يوليو; tammūz تموز

jump [jʌmp] 1. *n* qafza قفزة (qafazāt قفزات) 2. *v* qafaza قفز (i; qafazān قفزان)

jumper ['jʌmpə] *n* jirsīya جرسية (āt-)

junction ['jʌngkshən] *n* multaqan ملتقى (multaqayāt ملتقيات)

June [juːn] *n* yūniyū يونيو; ḥazīrān حزيران

jungle ['jʌnggəl] *n* daghal دغل (adghāl أدغال); ghāba غابة (āt-)

junior ['juːniə] *adj* aṣghar sinnan الأصغر سناً; al-aṣghar الأصغر

junk [jʌngk] *n* nufāya نفاية

jurisdiction [juəris'dikshən] *n* sulṭa سلطة (āt-)

juror ['juərə] *n* muḥallif محلف (ūn-)

jury ['juəri] *n* hay'at al-muḥallifīn هيئة المحلفين

just [jʌst] 1. *adj* 'ādil عادل 2. *adv* mujarrad مجرد 3. **just now** mundhu laḥaẓāt منذ لحظات 4. **just as** 'indamā عندما

justice ['jʌstis] *n* 1. 'adāla عدالة 2. 'adl عدل; inṣāf إنصاف

justify ['jʌstifai] *v* barrara برر

juvenile ['juːvənail] *adj* ḥadath حدث (aḥdāth أحداث)

kebab ['kibab] *n* kabāb كباب

keen ['ki:n] *adj* mutaḥammis متحمس

keep ['ki:p] *v* 1. ḥafiẓa حفظ (a; ḥifẓ حفظ) 2. **to keep a promise** wafā وفى (yafī يفي; wafā' وفاء) 3. **He kept on ...** wāṣala fī ... واصل في ....

keep away from *v* imtanaʿa ʿan امتنع عن

keeper ['ki:pə] *n* 1. ḥāfiẓ حافظ (-ūn) 2. *see* **goalkeeper**

keep on *v* astamarra fī استمر في

keep out of *v* amtanaʿa ʿan أمتنع عن

keep up with *v* istamarra bi استمر ب

kettle ['ketəl] *n* ghallāya غلاية (-āt)

key ['ki:] 1. *adj* ra'īsī رئيسي; asāsī أساسي 2. *n* miftāḥ مفتاح (mafātīḥ مفاتيح)

keyboard ['ki:bo:d] *n* (*mus./comp.*) lawḥat al-mafātīḥ لوحة المفاتيح

kick ['kik] 1. *n* rafsa رفسة (rafs رفس) 2. *v* rafasa رفس (u; rafs رفس)

kid ['kid] 1. *adj* (*col.*) aṣghar أصغر 2. *n* (*col.*) ṭifl طفل (aṭfāl أطفال) 3. *v* khadaʿa خدع (a)

kidnap ['kidnap] *v* khaṭafa خطف (i; khaṭf خطف); ikhtṭafa اختطف

kidnapper ['kidnapə] *n* khāṭif خاطف; mukhtaṭif مختطف (-ūn)

kidnapping ['kidnaping] *n* khaṭf خطف; ikhtiṭāf إختطاف

kidney ['kidni] *n* kulya كلية (kalāwī كلاوي)

kill ['kil] *v* qatala قتل (u; qatl قتل)

killer ['kilə] *n* qātil قاتل (qatala قتلة)

killing ['kiling] *n* qatil قتل

kilo; kilogramme, (*US*) **kilogram** ['ki:ləu; 'kiləgram] *n* kīlō كيلو kīlōgrām كيلوغرام

kilometre, (*US*) **kilometer** [ki'lomitə] *n* kīlōmitr كيلومتر

kind [kaind] 1. *adj* laṭīf لطيف 2. *n* nawʿ نوع (anwāʿ أنواع); ṣinf صنف (aṣnāf أصناف)

kindergarten ['kində'ga:dən] *n* dār al-ḥaḍāna دار الحضانة

kindness ['kaindnis] *n* luṭf لطف

kind of *adv* min nawʿin mā من نوع ما

king [king] *n* malik ملك (mulūk ملوك)

kingdom ['kingdəm] *n* mamlaka مملكة (mamālik ممالك)

kiosk ['ki:osk] *n* kushk كشك (akshāk أكشاك)

kiss [kis] 1. *n* qubla قبلة (qubulāt قبلات) 2. *v* qabbala قبل

kit [kit] *n* ṭaqm طقم (ṭuqūm طقوم)

kitchen ['kichin] *n* maṭbakh مطبخ (maṭābikh مطابخ)

kite [kait] *n* ṭā'ira waraqīya طائرة ورقية

kitten ['kitən] *n* hurayra هريرة

knack [nak] *n* barāʿa براعة

knee [ni:] *n* rukba ركبة (-āt; rukab ركب)

kneel; kneel down [ni:l] *v* rakaʿa ركع (a; rukūʿ ركوع)

knew [nyu:] *see* **know**

knickers ['nikəz] *n* malābis dākhilīya malāis nisā'īya ملابس داخلية نسائية

knife [naif] 1. *n* (*pl* **knives**) sikkīna

سكينة (sakākīn سكاكين) 2. v ṭaʿana
bi sikkīna طعن بسكينة (a; ṭaʿn طعن)

knight [nait] n fāris فارس (fursān
فرسان)

knit [nit] v ḥāka حاك (u; hiyāk حياك)

knives [naivz] see knife

knob [nob] n zirr زر (azrār أزرار)

knock [nok] v qaraʿa قرع (a; qarʿ قرع)

knock out v ḍaraba ḍarbatan
ḥāsimatan ضرب ضربة حاسمة (a;
ḍarb ضرب)

knot [not] n ʿuqda عقدة (ʿuqad عقد)

know [nəu] v (knew, known) 1.
ʿalima علم (a; ʿilm علم) 2. ʿarafa
عرف (i; maʿrifa معرفة; ʿirfān عرفان)

know-how ['nəuhau] n mahāra مهارة

know how to v ʿarafa عرف (i;
maʿrifa معرفة; ʿirfān عرفان)

knowledge ['nolij] n 1. ʿilm علم 2.
maʿrifa معرفة

known [nəun] adj 1. maʿrūf معروف 2.
see **know**

Koran [ko'ra:n] n al-qur'ān al-karīm
القرآن الكريم

kosher ['kəushə] adj mubāḥ مباح

k.p.h. (kilometres per hour)
kīlōmitr bi 's-sāʿa كيلومتر بالساعة

Kurd [kə:d] n kurdī كردي (kurd كرد)

Kurdish ['kə:dish] adj kurdī كردي

L

lab [lab] see **laboratory**

label ['leibəl] 1. n biṭāqa بطاقة
(-āt; baṭā'iq بطائق) 2. ʿalāma علامة
(-āt; ʿalā'im علائم) 3. v alṣaqa
biṭāqa ʿalā ألصق بطاقة على

laboratory [lə'borətri] n mukhtabar
مختبر (-āt)

laborious [lə'bo:riəs] adj shāqq شاق

labour, (US) **labor** ['leibə] 1. n
ʿamal عمل 2. **to be in labour**
makhiḍat مخضت (a; makhāḍ مخاض)
3. v kadaḥa كدح (a; kadḥ كدح)

labourer, (US) **laborer** ['leibərə] n
ʿāmil عامل (ʿummāl عمال)

Labour Party n ḥizb al-ʿummāl
حزب العمال

lack [lak] 1. n naqṣ نقص 2. v naqaṣa
نقص (u; naqṣ نقص)

lad [lad] n walad ولد (awlād أولاد);
ṣabīy صبي (ṣubyān صبيان)

ladder ['ladə] n sullam سلم (salālim
سلالم)

lady ['leidi] n sayyida سيدة (-āt)

lager ['la:gə] n bīra بيرة

laid [leid] see **lay**

lain [lein] see **lie**

lake [leik] n buḥaira بحيرة (-āt)

lamb [lam] n kharūf خروف (khirfān
خرفان)

lamp [lamp] n lamba لمبة (-āt)

lamp-post *n* ʿamūd al-’iḍā’a
عمود الإضاءة

land [land] **1.** *n* arḍ أرض (arāḍin
أراضٍ) **2. by land** barran برّاً **3.** *v*
habaṭa هبط (u/i; hubūṭ هبوط)

landing [ˈlanding] *n* (aviation)
hubūṭ هبوط

landlady [ˈlandleidi] *n* ṣāḥibat al-
bayt صاحبة البيت

landlord [ˈlandloːd] *n* ṣāḥib al-bayt
صاحب البيت

landmark [ˈlandmaːk] **1.** *n* maʿlam
معلم (maʿālim معالم) **2.** ḥadath
hāmm حدث هام

landowner [ˈlandəunə] *n* mallāk
arāḍin ملاك أراضٍ

landscape [ˈlandskeip] manẓar
ṭabīʿī منظر طبيعي

landslide [ˈlandslaid] *n* inhiyāl al-
arḍ إنهيال الأرض

lane [lein] *n* zuqāq زقاق (aziqqa
أزقة)

language [ˈlanggwij] *n* lugha لغة
(-āt)

lap [lap] **1.** *n* ḥiḍn حضن (aḥḍān
أحضان) **2.** (spor.) dawra دورة (-āt)

lapse [laps] *n* hafwa هفوة (hafawāt
هفوات)

laptop [ˈlaptop] *n* kombyūtar
maḥmūl كمبيوتر محمول

larder [ˈlaːdə] *n* ḥujra li ḥifẓ aṭ-ṭaʿām
حجرة لحفظ الطعام

large [laːj] *adj* ḍakhm ضخم; wāsiʿ واسع

large-scale *adj* wāsiʿ an-niṭāq
واسع النطاق

laser [ˈleizə] *n* ishʿāʿ al-layzer
إشعاع الليزر

laser printer *n* jihāz ṭibāʿat al-
layzer جهاز طباعة الليزر

last [laːst] **1.** *adj* akhīr أخير **2. last
night** laylat al-ams ليلة الأمس **3.**

last year al-sanat al-māḍīya
السنة الماضية **4. at last** akhīran
أخيراً **5. last of all** akhīran
أخيراً **6.** *adv* akhīran أخيراً **7.** *v* dāma
دام (u; dawām دوام)

lasting [ˈlaːsting] *adj* dā’im دائم;
bāqin باقٍ

lastly [ˈlaːstli] *adv* akhīran أخيراً

late [leit] *adj* **1.** muta’akhkhir متأخر
2. the late news nashrat al-akhbār
al-akhīra نشرة الأخبار الأخيرة **3. the
late Mr...** al-marḥūm... المرحوم ...
4. to be late ta’akhkhara تأخر

lately [ˈleitli] *adv* mu’akhkharan
مؤخراً

later [ˈleitə] **1.** *adv* lāḥiqan لاحقاً **2.**
see **late**

latest [ˈleitist] *adj* **1.** akhīr أخير **2.
the latest news** ākhir al-akhbār
آخر الأخبار

latitude [ˈlatityuːd] *n* khaṭṭ al-ʿarḍ
خط العرض

latter [ˈlatə] *adj* akhīr أخير

latterly [ˈlatəli] *adv* mu’akhkharan
مؤخراً

laugh [laːf] **1.** *n* ḍaḥk ضحك **2.** *v*
ḍaḥika ضحك (a; ḍaḥk ضحك)

laughable [ˈlaːfəbəl] *adj* muḍḥik
مضحك

laughter [ˈlaːftə] *n* ḍaḥk ضحك

launch [loːnch] *v* **1.** ʿawwama عوّم **2.**
aṭlaqa أطلق **3.** bāshara tarwīj
(silʿatin mā) باشر ترويج (سلعة ما)

launderette; laundrette [loːn-
dəˈret] *n* maghsala ʿāmma
مغسلة عامة

laundry [ˈloːndri] *n* **1.** ghasīl غسيل
2. maghsala مغسلة (-āt)

lava [ˈlaːvə] *n* ḥumam al-burkān
حمم البركان

lavatory ['lavətri] *n* 1. mirḥāḍ مرحاض; ḥammām حمام 2. **public lavatory** mirḥāḍ ʿumūmī مرحاض عمومي

lavish ['lavish] *adj* wāfir وافر; fākhir فاخر

law [lo:] *n* 1. qānūn قانون (qawānīn قوانين) 2. **against the law** mukhālif li 'l-qānūn مخالف للقانون 3. **to break the law** intahaka al-qānūn انتهك القانون 4. **to pass a law** marrara qānūnan مرر قانوناً

law court ['lo:ko:t] *n* maḥkama محكمة (maḥākim محاكم)

lawful ['lo:fəl] *adj* qānūnī قانوني

lawless ['lo:ləs] *adj* lā qānūnī لا قانوني

lawn [lo:n] *n* ʿushb عشب (aʿshāb أعشاب)

lawsuit ['lo:su:t] *n* daʿwā دعوى (daʿāwā دعاوى)

lawyer ['lo:yə] *n* muḥāmin محام (muḥāmūn محامون)

laxative ['laksətiv] *n* musahhil مسهل (-āt); mushil مسهل (-āt)

lay [lei] *v* 1. waḍaʿa وضع (yaḍaʿu يضع; waḍ' وضع) 2. **to lay an egg** bāḍa باض (i; bayḍ بيض) 3. *see* **lie**

layer ['leiə] *n* ṭabaqa طبقة (-āt)

lay off *v* sarraḥa ʿan al-ʿamal سرح عن العمل

lay-out *n* takhṭīṭ تخطيط

laziness ['leizinis] *n* kasal كسل

lazy ['leizi] *adj* kaslān كسلان

lead [led] *n* raṣāṣ رصاص

lead [li:d] *n* 1. ḥabl as-sīr حبل السير 2. *v* (led) qāda قاد (u; qiyāda قيادة)

leader ['li:də] *n* qā'id قائد (qāda قادة); zaʿīm زعيم (zuʿamā' زعماء)

leadership ['li:dəship] *n* qiyāda قيادة (-āt)

leading ['li:ding] *adj* ra'īsī رئيسي

leaf [li:f] *n* (*pl* **leaves**) waraqa ورقة (waraq ورق; awrāq أوراق)

leaflet ['li:flit] *n* manshūr منشور (-āt)

league [li:g] *n* (*spor.*) dawr دور (adwār أدوار)

leak [li:k] 1. *n* tasarrub تسرب 2. *v* tasarraba تسرب

lean [li:n] 1. *adj* qalīl ad-duhn قليل الدهن 2. naḥīf نحيف 3. *v* (leant/leaned) māla مال (i; mayl ميل) 4. **to lean on** ittaka'a ʿalā اتكأ على

leaning ['li:ning] *n* mā'il مائل

leant [lent] *see* **lean**

leap [li:p] 1. *n* qafza قفزة (qafazāt قفزات) 2. *v* (leapt/leaped) qafaza قفز (i; qafz قفز)

leap-year ['li:pyiə] *n* sana kabīsa سنة كبيسة

learn [lə:n] *v* (learnt/learned) 1. taʿallama تعلم 2. iktashafa اكتشف

learn about/of *v* ʿalima علم (a; ʿilm علم)

learned ['lə:nid] *adj* muthaqqaf مثقف

learner ['lə:nə] *n* tilmīdh تلميذ (talāmīdh تلاميذ; talāmidha تلامذة)

learn how *v* taʿallama تعلم

learning ['lə:ning] *n* maʿrifa معرفة

lease [li:s] 1. *n* ʿaqd عقد (ʿuqūd عقود); ījār إيجار 2. *v* ajjara أجّر 3. ista'jara استأجر

least [li:st] *adj* 1. aqall أقل 2. **at least** ʿalā 'l-aqall على الأقل

leather ['ledhə] *n* jild جلد (julūd جلود)

leave [li:v] 1. *n* idhn إذن 2. ajāza أجازة 3. *v* (left) taraka ترك (u; tark ترك) 4. ghādara غادر 5. *see* **left**

leaves [li:vz] *see* **leaf**

lecture ['lekchə] 1. *n* muḥāḍara محاضرة (-āt) 2. *v* ḥāḍara حاضر 3. *v* wabbakha وبخ

lecturer ['lekchərə] *n* 1. muḥāḍir محاضر 2. ustādh jāmi'ī أستاذ جامعي

led [led] *see* **lead**

left [left] 1. *n* yasār يسار 2. *(pol.)* al-yasār اليسار 3. **on the left** 'alā 'l-yasār على اليسار 4. *adj* yasārī يساري 5. **There is no time left.** nafida al-waqt نفد الوقت 6. *adv* yasāran يساراً 7. *see* **leave**

left-handed *adj* a'sar أعسر

left over *adj* mutabaqqin متبقٍ

left-wing *adj (pol.)* yasārī يساري

left wing *n (pol.)* al-yasār اليسار

left-winger *n (pol.)* yasārī يساري

leg [leg] *n* 1. rijl رجل (arjul أرجل) 2. *(spor.)* marḥala مرحلة (marāḥil مراحل)

legacy ['legəsi] *p* irth إرث; mirāth مراث

legal ['li:gəl] *adj* 1. qānūnī قانوني; shar'ī شرعي 2. qaḍā'ī قضائي

legalization [li:gəlai'zeishən] *n* tashrī' تشريع

legalize ['li:gəlaiz] *v* sharra'a شرّع

legend ['lejənd] *n* usṭūra أسطورة (asāṭīr أساطير)

legendary ['lejəndri] *adj* usṭūrī أسطوري

legible ['lejibəl] *adj* maqrū' مقروء

legislation [lejis'leishən] *n* tashrī' تشريع

legislative ['lejislətiv] *adj* tashrī'ī تشريعي

legitimacy [li'jitiməsi] *n* shar'īya شرعية

legitimate [li'jitimət] *adj* shar'ī شرعي

leisure ['lezhə] *n* waqt al-farāgh وقت الفراغ; tarfīh ترفيه

leisurely ['lezhəli] 1. *adj* mutamahhil متمهل 2. *adv* 'alā mahl على مهل; mahlan مهلاً

lemon(s) ['lemən] *n* laimūn ليمون *collective*

lend [lend] *v* (lent) aqraḍa أقرض

lender ['lendə] *n* muqriḍ مقرض (-ūn)

length [length] *n* 1. ṭūl طول 2. **at length** ṭawīlan طويلاً

lengthen ['lengthən] *v* ṭawwala طوّل

lengthy ['lengthi] *adj* ṭawīl طويل

lenient ['li:niənt] *adj* mutasāhil متساهل

lens [lenz] *n* (pl lenses) 'adasa عدسة (-āt)

lent [lent] *see* **lend**

lesbian ['lezbiən] 1. *adj* siḥāqī سحاقي 2. *n* siḥāqīya سحاقية (-āt)

lesbianism ['lezbiənizm] *n* siḥāq سحاق; musāḥaqa مساحقة

less [les] *adj* 1. aqall أقل 2. **more or less** taqrīban تقريباً

lessen ['lesən] *v* qallala قلّل

lesser ['lesə] *adj* aqall أقل

lesson ['lesən] *n* dars درس (durūs دروس)

lest [lest] *adv* kay lā كي لا; likay lā لكي لا

let [let] *v* (let) 1. yada'u يدع 2. taraka ترك (u; tark ترك); samuḥa سمح (u; samāḥ سماح) 3. ajjara أجر

let alone *conj* tarakah waḥdah تركه وحده

let down *v* khadhala خذل (u; khadhl خذل)

lethal ['li:thəl] *adj* mumīt مميت; qātil قاتل

let in v adkhala أدخل

let off v aʿfā ʿan أعفى عن

let's... v daʿna... ...دعنا

letter ['letə] n 1. ḥarf حرف (ḥurūf حروف) 2. risāla رسالة (rasāʾil رسائل)

letterbox ['letəboks] n (UK) ṣundūq al-barīd صندوق البريد

let up v kaffa كف (u; kaff كف)

level ['levəl] 1. n mustawan مستوى 2. sea level mustawā saṭḥ al-baḥr مستوى سطح البحر 3. adj mustawin مستو 4. v sawwā سوى

lever ['liːvə] n rāfiʿa رافعة (rawāfiʿ روافع)

liable ['laiəbəl] adj masʾūl qānūnīyan مسؤول قانونياً

liable to adj ʿurḍa li عرضة ل

liar ['laiə] n kadhdhāb كذّاب (-ūn)

libel ['laibəl] 1. n nashr aqwāl qadhfīya نشر أقوال قذفية 2. v nashara aqwāl qadhfīya نشر أقوال قذفية (u; nashr)

liberal ['libərəl] 1. adj librālī ليبرالي 2. n librālī ليبرالي 3. karīm كريم

liberate ['libəreit] v ḥarrara حرّر

liberation [libəˈreishən] n taḥrīr تحرير

liberty ['libəti] n ḥurrīya حرية (-āt)

library ['laibrəri] n maktaba مكتبة (-āt)

licence, (US) **license** ['laisəns] n 1. rukhṣa رخصة (rukhaṣ رخص) 2. driving licence rukhṣat qiyādat as-sayyārāt رخصة قيادة السيارات

license ['laisəns] v 1. rakhkhaṣa رخص 2. see licence

lick [lik] v laḥisa لحس (a; laḥs لحس)

lid [lid] n ghiṭāʾ غطاء (aghṭiya أغطية)

lie [lai] 1. n kidhb كذب; ukdhūba أكذوبة (akādhīb أكاذيب) 2. v (lay,

lain) tamaddada تمدد 3. (lied) kadhaba كذب (i; kidhb كذب)

lie down v tamaddada تمدد; istalqā استلقى

life [laif] n (pl lives) ḥayāh حياة; ʿumar عمر (aʿmār أعمار)

lifebelt n ḥizām al-ʾamān حزام الأمان

lifeboat n qārib an-najāh قارب النجاة

life insurance n taʾmīn ʿalā 'l-ḥayāh تأمين على الحياة

life jacket n sitrat an-najāh سترة النجاة

lifeless ['laifləs] adj mayyit ميت

lifestyle ['laifstail] n uslūb al-ḥayāh أسلوب الحياة

lifetime ['laiftaim] n mada 'l-ḥayāh مدى الحياة

lift [lift] 1. n miṣʿad مصعد (maṣāʿid مصاعد) 2. tawṣīla توصيلة 3. to give a lift waṣṣala وصل 4. v rafaʿa رفع (a; rafʿ رفع); raffaʿa رفع

light [lait] 1. adj khafīf خفيف 2. fātiḥ فاتح 3. n ḍawʾ ضوء (aḍwāʾ أضواء); nūr نور (anwār أنوار) 4. v (lit) aḍāʾa أضاء; anāra أنار; ashʿala أشعل

lightbulb ['laitbʌlb] n miṣbāḥ مصباح (maṣābīḥ مصابيح)

lighter ['laitə] n qaddāḥa قداحة (-āt); wallāʿa ولاعة (-āt)

lighthouse ['laithaus] n manār منار (manāwir مناور)

lightning ['laitning] n barq برق

like [laik] 1. prep/adv/conj ka ك; mithl مثل 2. v ḥabba حب (i; ḥubb حب)

likelihood ['laiklihud] n iḥtimāl إحتمال

likely ['laikli] adj/adv muḥtamal محتمل

likeness ['laiknis] *n* shabah شبه
(ashbāh أشباه); shabīh شبيه

likewise ['laikwaiz] *adv* kadhālik
كذالك; aydan أيضاً

liking ['laiking] *n* mayl ميل (muyūl
ميول)

limb [lim] *n* ʿudw عضو (aʿdāʾ أعضاء)

lime [laim] *n* **1.** laymūn ḥāmiḍ حامض
ليمون; kils كلس **2.** jīr جير
collective ليمون

limelight ['laimlait] *n* **in the
limelight** taḥt al-adwāʾ
تحت الأضواء

limit ['limit] **1.** *n* ḥadd حد (ḥudūd
حدود) **2. age limit** ḥadd ʿumarī
حد عمري **3. speed limit** ḥadd as-
surʿa حد السرعة **4.** *v* ḥaddada حدد

limitation [limi'teishən] *n* qayd قيد
(quyūd قيود); ḥadd حد (ḥudūd
حدود)

limited ['limitid] *adj* maḥdūd محدود

limited company *n* sharika
maḥdūda شركة محدودة

limitless ['limitləs] *adj* lā ḥadd lah
لا حد له

line [lain] *n* **1.** khaṭṭ خط (khuṭūṭ
خطوط) **2.** ḥabl حبل (ḥibāl حبال) **3.
telephone line** khaṭṭ tilifūnī
خط تلفوني

liner ['lainə] *n* bākhira باخرة
(bawākhir بواخر)

line up *v* ṣaffafa صفّف

lingerie ['lonzhəri] *n* malābis
muthīra li n-nisāʾ ملابس مثيرة للنساء

linguist ['lingwist] *n* lughawī لغوي
(-yūn)

linguistic [ling'gwistik] *adj* lughawī
لغوي

linguistics [ling'gwistiks] *n* ʿilm al-
lugha علم اللغة

link [lingk] *n* waṣl وصل (awṣāl
أوصال); ḥalaqa حلقة (-āt)

lino; linoleum ['lainəu; li'nəuliəm]
n mushammaʿ مشمع (-āt)

lion ['laiən] *n* asad أسد (usūd أسود)

lip [lip] *n* shafa شفة (shifāh شفاه)

lip-read *v* qaraʾa ash-shifāh
قرأ الشفاه (a; qirāʾa قراءة)

lipstick ['lipstik] *n* aḥmar ash-
shifāh أحمر الشفاه

liquid ['likwid] **1.** *adj* sāʾil سائل **2.** *n*
sāʾil سائل (sawāʾil سوائل); maḥlūl
محلول

liquor ['likə] *n* kuḥūl كحول

list [list] **1.** *n* qāʾima قائمة (qawāʾim
قوائم) **2.** *v* ʿaddada عدد

listen ['lisən] *v* samiʿa سمع (a; samʿ
سمع)

listener ['lisnə] *n* mustamiʿ مستمع
(-ūn)

listings ['listings] *pl* taṣnīfāt تصنيفات

lit [lit] *see* **light**

liter ['li:tə] *(US) n* litr لتر (-āt)

literacy ['litərəsi] *n* maʿrifat
al-qirāʾa wa ʾl-kitāba
معرفة القراءة والكتابة

literally ['litrəli] *adv* ḥarfīyan حرفياً

literate ['litərəl] *adj* mutaʿallim
متعلم

literature ['litrəchə] *n* adab أدب

litre ['li:tə] *n* litr لتر (-āt)

litter ['litə] *n* qumāma قمامة; zubāla
زبالة

little ['litəl] **1.** *adj* qalīl قليل; ṣaghīr
صغير **2.** *adv* qalīlan قليلاً **3. a little**
qalīlan قليلاً

little by little *adv* tadrījiyan
تدريجياً

live [laiv] **1.** *adj* ḥayy حي **2. a live
broadcast** bathth ḥayy بثّ حي **3.**
adv ḥayyan حياً; mubāsharatan
مباشرةً

live [liv] v 1. ʿāsha عاش (i; ʿaysh عيش) 2. ḥayiya حيي (yaḥyā يحيى; ḥayāh حياة)

livelihood ['laivlihud] n maʿīsha معيشة

lively ['laivli] adj 1. nashīṭ نشيط 2. ḥayawī حيوي

liver ['livə] n kabd كبد (akbād أكباد)

lives [laivz] see life

living ['living] 1. adj ḥayy حي 2. n maʿāsh معاش

living-room n ghurfat al-julūs غرفة الجلوس; ṣālōn صالون

lizard ['lizəd] n siḥlīya سحلية (saḥālin سحالٍ)

load [ləud] 1. n shaḥna شحنة (shaḥanāt شحنات); ʿadad kabīr عدد كبير 2. v ḥammala حمّل; shaḥana شحن (a; shaḥn شحن)

loaf [ləuf] n (pl loaves [ləuvz]) raghīf رغيف (arghifa أرغفة)

loan [ləun] 1. n qarḍ قرض (qurūḍ قروض) 2. v aqraḍa أقرض

loathe [ləudh] v kariha كره (a; kurh كره)

loaves [ləuvz] see loaf

lobby ['lobi] 1. n (pol.) ḍaghṭ ضغط 2. hotel lobby istiqbāl al-funduq إستقبال الفندق 3. v (pol.) ḍaghaṭa ضغط (u; ḍaghṭ ضغط)

local ['ləukəl] adj maḥallī محلي

local government n al-ḥukm al-maḥallī الحكم المحلي

locate [ləu'keit] v 1. to locate (sth/so) ḥaddada mawqiʿ (shay'/shakhṣ) حدد موقع (شيء\شخص) 2. see located

located [ləu'keitid] adj to be located wujida وجد

location [ləu'keishən] n mawqiʿ موقع (mawāqiʿ مواقع)

lock [lok] n 1. n qufl قفل (aqfāl أقفال) 2. v aqfala أقفل

locked [lokt] adj maqfūl مقفول

lodge [loj] 1. n manzil منزل (manāzil منازل) 2. v to lodge a complaint qaddama shakwa قدم شكوة

lodgings ['lojingz] n sakan سكن

lofty ['lofti] adj ʿālī عالي

log [log] 1. n khashab خشب (akhshāb أخشاب) 2. v to log in ashghala jihāz al-kombyūtar أشغل جهاز الكمبيوتر

logic ['lojik] n manṭiq منطق

logical ['lojikəl] adj manṭiqī منطقي

logo ['ləugəu] n shiʿār شعار (-āt)

loneliness ['ləunlinəs] n waḥda وحدة

lonely ['ləunli] adj waḥīd وحيد

long [long] 1. adj ṭawīl طويل 2. adv ṭawīlan طويلاً 3. before long qarīban قريباً 4. in the long run fi 'n-nihāya في النهاية 5. as long as mā dām ما دام; ṭālamā طالما 6. how long? kam al-mudda كم المدة؟ 7. long ago mundhu ʿahd baʿīd منذ عهد بعيد 8. not long ago ḥadīthan حديثاً 9. v to long for ishtāqa ilā اشتاق إلى

longer see long, no longer

longing ['longing] n shawq شوق (ashwāq أشواق)

longitude ['longgityu:d] khaṭṭ aṭ-ṭūl خط الطول

long-lasting adj dā'im دائم

long-range adj baʿīd al-madā بعيد المدى

long-sighted adj ṭawīl an-naẓar طويل النظر

long-term adj ṭawīl al-amad طويل الأمد

look [luk] 1. *n* naẓra نظرة (naẓarāt نظرات) 2. *v* naẓara نظر (u; naẓr نظر) 3. badā بدا (u)

look after *v* iʿtanā bi اعتنى ب

look ahead *v* taṭallaʿa ilā تطلع إلى

look back *v* fakkara fi 'l-māḍī فكر في الماضي

look for *v* baḥatha ʿan بحث عن (a; baḥth بحث)

look forward to *v* taṭallaʿa ilā تطلع إلى

looking-glass ['lukinggla:s] *n* mir'āh مرآة (marāyā مرايا)

look into *v* naẓara fī نظر في (u; naẓar نظر); baḥatha fī بحث في (a; baḥth بحث)

look like *v* shābaha شابه

look out! *v* intabih! !انتبه

look over *v* alqā naẓra ʿalā ألقى نظرة على

looks [luks] *pl* maẓāhir مظاهر

look up *v* 1. baḥatha ʿan بحث عن 2. taḥassana تحسن

look up to *v* taṭallaʿa ilā تطلع إلى

loop [lu:p] *n* ḥalaqa حلقة (-āt)

loose [lu:s] *adj* 1. maḥlūl محلول 2. ṭalīq طليق

loosen ['lu:sən] *v* fakka فك (u; fakk فك)

lord [lo:d] *n* sayyid سيد (sāda سادة)

lorry ['lori] *n* (UK) sayyārat shaḥn سيارة سحن

lose [lu:z] *v* 1. (lost [lost]) ḍayyaʿa ضيع; khasira خسر (a; khasr خسر) 2. to lose a key faqada al-miftāḥ فقد المفتاح (i; faqd فقد; fiqdān فقدان) 3. to lose a game khasira al-mubārāh خسر المباراة 4. to lose a war khasira al-ḥarb خسر الحرب 5. see lost

loser ['lu:zə] *n* khāsir خاسر (-ūn)

loss [los] *n* khasāra خسارة (khasā'ir خسائر)

losses ['losiz] *pl* (mil./fin.) khasā'ir خسائر

lost [lost] *adj* 1. I am lost. anā ḍā'iʿ أنا ضائع 2. see lose

lot [lot] *n* 1. ʿadad kabīr عدد كبير 2. qiṭʿat arḍ قطعة أرض 3. naṣīb نصيب 3. lots, a lot (of) kathīr (min) كثير (من) 4. the whole lot al-jamīʿ الجميع

lotion ['ləushən] *n* sā'il al-jamāl سائل الجمال

lots [lots] see lot

lottery ['lotəri] *n* yā naṣīb يا نصيب

loud [laud] *adj* murtafiʿ aṣ-ṣawt مرتفع الصوت

loudly ['laudli] *adv* bi ṣawt ʿālin بصوت عال

loudness ['laudnəs] *n* irtifāʿ aṣ-ṣawt إرتفاع الصوت

loudspeaker [laud'spi:kə] *n* mukabbir aṣ-ṣawt مكبر الصوت

lounge [launj] *n* ḥujrat al-julūs حجرة الجلوس; ṣālōn صالون

love [lʌv] 1. *n* ḥubb حب 2. *v* ḥabba حب (i; ḥubb حب) 3. to make love jāmaʿa جامع 4. to fall in love waqaʿa fī 'l-ḥubb وقع في الحب (with maʿa مع)

lovely ['lʌvli] *adj* 1. jamīl جميل 2. maḥbūb محبوب

lover ['lʌvə] *n* ʿāshiq عاشق (ūn; ʿushshāq عشاق)

loving ['lʌving] *adj* ḥanūn حنون; muḥibb محب

low [ləu] *adj* 1. munkhafiḍ منخفض 2. waḍīʿ وضيع 3. danī' دنيء

lower ['ləuə] 1. *adj* asfal أسفل 2. *v* khafaḍa خفض (i; khafḍ خفض)

loyal ['loiəl] *adj* mukhliṣ مخلص; wafī وفي

loyalty ['loiəlti] *n* ikhlāṣ إخلاص; wafā' وفاء

ltd *see* limited

lubricant ['lu:brikənt] *n* mazalliq مزلق

luck [lʌk] *n* ḥaẓẓ حظ

luckily ['lʌkili] *adv* li ḥusn al-ḥaẓẓ لحسن الحظ

lucky ['lʌki] *adj* maḥẓūẓ محظوظ

lucrative ['lu:krətiv] *adj* murbiḥ مربح

luggage ['lʌgij] *n* ḥaqā'ib حقائب; amti°a أمتعة

lump [lʌmp] *n* 1. qiṭ°a قطعة (qiṭa° قطع) 2. *(med.)* waram ورم (awrām أورام)

lunacy ['lu:nəsi] *n* junūn جنون

lunar ['lu:nə] *adj* qamarī قمري

lunatic ['lu:nətik] 1. *adj* majnūn مجنون 2. *n* majnūn مجنون (majānīn مجانين)

lunch [lʌnch] 1. *n* al-ghadā' الغداء (aghdiya أغدية) 2. *v* taghaddā تغدى

luncheon ['lʌnshən] *n* ghadā' rasmī غداء رسمي

lunchtime ['lʌnchtaim] *n* waqt al-ghadā' وقت الغداء

lung [lʌng] *n* ri'a رئة (ri'āt رئات)

lure [luə] *v* aghrā أغرى

lust [lʌst] *n* shahwa شهوة (shahawāt شهوات)

luxurious [lʌg'zhuəriəs] *adj* mutraf مترف; fakhm فخم

luxury ['lʌkshəri] *n* taraf ترف; fakhām فخامة

lying ['la:ing] 1. *adj* kādhib كاذب 2. *see* lie

lynch [linch] *v* a°dama (bidūn muḥākama) أعدم (بدون محاكمة)

lyrics ['liriks] *pl* kalimāt aghānī كلمات أغاني

lyricist ['lirisist] *n* mu'allif kalimāt al-aghānī مؤلف كلمات الأغاني

M

mac *see* mackintosh

machine [mə'shi:n] *n* āla آلة (-āt); makina/mākīna ماكينة (āt; makā'in مكائن)

machine-gun *n* rashshash ālī رشاش آلي (rashshashāt ālīya رشاشات آلية)

machinery [mə'shi:nəri] *n* 1. ālāt آلات; mākīnāt ماكينات 2. *(pol.)* ajhiza أجهزة

mackintosh ['makintosh] *n (UK)* mi°ṭaf mushamma° معتف مشمع; qumāsh mushamma° قماش مشمع

mad [mad] *adj* 1. majnūn مجنون 2.

ghaḍbān غضبان 3. **He's mad about football.** huwa shaghūf bi kurat al-qadam. هو شغوف بكرة القدم.

madam ['madəm] n madām مدام; sayyida سيّدة

madden ['madən] v jannana جنّن

made [meid] see **make**

madman ['madmən] n majnūn مجنون (majānīn مجانين)

madness ['madnəs] n junūn جنون

magazine [magə'zi:n] n 1. majalla مجلة (-āt) 2. (mil.) dhakhīra ذخيرة (dhakhā'ir ذخائر)

magic ['majik] 1. adj siḥrī سحري 2. n siḥr سحر

magical ['majikəl] adj siḥrī سحري

magician [mə'jishən] n sāḥir ساحر (-ūn; saḥara سحرة)

magistrate ['majistreit] n qāḍin قاض (quḍāh قضاة)

magnificent [mag'nifisənt] adj ʿaẓīm عظيم; fakhm فخم

mail [meil] 1. n barīd بريد 2. v arsala bi 'l-barīd أرسل بالبريد

mailbox ['meilboks] n ṣundūq al-barīd صندوق البريد

mailman ['meilman] n sāʿī al-barīd ساعي البريد

main [mein] adj raʾīsī رئيسي

mainland ['meinland] n al-barr ar-raʾīsī البر الرئيسي; al-waṭan al-umm الوطن الأم

mainly ['meinli] adv ghāliban غالباً

maintain [mein'tein] v 1. ṣāna صان (u; ṣiyāna صيانة) 2. (fin.) mawwala موّل

maintenance ['meintənəns] n 1. ṣiyāna صيانة 2. (fin.) nafaqa نفقة (-āt)

major ['meijə] 1. adj raʾīsī رئيسي;

hāmm هام; kabīr كبير 2. khaṭīr خطير 3. n (mil.) rāʾid رائد (ruwwād رواد)

majority [mə'jorəti] n aghlabīya أغلبية

make [meik; meid] 1. n ṣināʿa صناعة (-āt) 2. v (made) ʿamila عمل (a; ʿamal عمل); ṣanaʿa صنع (a; ṣanʿ صنع) 3. ajbara أجبر 4. **to make love** jāmaʿa جامع 5. **to make out** fahima فهم (a; fahm فهم) 6. zaʿama زعم (u; zaʿm زعم) 7. **to make up** taṣālaḥa تصالح 8. ikhtaraʿa اخترع 9. **to make up one's mind** qarrara قرّر; ḥasama حسم (i; ḥasm حسم)

maker ['meikə] n ṣāniʿ صانع (ṣunnāʿ صناع)

make-up ['meikəp] n mākiyāj ماكياج

male [meil] 1. adj dhakarī ذكري 2. n dhakar ذكر (dhukūr ذكور)

malice ['malis] n ḥiqd حقد (aḥqād أحقاد)

malignant [mə'lignənt] adj khabīth خبيث

mall [mol] n mujammaʿ tijārī مجمع تجاري

malnutrition [malnyu:'trishən] n sūʾ at-taghdhiya سوء التغذية

mammal ['maməl] n thadyī ثديي (thadyīyāt ثدييات)

man [man] n (pl men) rajul رجل (rijāl رجال)

manage ['manij] v 1. adāra أدار 2. taghallaba تغلب 3. najaḥa نجح (a; najāḥ نجاح)

management ['manijmənt] n idāra إدارة

manager ['manijə] n mudīr مدير (mudarā' مدراء)

managing director n mudīr ʿāmm مدير عام

maneuver [mə'nu:və] see **manoeuvre**

manhunt ['manhʌnt] *n* muṭārada
مطاردة

mania ['meiniə] *n* junūn جنون

maniac ['meiniak] *n* majnūn مجنون

manipulate [mə'nipyuleit] *v*
istaghalla استغل

mankind [man'kaind] *n* al-
basharīya البشرية

man-made [man'meid] *adj* iṣṭināʿī
إصطناعي

manner ['manə] *n* 1. ṭarīqa طريقة;
uslūb أسلوب 2. *see* manners

manners ['manəz] *pl* sulūk سلوك;
ādāb آداب; akhlāq أخلاق

manoeuvre [mə'nu:və] 1. *n* munāwara
مناورة (-āt) 2. *see* manoeuvres

manoeuvres [mə'nu:vəz] *pl (mil.)*
munāwarāt مناورات

manor ['manə] *n* bayt as-sayyid
بيت السيد; bayt dhū sha'n بيت ذو شأن

manpower ['manpauə] *n* al-qūwa
al-basharīya القوة البشرية

mansion ['manshən] *n* bayt kabīr
بيت كبير; qaṣr قصر (quṣūr قصور)

manslaughter ['manslo:tə] *n* al-
qatl ghayr al-mutaʿammid القتل غير
المتعمد

manual ['manyuəl] 1. *adj* yadawī
يدوي 2. *n* dalīl دليل (adilla أدلة)

manufacture [manyu'fakchə] 1. *n*
ṣanāʿa صناعة 2. *v* ṣanaʿa صنع (a;
ṣanʿ صنع)

manufacturer [manyu'fakchərə] *n*
ṣāniʿ صانع (ṣunnāʿ صناع)

manufacturing [manyu'fakchə-
ring] *n* ṣanāʿa صناعة

manure [mənyuə] *n* samād سماد
(asmida أسمدة)

manuscript ['manyuskript] *n*
makhṭūṭ مخطوط (-āt)

many ['meni] *adj* 1. kathīr كثير; ʿadīd
عديد 2. how many? kam? كم؟;
kam ʿadad? كم عدد؟

map [map] *n* kharīṭa خريطة (kharā'iṭ
خرائط)

marathon ['marəthən] *n* sibāq al-
marathōn سباق المرثون

marble ['ma:bəl] *n* rukhām رخام;
marmar مرمر

march [ma:ch] 1. *n* zaḥf زحف 2.
masīra مسيرة 2. *v (mil.)* zaḥafa زحف
(a; zaḥf زحف)

March [ma:ch] *n* māris مارس; ādhār
آذار

margarine [ma:jə'ri:n] *n* az-zubda
an-nabātīya الزبدة النباتية

margin ['ma:jin] *n* hāmish هامش
(hawāmish هوامش)

marginal ['ma:jinəl] *adj* hāmishī
هامشي

marijuana [mari'wa:nə] *n* ḥashīsh
حشيش

marine [mə'ri:n] 1. *adj* baḥrī بحري 2.
n jundī al-baḥrīya جندي البحرية
(junūd جنود)

maritime ['maritaim] *adj* baḥrī بحري

mark [ma:k] 1. *n* ʿalāma علامة (-āt) 2.
(acad.) ʿalāma علامة (-āt) 3. *v*
ʿallama علّم 4. *(acad.)* ṣaḥḥaḥa صحّح

marker ['ma:kə] *n* muṣaḥḥiḥ مصحّح

market ['ma:kit] 1. *n* sūq سوق
(aswāq أسواق) 2. *v* sawwaqa سوّق
3. *see* black market

marketing ['ma:kiting] *n* taswīq
تسويق

marriage ['marij] *n* ziwāj زواج

married ['marid] *adj* 1. a married
woman mutazawwija متزوّجة 2. a
married man mutazawwij متزوج

marry ['mari] *v* 1. to marry

zawwaja زَوَّجَ 2. **to get married**
tazawwaja تزوَّج

marsh [ma:sh] *n* mustanqaʿ مستنقع
(-āt)

martyr ['ma:tə] *n* shahīd شهيد
(shuhadā' شهداء)

marvellous ['ma:vələs] *adj* rā'iʿ رائع

masculine ['maskyulin] *adj*
mudhakkar مذكَّر

mask [ma:sk] 1. *n* qināʿ قناع (aqniʿa
أقنعة). 2. *v* qannaʿa قنَّع

mass [mas] 1. *adj* jamāhīrī جماهيري;
jamāʿī جماعي; ijmālī إجمالي; jumlī
جملي; ḥāshid حاشد 2. *n* kutla كتلة 3.
jumhūr جمهور (jamāhīr جماهير) 4.
(rel.) quddās قدَّاس (-āt) 5. *v* kattala
كتَّل; takattala تكتَّل; tajammaʿa
تجمَّع

massacre ['masəkə] 1. *n* madhbaḥa
مذبحة (madhābiḥ مذابح); majzara
مجزرة (majāzir مجازر) 2. *v* dhabaḥa
ذبح (a; dhabḥ ذبح)

massage ['masa:zh] 1. *n* tadlīk
تدليك 2. *v* dallaka دلَّك

massive ['masiv] *adj* ḍakhm ضخم

mass meeting *n* ijtimāʿ ḥāshid
إجتماع حاشد

mass production *n* al-intāj al-
jumlī الإنتاج الجملي

master ['ma:stə] 1. *n* sayyid سيِّد
(sāda سادة) 2. *v* tamakkana min
تمكَّن من 3. *see* **schoolmaster**

masterpiece ['ma:stəpi:s] *n* qiṭʿa
nādira قطعة نادرة

mat [mat] *n* ḥaṣīr حصير (ḥuṣur حصر);
sajjāda سجَّادة (sajājīd سجاجيد)

match [mach] 1. *n* mathīl مثيل
(muthul مثل); naẓīr نظير (nuẓarā'
نظراء) 2. *(spor.)* mubāra مباراة
(mubārayāt مباريات) 3. *v* tamāthala
تماثل; tasāwā تساوى

mate [meit] 1. *n* zawj زوج (azwāj
أزواج) 2. ṣadīq صديق (aṣdiqā'
أصدقاء) 3. *v* tazawwaja
تزوَّج

material [mə'tiəriəl] *n* 1. mādda
مادَّة (mawādd مواد) 2. qumāsh
قماش (aqmisha أقمشة) 3. *see*
materials

materialize [mə'tiəriəlaiz] *v* ẓahara
ظهر (a; ẓuhūr ظهور); bāna بان (i;
bayān بيان)

materials [mə'tiəriəlz] *pl* 1.
building materials mawādd bināʾ
مواد بناء 2. **raw materials** mawādd
khām مواد خام

maternal [mə'tə:nəl] *adj* umūmī
أمومي; ummī أمّي

maternity [mə'tə:nəti] *n* umūma
أمومة

maternity clinic *n* mustawṣaf al-
wilāda مستوصف الولادة

maths; mathematics [maths;
mathə'matiks] *n* riyāḍīyāt رياضيات

matinee ['matinei] *n* ʿarḍ baʿd aẓ-
ẓuhr عرض بعد الظهر; ḥafla mahārīya
حفلة مهارية

matrimonial [matri'məuniəl] *adj*
zawjī زوجي

matter ['matə] 1. *n* mas'ala مسألة
(masā'il مسائل); amr أمر (umūr
أمور) 2. mādda مادَّة (mawādd
مواد) 3. **What's the matter?** mā al-
amr? ما الأمر؟ 4. *v* ahamma أهمّ 5. **It
doesn't matter.** lā yuhimm لا يهم

mattress ['matris] *n* firāsh فراش
(furush فرش)

mature [mə'tyuə] 1. *adj* nāḍij ناضج
2. bāligh بالغ 3. *v* naḍija نضج (a;
naḍj نضج)

maximum ['maksiməm] *n/adj* aqṣā
أقصى

May [mei] *n* māyū مايو; nawwār نوار

may [mei] *v* (**might** [mait]) **1. May I come with you?** mumkin urāfiquka? ممكن أرافقك؟ **2. I may come with you.** qad urāfiquka قد أرافقك

maybe ['meibi] *adv* rubbamā ربما

mayonnaise [meyə'naiz] *n* ṣalṣat al-mayūnīz صلصة المايونيز

mayor [meə] *n* ra'īs al-baladīya رئيس البلدية; 'umda عمدة

me [mi:] *pronoun* -nī ني

meal [mi:l] *n* wajba وجبة (-āt)

mean [mi:n] **1.** *adj* ḥaqīr حقير **2.** bakhīl بخيل **3.** (fin.) wasaṭī وسطي **4.** *n* (fin.) wasaṭ وسط **5.** *v* (**meant**) 'anā عنى (i; 'any عني) **6.** qaṣada قصد (u; qaṣd قصد)

meaning ['mi:ning] *n* ma'nā معنى (ma'ānin معان)

meaningless ['mi:ningləs] *adj* bi lā ma'nā بلا معنى

means [mi:nz] *n* **1.** wasā'il وسائل **2.** imkānīyāt mālīya إمكانيات مالية

meant [ment] *see* **mean**

meantime ['mi:ntaim] *n* **in the meantime** fī ghuḍūn dhālik في غضون ذلك; fī dhālik al-waqt في ذلك الوقت

meanwhile ['mi:nwail] *adv* fī ghuḍūn dhālik في غضون ذلك

measure ['mezhə] **1.** *n* qiyās قياس (-āt); miqdār مقدار (maqādīr مقادير) **2.** *v* qāsa قاس (i; qiyās قياس) **3.** *see* **measures**

measurement ['mezhəmənt] *n* miqyās مقياس (maqāyīs مقاييس); maqās مقاس (-āt)

measures ['mezhəz] *pl* **to take measures** ittakhadha ijrā'āt اتخذ إجراءات

meat [mi:t] *n* laḥm لحم (luḥūm لحوم)

mechanic [mi'kanik] *n* mīkānīkī ميكانيكي (-yūn)

mechanical [mi'kanikəl] *adj* ālī آلي; mīkānī ميكاني

mechanics [mi'kaniks] *n* mīkānīka ميكانيكة

mechanism ['mekənizəm] *n* ālīya آلية (-āt)

medal ['medəl] *n* madalya مدلية (-āt)

media ['mi:diə] *n/pl* i'lām إعلام

mediaeval ['mi:diə] *see* **medieval**

mediate ['mi:dieit] *v* tawassaṭa توسط

mediation [mi:di'eishən] *n* tawassuṭ توسط

mediator ['mi:dieitə] *n* wasīṭ وسيط (wusaṭā' وسطاء)

medical ['medikəl] *adj* ṭibbī طبي

medical school *n* kullīyat aṭ-ṭibb كلية الطب

medication [medi'keishən] *n* dawā' دواء (adwiya أدوية)

medicinal [mə'disinəl] *adj* ṭibbī طبي

medicine ['medsən] *n* **1.** ṭibb طب **2.** dawā' دواء (adwiya أدوية)

medieval [me'di:vəl] *adj* muta'alliq bi متعلق بالقرون الوسطى 'l-qurūn al-wusṭā

mediocre [mi:di'əukə] *adj* mutawassiṭ al-jūda متوسط الجودة

Mediterranean Sea [meditə'reiniən 'si:] *n* al-baḥr al-abyaḍ al-mutawassiṭ البحر الأبيض المتوسط

medium ['mi:diəm] **1.** *adj* mutawassiṭ متوسط **2.** *n* mutawassiṭ متوسط **3.** (fin.) wasīṭ وسيط (wusaṭā' وسطاء)

medium-sized *adj* mutawassiṭ al-ḥajm متوسط الحجم

metaphor

meek [mi:k] *adj* حليم; khanū‘ خنوع

meet [mi:t] 1. *n (spor.)* sibāq سباق 2. *v* (met [met]) laqiya لقي (a; liqā’ لقاء)

meeting ['mi:ting] *n* 1. liqā’ لقاء 2. ijtimā‘ إجتماع (-āt) 3. maw‘id موعد (mawā‘īd مواعيد)

melody ['melədi] *n* laḥn لحن (alḥān ألحان)

melon(s) ['melən] *n* shammām شمّام *collective*

melt [melt] *v* dhāba ذاب (u; dhawb ذوب; dhawwaba ذوّب)

member ['membə] *n* ‘uḍw عضو (a‘ḍā’ أعضاء)

member of parliament *n* nā’ib barlamān نائب برلمان (nuwwāb نواب)

membership ['membəship] *n* ‘uḍwīya عضوية

memo [meməu] *see* **memorandum**

memoirs ['memua:z] *pl* mudhakkarāt مذكرات

memorable ['memərəbəl] *adj* lā yumkin nisyānuh لا يمكن نسيانه; bāriz بارز

memorandum [memə'randəm] *n* mudhakkara مذكرة (-āt)

memorial [mə'mo:riəl] *n* nuṣub tadhkārī نصب تذكاري

memorize ['meməraiz] *v* ḥafiẓa حفظ (a; ḥifẓ حفظ)

memory ['meməri] *n* 1. dhikrā ذكرى (dhikrayāt ذكريات) 2. dhākira ذاكرة

men [men] *see* **man**

menace ['menəs] 1. *n* tahdīd تهديد (-āt) 2. *v* haddada هدد

mend [mend] *v* aṣlaḥa أصلح

menstruation [menstru'eishən] *n* ḥiyāḍ حياض

mental ['mentəl] *adj* ‘aqlī عقلي

mental health *n* aṣ-ṣiḥḥa an-nafsānīya الصحة النفسانية

mental home *n* mustashfā ’l-amrāḍ al-‘aqlīya مستشفى الأمراض العقلية

mental hospital *n* mustashfā ’l-amrāḍ al-‘aqlīya مستشفى الأمراض العقلية

mentality [men'taləti] *n* ‘aqlīya عقلية; dhihnīya ذهنية

mention ['menshən] 1. *n* dhikr ذكر 2. *v* dhakara ذكر (u; dhikr ذكر)

menu ['menyu:] *n* qā’imat aṭ-ṭa‘ām قائمة الطعام

merchandise ['mə:shəndaiz] *n* sila‘ سلع

merchant ['mə:chənt] *n* tājir تاجر (tujjār تجار)

mercy ['mə:si] *n* raḥma رحمة

merely ['miəli] *adv* laysa illā ليس إلا; laysa ghayr ليس غير; fa ḥasb فحسب; faqaṭ فقط

merge [mə:j] *v* indamaja اندمج

merit ['merit] 1. *n* mīza ميزة (-āt) 2. *v* istaḥaqqa استحق; ista‘hala استأهل

merry ['meri] *adj* mariḥ مرح

mesh [mesh] *n* shabaka شبكة (-āt)

mess [mes] *n* fawḍā فوضى

message ['mesij] *n* risāla رسالة (rasā’il رسائل)

messenger ['mesinjə] *n* rasūl رسول (rusul رسل)

messy ['mesi] *adj* fawḍawī فوضوي

met [met] *see* **meet**

metal ['metəl] 1. *adj* ma‘dinī معدني 2. *n* ma‘din معدن (ma‘ādin معادن)

metaphor ['metəfo:] *n* majāz مجاز

meteor ['mi:tiə] *n* shihāb شهاب
(shuhub شهب); nayzak نيزك
(nayāzik نيازك)

meter ['mi:tə] *n* 1. ʿaddād عداد 2. *see*
metre

method ['methəd] *n* ṭarīqa طريقة
(ṭuruq طرق); uslūb أسلوب (asālīb
أساليب)

meticulous [mi'tikyuləs] *adj* daqīq
دقيق

metre ['mi:tə] *n* mitr متر (amtār
أمتار)

metro ['metrəu] *n* mitrō al-anfāq
مترو الأنفاق

metropolis [mə'tropəlis] *n* ʿāṣima
عاصمة (ʿawāsim عواصم)

mice [mais] *see* mouse

microphone ['maikrəfəun] *n*
mīkrūfōn ميكروفون (-āt)

microscope ['maikrəskəup] *n*
mīkrūskōb ميكروسكوب

mid [mid] *adj* muntaṣif منتصف

midday [mid'dei] *n* muntaṣif an-
nahār منتصف النهار

middle ['midəl] 1. *adj* mutawassiṭ
متوسط 2. *n* wasaṭ وسط (awsāṭ
أوساط); wasīṭ وسيط (wusaṭā'
وسطاء) 3. in the middle of bayna
بين

middle-age *n* muntaṣif al-ʿumr
منتصف العمر

middle-aged *adj* muntaṣif al-ʿumr
منتصف العمر

middle class *n* aṭ-ṭabaqa al-wusṭā
الطبقة الوسطى

Middle East *n* ash-sharq al-awsaṭ
الشرق الأوسط

midnight ['midnait] *n* muntaṣif al-
layl منتصف الليل

midst [midst] *n* in the midst of fī
wasaṭ min في وسط من

midsummer [mid'sʌmə] *n*
muntaṣif aṣ-ṣayf منتصف الصيف

midway [mid'wei] *adv* muntaṣif aṭ-
ṭarīq منتصف الطريق

midweek [mid'wi:k] *n* muntaṣif al-
usbūʿ منتصف الأسبوع

midwife ['midweif] *n* qābila قابلة
(-āt); muwallida مولدة (-āt)

might [mait] 1. *n* qūwa قوة; jabr جبر
2. *see* may

mighty ['maiti] *adj* qawī قوي; jabbār
جبار

migraine ['maigrein; 'mi:grein] *n*
ṣudāʿ niṣfī صداع نصفي

migrant ['maigrənt] *n* muhājir مهاجر
(-ūn)

migrate [mai'greit] *v* hājara هاجر

migration [mai'greishən] *n* hijra
هجرة

mild [maild] *adj* ḥalīm حليم; laṭīf
لطيف

mile [mail] *n* mīl ميل (amyāl أميال)

militant ['militənt] *n* munāḍil مناضل
(-ūn)

military ['militri] 1. *adj* ʿaskarī
عسكري 2. *n* al-qūwāt al-musallaḥa
القوات المسلحة

milk [milk] *n* ḥalīb حليب; laban
لبن

millennium [mi'leniəm] *n* alfīya
ألفية (-āt)

million ['milyən] *n* malyūn مليون
(malāyīn ملايين)

millionaire [milyə'neə] *n* malyūnīr
مليونير; ṣāḥib malāyīn صاحب ملايين

mind [maind] 1. *n* ʿaql عقل 2. to
change one's mind ghayyara
ra'yah غير رأيه 3. *v* raʿā رعى (i;
raʿy رعي); iʿtanā bi اعتنى ب
4. mānaʿa مانع 5. Never mind!

lā ba's! ‏لا بأس!‏ 6. **I don't mind!**
lā umāni‛! ‏لا أمانع!‏ 7. **Mind your
own business!** lā tatadakhkhal!
‏لا تتدخل!‏

mind-altering adj 1. mu'aththir li
'l-aql ‏مؤثر للعقل‏ 2. **mind-altering
drugs** al-mukhaddarāt al-
mu'aththira ‏المخدرات المؤثرة‏

mindful ['maindfəl] adj ḥadhir ‏حذر‏

mine [main] 1. pronoun lī ‏لي‏ 2. n
manjam ‏منجم‏ (manājim ‏مناجم‏) 3.
(mil.) laghm ‏لغم‏ (alghām ‏ألغام‏) 4. v
istakhraja ‏استخرج‏; ‛addana ‏عدن‏ 5.
(mil.) laghama ‏لغم‏ (a; laghm ‏لغم‏)

mine detector n jihāz al-kashf ‛an
al-alghām ‏جهاز الكشف عن الألغام‏

mine disposal n at-takhalluṣ min
al-alghām ‏التخلص من الألغام‏

miner ['mainə] n ‛āmil al-manājim
‏عامل المناجم‏

minefield ['mainfi:ld] n ḥaql al-
alghām ‏حقل الألغام‏

mineral ['minərəl] 1. adj ma‛dinī
‏معدني‏ 2. n ma‛din ‏معدن‏ (ma‛ādin
‏معادن‏)

mineral water n mā' ma‛dinī
‏ماء معدني‏

mini ['mini] adj saghīr ‏صغير‏

miniature ['minəchə] adj
musaghghar ‏مصغر‏

minibus ['minibʌs] n ḥāmilat
rukkāb ṣaghīra ‏حاملة ركاب صغيرة‏

minimize ['minimaiz] v qallala ‏قلل‏

minimum ['miniməm] adj/n al-ḥadd
al-adnā ‏الحد الأدنى‏

mining ['maining] 1. adj ta‛dīnī
‏تعديني‏ 2. n ta‛dīn ‏تعدين‏

minister ['ministə] n 1. (pol.) wazīr
‏وزير‏ (wuzarā' ‏وزراء‏) 2. (rel.) rā‛ī
kanīsa ‏راعي كنيسة‏

ministry ['ministri] n wizāra ‏وزارة‏ (-āt)

minor ['mainə] 1. adj ghayr hāmm
‏غير هام‏; ghayr khaṭīr ‏غير خطير‏ 2. n
qāṣir ‏قصير‏ (-ūn)

minority [mai'norəti] n 1. aqallīya
‏أقلية‏ (-āt) 2. **ethnic minority**
aqallīya ‛irqīya ‏أقلية عرقية‏

mint [mint] 1. n nā‛nā‛ ‏نعناع‏ 2. (fin.)
dār sakk al-‛umla ‏دار سك العملة‏ 3. v
(fin.) sakka ‏سك‏ (u; sakk ‏سك‏)

minus ['mainəs] prep nāqiṣ ‏ناقص‏

minute [mai'nyu:t] adj saghīr jiddan
‏صغير جداً‏

minute ['minit] n daqīqa ‏دقيقة‏
(daqā'iq ‏دقائق‏)

minutes ['minits] pl **minutes of a
meeting** waqā'i‛ ijtimā‛ ‏وقائع إجتماع‏

miracle ['mirəkəl] n mu‛jiza ‏معجزة‏
(-āt)

mirror ['mirə] n mir'āh ‏مرآة‏ (marā'in
‏مراء‏; marāyā ‏مرايا‏)

misbehave [misbi'heiv] v sā'a at-
taṣarruf ‏ساء التصرف‏ (i)

misbehaviour, (US) **misbe-
havior** [misbi'heiviə] n saw' at-
taṣarruf ‏سوء التصرف‏

miscalculate [mis'kalkyuleit] v
akhṭa'a al-ḥisāb ‏أخطأ الحساب‏

miscarriage [mis'karij] n (med.)
ijhāḍ ‏إجهاض‏

miscarry [mis'kari] v (med.) ajhaḍa
‏أجهض‏

miscellaneous [misə'leiniəs] adj
mutanawwi‛ ‏متنوع‏

mischievous ['mischivəs] adj
shaqī ‏شقي‏; la‛ūb ‏لعوب‏

miserable ['mizrəbəl] adj bā'is
‏بائس‏ (bu'asā' ‏بؤساء‏)

misery ['mizəri] n bu's ‏بؤس‏

misfire [mis'faiəd] v akhfaqa ‏أخفق‏

misfortune [mis'fo:chu:n] *n* sū' al-
ḥaẓẓ سوء الحظ

misjudge [mis'jʌj] *v* akhṭa'a at-
taqdīr أخطأ التقدير

mismanagement [mis'manijmənt]
n sū' al-idāra سوء الإدارة

misplace [mis'pleis] *v* ḍayya'a ضيّع;
aḍā'a أضاع

misprint [mis'print] *n* khaṭa'
maṭba'ī خطأ مطبعي (akhṭā' أخطاء)

miss [mis] **1.** *n* 'adm iṣāba عدم إصابة;
ikhfāq إخفاق **2. Miss** ānisa آنسة
(-āt) **3.** *v* iftaqada افتقد **4. They
missed the plane.** ta'akhkharū 'an
aṭ-ṭā'ira تأخروا عن الطائرة

missile ['misail] *n* ṣārūkh صاروخ
(ṣawārīkh صواريخ)

missing ['mising] *adj* mafqūd مفقود;
ḍā'i' ضائع

mission ['mishən] *n* **1.** mahamma
مهمة (mahāmm); muhimma مهمة
(-āt) **2.** (*rel.*) irsālīya tabshīrīya
إرسالية تبشيرية **3. diplomatic
mission** bu'tha diblomāsīya
بعثة دبلوماسية

mist [mist] *n* sadīm سديم (sudum
سدم); ḍabāb دباب

mistake [mi'steik] **1.** *n* khaṭa' خطأ
(akhṭā' أخطاء); ghalaṭ غلط (aghlāṭ
أغلاط) **2. by mistake** khaṭa'an خطأ
3. to make a mistake akhṭa'a أخطأ
4. *v* (mistook, mistaken) akhṭa'a
أخطأ

mistaken [mi'steikən] *adj* **1.**
mukhṭi' مخطئ **2.** *see* mistake

mister ['mistə] *see* Mr

mistook ['mistuk] *see* mistake

mistreatment [mis'tri:tmənt] *n*
sū' al-mu'āmala سوء المعاملة

mistress ['mistris] *n* **1.** 'ashīqa
عاشقة (-āt) **2. schoolmistress**
mudarrisa مدرسة (-āt) **3.** *see* Mrs

mistrust [mis'trʌst] **1.** *n* irtiyāb
إرتياب; shakk شك **2.** *v* irtāba ارتاب;
shakka شك (u; shakk شك)

misty ['misti] *adj* sadīmī سديمي;
ḍabābī دبابي

misunderstand [misʌndə'stand] *v*
(**misunderstood**) sā'a al-fahm
ساء الفهم; sā'a at-tafāhum ساء التفاهم

misunderstanding [misʌndə-
standing] *n* sū' al-fahm سوء الفهم;
sū' at-tafāhum سوء التفاهم

misuse [mis'yu:z] *v* sā'a al-isti'māl
ساء الإستعمال

mix [miks] *v* mazaja مزج (u; mazj
مزج); khalaṭa خلط (i; khalṭ خلط)

mixer ['miksə] *n* khallāṭ خلاط (-āt)

mixture ['mikschə] *n* mazij مزج;
khalīṭ خليط

mix-up *n* irtibāk إرتباك; tashwīsh
تشويش

moan [məun] **1.** *n* anīn أنين **2.** *v* anna
أنّ (i; anīn أنين)

mob [mob] *n* ghawghā' غوغاء

mobile ['məubail] *adj* mutaḥarrik
متحرك; qābil li 'l-ḥaraka
قابل للحركة

mobile phone *n* tilifūn naqqāl
تلفون النقّال; tilifūn maḥmūl
تلفون محمول; tilifūn khalawī
تلفون خلوي

mobility [məu'biləti] *n* qābilīya li 'l-
ḥaraka قابلية للحركة

mock [mok] *v* haza'a min/bi
هزأ من\ب (a; haz' هزء); sakhira
min/bi سخر من\ب (a; sukhr سخر)

mode [məud] *n* uslūb أسلوب (asālīb
أساليب)

model ['modəl] **1.** *n* namūdhaj نموذج

(-āt) **2. fashion model** ʿāriḍ al-azyā' عارض للأزياء **3.** v ʿaraḍa 'l-azyā' عرض الأزياء (a; ʿarḍ عرض)

modem ['məudem] n mōdem مودم; jihāz wasīṭ جهاز وسيط

moderate [modəret] adj muʿtadil معتدل

modern ['modən] adj ḥadīh حديث; muʿāṣir معاصر

modernize ['modənaiz] v ḥaddatha حدث; jaddada جدد

modest ['modist] adj mutawāḍiʿ متواضع

modesty ['modisti] n tawāḍuʿ تواضع

modification [modifi'keishən] n taʿdīl تعديل (-āt)

modify ['modifai] v ʿaddala عدل

moist [moist] adj raṭb رطب

moisture ['moischə] n ruṭūba رطوبة

moisturize ['moischəraiz] v raṭṭaba رطب

moisturizing cream ['moischə] n mashūq tajmīl li 'l-jild مسحوق تجميل للجلد

mold [məuld] see **mould**

molest [mo'lest] v iʿtadā ʿalā اعتدى على

moment ['məumənt] n **1.** laḥẓa لحظة (laḥaẓāt لحظات) **2. at the moment** al-'ān الآن **3. in a moment** baʿd laḥẓa بعد لحظة **4. for the moment** al-'ān الآن

momentary ['məuməntri] adj ānī آني; khāṭif خاطف

momentum [məu'mentum] n qūwat al-dafʿ قوة الدفع

monarch ['monək] n malik ملك (mulūk ملو)

monarchy ['monəki] n malakīya ملكية

Monday ['mʌndei] n (yawm) al-ithnayn (يوم) الإثنين

monetary ['mʌnitri] adj naqdī نقدي

money ['mʌni] n naqd نقد

monitor ['monitə] n (tel.) shāsha شاشة (-āt)

monkey ['mʌngki] n qird قرد (qurūd قرود)

mono- ['monəu] adj wāḥid واحد

monopoly [mə'nopəli] n iḥtikār إحتكار (-āt)

monotonous [mə'notənəs] adj mumill ممل

monster ['monstə] n waḥsh وحش (wuḥūsh وحوش)

month [mʌnth] n shahr شهر (shuhūr شهور; ashhur أشهر)

monthly ['mʌnthli] adj shahrī شهري

monument [monyumənt] n nuṣub tadhkārī نصب تذكاري

mood [mu:d] n **1. a good mood** mizāj jayyid مزاج جيد **2. a bad mood** mizāj sayyi' مزاج سيئ **3. I am in the mood to...** mizājī an... مزاجي أن...

moon [mu:n] n qamar قمر (aqmār أقمار)

moonlight ['mu:nlait] n ḍaw' al-qamar ضوء القمر

moral ['morəl] adj **1.** akhlāqī أخلاقي **2.** see **morals**

morale [mə'ra:l] n maʿnawīyāt معنويات

morality [mə'raləti] n akhlāqīya أخلاقية

morals ['morəlz] n akhlāq أخلاق

more [mo:] adj/adv **1.** akthar أكثر **2. more or less** taqrīban تقريباً **3. more than** akthar min أكثر من **4. more than ever** akthar min ayy waqt maḍā أكثر من أي وقت مضى

moreover [mo:'rəuvə] ʿilāwatan
علاوةً على ذلك ʿalā dhālik

morning ['mo:ning] n 1. ṣabāḥ صباح
2. **Good morning!** ṣabāḥ al-
khayr! !صباح الخير

mortal ['mo:təl] adj/n fānin فان

mortality [mo:'taləti] n fanā' فناء

mortgage ['mo:gij] n qarḍ li 'l-
ʿaqqārāt قرض للعقارات

mortuary ['mo:chəri] n ghurfat al-
amwāt غرفة الأموات; mashraḥa
مشرحة

Moslem ['mʌzlim] 1. adj muslim
مسلم 2. n muslim مسلم (-ūn)

mosque [mosk] n jāmiʿ جامع
(jawāmiʿ جوامع); masjid مسجد
(masājid مساجد)

mosquito(es) [mos'ki:təu] n baʿūḍ
بعوض ; collective nāmūs collective
ناموس

most [məust] adj/adv 1. muʿaẓẓam
معظم 2. akthar أكثر 3. **for the
most part** ghāliban غالباً 4. **to
make the most of** intahaza al-
furṣa انتهز الفرصة

mostly ['məustli] adv ghāliban غالباً;
fi 'l-ghālib في الغالب

motel [məutel] n nazl نزل (nuzūl
نزول)

mother ['mʌdhə] n umm أم
(ummahāt أمهات)

mother-in-law n ḥamāh حماة
(ḥamawāt حموات)

mother-tongue n al-lughat al-
umm اللغة الأم

motion ['məushən] n 1. ḥaraka حركة
2. (pol.) iqtirāḥ إقتراح

motionless ['məushnləs] adj sākin
ساكن

motivate ['məutiveit] v shajjaʿa شجّع

motivation [məuti'veishən] n ḥāfiz
حافز (ḥawāfiz حوافز)

motive ['məutiv] n bāʿith باعث
(bawāʿith بواعث)

motor ['məutə] n muḥarrik محرك
(-āt)

motorbike ['məutəbaik] n darrāja
nārīya دراجة نارية

motorcycle ['məutəsaikəl] n darrāja
nārīya دراجة نارية

motorist ['məutərist] n sāʾiq سائق
(-ūn)

motor scooter n darrāja nārīya
دراجة نارية

motorway ['məutəwei] n otostrād
أتوستراد (-āt)

mould [məuld] 1. n qālib قالب
(qawālib قوالب) 2. ʿafan عفن 3. v
ʿafina (a; ʿafn عفن) عفن

mound [maund] n kawma كومة
(akwām أكوام)

mount [maunt] 1. n rakūb ركوب 2. v
rakiba ركب (a; rukūb ركوب)

mountain ['mauntin] n jabal جبل
(jibāl جبال)

mountaineer [maunti'niə] n
mutasalliq al-jibāl متسلق الجبال
(-ūn)

mountainous ['mauntinəs] adj
jabalī جبلي

mourner ['mo:nə] n nādib نادب
(nawādib نوادب)

mourning ['mo:ning] n ḥidād حداد;
nadb ندب

mouse [maus] n (pl mice [mais])
faʾra فأرة (collective faʾr فأر; pl
fiʾrān فئران)

moustache [məs'ta:sh] n shārib شارب
(shawārib شوارب)

mouth [mauth] n fam فم (afwāh
أفواه)

mouthful ['mauthful] n ʿibāra ṣaʿb al-lafẓ عبارة صعب اللفظ

movable ['muːvəbəl] adj manqūl منقول (āt-)

move [muːv] 1. n dawr al-lāʿib دور اللاعب 2. khaṭwa خطوة (khaṭawāt خطوات) 3. v naqala نقل (u; naql نقل); intaqala انتقل 4. ḥarraka حرّك 5. athāra al-mashāʿir أثار المشاعر

movement ['muːvmənt] n ḥaraka حركة (āt-)

movie; movies ['muːvi; 'muːviz] n film فلم (aflām أفلام)

movie theatre n sīnama سينما (sīnimahāt سينمهات)

moving ['muːving] adj muʾaththir مؤثر

mow [məu] v (mowed, mown) qaṣṣa al-ʿushb قص العشب (u; qaṣṣ قص)

MP (= member of parliament) n nāʾib barlamān نائب برلمان (nuwwāb نوّاب)

m.p.h. (= miles per hour) mīl fi 's-sāʿa ميل في الساعة

Mr (= mister) ['mistə] as-sayyid السيد

Mrs (= mistress) ['misiz] as-sayyida السيدة

Mt see mount

much [mʌch] adj/adv 1. kathīr كثير 2. kathīran أ كثيراً; bi kathīr بكثير 3. much more akthar bi kathīr أكثر بكثير 4. how much? kam? كم؟

mud [mʌd] n ṭīn طين; waḥl وحل

muddle ['mʌdəl] n irtibāk إرتباك; tashawwush تشوّش; lakhbaṭa لخبطة

muddy ['mʌdi] adj waḥlī وحلي

mug [mʌg] 1. n qadaḥ قدح (aqdāḥ أقداح) 2. v sariqa bi ʿunf fī makān ʿāmm سرق بعنف في مكان عام (a; sarq سرق)

mugger ['mʌgə] n ṣāriq سارق (ūn-)

multi- ['mʌlti] adj mutaʿaddid al- متعدد الـ

multilingual [mʌlti'lingwəl] adj mutaʿaddid al-lughāt متعدد اللغات

multimedia [mʌlti'miːdia] n taʿaddud wasāʾil al-iʿlām تعدد وسائل الإعلام

multinational [mʌlti'nashənəl] adj mutaʿaddid al-jinsīyāt متعدد الجنسيات

multi-party [mʌlti'paːti] adj mutaʿaddid al-aḥzāb متعدد للأحزاب

multiple ['mʌltipəl] adj mutaʿaddid متعدد

multiplication [mʌltipli'keishən] n ḍarb ضرب

multiply ['mʌltiplai] v ḍāʿafa ضاعف

multi-racial [mʌlti'reishəl] adj mutaʿaddid al-ajnās متعدد الأجناس

multistorey, (US) **multistory** [mʌlti'stoːri] adj mutaʿaddid al-ṭabaqāt متعدد الطبقات

multitude ['mʌltityuːd] n jumhūr جمهور; (jamāhīr جماهير); ḥashd حشد (ḥushūd حشود)

mum [mʌm] n māma مامة

mummy ['mʌmi] n māma مامة

municipal [myuː'nisipl] adj baladī بلدي

municipality [myuːnisi'paləti] n baladīya بلدية (āt-)

murder ['məːdə] 1. n al-qatl al-ʿamd القتل العمد 2. v qatala bi 'l-ʿamd قتل بالعمد

murderer ['məːdərə] n qātil bi 'l-ʿamd قاتل بالعمد

murderess ['məːdəris] n qātila bi 'l-ʿamd قاتلة بالعمد

murmur ['məːmə] v hamasa همس (i; hams همس)

muscle ['mʌsəl] n ʿaḍala عضلة (āt-)

museum [myu:'ziəm] *n* mathaf
(matāhif) متاحف متحف

mushroom ['mʌshrum] *n* futr
فطر *collective*

music ['myu:zik] *n* mūsīqā موسيقى

musical ['myu:zikəl] 1. *adj* mūsīqī
موسيقي 2. *n* masrahīya mūsīqīya
مسرحية موسيقية

musician [myu:'zishən] *n* mūsīqār
موسيقار

Muslim ['mʌzlim] 1. *adj* muslim
مسلم 2. *n* muslim مسلم (-ūn)

must [məst; mʌst] *v* yajibu يجب

mustache ['məsta:sh] *see* **moustache**

mutilate ['myu:tileit] *v* shawwaha
شوه

mutilation [myu:ti'leishən] *n*
tashwīh تشويه

mutiny ['myu:tini] 1. *n* tamarrud
تمرد; 2. *v* tamarrada عصيان işyān

(عصيان işyān (i; تمرد 'aşā عصى

mutter ['mʌtə] *v* hamasa همس (i;
hams همس)

mutton ['mʌtən] *n* lahm ad-da'n
لحم الضأن

mutual ['myu:chuəl] *adj* mutabādal
متبادل

my [mai] -ī ي

myself [mai'self] nafsī نفسي

mysterious [mis'tiəriəs] *adj*
ghāmiḍ غامض

mystery ['mistəri] *n* lughz لغز
(alghāz الألغاز)

mystify ['mistifai] *n* hayyara حيّر

myth [mith] *n* ustūra أسطورة (asātīr
أساطير)

mythical ['mithikəl] *adj* ustūrī
أسطوري

mythology [mi'tholəji] *n* 'ilm al-
asātīr علم الأساطير

N

nail [neil] 1. *n* mismār مسمار
(masāmīr مسامير) 2. ẓufr ظفر
(aẓāfir أظافر) 3. *v* sammara سمر

naive [nai'i:v] *adj* sādhij ساذج

naivety; naivete [nai'i:viti] *n*
sadhāja سذاجة

naked ['neikid] *adj* 'ārin عار; 'uryān
عريان

name [neim] 1. *n* ism اسم (asmā'
أسماء) 2. *v* sammā سمى

namely ['neimli] *adv* ay أي

nanny ['nani] *n* murabbīyat aṭfāl
مربية أطفال

nap [nap] *n* ghafwa غفوة (-āt)

nappy ['napi] *n* hifāẓat al-aṭfāl
حفاظة الأطفال

narcotic [na:'kotik] 1. *adj*
mukhaddir مخدر 2. *n* mukhaddir
مخدر (-āt)

narrate [nəˈreit] *n* rawā روى (i; riwāya رواية)

narration [nəˈreishən] *n* riwāya رواية (-āt)

narrator [nəˈreitə] *n* rawin راوٍ (rawiyūn راويون; ruwāh رواة)

narrow [ˈnarəu] *adj* ḍayyiq ضيق

narrow-minded *adj* ḍayyiq al-ufuq ضيق الأفق

nasty [ˈnaːsti] *adj* karīh كريه; radīʾ al-qalb ردىء القلب; ghalīẓ al-qalb غليظ القلب

natal [ˈneitəl] *adj* wilādī ولادي

nation [ˈneishən] *n* **1.** umma أمة (umam أمم) **2.** shaʿb شعب (shuʿūb شعوب)

national [ˈnashənəl] **1.** *adj* qawmī قومي **2.** *n* muwāṭin مواطن (-ūn)

nationalism [ˈnashnəlizm] *n* qawmīya قومية (-āt)

nationalist [ˈnashnəlist] **1.** *adj* qawmī قومي **2.** *n* qawmī قومي (-yūn)

nationality [nashəˈnaliti] *n* jinsīya جنسية (-āt)

nationalization [nashnəlaiˈzeishən] *n* taʾmīm تأميم

nationalize [ˈnashnəlaiz] *v* ammama أمم

nationwide [neishənˈwaid] *adv* ʿalā niṭāq al-waṭan kulluh على نطاق الوطن كله

native [ˈneitiv] **1.** *adj* aṣlī أصلي; maḥallī محلي **2.** *n* ibn al-balad ابن البلد

native country *n* al-waṭan al-aṣlī الوطن الأصلي

natural [ˈnachrəl] *adj* ṭabīʿī طبيعي

naturalize [ˈnachrəlaiz] *v* jannasa جنس

naturally [ˈnachrəli] *adv* **1.** ṭabʿan طبعاً; bi ʾṭ-ṭabʿ بالطبع **2.** fiṭratan فطرة

nature [ˈneichə] *n* **1.** ṭabīʿa طبيعة **2.** fiṭra فطرة **3. human nature** al-fiṭrat al-insānīya الفطرة الإنسانية

naughty [ˈnoːti] *adj* shaqī شقي

nausea [ˈnoːsiə] *n* dawkha دوخة

nauseous [ˈnoːsiəs] *adj* dāʾikh دائخ

nautical [ˈnoːtikəl] *adj* milāḥī ملاحي; baḥrī بحري

naval [ˈneivəl] *adj* baḥrī بحري

navigation [naviˈgeishən] *n* milāḥa ملاحة

navigator [ˈnavigeitə] *n* mallāḥ ملاح (-ūn)

navy [ˈneivi] *n* al-qūwāt al-baḥrīya القوات البحرية

near; near to [ˈniə] **1.** *adj* qarīb (min) قريب (من); bi ʾl-qurb min بالقرب من **2.** *adv* qarīban تقريباً; taqrīban قريباً **3. to draw near** qarraba قرب **4.** *prep* qurb قرب

nearby [niəˈbai] *adv* qarīb قريب

nearly [ˈniəli] *adv* taqrīban تقريباً

nearness [ˈniənis] *n* qurb قرب

near-sighted *adj* qaṣīr an-naẓar قصير النظر

neat [niːt] *adj* murattab مرتب

necessarily *adv* ḍurūrīyan ضرورياً

necessary [ˈnesəsəri] *adj* **1.** ḍurūrī ضروري **2. it is necessary that...** yajib an... يجب أن...

necessity [niˈsesəti] *n* ḍurūra ضرورة (-āt)

neck [nek] *n* ʿunq عنق (aʿnāq أعناق); raqaba رقبة (-āt)

necklace ['neklis] *n* ʿiqd عقد (ʿuqūd عقود)

need [niːd] **1.** *n* ḥāja حاجة (-āt); ḍurūra ضرورة (-āt) **2. in need** faqīr فقير; maḥrūm محروم **3.** *v* iḥtāja ilā احتاج إلى **4. You need to ...** ʿalayka an... عليك أن...

needle ['niːdəl] *n* ibra إبرة (ibar إبر)

needless ['niːdlis] *adj* ghayr ḍurūrī غير ضروري

needy ['niːdi] *adj* faqīr فقير; maḥrūm محروم

negative ['negətiv] **1.** *adj* salbī سلبي **2.** *n* salbī سلبي

neglect [ni'glekt] **1.** *n* ihmāl إهمال **2.** *v* ahmala أهمل

negligence ['neglijəns] *n* ihmāl إهمال

negotiate [ni'gəushieit] *v* tafāwaḍa تفاوض

negotiation [nigəushi'eishən] *n* mufawāḍa مفاوضة (-āt)

negotiator [ni'gəushieitə] *n* mufāwiḍ مفاوض (-ūn)

neighbour, *(US)* **neighbor** ['neibə] *n* jār جار (jīrān جيران)

neighbourhood, *(US)* **neighborhood** ['neibəhud] *n* ḥayy حي (aḥyāʾ أحياء)

neighbouring, *(US)* **neighboring** ['neibəring] *adj* mujāwir مجاور

neither ['naidhə; 'niːdhə] **1.** wa lā ولا **2.** kilā al-amrayn كلا الأمرين **3.** **neither nor** lā.... wa lā لا ... ولا

neo- [niːəu] *adj* jadīd جديد

neon ['niːyon] *adj* niyūn نيون

nephew ['nefyuː] *n* ibn akh ابن أخ; ibn ukht ابن أخت

nerve [nəːv] *n* ʿaṣab عصب (aʿṣāb أعصاب)

nervous ['nəːvəs] *adj* ʿaṣabī عصبي; mutawattir al-aʿṣāb متوتر الأعصاب

nervousness ['nəːvəsnis] *n* ʿaṣabīya عصبية; tawattur al-aʿṣāb توتر الأعصاب

nest [nest] *n* ʿushsh عش (aʿshāsh أعشاش)

net [net] **1.** *adj (fin.)* ṣāfin صاف **2.** *n* shabaka شبكة (-āt)

Netherlands ['nedhələndz] *n/pl* holanda هولاندا

network ['netwəːk] **1.** *n* shabaka شبكة (-āt) **2. communications network** shabakat ittiṣālāt شبكة إتصالات

neutral ['nyuːtrəl] *adj* muḥāyid محايد; ḥiyādī حيادي

never ['nevə] *adv* **1.** abadan أبداً; qaṭṭ قط **2. never mind!** lā baʾs! لا بأس!

never-ending [nevə'ending] *adj* lā yantahī لا ينتهي

nevermore [nevə'moː] *adv* abadan أبداً

nevertheless [nevədhə'les] *conj* wa maʿa dhālik ومع ذلك; wa raghma dhālik ورغم ذلك

new [nyuː] *adj* **1.** jadīd جديد **2. brand new** jadīd tamāman جديد تماماً

newborn ['nyuːbon] *adj* mawlūd jadīd مولود جديد

newcomer ['nyuːkʌmə] *n* qādim jadīd قادم جديد

newly ['nyuːli] **1.** *adj* jadīd جديد **2.** *adv* min jadīd من جديد

news [nyuːz] *n* akhbār أخبار; anbāʾ أنباء

news agency *n* wikālat anbā' وكالة أنباء

newscast ['nyu:zca:st] *n* nashrat al-akhbār نشرة الأخبار

newscaster; newsreader ['nju:zca:stə; -ri:də] *n* mudhī' nashrat al-akhbār مذيع نشرة الأخبار

newspaper ['nyu:speipə] *n* jarīda جريدة (jarā'id جرائد)

newsstand ['nyu:zstand] *n* kushk aṣ-ṣuḥuf كشك الصحف

New Year [nyu:'yiːə] *n* ra's al-sana رأس السنة

New Year's Eve *n* laylat ra's al-sana ليلة رأس السنة

New Zealand [nyu:'zi:lənd] *n* nyū zīlanda نيو زيلاندا

next [nekst] **1.** *adj* qādim قادم **2.** next to janb جنب

nice [nais] *adj* laṭīf لطيف; ḥilw حلو

nick [nik] in the nick of time fī ākhir laḥẓa في آخر لحظة

nickname ['nikneim] *n* laqab لقب (alqāb ألقاب)

niece [ni:s] *n* bint akh بنت أخ; bint ukht بنت أخت

night [nait] *n* **1.** layla ليلة (layālin ليال) **2. at night** laylan ليلاً **3. good night!** tuṣbiḥ ʿalā khayr! تصبح على خير! **4. to spend the night** bāta بات (i; mabīt مبيت)

nightclub *n* malhan laylī ملهى ليلي

nightly ['naitli] *adv* kull layla كل ليلة

nightmare ['naitmeə] *n* kābūs كابوس (kawābīs كوابيس)

night school *n* kullīya masā'iya كلية مسائية

night shift *n* nawbat al-layl نوبة الليل

nil [nil] *n* ṣifr صفر; lā shay' لا شيء

nine [nain] *n/adj* tisʿa تسعة

nineteen [nain'ti:n] *n/adj* tisʿat ʿashar تسعة عشر

nineteenth [nain'ti:nth] *adj* tāsiʿ ʿashar تاسع عشر

ninetieth ['naintiəth] *adj* at-tisʿūn التسعون

ninety ['nainti] *n/adj* tisʿūn تسعون

ninth [nainth] *adj* tāsiʿ تاسع

nip [nip] *v* qaraṣa قرص (u; qarṣ قرص)

nipple ['nipəl] *n* ḥalama حلمة (-āt)

no [nəu] **1.** lā لا; kallā كلا **2.** *adj* lā لا

nobility [nəu'biləti] *n* **1.** nubl نبل **2.** al-ashrāf الأشراف

noble ['nəubəl] *adj* **1.** nabīl نبيل **2.** sharīf شريف

nobody ['nəubədi] lā aḥad لا أحد

nod [nod] *v* awma'a bi 'r-ra's أومأ بالرأس

noise [noiz] *n* ḍajja ضجة; ḍajīj ضجيج

noiseless ['noizlis] *adj* ṣāmit صامت

noisy ['noizi] *adj* ḍājj ضاج

no longer [nəu'lɔngə] *adv* mā ʿāda ما عاد

nomination [nomi'neishən] *n* tarshīḥ ترشيح

non- [non] ghayr غير; ʿadm عدم

none [nʌn] **1.** lā aḥad لا أحد; lā shay' لا شيء **2.** al-batta البتة

nonetheless [nʌndhə'les] *adv* wa maʿa dhālik ومع ذلك; wa raghma dhālik ورغم ذلك

nonsense ['nonsəns] *n* hurā' هراء

non-stop [non'stop] *adj/adv* bidūn tawaqquf بدون توقف

noodles ['nu:dəlz] *n* maʿkarūna shiʿrīya ṣīnīya معكرونة شعرية صينية

noon [nu:n] *n* ẓuhr ظهر

no one ['nəuwʌn] lā aḥad لا أحد

nor [no:] *see* **neither... nor**

norm [no:m] *n* miʿyār معيار (maʿāyīr معايير)

normal ['no:məl] *adj* ʿādī عادي

normally ['no:məli] *adv* ʿādatan عادةً

north [no:th] 1. *adj* shamālī شمالي 2. *n* shamāl شمال

northeast 1. *adj* shamāl sharqī شمال شرقي 2. *n* shamāl sharqī شمال شرقي

northern ['no:dhən] *adj* shamālī شمالي

northerner ['no:dhənə] *n* shamālī شمالي (-yūn)

Northern Ireland *n* āyrlandā ash-shamālīya آيرلندا الشمالية

northward(s) ['no:thwədz] *adv* shamālan شمالاً; naḥw ash-shamāl نحو الشمال

northwest 1. *adv* shamāl gharbī شمال غربي 2. *n* shamāl gharbī شمال غربي

Norway ['no:wei] *n* nurwīj نرويج

Norwegian [no:'wi:jən] 1. *adj* nūrwījī نورويجي 2. *n* nūrwījī نورويجي (-yūn)

nose [nəuz] *n* 1. anf أنف (ānāf آناف; unūf أنوف) 2. to blow one's nose makhaṭa مخط (u; makhṭ مخط)

nostalgia [nos'taljə] *n* al-ḥanīn ilā 'l-māḍī الحنين إلى الماضي

nostril ['nostrəl] *n* fatḥat al-anf فتحة الأنف

not [not] 1. lā لا 2. lā لا; lam لم; lan لن; laysa ليس 3. ghayr غير

notable ['nəutəbəl] *adj* bāriz بارز; mumayyaz مميز

note [nəut] 1. *n* mudhakkara مذكرة (-āt); mulāḥaẓa ملاحظة (-āt) 2. *(mus.)* naghama نغمة (-āt) 3. *v* lāḥaẓa لاحظ 4. *see* **banknote**

notebook ['nəutbuk] *n* mufakkira مفكرة (-āt)

noted ['nəutid] *adj* shahīr شهير

noteworthy ['nəutwə:dhi] *adj* jadīr bi 'l-mulāḥaẓa جدير بالملاحظة

nothing ['nʌthing] 1. lā shay' لا شيء 2. next to nothing qalīl jiddan قليل جداً

notice ['nəutis] *n* 1. iʿlām إعلام; iʿlān إعلان 2. to take notice of intibaha انتبه 3. *v* lāḥaẓa لاحظ

notice-board *n* lawḥat al-iʿlānāt لوحة الإعلانات

notify ['nəutifai] *v* aʿlama أعلم; ablagha أبلغ

notion ['nəushən] *n* fikra فكرة (afkār أفكار)

notorious [nəu'to:riəs] *adj* mashhūr مشهور; mashahhar مشهّر

nought [no:t] *n* ṣifr صفر

noun [naun] *n* ism اسم (asmā' أسماء)

nourishing ['nʌrishing] *adj* mughadhdhin مغذّ

nourishment ['nʌrishmənt] *n* ghidhā' غذاء

novel ['novəl] 1. *adj* jadīd wa gharīb جديد وغريب 2. *n* riwāya رواية (-āt)

novelist ['novəlist] *n* riwā'ī روائي (-yūn)

November [nəu'vembə] *n* novembir نوفمبر; tishrīn ath-thānī تشرين الثاني

now [nau] 1. al'ān الآن 2. just now mundhu laḥẓa منذ لحظة

nowadays ['nauədeiz] *adv* fī hādhihi 'l-ayyām في هذه الأيام

nowhere ['nəuweə] lā makān لا مكان

nuclear ['nyu:kliə] *adj* nawawī نووي

nude [nyu:d] *adj* ʿārin عارٍ; ʿuryān عريان

nuisance ['nyu:səns] *n* izʿāj إزعاج

numb [nʌm] *adj* khadir خدر

number ['nʌmbə] *n* **1.** raqm رقم
(arqām أرقام) **2.** ʿadad عدد (aʿdād
أعداد) **3.** *v* ʿadda عد (u; ʿadd عد)

numeral ['nyu:mərəl] *n* raqm رقم
(arqām أرقام)

numerous ['nyu:mərəs] *adj* ʿadīd
عديد

nurse [nəːs] **1.** *n (med.)* mumarriḍ
ممرّض **2.** *v* raʿā رعى (a; raʿy رعي) **3.**
(med.) marraḍa مرّض

nursery ['nəːsəri] *n* ḥiḍāna حضانة
(-āt)

nursing ['nəːsing] *n (med.)* tamrīḍ
تمريض

nuts [nʌts] *pl* mukassarāt مكسّرات

oak [əuk] *n* ballūṭ بلوط

oasis [əu'eisis] *(pl* **oases)** wāḥa واحة
(-āt)

oath [əuth] *n* yamīn يمين *f* (aymān
أيمان); qasam قسم (aqsām أقسام)

obedience [ə'biːdiəns] *n* ṭāʿa طاعة

obedient [ə'biːdiənt] *adj* muṭīʿ مطيع

obey [ə'bei] *v* aṭāʿa أطاع

object ['objikt] *n* **1.** shay' شيء
(ashyā' أشياء) **2.** hadaf هدف (ahdāf
أهداف)

object [əb'jekt] *v* iʿtaraḍa اعترض (to
ʿalā على)

objection [əb'jekshən] *n* **1.** iʿtirāḍ
إعتراض **2. to raise an objection to**
ʿāraḍa عارض

objective [əb'jəktiv] **1.** *adj*
mawḍūʿī موضوعي **2.** *n* hadaf هدف
(ahdāf أهداف)

obligation [obli'geishən] *n* wājib
واجب (-āt)

obligatory [ə'bligətri] *adj* wājib
واجب

oblige [ə'blaij] *v* **1.** awjaba أوجب **2.**
labbā لبى; istajāba استجاب

obscene [ob'siːn] *adj* dāʿir داعر;
fāḥish فاحش

obscure [əb'skyuə] **1.** *adj* ghāmiḍ
غامض **2.** *v* ghammaḍa غمض; ghaṭṭā
غطى

observant [əb'zəːvənt] *adj* yaqiẓ
يقظ

observation [obzə'veishən] *n* **1.**
murāqaba مراقبة **2.** mulāḥaẓa
ملاحظة

observe [əb'zəːv] *v* **1.** lāḥaẓa لاحظ;
rāqaba راقب **2. to observe the law**
aṭāʿa al-qānūn أطاع القانون

observer [əb'zəːvə] *n* murāqib
مراقب (-ūn)

obsess [əb'ses] *v* **to be obsessed
with** ashghala tamāman bi
أشغل تماماً ب

obsession [əb'seshən] *n* ishghāl إشغال

obsolete ['obsəliːt] *adj* mumāt ممات

obstacle ['obstəkəl] *n* ʿāʾiqa عائقة (ʿawāʾiq عوائق)

obstinate ['obstənət] *adj* ʿanīd عنيد

obstruction [əb'strʌkchən] *n* 1. ʿāʾiqa عائقة (ʿawāʾiq عوائق) 2. *(med.)* insidād إنسداد

obtain [əb'tein] *v* ḥaṣala ʿalā حصل على (u; ḥuṣūl حصول)

obvious ['obviəs] *adj* bayyin بين; wāḍiḥ واضح

obviously ['obviəsli] *adv* bi wuḍūḥ بوضوح

occasion [ə'keizhən] *n* munāsaba مناسبة (-āt)

occasional [ə'keizhənəl] *adj* bayn ḥīn wa ākhir بين حين وآخر

occasionally [ə'keizhənli] *adv* aḥyānan أحياناً

occidental [əksi'dentəl] *adj* gharbī غربي

occupant ['okyupənt] *n* sākin ساكن (sukkān سكان); muqīm مقيم (-ūn)

occupation [okyu'peishən] *n* 1. shughl شغل (ashghāl أشغال); mihna مهنة (mihan مهن) 2. *(mil.)* iḥtilāl إحتلال

occupier ['okyupaiyə] *n* muḥtall محتل (-ūn)

occupy ['okyupai] *v* 1. shaghala شغل (a; shughl شغل) 2. iḥtalla احتل

occur [ə'kəː] *v* (occurred) waqaʿa وقع (yaqaʿu يقع; wuqūʿ وقوع)

occurrence [ə'kʌrəns] *n* waqīʿa وقيعة (waqāʾiʿ وقائع)

ocean ['əushən] *n* muḥīṭ محيط (-āt)

o'clock [əu'klok] *adv* as-sāʿa الساعة

October [ok'təubə] *n* oktōbir أكتوبر;

tishrīn al-awwal تشرين الأول

octopus ['oktəpəs] *n* ukhṭabūṭ أخطبوط *collective*

odd [od] *adj* 1. gharīb غريب 2. watrī وتري 3. *(maths)* watrī; fardī فردي

odour, *(US)* **odor** ['əudə] *n* rāʾiḥa رائحة (rawāʾiḥ روائح)

of [əv] *prep* 1. *[adāt iḍāfa* أداة إضافة*]* 2. min من; ʿan عن; bi ب

off [of] *adj/adv/prep* 1. far off baʿīd بعيد 2. off the coast qurb al-shāṭiʾ قرب الشاطئ 3. a day off yawm ʿuṭla يوم عطلة 4. to take off aqlaʿa أقلع 5. to set off on a trip badaʾa riḥla بدأ رحلة 6. to switch off aghlaqa أغلق

offence, *(US)* **offense** [ə'fens] *n* 1. mukhālafa مخالفة (-āt) 2. jarḥ al-mashāʿir جرح المشاعر

offend [ə'fend] *v* ajraḥa mashāʿir ghayrih أجرح مشاعر غيره

offense [ə'fens] *see* offence

offensive [ə'fensiv] *adj* jāriḥ mashāʿir al-ghayr جارح مشاعر الغير

offer ['ofə] 1. *n* ʿarḍ عرض (ʿurūḍ عروض) 2. *v* qaddama قدم 3. ʿaruḍa عرض (u; ʿarḍ عرض)

office ['ofis] 1. *adj* maktabī مكتبي 2. *n* maktab مكتب (makātib مكاتب) 3. manṣib منصب (manāṣib مناصب)

officer ['ofisə] *n* 1. ḍābiṭ ضابط (ḍubbāṭ ضباط) 2. *(mil.)* ḍābiṭ ضابط (ḍubbāṭ ضباط)

official [ə'fishəl] 1. *adj* rasmī رسمي 2. *n* masʾūl مسؤول (-ūn)

officially [ə'fishəli] *adv* rasmīyan رسمياً

offshore [of'shoː] *adj/adv* khārij niṭāq ar-raqāba خارج نطاق الرقابة

often ['ofən; 'oftən] *adv* kathīran
كثيراً

oil [oil] *n* 1. zayt زيت (zuyūt زيوت) 2.
nafṭ نفط

oilfield ['oilfi:ld] *n* ḥaql nafṭ حقل نفط
(ḥuqūl حقول)

oil painting *n* lawḥa zaytīya زيتية
لوحة (-āt)

oil well *n* bi'r nafṭ بئر نفط (ābār آبار)

okay; OK [əu'kei] 1. ṭayyib طيب 2.
maḍbūṭ مضبوط

old [əuld] *adj* 1. qadīm قديم 2. ʿajūz
عجوز 3. *see* how old?

old age *n* shaykhūkha شيخوخة

olden times *pl* ayyām zamān
أيام زمان

old-fashioned *adj* ʿatīq al-namaṭ
عتيق النمط

olive ['oliv] *n* zaytūna زيتونة
(*collective* zaytūn زيتون)

Olympics; Olympic games *pl*
olimbiyād أولمبياد

omission [ə'mishən] *n* ḥadhf حذف

omit [ə'mit] *v* (**omitted**) ḥadhafa
حذف (i; ḥadhf حذف)

on [on] *prep* 1. ʿalā على; fawqa فوق;
aʿlā أعلى 2. on the table ʿalā 'ṭ-
ṭāwula على الطاولة 3. on the radio
ʿalā 'r-rādiyō على الراديو 4. on foot
ʿalā al-aqdām على الأقدام 5. on
purpose ʿamdan عمداً 6. on his
arrival ladā wuṣūlihi لدى وصوله
7. on Monday yawm al-ithnayn
يوم الإثنين 8. a book on Shakespeare kitāb ʿan shakespeare
كتاب عن شيكسبير 9. to get on
insajama انسجم 10. to put on
labisa لبس (a; lubs لبس) 11. to put
the light on aḍā'a an-nūr أضاء النور
12. What's going on? mādhā

yaḥduth? ماذا يحدث؟ 13. on
account of bisabab بسبب 14. on
behalf of niyābatan ʿan نيابة عن

once [wʌns] 1. *adv* marra مرة; marra
wāḥida مرة واحدة 2. at once ḥālan
حالاً; fawran فوراً 3. all at once
faj'atan فجأة 4. *conj* mā in ما إن;
ḥāla mā حالما

one [wʌn] *n/adj* 1. wāḥid واحد; aḥad
أحد 2. one another *adv* baʿḍuhum
al-baʿḍ بعضهم البعض

oneself [wʌn'self] nafsuh نفسه

one-way street *n* shāriʿ wāḥid al-
ittijāh شارع واحد الإتجاه

one-way ticket *n* tadhkara li 'l-
dhihāb faqaṭ تذكرة للذهاب فقط

onion ['ʌnyən] *n* baṣala بصلة
(*collective* baṣal بصل)

on-line [on'lain] *adj* muttaṣil bi 'l-
internet متصل بالإنترنيت

onlooker ['onlukə] *n* mushāhid
مشاهد (-ūn); mutafarrij متفرج (-ūn)

only ['əunli] 1. *adj* waḥīd وحيد 2. an
only child ṭifl waḥīd طفل وحيد
3. *adv* faqaṭ فقط 4. only one wāḥid
faqaṭ واحد فقط 5. not only... but
also laysa faqaṭ... lākin... ayḍan
ليس فقط... لكن... أيضاً 6. if only...
layta... ليت...

on to; onto *prep* ʿalā على

on top of *prep* ʿalā على; fawqa فوق

onward; onwards ['onwəd;
'onwədz] *adv* ilā 'l-amām
إلى الأمام

open ['əupən] 1. *adj* maftūḥ مفتوح 2.
v fataḥa فتح (a; fatḥ فتح)

open-air *adj* maftūḥ مفتوح; bi 'l-
hawā' aṭ-ṭalq بالهواء الطلق

opening ['əupəning] 1. *adj* iftitāḥī
إفتتاحي 2. *n* fatḥ فتح; iftitāḥ إفتتاح
3. futḥa فتحة (-āt)

openly ['əupənli] *adv* ʿalanan علناً

opera ['oprə] **1.** *adj* ūbrawī أوروي **2.** *n* ūbrā أوبرا

opera house *n* dār al-ūbrā دار الأوبرا

operate ['opəreit] *v* **1.** shaghghala شغل؛ **2.** istaʿmala استعمل **2.** *(med.)* ajrā عملية جراحية ʿamalīya jarāḥīya أجرى

operatic [opə'ratik] *adj* ubrawī أوروي

operating theatre, *(US)* **operating room** *n* ghurfat al-ʿamalīyāt غرفة العمليات

operation [opə'reishən] *n* **1.** ʿamalīya عملية (-āt) **2.** (med/mil.) ʿamalīyāt عمليات

operations [opə'reishənz] *pl* ʿamalīyāt عمليات

operator ['opəreitə] *n* **1.** ʿāmil عامل (ʿummāl عمال)؛ mushaghghil مشغل (-ūn)

opinion [ə'piniən] *n* **1.** ra'y رأي (ārā' آراء) **2. in my opinion** fī ra'yī في رأيي

opponent [ə'pəunənt] *n* khaṣm خصم (khuṣūm خصوم)

opportunity [opə'tyu:nəti] *n* furṣa فرصة (furaṣ فرص)

oppose [ə'pəuz] *v* ʿāraḍa عارض

opposing [ə'pəuzing] *adj* muʿāriḍ معارض

opposite ['opəzit] **1.** *adj* muwājih مواجه؛ muqābil مقابل **2.** *prep* amām أمام

opposite to *adj* muwājih مواجه؛ muqābil مقابل

opposition [opə'zishən] **1.** *adj (pol.)* muʿāriḍ معارض **2.** *n* taʿāruḍ تعارض **3.** *(pol.)* muʿāraḍa معارضة

opposition party *n* ḥizb muʿāriḍ حزب معارض

oppress [ə'pres] *v* qamaʿa قمع (a; qamʿ قمع)؛ ẓalama ظلم (i; ẓulm ظلم)

oppressive [ə'presiv] *adj* ẓālim ظالم؛ jā'ir جائر

opt for [opt] *v* ikhtāra اختار

optical ['optikəl] *adj* baṣarī بصري

optician [op'tishən] *n* ṭabīb al-ʿuyūn طبيب العيون

optimism ['optimizəm] *n* tafā'ul تفاؤل

optimist ['optimist] *n* mutafā'il متفائل (-ūn)

optimistic [opti'mistik] *adj* mutafā'il متفائل

optimum ['optiməm] *n* amthal أمثل

option ['opshən] *n* khiyār خيار؛ ikhtiyār إختيار

optional ['opshnəl] *adj* khiyārī خياري؛ ikhtiyārī إختياري

or [o:] *conj* **1.** aw أو **2. either... or** immā.... aw إمّا.... أو

oral ['o:rəl] *adj* **1.** shifahī شفهي؛ shafawī شفوي **2.** ʿan ṭarīq al-fam عن طريق الفم

orange ['orinj] **1.** *adj* burtaqālī برتقالي **2.** *n* burtuqāla برتقالة (collective burtuqāl برتقال)

orbit ['o:bit] **1.** *n* madār مدار (-āt) **2.** *v* dāra دار (u; dawr دور)

orchard ['o:chəd] *n* bustān بستان (basātīn بساتين)

orchestra ['o:kistrə] *n* orkestrā أوركسترا

ordeal [o:'di:l] *n* miḥna محنة (miḥan محن)

order ['o:də] **1.** *n* amr أمر (awāmir أوامر) **2.** tartīb ترتيب **3.** niẓām نظام (anẓima أنظمة) **4.** *(com.)* ṭalab طلب (-āt) **4. law and order** an-niẓām النظام؛ al-amn wa 'l-amān

5. الأمن والأمان **in order** murattab مرتب. 6. **out of order** ʿaṭlān عطلان 7. **in order to** kay كي; likay لكي 8. *v* amara أمر (u; amr أمر) 9. *(com.)* ṭalaba طلب (u; ṭalab طلب)

ordinary [ˈoːdənri] *adj* ʿādī عادي

ore [oː] *n* miʿdan معدن (maʿādin معادن)

organ [ˈoːgən] *n* 1. ʿuḍw عضو (aʿḍāʾ أعضاء). 2. *(mus.)* urghun أرغن (arāghin أراغن)

organism [ˈoːgənizəm] *n* kāʾin كائن ḥayy حي (-āt)

organization [oːgənaiˈzeishən] 1. *n* tanẓīm تنظيم 2. munaẓẓama منظمة (-āt)

organize [ˈoːgənaiz] *v* naẓẓama نظم

oriental [ˌoːriˈentəl] *adj* sharqī شرقي

origin [ˈorijin] *n* aṣl أصل (uṣūl أصول)

original [əˈrijənəl] 1. *adj* aṣlī أصلي 2. *n* aṣl أصل (uṣūl أصول)

originality [ərijəˈnaliti] *n* ibdāʿ إبداع

originally [əˈrijənli] *adv* aṣlan أصلاً

ornament [ˈoːnəmənt] *n* zīna زينة (-āt); zukhruf زخرف (zakhārif زخارف)

ornamental [ˌoːnəˈmentl] *adj* zukhrufī زخرفي

orphan [ˈoːfən] *n* yatīm يتيم (aytām أيتام)

orphanage [ˈoːfənij] *n* dār al-aytām دار الأيتام

other [ˈʌdhə] *adj/-i n* 1. ākhar آخر 2. **each other** baʿḍuhum al-baʿḍ بعضهم البعض 3. **the other day** qabl ʿiddat ayyām قبل عدة أيام 4. **every other day** yawm baʿda yawm يوم بعد يوم 5. **one after the other** al-wāḥid baʿd al-ākhar الواحد بعد الآخر 6. **on the one hand..., and on the other** min

nāḥiya... wa min nāḥiya ukhrā من ناحية... ومن ناحية أخرى

otherwise [ˈʌdhəwaiz] *adv* wa illā وإلا; mādhā wa illā ماذا وإلا

ought [oːt] *v* yajibu يجب; yanbaghī ينبغي

ounce [auns] *n* awns أونس

our [aː] -nā نا

ours [aːz] lanā لنا

ourselves [aːˈselvz] anfusunā أنفسنا

out [aut] 1. *adj* khārijī خارجي 2. *adv* khārijan خارجاً; fi ʾl-khārij في الخارج 3. **way out** makhraj مخرج 4. **inside out** bi ʾl-maqlūb بالمقلوب 5. **to go out** kharaja خرج (u; khurūj خروج) 6. **The fire's gone out.** khamadat an-nār خمدت النار

outbreak [ˈautbreik] *n* nushūb نشوب

outcome [ˈautkʌm] *n* natīja نتيجة (natāʾij نتائج)

outdated [autˈdeitid] *adj* ʿatīq an-namaṭ عتيق النمط

outdoor [ˈautˈdoː] *adj* khārijī خارجي

outdoors [ˈautdoːz] *adv* fi ʾl-khārij في الخارج

outer [ˈautə] *adj* khārijī خارجي

outer space *n* al-faḍāʾ al-khārijī الفضاء الخارجي

outfit [ˈautfit] *n* zayy زي (azyāʾ أزياء)

outing [ˈauting] *n* nuzha نزهة (nuzah نزه)

outlast [autˈlaːst] *v* ṣamida akthar صمد أكثر (u; ṣumūd صمود)

outlaw [ˈautloː] 1. *n* ṭarīd طريد 2. *v* ḥaẓara حظر (u; ḥaẓr حظر)

outline [ˈautlain] 1. *n* khaṭṭ kifāfī خط كفافي 2. *v* ikhtaṣara اختصر

outlook ['autluk] *n* **1.** wajhat naẓar
وجهة نظر **2.** al-mustaqbal al-
mutawaqqa' المستقبل المتوقع

outnumber [aut'nʌmbə] *v*
fawwaqah 'adadan فوّقه عدداً

out of date *adj* **1.** 'adā 'alayh az-
zaman عدا عليه الزمن **2.** 'atīq aṭ-
ṭarāz عتيق الطراز

out of work *adj* 'āṭil 'an al-'amal
عاطل عن العمل

output ['autput] *n* intāj إنتاج

outrage ['autreij] **1.** *n* faẓī'a فظيعة
(faẓā'i' فظائع) **2.** *v* afẓa'a أفظع

outrageous [aut'reijəs] *adj* faẓī'
فظيع

outright ['autrait] **1.** *adj* muṭlaq
مطلق; tāmm تام **2.** *adv* kullīyatan
كلّية

outside [aut'said] **1.** *n* khārij خارج
2. *adj* khārijī خارجي **3.** *adv* khārijan
خارجاً; fi 'l-khārij في الخارج **4.** *prep*
khārij خارج

outsize ['autsaiz] *adj* akbar min al-
ma'lūf أكبر من المألوف

outspoken [aut'spəukən] *adj* ṣarīḥ
صريح

outstanding [aut'standing] *adj* **1.**
bāriz بارز **2.** *(fin.)* ghayr madfū'
غير مدفوع

outward ['autwəd] *adj* khārijī
ظاهري; ẓāhirī خارجي

outwards ['autwədz] *adv* naḥw al-
khārij نحو الخارج

oven ['ʌvən] *n* furn فرن (afrān أفران)

over ['əuvə] **1.** *adv* fawq فوق **2.** *prep*
akthar min أكثر من

overall [əuvər'o:l] *adj* 'umūman
عموماً

overcast ['əuvəka:st] *adj* mulabbad
bi 'l-ghuyūm ملبد بالغيوم

overcharge [əuvə'cha:j] *v* ṭalaba
thamanan akthar min al-lāzim
طلب ثمناً أكثر من اللازم

overcoat ['əuvəkəut] *n* mi'ṭaf معطف
(ma'āṭif معاطف)

overcome [əuvə'kʌm] *v* **(over-
came, overcome)** taghallaba 'alā
تغلب على

overdo [əuvə'du:] *v* **(overdid,
overdone)** afraṭa fī أفرط في;
bālagha fī بالغ في

overdose ['əuvədəus] *n* jur'a
mufriṭa جرعة مفرطة (-āt)

overdue [əuvə'dyu:] *adj* fāt maw'id
istiḥqāquh فات موعد إستحقاقه; fāt
maw'id wuṣūluh فات موعد وصوله

overflow [əuvə'fləu] *v* fāḍa فاض (i;
fayḍ فيض)

overhear [əuvə'hi:ə] *v* sami'a
muṣādafatan سمع مصادفةً (a; sam'
سمع)

overland ['əuvələnd] **1.** *adj* barrī بري
2. *adv* barran براً

overload [əuvə'ləud] *v* ḥammala bi
ifrāṭ حمل بإفراط

overlook [əuvə'luk] *v* **1.** ashrafa 'alā
أشرف على **2.** aghfala أغفل

overnight [əuvə'nait] *adv* laylan
ليلاً

overpower [əuvə'pauə] *v* taghallaba
'alā تغلب على

overseas [əuvə'si:z] *adj/adv* 'abr al-
biḥār عبر البحار

oversee [əuvə'si:] *v* ashrafa 'alā
أشرف على

oversight [əuvə'sait] *n* ishrāf إشراف

overspend [əuvə'spend] *v*
anfaqa akthar min al-lāzim
أنفق أكثر من اللازم

overstay [əuvə'stei] *v* makatha akthar

min al-lāzim مكث أكثر من اللازم (u; makth مكث)

overstep [əuvə'step] v tajāwaza تجاوز

overtake [əuvə'teik] v tajāwaza تجاوز

overthrow [əuvə'thrəu] (pol.) qalaba قلب (i; qalb قلب)

overturn [əuvə'tə:n] v qalaba قلب (i; qalb قلب)

overuse [əuvə'yu:s] n afraṭa fī isti'māl shay' أفرط في إستعمال شيء

overwhelm [əuvə'welm] v ghamura غمر (u; ghamāra غمارة)

overwork [əuvə'wə:k] n 'amala akthar min al-lāzim عمل أكثر من اللازم

owe [əu] v kāna mudīnan lah bi دان ل\ب; dāna li/bi كان مديناً له ب (i; dayn دين)

owing to ['əuing tu] prep bisabab بسبب

owl [aul] n būm bom collective

own [əun] 1. adj milkuh ملكه 2. v imtalaka امتلك

owner ['əunə] n mālik مالك (mullāk ملاك); ṣāḥib صاحب (aṣḥāb أصحاب)

ownership ['əunəship] n mulk ملك

ox [oks] n thawr ثور (thīrān ثيران)

oxygen ['oksijən] n oksizhen أكسجين

oz. see **ounce**

P

pace [peis] 1. n khaṭwa خطوة (khaṭawāt خطوات) 2. sur'a سرعة 3. v khaṭā خطا (u; khaṭw خطو)

pack [pak] 1. n ṣurra صرة (ṣurar صرر); rizma رزمة (rizam رزم) 2. majmū'a مجموعة; jamā'a جماعة (-āt) 3. v ḥazama حزم (i; ḥazm حزم); waḍḍaba وضب 4. see **packed**

package ['pakij] n ṣurra صرة (ṣurar صرر); rizma رزمة (rizam رزم)

package tour n riḥla jamā'īya رحلة جماعية

packed [pakt] adj muzdaḥim مزدحم

packet ['pakit] n rizma ṣaghīra رزمة صغيرة

pact [pakt] n mīthāq ميثاق (mawāthīq مواثيق); mu'āhada معاهدة (-āt)

pad [pad] n launch pad minaṣṣat al-iṭlāq منصة الإطلاق

padlock ['padlok] n qufl قفل (aqfāl أقفال)

page [peij] n ṣafḥa صفحة (ṣafaḥāt صحفات)

paid [peid] see **pay**

pain [pein] 1. *n* alam ألم (ālām آلام) 2. *v* ālama آلم; awja'a أوجع

painful ['peinfəl] *adj* mu'lim مؤلم

painkiller ['peinkilə] *n* musakkin مسكن (-āt)

painless ['peinləs] *adj* ghayr mu'lim غير مؤلم

paint [peint] 1. *n* ṭilā' طلاء 2. *v* ṭalā طلى (i; ṭaly طلي)

paintbrush ['peintbrʌsh] *n* furshāt ṭilā' فرشاة طلاء

painter ['peintə] *n* 1. dahhān دهان (-ūn) 2. rassām رسام (-ūn)

painting ['peinting] *n* lawḥa لوحة (-āt)

pair [peə] *n* zawj زوج

palace ['palis] *n* qaṣr قصر (quṣūr قصور)

pale [peil] *adj* shāḥib شاحب

palm [pa:m] *n* 1. *collective* nakhl نخل 2. kaff *f* كف (kufūf كفوف)

pamphlet ['pamflit] *n* kutayyib كتيب (-āt); manshūr منشور (-āt)

pan [pan] *n* frying pan miqlāh مقلاة (maqālin مقال)

panel ['panəl] *n* 1. lawḥ لوح (alwāḥ ألواح) 2. nadwa ندوة

panic ['panik] 1. *n* dhu'r ذعر 2. *v* uṣība bi 'dh-dhu'r أصيب بالذعر

pant [pant] *v* lahatha لهث (a; lahth لهث)

panties ['pantiz] *pl* sirwāl dākhilī nisā'ī سروال داخلي نسائي

pantry ['pantri] *n* mustawdi' li 'l-akl مستودع للأكل

pants [pants] *pl* 1. sirwāl dākhilī سروال داخلي 2. *(US)* banṭalōn بنطلون

papal ['peipəl] *adj* bābawī بابوي

paper ['peipə] *n* 1. waraqa ورقة 2. awrāq أوراق; awrāq أوراق (waraq ورق) 2. jarīda جريدة (jarā'id جرائد) 3. *(acad.)* maqāla مقالة (-āt) 4. **toilet paper** waraq al-mirḥāḍ ورق المرحاض

par [pa:] *n* on a par with mutasāwin متساو مع ma'a

parachute ['parəshu:t] 1. *n* miẓalla مظلة (-āt) 2. *v* anzala bi 'l-miẓalla أنزل بالمظلة

parade [pə'reid] *n* 'arḍ عرض ('urūḍ عروض); isti'rāḍ إستعراض

paradise ['parədais] *n* firdaws فردوس; al-janna الجنة

paragraph ['parəgra:f] *n* fiqra فقرة (fiqarāt فقرات)

parallel ['parəlel] *adj* muwāzin موازن; mutawāzin متوازن

paralyze ['parəlaiz] *v* ashalla أشل

paranoia [parə'noyə] *n* maraḍ ash-shakk مرض الشك

paranoid [parənoid] *adj/n* muṣīb bi maraḍ al-shakk مصيب بمرض الشك

paratroops ['parətru:ps] *pl* jund al-miẓalliyīn جند المظليين

parcel ['pa:səl] *n* rizma رزمة (rizam رزم)

pardon ['pa:dən] 1. *n* maghfira مغفرة 2. *(leg.)* 'afw عفو 3. **I beg your pardon!** 'afwan! عفواً! 4. **I beg your pardon?** 'afwan? عفواً؟ 5. *v* ghafara غفر (i; ghafr غفر) 6. *(leg.)* 'afā عفا (u; 'afw عفو)

parent ['peərənt] *n* wālid والد (-ūn)

parents ['peərənts] *pl* al-wālidān الوالدان

parish ['parish] *n* dā'ira idārīya kanīsīya دائرة إدارية كنيسية

park [pa:k] 1. *n* ḥadīqa حديقة (ḥadā'iq حدائق) 2. **car-park** mir'ab al-sayyārāt مرأب السيارات 3.

amusement park malāʿib tarfīh ملاعب ترفيه 4. *v* to park a car rakana (ركون rukūn) ركن

parking [ˈpaːking] *n* makān wuqūf as-sayyārāt مكان وقوف السيارات

parking lot; parking space *n* makān wuqūf as-sayyārāt مكان وقوف السيارات

parliament [ˈpaːləmənt] 1. *adj* barlamānī برلماني 2. *n* barlamān برلمان

parody [ˈparodi] *n* muhākā sukhrīya محاكاة سخرية

parrot [ˈparət] *n* babghāʾ ببغاء (babghawāt ببغوات)

part [paːt] 1. *n* juzʾ جزء (ajzāʾ أجزاء); qism قسم (aqsām أقسام) 2. dawr دور (adwār أدوار) 3. **spare parts** qiṭaʿ ghiyār قطع غيار 4. **for the most part** muʿaẓẓam al-aḥyān معظم الأحيان; ghāliban غالباً 5. **to take part in** shāraka شارك 6. *v* iftaraqa افترق

participant [paːˈtisipənt] *n* mushārik مشارك (-ūn)

participate [paːˈtisipeit] *v* shāraka شارك (**in** fī في)

participation [paːˌtisiˈpeishən] *n* mushāraka مشاركة (**in** fī في); ishtirāk إشتراك (**in** fī في)

particle [ˈpaːtikəl] *n* dharra ذرة (*collective* dharr ذر)

particular [pəˈtikyulə] 1. *adj* khāṣṣ خاص 2. *n* **in particular** khāṣṣatan خصوصاً; khuṣūṣan خاصةً

particularly [pəˈtikyuləli] *adv* khāṣṣatan خصوصاً; khuṣūṣan خاصةً

partly [ˈpaːtli] *adv* juzʾīyan جزئياً

partner [ˈpaːtnə] *n* sharīk شريك (shurakāʾ شركاء)

partnership [ˈpaːtnəship] *n* shirāka شراكة

part-time *adj* **part-time job** ʿamal ghayr dāʾim عمل غير دائم

party [ˈpaːti] *n* 1. ḥafla حفلة (-āt) 2. (*leg.*) ṭaraf طرف (aṭrāf أطراف) 3. (*pol.*) ḥizb حزب (aḥzāb أحزاب)

pass [paːs] 1. *n* tadhkirat al-murūr تذكرة المرور 2. **mountain pass** shiʿb شعب (shiʿāb شعاب) 3. *v* marra مر (u; murūr مرور) 4. marrara مرّر; amarra أمر 5. **to pass time** qaḍā قضى (i; qaḍāʾ قضاء) 6. **to pass an exam** najaḥa نجح (a; najāḥ نجاح)

passage [ˈpasij] *n* 1. murūr مرور 2. mamarr ممر (-āt) 3. riḥla رحلة 4. fiqra فقرة (fiqrāt فقرات)

passenger [ˈpasinjə] *n* rākib راكب (rukkāb ركاب)

passion [ˈpashən] *n* shaghaf شغف

passionate [ˈpashənət] *adj* shaghif شغف

passport [ˈpaːspoːt] *n* jawāz safar جواز سفر (-āt)

past [ˈpaːst] 1. *adj* māḍin ماض 2. *n* al-māḍi الماضي 3. *adv* **to go past** marra مر (u; murūr مرور) 4. *prep* baʿd بعد; mutajāwiz متجاوز 5. **half past four** arbaʿ wa niṣf أربع ونصف

pasta [ˈpastə] *n* maʿkarūna معكرونة

paste [peist] *n* maʿjūn معجون (maʿājīn معاجين)

pastime [ˈpaːstaim] *n* taslīya تسلية; hawāya هواية (-āt)

pat [pat] *v* rabbata ربت

patch [pach] 1. *n* ruqʿa رقعة (ruqaʿ رقع)

path [paːth] *n* sabīl سبيل (subul سبل)

pathetic [pəˈthetik] *adj* mushajjin مشجٍ; muthīr li ʾsh-shafaqa مثير للشفقة

patience ['peishəns] n ṣabr صبر

patient ['peishənt] 1. adj ṣābir صابر
2. n marīḍ مريض (marḍā مرضى)

patriotic [patri'otik] adj waṭanī
وطني

patrol [pə'trəul] 1. n dawrīya دورية
(-āt) 2. v qāma bi dawrīya (u)
قام بدورية

patron ['peitrən] n rā'in راع (ru'āh
رعاة); naṣīr نصير (nuṣurā' نصراء);

pattern ['patən] n 1. mithāl مثال
(amthila أمثلة; muthul مثل) 2.
shakl شكل (ashkāl أشكال) 3.
namūdhaj نموذج (-āt)

pause [po:z] 1. n tawaqquf qaṣīr
توقف قصير 2. v tawaqqafa qaṣīran
توقف قصيراً

pavement ['peivmənt] n (UK) raṣīf
رصيف (arṣifa أرصفة)

paw [po:] n mikhlab مخلب (makhālib
مخالب)

pay [pei] 1. n rātib راتب (rawātib
رواتب) 2. v dafa'a دفع (a; daf'
دفع) 3. to pay attention intabaha
انتبه (to ilā إلى) 4. to pay a visit zāra زار
(u; ziyāra زيارة)

payment ['peimənt] n daf' دفع

peace [pi:s] n 1. adj silmī سلمي 2. n
salām سلام

peaceful ['pi:sfəl] adj 1. silmī سلمي
2. hādi' هادئ

peach [pi:ch] n khawkha خوخة
(collective khawkh خوخ)

peak [pi:k] 1. adj bāligh adh-dharwa
بالغ الذروة 2. n qimma قمة (qimam
قمم) 3. dharwa ذروة (dhuran ذرى) 4.
v balagha 'l-dharwa بلغ الذروة (u;
bulūgh بلوغ)

peanuts ['pi:nʌts] pl fūl sūdānī
فول سوداني collective

pear [peə] n kummathra كمثرة
(kummathrayāt كمثريات)

pearl [pə:l] n lu'lu'a لؤلؤة (collective
lu'lu' لؤلؤ)

peculiar [pi'kyu:liə] adj 1. khuṣūṣī
خصوصي 2. gharīb غريب; gharīb al-
aṭwār غريب الأطوار

pedal ['pedəl] n dawwāsa دواسة (-āt)

pedestal ['pedistəl] n qā'idat
timthāl قاعدة تمثال

pedestrian [pi'destriən] n māshin
ماش (mushāh مشاة)

peel [pi:l] 1. n qishra قشرة 2. v
qashshara قشّر

peg [peg] n 1. watad وتد (awtād
أوتاد) 2. milqaṭ ملقط (malāqiṭ
ملاقط)

pen [pen] n qalam قلم (aqlām أقلام)

penalty ['penəlti] n 1. 'iqāb عقاب;
'uqūba عقوبة (-āt) 2. (spor.) ḍarbat
al-jazā' ضربة الجزاء

pence [pens] see penny

pencil ['pensəl] n qalam raṣāṣ
قلم رصاص (aqlām أقلام)

penetrate ['penitreit] v 1. dakhala
دخل (u; dukhūl دخول); ikhtaraqa
اخترق 2. takhallala تخلل

peninsula [pə'ninsyulə] n shibh
jazīra شبه جزيرة

penis ['pi:nis] n qaḍīb قضيب
(quḍbān قضبان); al-'uḍw adh-
dhakarī العضو الذكري

penknife ['penaif] n sikkīn al-
qalam سكين القلم

penny ['peni] n (pl pence/pennies)
qirsh قرش (qurūsh قروش)

pension ['penshən] n ma'āsh معاش
(-āt)

pension [pon'syon] n bansiyūn
بنسيون

people ['pi:pəl] pl **1.** ناس nās **2.** shaᶜb شعب (shuᶜūb شعوب)

pepper(s) ['pepə] n filfil/fulful collective فلفل

per [pə; pɑ:] prep **1.** في fī; لكل likull **2.** wifqan li وفقاً لـ

perceive [pə'si:v] v أدرك adraka; وعي waᶜā (وعي); يعي yaᶜī; waᶜy (وعي)

per cent; percent [pə'sent] fi 'l-mi'a في المئة

perception [pə'sepshən] n idrāk إدراك

percussion [pə'kʌshən] n (mus.) naqr نقر

perfect ['pə:fikt] adj **1.** كامل kāmil **2.** tāmm تام; muṭlaq مطلق

perfect [pə'fekt] v kammala كمّل

perfection [pə'fekshən] n kamāl كمال

perfectly ['pə:fektli] adv **1.** tamāman تماماً **2.** bi shakl kāmil بشكل كامل

perform [pə'fo:m] v **1.** addā أدّى **2.** maththala مثّل

performance [pə'fo:məns] n **1.** adā' أداء (-āt) **2.** tamthīl تمثيل

perfume ['pə:fyu:m] n ᶜiṭr عطر (ᶜuṭūr عطور)

perhaps [pə'haps] adv rubbamā ربما; laᶜalla لعل; qad yakūn قد يكون

peril ['perəl] n khaṭar خطر (akhṭār أخطار)

period ['piəriyəd] n **1.** fatra فترة (fatarāt فترات) **2.** ᶜaṣr عصر (aᶜṣār أعصار) **3.** ᶜahd عهد (ᶜuhūd عهود) **4.** (ed.) ḥiṣṣa حصة (ḥiṣaṣ حصص) **4.** (med.) ad-dawra ash-shahrīya li 'n-nisā' الدورة الشهرية للنساء

perish ['perish] v halaka هلك (i; halāk هلاك)

permanent ['pə:mənənt] adj dā'im دائم

permanently ['pə:mənəntli] adv ilā 'l-abad إلى الأبد; dā'iman دائماً

permission [pə:mishən] n idhn إذن

permit ['pə:mit] n rukhṣa رخصة (rukhaṣ رخص)

permit [pə'mit] v (**permitted**) adhina أذن (a; idhn إذن); samuḥa سمح (u; samāḥ سماح)

perpetrate ['pə:pətreit] v irtakaba ارتكب

perpetual [pə:'pechuəl] adj abadī أبدي

persecute ['pə:sikyu:t] v iḍṭahada اضطهد

persecution [pə:si'kyu:shən] n iḍṭihād إضطهاد

perseverance [pə:si'viərəns] n muwāẓaba مواظبة

persevere [pə:si'viə] v wāẓaba واظب; wāṣala واصل (in ᶜalā على)

persist [pə'sist] v **1.** thābara ثابر **2.** istamarra استمر; wāṣala واصل

persistence [pə'sistəns] n muthābara مثابرة

persistent [pə'sistənt] adj muthābir مثابر; muwāẓib مواظب; mustamirr مستمر

person ['pə:sən] n shakhṣ شخص (ashkhāṣ أشخاص)

personal ['pə:sənəl] adj shakhṣī شخصي

personality [pə:sə'naləti] n shakhṣīya شخصية (-āt)

personally ['pə:sənli] adv shakhṣīyan شخصياً

personal organizer n munaẓẓim shakhṣī منظم شخصي

personnel [pə:sənel] n ash-shu'ūn

al-idārīya الإدارية الشؤون; majmūʿat
al-muwaẓẓafīn مجموعة الموظفين

perspective [pə'spektiv] n manẓūr
منظور

perspiration [pə:spə'reishən] n 1.
ʿaraq عرق 2. taʿarruq تعرق

persuade [pə'sweid] v aqnaʿa أقنع

persuasion [pə'sweizhən] n iqnāʿ
إقناع

persuasive [pə'sweisiv] adj muqniʿ
مقنع

pervert ['pə:və:t] n munḥarif منحرف

pessimism ['pesimizəm] n
tashā'um تشاؤم

pessimist ['pesimist] n mutashā'im
متشائم (-ūn)

pessimistic [pesi'mistik] adj
mutashā'im متشائم

pest [pest] n shay' muzʿij شيء مزعج;
shakhṣ muzʿij شخص مزعج

pester ['pestə] v azʿaja أزعج

petal ['petəl] n tuwayjīya تويجية

petition [pə'tishən] 1. n ʿarīḍa
عريضة (ʿarā'iḍ عرائض) 2. v qaddama
ʿarīḍa قدّم عريضة

petrochemical [petrəu'kemikəl]
adj bītrūkīmyā'ī بيتروكيميائي

petrol ['petrəl] n binzīn بنزين

petrol station n maḥaṭṭat binzīn
محطة بنزين

phantom ['fantəm] n shabaḥ شبح
(ashbāḥ أشباح)

pharmaceutical [fa:mə'syu:tikəl]
adj ṣaydalī صيدلي

pharmacist ['fa:məsist] n ṣaydalī
صيدلي (-yūn)

pharmacy ['fa:məsi] n ṣaydalīya
صيدلية (-āt)

phase [feiz] n marḥala مرحلة
(marāḥil مراحل)

phenomenon [fə'nominən] n (pl
phenomena) ẓāhira ظاهرة (ẓawāhir
ظواهر)

philosopher [fi'losəfə] n faylasūf
فيلسوف (falāsifa فلاسفة)

philosophy [fi'losəfi] n falsafa
فلسفة (-āt)

phone [fəun] 1. n tilifūn تلفون; hātif
هاتف 2. **car phone** hātif as-sayyāra
هاتف السيّارة 3. **mobile phone** hātif
naqqāl هاتف نقّال; hātif maḥmūl
هاتف محمول 4. v talfana تلفن

phony ['fəuni] adj zā'if زائف;
muzawwir مزوّر

photo ['fəutəu] 1. n ṣūra صورة
(ṣuwar صور) 2. v ṣawwara صوّر

photocopier ['fəutəukopiə] n jihāz
at-taṣwīr جهاز التصوير

photocopy ['fəutəukopi] 1. n
nuskha نسخة (nusakh نسخ) 2. v
nasakha نسخ (a; naskh نسخ)

photograph ['fəutəgra:f] 1. n ṣūra
صورة (ṣuwar صور) 2. v ṣawwara
صوّر

photographer [fə'togrəfə] n
muṣawwir مصوّر (-ūn)

photography [fə'togrəfi] n taṣwīr
تصوير

phrase [freiz] n ʿibāra عبارة (-āt)

physical ['fizikəl] 1. adj māddī مادي
2. badanī بدني 3. n (med.) faḥṣ ṭibbī
فحص طبّي

physician [fi'zishən] n ṭabīb طبيب
(aṭibbā' أطبّاء)

physicist ['fizisist] n fīzyā'ī فيزيائي
(-yūn)

physics ['fiziks] n al-fīzyā' الفيزياء

physiotherapy [fiziəu'therəpi] n
al-ʿilāj al-ṭabīʿī العلاج الطبيعي

piano; pianoforte [pi'yanəu;

pianəu'fo:tei] *n* biyānū بيانو

pick [pik] *v* 1. ikhtāra اختار 2. qaṭafa قطف (i; qaṭf قطف)

pickpocket ['pikpokit] *n* nashshāl نشال (-ūn)

pick-up (truck) *n* shāḥinat naql ṣaghīra شاحنة نقل صغيرة

pick up *v* iltaqaṭa التقط

picnic ['piknik] *n* nuzha khalawīya نزهة خلوية

picture ['pikchə] *n* ṣūra صورة (ṣuwar صور)

pie [pai] *n* faṭīra فطيرة (faṭā'ir فطائر)

piece [pi:s] *n* qiṭʿa قطعة (qiṭaʿ قطع)

pierce [piəs] *n* kharaqa خرق (u/i; kharq خرق); thaqaba ثقب (u; thaqb ثقب)

pig [pig] *n* khinzīr خنزير (khanāzīr خنازير)

pigeon ['pijin] *n* ḥamāma حمامة (collective ḥamām حمام)

pile [pail] 1. *n* kawm كوم (akwām أكوام) 2. *v* to pile up kawwama كوم

pill [pil] *n* 1. ḥabba حبة (collective ḥabb حب; pl ḥubūb حبوب) 2. contraceptive pill ḥabb manʿ al-ḥaml حب منع الحمل

pillar ['pilə] *n* ʿamūd عمود (aʿmida أعمدة)

pillow ['piləu] *n* wisāda وسادة (āt; wasā'id وسائد)

pilot ['pailət] 1. *n* ṭayyār طيار (-ūn) 2. *v* qāda ṭā'ira قاد طائرة (u; qiyāda قيادة)

pin [pin] *n* dabbūs دبوس (dabābīs دبابيس)

pinch [pinch] *v* qaraṣa قرص (u; qarṣ قرص)

pink [pingk] *adj* aḥmar zahrī أحمر زهري

pint [paint] *n* bāynt باينت (-āt)

pious ['paiəs] *adj* taqī تقي

pip [pip] *n* badhra بذرة (collective badhr بذر)

pipe [paip] *n* 1. unbūba أنبوبة (anābīb أنابيب); māsūra ماسورة (mawāsīr مواسير) 2. bība بيبة (-āt); ghalyūn غليون (ghalāyīn غلايين)

pipeline ['paiplain] *n* khaṭṭ anābīb خط أنابيب

pistol ['pistəl] *n* musaddas مسدس (-āt)

pit [pit] *n* ḥufra حفرة (ḥufar حفر)

pitch [pich] 1. *n* (mus.) darajat an-naghm درجة النغم 2. (spor.) malʿab ملعب (malāʿib ملاعب)

pitiful ['pitifəl] *adj* yurthā lah يرثى له

pity ['piti] 1. *n* shafaqa شفقة 2. what a pity! yā khasāra! يا خسارة! 3. *v* ashfaqa أشفق

pizza ['pi:tsə] *n* bītsa بيتسا

place [pleis] 1. *n* makān مكان (amākin أماكن); mawḍiʿ موضع (mawāḍiʿ مواضع) 2. maḥall محل (-āt) 3. in place of badalan min بدلا من 4. out of place fī ghayr maḥallihi في غير محله 5. in the first place awwalan أولا 6. to take place ḥadatha حدث (u; ḥudūth حدوث); waqaʿa وقع (yaqaʿu يقع; wuqūʿ وقوع) 7. *v* waḍaʿa وضع (yaḍaʿu يضع; waḍʿ وضع)

plain [plein] 1. *adj* basīṭ بسيط; ghayr muzakhrif غير مزخرف 2. wāḍiḥ واضح; ṣarīḥ صريح 3. *n* sahl سهل (suhūl سهول)

plainly ['pleinli] *adv* bi wuḍūḥ بوضوح; bi ṣarāḥa بصراحة

plan [plan] 1. *n* khiṭṭa خطة (khiṭaṭ خطط) 2. *v* (planned) khaṭṭaṭa خطط

plane [plein] n 1. saṭḥ سطح (suṭūḥ سطوح) 2. ṭā'ira طائرة (-āt)

planet ['planit] n kawkab كوكب (kawākib كواكب)

planning ['planing] n takhṭīṭ تخطيط

plant [plaːnt] 1. n nabata نبتة (-āt) 2. maṣnaʿ مصنع (maṣāniʿ مصانع) 3. v zaraʿa زرع (a; zarʿ زرع)

plaster ['plaːstə] 1. n jiṣṣ جص 2. (med.) laṣūq لصوق 3. v jaṣṣaṣa جصص

plastic ['plastik] 1. adj blāstīkī بلاستيكي 2. n blāstīk بلاستيك

plate [pleit] n 1. ṭabaq طبق (aṭbāq أطباق); ṣaḥn صحن (ṣuḥūn صحون) 2. gold plate ṭilā' dhahabī طلاء ذهبي

platform ['platfoːm] n minaṣṣa منصة (-āt)

play [plei] 1. n laʿb لعب 2. masraḥīya مسرحية (-āt) 3. v (spor.) laʿiba لعب (a; laʿb لعب) 4. (mus.) ʿazafa عزف (i; ʿazf عزف)

player ['pleiə] n 1. lāʿib لاعب (-ūn) 2. ʿāzif عازف (-ūn)

plaza ['plaːzə] n maydān ميدان (mayādīn ميادين); sāḥa ʿāmma ساحة عامة

plead [pliːd] v nāshada ناشد

pleasant ['plezənt] adj laṭīf لطيف

please [pliːz] 1. min faḍlak فضلك من 2. please! arjūk! أرجوك! 3. v asarra أسر

pleased [pliːzd] adj masrūr مسرور

pleasing ['pliːzing] adj sārr سار

pleasure ['pleʒə] n mutʿa متعة (mutaʿ متع)

plenty ['plenti] 1. adj wāfir وافر 2. n wafra وفرة 3. adv kathīran كثيراً

plot [plot] 1. (pol.) mu'āmara مؤامرة (-āt) 2. plot of land qiṭʿat arḍ قطعة أرض 3. story plot riwāya رواية (-āt) 4. v (pol.) ta'āmara تآمر

plough, (US) **plow** [plau] 1. n miḥrāth محراث (maḥārīth محاريث) 2. v ḥaratha حرث (i/u; ḥarth حرث)

pluck [plʌk] v iqtalaʿa اقتلع

plug [plʌg] n 1. sidāda سدادة (-āt) 2. electric plug qābis kahrabā'ī قابس كهربائي 3. v sadda سد (u; sadd سد)

plug in v adkhala al-qābis fi 'l-ma'khadh أدخل القابس في المأخذ

plum [plʌm] n barqūqa برقوقة (collective barqūq برقوق)

plumber ['plʌmə] n sabbāk سباك (-ūn)

plunge [plʌnj] v 1. ghāṣa غاص (u; ghawṣ غوص); ghaṭasa غطس (i; ghaṭs غطس) 2. khāḍa خاض (u; khawḍ خوض)

plural ['pluərəl] 1. adj jamʿī جمعي 2. n jamʿ جمع

plus [plʌs] conj zā'id زائد

p.m. (= post meridiem) ['piː'em] baʿd al-ẓuhr بعد الظهر

pneumonia [nyuː'məuniə] n dhāt ar-ri'a ذات الرئة

PO (post office) [piːəu] n maktab al-barīd مكتب البريد (makātib مكاتب)

poach [pəuch] v 1. salaqa سلق (u; salq سلق) 2. saraqa aṣ-ṣayd/as-samak سرق الصيد\السمك (i; saraqa سرقة)

PO box n ṣundūq al-barīd صندوق البريد (ṣanādīq al-barīd صناديق البريد)

pocket ['pokit] n jayb جيب (juyūb جيوب)

pocketful ['pokitful] n mil' jayb ملء جيب

poem ['pəuim] n shiʿr شعر (ashʿār أشعار)

poet [pəuit] n shā'ir شاعر (shu'arā' شعراء)

poetic [pəu'etik] adj shi'rī شعري

poetry ['pəuitri] n shi'r شعر

point [point] **1.** n (pencil, etc) ra's رأس **2.** nuqta نقطة (nuqaṭ نقط; niqāṭ نقاط) **3.** qaṣd قصد **4.** (spor.) nuqta نقطة (nuqaṭ نقط) **5.** assembly point makān al-ijtimā' مكان الإجتماع **6.** at that point fī tilka al-laḥẓa في تلك اللحظة **7.** on the point of 'alā washak an على وشك أن **8.** zero point three (0.3) ṣifr nuqta thalātha صفر نقطة ثلاثة **9.** v ashāra أشار (at ilā إلى) **10.** to point (a gun) ṣawwaba صوّب (at naḥw نحو)

pointless ['pointləs] adj bilā ma'nā بلا معنى

poison ['poizən] **1.** n samm سم (sumūm سموم) **2.** v sammama سمم

poisonous ['poizənəs] adj sāmm سام

pole [pəul] n **1.** quṭb قطب (aqṭāb أقطاب) **2.** the North Pole al-quṭb ash-shamālī القطب الشمالي **3.** the South Pole al-quṭb al-janūbī القطب الجنوبي

police [pə'li:s] pl **1.** shurṭa شرطة **2.** secret police būlīs sirrī بوليس سري

police force n ash-shurṭa الشرطة

policeman; police officer [pə'li:smən] n shurṭī شرطي (-yūn)

police station n markaz ash-shurṭa مركز الشرطة

policewoman [pə'li:swumən] n shurṭiya شرطية (-āt)

policy ['poləsi] n (pol.) siyāsa سياسة (-āt)

polish ['polish] **1.** n lum'a لمعة **2.** v lamma'a لمّع

polite [pə'lait] adj mu'addab مؤدّب

political [pə'litikəl] adj siyāsī سياسي

politician [poli'tishən] n siyāsī سياسي (-yūn); sāsa ساسة (ساسة)

politics ['polətiks] n as-siyāsa السياسة

poll [pəul] **1.** n iqtirā' إقتراع **2.** istiftā' إستفتاء **3.** v ajrā istiftā' أجرى إستفتاء **4.** see polls

polls [pəulz] pl intikhābāt إنتخابات

pollute [pə'lu:t] v lawwatha لوّث

pollution [pə'lu:shən] n talawwuth تلوّث

pond [pond] n birka بركة (birak برك)

pony ['pəuni] n ḥiṣān ṣaghīr حصان صغير

pool [pu:l] **1.** n birka بركة (birak برك) **2.** see swimming-pool

poor [po:] adj **1.** faqīr فقير **2.** radī' ردي **3.** miskīn مسكين **4.** the poor al-fuqarā' الفقراء

poorly ['po:li] **1.** adj marīḍ مريض **2.** adv bi ṭarīqa sayyi'a بطريقة سيئة

pop [pop] v farqa'a فرقع

pope [pəup] n bābā بابا (bābawāt بابوات)

pop in v marr 'alā مرّ على (u; murūr مرور)

popular ['popyulə] adj **1.** sha'bī شعبي **2.** maḥbūb محبوب

popularity [popyu'larəti] n sha'bīya شعبية

populated ['popyuleitid] adj This area is densely populated. hādhihi 'l-minṭaqa kathīfat as-sukkān هذه المنطقة كثيفة السكان

population [popyu'leishən] n **1.** sukkān سكان **2.** 'adad al-sukkān عدد السكان

porcelain ['po:səlin] adj/n ṣīnī صيني

porch [po:ch] n (US) riwāq رواق
(arwiqa أروقة)

pork [po:k] n laḥm al-khinzīr
لحم الخنزير

porn [po:n] see pornography

pornographic [po:nə'grafik] adj
ibāḥī إباحي

pornography [pɔ:'nogrəfi] n
ibāḥīya إباحية

port [po:t] n marfa' مرفأ (marāfi'
مرافئ); mīnā' f ميناء (mawānin
موان)

portable ['po:təbəl] adj qābil li 'l-
ḥaml قابل للحمل; maḥmūl محمول

porter ['po:tə] n 1. ḥammāl حمال
(-ūn); ʿattāl عتال (-ūn) 2. (UK)
bawwāb بواب (-ūn)

portion ['po:shən] n 1. ḥiṣṣa حصة
(ḥiṣaṣ حصص); naṣīb نصيب 2. juz'
جزء (ajzā' أجزاء)

portrait ['po:treit] n lawḥa لوحة
(-āt); ṣūra صورة (ṣuwar صور)

portray [po:'trei] v waṣafa وصف
(yaṣifu يصف); waṣf وصف)

Portugal ['pochugəl] n burtughāl
برتغال

Portuguese [pochu'gi:z] 1. adj
burtughālī برتغالي 2. n burtughālī
برتغالي

pose [pəuz] v 1. to pose a question
qaddama su'ālan قدم سؤالاً 2. to
pose a threat maththala khaṭaran
مثل خطراً

posh [posh] adj rāqī راقي

position [pə'zishən] n 1. mawḍiʿ
موضع (mawāḍiʿ مواضع); mawqiʿ
موقع (mawāqiʿ مواقع) 2. mawqif
موقف (mawāqif مواقف) 3. markaz
مركز 4. waẓīfa وظيفة (waẓā'if وظائف)

positive ['pozətiv] adj 1. ījābī
إيجابي 2. waḍʿī وضعي 3. Are you
(m) positive? hal anta muta'akkid?
هل أنت متأكد؟

positively ['pozətivli] adv tamāman
تماماً

possess [pə'zes] v malaka ملك (u;
mulk ملك)

possession [pə'zeshən] n mumtalak
ممتلك (-āt)

possessions [pə'zeshənz] pl
mumtalakāt ممتلكات

possessive [pə'zesiv] adj ghayūr
غيور

possessor [pə'zesə] n ṣāḥib صاحب
(aṣḥāb أصحاب); mālik مالك

possibility [posi'biləti] n imkānīya
إمكانية (-āt)

possible ['posəbəl] adj mumkin
ممكن

possibly ['posəbli] adv rubbamā ربما

post [pəust] 1. n ʿamūd عمود (aʿmida
أعمدة) 2. barīd بريد 3. waẓīfa وظيفة
4. v arsala bi 'l-barīd أرسل بالبريد
5. alṣaqa iʿlānan ألصق إعلاناً

postage ['pəustij] adj barīdī بريدي

postbox ['pəustboks] n ṣundūq al-
barīd صندوق البريد (ṣanādīq
صناديق)

postcard ['pəustka:d] n biṭāqa
barīdīya بطاقة بريدية

post code n (UK) ramz barīdī
رمز بريدي (rumūz رموز)

poster ['pəustə] n mulṣaq ملصق (-āt)

postgraduate [pəustgradjuət] adj
postgraduate studies dirāsāt
ʿālīya دراسات عالية

postman ['pəustmən] n sāʿi 'l-barīd
ساعي البريد

post office n maktab al-barīd
مكتب البريد

postpone [pəs'pəun] v ajjala أجّل

pot [pot] n qidr قدر (qudūr (قدور);
wiʿāʾ وعاء (awʿiya (أوعية

potato [pə'teitəu] n (pl **potatoes**)
baṭāṭis بطاطس

potent ['pəutənt] adj qawī قوي

potential [pə'tensəl] 1. adj ihtimalī
إحتمالي 2. n imkānīya إمكانية

potter ['potə] n ṣāniʿ al-fakhkhār
صانع الفخار (ṣunnāʿ (صنّاع

pottery ['potəri] n fakhkhār فخار

pouch [pauch] n kīs كيس (akyās
(أكياس

poultry ['pəultri] pl dawājin دواجن

pound [paund] 1. n bawnd باوند (-āt)
2. v saḥaqa سحق (a; saḥq (سحق

pour [po:] v sakaba سكب (u; sakb
(سكب ṣabba صب (u; ṣabb (صبّ

poverty ['povəti] n faqr فقر

POW [piyəu'dʌbəlyu] see **prisoner
of war**

powder ['paudə] n dharūr ذرور;
mashūq مسحوق

powdered ['paudəd] adj dharūrīya
ذرورية; mashūq مسحوق

power ['pauə] 1. n qudra قدرة (-āt) 2.
qūwa قوة 3. ṭāqa طاقة 4. **in power**
fī 's-sulṭa في السلطة

powerbook ['pauəbuk] n
kombyūtar naqqāl كمبيوتر نقال;
kombyūtar maḥmūl كمبيوتر محمول

powerful ['pauəfəl] adj qawī قوي

powerless ['pauələs] adj ḍaʿīf
ضعيف; ʿājiz عاجز

power plant; power station n
maḥaṭṭat aṭ-ṭāqa محطة الطاقة

practical ['praktikəl] adj ʿamalī
عملي

practically ['praktikli] adv 1.
taqrīban تقريباً 2. ʿamalīyan عملياً

practice ['praktis] n 1. mumārasa
ممارسة 2. tadarrub تدرب 3. ʿāda
عادة (-āt); ʿurf عرف 4. **to put into
practice** ṭabbaqa طبّق 5. see
practise

practise ['praktis] v 1. mārasa
مارس 2. darraba درّب

praise [preiz] 1. n madḥ مدح 2. v
madaḥa مدح (a; madḥ (مدح

pray [prei] v ṣallā صلى; daʿā دعا (u;
duʿāʾ (دعاء

prayer ['preə] n ṣalāh صلاة (ṣalawāt
(صلوات; duʿāʾ دعاء (adʿiya (أدعية

preach [pri:ch] v waʿaẓa وعظ
(yaʿiẓu يعظ; waʿẓ وعظ), ʿiẓa
عظة

precaution [pri'ko:shən] n iḥtiyāṭ
إحتياط (-āt)

preceding [pri'si:ding] adj sābiq
سابق

precinct ['pri:singkt] n 1. (US)
markaz shurṭa مركز شرطة 2. (UK)
shopping precinct mujammaʿ
tijārī مجمع تجاري

precious ['preshəs] adj qayyim قيم;
ghālin غال

precise [pri'sais] adj daqīq دقيق

precisely [pri'saisli] adv bi diqqa
بدقة bi 'ḍ-ḍabṭ; بالضبط

precision [pri'sizhən] n diqqa دقة

predict [pri'dikt] v tanabba'a تنبأ

predictable [pri'diktəbəl] adj
1. yumkin at-tanabbu' bih
يمكن التنبّؤ به 2. mutawaqqaʿ
متوقع

prediction [pri'dikshən] n tanabbu'
تنبؤ (-āt)

prefer [pri'fə:] v faḍḍala فضّل;
rajjaḥa رجّح; arjaḥa أرجح

preferable ['prefrəbəl] adj
mufaddal مفضل

preference ['prefrəns] n tarjīḥ ترجيح

pregnancy ['pregnənsi] n ḥaml حمل

pregnant ['pregnənt] adj ḥāmil حامل

prejudice ['prejudis] n 1. ḍarar ضرر 2. ḥukm sabaqī حكم سبقي

preliminary [pri'liminəri] adj tamhīdī تمهيدي

premature [premə'chyuə] adj sābiq al-awān سابق الأوان

premeditated [pri:'mediteitid] adj muta'ammad متعمد

premier ['premiə] n ra'īs al-wuzarā' رئيس الوزراء

premiere ['premieə] n 'arḍ awwal عرض أول

premises ['premisiz] pl mabnan wa 'l-arāḍī at-tābi'a lah مبنى والأراضي التابعة له

preparation [prepə'reishən] n i'dād إعداد; isti'dād استعداد

preparatory [pri'parətri] adj i'dādī إعدادي

prepare [pri'peə] v a'adda أعد; ista'adda استعد

prepared [pri'peəd] adj musta'idd مستعد

preposition [prepə'zishən] n ḥarf jarr حرف جر

prescription [pri'skripshən] n (med.) waṣfa ṭibbīya وصفة طبية

presence ['prezəns] n ḥuḍūr حضور; wujūd وجود

present ['prezənt] 1. adj ḥālī حالي 2. ḥāḍir حاضر; mawjūd موجود 3. n hadīya هدية (hadāyā هدايا); hiba هبة (-āt) 4. al-ḥāḍir الحاضر 5. at present al-ān الآن

present [pri'zent] v 1. qaddama قدّم 2. a'ṭā أعطى

presentation [prezən'teishən] n 1. taqdīm تقديم 2. 'arḍ عرض ('urūḍ); 3. muḥāḍara محاضرة (-āt)

present-day [preznt'dei] adj mu'āṣir معاصر

presenter [pre'zentə] n muqaddim مقدم (-ūn)

presently ['prezntli] adv 1. ba'd qalīl بعد قليل 2. tawwan توّاً; al-'ān الآن

preservation [prezə'veishən] n ḥifẓ حفظ

preserve [pri'zə:v] v ḥafiẓa حفظ (a; ḥifẓ حفظ)

presidency ['prezidənsi] n ri'āsa رئاسة

president ['prezidənt] n 1. ra'īs رئيس (ru'asā' رؤساء) 2. (com.) ra'īs majlis al-idāra رئيس مجلس الإدارة

presidential ['prezidənshəl] n ri'āsī رئاسي

press [pres] 1. n mi'ṣara معصرة (ma'āṣir معاصر) 2. the Press aṣ-ṣaḥāfa الصحافة 3. v ḍaghaṭa ضغط (a; ḍaghṭ ضغط) 4. 'aṣara عصر (i; 'aṣr عصر)

press agency n wikālat al-anbā' وكالة الأنباء

press conference n mu'tamar ṣuḥufī مؤتمر صحفي

pressure ['preshə] n 1. ḍaghṭ ضغط (ḍughūṭ ضغوط) 2. under pressure taḥt al-ḍaghṭ تحت الضغط

prestige [pres'ti:zh] n hayba هيبة; makāna مكانة

presume [pri'zyu:m] v iftaraḍa افترض

pretence [pri'tens] n taẓāhur تظاهر

pretend [pri'tend] v taẓāhara تظاهر

pretense [pri'tens] *see* **pretence**

pretty ['priti] *adj* **1.** ḥilw ;حلو jamīl جميل **2.** *(sl.)* jiddan جداً

prevail [pri'veil] *v* sāda ساد (u; siyāda سيادة)

prevent [pri'vent] *v* manaʿa منع (a; manʿ منع)

prevention [pri'venshən] *n* manʿ منع; waqāʾ وقاء

preventive; preventative [pri'ventiv; pri'ventətiv] *adj* waqāʾī وقائي

preview ['pri:vyu] *n* ʿarḍ musabbaq عرض مسبق

previous ['pri:viəs] *adj* sābiq سابق

previously ['pri:vyəsli] *adv* sābiqan سابقاً

prey [prei] *n* farīsa فريسة

price [prais] **1.** *n* thaman ثمن (athmān أثمان) **2. at half price** bi niṣf as-siʿr بنصف السعر **3.** *v* saʿʿara سعّر

priceless ['praislis] *adj* lā yuqaddir bi ʾl-māl لا يقدر بالمال

prick [prik] *v* wakhaza وخز (yakhizu يخز; wakhz وخز)

pride [praid] *n* fakhr فخر

priest [pri:st] *n* qissīs قسيس (-ūn)

primarily [prai'merili] *adv* asāsan أساساً; qabl kull shayʾ قبل كل شيء

primary ['praiməri] *adj* **1.** asāsī أساسي **2.** ibtidāʾī إبتدائي

primary school *n* madrasa ibtidāʾīya مدرسة إبتدائية

prime [praim] *adj* raʾīsī رئيسي

prime minister *n* raʾīs al-wuzarāʾ رئيس الوزراء

primitive ['primitiv] *adj* bidāʾī بدائي

prince [prins] *n* amīr أمير (umarāʾ أمراء)

princess ['prinses] *n* amīra أميرة (-āt)

principal ['prinsəpəl] **1.** *adj* raʾīsī رئيسي **2.** *n (ed.)* mudīr kullīya مدير كلّية

principality [prinsi'paləti] *n* imāra إمارة (-āt)

principle ['prinsəpəl] *n* mabdaʾ مبدأ (mabādiʾ مبادئ)

print [print] **1.** *n* ḥurūf حروف **2.** *v* ṭabaʿa طبع (a; ṭabʿ طبع) **3. Please print your name.** uktub ismak bi ʾl-ḥurūf al-munfaṣila. أكتب اسمك بالحروف المنفصلة.

printer ['printə] *n* **1.** ṭabbāʿ طبّاع (-ūn) **2.** *(comp.)* ṭabbāʿa طباعة (-āt)

printing ['printing] *n* ṭabʿ طبع

priority [prai'orəti] *n* awlawīya أولوية (-āt)

prior to ['praiə tu] *prep* qabl قبل

prison ['prizən] *n* sijn سجن (sujūn سجون)

prisoner ['priznə] *n* sajīn سجين (sujanāʾ سجناء)

prisoner of war (POW) *n* asīr al-ḥarb أسير الحرب (asrā أسرى)

privacy ['privəsi] *n* ʿuzla عزلة

private ['praivit] **1.** *adj* khuṣūṣī خصوصي; khāṣṣ خاص **2.** fī ḥālihi في حاله **3. in private** sirrīyan سرياً **4.** *n (mil.)* jundī جندي

private detective; private investigator *n* muḥaqqiq khāṣṣ محقّق خاص

privately ['praivitli] *adv* sirran سرّاً

privilege ['privəlij] *n* imtiyāz إمتياز (-āt)

prize [praiz] *n* jāʾiza جائزة (jawāʾiz جوائز)

pro [prəu] **1.** *adv/adj* muʾayyid li مؤيد ل **2.** *see* **professional**

probability [probə'biləti] n iḥtimāl
إحتمال

probable ['probəbəl] adj muḥtamal
محتمل

probably ['probəbli] adv min al-muḥtamal من المحتمل

probe [prəub] v faḥaṣa ;فحص
ḥaqqaqa حقّق

problem ['probləm] n 1. mushkila
مشكلة (-āt; mashākil مشاكل) 2. to
solve a problem ḥalla mushkila
حل مشكلة 3. no problem! lā ba's!
لا بأس!

procedure [prə'si:jə] n ijrā' إجراء
(-āt)

proceed [prə'si:d] v wāṣala ;واصل
istamarra استمر

proceeds ['prəsi:dz] pl ʿawā'id
عوائد

process ['prəuses] 1. n ʿamalīya
عملية (-āt) 2. in process jāri al-
ʿamal fīh جاري العمل فيه 3. v ʿālaja
عالج ṣināʿīyan صناعياً

procession [prə'seshən] n mawkib
موكب (mawākib مواكب)

proclaim [prə'kleim] v aʿlana أعلن;
ṣarraḥa صرح

produce ['prodyu:s] n maḥṣūl
محصول; intāj إنتاج

produce [prə'dyu:s] v 1. antaja ;أنتج
ṣanaʿa صنع (a; ṣanʿ صنع) 2. to
produce a film antaja filman فلماً
أنتج

producer [prə'dyu:sə] n 1. muntij
منتج 2. film producer muntij
sīinamāʾī منتج سينمائي

product ['prodʌkt] n muntaj منتج (-
āt)

production [prə'dʌkshən] n intāj
إنتاج

profession [prə'feshən] n mihna
مهنة (mihan مهن)

professional [prə'feshənəl] 1. adj
muḥtarif محترف 2. mihnī مهني 3. n
mihnī مهني (-yūn)

professor [prə'fesə] n ustādh أستاذ
(asātidha أساتذة)

proficiency [prə'fishənsi] n barāʿa
براعة; itqān إتقان (-āt)

profile ['prəufail] n 1. maẓhar jānibī
مظهر جانبي 2. tarjuma shakhṣīya
ترجمة شخصية

profit ['profit] 1. n ribḥ ربح (arbāḥ
أرباح); ʿā'ida عائدة (-āt; ʿawā'id
عوائد) 2. v istafāda استفاد; intafaʿa
إنتفع

profitable [profitəbəl] adj 1.
murbiḥ مربح 2. mufid مفيد

profound [prə'faund] adj ʿamīq
عميق

programme; program ['prəugram]
n 1. barnāmij برنامج (barāmij برامج)
2. minhāj منهاج (manāhīj مناهيج) 3.
v barmaja برمج

programmer ['prəugramə] n
mubarmij مبرمج (-ūn)

progress ['prəugres] n 1. taqaddum
تقدم; irtiqāʾ إرتقاء 2. to make
progress taqaddama تقدم

progression [prə'greshən] n
taqaddum تقدم

progressive [prə'gresiv] adj
taqaddumī تقدمي

prohibit [prə'hibit] v ḥarrama ;حرم
ḥaẓẓara حظر; manaʿa منع (a; manʿ
منع)

prohibition [prəuhibishən] n manʿ
منع

project [projekt] n mashrūʿ مشروع
(mashārīʿ مشاريع)

projection [prə'jekshən] *n (fin.)* tanabbu' تنبؤ; tawaqquʿ توقع

projector [prə'jektə] *n* jihāz al-ʿarḍ جهاز العرض

prolific [prə'lifik] *adj* muthmir مثمر; wafīr al-intāj وفير الإنتاج

prolong [prə'long] *v* maddada مدّد

prominent ['prominənt] *adj* bāriz بارز; mutamayyiz متميّز

promise ['promis] **1.** *n* waʿd وعد (wuʿūd وعود) **2.** *v* waʿada وعد (yaʿidu يعد; waʿd وعد)

promising ['promising] *adj* mubashshir bi 'l-khayr مبشر بالخير

promote [prə'məut] *v* **1.** raqqā رقى **2.** shajjaʿa شجّع **3.** *(com.)* rawwaja روج

promoter [prə'məutə] *n* murawwij مروّج (-ūn)

promotion [prə'məushən] *n* **1.** tarqīya ترقية **2.** *(com.)* tarwīj ترويج

prompt [prompt] *adj* ḥaththa حث (u; ḥathth حث)

pronoun ['prəunaun] *n* ḍamīr ضمير (ḍamā'ir ضمائر)

pronounce [prə'nauns] *v* **1.** talaffaẓa تلفظ **2.** aʿlana أعلن

pronunciation [prənʌnsi'eishən] *n* talaffuẓ تلفظ

proof [pru:f] *n* **1.** burhān برهان (barāhīn براهين); dalīl دليل (adilla أدلة); ithbāt إثبات **2.** *see* **waterproof**

prop; prop up [prop] *v* daʿʿama دعم; sānada ساند

propaganda [propə'gandə] *n* daʿāya دعاية (-āt)

propeller [prə'pelə] *n* mirwaḥa مروحة (marāwiḥ مراوح)

proper ['propə] *adj* **1.** daqīq دقيق **2.**

munāsib مناسب **3.** muḥtaram محترم

properly ['propəli] *adv* kamā yanbaghī كما ينبغي

property ['propəti] **1.** *adj* milkī ملكي; ʿaqārī عقاري **2.** *n* milk ملك (amlāk أملاك); ʿaqār عقار (-āt)

prophet ['profit] *n* nabī نبي (anbiyā' أنبياء)

proportion [prə'po:shən] *n* **1.** nisba نسبة **2.** ittisāq إتساق

proposal [prə'pəuzəl] *n* iqtirāḥ إقتراح (-āt)

propose [prə'pəuz] *v* iqtaraḥa اقترح

proposition [propə'zishən] *n* muqtaraḥ مقترح (-āt); iqtirāḥ إقتراح (-āt)

prosecute ['prosikyu:t] *v* **1.** ḥākama حاكم **2.** qāma bi ب قام (u; qiyām قيام)

prosecution [prosi'kyu:shən] *n* muḥākama محاكمة (-āt)

prosecutor ['prosikyu:tə] *n (leg.)* muddaʿin مدّع (muddaʿūn مدعون)

prospective [prə'spektiv] *adj* **1.** mustaqbalī مستقبلي **2.** mutawaqqaʿ متوقع

prospectus [prə'spektəs] *n* dalīl دليل (adilla أدلة); kutayyib كتيب (-āt)

prosper ['prospə] *v* izdahara ازدهر

prosperity [pro'sperəti] *n* rakhā' رخاء

prosperous [pro'sperəs] *adj* tharī ثري; muzdahir مزدهر

prostitute [pro'stityu:t] *n* mūmis مومس (-āt); dāʿira داعرة (-āt)

protect [prə'tekt] *v* ḥamā حمي (i; ḥimāya حماية)

protection [prə'tekshən] *n* ḥimāya حماية

protective [prə'tektiv] *adj* wāqin
واقٍ

protector [prə'tektə] *n* ḥāmin حامٍ
(ḥumāh حماة)

protein ['prəutiːn] *n* brōtīn بروتين
(-āt)

protest ['prəutest] **1.** *adj* iḥtijājī
إحتجاجي **2.** *n* iḥtijāj إحتجاج; i'tirāḍ
إعتراض

protest [prə'test] *v* iḥtajja احتج;
i'taraḍa اعترض (**against** 'alā على)

Protestant ['protistənt] **1.** *adj*
brotostantī بروتستانتي **2.** *n*
brotostantī بروتستانتي (-yūn)

protester [prə'testə] *n* mutaẓāhir
متظاهر (-ūn)

prototype ['prəutətaip] *n* namūdhaj
awwalī نموذج أولي

protrude [prə'truːd] *v* nata'a نتأ (a;
nutū' نتوء)

proud [praud] *adj* **1.** fakhūr فخور
(**of** bi ب) **2.** maghrūr مغرور;
mutakabbir متكبر; mutaghaṭris
متغطرس

prove [pruːv] *v* (**proved,
proved/proven**) athbata أثبت

proverb ['provɜːb] *n* mathal مثل
(amthāl أمثال)

provide [prə'vaid] *v* manaḥa منح (a;
manḥ منح); zawwada زوّد

provided [prə'vaidid] *conj* 'alā sharṭ
على شرط (**that an** أن)

provide for [prə'vaid] *v* 'āla عال (u;
'awl عول); 'iyāla عيالة)

providing [prə'vaiding] *see*
provided

province ['provins] *n* muqāṭa'a
مقاطعة (-āt); iqlīm إقليم (aqālīm
أقاليم); wilāya ولاية (-āt)

provincial [pro'vinshəl] *adj* rīfī
ريفي; qarawī قروي

provision [prə'vizhən] *n* **1.**
(leg./pol.) sharṭ شرط (shurūṭ
شروط) **2. on the provision that** alā sharṭ
an على شرط أن

provisional [prə'vizhənəl] *adj*
mu'aqqat مؤقت

provisions [prə'vizhənz] *n* mawādd
ghidhā'īya مواد غذائية

provocative [prə'vokətiv] *adj*
istifzāzī إستفزازي

provoke [prə'vəuk] *v* istafazza إستفز

prudent [pruːdnt] *adj* ḥadhir حذر

pseudo- [syu:dəu] *adj* zā'if زائف

psychiatric [saikaiətrik] *adj*
muta'alliq bi 'ṭ-ṭibb an-nafsī
متعلق بالطب النفسي

psychiatrist [saikaiətrist] *n* ṭabīb
nafsī طبيب نفسي

psychiatry [saikaiətri] *n* ṭibb nafsī
طب نفسي

psycho [saikəu] *n* majnūn مجنون
(majānīn مجانين)

psychological [saikələojikəl] *adj*
nafsī نفسي; sīkolūjī سيكولوجي

psychologist [saikoləjist] *n* 'ālim
an-nafs عالم النفس

psychology [saikoləji] *n* 'ilm an-
nafs علم النفس

pub [pʌb] *n (UK)* ḥāna حانة (-āt)

public ['pʌblik] **1.** *adj* 'āmm عام;
ḥukūmī حكومي **2.** ḥukūmī
'umūmī عمومي **3.** *n* jumhūr جمهور **4. in public**
'alāniyatan علانيةً; jahran جهراً

publication [pʌbli'keishən] *n*
manshūr منشور (-āt)

publicity [pʌblisəti] *n* di'āya دعاية

publicize [pʌblisaiz] *v* a'lana أعلن;
ashāra أشار

publicly [pʌblikli] *adv* ʿalāniyatan علانيةً; jahran جهراً

publish [pʌblish] *v* nashara نشر (u; nashr نشر)

publisher [pʌblishə] *n* nāshir ناشر (-ūn)

publishing [pʌblishing] *n* nashr نشر

pudding ['puding] *n* nawʿ min al-ḥalawiyāt نوع من الحلويات

puddle [pʌdl] *n* ḥufra mamlū'a bi 'l-mā' حفرة مملوءة بالماء

puff [pʌf] *v* nafakha نفخ (u; nafkh نفخ)

pull [pul] *v* jarr جر (u; jarr جر); shadda شد (i; shadd شد)

pull back *v* insaḥaba إنسحب

pullover [puləuvə] *n* sitra سترة (-āt)

pull through *v* najā نجا (u; najāh نجاة)

pulp [pʌlp] *n* 1. labb ath-thamra لب الثمرة 2. maʿjūn معجون

pulse [pʌls] *n* nabḍ نبض (anbāḍ أنباض)

pump [pʌmp] 1. *n* miḍakhkha مضخة (-āt) 2. *v* ḍakhkha ضخ (u; ḍakhkh ضخ)

punch [pʌnch] 1. *n* lakma لكمة (lakamāt الكمات) 2. *v* lakama لكم (u; lakm لكم)

punctual ['pʌngkchuəl] *adj* murāʿī 'l-mawāʿīd مراعي المواعيد; daqīq دقيق

punctuality ['pʌngkchu'aləti] *n* murāʿat al-mawāʿīd مراعاة المواعيد; diqqa دقة

punctuation [pʌngkchu'eishən] *n* tarqīm ترقيم

puncture ['pʌngkchə] 1. *n* thaqb ثقب (thuqūb ثقوب) 2. *v* thaqaba ثقب (u; thaqb ثقب)

punish ['pʌnish] *v* ʿāqaba عاقب

punishable ['pʌnishəbəl] *adj* yuʿāqab ʿalayh يعاقب عليه

punishment ['pʌnishmənt] *n* muʿāqaba معاقبة; ʿiqāb عقاب

pupil ['pyu:pəl] *n* 1. insān al-ʿayn إنسان العين 2. (*ed.*) tilmīdh تلميذ (talāmidha تلامذة)

puppet ['pʌpit] *n* dumya muta-ḥarrika دمية متحركة (duman دمى)

puppy ['pʌpi] *n* jarw جرو (jirāʾ جراء)

purchase ['pə:chəs] 1. *n* shirāʾ شراء 2. *v* ishtarā اشترى

purchaser ['pə:chəsə] *n* mushtarin مشتر (-yūn)

pure [pyuə:] *adj* khāliṣ خالص; naqī نقي; ṭāhir طاهر

purely ['pyuə:li] mujarrad مجرّد

purify ['pyuərifai] *v* ṭahhara طهّر

purity ['pyuərəti] *n* ṭahāra طهارة

purple ['pə:pəl] *adj* urjuwānī أرجواني

purpose ['pə:pəs] *n* 1. ghāya غاية (-āt) 2. ʿazm عزم 3. **on purpose** ʿamadan عمداً; qaṣdan قصداً

purse [pə:s] *n* maḥfaza محفظة (-āt)

pursue [pə'syu:] *v* lāḥaqa لاحق; taʿaqqaba تعقب

pursuit [pə'syu:t] *n* mulāḥaqa ملاحقة

push [push] *v* dafaʿa دفع (a; dafʿ دفع); ḍaghaṭa ضغط (a; ḍaghṭ ضغط)

put [put] *v* (**put**) waḍaʿa وضع (yaḍaʿu يضع; waḍʿ وضع)

put away *v* aʿāda ilā makānih al-ma'lūf أعاد إلى مكانه المألوف

put back *v* akhkhara أخّر

put down *v* qamaʿa قمع (a; qamʿ قمع)

put off *v* ajjala أجّل; arja'a أرجأ

put on v *(clothes)* labisa لبس (a; labs لبس)

put out v *(a fire/light)* aṭfa'a أطفأ

put up with v taḥammala تحمل

puzzle ['pʌzəl] **1.** n lughz لغز (alghāz ألغاز) **2.** v ḥayyara حيّر

puzzling ['pʌzling] adj ḥā'ir حائر

pyjamas [pə'ja:məz] pl bījāma بيجامة

quaint [kweint] adj ṭarīf طريف

quake [kweint] v **1.** ihtazza اهتز **2.** see **earthquake**

qualification [kwolifi'keishən] n mu'ahhil مؤهل (-āt)

qualified ['kwolifaid] adj mu'ahhal مؤهل

qualify ['kwolifai] v ahhala أهل

quality ['kwoləti] n **1.** ṣifa صفة (-āt); mīza ميزة (-āt) **2.** naw'īya نوعية

quantity ['kwontəti] n kamīya كمية (-āt); miqdār مقدار (maqādīr مقادير)

quarrel ['kworəl] **1.** n mushājara مشاجرة (-āt) **2.** v shājara شاجر (**with** ma'a مع)

quarter ['kwo:tə] n **1.** rub' ربع (arbā' أرباع) **2.** ḥayy حي (aḥyā' أحياء)

quarterly ['kwo:təli] adv rub' sanawīyan ربع سنوياً

quarters ['ko:təz] pl *(mil.)* sakan al-junūd سكن الجنود

queen [kwi:n] n malika ملكة (-āt)

queer [kwiə] adj gharīb غريب

query ['kwi:ri] n istifhām إستفهام (-āt)

question ['kweschən] **1.** n su'āl سؤال (as'ila أسئلة) **2.** qaḍīya قضية (qaḍāyā قضايا) **3.** v istajwaba استجوب; istafhama استفهم **4.** shakka شك (u; shakk شك)

question mark n 'alāmat istifhām علامة إستفهام

questionnaire [kweschə'neə] n istiṭlā' ra'y إستطلاع رأي

queue [kyu:] **1.** n ṭābūr طابور (ṭawābir طوابير); ṣaff صف (ṣufūf صفوف) **2.** v waqafa fi 'ṭ-ṭābūr وقف في الطابور (yaqifu يقف; waqf وقف)

quick [kwik] adj **1.** sarī' سريع **2.** see **quickly**

quicken ['kwikən] v asra'a أسرع

quickly ['kwikli] adv bi sur'a بسرعة

quid [kwid] n *(UK)* bawnd باوند

quiet [kwaiət] **1.** adj hādi' هادئ **2.** n hudū' هدوء

quieten down ['kwaiətən] v sakata سكت (u; sakt سكت; sukūt سكوت)

quietly ['kwaiətli] adv bi hudū' بهدوء

quilt [kwilt] n liḥāf لحاف (luḥuf لحف; alḥifa ألحفة)

quit [kwit] v **1.** taraka ترك (u; tark ترك); ghādara غادر **2.** istaqāla استقال

quite [kwait] adv **1.** liḥaddin mā لحد ما **2.** bi 'ḍ-ḍabṭ بالضبط

quiz [kwiz] **1.** n musābaqa maʿlūmātīya مسابقة معلوماتية; ikhtibār al-maʿlūmāt إختبار المعلومات **2.** v istajwaba استجوب

quota ['kwəutə] n naṣīb نصيب

(nuṣub نصب; anṣiba أنصنة); ḥiṣṣa حصة (ḥiṣaṣ حصص)

quotation [kwəu'teishən] n iqtibās إقتباس (-āt)

quote [kwəut] **1.** n iqtibās إقتباس (-āt) **2.** (com.) siʿr سعر (asʿār أسعار) **3.** v iqtabasa اقتبس

Qur'an; Quran [kəˈrɑːn] n al-qurʾān al-karīm القرآن الكريم

R

rabbi ['rabai] n (rel.) ḥākhām حاخام (-ūn)

rabbit ['rabit] n arnab أرنب (arānib أرانب)

race [reis] **1.** n ʿirq عرق (ʿurūq عروق) **2.** (spor.) sibāq سباق; musābaqa مسابقة (-āt) **3.** arms race sibāq al-tasalluḥ سباق التسلح **4.** v sābaqa سابق

racecourse; racetrack [reiskoːs; reistrak] n midmār مضمار (maḍāmīr مضامير)

race horse n ḥuṣān as-sibāq حصان السباق

racetrack [reistrak] n midmār مضمار (maḍāmīr مضامير)

racial ['reishəl] adj ʿirqī عرقي

racing ['reising] n musābaqa مسابقة

racism ['reisizəm] n ʿirqīya عرقية; ʿunṣurīya عصرية

racist ['reisist] **1.** adj ʿirqī عرقي; ʿunṣurī عنصري **2.** n ʿirqī عرقي (yūn); ʿunṣurī عنصري (yūn)

rack [rak] n **1.** clothes rack manshar منشر **2.** to go to rack and ruin intahā ilā kharāb انتهى إلى خراب

racket [rakit] n **1.** ḍajja ضجة **2.** ʿamal iḥtiyālī عمل احتيالي **3.** (spor.) tennis racket midrab al-tanis مضرب التنس (maḍārib مضارب)

racquet see **racket**

radar ['reidaː] n rādār رادار

radiant ['reidiənt] adj mushiʿʿ مشع; mushriq مشرق

radiate ['reidiyeit] v ashaʿʿa أشع

radiation [reidi'eishən] n ishʿāʿ إشعاع

radical ['radikəl] **1.** adj jidhrī جذري **2.** n (pol.) rādikālī رادكالي

radio ['reidiəu] n rādiyo راديو

rage [reij] 1. *n* ghayẓ غيظ 2. *v* ightāẓa اغتاظ

raid [reid] 1. *n* ghāra غارة (-āt) 2. *v* shanna ghāra ʿalā شن غارة على (u; shann شن) 3. **police raid** mudāhama مداهمة (-āt)

raider ['reidə] *n* mughīr مغير (-ūn)

rail [reil] *n* qaḍīb قضيب (quḍbān قضبان)

railway, (US) **railroad** ['reilwei] *n* sikka ḥadīdīya سكة حديدية

rain [rein] 1. *n* maṭar مطر (amṭār أمطار) 2. *v* maṭara مطر (u; maṭar مطر)

rainbow ['reinbəu] *n* qaws quzaḥ قوس قزح

raincoat ['reinkəut] *n* miṭmar مطمر (maṭāmir مطامر)

rainy ['reini] *adj* maṭir مطر; mumṭir ممطر

raise [reiz] *v* 1. rafaʿa رفع (a; rafʿ رفع) 2. zawwada زود 3. jamaʿa جمع (a; jamʿ جمع) 4. rabbā ربى

rally [rali] *n* 1. ijtimāʿ ḥāshid اجتماع حاشد 2. (spor.) sibāq sayyārāt سباق سيارات

ran [ran] *see* **run**

random ['randəm] *adj* 1. ʿashwāʾī عشوائي 2. **at random** ʿashwāʾiyan عشوائياً

rang [rang] *see* **ring**

range [reinj] *n* 1. madan مدىً 2. **mountain range** silsilat jibāl سلسلة جبال 3. (mil.) marman مرمىً 4. **rifle range** maydān li 'r-rimāya ميدان للرماية

rank [rangk] *n* (mil.) rutba رتبة (rutab رتب)

ransom ['ransəm] 1. *n* fidya فدية (fidāyāt فدايات) 2. *v* iftadā افتدى

rap [rap] *v* ṭaraqa طرق (u; ṭarq طرق)

rape [reip] 1. *n* ightiṣāb اغتصاب 2. *v* ightaṣaba اغتصب

rapid ['rapid] *adj* sarīʿ سريع

rapidly ['rapidli] *adv* bi surʿa بسرعة

rapist ['reipist] *n* mughtaṣib مغتصب (-ūn)

rare [reə] *adj* 1. nādir نادر 2. ghayr naḍīj غير نضيج

rarely ['reəli] *adv* nādiran نادراً

raspberry ['ra:zbəri] *n* tūt al-ʿullayq توت العليق

rash [rash] 1. *adj* mutahawwir متهور 2. *n* ṭafḥa طفحة

rat [rat] *n* juradh جرذ (jirdhān جرذان)

rate [reit] 1. *n* nisba نسبة (nisab نسب) 2. (fin.) siʿr سعر (asʿār أسعار) 3. **first rate** mumtāz ممتاز 4. **at any rate** ʿalā ayyati ḥāl على أية حال 5. **birth rate** nisbat al-mawālīd نسبة المواليد 6. **interest rate** muʿaddal al-fāʾida معدل الفائدة 7. **rate of exchange** *n* siʿr taḥwīl al-ʿumla سعر تحويل العملة 8. *v* qaddara قدر

rather [ra:dhə] *adv* 1. ilā ḥaddin mā إلى حد ما 2. bi 'l-aḥrā بالأحرى 3. ʿalā 'l-ʿaks على العكس

ration ['rashən] *v* ḥiṣṣat tamwīn حصة تموين

rational ['rashənəl] *adj* ʿaqlī عقلي

rattle ['ratəl] *v* khashkhasha خشخش

ravage ['ravij] *v* nahaba نهب (a; nahb نهب)

rave [reiv] 1. *n* ḥafla ḥamīya حفلة حمية 2. *v* **to rave about** takallama bi iʿjāb shadīd ʿan تكلم بإعجاب شديد عن

raw [ro:] *adj* nīʾ نيء

ray [rei] *n* shuʿāʿa (شعاعة (shuʿāʿ; ashiʿʿa (أشعة

razor [reizə] *n* mūsā موسى (mawāsin موسى (أمواس amwās (مواس

razor-blade *n* shafrat al-ḥilāqa شفرة الحلاقة

reach [riːch] *v* 1. madda مد (u; madd مد) 2. balagha بلغ (u; bulūgh بلوغ) 3. waṣala وصل (yaṣilu يصل; waṣl وصل) 4. tanāwala تناول

react [riˈakt] *v* kāna radd fiʿluh كان رد فعله

reaction [riˈakshən] *n* radd رد (rudūd ردود)

read [riːd] *v* (**read** [red]) qaraʾa قرأ (a; qirāʾa قراءة)

reader [ˈriːdə] *n* qāriʾ قارئ (ūn; qurrāʾ قراء)

readiness [ˈredinis] *n* istiʿdād استعداد

reading [ˈriːding] *n* qirāʾa قراءة

ready [ˈredi] *adj* 1. mustaʿidd مستعد; mutaʾahhib متأهب; jāhiz جاهز 2. **to get ready** istaʿadda استعد

real [ˈriəl] *adj* ḥaqīqī حقيقي

real estate *n* ʿaqār عقار

realistic [riəˈlistik] *adj* wāqiʿī واقعي

reality [riˈaləti] *n* 1. al-wāqiʿ الواقع 2. **in reality** fi ʾl-wāqiʿ في الواقع

realization [riəlaiˈzeishən] *n* 1. taḥqīq تحقيق 2. idrāk إدراك

realize [ˈriəlaiz] *v* 1. ḥaqqaqa حقق 2. adraka أدرك

really [ˈriəli] *adv* 1. ḥaqqan حقاً 2. jiddan جداً

realm [relm] *n* mamlaka مملكة (mamālik ممالك)

realtor [ˈriːəltə] *n* simsār ʿaqārī سمسار عقاري

rear [ˈriə] 1. *adj* khalfī خلفي 2. *n* muʾakhkhar مؤخر 3. *v* rabbā ربى

rearrange [riːəˈreinj] *v* aʿāda al-tartīb أعاد الترتيب

reason [ˈriːzən] *n* 1. ʿaql عقل 2. sabab سبب (asbāb أسباب) 3. **by reason of** bi sabab بسبب

reasonable [ˈriːznəbəl] *adj* maʿqūl معقول

reassure [riːəˈshoː] *v* ṭamʾana طمأن

rebel [ˈrebəl] *n* ʿaṣīy عصي (ūn; aʿṣiyāʾ أعصياء); mutamarrid متمرد

rebel [riˈbel] *v* ʿaṣā عصى (i; ʿiṣyān عصيان); tamarrada تمرد (**against** ʿalā على)

rebellion [riˈbeliən] *n* ʿiṣyān عصيان; tamarrud تمرد

rebellious [riˈbeliəs] *adj* mutamarrid متمرد

rebirth [ˈriːbəːth] *n* nahḍa نهضة

rebuild [riːˈbild] *v* aʿāda al-bināʾ أعاد البناء

rebuke [riˈbyuːk] *v* wabbakha وبخ

recall [riˈkoːl] *v* 1. tadhakkara تذكر 2. istaradda استرد

recede [rˈisiːd] *v* tarājaʿa تراجع

receipt [riˈsiːt] *n* 1. istilām إستلام 2. waṣl istilām وصل إستلام

receive [riˈsiːv] *v* istalama استلم

receiver [riˈsiːvə] *n* 1. mustalim مستلم 2. *(tech.)* jihāz جهاز (ajhiza أجهزة) 3. sammāʿa سماعة (-āt) 2. **to replace the receiver** waḍaʿa as-sammāʿa وضع السماعة (yaḍaʿu يضع; waḍʿ وضع)

recent [ˈriːsənt] *adj* ḥadīth حديث

recently [ˈriːsəntli] *adv* ḥadīthan حديثاً; muʾakhkharan مؤخراً

reception [riˈsepshən] *n* istiqbāl إستقبال

receptionist [riˈsepshənist] *n* muwaẓẓaf al-istiqbāl موظف الإستقبال

recession [ri'seshən] *n (ec.)* rukūd iqtiṣādī ركود اقتصادي

recipe ['resipi] *n* waṣfa وصفة (-āt)

recipient [re'sipiyənt] *n* mustalim مستلم

recital [ri'saitəl] *n* **1.** tilāwa تلاوة **2.** ḥafla mūsiqīya حفلة موسيقية

recite [ri'sait] *v* talā تلا (u; tulūw تلو)

reckless ['reklis] *adj* ṭā'ish طائش

reckon ['rekən] *v* **1.** ḥasaba حسب (u; ḥisāb حساب) **2.** i'tabara اعتبر; ẓanna ظن (u; ẓann ظن)

reclaim [ri'kleim] *v* **1.** istaradda استرد **2. to reclaim land** istaṣlaḥa arāḍin استصلح أراض

recognition [rekəg'nishən] *n* **1.** taqdīr تقدير **2.** *(pol.)* i'tirāf اعتراف

recognize ['rekəgnaiz] *v* **1.** 'arafa عرف (i; ma'rifa معرفة; 'irfān عرفان) **2.** qaddara قدر **3.** *(pol.)* i'tarafa bi اعترف ب

recollect [rekə'lekt] *v* dhakara ذكر (u; dhikr ذكر; tadhkār تذكار)

recollection [rekə'lekshən] *n* dhikr ذكر

recommend [rekə'mend] *v* waṣṣā وصى

recommendation [rekəmen'deishən] *n* tawṣīya توصية

recompense ['rekəmpens] **1.** *n* jazā' جزاء; mukāfa'a مكافأة (-āt) **2.** *v* jazā جزي (i; jazā' جزاء); kāfa'a كافأ

reconcile [rekən'sail] *v* aṣlaḥa أصلح

reconciliation [rekənsili'eishən] *n* iṣlāḥ إصلاح

reconsider [ri:kən'sidə] *v* a'āda al-naẓar fī أعاد النظر في

reconstruct [ri:kən'strʌkt] *v* a'āda al-binā' أعاد البناء

reconstruction [ri:kən'strʌkchən] *n* i'ādat al-binā' إعادة البناء

record ['reko:d] **1.** *adj* qiyāsī قياسي **2.** *n* raqm qiyāsī رقم قياسي (arqām أرقام) **3.** mudawwana مدونة (-āt) **4.** *(leg.)* sijill سجل (-āt) **5.** *(mus.)* usṭuwāna أسطوانة (-āt) **6. for the record** li 'n-nashr للنشر **7. off the record** laysa li n-nashr ليس للنشر **8. world record** raqm qiyās 'ālamī رقم قياس عالمي **9. to break a record** kasara raqman qiyāsīyan كسر رقماً قياسياً (i; kasr كسر) **10.** *see* **records**

record [ri'ko:d] *v* **1.** sajjala سجل; dawwana دون **2.** *(mus.)* sajjala سجل **3.** *see* **records**

recording [ri'ko:ding] *n (mus.)* tasjīl تسجيل

records ['reko:dz] *pl* sijillāt سجلات

recover [ri'kʌvə] *v* **1.** istaradda استرد **2.** *(med.)* ista'āda استعاد; shafā شفى (i; shifā' شفاء)

recovery [ri'kʌvəri] *n* **1.** istirdād استرداد; istirjā' إسترجاع **2.** *(med.)* shifā' شفاء

recreation [rekri'eishən] *n* istijmām إستجمام; tasliya تسلية (-āt)

recruit [ri'kru:t] **1.** *n* 'uḍw jadīd عضو جديد (a'ḍā' أعضاء); **2.** *(mil.)* mujannad jadīd مجند جديد (-ūn) **3.** *v* jannada جند

recruitment [ri'kru:tmənt] *n* tajnīd تجنيد

rectangle ['rektanggəl] *n* mustaṭīl مستطيل (-āt)

recuperation [riku:pə'reishən] *n* shifā' شفاء

recur [ri'kə:] *v* takarrara تكرر

recurrence [ri'kʌrəns] *n* takarrur تكرر

recycle [ri'saikəl] *v* aᶜāda istiᶜmāl
أعاد إستعمال

red [red] *adj* aḥmar أحمر

redeem [ri'di:m] *v* istaradda استرد;
istarjaᶜa استرجع

red-handed [red'handid] *adj*
mutalabbis متلبس

red-hot *adj* mutawahhij متوهج

red tape *n* al-rūtīn al-ḥukūmī
الروتين الحكومي

reduce [ri'dyu:s] *v* qallala قلل;
khaffaḍa خفض

reduction [ri'dʌkshən] *n* takhfīḍ
تخفيض

redundancy [ri'dʌndənsi] *n* faṣl ᶜan
al-ᶜamal فصل عن العمل

redundant [ri'dʌndənt] *adj* fāṣil ᶜan
al-ᶜamal فاصل عن العمل

reduplicate [ri'dyuplikeit] *v*
karrara كرر

reef [ri:f] *n* shiᶜb marjānī شعب مرجاني
(shiᶜāb marjānīya شعاب مرجانية)

re-elect ['ri:ə'lekt] *v* aᶜāda intikhāb
أعاد انتخاب

refer [ri'fə:] *v* 1. rājaᶜa راجع (to ilā
إلى). 2. ashāra أشار (to ilā إلى). 3.
aḥāla أحال (to ilā إلى)

referee [refə'ri:] *n* ḥakam حكم
(ḥukkām حكام)

reference ['refərəns] *n* 1. marjaᶜ
مرجع (marājiᶜ مراجع). 2. **with
reference to...** bi khuṣūṣ بخصوص

referendum [refə'rendəm] *n*
istiftā' (al-shaᶜb) إستفتاء (الشعب)

refill [ri:'fil] *v* aᶜāda al-mal'
أعاد الملء

refine [ri'fain] *v* naqqā نقى

refined [ri'faind] *adj* 1. munaqqan
منقى. 2. muhadhdhab مهذب

refinery [ri'fainəri] *n* miṣfāh مصفاة
(maṣāfin مصاف)

reflect [ri'flekt] *v* 1. ᶜakasa عكس (i;
ᶜaks عكس). 2. tafakkara تفكر

reflection [ri'flekshən] *n* 1. inᶜikās
إنعكاس (-āt). 2. tafakkur تفكر

reflex ['ri:fleks] *n* inᶜikās lā irādī
إنعكاس لا إرادي (-āt)

reform [ri'fo:m] 1. *n* iṣlāḥ إصلاح
(-āt). 2. *v* aṣlaḥa أصلح

refrain [ri'frein] 1. *n* ᶜibāra عبارة
mutakarrira متكررة. 2. *v*
imtanaᶜa امتنع (**from** ᶜan عن)

refresh [ri'fresh] *v* anᶜasha أنعش

refreshing [ri'freshing] *adj* munᶜish
منعش

refreshments [ri'freshmənts] *pl*
muraṭṭibāt مرطبات

refrigeration [rifrijə'reishən] *n*
tathlīj تثليج

refrigerator [ri'frijəreitə] *n*
thallāja ثلاجة (-āt)

refuge ['refyu:j] *n* malja' ملجأ
(malāji' ملاجئ)

refugee [refyu'ji:] *n* lāji' لاجئ (-ūn)

refund ['ri:fʌnd] 1. *n* iᶜādat māl
إعادة مال. 2. *v* aᶜāda mālan أعاد مالاً

refurbishment [ri'fə:bishmənt] *n*
tajdīd تجديد

refusal [ri'fyu:zəl] *n* rafḍ رفض

refuse ['refyu:s] *n* nufāya نفاية
(-āt)

refuse [ri'fyu:z] *v* rafaḍa رفض (u;
rafḍ رفض)

regain [ri'gein] *v* istaradda استرد;
istaᶜāda استعاد

regard [ri'ga:d] 1. *n* iḥtirām إحترام
(-āt). 2. **with regard to** bi 'n-
nisbati ilā بالنسبة إلى. 3. *v* iᶜtabara
اعتبر. 4. naẓara ilā نظر إلى (u; naẓar
نظر). 5. *see* **regards**

regarding [ri'ga:ding] *prep* bi 'n-nisbati ilā بالنسبة إلى

regardless [ri'ga:dlis] *adv* mahmā yakun مهما يكن

regardless of *prep* bi 'r-raghmi min بالرغم من; bi ṣarf an-naẓar ʿan بصرف النظر عن

regards [ri'ga:dz] *pl* 1. taḥayyāt تحيات; tamanniyāt تمنيات 2. **as regards** bi 'n-nisbati ilā بالنسبة إلى

regime [rei'zhi:m] *n* niẓām نظام (anẓima أنظمة)

regiment ['rejimənt] *n* fawj فوج (afwāj أفواج)

region ['ri:jən] *n* iqlīm إقليم (aqālīm أقاليم); minṭaqa منطقة (manāṭiq مناطق)

register ['rejistə] 1. *n* sijill سجل (-āt) 2. **cash till** ṣundūq ḥāsib صندوق حاسب 3. *v* sajjala سجل

registration [reji'streishən] *n* tasjīl تسجيل

regret [ri'gret] 1. *n* asaf أسف; nadam ندم 2. *v* asifa أسف (a; asaf أسف); nadima ندم (a; nadam ندم)

regretfully [ri'gretfuli] *adv* li 'l-asaf للأسف

regrettable [ri'gretəbəl] *adj* mu'sif مؤسف

regular ['regyulə] *adj* 1. iʿtiyādī إعتيادي 2. munaẓẓam منظم

regularity [regyu'lærəti] *n* intiẓām إنتظام

regularly ['regyuləli] *adv* bi intiẓām بإنتظام

regulate ['regyuleit] *v* naẓẓama نظم; ʿaddala عدل

regulation [regyu'leishən] *n* 1. qānūn قانون (qawānīn قوانين) 2. tanẓīm تنظيم; taʿdīl تعديل

rehearsal [ri'hə:səl] *n* tamrīn تمرين

rehearse [ri'hə:s] *v* marrana مرن

reign [rein] 1. *n* mulk ملك; ʿahd عهد (ʿuhūd عهود) 2. *v* malaka ملك (u; mulk ملك)

rein [rein] *n* ʿinān عنان (aʿinna أعنة)

reinforcements [ri:in'fo:smənts] *pl (mil.)* taʿzīzāt تعزيزات

reject [ri'jekt] *v* rafaḍa رفض (u; rafḍ رفض)

rejection [ri'jekshən] *n* rafḍ رفض

rejoice [ri'jois] *v* fariḥa فرح (a; faraḥ فرح)

relapse ['rilaps] *n (med.)* intikās إنتكاس

relate [ri'leit] *v* 1. rawā روى (i; riwāya رواية) 2. *see* **related**

related [ri'leitid] *adj* 1. mutaʿalliq متعلق (to ب) 2. murtabiṭ bi ṣilat al-qarāba مرتبط بصلة القرابة

relation [ri'leishən] *n* 1. qarīb قريب (aqribā' أقرباء); nasīb نسيب (ansāb أنساب) 2. ʿalāqa علاقة (-āt); ṣila صلة (-āt); rābiṭa رابطة (rawābiṭ روابط) 3. **in relation to** fī mā yataʿallaq bi في ما يتعلق ب 4. *see* **relations**

relations [ri'leishənz] *pl* **diplomatic relations** al-ʿalāqāt al-diblōmāsīya العلاقات الدبلوماسية

relationship [ri'leishənship] *n* 1. ṣila صلة (-āt); ʿalāqa علاقة (-āt) 2. qurāba قرابة; nasab نسب

relative ['relətiv] 1. *adj* nisbī نسبي 2. *n see* **relation**

relatively ['relətivli] *adv* nisbīyan نسبياً

relax [ri'laks] *v* arkhā أرخى; istarkhā استرخى

relaxation [ri:lak'seishən] n irkhā' إرخاء; istirkhā' إسترخاء

relaxed [ri'lakst] adj 1. mustarkhin مسترخ 2. mustarīḥ مستريح

release [ri'li:s] 1. n iṭlāq إطلاق; taḥrīr تحرير 2. **press release** bayān ṣaḥafī بيان صحفي; 3. v aṭlaqa أطلق; ḥarrara حرر

relevance; relevancy ['reləvəns; -si] n wathāqat aṣ-ṣila وثاقة الصلة

relevant ['reləvənt] adj wathīq aṣ-ṣila وثيق الصلة

reliability [rilaiə'biləti] n jidāra bi 'th-thiqa جدارة بالثقة

reliable [ri'laiəbəl] adj jadīr bi 'th-thiqa جدير بالثقة

reliant on [re'laiənt] adj muttakil ʿalā متكل على; muʿtamid ʿalā معتمد على

relic ['relik] n athar أثر (āthār آثار)

relief [ri'li:f] n 1. faraj فرج; irtiyāḥ إرتياح 2. iʿāna إعانة (-āt)

relieve [ri'li:v] v 1. arāḥa أراح 2. sakkana سكن 3. ḥalla maḥall حل محل (u; ḥall حل)

relieved [ri'li:vd] adj mirtāḥ مرتاح

religion [ri'lijən] n dīn دين (adyān أديان)

religious [ri'lijəs] adj mutadayyin متدين

relish ['relish] v tadhawwaqa تذوق

reluctance [ri'lʌktəns] n taraddud تردد

reluctant [ri'lʌktənt] adj taraddada تردد

rely [ri'lai] v iʿtamada اعتمد (on ʿalā على)

remain [ri'mein] v baqiya بقي (a; baqā' بقاء); makatha مكث (u; makth مكث); ẓalla ظل (a; ẓall ظل)

remainder [ri'meində] n baqīya بقية (baqāyā بقايا)

remains [ri'meinz] pl 1. baqāya بقايا 2. āthār آثار 3. juththa جثة; juthmān جثمان

remake ['ri:meik] v aʿāda intāj/taskīl... أعاد إنتاج\تشكيل...

remark [ri'ma:k] 1. n taʿlīq تعليق 2. v ʿallaqa علق (**upon** ʿalā على)

remarkable [ri'ma:kəbəl] n rā'iʿ رائع; istithnā'ī إستثنائي

remedy ['remədi] n ʿilāj علاج; dawā' دواء

remember [ri'membə] v dhakara ذكر (u; tadhkār تذكار); tadhakkara تذكر

remind [ri'maind] v dhakkara ذكر

reminder [ri'maində] n mudhakkara مذكرة (-āt)

remote [ri'məut] adj baʿīd بعيد; maʿzūl معزول

removal [ri'mu:vəl] n nazʿ نزع

remove [ri'mu:v] v 1. nazaʿa نزع (i; nazʿ نزع) 2. naqala نقل (u; naql نقل)

renaissance [ri'neisəns] n nahḍa نهضة (-āt)

render ['rendə] v jaʿala جعل (a; jaʿl جعل)

renew [ri'nyu:] v jaddada جدد

renounce [ri'nauns] v takhallā ʿan تخلى عن

renovate ['renəveit] v jaddada جدد; aṣlaḥa أصلح

rent [rent] 1. n ujra أجرة 2. v ajjara أجر 3. istaʾjara استأجر

rental ['rentəl] n ujra أجرة

reorganize [ri:'o:gənaiz] v aʿāda al-tanẓīm أعاد التنظيم

repair [ri'peə] 1. n tarmīm ترميم 2. v ṣallaḥa صلح; aṣlaḥa أصلح

repay [ri:'pei] v عوّض; wafā daynan وفى ديناً (i; wafā' وفاء; wafiy وفي)

repayment [ri:'peimənt] n ta'awwuḍ تعوّض; wafā' ad-dayn وفاء الدين

repeat [ri'pi:t] v karrara كرّر

repeatedly [ri'pi:tidli] adv takrāran تكراراً

repel [ri'pel] v ṣadda صدّ (u; ṣadd صدّ)

repetition [repi'tishən] n takrār تكرار

replace [ri'pleis] v 1. arja'a أرجع 2. istabdala استبدل

replacement [ri'pleismənt] n badīl بديل (budalā' بدلاء)

reply [ri'plai] 1. n jawāb جواب (ajwiba أجوبة); 2. v jāwaba جاوب; ajāba أجاب (to ilā إلى; 'alā على)

report [ri'po:t] 1. n taqrīr تقرير (taqārīr تقارير) 2. v ballagha 'an بلغ عن

reporter [ri'po:tə] n murāsil مراسل (-ūn)

represent [repri'zent] v maththala مثّل

representation [reprizen'teishən] n tamthīl تمثيل

representative [repri'zentətiv] n 1. mumaththil ممثّل (-ūn) 2. see House of Representatives; sales representative

reprieve [ri'pri:v] v (leg.) arja'a tanfīdh hukm bi 'l-i'dām أرجأ تنفيذ حكم بالاعدام

reprint ['ri:print] v a'āda al-ṭab' أعاد الطبع

reproduce [ri:prə'dyu:s] v 1. nasakha نسخ (a; naskh نسخ) 2. to

sexually reproduce tawālada توالد

reproduction [ri:prə'dʌkshən] n 1. naskh نسخ; nuskha نسخة 2. **sexual reproduction** tawālud توالد

reptile [reptail] n zāḥif زاحف (zawāḥif زواحف)

republic [ri'pʌblik] n jumhūrīya جمهورية (-āt)

republican [ri'pʌblikən] 1. adj jumhūrī جمهوري 2. n jumhūrī جمهوري (yūn)

repulsive [ri'pʌlsiv] adj karīh كريه

reputation [repyu'teishən] n sum'a سمعة

request [ri'kwest] 1. n ṭalab طلب (-āt) 2. v ṭalaba طلب (u; ṭalab طلب)

require [rikwaiə] v taṭallaba تطلّب; iḥtāja ilā احتاج إلى

requirement [ri'kwaiəmənt] n 1. ḥāja حاجة (-āt) 2. mutaṭallab متطلّب (-āt)

rescue ['reskyu:] 1. n inqādh إنقاذ 2. v anqadha أنقذ

research ['ri:sə:ch] 1. n baḥth بحث (buḥūth بحوث; abḥāth أبحاث) 2. **research centre** markaz li 'l-buḥūth مركز للبحوث 3. v baḥatha بحث (a; baḥth بحث)

researcher [ri'sə:chə] n bāḥith باحث (-ūn)

resemblance [ri'zembləns] n shibh شبه (ashbāh أشباه)

resemble [ri'zembəl] v shābaha شابه

resent [ri'zent] v imta'aḍa امتعض

resentment [ri'zentmənt] n imti'āḍ إمتعاض

reservation [rezə'veishən] n ḥajz حجز

reserve [ri'zə:v] 1. adj iḥtiyāṭī احتياطي

2. *v* ḥajaza حجز (u/i; ḥajz حجز) 2. إحتياطي
3. *see* reserves حجز

reserved [ri'zə:vd] *adj* mutaḥaffiẓ
متحفظ

reserves [ris'sə:vz] *pl* **oil reserves**
iḥtiyāṭāt an-nafṭ
إحتياطات النفط

reservoir ['rezəvwa:] *n* 1. buḥayra
iṣṭināʿīya بحيرة إصطناعية .2
mustawdaʿ مستودع

reset [ri:'set] *v* aʿāda aḍ-ḍabṭ
أعاد الضبط

residence ['rezidəns] *n* 1. iqāma
إقامة .2 manzil منزل (manāzil منازل)

resident ['rezidənt] *n* 1. muqīm
مقيم .2 sākin ساكن (sukkān سكان)

residential [rezi'denshəl] *adj*
sakanī سكني

resign [ri'zain] *v* 1. istaqāla إستقال .2
istaslama li استسلم لـ

resignation [rezig'neishən] *n*
istiqāla إستقالة (-āt)

resist [ri'zist] *v* qāwama قاوم

resistance [ri'zistəns] *n* muqāwama
مقاومة

resistant [ri'zistənt] *adj* wāqin واقٍ
(to ḍidd ضد)

resolution [rezə'lu:shən] *n* 1. ḥall
حل (ḥulūl حلول) 2. taṣmīm تصميم .3
(pol.) qarār قرار (-āt)

resolve [ri'zolv] 1. *n* taṣmīm تصميم
2. *v* ṣammama صمم (to ʿalā على)

resort [ri'zo:t] 1. *n* **holiday resort**
qarya siyāḥīya قرية سياحية .2 **as a
last resort** ka malādh akhīr
كملاذ أخير .3 *v* **to resort to force**
laja'a ilā 'l-qūwa لجأ إلى القوة (a;
lujū' لجوء)

resource [ri'so:sfəl] *n* 1. mawrid
مورد (mawārīd موارد) 2. *see*
resources

resourceful [ri'zo:sfəl] *adj* dāhin
داه

resources [ri'zo:siz] *pl* mawārid
موارد

respect [ri'spekt] 1. *n* iḥtirām إحترام
(-āt) 2. **with respect to** bi 'n-
nisbati ilā بالنسبة إلى 3. **to show
respect to** iḥtarama احترم 4. *v*
iḥtarama احترم

respectability [rispektə'biləti] *n*
makāna مكانة

respectable [ris'pektəbəl] *adj*
muḥtaram محترم

respectful [ris'pektfəl] *adj*
muḥtarim متحرم

respects [ris'pekts] *pl* iḥtirāmāt
إحترامات

respond [ris'pond] *v* ajāba أجاب (to
ilā إلى/ʿalā على)

response [ris'pons] *n* ijāba إجابة
(-āt)

responsibility [risponsə'biləti] *n*
mas'ūlīya مسؤولية (-āt)

responsible [ris'ponsəbəl] *adj*
mas'ūl مسؤول (for ʿan عن)

rest [rest] 1. *n* rāḥa راحة; istirāḥa
استراحة 2. baqīya بقية 3. *v* irtāḥa
ارتاح; istarāḥa استراح

restaurant ['restront] *n* maṭʿam
مطعم (maṭāʿim مطاعم)

restless ['restlis] *adj* mutamalmil
متململ

restoration [restə'reishən] *n* 1.
iʿāda إعادة 2. tajdīd تجديد; tarmīm
ترميم

restore [ri'sto:] *v* 1. aʿāda أعاد 2.
rammama رمم; jaddada جدد 3.
shafā شفى (i; shifā' شفاء)

restraint [ri'streint] *n* kabḥ كبح

restrict [ri'strikt] *v* qayyada قيد

restriction [ri'strikchən] n qayd قيد (quyūd) تقييد; taqyīd (-āt); تضييق tadyīq

result [ri'zʌlt] n 1. natīja نتيجة (natā'ij نتائج) 2. **as a result of** natījatan li نتيجةً ل 3. **to result in** addā ilā أدى إلى 4. **to result from** nataja ʿan نتج عن (i; nutūj نتوج); nasha'a ʿan نشأ عن (a; nash')

resume [ri'zyu:m] v ista'nafa استأنف

retail ['ri:teil] 1. adj tajzi'ī تجزيئي 2. n bayʿ bi 't-tajzi'a بيع بالتجزئة 3. v bāʿa bi 't-tajzi'a باع بالتجزئة (i; bayʿ بيع)

retailer ['ri:teilə] n bāʾiʿ bi 't-tajzi'a بائع بالتجزئة

retain [ri'tein] v iḥtafaẓa bi احتفظ ب; istabqā استبقى

retaliation [ritalieishən] n al-muqābala bi 'l-mithl المقابلة بالمثل

retire [ri'taiə] v 1. taqāʿada تقاعد 2. āwā آوى (**to** ilā إلى)

retired [ri'taiəd] adj mutaqāʿid متقاعد

retirement [ri'taiəmənt] n taqāʿud تقاعد

retreat [ri'tri:t] 1. n insiḥāb انسحاب; tarājuʿ تراجع 2. v insaḥaba انسحب; tarāja'a تراجع

retrieve [ri'tri:v] v istaradda استرد; istarja'a استرجع

return [ri'tə:n] 1. n ʿawda عودة; rujūʿ رجوع 2. (spor.) radd رد 3. ʿā'id عائد (-āt); ʿawā'id عوائد 4. **in return for** muqābila مقابلة 5. v ʿāda عاد (u; ʿawda عودة); raja'a رجع (i; rujūʿ رجوع)

return ticket n tadhkirat dhihāb īhāb تذكرة ذهاب إيهاب

reunion [ri'yu:nyən] n jamʿ ash-

shaml جمع الشمل; ijtimāʿ ash-shaml اجتماع الشمل

reunite [ri:yu:'nait] v waḥḥada thāniyatan وحد ثانيةً; ijtama'a baʿd firāq اجتمع بعد فراق

reveal [ri'vi:l] v aẓhara أظهر

revenge [ri'venj] n intiqām انتقام

revenue ['revənyu:] n dakhl دخل

reverence ['revərəns] n tawqīr توقير

reverse [ri'və:s] 1. adj irtidādī إرتدادي 2. n naksa نكسة 3. v taḥarraka ilā 'l-warā' تحرك إلى الوراء

review [ri'vyu:] 1. n murāja'a مواجعة 2. (media) naqd نقد; murāja'a مراجعة 4. v isti'rāḍ إستعراض 3. rāja'a راجع 5. (media) naqada نقد (u; naqd نقد); rāja'a راجع 6. (mil.) ista'raḍa استعرض

reviewer [ri'vyu:ə] n murāji' مراجع (-ūn); nāqid ناقد (nuqqād نقاد)

revise [ri'vaiz] v 1. naqqaḥa نقح 2. (ed.) rāja'a راجع

revision [ri'vizhən] n 1. tanqīḥ تنقيح 2. (ed.) murāja'a مراجعة

revival [ri'vaivəl] n iḥyā' إحياء

revolt [ri'vəult] 1. n tamarrud تمرد 2. v tamarrada تمرد 3. qarrafa قرّف

revolting [ri'vəulting] adj muqrif مقرف

revolution [revə'lu:shən] n 1. dawra دورة (-āt) 2. (pol.) thawra ثورة (-āt)

revolutionary [revə'lu:shənəri] 1. adj thawrī ثوري 2. n thawrī ثوري (-yūn)

revolve [ri'vɔlv] v dāra دار (u; dawr دور)

revolver [ri'vɔlvə] n musaddas مسدس (-āt)

reward [ri'wo:d] 1. *n* mukāfa'a مكافأة (-āt) 2. *v* kāfa'a كافأ (with bi ب; for li لـ)

rewind [ri:'waind] *v* aʿāda ash-sharīṭ أعاد الشريط

rewrite [ri:'rait] *v* aʿāda al-kitāba أعاد الكتابة

rhubarb ['ru:ba:b] *n* rāwand راوند

rhyme [raim] *n* qāfiya قافية (qawāfin قواف)

rhythm ['ridhəm] *n* īqāʿ إيقاع (-āt)

rib [rib] *n* ḍilʿ ضلع (ḍulūʿ ضلوع)

ribbon ['ribən] *n* sharīṭ شريط (ashriṭa أشرطة)

rice [rais] *n* aruzz أرز

rich [rich] *adj* ghanī غني

riches ['richiz] *pl* tharwa ثروة

rid [rid] *v* 1. khallaṣa خلص 2. to get rid of takhallaṣa min تخلص من

ridden ['ridən] *see* ride

ride [raid] 1. *n* rukūb ركوب 2. *v* (rode, ridden) rakiba (a) ركب (rukūb ركوب)

rider ['raidə] *n* rākib راكب (rukkāb ركاب)

ridiculous [ri'dikyuləs] *adj* sakhīf سخيف; muḍhik مضحك

rifle ['raifəl] *n* bunduqīya بندقية (-āt)

rig [rig] *see* oil rig

rig an election *v* talāʿaba bi intikhāb تلاعب بانتخاب

right [rait] 1. *adj* ayman أيمن; yamīn يمين 2. ṣaḥīḥ صحيح; ḥaqīqī حقيقي 3. munāsib مناسب 4. *n* (pol.) ḥaqq حق (ḥuqūq حقوق) 5. *adv* bi ṭarīqa ṣaḥīḥa بطريقة صحيحة 6. right away fawran فوراً; ḥālan حالاً 7. *see* rights

right-hand *adj* ayman أيمن

right-handed *adj* ayman أيمن

rights [raits] *pl* 1. huqūq حقوق 2. human rights huqūq al-insān حقوق الإنسان

right-wing *adj* (pol.) yamīnī يميني

right wing *n* (pol.) al-yamīn اليمين

right-winger *n* (pol.) yamīnī يميني

rigid ['rijid] *adj* ṣulb صلب

rigorous ['rigərəs] *adj* 1. ṣārim صارم; qāsin قاس 2. daqīq jiddan دقيق جداً

rim [rim] *n* ḥāffa حافة (-āt)

ring [ring] 1. *n* khātim خاتم (khawātim خواتم) 2. mukālama tilifōnīya مكالمة تلفونية 3. boxing ring malʿab al-mulākama ملعب الملاكمة 4. *v* (rang, rung) ranna رن (i; ranīn رنين) 5. talfana تلفن

ring a bell *v* qaraʿa قرع (a; qarʿ قرع)

ringleader ['ringli:də] *n* zaʿīm fitna زعيم فتنة (zuʿamā' زعماء)

ring up *v* talfana تلفن

rink [ringk] *n* skating rink mazlaja مزلجة

riot ['raiət] 1. *n* shaghab شغب 2. *v* shāghaba شاغب

rioter ['raiətə] *n* mushāghib مشاغب (-ūn)

rip [rip] 1. *n* mazq مزق 2. *v* mazaqa مزق (i; mazq مزق)

ripe [raip] *n* nāḍij ناضج

ripple ['ripəl] *n* mawj موج (amwāj أمواج); muwayja مويجة (-āt)

rise [raiz] 1. *n* ṣaʿda صعدة (-āt) 2. (fin.) irtifāʿ إرتفاع 3. pay rise ʿilāwa علاوة 4. sunrise shurūq شروق 5. *v* (rose, risen) ṣaʿida صعد (a; ṣuʿūd صعود) 6. ṭalaʿa طلع (a; ṭulūʿ طلوع; maṭlaʿ مطلع) 7. irtafaʿa ارتفع (مطلع)

risk [risk] 1. *n* mukhāṭira مخاطرة (-āt) 2. *v* khāṭara خاطر

risky ['riski] *adj* maḥfūf bi 'l-
makhāṭir محفوف بالمخاطر

ritual ['rityul] 1. *adj* ṭaqsī طقسي;
sha'ā'irī شعائري 2. *n* ṭaqs طقس
(ṭuqūs طقوس); sha'īra شعيرة
(sha'ā'ir شعائر)

rival ['raivəl] 1. *adj* munāfis منافس 2.
n munāfis منافس (-ūn) 3. *v* nāfasa
نافس

river ['rivə] *n* nahr نهر (anhār أنهار)

river bank *n* ḍiffa/ḍaffa ضفة (ḍifāf
ضفاف)

road [rəud] *n* ṭarīq طريق (ṭuruq
طرق)

road sign *n* ishārat ṭarīq إشارة طريق

roam [rəum] *v* jāla جال (u; jawla
جولة)

roar [ro:] 1. *n* hadīr هدير 2. *v* hadara
هدر (i; hadr هدر; hadīr هدير)

roast [rəust] 1. *adj* shawī شوي 2. *v*
shawā شوى (i; shayy شي)

rob [rob] *v* (**robbed**) saraqa سرق (i;
sariqa سرقة)

robber ['robə] *n* sāriq سارق (-ūn;
saraqa سرقة)

robbery ['robəri] *n* sariqa سرقة
(-āt)

robe [rəub] *n* ridā' رداء (ardiya أردية)

robot ['rəubot] *n* rōbōṭ روبوط; insān
ālī إنسان آلي

rock [rok] 1. *n* ṣakhra صخرة (ṣakhr
صخر; ṣukhūr صخور) 2. *v* ta'arjaḥa
تأرجح; hazza هز (u; hazz هز)

rocket ['rokit] *n* ṣārūkh صاروخ
(ṣawārīkh صواريخ)

rock'n'roll [rokən'rol] *n (mus.)* rōk
and rōll روك أند رول

rocky ['roki] *adj* ṣakhrī صخري

rod [rod] *n* 1. 'ūd عود (a'wād أعواد);
qaḍīb قضيب (quḍbān قضبان) 2.

fishing rod ṣinnāra li ṣayd as-
samak صنارة لصيد السمك (ṣanānīr
صنانير)

rode [rəud] *see* ride

role [rəul] *n* dawr دور (adwār أدوار)

roll [rəul] 1. *n* roll of cloth laffat
qumāsh لفة قماش 2. roll of bread
qurṣ قرص (aqrāṣ أقراص) 3. *v* to roll
along tadaḥnaja تدحنج 4. to roll
up ṭawā طوى (i; ṭayy طي)

romance ['rəumans] *n* 1. rōmāns
رومانس 2. qiṣṣat ḥubb قصة حب

romantic [rəu'mantik] *adj*
rōmāntikī رومانتكي

roof [ru:f] *n* saqf سقف (suqūf سقوف)

room [ru:m; rum] *n* 1. ghurfa غرفة
(āt; ghuraf غرف); ḥujra حجرة
(ḥujarāt حجرات) 2. muttasa' متسع
3. majāl مجال

rooster ['ru:stə] *n (US)* dīk ديك
(duyūk ديوك)

root [ru:t] *n* jidhr جذر (judhūr
جذور)

rope [rəup] *n* ḥabl حبل (ḥibāl حبال)

rose [rəuz] 1. *n* warda وردة (ward
ورد) 2. *see* rise

rot [rot] 1. *n* ta'affun تعفن 2. *v*
(**rotted**) ta'affana تعفن

rotate [rəu'teit] *v* 1. dāra دار (u;
dawr دور) 2. tanāwaba تناوب

rotation [rəu'teishən] *n* dawra دورة
(-āt)

rotten ['rotən] *adj* 1. natin نتن;
muta'affin متعفن 2. ḥaqīr حقير

rough [rʌf] *adj* 1. khashin خشن 2.
ghayr muhadhdhab غير مهذب 3.
qāsin قاس 4. rough weather ṭaqs
'āṣif طقس عاصف

roughly ['rʌfli] *adv* 1. bi qaswa
بقسوة 2. taqrīban تقريباً

round [raund] 1. *adj* mudawwar مدور؛ mustadīr مستدير 2. tāmm تام 3. *n (spor.)* dawra دورة (-āt) 4. **round of ammunition** ṭalaqa طلقة (-āt) 5. *adv* **all year round** ṭiwāl as-sana طوال السنة 6. *see* **around**

roundabout ['raundəbaut] *n* dawwāra دوارة

route [ru:t; *(US)* raut] *n* ṭarīq طريق (ṭuruq طرق)

routine [ru:'ti:n] 1. *adj* rūtīnī روتيني 2. *n* rūtīn روتين

row [rau] *n* 1. mushājara مشاجرة 2. *v* shājara شاجر

row [rəu] 1. *n* ṣaff صف (ṣufūf صفوف) 2. *v* jadhdhafa جذف

royal ['roiəl] *adj* malakī ملكي

royalty ['roiəlti] *n* 1. malakīya ملكية 2. *(fin.)* juʿāla جعالة

rub [rʌb] *v* ḥakka حك (u; ḥakk حك)

rubber ['rʌbə] 1. *adj* maṭṭāṭī مطاطي 2. *n* maṭṭāṭ مطاط 3. maḥayya محية (-āt)

rubber band *n* sharīṭ maṭṭāṭī شريط مطاطي

rubber stamp *n* khatm maṭṭāṭī ختم مطاطي

rubbish ['rʌbish] *n* nufāya نفاية (-āt)

rucksack ['rʌksak] *n* ḥaqībat al-ẓahr حقيبة الظهر

rude [ru:d] *adj* faẓẓ فظ

rudeness ['ru:dnis] *n* faẓāẓa فظاظة

rug [rʌg] *n* sajjāda سجادة (sajjād سجاد)

rugby ['rʌgbi] *n* rughbī رغبي

rugged ['rʌgid] *adj* 1. waʿir وعير 2. mutajaʿʿid متجعد

ruin ['ru:in] 1. *n* kharāb خراب 2. *v* kharraba خرب 3. *see* **ruins**

ruined ['ru:ind] *adj* muflis مفلس

ruins ['ru:inz] *pl* āthār آثار

rule [ru:l] 1. *n* qāʿida قاعدة (qawāʿid قواعد) 2. ḥukm حكم 3. **as a rule** ʿādatan عادة 4. *v* ḥakama حكم (u; ḥukm حكم)

ruler ['ru:lə] *n* 1. ḥākim حاكم (-ūn; ḥukkām حكام) 2. misṭara مسطرة (masāṭir مساطر)

ruling ['ru:ling] 1. *adj* ḥākim حاكم 2. *n (leg.)* ḥukm حكم (aḥkām أحكام)

rum [rʌm] *n* rumm رم

rumour, *(US)* **rumor** ['ru:mə] *n* ishāʿa إشاعة (-āt)

run [rʌn] 1. *n* ʿadw عدو 2. *v* (**ran, run**) ʿadā عدا (i; adw عدو); rakaḍa ركض (u; rakḍ ركض) 3. adāra أدار

run away *v* farra فر (i; firār فرار)

runner ['rʌnə] *n* rākiḍ راكض (-ūn)

runner-up [rʌnə'ʌp] *n* al-mutasābiq alladhī yatlū al-fā'iz المتسابق الذي يتلو الفائز

run out *v* nafida نفد (a; nafād نفاد)

run over *v* 1. rājaʿa راجع 2. *see* **overflow**

rung [rʌng] *see* **ring**

runway ['rʌnwei] *n* madraj مدرج (madārij مدارج)

rural ['ruərəl] *adj* rīfī ريفي؛ qarawī قروي

rush [rʌsh] 1. *n* indifāʿ إندفاع؛ harwala هرولة 2. *v* indafaʿa إندفع؛ harwala هرول

Russia ['rʌshə] *n* rūsiyā روسيا

Russian ['rʌshən] 1. *adj* rūsī روسي 2. *n* rūsī روسي (-yūn)

rusty ['rʌsti] *adj* ṣadiʾ صديء

ruthless ['ru:thlis] *adj* lā yarḥam لا يرحم

S

sabbath ['sabəth] *n* al-sabt السبت

sabotage ['sabəta:zh] **1.** *n* takhrīb
تخريب **2.** *v* kharraba خرب

sack [sak] **1.** *n* kīs كيس (akyās
أكياس) **2.** *v* ṭaradah min manṣibih
طرده من منصبه

sacred ['seikrid] *adj* muqaddas
مقدس

sacrifice ['sakrifais] **1.** *n* taḍḥīya
تضحية **2.** *v* ḍaḥḥā ضحى

sad [sad] *adj* ḥazīn حزين

sadden ['sadən] *v* ḥazzana حزن;
aḥzana أحزن

sadistic [sə'distik] *adj* sādī سادي

sadness ['sadnis] *n* ḥuzn حزن
(aḥzān أحزان)

safe [seif] **1.** *adj* āmin آمن; sālim سالم
2. amīn أمين; salīm سليم **3.** *n*
khizāna خزانة (khazā'in خزائن)

safeguard ['seifga:d] *v* ammana أمن

safely ['seifli] *adv* sāliman سالماً

safety ['seifti] *n* amān أمان; amn
أمن; salāma سلامة

said [sed] *see* say

sail [seil] **1.** *n* shirāʿ شراع (ashriʿa
أشرعة) **2.** *v* abḥara أبحر **3. to set sail**
abḥara أبحر

sailing ['seiling] *n* ibḥār إبحار

sailing-boat; sailing-ship
['seilingbəut; -ship] *n* markab shirāʿī
مركب شراعي (marākib مراكب)

sailor ['seilə] *n* baḥḥār بحار (-ūn);
mallāḥ ملاح (-ūn)

saint [seint] *n* qiddīs قديس (-ūn);

walī ولي (awliyā' أولياء)

sake [seik] *n* **1. for the sake of** min
ajl من أجل **2. for my sake** min ajlī
من أجلي; ikrāman lī إكراماً لي

salad ['saləd] *n* salaṭa سلطة (-āt)

salary ['saləri] *n* ajr أجر (ujūr أجور);
rātib راتب (rawātib رواتب)

sale [seil] *n* **1.** bīʿ بيع; mabīʿ مبيع **2.**
okāzyūn أكازيون **3. for sale** li 'l-bīʿ
للبيع

salesman; salesperson ['seilz-
mən; 'seilzpə:sn] *n* bā'iʿ بائع (-ūn)

saleswoman ['seilzwumən] *n*
bā'iʿa بائعة (-āt)

saline ['seilain] *adj* māliḥ مالح

salmon ['samən] *n* samak sulaymān
سمك سليمان

salt [so:lt] *n* malḥ ملح

salty ['so:lti] *adj* māliḥ مالح

salute [sə'lu:t] **1.** *n* taḥīya تحية (-āt)
2. *v* ḥayyā حيى

salvage ['salvij] *v* anqadha أنقذ

salvation [sal'veishən] *n* inqādh
إنقاذ; khalāṣ خلاص

same [seim] *adj* nafsuh نفسه; ʿaynah
عينه

sample ['sa:mpəl] *n* ʿayyina عينة
(-āt)

sanction ['sangkshən] **1.** *n* ʿuquba
عقوبة (-āt) **2.** *v* ajāza أجاز

sand [sand] *n* raml رمل

sandwich ['sandwij] *n* sandwīch
سندويتش (-āt)

sandy ['sandi] *adj* ramlī رملي

sane [sein] *adj* salīm al-ʿaql
سليم العقل

sang [sang] *see* **sing**

sanitary ['sanitri] *adj* ṣiḥḥī صحي

sanitation [sani'teishən] *n* **1.**
aṣ-ṣiḥḥa al-ʿāmma الصحة العامة
2. ṣiyānat aṣ-ṣiḥḥa al-ʿāmma
صيانة الصحة العامة

sanity ['saniti] *n* salāmat al-ʿaql
سلامة العقل

sank [sangk] *see* **sink**

sarcastic [saːˈkastik] *adj* sukhrī
سخري

sardine(s) [saːˈdiːn] *n* sardīn
سردين *collective*

Sardinia [saːˈdiniyə] *n* sardāniya
سردانية

Sardinian [saːˈdiniyən] **1.** *adj*
sardānī سرداني **2.** *n* sardānī
(-yūn)

sat [sat] *see* **sit**

Satan [seitn] *n* ash-shayṭān الشيطان

satellite ['satəlait] *n* **1.** qamar قمر
(aqmār أقمار) **2. communications
satellite** qamar ṣināʿī
قمر صناعي

satire ['sataiə] *n* hijāʾ هجاء

satirical [səˈtirikəl] *adj* hijāʾī هجائي

satisfaction [satisˈfakshən] *n*
qanāʿa قناعة; riḍan رضًى

satisfactory [satisˈfaktəri] *adj*
murḍin مرضٍ

satisfied ['satisfaid] *adj* rāḍin راضٍ
(**with** bi بـ; fī في)

satisfy ['satisfai] *v* arḍā أرضى

Saturday ['satədei] *n* yawm al-sabt
يوم السبت

sauce [soːs] *n* ṣalṣa صلصة (-āt)

saucer ['soːsə] *n* ṣaḥn al-finjān
صحن الفنجان

sausage ['sosij] *n* sujuq سجق

savage ['savij] *adj* mutawaḥḥish
متوحش

save [seiv] **1.** *prep* illā إلّا **2.** *v*
anqadha أنقذ; najjā نجّى **3. to save
money** iddakhara ادّخر **4. to save
(a document)** *(comp.)* ḥafiẓa حفظ
(a; ḥifẓ حفظ)

saver ['seivə] *n* *(fin.)* muddakhir
مدّخر (-ūn)

savings ['seivingz] *pl* **1.**
muddakharāt مدّخرات **2. savings
bank** bank al-iddikhār بنك الإدّخار

savour, *(US)* **savor** ['seivə] *v* **1.**
tadhawwaqa تذوّق **2.** istamtaʿa bi
استمتع بـ

savoury, *(US)* **savory** ['seivəri] *adj*
1. ladhīdh لذيذ **2.** māliḥ مالح

saw [soː] **1.** *n* minshār منشار
(manāshīr مناشير) **2.** *v* (**sawed,
sawn/sawed**) nashara نشر (u;
nashr نشر) **3.** *see* **see**

sawn [soːn] *see* **saw**

say [sei; sed] *v* (**said**) **1.** qāla قال (u;
qawl قول) **2. that is to say** yaʿnī
يعني

saying ['seying] *n* mathal مثل
(amthāl أمثال)

scale [skeil] **1.** *n* niẓām darajī
نظام درجي **2.** miqyās مقياس **3.** *(mus.)*
sullam mūsīqī سلم موسيقي **4.** *v* **to
scale a mountain** ṣaʿida صعد (a;
ṣuʿūd صعود) **5.** *see* **scales**

scales [skeilz] *pl* **1.** mīzān ميزان **2.
fish scale(s)** ḥarshaf حرشف
(ḥarāshif حراشف)

scan [skan] *v* **1.** *(comp.)* masaḥa ṣūra
مسح صورة (a; masḥ مسح) **2.** *(med.)*
ʿamila ashiʿʿa عمل أشعة (a; ʿamal
عمل)

scandal ['skandəl] *n* faḍīḥa فضيحة (faḍā'iḥ فضائح)

scanner [skanə] *n* **1.** *(comp.)* māsiḥ ماسح **2.** *(med.)* māsiḥ ṭibbī ماسح طبي

scapegoat ['skeipgəut] *n* kabsh al-fidā' كبش الفداء

scar [ska:] *n* nadab ندب (andāb أنداب)

scarce [skeəs] *adj* nādir نادر; qalīl قليل

scarcely ['skeəsli] *adv* nādiran نادراً

scarcity ['skeəsəti] *n* nadra ندرة (-āt); qilla قلة (-āt)

scare [skeə] **1.** fazaʿ فزع (afzāʿ أفزاع) **2.** *v* afzaʿa أفزع; rawwaʿa روع

scarecrow ['skeəkrəu] *n* fazzāʿa فزاعة

scared [skeəd] *adj* khā'if خائف

scarf [ska:f] *n* wishāḥ وشاح (awshiḥa أوشحة)

scarlet ['ska:lət] *adj* qirmizī قرمزي

scary ['skeəri] *adj* murawwiʿ مروع

scatter ['skatə] *v* **1.** baʿthara بعثر **2.** baddada بدد

scene [si:n] *n* mashhad مشهد (mashāhid مشاهد)

scenery ['si:nəri] *n* manẓar منظر

scent [sent] *n* **1.** ʿiṭr عطر **2.** *see* **smell**

sceptic ['skeptik] *n* shākk شاك

sceptical ['skeptiəkəl] *adj* shākk شاك

schedule ['shedyu:l; 'skedyu:l] **1.** *n* barnāmij برنامج (barāmij برامج) **2.** *v* ḥaddada mawāʿīd حدد مواعيد

scheme [ski:m] **1.** *n* khiṭṭa خطة (khiṭaṭ خطط); mashrūʿ مشروع (mashārīʿ مشاريع) **2.** makīda مكيدة (makāyid مكايد) **3.** *v* dabbara makīda دبر مكيدة; taʾāmara تآمر

scholar ['skolə] *n* ʿālim عالم (ʿulamā' علماء)

scholarship ['skoləship] *n* **1.** jawda akādīmīya جودة أكاديمية **2.** minḥa taʿlīmīya منحة تعليمية

school [sku:l] **1.** *adj* madrasī مدرسي **2.** *n* madrasa مدرسة (madāris مدارس) **3.** *(US)* kullīya كلية (-āt)

schoolboy ['sku:lboi] *n* tilmīdh madrasi تلميذ مدرسي

schoolgirl ['sku:lgə:l] *n* tilmīdha madrasīya تلميذة مدرسية

schoolmaster *n* mudarris مدرس (-ūn)

schoolmistress *n* mudarrisa مدرسة (-āt)

schoolteacher *n* mudarris مدرس (-ūn)

science ['saiəns] *n* ʿilm علم (ʿulūm علوم)

scientific [saiən'tifik] *adj* ʿilmī علمي

scientist ['saiəntist] *n* ʿālim عالم (ʿulamā' علماء)

scissors ['sizəz] *pl* miqaṣṣ مقص

scooter ['sku:tə] *n* darrājat ar-rijl دراجة الرجل

scope [skəup] *n* majāl مجال

score [sko:] **1.** *(ed.)* natīja نتيجة (natā'ij نتائج) **2.** *(spor.)* majmūʿ al-iṣābāt مجموع الإصابات **3.** *v* sajjala iṣāba سجل إصابة

scorer ['sko:rə] *n* musajjil iṣāba مسجل إصابة

scorn [sko:n] **1.** *n* iḥtiqār إحتقار; istihzā' إستهزاء **2.** *v* iḥtaqara إحتقر; istahza'a إستهزأ

scornful ['sko:nfəl] *adj* hāzi' هازئ (of min من; bi ب)

Scot [skot] *n* iskotlandī اسكتلندي

Scotch [skoch] *adj* iskotlandī اسكتلندي

Scotland ['skotlənd] n iskotlandā
اسكتلندا

Scotsman ['skotsmən] n iskotlandī
اسكتلندي

Scottish [skotish] adj iskotlandī
اسكتلندي

scout [skaut] **1.** (mil.) kashshāf
كشاف (kashshāfa كشافة) **2.** see boy
scout

scrap [skrap] **1.** n qiṭʿa قطعة (qitaʿ
قطع) **2.** nufāyāt نفايات **3.** mushājara
مشاجرة **4.** v nabadha نبذ (i; nabdh
نبذ)

scratch [skrach] v kharbasha خربش

scream [skri:m] **1.** n ṣarkha صرخة
(-āt) **2.** v ṣarakha صرخ (u; ṣurākh
صراخ)

screen [skri:n] **1.** n ḥājiz حاجز
(ḥawājiz حواجز) **2.** (tel.) shāsha
شاشة (-āt) **3.** v ḥajaba حجب (u; ḥajb
حجب)

screw [skru:] **1.** n lawlab لولب
(lawālib اللوالب) **2.** v athbata bi
lawlab أثبت بلولب

screwdriver ['skru:draivə] n
mifakk مفك (-āt)

script [skript] n **1.** kitāba كتابة **2.**
film script naṣṣ film نص فلم **3.**
stage script naṣṣ masraḥīya
نص مسرحية

scrutiny ['skru:tini] n tafaḥḥuṣ تفحص

sculptor ['skʌlptə] n naḥḥāt نحات
(-ūn); maththāl مثال (-ūn)

sculpture ['skʌlpchə] n timthāl
تمثال (tamāthīl تماثيل)

scum [skʌm] n zabad زبد

sea [si:] **1.** adj baḥrī بحري **2.** n baḥr
بحر (biḥār بحار) **3.** by sea baḥran
بحراً **4.** at sea ʿalā 'l-baḥr على البحر

seafood ['si:fu:d] n ma'kūlāt al-

baḥr مأكولات البحر

seagull(s) ['si:gʌl] n nawraza نورزة
(collective nawraz نورز)

seal [si:l] **1.** n khatm ختم (akhtām
أختام) **2.** fuqqam; fuqm collective
فقم **3.** v khatama ختم (i; khatm
ختم)

sea-level ['si:levəl] n mustawā saṭḥ
al-baḥr مستوى سطح البحر

seaman ['si:mən] n baḥḥār بحار
(-ūn); mallāḥ ملاح (-ūn)

search [sə:ch] **1.** n baḥth بحث
(buḥūth بحوث) **2.** (police) search
taftish تفتيش **3.** v baḥatha بحث (a;
baḥth بحث) (for ʿan عن)

seashells ['si:shel] n ṣadaf صدف
collective (aṣdāf أصداف)

seashore ['si:sho:] n sāḥil ساحل
(sawāḥil سواحل); shāṭiʾ شاطئ
(shawāṭiʾ شواطئ)

seasick ['si:sik] n duwār al-baḥr
دوار البحر

seaside ['si:said] n at the seaside
ʿalā s-sāḥil على الساحل; ʿalā 'sh-
shāṭiʾ على الشاطئ

season ['si:zən] n mawsim موسم
(mawāsim مواسم)

seasonal ['si:zənəl] adj mawsimī
موسمي

seat [si:t] **1.** n maqʿad مقعد (maqāʿid
مقاعد) **2.** v aqʿada أقعد

seatbelt ['si:tbelt] n ḥizām al-amn
حزام الأمن

secede [sə'si:d] v insaḥaba انسحب
(from min من)

second ['sekənd] **1.** adj thānin ثان **2.**
n thāniya ثانية (thawānin ثوان) **3.**
laḥẓa لحظة (laḥaẓāt اللحظات) **4.** v
(pol.) sānada ساند

secondary ['sekəndri] adj thānawī
ثانوي

secondary school *n* madrasa thānawīya مدرسة ثانوية

second class *n* ad-daraja 'th-thāniya الدرجة الثانية

second-hand *adj* mustaʿmal مستعمل

secrecy ['si:krəsi] *n* sirrīya سرية

secret ['si:krit] **1.** *adj* sirrī سري **2.** *n* sirr سر (asrār أسرار) **3. military secret** sirr ʿaskarī سر عسكري **4. in secret** sirran سراً

secret agent *n* ʿamīl sirrī عميل سري

secretarial [sekrə'teəriəl] *adj* maktabī مكتبي; sekretīrī سكرتيري

secretary ['sekrətri] *n* sekretēr سكرتير

secretary of state *n* **1.** (UK) wazīr وزير (wuzarā' وزراء) **2.** (US) wazīr al-khārijīya وزير الخارجية

secret police *pl* al-būlis as-sirrī البولس السري

secret service *n* al-mukhābarāt المخابرات

secretly ['si:kritli] *adv* sirran سراً

sect [sekt] *n* ṭā'ifa طائفة (ṭawā'if طوائف)

section ['sekshən] *n* qism قسم (aqsām أقسام)

sector ['sektə] *n* qiṭāʿ قطاع (-āt)

secure [si'kyuə] **1.** *adj* āmin آمن; ma'mūn مأمون **2.** *v* ammana أمن

securely [si'kyuəli] *adv* jayyidan جيداً

security [si'kyuərəti] *n* **1.** amn أمن; amān أمان **2.** (fin.) sanad سند (-āt)

seduce [si'dyu:s] *v* aghrā أغرى; ghawā غوى (i; ghayy غي)

see [si:] *v* (saw, seen) ra'ā رأى (imperfect yarā يرى; ru'ya رؤية)

seed [si:d] *n* bizr بزر collective (buzūr بزور); badhr بذر collective (budhūr بذور); ḥabb حب collective (ḥubūb حبوب)

seeing that *conj* naẓaran li نظراً لـ

seek [si:k] *v* (sought) baḥatha ʿan بحث عن (a; baḥth بحث)

seem [si:m] *v* badā بدا (u)

seemingly ['si:mingli] *adv* fī mā yabdū في ما يبدو

seen [si:n] *see* see

seize [si:z] *v* istawlā ʿalā استولى على; masaka b مسك ب (u; i; mask مسك)

seldom ['seldəm] *adv* nādiran نادراً

select [si'lekt] *v* ikhtāra اختار; intaqā انتقى

selection [si'lekchən] *n* ikhtiyār اختيار; intiqā' إنتقاء

selective [si'lektiv] *adj* intiqā'ī إنتقائي

self [self] *n/pronoun* (pl selves) **1.** nafs نفس (anfus أنفس) **2. myself** nafsī نفسي

self-centred, (US) **self-centered** [self'sentəd] *adj* anānī أناني

self-confidence [self'konfidəns] *n* ath-thiqa bi 'n-nafs الثقة بالنفس

self-control [selfkən'trəul] *n* ḍabṭ an-nafs ضبط النفس

self-defence, (US) **self-defense** [selfdi'fens] *n* ad-difāʿ ʿan an-nafs الدفاع عن النفس

self-government [self'gʌvnmənt] *n* al-ḥukm adh-dhātī الحكم الذاتي

self-interest [self'intrest] *n* al-maṣlaḥa ash-shakhṣīya المصلحة الشخصية

selfish ['selfish] *adj* anānī أناني

selfishness ['selfishnis] *n* anānīya أنانية

selfless ['selfləs] *n* ghayr anānī
غير أناني

self-respect [selfri'spekt] *n*
iḥtirām an-nafs إحترام النفس

self-rule [self'ru:l] *n* istiqlāl إستقلال

self-sufficient [selfsə'fishənt] *adj*
muktafin dhātiyan مكتف ذاتياً

sell [sel] *v* (sold) bāʿa باع (i; bayʿ بيع)

seller ['selə] *n* 1. bāʾiʿ بائع 2.
(-ūn) best-seller rāʾij رائج

sell out *v* bāʿa jamīʿ biḍāʿatih
باع جميع بضاعته

semblance ['sembləns] *n* maẓhar
مظهر

semen ['si:mən] *n* minan منى

semi- ['semi] *adj* 1. niṣf نصف 2.
shibh شبه

semi-final [semi'fainəl] *n* shibh
nihāʾī شبه نهائي

seminar ['semina:] *n* 1. dars
fī jāmiʿa درس في جامعة 2.
dawra taʿlīmīya muṣghghara دورة تعليمية مصغرة 3. muʾtamar
khubarāʾ مؤتمر خبراء

senate [senit] *n* majlis ash-shuyūkh
مجلس الشيوخ

senator ['senətə] *n* shaykh شيخ
(shuyūkh شيوخ)

send [send] *v* (sent) arsala أرسل;
baʿatha بعث (a; baʿth بعث)

send back *v* arjaʿa أرجع; aʿāda أعاد;
radda رد (u; radd رد)

sender ['sendə] *n* murāsil مراسل

senile ['si:nail] *adj* kharif خرف;
kharfān خرفان

senior ['si:niə] 1. *adj* akbar أكبر; aʿlā
أعلى 2. *n* akbar sinnan أكبر سناً; aʿlā
makānatan أعلى مكانةً

sensation [sen'seishən] *n* 1. iḥsās
إحساس (aḥāsīs أحاسيس) 2.

ḥadath/shakhṣ muthīr li 'l-ghāya
حدث\شخص مثير للغاية

sensational [sen'seishənəl] *adj*
muthīr li 'l-ghāya مثير للغاية

sense ['sens] 1. *n* maʿnan معنى 2.
ḥāssa حاسة (ḥawāss حواس) 3. idrāk
إدراك 4. *v* ḥassa حس (u; ḥass حس)

senseless ['sensləs] *adj* 1. fāqid al-
waʿy فاقد الوعي 2. bi lā maʿnan
بلا معنى

sensibility [sensi'biləti] *n* ḥassāsīya
حساسية

sensible ['sensəbl] *n* ʿāqil عاقل

sensitive ['sensətiv] *adj* ḥassās
حساس

sensitivity ['sensətiviti] *n*
ḥassāsīya حساسية

sent [sent] *see* **send**

sentence ['sentəns] 1. *n* jumla جملة
(jumal جمل) 2. (*leg.*) ḥukm حكم
(aḥkām أحكام) 3. **death sentence**
ḥukm al-iʿdām حكم الإعدام 4. *v* (*leg.*)
ḥakama حكم (u; ḥukm حكم)

sentiment ['sentimənt] *n* 1. shuʿūr
شعور *pl* (ārāʾ آراء) 2. raʾy رأي

sentry ['sentri] *n* ḥāris حارس; ḥurrās
حراس

separate ['seprət] *adj* munfaṣil
منفصل

separate ['sepəreit] *v* 1. fāṣala
فاصل 2. iftaraqa افترق

separately ['sepəreitli] *adv*
munfaṣilan منفصلاً

separation [sepə'reishən] *n* firāq
فراق

separatist ['seprətist] *n* infiṣālī
إنفصالي

September [sep'tembə] *n* sibtambir
سبتمبر; aylūl أيلول

septic ['septik] *adj* ʿafin عفن

sequel ['si:kwəl] *n* mā yatbaᶜ ما يتبع

sequence [si:kwəns] *n* tasalsul تسلسل

sergeant ['sa:jənt] *n* raqīb رقيب; shāwīsh شاويش

serial ['siəriəl] 1. *adj* musalsal مسلسل 2. *n* musalsal مسلسل (-āt)

serial killer *n* qātil musalsal قاتل مسلسل

series ['siəri:z] *n* 1. silsila سلسلة (-āt) 2. TV series musalsal مسلسل (-āt)

serious ['siəriəs] *adj* jiddī جدي

serpent ['sə:pənt] *n* ḥayya حية (-āt); afᶜan أفعى (afāᶜin أفاع)

servant ['sə:vənt] *n* 1. khādim خادم (khuddām خدام; khadama خدمة) 2. civil servant muwaẓẓaf ḥukūmī موظف حكومي

serve [sə:v] *v* 1. khadama خدم (i/u; khidma خدمة) 2. nafaᶜa نفع (a; nafᶜ نفع) 3. aṣlaḥa li ل أصلح; qaḍā قضى (i; qaḍā' قضاء)

service ['sə:vis] 1. *adj* mirfaq مرفق (marāfiq مرافق) 2. *(mil.)* mutaᶜalliq bi 'l-qūwāt al-musallaḥa متعلق بالقوات المسلحة 3. *n* khidma خدمة (khadamāt خدمات) 4. ṣiyāna صيانة (-āt) 5. ṭaqs dīnī طقس ديني 6. secret service al-mukhābarāt المخابرات

service station *n* muḥaṭṭat banzīn محطة بنزين

session ['seshən] *n* 1. inᶜiqād إنعقاد; jalsa جلسة (-āt) 2. dawr al-inᶜiqād دور الإنعقاد

set [set] 1. *adj* muḥaddad محدد; muᶜayyan معين 2. muthabbat مثبت; lā yataghayyar لا يتغير 3. *n* ṭaqm طقم (ṭuqūm طقوم; majmūᶜa مجموعة) (-āt) 4. tea set ṭaqm shāy طقم شاي 5. television set jihāz tilifizyōn جهاز تلفزيون 6. *v* (set) waḍaᶜa وضع

(yaḍaᶜu يضع; waḍᶜ وضع) 7. ẓabbaṭa ضبط 8. to set a table rattaba sufra رتب سفرة 9. to set a time ḥaddada mawᶜidan حدد موعداً 9. to set an example iḥtadhā احتذى 10. *see* **sunset**

setback ['setbak] *n* naksa نكسة

set fire to *v* ḍarrama al-nār fī ضرم النار في

set free *v* aṭlaqa أطلق

set off; set out *v* bada'a riḥla بدأ رحلة

set sail *v* baḥḥara بحر

setting ['seting] *n* 1. muḥīṭ محيط 2. *(tech.)* ḍabṭ ضبط

settle ['setəl] *v* 1. istaqarra استقر 2. istawṭana استوطن

settlement ['setəlmənt] *n* 1. mustawṭan مستوطن (-āt) 2. *(fin.)* tasdīd تسديد 3. *(leg.)* ḥall حل

settler [setlə] *n* mustawṭin مستوطن (-ūn)

set up *v* 1. aqāma أقام 2. assasa أسس; ansha'a أنشأ

seven ['sevən] *n/adj* sabᶜa سبعة

seventeen [sevən'ti:n] *n/adj* sabᶜata ᶜashar سبعة عشر

seventeenth [sevən'ti:nth] *adj* sābiᶜ ᶜashar سابع عشر

seventh ['sevnth] *adj* sābiᶜ سابع

seventy ['sevənti] *n/adj* sabᶜūn سبعون

sever ['sevə] *v* faṣala فصل (i; faṣl فصل); qaṭaᶜa قطع (a; qaṭᶜ قطع)

several ['sevrəl] *adj* ᶜidda عدة; biḍ ᶜ بضع

severe [si'viə] *adj* 1. ṣārim صارم 2. qāsin قاس 3. khaṭīr خطير

severity [si'verəti] *n* 1. ṣarāma صرامة 2. qaswa قسوة; qasāwa قساوة

sew [səu] v (sewed, sewn/sewed) khayyaţa خيط

sewer ['su:ə] n bālū‘a بالوعة (-āt; bawālī‘ بواليع)

sewing machine n ālat al-khiyāţa آلة الخياطة

sex [seks] 1. adj jinsī جنسي 2. n (pl sexes ['seksiz]) jins جنس (ajnās أجناس) 3. al-ittişāl al-jinsī الإتصال الجنسي

sexism ['seksizm] n jinsānīya جنسانية

sexist ['seksist] 1. adj jinsānī جنساني 2. n jinsānī جنساني (-yūn)

sexual ['sekshuəl] adj 1. jinsī جنسي 2. tanāsulī تناسلي

sexuality [sekshu'aliti] n jinsānīya جنسانية ; junūsīya جنوسية

sexy ['seksi] adj muthīr al-gharīza ’l-jinsīya مثير الغريزة الجنسية

shade [sheid] n ẓill ظل

shadow ['shadəu] n ẓill ظل (ẓilāl ظلال)

shadowy ['shadəui] adj 1. muẓallil مظلل 2. ghāmiḍ غامض

shaft [sha:ft] n 1. ‘amūd عمود (a‘mida أعمدة) 2. miqbaḍ مقبض (maqābiḍ مقابض) 3. **mining shaft** madkhal ‘amūdī li manjam مدخل عمودي لمنجم

shake [sheik] v (shook, shaken) hazza هز (u; hazz هز); za‘za‘a زعزع

shake hands v şāfaḥa صافح

shaken ['sheikən] see shake

shake-up n i‘ādat tanẓīm إعادة تنظيم

shaky ['sheiki] adj mutaza‘zi‘ متزعزع; murta‘ish مرتعش

shall [shəl; shal] see be

shallow ['shaləu] adj 1. ḍaḥl ضحل 2. saţḥī سطحي

shame [sheim] 1. n ‘ār عار; ‘ayb عيب 2. ḥayā’ حياء; khajl خجل 3. **what a shame!** yā khasāra! يا خسارة! 4. v khajjala خجل; akhjala أخجل

shameful ['sheimfəl] adj mukhjil مخجل

shameless ['sheimlis] adj waqiḥ وقح; bi lā ḥayā’ بلا حياء

shampoo ['shampu:] n shāmbū شامبو

shape [sheip] 1. n shakl شكل (ashkāl أشكال) 2. v shakkala شكل

share [sheə] 1. n naşīb نصيب (nuşub نصب); 2. ḥişşa حصة (ḥişaş حصص) (fin.) sahm سهم (ashum أسهم) 3. v qāsama قاسم; 4. shāraka شارك; ishtaraka اشترك

shark [sha:k] n qirsh قرش (qurūsh قروش)

sharp [sha:p] adj ḥādd حاد

sharpen ['sha:pən] v ḥaddada حدد

shatter ['shatə] v kassara كسر; ḥaţţama حطم

shave [sheiv] v ḥalaqa حلق (i; ḥalq حلق)

she [shi:] pronoun hiya هي

shed [shed] 1. n ḥazīra حزيرة (ḥazā’ir حزائر) 2. v asqaţa أسقط 3. sayyala سيل

shed blood v safaka ad-dimā’ سفك الدماء (i/u; safk سفك)

sheep [shi:p] n (pl sheep) kharūf خروف (khirfān خرفان)

sheepdog ['shi:pdog] n kalb al-rā‘ī كلب الراعي

sheer ['shiə] adj muţlaq مطلق; maḥḍ محض; mujarrad مجرد; şirf صرف

sheet [shi:t] n 1. mulā’a ملاءة (-āt); milāya ملاية (-āt) 2. lawḥ لوح (alwāḥ ألواح) 3. **a sheet of**

paper ṣaḥīfa min al-waraq
صحيفة من الورق

shelf [shelf; shelvz] *n* (**shelves**) raff
رف (rufūf رفوف)

shell [shel] 1. *n* qawqaʿ قوقع; ṣadaf
collective صدف 2. (aṣdāf أصداف)
qishra قشرة 3. (*mil.*) qadhīfa قذيفة
(qadhā'if قذائف) 4. *v* (*mil.*) qadhafa
قذف (i; qadhf قذف)

shellfish ['shelfish] *n* ḥayawānāt
ṣadafīya حيوانات صدفية

shelter ['sheltə] 1. *n* ma'wā مأوى
(ma'āwin مآو); malja' ملجأ
(malāji' ملاجئ) 2. **to take shelter**
awā أوى (i); laja'a لجأ (a; lujū'
لجوء); alja'a ألجأ 4. *v* awwā أوى;
alja'a ألجأ (اللجوء)

shelve [shelv] *v* to shelve (**a plan**)
ajjala أجل

shelves [shelvz] *see* **shelf**

sheriff ['sherif] *n* (*US*) ḍābiṭ shurṭī
ضابط شرطي

shield [shi:ld] 1. *n* turs ترس (atrās
أتراس) 2. *v* ḥajaba حجب (i; ḥijāb
حجاب) 3. ḥamā حمى (i; ḥimāya
حماية)

shift [shift] 1. *n* munāwaba مناوبة
(-āt) 2. *v* naqala نقل (u; naql نقل)

Shi'i; Shi'ite ['shi:i:; 'shi:ayt] *adj/n*
shī'ī شيعي

shine [shain] 1. *n* lamʿ لمع; lamaʿān
لمعان 2. *v* (**shone**) lamaʿa لمع (a;
lamʿ لمع; lamaʿān لمعان)

shiny ['shaini] *adj* lāmiʿ لامع;
mutalammiʿ متلمع

ship [ship] 1. *n* safīna سفينة (sufun
سفن); markab مركب (marākib
مراكب) 2. *v* shaḥana شحن (a; shaḥn
شحن)

shipping ['shiping] 1. sufun سفن 2.
n shaḥn شحن

shire ['shaiə] *n* (*UK*) muqāṭaʿa مقاطعة
(-āt)

shirt [shə:t] *n* qamīṣ قميص (qumṣān
قمصان)

shiver ['shivə] 1. *n* rajfa رجفة (-āt);
raʿsha رعشة 2. *v* irtajafa ارتجف;
irtaʿasha ارتعش

shock [shok] 1. *n* ṣadma صدمة
(ṣadamāt صدمات); iṣṭidām
إصطدام 2. **electric shock** ṣadma
kahrubā'īya صدمة كهربائية 3. **to be
in shock** (*med.*) uṣība bi ṣadma
أصيب بصدمة 4. *v* afzaʿa أفزع

shocking ['shoking] *adj* faẓīʿ فظيع;
murawwiʿ مروع

shoe [shu:] *n* ḥidhā' حذاء (aḥdhiya
أحذية)

shone [shon] *see* **shine**

shook [shuk] *see* **shake**

shoot [shu:t] 1. *n* burʿum برعم
(barāʿim براعم) 2. riḥlat ṣayd
رحلة صيد 3. *v* (**shot**) aṭlaqa أطلق;
aṭlaqa an-nār ʿalā أطلق النار على

shooting ['shu:ting] *n* iṭlāq an-nār
إطلاق النار

shop [shop] 1. *n* dukkān دكان
(dakākīn دكاكين) 2. *v* tasawwaqa
تسوق

shopkeeper ['shopki:pə] *n* ṣāḥib
dukkān صاحب دكان

shoplifting ['shoplifting] *n*
as-sariqa min ad-dakākīn
السرقة من الدكاكين

shopping ['shoping] *n* 1. tasawwuq
تسوق 2. mushtarayāt مشتريات

**shopping centre; shopping
mall** *n* tajammuʿ tijārī تجمع تجاري

shore [sho:] *n* shāṭi' شاطئ (shawāṭi'
شواطئ)

short [sho:t] 1. *adj* qaṣīr قصير 2.
nāqiṣ ناقص 3. **to be short of**

naqaṣa نقص (u; naqṣ نقص) 4. **in short** bi 'l-ikhtiṣār بالإختصار

shortage ['sho:tij] *n* naqṣ نقص; qilla قلة

shortcut *n* ṭarīq mukhtaṣara طريق مختصرة

shorten ['sho:tən] *v* qaṣṣara قصر

shortly ['sho:tli] *adv* baʿd qalīl بعد قليل

shorts [sho:ts] *pl* 1. (UK) banṭalōn qaṣīr بنطلون قصير 2. (US) see **underwear**

short-sighted [sho:t'saitid] *adj* ḥasīr al-baṣar حسير البصر

short-term [sho:t'tə:m] *adj* qaṣīr al-ajal قصير الأجل

shot [shot] 1. *n* ṭalaqa طلقة (-āt) 2. (med.) ḥuqna حقنة (ḥuqan حقن) 3. see **shoot**

should [shud] *v* yajib يجب; yanbaghī ينبغي

shoulder ['shəuldə] *n* katf كتف (aktāf أكتاف)

shout [shaut] 1. *n* ṣayḥa صيحة (-āt) 2. *v* ṣāḥa صاح (i; ṣayḥa صيحة)

shove [shʌv] *v* dafaʿa دفع (a; dafʿ دفع)

shovel ['shʌvəl] *n* mijrāf مجراف (majārīf مجاريف)

show [shəu] 1. *n* iẓhār إظهار 2. ʿarḍ عرض 3. istiʿrāḍ masraḥī إستعراض مسرحي 4. **television show** barnāmij tilivizyōnī برنامج تلفزيوني 5. *v* (showed, shown) aẓhara أظهر 6. ʿaraḍa عرض (i; ʿarḍ عرض)

show business *n* ʿālam al-masraḥ عالم المسرح

shower [shauə] *n* 1. dush دوش 2. wābil وابل

shown [shəun] see **show**

show off *v* fākhara فاخر; bāhā باهى

showroom ['shəurum] *n* maʿraḍ معرض (maʿāriḍ معارض)

shrank [shrangk] see **shrink**

shrimp [shrimp] *n* quraydis قريدس

shrine [shrain] *n* mazār مزار (-āt)

shrink [shringk] *v* (shrank, shrunk) qalaṣa قلص (i; qulūṣ قلوص)

shrunk [shrʌngk] see **shrink**

shuffle ['shʌfəl] *v* (pol.) aʿāda tartīb al-manāṣib أعاد ترتيب المناصب

shut [shʌt] 1. *adj* maqfūl مقفول 2. *v* (shut) aqfala أقفل

shutdown ['shʌtdaun] *n* waqf al-ʿamal وقف الأمل

shuttle ['shʌtəl] *n* makkūk مكوك (makākīk مكاكيك)

shy [shai] *adj* khajūl خجول

sick [sik] *adj* marīḍ مريض

sicken ['sikən] *v* amraḍa أمرض

sickness ['siknis] *n* maraḍ مرض (amrāḍ أمراض)

side [said] 1. *n* janb جنب (ajnāb أجناب); jānib جانب (jawānib جوانب) 2. (pol./spor.) ṭaraf طرف (aṭrāf أطراف) 3. **side by side** janban ilā janb جنباً إلى جنب 4. *v* anḥāza أنحاز (with ilā إلى)

sidewalk ['saidwo:k] *n* (US) raṣīf رصيف (arṣifa أرصفة)

sideways ['saidweiz] *adv* jānibīyan جانبياً

siege [si:j] *n* 1. ḥiṣār حصار 2. **to lay/set siege to** ḥāṣara حاصر; afraḍa al-ḥiṣār ʿalā أفرض الحصار على

sigh [sai] 1. *n* āha آهة (-āt) 2. *v* awwaha أوه

sight [sait] 1. *n* baṣar بصر 2. mashhad مشهد (mashāhid مشاهد);

manẓar منظر (manāẓir مناظر) 3.
maʿlam معلم (maʿālim معالم) 4. v
raʾā رأى (a; raʾy رأي)

sightless ['saitlis] *adj* aʿmā أعمى

sightseeing ['saitsiːing] *n* ziyārat al-maʿālim زيارة المعالم

sign [sain] 1. *n* ishāra إشارة (-āt); 2.
ʿallāma علامة (-āt) 3. muʿjiza معجزة (-āt) 4. ramz رمز (rumūz رموز) 5.
road sign ishārat ṭarīq إشارة طريق
6. v waqqaʿa وقّع; amḍā أمضى

signal ['signəl] 1. *n* ishāra إشارة (-āt)
2. v shawwara شوّر; ashāra أشار

signature ['signəchə] *n* tawqīʿ
توقيع; imḍāʾ إمضاء

signboard ['sainboːd] *n* lawḥa لوحة (-āt)

significance [sig'nifikəns] *n* 1.
maʿnan معنى (maʿānin معان) 2.
ahammīya أهمية (-āt)

significant [sig'nifikənt] *adj* 1. dhū maʿnā هام 2. hāmm ذو معنى

signify ['signifai] v ʿanā عنى (i; ʿany عني)

sign language *n* lughat al-ṣumm لغة الصم

signpost ['sainpəust] *n* maʿlam معلم (maʿālim معالم)

silence ['sailəns] *n* ṣamt صمت; ṣumūt صموت

silent ['sailənt] *adj* ṣāmit صامت

silk [silk] *n* ḥarīr حرير

silly ['sili] *adj* sakhīf سخيف

silver ['silvə] 1. *adj* fiḍḍī فضي 2. *n* fiḍḍa فضة

similar ['similə] *adj* mushābih مشابه; mutashabih متشابه

similarity [simə'lariti] *n* shabah شبه; tashābuh تشابه

simple ['simpəl] *adj* 1. basīṭ بسيط 2. ablah أبله

simplicity [sim'plisiti] *n* basāṭa بساطة

simplify ['simplifai] v bassaṭa بسّط; sahhala سهّل

simply ['simpli] *adv* 1. bi basāṭa بساطة 2. mujarrad مجرد; laysa ghayr ليس غير; laysa illā ليس إلا 3. ḥaqqan حقاً

simulation [simyu'leishən] *n* 1.
taẓāhur تظاهر 2. taqlīd تقليد

simultaneous [siməl'teiniəs] *adj* mutazāmin متزامن

sin [sin] 1. *n* ithm إثم (āthām آثام);
khaṭīʾa خطيئة (khaṭāyā خطايا) 2. v
athima أثم (a; ithm إثم)

since [sins] 1. *adv* mundhu dhālik al-waqt منذ ذلك الوقت; fī mā maḍā في ما مضى 2. *prep* mundhu منذ 3. *conj* min ḥīn من حين 4. bi mā anna نظراً ل; naẓaran li بما أن

sincere [sin'siə] *adj* mukhliṣ مخلص; ṣādiq صادق

sincerely [sin'siəli] *adv* bi 'ikhlāṣ بإخلاص; bi ṣidq بصدق

sing [sing] v (**sang, sung**) ghannā غنى

singer ['singə] *n* mughannin مغن (mughanniyūn مغنيون)

singing ['singing] *n* ghināʾ غناء

single ['singgəl] 1. *adj* waḥīd وحيد; munfarid منفرد 2. aʿzab أعزب 3. *n* shay'/shakhṣ waḥīd شيء\شخص وحيد 4. tadhkara li 'dh-dhihāb faqaṭ تذكرة للذهاب فقط 5. *(mus.)* usṭuwāna أسطوانة (-āt)

singular ['singgyulə] *n* 1. mufrad مفرد 2. istithnāʾī إستثنائي

sinister ['sinistə] *adj* mashʾūm مشؤوم

sink [singk] 1. *n* ḥawḍ حوض (aḥwāḍ أحواض

أحواض) 2. v (sank, sunk) ghariqa
غرق (a; gharaq غرق) 3. gharraqa
غرق 4. ḥabaṭa حبط (u/i; ḥubūṭ
حبوط)

sir [sə:] n sayyid سيّد

siren ['saiərən] n ṣaffārat al-indhār
صفارة الإنذار

sister ['sistə] n 1. ukht أخت (akhawāt
أخوات) 2. (rel.) rāhiba راهبة (-āt)

sit [sit] v (sat) qaʿada قعد (u; quʿūd
قعود)

sit down v 1. jalasa جلس (i; julūs
جلوس) (on ʿalā على; at ilā إلى) 2.
aqʿada أقعد

site [sait] n mawqiʿ موقع (mawāqiʿ
مواقع)

sitting ['siting] n jalsa جلسة (-āt)

sitting-room n ghurfat al-julūs
غرفة الجلوس

situate ['sityueit] v 1. waḍaʿa وضع
(yaḍaʿu يضع; waḍʿ وضع) 2. to be
situated yūjad يوجد

situation [sityu'eishən] n 1. mawqiʿ
موقع (mawāqiʿ مواقع) 2. waḍʿ وضع
(awḍāʿ أوضاع)

six [siks] n/adj sitta ستة

sixteen [siks'ti:n] n/adj sittat ʿashar
ستة عشر

sixteenth [siks'ti:nth] adj sādis
ʿashar سادس عشر

sixth [siksth] adj sādis سادس

sixty ['siksti] n/adj sittūn ستون

size [saiz] n 1. ḥajm حجم (aḥjām
أحجام) 2. maqās مقاس (-āt)

skate [skeit] 1. n mizlaj مزلج
(mazālij مزالج) 2. v tazallaja ʿalā 'l-
jalīd تزلج على الجليد

skater ['skeitə] n mutazallij ʿalā 'l-
jalīd متزلج على الجليد (-ūn)

skating ['skeiting] n at-tazalluj ʿalā
'l-jalīd التزلج على الجليد

skeleton ['skelitən] n haykal ʿaẓmī
هيكل عظمي

skeptic; skeptical; skepticism
(US) see sceptic, sceptical, scepticism

sketch [skech] 1. n rasm رسم
(rusūm رسوم) 2. v rasama رسم (u;
rasm رسم)

ski [ski:] 1. n mizlaj مزلج (mazālij
مزالج) 2. v tazaḥlaqa ʿalā 'th-thalj
تزحلق على الثلج

skid [skid] v inzalaqa انزلق

skier ['ski:ə] n mutazaḥliq ʿalā 'th-
thalj متزحلق على الثلج

skiing ['ski:ing] n at-tazaḥluq ʿalā
'th-thalj التزحلق على الثلج

skilful, (US) **skillful** ['skilfəl] adj
māhir ماهر; bāriʿ بارع

skill [skil] n mahāra مهارة; barāʿa
براعة

skilled [skild] adj 1. māhir ماهر 2.
mutaṭallib al-mahāra متطلب المهارة

skin [skin] 1. n jild جلد (julūd
جلود) 2. v salakha سلخ (a, u; salkh
سلخ)

skinny ['skini] adj naḥīf نحيف; naḥīl
نحيل

skip [skip] v 1. takhaṭṭā qāfizan
تخطى قافزاً 2. taghayyaba bi dūn
idhn تغيب بدون إذن

skirt [skə:t] n tannūra تنورة (-āt)

skull [skʌl] n jumjuma جمجمة
(jamājim جماجم)

sky [skai] n samā' سماء (samawāt
سموات)

skyscraper ['skaiskreipə] n nāṭiḥat
saḥāb ناطحة سحاب (nawāṭiḥ نواطح)

slain [slein] see slay

slam [slam] v (slammed) aghlaqa bi
qūwa أغلق بقوة

slang [slang] n lugha ʿāmmīya
لغة عامية

slant [sla:nt] 1. *n* inḥidār إنحدار 2. *v* inḥadara انحدر

slap [slap] 1. *n* ṣafʿa صفعة; laṭma لطمة (laṭamāt لطمات) 2. *v* (**slapped**) ṣafaʿa صفع (a; ṣafʿ صفع); laṭama لطم (i; laṭm لطم)

slash [slash] *v* 1. shaqqa bi 'ṭ-ṭūl شق بالطول (u; shaqq شق) 2. (*fin.*) khaffaḍa takhfīḍan kabīran خفض تخفيضاً كبيراً

slaughter ['slo:tə] 1. *n* dhabḥ ذبح 2. *v* dhabaḥa ذبح (a; dhabḥ ذبح)

slaughterhouse ['slo:təhaus] *n* maslakh مسلخ (masālikh مسالخ)

slave [sleiv] *n* ʿabd عبد (ʿabīd عبيد)

slavery ['sleivəri] *n* ʿubūdīya عبودية (-āt)

slay [slei] *v* (**slew, slain**) dhabaḥa ذبح (a; dhabḥ ذبح)

sled; sledge [sled; slej] *n* zallāqa زلاقة (-āt)

sleep [sli:p] 1. *n* nawm نوم 2. *v* (**slept**) nāma نام (a; nawm نوم)

sleepiness [sli:pinis] *n* nuʿās نعاس

sleeping bag *n* kīs li 'n-nawm *m/f* كيس للنوم (akyās أكياس)

sleeping pill *n* ḥabba munawwima حبة منومة

sleepless ['sli:pləs] *adj* āriq أرق; ariq أرق

sleepy ['sli:pi] *adj* naʿsān نعسان

sleeve [sli:v] *n* kumm كم (akmām أكمام)

sleigh [slei] *see* **sled**

slender ['slendə] *adj* naḥīl نحيل

slept [slept] *see* **sleep**

slew [slu:] *see* **slay**

slice [slais] 1. *n* sharīḥa شريحة (sharāʾiḥ شرائح) 2. *v* sharraḥa شرح شرائح; qaṭṭaʿa sharāʾiḥ قطع شرائح

slick [slik] *n* oil slick buqʿat zayt بقعة زيت

slide [slaid] 1. *n* mazlaq مزلق (mazāliq مزالق) 2. *v* (**slid**) inzalaqa انزلق 3. (*fin.*) habaṭa هبط (u/i; hubūṭ هبوط)

slight [slait] *adj* tāfih تافه

slightly ['slaitli] *adv* qalīlan قليلاً

slim [slim] *adj* naḥīl نحيل

slimy [slaimi] *adj* lazij لزج; ghirawī غروي

slip [slip] 1. *n* **slip of paper** qiṭʿat waraqa قطعة ورقة 2. **to make a slip** akhṭaʾa أخطأ 3. *v* (**slipped**) inzalaqa انزلق

slippery ['slipəri] *adj* zaliq زلق

slit [slit] 1. *n* shaqq tawīl شق طويل 2. *v* shaqqa bi 'ṭ-ṭūl شق بالطول (u; shaqq شق)

slogan ['sləugən] *n* shiʿār شعار (-āt)

slope [sləup] 1. *n* munḥadar منحدر (-āt) 2. *v* inḥadara انحدر

slot [slot] *n* shaqq شق (shuqūq شقوق)

slow [sləu] 1. *adj* baṭīʾ بطيء 2. **This clock is slow.** hādhihi 's-sāʿa mutaʾakhkhira هذه الساعة متأخرة 3. *adv* bi buṭʾ ببطء

slow down *v* baṭṭaʾa بطأ; abṭaʾa أبطأ

slowly ['sləuli] *adv* bi buṭʾ ببطء

slowness ['sləunis] *n* buṭʾ بطء

slum ['slʌmə] *n* ḥayy al-fuqarāʾ حي الفقراء

slump [slʌmp] 1. *n* (*ec.*) hubūṭ iqtiṣādī هبوط إقتصادي 2. *v* saqaṭa fajʾatan سقط فجأة

slums [slʌmz] *see* **slum**

smack [smak] 1. *n* ṣafq صفق 2. *v* ṣafaqa صفق (i; ṣafq صفق)

small [smo:l] *adj* saghīr صغير

smart [sma:t] *adj* **1.** dhakī ذكي;
shāṭir شاطر **2.** anīq أنيق

smash [smash] *v* ḥaṭṭama حطم

smell [smel] **1.** *n* rā'iḥa رائحة
(rawā'iḥ روائح) **2.** *v* (**smelt/
smelled**) shamma شم (u; shamm
شم)

smile [smail] **1.** *n* ibtisām إبتسام **2.** *v*
ibtasama ابتسم

smoke [sməuk] **1.** *n* dukhān دخان
(adkhina أدخنة) **2.** *v* dakhana دخن
(u) **3. to smoke food** dakhkhana
دخن

smoker ['sməukə] *n* mudakhkhin
مدخن (-ūn)

smoking ['sməuking] *n* **1.** tadkhīn
تدخين **2. no smoking!** mamnūᶜ at-
tadkhīn ممنوع التدخين

smooth [smu:dh] **1.** *adj* nāᶜim ناعم
2. salis سلس **3.** *v* naᶜᶜama نعم

smoothly ['smu:dhli] *adv* bi salāsa
بسلاسة

smuggle ['smʌgəl] *v* harraba هرب

smuggler ['smʌglə] *n* muharrib
مهرب (-ūn)

smuggling ['smʌgling] *n* tahrīb
تهريب

snack [snak] *n* wajba khafīfa
وجبة خفيفة

snack bar *n* maṭᶜam li 'l-wajbāt al-
khafīfa مطعم للوجبات الخفيفة

snail [sneil] *n* qawqaᶜa قوقعة
(qawāqiᶜ قواقع); ḥalazūn *collective*
حلزون

snake [sneik] *n* ḥayya حية (-āt);
afᶜan أفعى (afāᶜin أفاع)

snap [snap] *v* (**snapped**) inqaṭaᶜa
انقطع faj'atan فجأة

snapshot ['snapshot] *n* ṣūra
fotōghrāfīya صورة فتوغرافية

snatch [snach] *v* intazaᶜa انتزع;
ikhtaṭafa اختطف

sneak [sni:k] *v* tasallala تسلل

sneeze [sni:z] **1.** *n* ᶜaṭsa عطسة **2.** *v*
ᶜaṭasa عطس (i, u; ᶜaṭs عطس)

sniff [snif] *v* **1.** tanashshaqa تنشق **2.**
shamma شم (u; shamm شم)

snip [snip] *v* qaṣṣa bi miqaṣṣ
قص بمقص (u; qaṣṣ قص)

snob [snob] *n* naffāj نفاج (-ūn);
mutakabbir متكبر (-ūn)

snore [sno:] *v* shakhara شخر (i;
shakhīr شخير); ghaṭṭa غط (i; ghaṭīṭ
غطيط)

snow [snəu] **1.** *n* thalj ثلج (thulūj
ثلوج) **2.** *v* **It's snowing.** yathluju
as-samā' يثلج السماء

so [səu] **1.** *adv* ilā hādha 'l-ḥadd
إلى هذا الحد; li hādhihi 'd-daraja
لهذه الدرجة **2.** *conj* (**and**) **so** lihādha
لهذا; lidhālik لذلك **3. so (that)** ḥattā
حتى; kay كي; likay لكي

soak [səuk] *v* anqaᶜa أنقع

so-and-so ['səuənsəu] *n* fulān فلان

soap [səup] *n* ṣābūn صابون

soap opera *n* musalsal مسلسل
(-āt)

sob [sob] *v* nashaja نشج (i; nashīj
نشيج)

sober ['səubə] *adj* **1.** muqtaṣid
مقتصد **2.** ghayr sakrān غير سكران

soccer ['sokə] *n* kurat al-qadam
كرة القدم

social ['səushəl] *adj* ijtimāᶜī إجتماعي

socialism ['səushəlizəm] *n*
ishtirākīya إشتراكية

socialist ['səushəlist] *adj* ishtirākī
إشتراكي

society [sə'saiəti] *n* mujtamaᶜ مجتمع
(-āt)

sock [sok] *n* jawrab جورب (jawārib جوارب)

socket ['sokit] *n* 1. ḥuqq حق 2. **power socket** ma'khadh مأخذ (ma'ākhidh مآخذ) 3. **eye socket** maḥjir al-ʿayn محجر العين (maḥājir محاجر)

soda water *n* mā' ghāzīya ماء غازية

sofa [səufa] *n* arīka أريكة (arā'ik أرائك)

soft [soft] *adj* nāʿim ناعم

soften ['sofən] *v* layyana لين

softly ['softli] *adv* bi hudū' بهدوء

software ['softwea] *n* barāmij kombyūtir برامج كومبيوتر *pl*

soil [soil] 1. *n* turba تربة (turāb تراب) 2. *v* lawwatha لوث; wassakha وسخ

solar [səulə] *adj* shamsī شمسي

sold [səuld] *see* **sell**

soldier ['səuljə] *n* jundī جندي (jund جند; junūd جنود)

sole [səul] 1. *adj* waḥīd وحيد 2. *n* akhmaṣ al-qadam أخمص القدم 3. samak mūsā سمك موسى

solely ['səuli] *adv* faḥasb فحسب

solemn ['soləm] *adj* muhīb مهيب; waqūr وقور

solicitor [sə'lisitə] *n (UK)* muḥāmin محامٍ (muḥāmūn محامون)

solid ['solid] 1. *adj* muṣmat مصمت 2. matīn متين; ṣulb صلب 3. *n* mādda ṣulba مادة صلبة

solitary ['solitri] *adj* waḥdānī وحداني

solo ['səuləu] *adj/n/adv* munfarid منفرد

so long as *conj* 1. ṭālamā طالما 2. sharṭ an أن شرط

solution [sə'lu:shən] *n* 1. ḥall حل (ḥulūl حلول) 2. sā'il سائل (sawā'il سوائل)

solve [solv] *v* ḥalla حل (u; ḥall حل)

some [səm; sʌm] 1. *pronoun/adj* baʿḍ بعض 2. biḍʿa بضعة; biḍʿ بضع 3. mā ما 4. *adv* ḥawālā حوالى; naḥw نحو

somebody ['sʌmbədi] 1. shakhṣ mā شخص ما 2. shakhṣ hāmm شخص هام

someday ['sʌmdei] *adv* yawman mā يوماً ما

somehow ['sʌmhau] *adv* bi ṭarīqa aw bi 'ukhrā بطريقة أو بأخرى

someone ['sʌmwʌn] shakhṣ mā شخص ما

someplace ['sʌmpleis] *adv* makān mā مكان ما

something ['sʌmthing] shay' mā شيء ما

sometime ['sʌmtaim] *adv* fī waqt ghayr muḥaddad في وقت غير محدد; yawman mā يوماً ما

sometimes ['sʌmtaimz] *adv* aḥyānan أحياناً

someway ['sʌmwei] *adv* bi ṭarīqa aw bi 'ukhrā بطريقة أو بأخرى

somewhat ['sʌmwot] *adv* baʿḍ ash-shay' بعض الشيء; ilā ḥaddin mā إلى حد ما

somewhere ['sʌmwea] *adv* makān mā مكان ما

son [sʌn] *n* ibn ابن (abnā' أبناء; banūn بنون)

song [song] *n* ughniya أغنية (aghānin أغانٍ)

soon [su:n] *adv* 1. qarīban قريباً 2. **as soon as** ḥālamā حالما

sooner or later *adv* ʿājilan aw ājilan عاجلاً أو آجلاً

sophisticated [sə'fistikeitid] *adj* muḥannak محنك

sore [so:] **1.** *adj* alīm عليم **2.** *n* qarḥa قرحة (qiraḥ قرح)

sorrow ['sorəu] *n* ḥuzn حزن (aḥzān أحزان); asan أسًى

sorry ['sori] *adj* **1.** āsif آسف **2.** ḥazīn حزين; mu'sif مؤسف **3.** sorry! āsif آسف

sort [so:t] **1.** *n* nawʿ نوع (anwāʿ أنواع); ṣanf صنف (aṣnāf أصناف) **2.** *v* ṣannafa صنف

so-so [səu səu] *adv* bayn bayn بين بين

so that *conj* kay كي; likay لكي

sought [so:t] *see* **seek**

soul [səul] *n* nafs نفس (anfus أنفس); rūḥ روح (arwāḥ أرواح)

sound [saund] **1.** *adj* salīm سليم **2.** *n* ṣawt صوت (aṣwāt أصوات)

soundless ['saundlis] *adj* ṣāmit صامت

soundtrack ['saundtrak] *n* mūsīqā film موسيقى فلم

soup [su:p] *n* ḥasā' حساء

sour [sauə] **1.** *adj* ḥāmiḍ حامض **2.** The milk is sour. al-ḥalīb fāsid الحليب فاسد **3.** *v* ḥammaḍa حمض **4.** afsada أفسد

source [so:s] *n* maṣdar مصدر (maṣādir مصادر); manbaʿ منبع (manābiʿ منابع)

south [sauth] **1.** *adj* janūbī جنوبي **2.** *n* janūb جنوب

southeast [sauth'i:st] **1.** *adj* janūbī sharqī جنوبي شرقي **2.** *n* janūb sharqī جنوب شرقي

southerly ['sʌdhəli] *adj* janūbī جنوبي

southern ['sʌdhən] *adj* janūbī جنوبي

southerner ['sʌdhənə] *n* janūbī جنوبي (-yūn)

southwards ['sauthwə:ds] *adv* janūban جنوباً; naḥw al-janūb نحو الجنوب

southwest [sauth'west] **1.** *adj* janūbī gharbī جنوبي غربي **2.** *n* janūb gharbī جنوب غربي

souvenir [su:və'niə] *n* tadhkār تذكار

sovereign ['sovrin] *n* ʿāhil عاهل (ʿawāhil عواهل)

sow [səu] *v* (sowed, sown) zaraʿa زرع (a; zarʿ زرع)

space [speis] **1.** *adj* faḍā'ī فضائي **2.** *n* farāgh فراغ **3.** masāḥa مساحة (-āt); makān مكان (amākin أماكن) **4.** saʿa سعة **5.** outer space al-faḍā' al-khārijī الفضاء الخارجي

spacecraft ['speiskra:ft] *n* safīnat al-faḍā' سفينة الفضاء

spaceman ['speisman] *n* rā'id al-faḍā' رائد الفضاء

spaceship ['speisship] *n* safīnat al-faḍā' سفينة الفضاء

space shuttle ['speis'shʌtəl] *n* al-makkūk al-faḍā'ī المكوك الفضائي

spacious ['speishəs] *adj* wāsiʿ واسع

spade [speid] *n* misḥāh مسحاة (masāḥin مساح)

spaghetti [spə'geti] *n* maʿkarōnat as-spaghītī معكرونة السبغيتي

Spain [spein] *n* isbānyā إسبانيا

span [span] *n* **1.** shibr شبر (ashbār أشبار) **2.** mudda مدة **3.** imtidād إمتداد

Spanish ['spanish] *adj* isbānī إسباني

spanner ['spanə] *n* miftāḥ rabṭ مفتاح ربط

spare [speə] **1.** *adj* iḍāfī إضافي **2.** iḥtiyāṭī إحتياطي **3.** *v* istabqā استبقى **4.** raḥima رحم (a; raḥma رحمة)

spark [spa:k] *n* sharāra شرارة (-āt)

spat [spat] *see* **spit**

speak [spi:k] *v* (**spoke, spoken**)
takallama تكلم

speaker ['spi:kə] 1. mutakallim
متكلم; nāṭiq ناطق 2. *see*
loudspeaker

spear ['spiə] *n* rumḥ رمح (rimāḥ
(رماح

special ['speshəl] *adj* 1. istithnā'ī
إستثنائي 2. khāṣṣ خاص

specialist ['speshəlist] *n* ikhtiṣāṣī
إختصاصي (-yūn)

specialty; speciality ['speshəlti;
speshi'aləti] *n* ikhtiṣāṣ إختصاص

specialize ['speshəlaiz] *v* takhaṣṣaṣa
تخصص (**in** li/bi/fī في/ب/ل)

specially ['speshəli] *adv* khuṣūṣan
خصوصاً

species ['spi:shi:z] *n* jins جنس
(ajnās أجناس)

specific [spə'sifik] *adj* mu'ayyin
معين; muḥaddad محدد

specifically [spə'sifikli] *adv* bi 't-
taḥdīd بالتحديد

specification [spəsifi'keishən] *n*
muwāṣafa مواصفة (-āt)

specimen ['spesimən] *n* 'ayyina
عينة (-āt); namūdhaj نموذج (-āt)

spectacle ['spektəkəl] *n* isti'rāḍ
'āmm إستعراض عام

spectacles ['spektəklz] *pl* naẓẓāra
نظارة (-āt); 'uwaynāt عوينات

spectacular [spek'takyulə] *adj*
mudhhil مذهل

spectator [spek'teitə] *n* mushāhid
مشاهد (-ūn)

speculate ['spekyuleit] *v* 1.
tafakkara تفكر 2. *(fin.)* ḍāraba
ضارب

speculation [spekyu'leishən] *n* 1.

tafakkur تفكر 2. *(fin.)* muḍāraba
مضاربة

speech [spi:ch] *n* 1. kalām كلام 2.
khiṭāb خطاب (akhṭiba أخطبة);
khuṭba خطبة (khuṭab خطب) 3. **to
make a speech** alqā khiṭāban خطاباً
ألقى

speechless ['spi:chlis] *adj* 'ājiz 'an
al-kalām عاجز عن الكلام

speed [spi:d] 1. *n* sur'a سرعة 2. **at
top speed** bi aqṣā sur'a بأقصى سرعة
3. *v* sarra'a سرع

speeding ['spi:ding] *n* al-ḥadd
al-masmūḥ bih li 's-sur'a
الحد المسموح به للسرعة

speedy ['spi:di] *adj* sarī' سريع; 'ājil
عاجل

spell [spel] 1. *n* fatra فترة (fatarāt
فترات) 2. ruqya رقية (ruqan رقى)
3. *v* (**spelt/spelled**) tahajjā تهجى

spelling ['speling] *n* tahjiya تهجية;
hijā' هجاء

spend [spend] *v* (**spent**) 1. anfaqa
أنفق 2. **to spend time** qaḍā قضى
(i; qaḍā' قضاء)

spent [spent] *see* **spend**

sperm [spə:m] *n* minan منى; as-sā'il
al-manawī السائل المنوي

sphere ['sfiə] *n* kura كرة (-āt)

spice [spais] *n* tābil تابل (tawābil
توابل)

spicy ['spaisi] *adj* mutabbal متبل

spider ['spaidə] *n* 'ankabūt عنكبوت
('anākīb عناكيب)

spike [spaik] *n* mismār ḍakhm
مسمار ضخم

spill [spil] 1. *n* **oil spill** irāqat an-nafṭ
إراقة النفط 2. *v* (**split/spilled**) arāqa
أراق

spin [spin] *v* (**spun**) ghazala غزل (i;
ghazl غزل)

spinal ['spainǝl] *adj* faqrī فقري;
shawkī شوكي

spine [spain] *n* al-ʿamūd al-faqrī
العمود الفقري

spirit ['spirit] *n* **1.** rūḥ روح (arwāḥ
أرواح); shabaḥ شبح (ashbāḥ
أشباح) **2.** kuḥūl كحول **3.** *and see*
spirits

spirits ['spirits] *pl* **1. alcoholic
spirits** kuḥūl كحول **2. to be in
good spirits** ibtahaja ابتهج

spiritual ['spirichuǝl] *adj* rūḥānī
رحاني

spit [spit] **1.** *n* başqa بصقة **2.** *v* (*[UK]*
spat; *[US]* **spit**) başaqa (a) بصق

spite [spait] **1.** *n* ḥiqd حقد (aḥqād
أحقاد) **2. in spite of** ʿalā r-raghmi
min على الرغم من

spiteful ['spaitfǝl] *adj* ḥāqid حاقد

splash [splash] **1.** *n* rashsh رش **2.** *v*
rashsha رش (u; rashsh رش)

splendid ['splendid] *adj* rāʾiʿ رائع

splendour, *(US)* **splendor**
['splendǝ] *n* sanāʾ سناء; rawʿa روعة

split [split] **1.** *n* shaqq شق (shuqūq
شقوق) **2.** *v* (**split**) shaqqaqa شقق **3.**
inshaqqa انشق

spoil [spoil] *v* (**spoilt/spoiled**) **1.**
afsada أفسد **2.** *see* **spoils**

spoiled [spoild] *adj* **a spoiled child**
ṭifl mudallaʿ طفل مدلع

spoilt [spoilt] *see* **spoil, spoiled**

spoke; spoken [spǝuk; spǝukǝn]
see **speak**

spokesman ['spǝuksmǝn] *n*
mutaḥaddith متحدث; nāṭiq ناطق
(**for/of** bi lisān بلسان)

spokesperson ['spǝukspǝ:sǝn] *n*
mutaḥaddith متحدث; mutaḥadditha
متحدثة

spokeswoman ['spǝukswumǝn] *n*
mutaḥadditha متحدثة; nāṭiq ناطق
(**for/of** bi lisān بلسان)

sponsor [sponsǝ] **1.** *n* ʿarrāb عراب
(-ūn); rāʾī راعي **2.** *v* rāʿā راعى

spontaneous [spon'teiniǝs] *adj*
ʿafwī عفوي; tilqāʾī تلقائي

spool [spu:l] *n* mikabb مكب (-āt)

spoon [spu:n] *n* milʿaqa ملعقة
(malāʿiq ملاعق)

sport; sports [spo:t; -s] **1.** *adj*
riyāḍī رياضي **2.** *n* riyāḍa رياضة

sportsman ['spo:tsmǝn] *n* riyāḍī
رياضي

sportswear ['spo:tsweǝ] *n* malābis
riyāḍīya ملابس رياضية

sportswoman ['spo:tswumǝn] *n*
riyāḍīya رياضية

spot [spot] **1.** *n* buqʿa بقعة (buqaʿ
بقع); laṭkha لطخة (laṭakhāt
لطخات) **2.** makān مكان (amākin
أماكن) **3.** (*med.*) buqʿa بقعة (buqaʿ
بقع) **4.** *v* (**spotted**) raʾā رأى (yarā
يرى); raʾy رأي)

spotless [spotlis] *adj* naẓīf jiddan
نظيف جداً

spotlight ['spotlait] *n* ḍawʾ al-
masraḥ ضوء المسرح; ḍawʾ kāshif
ضوء كاشف

spout [spaut] *n* mizrāb مزراب
(mazārib مزارب)

sprang [sprang] *see* **spring**

spray [sprei] **1.** *n* rashāsh رشاش **2.** *v*
rashsha رش (u; rashsh رش)

spread [spred] **1.** *n* basṭ بسط; nashr
نشر **2.** *v* (**spread**) basaṭa بسط (u;
basṭ بسط); nashara نشر (u; nashr
نشر)

spring [spring] **1.** *n* rabīʿ ربيع **2.**
manbaʿ منبع (manābiʿ منابع); yanbūʿ

عين (yanābīʿ ينابيع); ʿayn عين
(ʿuyūn عيون) **3. metal spring**
zanbarak زنبرك (zanābik زنابك) **4.** v
(sprang, sprung) qafaza قفز (i;
qafz قفز); wathaba وثب (yathibu
يثب; wathb وثب)

sprinkle ['springkəl] v nathara نثر
(u; nathr نثر); rashsha رش (u;
rashsh رش)

sprint [sprint] v rakaḍa bi aqṣā surʿa
(u; rakḍ ركض بأقصى سرعة)

sprung [sprʌng] see **spring**

spy [spai] **1.** n jāsūs جاسوس (jawāsīs
جواسيس) **2.** v tajassasa تجسس

spying ['spa:ying] n tajassus تجسس

squad [skwod] n firqa فرقة (firaq
فرق)

squalid ['skwolid] adj **1.** qadhir قذر
jiddan جداً **2.** khasīs خسيس

square ['skweə] **1.** adj murabbaʿ
مربع **2.** n murabbaʿ مربع (-āt) **3.**
town square maydān ميدان
(mayādīn ميادين)

square metre, (US) **square
meter** n mitr murabbaʿ متر مربع

square kilometre, (US) **square
kilometer** n kīlōmitr murabbaʿ
كيلومتر مربع

squash [skwosh] **1.** ziḥām زحام **2.**
qarʿ collective قرع **3.** ʿaṣīr عصير **4.**
(spor.) iskwāsh إسكواش **5.** v harasa
هرس (u; hars هرس)

squat [skwot] v qarfaṣa قرفص

squeak [skwi:k] v **1.** ṣarafa صرف (i;
ṣarīf صريف) **2.** ṣawwā صوى

squeeze [skwi:z] v **1.** ḍaghaṭa ضغط
(a; ḍaght ضغط); kabasa ʿalā كبس على
(i; kabs كبس) **2.** ʿaṣara عصر (i;
ʿaṣr عصر)

St. see **saint, street**

stab [stab] v **(stabbed)** ṭaʿana طعن
(a/u; ṭaʿn طعن)

stability [stə'biləti] n istiqrār
إستقرار

stabilize ['steibəlaiz] v istaqarra
استقر

stable ['steibəl] **1.** adj mustaqirr
مستقر; rāsikh راسخ **2.** n iṣṭabl
إصطبل (-āt)

stack [stak] **1.** n kawma كومة (-āt) **2.**
v kawwama كوم

stadium ['steidiəm] n istād إستاد

staff [sta:f] n **1.** ʿaṣan f عصا (ʿuṣīy
عصي) **2.** majmūʿ muwaẓẓafīn
مجموع موظفين

stage [steij] **1.** adj masraḥī مسرحي **2.**
n masraḥ مسرح (masāriḥ مسارح) **3.**
marḥala مرحلة (marāḥil مراحل)

stain [stein] **1.** n buqʿa بقعة (buqaʿ
بقع); laṭkha لطخة (laṭakhāt لطخات)
2. v baqqaʿa بقع; laṭakha لطخ (a;
laṭkh لطخ)

stainless ['steinlis] adj **1.** dūn
buqʿa دون بقعة **2.** lā yatalaṭṭakh
لا يتلطخ

stair [steə] n daraja درجة (-āt)

staircase ['steəkeis] n sullam سلم
(salālim سلالم)

stairs [steəz] pl darajāt درجات;
sullam سلم

stairway ['steəwei] see **stairs**

stake [steik] n **1.** watad وتد (awtād
أوتاد) **2. at stake** rahn al-aḥdāth
رهن الأحداث

stale [steil] adj ghayr ṭāzij غير طازج

stalk [sto:k] **1.** n suwayqa سويقة **2.** v
ittabaʿa rāṣidan اتبع راصداً

stall [sto:l] **1.** n kushk كشك (akshāk
أكشاك) **2.** v ajjala أجل **3.** tawaqqafa
faj'atan توقف فجأة

stamina ['staminə] *n* qudra ᶜalā 'l-iḥtimāl قدرة على الإحتمال

stamp [stamp] **1.** *n* khatm ختم (akhtām أختام); damgha دمغة **2.** postage stamp ṭābiᶜ barīdī طابع بريدي (ṭawābiᶜ طوابع) **3.** *v* dāsa bi qūwa داس بقوة (u; daws دوس) **4.** khatama ختم (i; khatm ختم)

stance [sta:ns] *n* **1.** waqfa وقفة (-āt) **2.** mawqif موقف (mawāqif مواقف)

stand [stand] **1.** *n* trade stand janāḥ جناح **2.** to make a stand against ittakhada mawqif ḍidd إتخذ موقف ضد **3.** *v* (stood) waqafa وقف (yaqifu يقف; waqūf وقوف)

standard ['standəd] **1.** *adj* miᶜyārī معياري **2.** muᶜtarif bih معترف به **3.** *n* miᶜyār معيار (maᶜāyīr معايير); miqyās مقياس (maqāyīs مقاييس) **4.** mustawan مستوى **5.** rāya راية (-āt)

standardize ['standedaiz] *v* waḥḥada 'l-maᶜāyīr وحد المعاير

stand-by ['standbai] *n* iḥtiyāṭī إحتياطي

stand down *v* insaḥaba انسحب

stand for *v* ayyada أيد

stand for election *v* tarashshaḥa ترشح

stand out *v* bariza برز (u)

standpoint ['standpoint] *n* wajhat naẓar وجهة نظر

standstill ['standstil] *n* tawaqquf tāmm توقف تام

stand up *v* waqafa وقف (yaqifu يقف; waqūf وقوف)

stank [stangk] *see* stink

staple ['steipəl] **1.** *adj* ra'īsī رئيسي **2.** *n* silᶜa ra'īsīya سلعة رئيسية **3.** *v* dabbasa دبس

stapler ['steiplə] *n* dabbāsa دباسة

star [sta:] *n* najm نجم (nujūm نجوم)

stare [steə] *v* ḥaddaqa حدق (at ilā إلى/fī في)

start [sta:t] **1.** *n* bidāya بداية (-āt) **2.** *v* bada'a بدأ (a; bad' بدء)

starvation [sta:'veishən] *n* jawᶜ جوع

starve [sta:v] *v* jāᶜa جاع (u; jawᶜ جوع)

state [steit] **1.** *adj* ḥukūmī حكومي **2.** rasmī رسمي **3.** *n* ḥāl حال (aḥwāl أحوال); ḥāla حالة (-āt) **4.** dawla دولة (duwal دول) **5.** federal state wilāya ولاية (-āt) **6.** *v* ṣarraḥa صرح; aᶜlana أعلن

stately ['steitli] *adj* jalīl جليل; fakhm فخم

statement ['steitmənt] *n* **1.** bayān بيان; taṣrīḥ تصريح **2.** ifāda إفادة **3.** bank statement kashf al-ḥisāb كشف الحساب **4.** to make a statement aᶜṭā ifāda أعطى إفادة

States [steits] *pl* the States al-wilāyāt al-muttaḥida الولايات المتحدة

statesman ['steitsmən] *n* rajul dawla رجل دولة

static ['statik] *adj* sākin ساكن

station ['steishən] **1.** *n* maḥaṭṭa محطة (-āt); markaz مركز (marākiz مراكز) **2.** *v* waḍaᶜa وضع (yaḍaᶜu يضع; waḍᶜ وضع)

stationary ['steishənri] *adj* wāqif واقف; sākin ساكن

stationer's ['steishənəz] *n* maktaba مكتبة

stationery ['steishənri] *n* adawāt maktabīya أدوات مكتبية; qirṭāsīya قرطاسية

statistical [stə'tistikəl] *adj* iḥṣā'ī إحصائي

statistics [stə'tistiks] *pl* iḥṣā'īyāt إحصائيات; 'ilm al-iḥṣā' علم الإحصاء

statue ['stachu:] *n* timthāl تمثال (tamāthīl تماثيل)

status ['steitəs] *n* 1. manzila منزلة; makāna مكانة; markaz مركز 2. *(leg.)* waḍʿ sharʿī وضع شرعي

stay [stei] 1. *n* iqāma إقامة 2. *v* aqāma أقام 3. baqiya بقي (i; baqā' بقاء)

stead [sted] *n* in his stead badaluh بدله

steady ['stedi] *adj* 1. thābit ثابت 2. mustaqirr مستقر 3. hādi' هادئ

steak [steik] *n* sharīḥat laḥm/samak شريحة لحم\سمك

steal [sti:l] *v* (stole, stolen) saraqa سرق (i; sariqa سرقة) (from min من)

stealth [stelth] *n* insilāl إنسلال

steam [sti:m] *n* bukhār بخار

steel [sti:l] *n* ṣulb صلب

steep [sti:p] *adj* shadīd al-inḥidār شديد الإنحدار

steer [stiə] *v* wajjaha وجه

steering wheel *n* ʿajalat al-qiyāda عجلة القيادة

stem [stem] 1. *n* suwayqa سويقة (-āt) 2. *v* ṣadda صد (u; ṣadd صد) 3. najama نجم (u; nujūm نجوم) (from min من)

step [step] 1. *n* daraja درجة (-āt) 2. khaṭwa خطوة (khaṭawāt خطوات) 3. a step forward khaṭwa ilā 'l-amām خطوة إلى الأمام 4. step by step khaṭwa fa khaṭwa خطوة فخطوة 5. *v* (stepped) khaṭā خطا (u; khaṭw خطو)

stereo ['steriəu] 1. *adj* isteriyō إستريو 2. *n* jihāz isteriyō جهاز إستريو

stereotype ['steriəutaip] *n* muqawlab مقولب (-āt)

sterile ['sterail] *adj* ʿaqīm عقيم

sterilize ['sterəlaiz] *v* ʿaqqama عقم

sterling ['stə:ling] *adj (fin.)* istarlīnī إسترليني

stern [stə:n] 1. *adj* ṣārim صارم 2. *n* mu'akhkhar as-safīna مؤخر السفينة

stew [styu:] *n* yakhna يخنة

steward ['styuəd] *n* muḍīf مضيف

stewardess ['styuədes] *n* muḍīfa مضيفة

stick [stik] 1. *n* ʿaṣā عصا (ʿuṣīy عصي) 2. *v* (stuck) laṣiqa لصق (a; laṣq لصق); alṣaqa ألصق

stick to *v* iltazama التزم

sticker ['stikə] *n* waraqa muṣammagha ورقة مصمغة

sticky ['stiki] *adj* lazij لزج

stiff [stif] *adj* ṣulb صلب

still [stil] 1. *adj* hādi' هادئ; sākin ساكن 2. *adv* lā yazāl لا يزال 3. wa maʿa dhālik ومع ذلك 4. ḥatta al'ān حتى الآن

stimulant ['stimyulənt] *n* munabbih منبه (-āt)

stimulate ['stimyuleit] *v* athāra أثار; nabbaha نبه

stimulating ['stimyuleiting] *adj* muthīr مثير

sting [sting] *v* (stung) lasaʿa لسع (a; lasʿ لسع); ladagha لدغ (u; ladgh لدغ); qaraṣa قرص (u; qarṣ قرص)

stink [stingk] 1. *n* rā'iḥa karīha رائحة كريهة 2. *v* (stank, stunk) natana نتن (i; natn نتن)

stir [stə:] *v* (stirred) 1. ḥarraka حرك 2. ḥarraḍa حرض

stir up *v* 1. ḥarraḍa حرض 2. athāra أثار

stitch [stich] 1. *n (also med.)* ghurza غرزة

زة غرز (ghuraz غرز) 2. v daraza درز
(u; darz درز); khayyaṭa خيط

stoat [stəut] n ibn ʿirs abyaḍ
ابن عرس أبيض ; qāqum قاقم

stock [stok] 1. n baḍāʾiʿ بضائع ; silaʿ
سلع 2. (fin.) raʾsmāl رأسمال ; ashum
أسهم 3. **livestock** mawāshin مواش
4. aṣl أصل 5. maraq مرق 6. v
zawwada bi 'l-baḍāʾiʿ
زود بالبضائع

stockbroker [ˈstokbrəukə] n
simsār al-būrṣa سمسار البورصة ;
simsār al-ashum سمسار الأسهم

stock exchange n būrṣa بورصة (-āt)

stock market n būrṣa بورصة (-āt)

stole; stolen [stəul; ˈstəulən] see
steal

stomach [ˈstʌmək] n miʿda معدة
(miʿad معد); baṭn بطن (buṭūn بطون)

stomach ache n maghaṣ مغص

stone [stəun] 1. n ḥajar حجر (aḥjār
أحجار); ḥijāra حجارة 2. v rajama bi
'l-ḥijāra رجم بالحجارة (u; rajm رجم)

stoned [stəund] adj (sl.) masṭūl
مسطول

stony [ˈstəuni] adj ḥajarī حجري

stood [stud] see **stand**

stool [stuːl] n kursī bidūn ẓahr
كرسي بدون ظهر

stop [stop] 1. n waqf وقف 2. **bus-stop** mawqif al-otobīs موقف الأتوبيس
3. **to bring to a stop** awqafa أوقف
4. v (**stopped**) waqafa وقف (yaqifu
يقف; waqf وقف) 5. manaʿa منع (a;
manʿ منع)

storage [ˈstoːrij] n khazn خزن

store [stoː] 1. n dhakhīra ذخيرة
(dhakhāʾir ذخائر) 2. dukkān دكان
(dakākīn دكاكين); matjar متجر
(matājir متاجر) 3. v khazana خزن (u;
khazn خزن)

storekeeper [ˈstoːkiːpə] n ṣāḥib
dukkān صاحب دكان

storeroom [ˈstoːrum] n makhzan
مخزن (makhāzin مخازن)

storey [ˈstoːri] n (pl **storeys**) ṭabaqa
طبقة (-āt); dawr دور (adwār أدوار)

storm [stoːm] 1. n ʿāṣifa عاصفة
(ʿawāṣif عواصف) 2. v (mil.)
iqtaḥama اقتحم

stormy [ˈstoːmi] adj ʿāṣif عاصف

story [ˈstoːri] n 1. ḥikāya حكاية (-āt)
2. **to tell a story** rawā riwāya
روى رواية (i) 3. see **storey**

stove [stəuv] n mawqid موقد
(mawāqid مواقد)

straight [streit] 1. adj mustaqīm
مستقيم 2. adv ʿalā ṭūl على طول

straightaway [streitəˈwei] adv
fawran فوراً; ḥālan حالاً; tawwan
توّاً

straighten [ˈstreitən] v qawwama
قوم; sawwā سوى

straightforward [streitˈfoːwəd]
adj basīṭ بسيط

strain [strein] 1. n juhd جهد (juhūd
جهود) 2. v jahada جهد (a; jahd جهد)
3. ṣaffā صفى

straits [streits] n maḍīq مضيق
(maḍāyiq مضايق)

strange [streinj] adj gharīb غريب

stranger [ˈstreinjə] n gharīb غريب
(ghurabāʾ غرباء)

strangle [ˈstrangɡəl] v khanaqa خنق
(u; khanq خنق)

strap [strap] n sharīṭ شريط (sharāʾiṭ
أشرطة; ashriṭa شرائط)

strategic [strəˈtiːjik] adj istrātījī
إستراتيجي

strategy [ˈstratəji] n istrātījīya
إستراتيجية

straw [strɔ:] *n* 1. qashsh قش 2. **drinking straw** shārūqa شاروقة (-āt)

strawberry ['strɔ:bəri] *n* farāwala فراولة

stray [strei] *v* ḍalla ضل (i; ḍalāl ضلال)

streak [stri:k] *n* khaṭṭ خط (khuṭūṭ خطوط)

stream [stri:m] 1. *n* nahr نهر (anhār أنهار) 2. *v* fāḍa فاض (i; fayḍ فيض; fayaḍān فيضان)

streamlined ['stri:mlaind] *adj* 1. insiyābī إنسيابي 2. mubassaṭ مبسط

street [stri:t] *n* shāriʿ شارع (shawāriʿ شوارع)

streetlamp; streetlight *n* miṣbāḥ ash-shāriʿ مصباح الشارع

strength [strength] *n* 1. qūwa قوة 2. maqdira مقدرة

strengthen ['strengthən] *v* qawwā قوى; ʿazzaza عزز

stress [stres] 1. *n* ḍaght ضغط (ḍughūṭ ضغوط) 2. nabra نبرة (nabarāt نبرات) 3. *v* akkada أكد

stretch [strech] *v* 1. madda مد (u; madd مد) 2. tamaṭṭā تمطى

strict [strikt] *adj* ṣārim صارم

strike [straik] 1. *n (pol.)* iḍrāb ʿan al-ʿamal إضراب عن العمل 2. *(mil.)* ḍarba ضربة (ḍarabāt ضربات) 3. *v* (**struck**) ḍaraba ضرب (i; ḍarb ضرب) 4. *(pol.)* aḍraba ʿan al-ʿamal أضرب عن العمل

striking ['straiking] *adj* lāfit li 'n-naẓar لافت للنظر

string [string] *n* 1. khayṭ خيط (khuyūṭ خيوط) 2. silsila سلسلة (salāsil سلاسل)

strip [strip] 1. *n* qiṭʿa (ṭawīla ḍayyiqa) قطعة (طويلة ضيقة) 2. *v* jarrada جرد 3. ʿarrā عرى

stripe [straip] *n* khaṭṭ خط (khuṭūṭ خطوط); qalam قلم (aqlām أقلام)

striped [straipt] *adj* mukhaṭṭaṭ مخطط; muqallam مقلم

strive [straiv] *v* jāhada جاهد

stroke [strəuk] 1. *n* ḍarba ضربة (ḍarabāt ضربات) 2. *(med.)* sakta dimāghīya سكتة دماغية 3. *v* massada مسد; lāṭafa لاطف

strong [strong] *adj* qawī قوي; shadīd شديد

struck [strʌk] *see* **strike**

structural ['strʌkchərəl] *adj* binā'ī بنائي; inshā'ī إنشائي

structure ['strʌkchə] *n* binā' بناء (abniya أبنية)

struggle ['strʌgəl] 1. *n* kifāḥ كفاح; niḍāl نضال 2. *v* kāfaha كافح; nāḍala ناضل

stubborn ['stʌbən] *adj* ʿanīd عنيد

stuck [stʌk] *see* **stick**

student ['styu:dənt] *n* ṭālib طالب (ṭullāb طلاب); tilmīdh تلميذ (talāmidha تلامذة)

studio ['styu:diəu] *n* istūdiyō إستوديو (istūdiyōhāt إستوديوهات)

study ['stʌdi] 1. *n* baḥth بحث (buḥūth بحوث) 2. maktab مكتب (makātib مكاتب) 3. *v* darasa درس (u; dars درس) 4. ta'ammala تأمل

stuff [stʌf] 1. *n* ashyā' أشياء; amtiʿa أمتعة 2. *v* ḥashā حشا (u; ḥashw حشو)

stuffed [stʌft] *adj* muḥannaṭ محنط

stun [stʌn] *v* 1. dawwakha دوخ 2. adhhala أذهل

stung [stʌng] *see* **sting**

stunk [stʌngk] *see* **stink**

stunt [stʌnt] *n* ʿamal muthīr
عمل مثير

stupid [styu:pid] *adj* ghabī غبي;
aḥmaq أحمق

stupidity [styu:'pidəti] *n* ghabā'
غباء; ḥamāqa حماقة

sturdy ['stə:di] *adj* matin متين

sty [stai] *n* zarībat al-khanāzīr
زريبة الخنازير

style [stail] 1. *n* uslūb أسلوب (asālīb
أساليب); ṭirāz طراز (ṭuruz طرز) 2. *v*
sarraḥa سرح

stylish ['stailish] *adj* anīq أنيق

subject ['sʌbjikt] *n* 1. mawḍūʿ
موضوع (mawāḍīʿ مواضيع) 2. mādda
مادة (mawādd مواد) 3. tābiʿ تابع
(atbāʿ أتباع)

subject to *adj* ʿurḍa li عرضة ل

submarine [sʌbmə'ri:n] 1. *adj* tahta
saṭḥ al-baḥr تحت سطح البحر 2. *n*
ghawwāṣa غواصة (-āt)

submissive [səb'misiv] *adj* khaḍūʿ
خضوع

submit [səb'mit] *v* 1. khaḍaʿa خضع
(a; khuḍūʿ خضوع) 2. qaddama قدم

subordinate [sə'bo:dinət] *adj*
mar'ūs مرؤوس (-ūn); tābiʿ تابع
(tabaʿa تبعة)

subscribe [səb'skraib] *v* ishtaraka
اشترك

subscriber [səb'skraibə] *n*
mushtarik مشترك (-ūn)

subscription [səb'skripshən] *n*
ishtirāk إشتراك

subsequent ['sʌbsikwənt] *adj*
lāḥiq لاحق; tālin تال

subsequently ['sʌbsikwəntli] *adv*
fī mā baʿd في ما بعد

subsequent to *prep* baʿd بعد

subsidiary [səb'sidiəri] *adj* iḍāfī
إضافي; thānawī ثانوي

subsidy ['sʌbsidi] *n* iʿāna mālīya
إعانة مالية

substance ['sʌbstəns] *n* 1. mādda
مادة (mawādd مواد) 2. jawhar
جوهر

substantial [səb'stanshəl] *adj* 1.
hāmm هام 2. ḍakhm ضخم

substitute ['sʌbstityu:t] 1. *n* badīl
بديل 2. *(spor.)* badīl بديل 3. *v*
istabdala استبدل

substitution [sʌbsti'tyu:shən] *n* 1.
istibdāl إستبدال 2. *(spor.)* istibdāl
إستبدال

subterranean [sʌbtə'reiniən] *adj*
tahta saṭh al-arḍ تحت سطح الأرض

subtitles ['sʌbtaitlz] *pl* tarjamat
film ترجمة فلم

subtle ['sʌtəl] *adj* raqīq رقيق; laṭīf
لطيف

subtract [səb'trakt] *v* ṭaraḥa طرح
(a; ṭarḥ طرح)

subtraction [səb'trakshən] *n* ṭarḥ
طرح

suburbs ['sʌbə:bs] *pl* ḍawāḥin
ضواح

suburban [sə'bə:bən] *adj* mutaʿalliq
bi 'ḍ-ḍawāḥī متعلق بالضواحي

subversive [səb'və:siv] *adj*
mukharrib مخرب

subvert [sʌb'və:t] *v* kharraba خرب

subway ['sʌbwei] *n* 1. *(UK)* nafaq
نفق (anfāq أنفاق) 2. *(US)* metrō al-
anfāq ميترو الأنفاق

succeed [sək'si:d] *v* 1. najaḥa نجح
(a; najāḥ نجاح); aflaḥa أفلح 2.
khalafa خلف (u; khilāfa خلافة);
walā ولى (yalī يلي; wilāya ولاية)

success [sək'ses] *n* najāḥ نجاح

successful [sək'sesfəl] *adj* nājiḥ
ناجح

succession [sək'seshən] n 1. khilāfa خلافة 2. silsila سلسلة 3. in succession bi t-tatābi' بالتتابع

successive [sək'sesiv] adj mutawālin متوالٍ; mutatābi' متتابع

successor [sək'sesə] n khalīfa خليفة (khulafā' خلفاء)

such [sʌch] 1. mithl مثل 2. hādha هذا; hākadhā هكذا

such and such adj kadhā wa kadhā كذا وكذا

such as mithl مثل; amthāl أمثال; ka ك

suck [sʌk] v maṣṣa مص (a/u; maṣṣ مص)

sudden ['sʌdən] adj mufāji' مفاجئ

suddenly ['sʌdənli] adv faj'atan فجأة

sue [su:] v rafaʿa daʿwā ʿalā رفع دعوى على (a; rafʿ رفع)

suffer ['sʌfə] v 'ānā عانى; qāsā قاسى

suffering ['sʌfəring] n ʿadhāb عذاب; alam ألم (ālām آلام)

sufficiency [sə'fishənsi] n kifāya كفاية

sufficient [sə'fishənt] adj kāfin كاف

suffix ['sʌfiks] v aḍāfa أضاف; alḥaqa ألحق

suffocate ['sʌfəkeit] v 1. khanaqa خنق (u; khanq خنق) 2. ikhtanaqa اختنق

sugar ['shugə] n sukkar سكر

suggest [se'jest] v iqtaraḥa اقترح

suggestion [sə'jeschən] n iqtirāḥ اقتراح (-āt)

suicide ['su:isaid] n intiḥār إنتحار

suit [su:t] 1. n badla بدلة (bidal بدل); ṭaqm طقم (ṭuqūm طقوم) 2. (leg.) daʿwā دعوى 3. v lā'ama لاءم; nāsaba ناسب 4. arḍā أرضى

suitable ['su:təbəl] adj munāsib مناسب; mulā'im ملائم

suitcase ['su:tkeis] n ḥaqība حقيبة (ḥaqā'ib حقائب)

suite [swi:t] n 1. janāḥ جناح 2. ṭaqm athāth طقم أثاث

sum [sʌm] n mablagh مبلغ (mabāligh مبالغ)

summarize ['sʌməraiz] v lakhkhaṣa لخص

summary ['sʌməri] n mūjaz موجز

summer ['sʌmə] n ṣayf صيف (aṣyāf أصياف)

summit ['sʌmit] n qimma قمة (qimam قمم); dhurwa ذروة (dhuran ذرى)

summon ['sʌmən] v daʿā دعى (u; duʿā' دعاء); istadʿā استدعى

sum up v lakhkhaṣa لخص

sun [sʌn] n shams شمس (shumūs شموس)

sunbathe ['sʌnbeidh] v akhadha ḥammām shams أخذ حمام شمس (u; akhdh أخذ)

sunburn ['sʌnbə:n] n safʿ ash-shams سفع الشمس

sunburnt ['sʌnbə:nt] adj masfūʿ مسفوع

Sunday ['sʌndei] n yawm al-'aḥad يوم الأحد

sung [sʌng] see sing

sunglasses ['sʌngla:siz] pl naẓẓārat shams نظارة شمس

sunk [sʌngk] see sink

sunlight ['sʌnlait] n ḍaw' ash-shams ضوء الشمس

Sunni; Sunnite ['suni:; 'sunayt] adj/n sunnī سني

sunny ['sʌni] adj mushmis مشمس

sunrise ['sʌnraiz] n shurūq شروق

sunset ['sʌnset] n ghurūb غروب

sunshine ['sʌnshain] n ashiʿʿat al-shams أشعة الشمس

super ['su:pə] adj rāʾiʿ رائع; mumtāz ممتاز

super- ['su:pə] fawq فوق; akbar أكبر; aʿẓam أعظم

superb [su:'pəːb] adj rāʾiʿ رائع; mumtāz ممتاز

superficial [su:pə'fishəl] adj saṭḥī سطحي

superhighway ['su:pə'haiwei] n (US) otostrād أوتوستراد (-āt)

superhuman [su:pəhyu:mən] adj fawq al-basharī فوق البشري

superior [su:'piəriə] 1. adj fāʾiq فائق 2. arfaʿ rutbatan/manzilatan أرفع رتبةً\منزلةً 3. n mudīr مدير (mudarāʾ مدراء)

superiority [su:piəri'oriti] n 1. tafawwuq تفوق 2. istiʿlāʾ إستعلاء

supermarket ['su:pəma:kit] n matjar kabīr متجر كبير; sūpermārket سوبرماركت

supernatural [su:pə'nachrəl] adj khāriq aṭ-ṭabīʿa خارق الطبيعة

superpower ['su:pəpauə] n dawla ʿuẓmā دولة عظمى; qūwa ʿuẓmā قوة عظمى

superstar ['su:pəsta:] n najm kabīr نجم كبير

superstition [su:pə'stishən] n khurāfa خرافة (-āt)

superstitious [su:pə'stishəs] adj khurāfī خرافي

supervise ['su:pəvaiz] v ashrafa ʿalā أشرف على

supervision [su:pəvizhən] n ishrāf إشراف

supervisor ['su:pəvizhə] n mushrif مشرف (-ūn)

supper ['sʌpə] n ʿashāʾ عشاء

supplementary [sʌpli'mentri] adj iḍāfī إضافي

supplier [sə'plaiə] n muzawwid مزود (-ūn); mumawwin ممون (-ūn)

supplies [sə'plaiz] pl maʾūnāt مؤونات; muʾan مؤن

supply [sə'plai] 1. n tamwīn تموين 2. v zawwada زود 3. see supplies

support [sə'po:t] 1. n diʿāma دعامة (-āt) 2. (leg.) taʾyīd تأييد 3. v daʿama دعم; daʿʿama دعّم; (a; daʿm دعم); daʿʿama دعّم (leg.) ayyada أيد

supporter [sə'po:tə] n muʾayyid مؤيد (-ūn); naṣīr نصير (nuṣarāʾ نصراء)

suppose [sə'pəuz] v iftaraḍa افترض

supremacy [su:'preməsi] n 1. tafawwuq تفوق 2. siyāda سيادة; haymana هيمنة

supreme [su:'pri:m] adj aʿlā أعلى

sure [sho:] 1. adj akīd أكيد; mutaʾakkid متأكد 2. adv bi t-taʾkīd بالتأكيد 3. for sure bi t-taʾkīd بتأكيد 4. to make sure taʾakkada تأكد

surely ['sho:li] adv min ghayr shakk من غير شك

surface ['sə:fis] n saṭḥ سطح (suṭūḥ سطوح)

surge [sə:j] v indafaʿa اندفع

surgeon ['sə:jən] n jarrāḥ جراح (-ūn)

surgery ['sə:jəri] n 1. jirāḥa جراحة 2. doctor's surgery ʿiyāda عيادة (-āt)

surgical ['sə:jikəl] adj jirāḥa جراحة

surname ['sə:neim] n ism al-ʿāʾila اسم العائلة

surplus ['sə:pləs] n faḍl فضل; fāʾiḍ فائض

surprise [sə'praiz] 1. adj mufājiʾ

2. *n* mufāja'a مفاجأة (-āt) 3. *v* fāja'a فاجأ

surprising [sə'praizing] *adj* mufāji' مفاجئ

surrender [sə'rendə] *v* 1. istaslama استسلم 2. sallama سلم

surround [sə'raund] *v* ḥāṣara حاصر

surroundings [sə'raundingz] *pl* muḥīṭ محيط; bay'a بيئة

survey ['səvei] 1. *n* masḥ مسح 2. *v* masaḥa مسح (a; masḥ مسح)

surveyor [sə'veiə] *n* massāḥ مساح (-ūn)

survival [sə'vaivəl] *n* baqā' بقاء

survive [sə'vaiv] *v* 1. baqiya ḥayyan بقي حياً (a; baqā' بقاء) 2. najā نجا (u; najā' نجاء)

survivor [sə'vaivə] *n* nājin ناج (nājūn ناجون)

susceptible [sə'septəbəl] *adj* qābil li قابل ل

suspect ['sʌspekt] 1. *adj* mashbūh مشبوه 2. *n* mushtabih fīh مشتبه فيه

suspect [sə'spekt] *v* ishtabaha اشتبه

suspend [sə'spend] *v* 1. 'allaqa علق 2. *(ed.)* faṣala mu'aqqatan فصل مؤقتاً (a; faṣl فصل) 3. *(leg.)* arja'a tanfīdh ḥukm أرجأ تنفيذ حكم

suspension [sə'spenshən] *n* 1. ta'līq تعليق 2. *(ed.)* faṣl mu'aqqat فصل مؤقت 3. *(leg.)* irjā' tanfīdh ḥukm إرجاء تنفيذ حكم

suspicion [sə'spishən] *n* shakk شك (shukūk شكوك); shubha شبهة (shubuhāt شبهات); ishtibāh إشتباه; rayb ريب irtiyāb إرتياب

suspicious [sə'spishəs] *adj* 1. mashbūh مشبوه; murīb مريب 2. shākk شاك

sustain [sə'stein] *v* 1. sānada ساند 2. ghadhdhā غذى

swallow ['swoləu] 1. *n* sunūnū سنونو 2. *v* ibtala'a ابتلع

swam [swam] *see* swim

swap [swop] *v* (swapped) bādala بادل; tabādala تبادل

swear [sweə] *v* 1. aqsama أقسم; ḥallafa حلف 2. shatama شتم (i/u; shatm شتم); sabba سب (u; sabb سب)

sweat [swet] 1. *n* 'araq عرق 2. *v* 'ariqa عرق (a; 'araq عرق)

sweater ['swetə] *n* kinza كنزة

Swede [swi:d] *n* suwīdī سويدي (-yūn)

Sweden ['swi:dən] *n* as-suwīd السويد

Swedish ['swi:dish] *adj* suwīdī سويدي

sweep [swi:p] *v* (swept) kanasa كنس (u; kans كنس)

sweet [swi:t] 1. *adj* ḥulw حلو 2. *n* ḥalwayāt حلويات

sweetheart ['swi:tha:t] *n* ḥabīb حبيب (aḥibbā' أحباء; aḥbāb أحباب)

sweetness ['swi:tnis] *n* ḥalāwa حلاوة

sweets [swi:tz] *pl* ḥalwayāt حلويات

swell [swəl] *v* (swelled, swollen/swelled) shamma شم (a/u; shamm شم)

swept [swept] *see* sweep

swift [swift] *adj* sarī' سريع

swim [swim] 1. *n* sibāḥa سباحة 2. *v* (swam, swum) sabaḥa سبح (a; sabḥ سبح); sibāḥa سباحة)

swimmer ['swimə] *n* sābiḥ سابح (-ūn)

swimming pool ['swimingpu:l] *n* ḥammām sibāḥa حمام سباحة

swimsuit ['swimsu:t] *n* māyō مايو

swindle ['swindəl] v iḥtāla احتال;
khadaʿa خدع (a; khadʿ خدع);
ghashsha غش (u; ghashsh غش)

swine [swain] pl khanāzīr خنازير

swing [swing] **1.** n marjūḥa مرجوحة
(marājīḥ مراجيح) **2.** v irtajaḥa ارتجح

Swiss [swis] **1.** adj suwīsrī سويسري
2. n suwīsrī سويسري (-yūn)

switch [swich] **1.** n miftāḥ taḥwīl
مفتاح تحويل **2.** v baddala بدل

switchboard ['swichbo:d] n
lawḥat at-taḥwīl al-hātifī
لوحة التحويل الهاتفي

switch off v aqfala أقفل

switch on v fataḥa فتح (a; fatḥ فتح)

Switzerland ['switsələnd] n
suwīsrā سويسرا

swollen ['swəulən] adj **1.**
mutawarrim متورم **2.** see swell

swoop [swu:p] v inqaḍḍa انقض

sword [so:d] n sayf سيف (suyūf
سيوف)

swum [swʌm] see swim

syllable ['siləbəl] n maqṭaʿ lafẓī
مقطع لفظي (maqāṭiʿ مقاطع)

syllabus ['siləbəs] n manhaj at-
taʿlīm منهج التعليم (manāhij مناهج)

symbol ['simbəl] n ramz رمز (rumūz
رموز)

symmetry ['simətri] n tanāsuq
تناسق

sympathetic [simpə'thetik] adj
mutaʿāṭif متعاطف

sympathize ['simpəthaiz] v taʿāṭafa
تعاطف

sympathy ['simpəthi] n taʿāṭuf
تعاطف

symphony ['simfəni] n simfōnīya
سمفونية

symptom ['simptəm] n ʿaraḍ عرض
(aʿrāḍ أعراض)

synagogue ['sinəgog] n maʿbad
yahūdī معبد يهودي (maʿābid
معابد)

syndicate ['sindikət] n niqāba نقابة
(-āt)

syntax ['sintaks] n bināʾ al-jumla
بناء الجملة

synthesizer ['sinthə'saizə] n
lawḥat mafātīḥ iliktrōnīya
لوحة مفاتيح إلكترونية

synthetic [sin'thetik] adj iṣṭināʿī
إصطناعي

syringe [si'rinj] n miḥqana محقنة
(maḥāqin محاقن)

syrup ['sirəp] n sharāb شراب

system ['sistəm] n niẓām نظام
(anẓima أنظمة)

system software n barnāmij
niẓām at-tashghīl برنامج نظام التشغيل

table 402

T

table ['teibəl] *n* طاولة ṭāwula (-āt); مائدة mā'ida (-āt)

tablet ['tablit] *n* حبة ḥabba (حبّ ḥabb); قرص qurṣ (أقراص aqrāṣ)

tabloid ['tabloːid] *n* جريدة شعبية jarīda shaʿbīya

taboo [tə'buː] *adj/n* محرّم muḥarram (-āt)

tackle ['takəl] **1.** *n* أدوات adawāt **2.** *(spor.)* عرقلة ʿarqala (-āt) **3.** *v* عالج ʿālaja **4.** *(spor.)* عرقل ʿarqala

tact [takt] *n* رقة riqqa; لباقة labāqa

tactful ['taktfəl] *adj* رقيق raqīq; لبق labiq

tactic ['taktik] *n* تكتيك taktīk (-āt)

tactical ['taktikəl] *adj* تكتيكي taktīkī

tadpole ['tadpəul] *n* شرغوف shurghūf

tag [tag] *n* بطاقة biṭāqa (-āt)

tail [teil] *n* ذنب dhanab (أذناب adhnāb); ذيل dhayl (ذيول dhuyūl)

tailor ['teilə] *n* خياط khayyāṭ (-ūn)

take [teik] *v* (**took, taken**) أخذ akhadha (u; أخذ akhdh)

takeaway ['teikəwei] *adj (UK)* (akl) li 'l-akhdh (أكل للأخذ)

take away *v* ذهب ب dhahaba bi

take back *v* استردّ istaradda

take care of *v* اعتنى ب iʿtanā bi

take notice of *v* انتبه ل intabaha li

take off *v* **1.** قلع qalaʿa (a; قلع qalʿ) **2.** أقلع aqlaʿa **3.** نجح najaḥa (a; نجاح najāḥ)

take over ['teikəuvə] *v* استولى على istawlā ʿalā

take-out ['teikəwei] *adj (US)* (akl) li 'l-akhdh (أكل للأخذ)

take out *v* **1.** أخرج akhraja **2.** قتل qatala (قتل qatl)

take place *v* حدث ḥadatha (u; حدوث ḥudūth)

take up *v* **1.** بدأ badaʾa (a; بدء badʾ) **2.** بدأ يهتم ب badaʾa yahtamm bi **3.** استغرق istaghraqa

tale [teil] *n* قصة qiṣṣa (قصص qiṣaṣ)

talent ['talənt] *n* موهبة mawhiba (مواهب mawāhib)

talented ['taləntid] *adj* موهوب mawhūb

talk [toːk] **1.** *n* كلام kalām **2.** حديث ḥadīth **3.** *v* تكلم takallama **4.** محاضرة muḥāḍira **5.** *see* **talks**

talks [toːks] *pl* مباحثات mubāḥathāt

tall [toːl] *adj* طويل ṭawīl

tampon ['tampon] *n* فوطة صحية fūṭa ṣiḥḥīya (فوط fuwaṭ)

tan [tan] **1.** *n* sun tan سفع الشمس safʿ ash-shams **2.** *v* دبغ dabagha (a; دبغ dabgh)

tank [tangk] *n* **1.** خزان khazzān (-āt; خزازين khazāzīn) **2.** *(mil.)* دبابة dabbāba (-āt)

tanker ['tangkə] *n* ناقلة النفط nāqilat an-nafṭ

tap [tap] **1.** *n* حنفية ḥanafiya (-āt) **2.** *v* دق daqqa (u; دق daqq)

tape [teip] **1.** *n* شريط sharīṭ (أشرطة ashriṭa) **2.** *v* سجل sajjala

tape recorder ['teiprikoːdə] *n* مسجّل musajjil (-āt)

target [ta:git] *n* hadaf هدف (ahdāf أهداف)

tart [ta:t] *n* turta ترتة (-āt)

task [ta:sk] *n* mahamma مهمة (mahāmm مهام)

task force *n (mil.)* qūwa khāṣṣa قوة خاصة

taste [teist] 1. *n* dhawq ذوق (adhwāq أذواق) 2. *v* dhāqa ذاق (u; dhawq ذوق)

tasteful ['teistfəl] *adj* rafī‘ adh-dhawq رفيع الذوق

tasteless ['teistlis] *adj* lā ṭa‘m lah لا طعم له

tasty ['teisti] *adj* ladhīdh لذيذ

tattoo [tə'tu:] 1. *n* washm وشم (wishām وشام) 2. *v* washshama وشم

taught [to:t] *see* **teach**

tavern ['tavən] *n* ḥāna حانة (-āt)

tax [taks] 1. *adj* ḍarībī ضريبي 2. *n (pl* **taxes)** ḍarība ضريبة (ḍarā’ib ضرائب) 3. **value added tax (VAT)** ḍarībat al-qīmat al-muḍāfa ضريبة القيمة المضافة 4. **to pay tax** dafa‘a aḍ-ḍarā’ib دفع الضرائب (a) 5. *v* faraḍa aḍ-ḍarība ‘alā فرض الضريبة على (i; farḍ فرض) 6. arhaqa أرهق

tax-free *n* mu‘āfan min aḍ-ḍarā’ib معافىً من الضرائب

taxi ['taksi] *n* tāksī تاكسي; sayārat ujra سيارة أجرة

taxi driver *n* sawwāq tāksī سواق تاكسي (-ūn)

tea [ti:] *n* shāy شاي

teabag ['ti:bag] *n* kīs ash-shay كيس الشاي (akyās أكياس)

teach [ti:ch] *v* (taught) 1. ‘allama علم 2. darrasa درس

teacher ['ti:chə] *n* mudarris مدرس (-ūn); mu‘allim معلم (-ūn)

teaching ['ti:ching] *n* tadrīs تدريس

team [ti:m] *n* farīq فريق

teapot ['ti:pot] *n* ibrīq ash-shāy إبريق الشاي (abārīq أباريق)

tear ['tiə] *n* 1. dam‘a دمعة (dumū‘ دموع) 2. **in tears** bākiyan باكياً

tear [teə] 1. *n* kharq خرق (khurūq خروق) 2. *v* (tore, torn) kharaqa خرق (i/u; kharq خرق) 3. **to tear up** mazzaqa مزق

tear gas ['tiəgas] *n* al-ghāz al-musayyil li ’d-dumū‘ الغاز المسيّل للدموع

tease [ti:z] *v* dā‘aba داعب

teaspoon ['ti:spu:n] *n* mil‘aqat shāy ملعقة شاي

technical ['teknikəl] *adj* tiqnī تقني

technique [tek'ni:k] *n* tiqniya تقنية

technological [teknə'lojikəl] *adj* tiknolozhī تكنولوجي

technology [tek'noləji] *n* at-tiknōlōzhiya التكنولوجية

teenager ['ti:neijə] *n* murāhiq مراهق (-ūn)

teens [ti:nz] *pl* 1. sinn al-murāhaqa سن المراهقة 2. al-murāhiqūn المراهقون

tee-shirt ['ti:shə:t] *n* tī shirt تي شرت (-āt)

teeth [ti:th] *see* **tooth**

telecommunications [telikə-myu:ni'keishənz] *n* al-ittiṣālāt al-hātifīya الإتصالات الهاتفية

telepathic [telə'pathik] *adj* qāri’ ‘uqūl قارئ عقول

telephone ['telifəun] 1. *adj* hātifī هاتفي 2. *n* hātif هاتف (hawātif هواتف

هواتف)‏; tilifōn تلفون (āt-) ‎3. v talfana تلفن

telephone booth n kushk at-tilifōn ‏كشك التلفون‎; sundūq at-tilifōn ‏صندوق التلفون‎

telephone call n mukālama tilifōniya ‏مكالمة تلفونية‎

telescope ['teliskəup] n tiliskūb ‏تلسكوب‎

television [teli'vizhən] n **1.** tilivizyōn تلفزيون (āt-) **2. to watch television** tafarraja ʿalā t-tilivizyōn ‏تفرج على تلفزيون‎

television set n tilivizyōn تلفزيون (āt-)

tell [tel] v (**told**) qaṣṣa قص (u; qaṣṣ ‏قص‎); ḥakā حكى (i; ḥikāya ‏حكاية‎)

temp [temp] see **temporary worker**

temper ['tempə] n **1.** mizāj مزاج **2. bad temper** ghaḍab غضب **3. to lose one's temper** ghaḍiba غضب (a; ghaḍab ‏غضب‎)

temperature ['temprəchə] n **1.** darajat al-ḥarāra درجة الحرارة **2.** see **fever**

temple ['tempəl] n maʿbad معبد (maʿābid ‏معابد‎)

temporary ['temprəri] adj muʾaqqat مؤقت

temporary worker n ʿāmil muʾaqqat عامل مؤقت

tempt [tempt] v aghrā أغرى

temptation [temp'teishən] n ighrāʾ إغراء

ten [ten] n/adj ʿashara عشرة

tend [tend] v **1.** raʿā رعى (a; raʿy ‏رعي‎); riʿāya رعاية; marʿan مرعى (مراعى) **2.** māla ilā مال إلى (i; mayl ‏ميل‎)

tendency ['tendənsi] n mail ميل (muyūl ‏ميول‎)

tender ['tendə] **1.** adj ḥanūn حنون **2.** n (com.) ʿaṭāʾ عطاء **3.** v (com.) qaddama ʿaṭāʾ قدم عطاء

tenderness ['tendənis] n ḥanān حنان

tennis [tenis] n tanis تنس

tense [tens] **1.** adj mutawattir متوتر **2.** n **verb tense** zaman زمن (azmina ‏أزمنة‎)

tension ['tenshən] n tawattur توتر

tent [tent] n khayma خيمة (khiyam ‏خيم‎)

tenth [tenth] adj ʿāshir عاشر

term [təːm] **1.** n mudda مدة (mudad ‏مدد‎) **2.** nihāya نهاية (āt-) **3.** (ed.) faṣl dirāsī فصل دراسي **4. short-term** qaṣīr al-amad قصير الأمد **5. long-term** baʿīd al-amad بعيد الأمد **6.** see **terms**

terminal ['təːminəl] **1.** adj (med.) mumīt مميت **2.** n **airport terminal** bināyat al-musāfirīn بناية المسافرين **3. computer terminal** jihāz kombyūtar جهاز كمبيوتر

terminate ['təːmineit] v anhā أنهى

terminus ['təːminəs] n al-maḥaṭṭat al-akhīra المحطة الأخيرة

terms [təːmz] pl **1.** shurūṭ شروط **2. to be on good terms** kāna ʿalā ʿalāqa hasana كان على علاقة حسنة (**with** maʿa ‏مع‎)

terrace ['terəs] n **terrace of houses** ṣaff min al-manāzil al-muttaṣila صف من المنازل المتصلة

terrible ['terəbəl] adj rahīb رهيب; faẓīʿ فظيع

terrific [tə'rifik] adj hāʾil هائل; rāʾiʿ رائع

terrify ['terifai] v rawwa'a روّع;
arhaba أرهب

territorial [terə'to:riəl] adj iqlīmī
إقليمي

territory ['terətri] n iqlīm إقليم
(aqālīm أقاليم); minṭaqa منطقة
(manāṭiq مناطق)

terror ['terə] n ru'b رعب; irhāb إرهاب

terrorism ['terərizəm] n irhāb إرهاب

terrorist ['terərist] n irhābī إرهابي
(-ūn)

test [test] 1. n ikhtibār إختبار (-āt);
imtiḥān إمتحان (-āt) 2. v ikhtabar
إختبر; imtaḥana إمتحن

testify ['testifai] v shahida شهد (a;
shuhūd شهود) (**against** 'alā على; **on
behalf of** li لـ)

text [tekst] n naṣṣ نص (nuṣūṣ نصوص)

textbook ['tekstbuk] n kitāb
manhajī كتاب منهجي

textile ['tekstail] n nasīj نسيج
(ansija أنسجة)

texture ['tekschə] n nasīj نسيج

than [dhən] conj min من

thank [thangk] v shakara شكر (u;
shukr شكر;shukrān شكران)

thank you! shukran شكراً

thanks [thangks] pl shukran شكراً

thanks to prep bi sabab بسبب

that [dhət; dhat] 1. (pl those) dhāk
ذاك; dhālik ذلك/tilka تلك 2. conj
anna أنّ; alladhī الذي; allatī التي.
3. **so that; in order that** kay كي;
likay لكي

that is (= i.e.) ya'nī يعني

thaw [tho:] 1. n dhawabān ذوبان 2. v
dhāba ذاب (u; dhawb ذوب;
dhawabān ذوبان)

the [dhə; dhi; dhi:] al- الـ

theatre [thiətə] n 1. masraḥ مسرح
(masāriḥ مسارح) 2. **movie theatre**
sīnamā سينما 3. **operating theatre**
ghurfat al-'amaliyāt غرفة العمليات

theft [theft] n sariqa سرقة (-āt)

their [dheə] -hum هم; -hunna هن; -hā
ها

theirs [dheəz] milkuhum ملكهم

them [dhəm; dhem] pronoun -hum
هم; -hunna هن; -hā ها

theme [thi:m] n mawḍū' موضوع
(mawāḍī' مواضيع)

then [dhen] 1. adv thumma ثم;
idhan إذن\إذاك; ānadhāk آنذاك;
ḥīnadhāk حين ذاك 2. **now and then**
aḥyānan أحياناً

theory ['thiəri] n naẓariya نظرية (-āt)

therapist ['therapist] n 1. mu'ālij
معالج (-ūn) 2. ṭabīb nafsānī
طبيب نفساني

therapy ['therapi] n 1. 'ilāj علاج 2.
'ilāj nafsānī علاج نفساني

there [dheə] hunāka هناك

there is/are... hunāka هناك; yūjad
يوجد; thamma ثم; fī في

therefore ['dheəfo:] adv lidhālika
لذلك

thermometer [thə'momitə] n
mīzān al-ḥarāra ميزان الحرارة

these [dhi:z] see this

thesis ['thi:sis] n uṭrūḥa أطروحة (-āt)

they [dhei] pronoun hum هم; hunna
هن; hiya هي

thick [thik] adj 1. kathīf كثيف;
ghalīẓ غليظ 2. aḥmaq أحمق; ghabī
غبي

thief [thi:f] n (pl thieves) liṣṣ لص
(luṣūṣ لصوص)

thigh [thai] *n* fakhdh فخذ (afkhādh أفخاذ)

thin [thin] *adj* 1. raqīq رقيق 2. naḥīl نحيل; naḥīf نحيف

thing [thing] *n* shay' شيء (ashyā' أشياء)

think [thingk] *v* (thought) fakkara فكر (about/of fī في)

third [thə:d] 1. *adj* thālith ثالث 2. *n* thulth ثلث

thirst [thə:st] *n* ʿaṭash عطش

thirsty ['thə:sti] *adj* ʿaṭshān عطشان

thirteen [thə:'ti:n] *n/adj* thalāthata ʿashar ثلاثة عشر

thirteenth [thə:'ti:nth] *adj* thālith ʿashar ثالث عشر

thirtieth ['thə:tiəth] *adj* thalāthūn ثلاثون

thirty ['thə:ti] *n/adj* thalāthūn ثلاثون

this [dhis] (*pl* these) hādha هذا; hādhihi هذه (hā'ulā'i هؤلاء)

thorough ['thʌrə] *adj* shāmil شامل

thoroughly ['thʌrəli] *adv* tamāman تماماً

those [dhəuz] *see* that

though [dhəu] *adv* 1. raghma anna رغم أن 2. as though ka anna كأن

thought [tho:t] *n* 1. fikr فكر (afkār أفكار) 2. *see* think

thoughtful ['tho:tfəl] *adj* raqīq رقيق

thoughtless ['tho:tlis] *adj* ṭā'ish طائش

thousand ['thauzənd] *n/adj* alf ألف (ulūf ألوف; ālāf آلاف)

thousandth ['thauzənth] *adj* alf ألف

thread [thred] *n* khayṭ خيط (khuyūṭ خيوط)

threat [thret] *n* tahdīd تهديد (-āt)

threaten ['thretən] *v* haddada هدد

three [thri:] *n/adj* thalātha ثلاثة

threshold ['threshəuld] *n* ʿataba عتبة (aʿtāb أعتاب); bidāya بداية (-āt)

threw [thru:] *see* throw

thrill [thril] 1. *n* ithāra إثارة 2. *v* athāra أثار

thriller ['thrilə] *n* riwāya muthīra رواية مثيرة

thrive [thraiv] *v* izdahara ازدهر

throat [thrəut] *n* ḥanjara حنجرة (ḥanājir حناجر)

throne [thrəun] *n* ʿarsh عرش (ʿurush عروش); aʿrāsh أعراش

through [thru:] *prep* 1. khilāl خلال; min khilāl من خلال; ʿabra عبر 2. bi بـ; sabab بسبب 3. bi wāsiṭa بواسطة

throughout [thru:'aut] 1. *prep* ṭiwāl طوال 2. *adv* fī kull makān في كل مكان

throw [thrəu] *v* (throw, thrown) 1. ramā رمى (i; ramy رمي) 2. to throw away ramā رمى (i; ramy رمي) 3. to throw out ṭarada طرد (u) 4. to throw up taqayya'a تقيأ

thrust [thrʌst] *v* gharraza غرز

thumb [thʌm] *n* ibhām إبهام (abāhīm أباهيم)

thunder ['thʌndə] *n* raʿd رعد (ruʿūd رعود)

Thursday ['thə:zdei] *n* (yawm) al-khamīs (يوم) الخميس

thus [dhʌs] *adv* hakadha هكذا

tick [tik] 1. *n* qurāda قرادة (qurād قراد) 2. taktaka تكتكة 3. *v* taktaka تكتكة 4. waḍaʿa ishāra وضع إشارة

ticket ['tikit] *n* tadhkara تذكرة (tadhākir تذاكر); biṭāqa بطاقة (-āt)

ticket inspector *n* mufattish at-tadhākir مفتش التذاكر

ticket office *n* maktab at-tadhākir مكتب التذاكر; shubbāk at-tadhākir شباك التذاكر

tickle ['tikəl] *v* daghdagha دغدغ

tidal ['taidəl] *adj* maddī مدي; madd wa jazrī مد وجزري

tide [taid] *n* al-madd wa 'l-jazr المد والجزر

tidy ['taidi] 1. *adj* murattab مرتب 2. *v* rattaba رتب

tie [tai] 1. *n* şila صلة (-āt) 2. rabţat al-ʿunq ربطة العنق (-āt) 3. (spor.) taʿādul تعادل 4. *v* aqada عقد (i; ʿaqd عقد) 5. (spor.) taʿādala تعادل

tier ['tiə] *n* şaff صف (şufūf صفوف)

tight [tait] *adj* mashdūd مشدود; dayyiq ضيق

tighten ['taitən] *v* shadda شد (i; shadd شد)

tights [taits] *pl* shirwāl nisā'ī dayyiq شروال نسائي ضيق

'til [til] *see* until

tile [tail] 1. *n* balāţa بلاطة (balāţ بلاط); 2. *v* ballaţa بلط

till [til] 1. *n* **cash till** şundūq ḥāsib صندوق حاسب 2. *v* haratha حرث (u/i; ḥarth حرث) 3. *see* until

timber ['timbə] *n* khashab خشب

time [taim] 1. *n* waqt وقت; ʿaşr عصر; zaman زمن; zamān زمان 2. **on time** ʿalā 'l-mawʿid على الموعد 3. **at that time** fī dhālik al-waqt في ذلك الوقت 4. **at the same time** fī 'l-waqt nafsuh في الوقت نفسه 5. **from time to time** aḥyānan أحياناً 6. **to waste time** dayyaʿa al-waqt ضيع الوقت 7. **to spend time** qaḍā al-waqt قضى الوقت (i; qaḍā' قضى) 8. *v* waqqata وقت

times [taimz] *prep* fī في

timetable ['taimteibəl] *n* jadwal mawāʿīd جدول مواعيد

timid ['timid] *adj* khajūl خجول

tin [tin] *n* 1. qaşdīr قصدير 2. **tin can** ʿilba علبة (ʿilab علب)

tin-opener ['tinəupnə] *n* fattāḥat ʿilab فتاحة علب

tiny ['taini] *adj* şaghīr jiddan صغير جداً

tip [tip] 1. *n* qimma قمة (qimam قمم); ra's رأس (ru'ūs رؤوس) 2. baqshīsh بقشيش 3. **rubbish tip** mazbala مزبلة (mazābil مزابل) 4. *v* qalaba قلب (i)

tip-off *n* balāgh sirrī بلاغ سري

tire [taiə] *v* 1. taʿiba تعب (a; taʿab تعب) 2. *see* tyre

tired ['taiəd] *adj* taʿbān تعبان

tissue ['tishu:] *n* 1. nasīj نسيج (ansija أنسجة) 2. *see* tissue paper

tissue paper *n* mandīl waraqī منديل ورقي

title ['taitəl] *n* 1. ʿunwān عنوان (ʿanāwīn عناوين) 2. (spor.) buţūla بطولة

to [tə; tu; tu:] *prep* 1. ilā إلى 2. li ل 3. ʿalā على

toad [təud] *n* difdaʿ ضفدع (dafādiʿ ضفادع)

toast [təust] 1. *n* khubz muḥammaş خبز محمص 2. nakhb نخب 3. *v* ḥammaşa حمص 4. shariba nakhbuh شرب نخبه (a; shurb شرب)

tobacco [tə'bakəu] *n* tibgh تبغ (tubūgh تبوغ)

today [tə'dei] *adv* al-yawm اليوم

today's [tə'deiz] *adj* ...al-yawm ...الوم

toe [təu] *n* işbaʿ (al-qadam) أصابع (القدم) (aşābiʿ اصبع (القدم))

together [tə'gedhə] *adv* maᶜan
معاً

toilet ['toilit] *n* mirḥāḍ مرحاض
(marāḥīḍ مراحيض)

toilet paper *n* waraq al-mirḥāḍ
ورق المرحاض

told [təuld] *see* tell

tolerant ['tolərənt] *adj* mutasāmiḥ
متسامح

tolerate ['toləreit] *v* tasāmaḥa
تسامح

toleration [tolə'reishən] *n* tasāmuḥ
تسامح

toll [təul] *n* **1.** highway toll ḍarībat
aṭ-ṭuruq ضريبة الطرق **2.** death toll
ᶜadad al-mawtā عدد الموتى

tomato [tə'ma:təu] *n* (*pl* tomatoes)
ṭumāṭa طماطة (ṭamāṭim طماطم)

tomb [tu:m] *n* qabr قبر (qubūr قبور)

tomorrow [tə'morəu] *adv* **1.**
ghadan غداً **2.** the day after
tomorrow baᶜd ghad بعد غد

ton [tʌn] *n* ṭunn طن (aṭnān أطنان)

tone [təun] *n* nabra نبرة (-āt)

tongue [tʌng] *n* lisān لسان (alsina
ألسنة; alsun ألسن)

tonight [tə'nait] *adv* hādhihi 'l-layla
الليلة; al-layla هذه الليلة

tonne [tʌn] *n* ṭunn mitrī طن متري

too [tu:] *adv* **1.** ayḍan أيضاً **2.**
kadhālik كذلك **3.** akthar mimmā
yanbaghī أكثر مما ينبغي

took [tuk] *see* take

tool [tu:l] *n* adā أداة (adawāt أدوات)

tooth [tu:th] *n* sinn *f* سن (asnān
أسنان)

toothbrush ['tu:thbrʌsh] *n* furshāt
al-asnān فرشاة الأسنان

toothpaste ['tu:thpeist] *n* maᶜjūn
al-asnān معجون الأسنان

top [top] **1.** *adj* aᶜlā أعلى **2.** *n* qimma
قمة (qimam قمم) **3.** on top of fawq
فوق

topic ['topik] *n* mawḍūᶜ موضوع
(mawāḍīᶜ مواضيع)

topical ['topikəl] *adj* jārī جاري

topple ['topəl] *v* qallaba قلب

Torah ['to:rə] *n* at-tawrā التوراة

torch [to:ch] *n* mashᶜal مشعل
(mashāᶜil مشاعل); miṣbāḥ مصباح
(maṣābīḥ مصابيح)

tore; torn [to:; to:n] *see* tear

torment ['to:ment] *n* ᶜadhāb عذاب
(aᶜdhiba أعذبة)

torrent ['torənt] *n* sayl سيل (suyūl
سيول)

torture ['to:chə] **1.** *n* taᶜdhīb تعذيب
2. *v* ᶜadhdhaba عذب

torturer ['to:chərə] *n* muᶜadhdhib
معذب (-ūn)

toss [tos] *v* ramā رمى (i; ramy رمي)

total ['təutəl] **1.** *adj* kull كل; shāmil
شامل **2.** *n* majmūᶜ مجموع **3.** *v* jamaᶜa
جمع (a; jamᶜ جمع)

touch [tʌch] **1.** *n* lamsa لمسة (-āt) **2.**
v lamasa لمس (u,i; lams لمس)

touching ['tʌching] *adj* mu'aththir
مؤثر

tough [tʌf] *adj* **1.** qawī قوي **2.** matīn
متين **3.** ᶜasīr عسير

tour ['tuə; to:] **1.** *n* jawla جولة (-āt) **2.**
v jāla جال (u; jawla جولة)

tour guide *n* murshid siyāḥī
مرشد سياحي (-ūn)

tourism ['tu:rizəm] *n* siyāḥa سياحة

tourist ['tu:rist] *n* sā'iḥ سائح (-ūn;
suwwāḥ سواح)

tourist industry *n* as-siyāḥa
السياحة

tourist season n al-mawsim as-siyāḥī الموسم السياحي

tournament ['to:nəmənt] n mubārāh مباراة (mubārayāt مباريات); musābaqa مسابقة (-āt)

tour operator n sharikat as-siyāḥa شركة السياحة

tow [teu] v jarra جر (u; jarr جر)

toward; towards [tə'wo:d; -z] prep naḥw نحو

towel ['tauəl] n minshafa منشفة (manāshif مناشف)

tower ['tauə] n burj برج (abrāj أبراج; burūj بروج)

town [taun] n balda بلدة (-āt)

town council n baladiya بلدية (-āt)

town hall n dār al-baladiya دار البلدية

toxic ['toksik] adj sāmm سام

toy [toi] n luʿba لعبة (luʿab لعب)

trace [treis] 1. n athar أثر (āthār آثار) 2. v taʿaqqaba تعقب

track [trak] 1. n darb درب (durūb دروب) 2. (spor.) ḥalba حلبة (ḥalabāt حلبات) 3. railtrack khaṭṭ sikkat al-ḥadīd خط سكة الحديد 4. v ʿaqqaba عقب

tractor ['traktə] n jarrāra جرارة (-āt)

trade [treid] 1. n tijāra تجارة 2. ḥirfa حرفة (ḥiraf حرف) 3. v tajara تجر (u; tijāra تجارة) (**in** bi ب) 4. istabdala استبدل

trade fair n maʿraḍ tijārī معرض تجاري (maʿāriḍ معارض)

trader ['treidə] n tājir تاجر

trade union; trades union n niqābat ʿummāl نقابة عمال (-āt)

tradition [trə'dishən] n taqlīd تقليد (taqālīd تقاليد)

traditional [trə'dishənəl] adj taqlīdī تقليدي

traffic ['trafik] 1. n murūr مرور 2. (com.) tahrīb تهريب 3. v (com.) harraba هرب

traffic jam n izdiḥām al-murūr إزدحام المرور

traffic lights pl ishāra ḍaw'īya إشارة ضوئية

tragedy ['tradəji] n ma'sā مأساة (ma'āsin مآس)

tragic ['trajik] adj ma'sawī مأسوي

trail [treil] 1. n āthār آثار 2. darb درب (durūb دروب) 3. v jarjara جرجر

trailer ['treilə] n qāṭira majrūra قاطرة مجرورة

trailer park n mukhayyam al-qāṭirāt مخيم القاطرات

train [trein] 1. n qiṭār قطار (-āt) 2. **by train** bi 'l-qiṭār بالقطار 3. v darraba درب

trainer ['treinə] n mudarrib مدرب (-ūn)

trainers ['treinəz] pl (UK) aḥdhiya riyāḍiya أحذية رياضية

training ['treining] n tadrīb تدريب

traitor ['treitə] n khā'in خائن (khawana خونة)

tram [tram] n trāmwāy تراماوي

tramp [tramp] n mutasharrid متشرد (-ūn)

trance [tra:ns] n ghaybūba غيبوبة

tranquilliser, (US) tranquilizer ['trangkwilaizə] n musakkin مسكن (-āt); muhaddi' مهدئ (-āt)

transfer ['transfə:] 1. n naql نقل 2. v naqala نقل (u; naql نقل; naql نقل)

transform [trans'fo:m] v ḥawwala حول; ghayyara غير

transformation [transfə'meishən] n taḥwīl تحويل; taghyīr تغيير

transformer [trans'fo:mə] *n*
muḥawwil محول

transfusion [trans'fyu:zhən] *n*
blood transfusion naql ad-dam
نقل الدم

transit ['tranzit] *adj/n* tranzīt ترنزيت

transition ['tranzishən] *n* taḥawwul
تحول

transitional [tran'zishənəl] *adj*
intiqālī إنتقالي

translate [tranz'leit] *v* tarjama ترجم
(**from** min من; **into** ilā إلى)

translation [tranz'leishən] *n*
tarjama ترجمة (tarājim تراجم)

translator [tranz'leitə] *n* mutarjim
مترجم (-ūn)

transmission [tranz'mishən] *n*
irsāl إرسال

transmit [tranz'mit] *v* arsala أرسل

transmitter [tranz'mitə] *n* mursila
مرسلة (-āt)

transparency [tranz'parənsi] *n*
shaffāfiya شفافية

transparent [tranz'parənt] *adj*
shaffāf شفاف

transplant [tranz'pla:nt] 1. *n* zarʿ
زرع; zirāʿa زراعة 2. *v* zaraʿa زرع (a;
zarʿ زرع)

transport ['tranzpo:t] *n* naql نقل

transport [tranz'po:t] *v* naqala نقل
(u; naql نقل)

trap [trap] 1. *n* fakh فخ (fikhākh
فخاخ); maṣyada مصيدة (maṣāyid
مصايد) 2. *v* (**trapped**) ʿalaqa علق
(a; ʿalaq علق)

trash [trash] *n* zubāla زبالة; nafāyāt
نفايات

traumatic [tro'matik] *adj*
musabbib aṣ-ṣadma مسبب الصدمة

travel ['travəl] 1. *n* safar سفر (asfār

أسفار) 2. *v* (**travelled**) sāfara سافر

travel agency *n* wikālat as-safar
وكالة السفر

travel industry *n* qiṭāʿ as-siyāḥa
قطاع السياحة

travel insurance *n* taʾmīn siyāḥī
تأمين سياحي

traveller ['travlə] *n* musāfir مسافر
(-ūn)

traveller's cheque *n* ash-shīk as-
siyāḥī الشيك السياحي

travel sickness *n* duwār دوار

tread [tred] *v* (**trod, trodden**) dāsa
داس (u; daws دوس)

treason ['tri:zən] *n* khiyāna خيانة

treasure ['trezhə] *n* kanz كنز (kunūz
كنوز)

treasurer ['trezhərə] *n* amīn aṣ-
ṣundūq أمين الصندوق

treasury ['trezhəri] *n* 1. khizāna
خزانة (khazāʾin خزائن) 2. wizārat al-
māl وزارة المال

treat [tri:t] *v* 1. ʿāmala عامل 2. (*med.*)
ʿālaja عالج

treatment ['tri:tmənt] *n* 1.
muʿāmala معاملة 2. (*med.*) muʿālaja
معالجة

treaty ['tri:ti] *n* 1. muʿāhada معاهدة
2. **peace treaty** muʿāhadat as-
salām معاهدة السلام

treble ['trebəl] *v* zādah thalāthat
aḍʿāf زاده ثلاثة أضعاف (i; ziyāda
زيادة)

tree [tri:] *n* shajara شجرة (āt; shajar
شجر)

tremble ['trembəl] *v* irtajafa ارتجف

tremendous [trimendəs] *adj* hāʾil
هائل

tremor [tremə] *n* rajfa رجفة (-āt);
hazza هزة (-āt)

trend [trend] *n* ittijāh إتجاه

trial ['traiəl] *n* **1.** tajriba تجربة (tajārib تجارب) **2.** (leg.) muḥākama محاكمة (maḥākim محاكم)

triangle ['traianggəl] *n* muthallath مثلث (-āt)

tribe [traib] *n* qabīla قبيلة (qabā'il قبائل)

tribunal [trai'byu:nəl] *n* jalsat istimāʿ جلسة إستماع

tribute ['tribyu:t] *n* **to pay tribute to** madaḥa مدح (a; madḥ مدح)

trick [trik] *n* **1.** ḥīla حيلة (ḥiyal حيل) **2.** khudʿa خدعة (khudaʿ خدع) **3.** *v* khadaʿa خدع (a)

trigger ['trigə] **1.** *n* zinād زناد (aznida أزندة) **2.** *v* bāshara باشر

trim [trim] *v* qaṣṣa قص (u; qaṣṣ قص)

trip [trip] **1.** *n* riḥla رحلة **2.** *v* (tripped) taʿaththara تعثر

tripe [traip] *n* kurūsh كروش (pl of kirsh كرش); amʿā' أمعاء

triple ['tripəl] *v* ḍāʿafa thulāth marrāt ضاعف ثلاث مرات

tripper ['tripə] *n* sā'iḥ سائح (-ūn; suwwāḥ سواح)

triumph ['traiʌmf] **1.** *n* naṣr نصر; intiṣār إنتصار **2.** *v* intaṣara إنتصر

triumphant [trai'ʌmfənt] *n* muntaṣir منتصر

trivial ['triviəl] *adj* tāfih تافه

trod; trodden [trod; 'trodən] *see* **tread**

troop [tru:p] *n* jamāʿa جماعة (-āt)

troops [tru:ps] *pl* jund جند

trophy ['trəufi] *n* (spor.) ka's كأس (ku'ūs كؤوس)

tropical ['tropik] *adj* istiwā'ī إستوائي

tropics ['tropikəl] *pl* al-manāṭiq al-istiwā'iya المناطق الإستوائية

trot [trot] *v* jarā bayn al-mashī wa 'l-ʿadw جرى بين المشي والعدو (i; jary جري)

trouble ['trʌbəl] **1.** *n* mushkila مشكلة (-āt; mashākil مشاكل) **2.** *v* azʿaja أزعج **3.** izʿāj إزعاج

troubled ['trʌbəld] *adj* qaliq قلق

trough [trof] *n* ḥawḍ حوض (aḥwāḍ أحواض)

trousers ['trauzəz] *pl* banṭalūn بنطلون (-āt); sirwāl سروال (sarāwīl سراويل)

truce [tru:s] *n* hudna هدنة (-āt)

truck [trʌk] *n* shāḥina شاحنة (-āt)

true [tru:] *adj* ṣaḥīḥ صحيح

truly ['tru:li] *adv* ḥaqīqatan حقيقة

trumpet ['trʌmpit] *n* būq بوق (āt; abwāq أبواق)

trunk [trʌngk] *n* **1.** jidhʿ جذع (judhūʿ جذوع; ajdhāʿ أجذاع) **2.** badan بدن (abdān أبدان; أبدن abdun) **3.** ṣundūq صندوق (ṣanādīq صناديق) **4.** khurṭūm خرطوم (kharāṭīm خراطيم) **5. car trunk** ṣandūq sayyāra صندوق سيارة

trust [trʌst] **1.** *n* thiqa ثقة **2. on trust** wadīʿatan وديعة **3.** *v* wathiqa وثق (yathiqu يثق; thiqa ثقة)

trustworthy ['trʌstwə:dhi] *adj* mawthūq bih موثوق به

truth [tru:th] *n* ḥaqīqa حقيقة

truthful ['tru:thfəl] *adj* ṣādiq صادق

try [trai] *v* **1.** ḥāwala حاول **2.** jarraba جرب **3.** (leg.) ḥākama حاكم

try on *v* qāsa قاس (i; qiyās قياس)

try out *v* jarraba جرب

T-shirt *n* tī shirt تي شرت

tub [tʌb] *n* **1.** inā' mudawwar إناء مدور (āniya mudawwara آنية مدورة) **2.** *see* **bathtub**

tube [tyu:b] *n* **1.** anbūb أنبوب (anābīb أنابيب) **2. inner tube** iṭār dākhilī إطار داخلي **3.** *(UK)* **the Tube** metro al-anfāq مترو الأنفاق

tuck [tʌk] *v* adkhala أدخل

Tuesday ['tyu:zdei] *n* (yawm) ath-thalāthā' (يوم) الثلاثاء

tug [tʌg] *v* shadda bi qūwa (u; شد بقوة sadd شد)

tune [tyu:n] *n* nagham نغم (anghām أنغام)

tunnel ['tʌnəl] *n* nafaq نفق (anfāq أنفاق)

turbulence ['tə:byuləns] *n* munkhafaḍ jawwī منخفض جوي

turbulent ['tə:byulənt] *adj* ʿāṣif عاصف

turf [tə:f] *n* ʿushb عشب

Turk [tə:k] *n* turkī تركي (atrāk أتراك)

turkey ['tə:ki] *n* (*pl* **turkeys**) dīk rūmī ديك رومي

Turkey *n* turkiya تركية

Turkish ['tə:kish] *adj* turkī تركي

turn [tə:n] **1.** *n* dawr دور (adwār أدوار) **2. in turn** bi 'd-dawr بالدور **3. It's your turn.** dawruk. دورك. **4.** *v* dāra دار (u; dawr دور)

turn against *v* inqalaba ḍidda انقلب ضد

turn back *v* arjaʿa أرجع

turn down *v* rafaḍ رفض (u; rafḍ رفض)

turning ['tə:ning] *n* minʿaṭaf منعطف

turn into *v* ḥawwala ilā حول إلى

turn off *v* aqfala أقفل

turn on *v* **1.** fataḥa فتح (a) **2.** aḍā'a أضاء

turn-out *n* mushāraka مشاركة

turn out *v* **1.** shāraka شارك **2.** ṭalaʿa طلع (a; ṭulūʿ طلوع) **3.** ṭarada طرد (u; ṭard طرد)

turnover ['tə:nəuvə] *n* (*fin.*) qīmat al-mabīʿāt قيمة المبيعات

turn round *see* **turn around**

turn up *v* **1.** ḥaḍara حضر (u; ḥuḍūr حضور) **2.** rafaʿa aṣ-ṣawt رفع الصوت (a; rafʿ رفع)

TV [ti:'vi:] *n* tilivizyōn تلفزيون (-āt)

twelfth [twelfth] *adj* thāni ʿashar ثاني عشر

twelve [twelv] *n/adj* ithnā ʿashar إثنا عشر

twentieth ['twentiəth] *adj* ʿashrūn عشرون

twenty ['twenti] *n/adj* ʿishrūn عشرون

twice [twais] *adv* marratayn مرتين

twinkle ['twingkəl] *v* tala'la'a تلألأ

twins [twinz] *pl* tawā'im توائم (*sing* taw'am توأم; توأم)

twist [twist] *v* **1.** lawā لوى (i; luwīy لوي); jadala جدل (u; jadl جدل) **2.** fattala فتل **3.** *see* **sprain**

two [tu:] *n/adj* ithnān اثنان

two-faced [tu:'feist] *adj* dhū wajhayn ذو وجهين

type [taip] **1.** *n* nawʿ نوع (anwāʿ أنواع) **2.** *v* ṭabaʿa ʿalā 'l-āla al-kātiba طبع على الآلة الكاتبة (a; ṭabʿ طبع)

typewriter ['taipraitə] *n* al-āla al-kātiba الآلة الكاتبة

typical ['tipikəl] *adj* namūdhajī نموذجي

typically ['tipikli] *adv* namūdhajiyan نموذجياً

typist ['taipist] *n* ṭābiʿ ʿalā 'l-āla al-kātiba طابع على الآلة الكاتبة

tyranny ['tirəni] *n* ṭughyān طغيان

tyre [taiə] *n* iṭār إطار (-āt)

U

ugly ['ʌgli] *adj* qabīḥ قبيح

UK [yu:'kei] *see* **United Kingdom**

ulterior [ʌl'tiəriə] *adj* **ulterior motive** dāfiʿ khafī دافع خفي (dawāfiʿ khafiya دوافع خفية)

ultimate [ʌl'timət] *adj* abʿad أبعد; akhīr أخير

ultimately [ʌl'timətli] *adv* akhīran أخيراً; fi 'n-nihāya في النهاية

ultimatum [ʌlti'meitəm] *n* indhār akhīr إنذار أخير

ultra- ['ʌltrə] *adj* **1.** fawq فوق **2.** *(pol.)* mutaṭarrif متطرف

umbrella [ʌm'brelə] *n* shamsiya شمسية (-āt)

umpire ['ʌmpaiə] *n* ḥakam حكم (ḥukkām حكام)

unable [ʌn'eibəl] *adj* ʿājiz عاجز

unacceptable [ʌnə'kseptəbəl] *adj* ghayr maqbūl غير مقبول (**to** li ل)

unaccompanied [ʌnə'kʌmpənid] *adj* ghayr murāfaq غير مرافق; waḥadah وحده

unaccustomed to [ʌnə'kʌstəmd] *adj* ghayr muʿtād ʿalā غير معتاد على

unaffected [ʌnə'fektid] *adj* ghayr muta'aththar غير متأثر

unanimous [yu:'naniməs] *adj* ijmāʿī إجماعي

unarmed [ʌn'a:md] *adj* aʿzal أعزل

unattractive [ʌnə'traktiv] *adj* ghayr jadhdhāb غير جذاب

unavoidable [ʌnə'voidəbəl] *adj* lā mahrab minh لا مهرب منه

unaware [ʌnə'weə] *adj* ghāfil غافل

unbearable [ʌn'beərəbəl] *adj* lā yuṭāq لا يطاق

unbelievable [ʌnbi'li:vəbəl] *adj* lā yuṣaddaq لا يصدق

unbroken [ʌn'brəukən] *adj* **1.** ghayr munqaṭiʿ غير منقطع; mutawāṣil متواصل

uncertain [ʌn'sə:tən] *adj* **1.** mashkūk fīh مشكوك فيه **2.** ḥā'ir حائر

uncle ['ʌngkəl] *n* ʿamm عم; khāl خال

unclear [ʌn'kliə] *adj* **1.** ghayr wāḍiḥ غير واضح; ghāmiḍ غامض

uncomfortable [ʌn'kʌmftəbəl] *adj* **1.** ghayr murīḥ غير مريح **2.** mutaḍāyiq متضايق

uncommon [ʌn'komən] *adj* ghayr ʿādī غير عادي; gharīb غريب

unconcerned [ʌnkən'sə:nd] *adj* muṭma'inn مطمئن; mirtāḥ al-bāl مرتاح البال

unconditional [ʌnkən'dishənəl] *n* min ghayr sharṭ من غير شرط; muṭlaq مطلق

unconscious [ʌn'konshəs] *adj* **1.** mughmā ʿalayh مغمى عليه **2.** ghayr maqṣūd غير مقصود

uncover [ʌn'kʌvə] *v* kashafa كشف (i; kashf كشف)

undecided [ʌndi'saidid] *adj* mutaraddid متردد

undefeated [ʌndi'fi:tid] *adj* lam yuhzam لم يهزم

undeniable [ʌndɪ'naɪəbəl] *adj* lā
yumkin inkāruh لا يمكن إنكاره

under ['ʌndə] *prep* **1.** taḥt تحت
2. under fire taḥt al-qadhf
تحت القذف

undercover [ʌndə'kʌvə] *adj* sirrī
سري

underdeveloped [ʌndə'diveləpt]
n ghayr mutaṭawwir غير متطور

underestimate [ʌndə'restimeit] *v*
istakhaffa استخف; qallala min
ahammīyat... قلل من أهمية...

undergo [ʌndə'gəu] *v* khaḍaʿa li لـ
خضع (a)

undergraduate [ʌndə'grajuət]
n ṭālib ghayr mutakharrij
طالب غير متخرج

underground ['ʌndəgraund] *adj/adv*
1. taḥt al-arḍ تحت الأرض **2.** sirrī
سري **3.** *(UK)* **the Underground**
metrō al-anfāq مترو الأنفاق

underline [ʌndə'lain] *v* **1.** rasima
khaṭṭan taḥta رسم خطاً تحت (a) **2.**
akkada أكد

undermine [ʌndə'main] *v* aḍʿafa
(al-makāna) أضعف (المكانة)

underneath [ʌndə'ni:th] **1.** *prep*
taḥta تحت **2.** *adv* asfal أسفل

underpants, *(US)* **undershorts**
['ʌndəpants; 'ʌndəshoːts] *pl* sirwāl
dākhilī سروال داخلي

underside ['ʌndəsaid] *n* al-jānib al-
asfal الجانب الأسفل

understand [ʌndə'stand] *v* fahima
فهم (a; fahm فهم)

understandable [ʌndə'standəbəl]
adj mafhūm مفهوم

understanding [ʌndə'standing]
adj **1.** mutaʿāṭif متعاطف;
mutafahhim متفهم **2.** *n* fahm فهم

3. to come to an understanding
ittafaqa اتفق

undertake [ʌndə'teik] *v* qāma bi
قام بـ; taʿahhada bi تعهد بـ

underwater [ʌndə'woːtə] *adj* taḥt
saṭḥ al-māʾ تحت سطح الماء

underway [ʌndə'wei] *adv* jārī جاري

underwear ['ʌndəweə] *n* malābis
dākhilīya ملابس داخلية

undid [ʌn'did] *see* undo

undo [ʌn'duː] *v* (undid, undone)
ḥalla حل (u; ḥall حل)

undoubtedly [ʌn'dautidli] *adv* lā
shakk لا شك

undress [ʌn'dres] *v* qalaʿa قلع (a;
qalʿ قلع)

uneducated [ʌn'edyukeitid] *adj*
ghayr mutaʿallim غير متعلم

unemployed [ʌnim'ploid] *adj* **1.**
ʿāṭil (ʿan al-ʿamal) عاطل (عن العمل)
2. the unemployed al-baṭṭālūn
البطالون

unemployment [ʌnim'ploimənt] *n*
biṭāla بطالة

unequal [ʌn'iːkwəl] *adj* ghayr
mutasāwin غير متساوٍ; mutafāwit
متفاوت

uneven [ʌn'iːvən] *adj* ghayr
mutasāwin غير متساوٍ

unexpected [ʌniks'pektid] *adj*
mufāji' مفاجئ; ghayr
mutawwaqqaʿ غير متوقع

unexpectedly [ʌnik'spektili] *adv*
faj'atan فجأةً

unfair [ʌn'feə] *adj* ẓālim ظالم; ghayr
munṣif غير منصف

unfasten [ʌn'faːsən] *v* fakka فك (u;
fakk فك)

unfinished [ʌn'finisht] *adj* lam
yatimm لم يتم; nāqiṣ ناقص

unfit [ʌn'fit] *adj* ghayr munāsib غير مناسب; ghayr mu'ahhal مؤهل

unfold [ʌn'fəuld] *v* fakka فك (u; fakk فك)

unfortunate [ʌn'fo:chənət] *adj* manḥūs منحوس

unfortunately [ʌn'fo:chənətli] *adv* li 'l-asaf للأسف

unfriendly [ʌn'frendli] *adj* ʿudwānī عدواني

ungrateful [ʌn'greitfəl] *adj* jāḥid جاحد

unhappiness [ʌn'hapinis] *n* ḥuzn حزن

unhappy [ʌn'hapi] *adj* ḥazīn حزين; matʿūs متعوس

unhealthy [ʌn'helthi] *adj* 1. ghayr ṣiḥḥī غير صحي 2. ḍārr bi 'ṣ-ṣiḥḥa ضار بالصحة

unhurt [ʌn'hə:t] *adj* ghayr majrūḥ غير مجروح

unidentified [ʌnai'dentifaid] *adj* majhūl مجهول

unidentified flying object (UFO) *n* al-ajsām al-faḍā'iya al-majhūla الأجسام الفضائية المجهولة; al-aṭbāq aṭ-ṭā'ira الأطباق الطائرة

uniform ['yu:nifo:m] 1. *adj* muntaẓim منتظم 2. *n* ziyy rasmī زي رسمي 3. **school uniform** ziyy al-madāris زي المدارس

unify ['yu:nifai] *v* waḥḥada وحد

unimportant [ʌnim'po:tənt] *adj* ghayr muhimm غير مهم; tāfih تافه

uninhabited [ʌni'nhabitid] *adj* mahjūr مهجور

uninjured [ʌni'njəd] *adj* ghayr majrūḥ غير مجروح; salīm سليم

unintentional [ʌnin'tenshənəl] *adj* ghayr maqṣūd غير مقصود; ghayr mutaʿammid غير متعمد

uninteresting [ʌn'intəresting] *adj* mumill ممل

uninterrupted [ʌnintə'rʌptid] *adj* ghayr munqaṭiʿ غير منقطع; mutawāṣil متواصل

union ['yu:nyən] 1. *adj* niqābī نقابي 2. *n* tawḥīd توحيد; ittiḥād إتحاد. 3. **trade union** niqābat ʿummāl عمال نقابة

unionist ['yuniyənist] *adj/n* ittiḥādī إتحادي

Union Jack *n* al-ʿalam al-brīṭānī العلم البريطاني

unique [yu:ni:k] *adj* farīd فريد; mumayyaz مميز

unison ['yu:nisən] *v* insijām إنسجام

unit ['yu:nit] *n* 1. waḥda وحدة (-āt) 2. **military unit** waḥda ʿaskariya وحدة عسكرية

unite [yu:'nait] *v* waḥḥada وحد

united [yu:'naitid] *adj* muttaḥid متحد

United Kingdom [yu:'naitid 'kingdəm] *n* al-mamlaka al-muttaḥida المملكة المتحدة

United Nations (UN) *n* al-umam al-muttaḥida الأمم المتحدة

United States of America *n* al-wilāyāt al-amrīkīya al-muttaḥida الولايات الأمريكية المتحدة

unity ['yu:nəti] *n* waḥda وحدة

universal [yu:ni'və:səl] *adj* 1. kawnī كوني 2. jāmiʿ جامع

universe ['yu:nivə:s] *n* al-kawn الكون

university [yu:ni'və:səti] *n* jāmiʿa جامعة (-āt)

unjust [ʌn'jʌst] *adj* ẓālim ظالم

unkind [ʌn'kaind] *adj* qāsin قاس

unknown [ʌn'nəun] *adj/n* majhūl مجهول

unlawful [ʌn'loːfəl] *adj* ghayr qānūnī غير قانوني

unleash [ən'liːsh] *v* ḥarrara حرر

unless [ən'les] *conj* mā lam ما لم; illā إلا wa الا و

unlike [ʌn'laik] 1. *adj* mukhtalif مختلف. 2. *adv* ʿalā khilāf على خلاف

unlikely [ʌn'laikli] *adj* ghayr muḥtamal غير محتمل

unlimited [ʌn'limitid] *adj* ghayr maḥdūd غير محدود

unload [ʌn'ləud] *v* afragha أفرغ; farragha فرغ

unlock [ʌn'lok] *v* fataḥa 'l-qufl فتح القفل (a; fatḥ)

unlucky [ʌn'lʌki] *adj* mashʾūm مشؤوم; manḥūs منحوس

unmarried [ʌn'marid] *adj* ghayr mutazawwij غير متزوج; ʿāzib عازب

unmistakable [ʌnmis'teikəbəl] *adj* mubīn مبين; wāḍiḥ واضح

unnatural [ʌn'nachrəl] *adj* 1. ghayr ṭabīʿī غير طبيعي. 2. iṣṭināʿī إصطناعي

unnecessary [ʌn'nesəsri] *adj* ghayr ḍurūrī غير ضروري

unofficial [ʌnə'fishəl] *adj* ghayr rasmī غير رسمي

unpack [ʌn'pak] *v* farragha al-ḥaqība فرغ الحقيبة

unpaid [ʌn'peid] *adj* ghayr musaddad غير مسدد

unplanned [ʌn'pland] *adj* ghayr mukhaṭṭaṭ غير مخطط

unpleasant [ʌn'plezənt] *adj* karīh كريه

unplug [ʌn'plʌg] *v* akhraja 'l-qābis min al-maʾkhadh أخرج القابس من المأخذ

unpopular [ʌn'popyulə] *adj* ghayr maḥbūb غير محبوب

unpopularity [ʌnpopyu'larəti] *n* lā shaʿbīya لا شعبية

unpredictable [ʌnpri'diktəbəl] *adj* lā yumkin at-tanabbuʾ bih لا يمكن التنبؤ به

unprofitable [ʌn'profitəbəl] *adj* ghayr murbiḥ غير مربح

unprotected [ʌnprə'tektid] *adj* ghayr maḥmī غير محمي; aʿzal أعزل

unreal [ʌn'riːyəl] *adj* wahmī وهمي

unrealistic [ʌnri:yə'listik] *adj* ghayr wāqiʿī غير واقعي

unreasonable [ʌn'ri:znəbəl] *adj* ghayr maʿqūl غير معقول

unrelated [ʌnri'leitid] *adj* ghayr mutaʿalliq غير متعلق

unreliable [ʌnri'laiəbəl] *adj* lā yuʿtamad ʿalayh لا يعتمد عليه; ghayr jadīr bi 'th-thiqa غير جدير بالثقة

unrest [ʌn'rest] *n* shaghab شغب

unripe [ʌn'raip] *adj* ghayr nāḍij غير ناضج

unroll [ʌn'rol] *v* basaṭa بسط (u; basṭ بسط)

unruly [ʌn'ru:li] *adj* mutamarrid متمرد

unsafe [ʌn'seif] *adj* khaṭīr خطير; ghayr maʾmūn غير مأمون; ghayr salīm غير سليم

unsaid [ʌn'sed] *adj* ghayr muʿlin غير معلن

unsatisfactory [ʌnsatis'faktri] *adj* dūn al-mustawā دون المستوى

unsatisfied [ʌn'satisfaid] *adj* ghayr rāḍin غير راض; ghayr muqtanaʿ غير مقتنع

unscathed [ʌn'skeidhd] *adj* salīm سليم

unscrew [ʌn'skru:] *v* fakka فك (u; fakk فك)

unseen [ʌn'si:n] *adj* ghayr mar'ī
غير مرئي

unselfish [ʌn'selfish] *adj* ghayr
anānī غير أناني

unskilled [ʌn'skild] *adj* **1.** ghayr
bāri' غير بارئ **2.** ghayr muhtarif
غير محترف

unstable [ʌn'steibəl] *adj* ghayr
thābit غير ثابت; ghayr muwaṭṭad
غير موطد

unsteady [ʌn'stedi] *adj* mutazaʿzaʿ
متزعزع; ghayr mustaqirr غير مستقر

unsuccessful [ʌnsʌk'sesfəl] *adj*
fāshil فاشل; mukhfaq مخفق

unsuitable [ʌn'su:təbəl] *adj* ghayr
munāsib غير مناسب

untidy [ʌn'taidi] *adj* ghayr murattab
غير مرتب

untie [ʌn'tai] *v* halla (حل (u; hall حل

until [ən'til] **1.** *prep* hattā حتى **2.** *conj*
ilā anna إلى أن

untrue [ʌn'tru:] *adj* kādhib كاذب;
ghayr sahīh غير صحيح

unusual [ʌn'yu:zhəl] *adj* ghayr ʿādī
غير عادي; nādir نادر

unwelcome [ʌn'welkəm] *adj* ghayr
murahhab bih غير مرحب به

unwell [ʌn'wel] *adj* marīḍ مريض

unwilling [ʌn'wiling] *adj* ghayr
mustaʿidd غير مستعد

unwind [ʌn'waind] *v* istarkhā استرخى

unwise [ʌn'waiz] *adj* mutahawwir
متهور; ghayr ʿāqil غير عاقل

unwrap [ʌn'rap] *v* fakka al-ghiṭā'
(فك الغطاء (u; fakk فك

up [ʌp] *prep/adv* **1.** fawq فوق; aʿlā
أعلى **2. up to** hattā حتى **3.** ilā إلى

upbringing ['ʌpbringing] *n* tarbiya
تربية

update ['ʌpdeit] *n* bayān ākhir at-

taṭawwurāt بيان آخر التطورات

update [ʌp'deit] *v* jaddada جدد;
jaddada al-maʿlūmāt جدد المعلومات

uphill [ʌphil] *adj* **1.** ṣāʿid صاعد **2.**
ṣaʿb صعب

uphold [ʌp'həuld] *v* sānada ساند;
ayyada أيد

upon [ə'pon] *prep* ʿalā على; fawqa
فوق

upper ['ʌpə] *adj* aʿlā أعلى

upright ['ʌprait] *adj/adv* wāqif واقف;
mustaqīm مستقيم

uprising ['ʌpreizing] *n* tamarrud
تمرد

uproar [ʌp'ro:] *n* ḍajīj ضجيج

uproot [ʌp'ru:t] *v* jaththa جث (u;
jathth جث); ijtaththa اجتث

upset [ʌp'set] **1.** *adj* zaʿlān زعلان
(**about** min من) **2.** *v* (upset) zaʿʿala
زعل **3. to be upset** zaʿila زعل (a;
zaʿal زعل) **4.** qallaba قلب

upside-down [ʌpsaid'daun] *adv*
maqlūb مقلوب

upstairs [ʌp'steəz] *adv* fawq فوق

up-to-date [ʌptu'deit] *adj* hadīth
حديث

upward; upwards ['ʌpwəd; -z]
adv ṣāʿidan صاعداً; bi ittijāh al-aʿlā
باتجاه الأعلى

uranium [yu'reiniyəm] *n* yūrāniyūm
يورانيوم

urban ['ə:bən] *adj* madanī مدني

urbanisation [ə:bənai'zeishən] *n*
tamdīn تمدين

urge [ə:j] **1.** *n* dāfiʿ دافع (dawāfiʿ
دوافع) **2.** raghba رغبة **3.** *v* alahha
ألح; haththa حث (u; hathth حث)

urgency ['ə:jənsi] *n* ilhāh إلحاح

urgent ['ə:jənt] *adj* mulihh ملح

urgently ['ə:jəntli] *adv* ʿājilan عاجلاً

urine ['yuərin] *n* bawl بول

us [əs; ʌs] -nā نا

US; USA *see* United States (of America)

use [yu:s] *n* 1. nafʿ نفع 2. fā'ida فائدة (-āt) 3. What's the use of...? mā fā'idat...? ما فائدة ... ؟

use [yu:z] *v* 1. istaʿmala استعمل; istakhdama استخدم

used [yu:zd] *adj* mustaʿmal مستعمل; mustakhdam مستخدم

used to ['yu:s tu] 1. to get used to taʿawwada ʿalā تعود على 2. We used to live in London. kunnā naskun fī lundun كنا نسكن في لندن

useful ['yu:sfəl] *adj* nāfiʿ نافع; mufīd مفيد

usefulness ['yu:sfəlnis] *n* nafʿa نفعة

useless ['yu:slis] *adj* ghayr nāfiʿ عقيم ʿaqīm; ghayr nāfiʿ غير نافع

user ['yu:zə] *n* mustaʿmil مستعمل (-ūn)

usual ['yu:zhəl] *adj* muʿtād معتاد

usually ['yu:zhəli] *adv* ʿādatan عادةً

use up *v* istahlaka استهلك

utility [yu:'tiliti] *n* public utility mirfaq ʿāmm مرفق عام (marāfiq ʿāmma مرافق عامة)

utilize ['yu:tilaiz] *v* istakhdama استخدم; istaʿmala استعمل

utmost ['ʌtməust] *adj* abʿad أبعد; aqṣā أقصى

utter ['ʌtə] 1. *adj* tāmm تام; muṭlaq مطلق 2. *v* qāla قال (u; qawl قول); naṭaqa نطق (u; nuṭq نطق)

utterance ['ʌtərəns] *n* qawl قول (aqwāl أقوال)

V

v.; vs. *see* versus

vacancy ['veikənsi] *n* 1. khalā' خلاء 2. shughūr شغور

vacant ['veikənt] *adj* 1. khālin خال 2. shāghir شاغر

vacation [vei'keishən] *n* ʿutla عطلة (āt; ʿuṭal عطل); ijāza إجازة (-āt)

vaccinate ['vaksineit] *v* laqqaḥa لقح (against ḍidda ضد); ṭaʿʿama طعم

vaccination [vaksi'neishən] *n* talqīḥ تلقيح; taṭʿīm تطعيم

vaccine ['vaksi:n] *n* laqāḥ لقاح

vacuum ['vakyuəm] 1. *n* farāgh فراغ 2. *v* naẓẓafa bi miknasa kahrabā'iya نظف بمكنسة كهربائية

vacuum cleaner *n* miknasa kahrabā'iya مكنسة كهربائية (makānis مكانس)

vagina [və'jainə] *n* mahbal مهبل (mahābil مهابل)

vagrant ['veigrənt] *n* mutasharrad متشرد (-ūn)

vague [veig] *adj* ghayr wāḍiḥ غير واضح; ghāmiḍ غامض

vain [vein] *adj* **1.** narjisī نرجسي **2.** maghrūr مغرور **3. in vain** ʿabathan عبثاً

valiant ['valiənt] *adj* shujāʿ شجاع

valid ['valid] *adj* sārī al-mafʿūl ساري المفعول

valley ['vali] *n* wādin وادٍ (awdiya أودية)

valour, (US) valor ['valə] *n* shajāʿa شجاعة

valuable ['valyuəbəl] *adj* thamin ثمن; qayyim قيم

valuables ['valyuəbəlz] *pl* ashyāʾ qayyima أشياء قيمة

value ['valyu] **1.** *n* qīma قيمة (qiyam قيم) **2.** *v* qaddara قدر

valve [valv] *n* ṣimām صمام (-āt)

vampire ['vampayə] *n* maṣṣāṣ ad-dimāʾ مصاص الدماء

vampire slayer *n* qātil maṣṣāṣ ad-dimāʾ قاتل مصاص الدماء

van [van] *n* shāḥina ṣaghīra شاحنة صغيرة

vandal ['vandəl] *n* mukharrib مخرب (-ūn)

vanilla [vəˈnilə] *n* vanīllā فانيلا

vanish ['vanish] *v* ikhtafā اختفى

vanity ['vaniti] *n* **1.** narjasa نرجسة **2.** ghurūr غرور

vapour, (US) vapor ['veipə] *n* bukhār بخار

variant ['veəriənt] *n* mukhtalif مختلف

variation [veəriˈeishən] *n* taghayyur تغير

variety [vəˈraiəti] *n* **1.** nawʿ نوع (anwāʿ أنواع) **2.** tanawwuʿ تنوع

various ['veəriəs] *adj* mutanawwiʿ متنوع

varnish ['vaːnish] *n* dihān aṭ-ṭilāʾ دهان الطلاء (adhina أدهنة)

vary ['veəri] *v* **1.** nawwaʿa نوع **2.** ikhtalafa اختلف

vase [vaːz] *n* zuhriya زهرية (-āt); mazharīya مزهرية (-āt)

vaseline ['vazəliːn] *n* al-vāzalīn الفازلين

vast [vaːst] *adj* wāsiʿ واسع

vastly ['vaːstli] *adv* bi kathīr بكثير

V.A.T. *see* value-added tax

vault [voːlt] *n* **1.** qanṭara قنطرة (qanāṭir قناطر) **2.** sirdāb سرداب (saradīb سرديب)

veal [viːl] *n* laḥm al-ʿijl لحم العجل

vegetables ['vejtəbəlz] *pl* khuḍar خضر

vegetarian [vejiˈteəriən] **1.** *adj* nabātī نباتي **2.** *n* nabātī نباتي (nabātiyūn نباتيون)

vegetation [vejiˈteishən] *n* khuḍra خضرة

vehicle ['viəkəl] *n* sayyāra سيارة (-āt); markaba مركبة (-āt)

veil [veil] *n* ḥijāb حجاب (aḥjiba أحجبة); ḥujub حجب

vein [vein] *n* ʿirq عرق (ʿurūq عروق)

velocity [viˈlosəti] *n* surʿa سرعة

vender; vendor ['vendə] *n* bāʾiʿ بائع (bāʿa باعة)

venereal disease [vəˈniəriəl] *n* maraḍ tanāsulī مرض تناسلي

vengeance ['venjəns] *n* intiqām إنتقام; thaʾr ثأر

venom ['venəm] *n* **1.** samm سم (sumūm سموم) **2.** ḥiqd حقد (aḥqād أحقاد)

venomous ['venəməs] *adj* **1.** sāmm سام **2.** ḥāqid حاقد; ḥaqūd حقود

ventilation [venti'leishən] *n* tahwiya تهوية

ventilator ['ventileitə] *n* mihwāh مهواة; mukayyif hawā' مكيف هواء

venture ['venchə] **1.** *n* mukhāṭira مخاطرة (-āt) **2.** *(com.)* mashrū' مشروع (mashārī' مشاريع) **3.** *v* ghāmara غامر

venue ['venyu] *n* makān مكان (amākin أماكن)

veranda [və'randə] *n* shurfa شرفة (shurafāt شرفات; shuruf شرف)

verb [və:b] *n* fi'l فعل (af'āl أفعال)

verbal ['və:bəl] *adj* **1.** shafahī شفهي **2.** fi'lī فعلي

verdict ['və:dikt] *n* ḥukm حكم (aḥkām أحكام)

verge [və:j] *n* **1. road verge** ḥāfat aṭ-ṭarīq حافة الطريق **2. on the verge of** 'alā washk an على وشك أن

verify ['verifai] *v* akkada أكد; athbata أثبت

vermin ['və:min] *n* hawāmm هوام

verse [və:s] *n* **1.** naẓm نظم **2.** bayt بيت (abyāt أبيات) **3.** *(rel.)* **verse of the Qur'an** āya آية (-āt)

version ['və:shən] *n* **1.** riwāya رواية (-āt) **2.** tarjama ترجمة (tarājim تراجم)

versus ['və:səs] ḍidd ضد

vertebrate ['və:təbreit] *n* ḥayawān faqrī حيوان فقري

vertical ['vertikəl] **1.** *adj* 'amūdī عمودي **2.** *n* khaṭṭ 'amūdī خط عمودي

very ['veri] **1.** *adj* 'ayn عين; nafs نفس **2.** *adv* jiddan جداً

vessel ['vesəl] *n* **1.** wi'ā' وعاء

(aw'iya أوعية; awā'in أواعٍ) **2.** *(mar.)* safina سفينة (sufun سفن) **3. blood vessel** wi'ā' damawī وعاء دموي

vest [vest] *n* **1.** ṣudra صدرة **2.** *(US)* sutra سترة (sutar ستر)

vet [vet] *n* ṭabīb bayṭarī طبيب بيطري (aṭibbā' أطباء)

veteran ['vetərən] *adj/n* maris مرس (amrās أمراس)

veterinary ['vetineri] *adj* bayṭarī بيطري

veterinary medicine *n* aṭ-ṭibb al-bayṭarī الطب البيطري

veterinary surgeon *n* jarrāḥ bayṭarī جراح بيطري

veto ['vi:təu] **1.** *n (pl vetoes)* naqḍ نقض **2.** *v* ista'mala ḥaqq an-naqḍ استعمل حق النقض

vex [veks] *v* aghāẓa أغاظ

vexed [vekst] *adj* munza'ij منزعج

via ['vaiə] *prep* 'an ṭarīq عن طريق

vibrant ['vaibrənt] *adj* ḥayawī حيوي

vibrate [vai'breit] *v* tadhabdhaba تذبذب

vibration [vai'breishən] *n* dhabdhaba ذبذبة (-āt)

vibrator [vai'breitə] *n* jihāz mutadhabdhib جهاز متذبذب (ajhiza أجهزة)

vice [vais] *n* radhīla رذيلة (radhā'il رذائل)

vice president *n* nā'ib ar-ra'īs نائب الرئيس

vice versa [vaisi'və:sə] wa 'l-'aks والعكس

vicinity [vi'sinəti] *n* **1.** qurb قرب **2. in the vicinity of** bi jiwār بجوار

vicious ['vishəs] *adj* **1.** sharis شرس **2.** sharīr شرير **3.** 'udwānī عدواني

victim ['viktim] *n* ḍaḥīya ضحية
(ḍaḥāyā ضحايا)

victor ['viktə] *n* muntaṣir منتصر

victorious [vik'tо:riəs] *adj*
muntaṣir منتصر

victory ['viktəri] *n* naṣr نصر; intiṣār
إنتصار

video ['vidiəu] **1.** *n* vīdiyō فيديو
2. *v* ṣawwara ʿalā 'l-vīdiyo
صور على الفيديو

video game *n* laʿb al-vīdiyo
(alʿāb ألعاب الفيديو) لعب الفيديو

video recorder *n* jihāz al-vīdiyo
(ajhiza جهاز الفيديو) أجهزة

video tape *n* sharīṭ al-vīdiyo
(ashriṭa أشرطة) شريط الفيديو

video-tape *v* ṣawwara/sajjala ʿalā
al-vīdiyo صور\سجل على الفيديو

vie [vai] *v* nāfasa نافس (**for** ʿalā على)

view [vyu:] **1.** *n* manẓar منظر
(manāẓir مناظر) **2. point of view**
ra'y رأي (ārā' آراء); wijhat naẓar
وجهة نظر **3.** *v* naẓara نظر (u; naẓar
نظر)

viewer ['vyu:ə] *n* mushāhid مشاهد
(-ūn)

vigilant ['vijilənt] *adj* ḥadhir حذر;
muḥtaris محترس; muntabih منتبه

vigorous ['vigərəs] *adj* nashīṭ نشيط

vigour, *(US)* **vigor** ['vigə] *n* nashāṭ
نشاط

villa ['vilə] *n* villā فيلا (villāt فيلات)

village ['vilij] *n* qarya قرية (quran
قرى)

villager ['vilijə] *n* qarawī قروي
(-yūn)

villain ['vilən] *n* **1.** mujrim مجرم
(-ūn) **2.** waghd وغد (awghād أوغاد)

vindicate ['vindikeit] *v* barrara برر

vinegar ['vinigə] *n* khall خل

vineyard ['vinya:d] *n* karm كرم
(kurūm كروم)

vintage ['vintij] *adj* ʿatīq عتيق

violate ['vaiəleit] *v* **1.** intahaka انتهك
2. iʿtadā ʿalā اعتدى على

violation [vaiə'leishən] *n* **1.** intihāk
إنتهاك **2.** iʿtidāʾ إعتداء

violence ['vaiələns] *n* ʿunf عنف

violent ['vaiələnt] *adj* ʿanīf عنيف

violin [vaiə'lin] *n* kamān كمان

VIP [vi:ai'pi:] *n* shakhṣ muhimm
jiddan شخص مهم جداً

virgin ['və:jin] *n* ʿadhrāʾ عذراء
(ʿadhārā عذارى)

virility [vi'riləti] *n* rujūla رجولة

virtual ['və:chuəl] *adj* shābih al-
wāqiʿ شابه الواقع

virtually ['və:chuəli] *adv* taqrīban
تقريباً

virtue ['və:chu:] *n* faḍīla فضيلة
(faḍāʾil فضائل)

virus ['vairəs] *n* vayrūs فيروس
(-āt)

visa ['vi:zə] *n* taʾshīra تأشيرة (-āt)

visibility [vizə'biləti] *n* marʾīya
مرئية

visible ['vizəbəl] *adj* marʾī مرئي

vision ['vizhən] *n* **1.** ruʾya رؤية **2.**
(rel.) ruʾyā رؤيا (ruʾan رؤن)

visit ['vizit] **1.** *n* ziyāra زيارة (-āt) **2.** *v*
zāra زار (u; ziyāra زيارة)

visitor ['vizitə] *n* zāʾir زائر (ūn;
zuwwār زوار)

visual ['vizhuəl] *adj* baṣarī بصري

vital ['vaitəl] *adj* ḥayawī حيوي

vitality [vai'taləti] *n* ḥayawīya حيوية

vitamin ['vitəmin] *n* vītāmīn فيتامين
(-āt)

vivid ['vivid] *adj* mushriq مشرق

vocabulary [vəˈkabyuləri] *n*
مفردات mufradāt

vocal [ˈvəukəl] *adj* 1. şawtī صوتي 2.
şarīḥ صريح

vocalist [ˈvəukəlist] *n* mughannin
مغن (mughannīyūn مغنيون)

vocation [vəuˈkeishən] *n* mihna
مهنة (mihan مهن)

vogue [vəug] *n* in vogue dārij دارج

voice [vois] *n* şawt صوت (aşwāt
أصوات)

volatile [ˈvolətail] *adj* mutaqallib
متقلب

volcano [vɒlˈkeinəu] *n* (pl
volcanoes) burkān بركان (barākīn
براكين)

volt [vəult] *n* walṭ ولط

voltage [ˈvəultij] *n* walṭīya ولطية

volume [ˈvolyu:m] *n* 1. ḥajm حجم 2.
mujallad مجلد (-āt) 3. jahārat aş-
şawt جهارة الصوت

voluntary [ˈvoləntri] *adj* ikhtiyārī
إختياري; taṭawwaʿī تطوعي

volunteer [volənˈtiə] 1. *n*

mutaṭawwiʿ متطوع 2. *v* taṭawwaʿa
تطوع

vomit [ˈvomit] 1. *n* qayʾ قيء 2. *v*
taqayyaʾa تقيأ

vote [vəut] 1. *n* şawt صوت (aşwāt
أصوات) 2. **to take a vote on**
iqtaraʿa ʿalā اقترع على 3. *v* şawwata
صوت (**for** li لـ)

voter [ˈvəutə] *n* nākhib ناخب (-ūn);
muntakhib منتخب (-ūn)

voucher [ˈvauchə] *n* īşāl إيصال (-āt);
biṭāqa maʿawna بطاقة معونة (-āt)

vow [vau] 1. *n* qasam قسم (aqsām
أقسام) 2. *v* aqsama أقسم

vowel [ˈvauəl] *n* ḥaraka حركة (-āt);
şawt layyin صوت لين

voyage [ˈvoyij] *n* riḥla رحلة (-āt)

vs. *see* **versus**

vulgar [ˈvʌlgər] *adj* sūqī سوقي

vulnerability [vʌlnrəˈbiliti] *n*
qābiliya li ʾl-injirāḥ قابلية للإنجراح

vulnerable [ˈvʌlnrəbəl] *adj* qābil li
ʾl-injirāḥ قابل للإنجراح

vulture [ˈvʌlchə] *n* nasr نسر (nusūr
نسور)

W

wade [weid] *v* khāḍa خاض (u;
khawḍ خوض)

wag [wag] *v* hazza هز (u; hazz هز)

wage [weij] *n* 1. ajr أجر (ujūr أجور);
rātib راتب (rawātib رواتب)

wage earner *n* kāsib كاسب (-ūn);
muʿīl معيل (-ūn)

wage freeze *n* tajammud ar-
rawātib تجمد الرواتب

wage rise *n* ziyāda زيادة (-āt);
ʿilāwa علاوة (-āt)

wage war *v* shanna al-ḥarb
شن الحرب (u; shann شن)

wages [ˈweijiz] *pl* rawātib رواتب

waggon; wagon ['wagən] *n* ʿaraba
عربة (āt-)

wail [weil] *v* nahaba نحب (a/i; nahb
نحب; nahīb نحيب)

waist [weist] *n* khasr خصر (khuṣūr
خصور)

waistcoat ['weiskəut] *n* ṣudra
صدرة; sutra سترة (sutar ستر)

wait [weit] *v* intaẓara انتظر

waiter ['weitə] *n* garsōn غرسون;
nādil نادل

waitress ['weitris] *n* nādila نادلة

wake; wake up [weik] *v* (woke/
waked, woken/waked) istayqaẓa
استيقظ

waken ['weikən] *see* wake

Wales [weilz] *n* muqāṭaʿat waylz ويلز
مقاطعة

walk [wo:k] 1. *n* nuzha نزهة (āt;
nuzah نزه) 2. *v* mashā مشى (i;
mashy مشي)

walk out (of) *v* 1. insahaba
انسحب 2. aḍraba ʿan al-ʿamal
أضرب عن العمل

wall [wo:l] *n* ḥāʾiṭ حائط (ḥīṭān حيطان)

wallet ['wolit] *n* maḥfaẓa محفظة
(maḥāfiẓ محافظ)

wallpaper ['wolpeipə] *n* waraq al-
ḥīṭān ورق الحيطان

walnut ['wolnʌt] *n* jawza جوزة
(*collective* jawz جوز; *pl* -āt)

wander [wondə] *v* tajawwala تجول

wanderer ['wondərə] *n* mutajawwil
متجول

want [wont] 1. *n* ḥāja حاجة (āt-) 2. *v*
arāda أراد; raghiba fī رغب في (a;
raghba رغبة)

war [wo:] 1. *adj* ḥarbī حربي 2. *n* ḥarb
حرب *f* (ḥurūb حروب) 3. **civil war**
ḥarb ahlīya حرب أهلية 4. **the Cold**

War al-ḥarb al-bārida الحرب الباردة
5. *see* **wage war**

war crime *n* 1. jarāʾim ḥarb
جرائم حرب 2. **to commit a
war crime** irtakaba jarāʾim ḥarb
ارتكب جرائم حرب

war criminal *n* murtakib jarāʾim
ḥarb مرتكب جرائم حرب (ūn-)

ward [wo:d] *n* 1. (*pol.*) dāʾira
intikhābiya دائرة إنتخابية 2. (*med.*)
janāḥ جناح (ajniḥa أجنحة)

warden ['wo:dən] *n* amīn
أمين (umanāʾ أمناء); ḥāfiẓ
حافظ (ḥuffāẓ حفاظ); murāqib
مراقب (ūn-)

warder ['wo:də] *n* ḥāris حارس
(ḥurrās حراس)

wardrobe ['wo:drəub] *n* khazzāna
li 'l-malābis خزانة للملابس (āt-)

warehouse ['weəhaus] *n*
mustawdaʿ مستودع (āt-); makhzin
مخزن (makhāzin مخازن)

wares [weə] *pl* silaʿ li 'l-bayʿ
سلع للبيع

warfare ['wo:feə] *n* ḥarb حرب *f*

warm [wo:m] 1. *adj* dāfiʾ دافئ 2. *v*
daffaʾa دفأ

warmth [wo:mth] *n* difʾ دفء

warn [wo:n] *v* ḥadhdhara حذر;
andhara أنذر

warning ['wo:ning] *n* taḥdhīr تحذير;
indhār إنذار

warrior ['woriə] *n* muḥārib محارب
(ūn-)

wartime ['wo:taim] 1. *adj/n* zaman
al-ḥarb زمن الحرب

was [wəz; woz] *see* **be**

wash [wosh] *v* 1. ghasala غسل (i;
ghasl غسل) 2. **to wash up** jalā aṣ-
ṣuḥūn جلا الصحون (u; jaly جلي)

washing ['woshing] *n* ghasīl غسيل

washing powder *n* masḥūq al-ghasīl مسحوق الغسيل

washing up *n* jaly aṣ-ṣuḥūn جلي الصحون

washroom ['woshrum] *n* ghurfat al-ghasīl غرفة الغسيل

wasp [wosp] *n* dabbūr دبور (dabābīr دبابير)

waste [weist] **1.** *n* nufāya نفاية (-āt) **2.** *v* baddada بدد

wasteful ['weistfəl] *adj* musrif مسرف

watch [woch] **1.** *n* sāʿa ساعة (-āt) **2.** *v* rāqaba راقب; tafarraja ʿalā تفرج على

watcher ['wochə] *n* murāqib مراقب (-ūn)

water ['wo:tə] *n* māʾ ماء (miyāh مياه)

waterfall ['wo:təfo:l] *n* shallāl شلال (-āt)

watermelon ['wo:təmelən] *n* baṭṭīkha بطيخة (*collective* baṭṭīkh بطيخ)

waterproof ['wo:təpru:f] *adj* wāqin didd al-maṭar واق ضد المطر

watersports ['wo:təspo:ts] *pl* al-alʿāb al-māʾīya الألعاب المائية

wave [weiv] **1.** *n* mawja موجة (-āt) **2.** *v* lawwaḥa لوح

wavelength ['weivlength] *n* ṭūl mawjī طول موجي

wax [waks] *n* shamʿ شمع

way [wei] **1.** *n* sabīl سبيل (subul سبل); ṭarīq طريق (ṭuruq طرق) **2.** ʿāda عادة (-āt) **3. way of life** uslūb ḥayāh أسلوب حياة (asālīb أساليب) **4. by way of** ʿan ṭarīq عن طريق **5. on the way** fi ʾṭ-ṭarīq في الطريق **6. by the way** ʿalā fikra على فكرة **7.**

underway jārī جاري **8. to give way** aʿṭā aṭ-ṭarīq أعطى الطريق

we [wi:] *pronoun* naḥnu نحن

weak [wi:k] *adj* ḍaʿīf ضعيف

weaken [wi:kən] *v* aḍʿafa أضعف

weakness [wi:knis] *n* ḍuʿf ضعف

wealth [welth] *n* tharwa ثروة

wealthy ['welthi] *adj* ghanī غني; tharī ثري

weapon ['wepən] *n* silāḥ سلاح (asliḥa أسلحة)

wear [weə] *v* (**wore, worn**) **1.** labisa لبس (a; lubs لبس) **2. to wear out** baliya بلي (a; bilan بلى)

weasel ['wi:zəl] *n* ibn ʿirs ابن عرس (banāt ʿirs بنات عرس)

weather ['wedhə] **1.** *n* ṭaqs طقس; jaww جو **2.** *v* najā نجا (u; najāʾ نجاء)

weave [wi:v] *v* (**wove, woven**) nasaja نسج (u/i; nasīj نسيج)

web [web] *n* **1.** nasīj نسيج (ansija أنسجة) **2. the Web** al-internet الإنترنت

wed [wed] *v* zawwaja زوج

wedding ['weding] *n* ʿurs عرس (aʿrās أعراس); zifāf زفاف

Wednesday ['wenzdei] *n* (yawm) al-arbaʿāʾ (يوم) الأربعاء

week [wi:k] *n* usbūʿ أسبوع (asābīʿ أسابيع)

weekend [wi:k'end] *n* nihāyat al-usbūʿ نهاية الأسبوع

weekly ['wi:kli] **1.** *adj* usbūʿī أسبوعي **2.** *adv* usbūʿīyan أسبوعياً **3.** *n* usbūʿīya أسبوعية

weep [wi:p] *v* (**wept**) bakā بكى (i; bukāʾ بكاء)

weigh [wei] *v* wazana وزن (yazinu يزن; wazn وزن)

weight [weit] *n* wazn وزن (awzān أوزان)

weird [wiːəd] *adj* gharīb al-aṭwār غريب الأطوار

welcome [welkəm] **1.** *adj* muraḥḥab bih مرحب به **2.** *n* tarḥīb ترحيب **3.** *v* raḥḥaba رحب

welfare [welfeə] *n* **1.** rafāha رفاهة **2.** khidmāt ijtimāʿīya خدمات إجتماعية

well [wel] **1.** *adj* jayyid جيد **2.** *n* biʾr بئر (ābār آبار; biʾār بئار) **3. oil well** biʾr nafṭ بئر نفط **4. gas well** biʾr ghāz بئر غاز **5.** *adv* jayyid جيد **6. as well as** bi ʾl-iḍāfati ilā بالإضافة إلى; ayḍan أيضاً **7. well!** ḥasanan حسناً

well-being [welˈbiːying] *n* rafāha رفاهة

well-known [welˈnəun] *adj* maʿrūf معروف; mashhūr مشهور

Welsh [welsh] *adj* waylzī ويلزي

went [went] *see* **go**

wept [wept] *see* **weep**

were [wəː] *see* **be**

werewolf [ˈweəwulf] *n* rajul dhiʾb رجل ذئب

west [west] **1.** *adj* gharbī غربي **2.** *n* gharb غرب

western [ˈwestən] *adj/n* gharbī غربي

westerner [ˈwestənə] *n* gharbī غربي

wet [wet] **1.** *adj* mablūl مبلول **2.** *v* balla بل (u; ball بل)

whale [weil] *n* ḥūt حوت

what [wot] **1.** mā ما; mādhā ماذا **2.** alladhī الذي **3.** yā lah min... يا له من... **4. what for?** limādhā لماذا

whatever [woˈtevə] **1.** ayyu shayʾ أي شيء; **2.** ayyan kān أياً كان; mahmā yakun مهما يكن

wheat [wiːt] *n* qamḥ قمح

wheel [wiːl] *n* ʿajala عجلة (-āt)

wheelchair [ˈwiːlcheə] *n* kursī mutaḥarrik كرسي متحرك

when [wen] **1.** lamma لما; ʿindamā عندما **2.** matā متى **3. since when** mundhu matā منذ متى

whenever [wenˈevə] kullamā كلما

where [weə] **1.** ayna أين **2.** aynamā أينما **3. from where?** min ayna من أين

whereabouts [ˈweərəbauts] **1.** ayna أين **2.** makān مكان

whereas [weərˈaz] *conj* ḥaithu kān حيث كان

wherever [weərˈevə] **1.** ayna أين **2.** aynamā أينما

whether [ˈwethə] *conj* **1.** idhā إذا; mā idhā ما إذا **2. whether... or** a... am... أ... أم...

which [wich] ayy أي

whichever [wichˈevə] ayy أي; ayyumā أيما

while [wail] **1.** *n* fatra فترة (-āt) **2.** *prep* fī ḥīn في حين; ʿalā r-raghmi min على الرغم من **3.** *conj* baynamā بينما; mā dām ما دام **4. for a while** qalīlan قليلاً

whiskey; whisky [wiski] *n* wiskī وسكي

whisper [ˈwispə] *v* hamasa همس (i; hams همس)

whistle [ˈwisəl] *v* ṣafara صفر (i; ṣafīr صفير; ṣaffara صفر)

white [wait] *adj* abyaḍ أبيض

who [huː] **1.** man من **2.** alladhī الذي

whoever; whosoever [huːevə huːˈsəuevə] **1.** man من **2.** ayyan kān أياً كان

whole [həul] **1.** *n* kull كل **2.** *adj* kāmil

تام tāmm ;كامل 3. **on the whole** ijmālan إجمالاً

whom [hu:m] *see* who

whose [hu:z] 1. liman لمن 2. alladhī الذي

why [wai] 1. lima لم; limā لما; limādhā لماذا 2. **why not?** lima lā لم لا

wicked ['wikid] *adj* sharīr شرير

wide [waid] 1. *adj* wāsiʿ واسع 2. *adv* baʿīdan بعيداً

widen ['waidən] *v* wassaʿa وسع

widespread ['waidspred] *adj* muntashir منتشر

widow ['widəu] *n* armala أرملة (arāmil أرامل)

widower ['widəuə] *n* armal أرمل (arāmil أرامل)

width [width] *n* ʿarḍ عرض (ʿurūḍ عروض)

wield [wi:ld] *v* istakhdama استخدم

wife [waif] *n* (*pl* **wives**) zawja زوجة (-āt)

wild [waild] *adj* waḥshī وحشي

will [wil] 1. *n* irāda إرادة 2. (*leg.*) waṣīya وصية 3. *see* be

willing ['wiling] *adj* mustaʿidd مستعد

win [win] *v* (**won**) 1. fāza فاز (u; fawz فوز) 2. rabiḥa ربح (i; ribḥ ربح)

wind [wind] *n* rīḥ ريح *usually f* (riyāḥ رياح)

wind [waind] *v* (**wound**) laffa لف (u; laff لف)

window ['windəu] *n* shubbāk شباك (shabābīk شبابيك)

windy ['windi] *adj* ʿāṣif عاصف

wine [wain] *n* nabīdh نبيذ (anbidha أنبذة)

wing [wing] *n* janāḥ جناح (ajniḥa أجنحة)

wink [wink] *v* ghamaza غمز (i; ghamz غمز)

winner ['winə] *n* fāʾiz فائز (-ūn)

winter ['wintə] *n* shitāʾ شتاء

wipe [waip] *v* 1. masaḥa مسح (a; masḥ مسح) 2. **to wipe out** aqḍā أقضى على ʿalā

wire [waiə] *n* 1. silk سلك (aslāk أسلاك) 2. **barbed wire** aslāk shāʾika أسلاك شائكة

wisdom ['wizdəm] *n* ḥikma حكمة

wise [waiz] *n* ḥakīm حكيم

wish [wish] 1. *n* umnīya أمنية (amānin أمان) 2. *v* tamannā تمنى

wit [wit] *n* 1. ẓarāfa ظرافة 2. ʿaql عقل 3. *see* wits

witch [wich] *n* sāḥira ساحرة (-āt)

with [widh] *prep* 1. bi ب 2. maʿa مع 3. ʿinda عند 4. ladā لدى

withdraw [with'dro:] *v* (**withdrew, withdrawn**) 1. insaḥaba انسحب 2. tarājaʿa تراجع 3. **to withdraw money** saḥaba naqdan سحب نقداً (a; saḥb سحب)

withhold [widh'həuld] *v* iḥtabasa احتبس

within [wi'dhin] 1. *prep* dākhil داخل 2. *adv* dakhilan داخلاً

without [wi'dhaut] *prep* 1. min ghayr من غير; dūn دون 2. **without a doubt** dūna shakk دون شك 3. **without fail** bi t-taʾkīd بالتأكيد

withstand [widh'stand] *v* qāwama قاوم; taḥammala تحمل

witness ['witnis] *n* 1. *n* shāhid شاهد (shuhūd شهود) 2. *v* shāhada شاهد

wits [wit] *n* ʿaql عقل

wives [waivz] *see* wife

wizard ['wizəd] *n* sāḥir ساحر (ūn; saḥara ;سحرة; suḥḥār (سحار)

woke; woken [wəuk; 'wəukən] *see* **wake**

wolf [wulf] *n* (*pl* **wolves**) dhi'b ذئب (dhi'āb (ذئاب)

woman ['wumən] *n* (*pl* **women** ['wimin]) imra'a إمرأة (nisā ' نساء ; niswān ;نسوان; niswa (نسوة)

womb [wu:m] *n* raḥim رحم *f* (arḥām (أرحام)

women ['wimin] *see* **woman**

won [wʌn] *see* **win**

wonder ['wʌndə] 1. *n* a'jūba أعجوبة (a'ājīb (أعاجيب) 2. *v* ta'ajjaba تعجب 3. tasā'ala تساءل

wonderful ['wʌndəfəl] *adj* 'ajīb عجيب; mudhish ;مدهش; hā'il هائل

wood [wud] *n* 1. khashab خشب (akhshāb (أخشاب) 2. ghāba غابة (-āt)

wooden ['wudən] *adj* khashabī خشبي

wool [wul] *n* ṣūf صوف

word [wə:d] *n* kalima كلمة (-āt)

wore [wo:] *see* **wear**

work [wə:k] 1. *n* amal عمل (a'māl (أعمال) 2. *v* 'amila عمل (a; 'amal (عمل) 3. **out of work** 'āṭil عاطل 4. *and see* **work out**

worker ['wə:kə] *n* 'āmil عامل ('ummāl (عمال)

work force *n* al-qūwa al-'āmila القوة العاملة

work out *v* 1. ḥalla حل (u; ḥall (حل) 2. (*spor.*) tamarrana تمرن

workplace ['wə:kpleis] *n* makān al-'amal مكان العمل

workshop ['wə:kshop] *n* warshat 'amal ورشة عمل (-āt)

world [wə:ld] 1. *adj* 'ālamī عالمي 2. *n*

the world al-'ālam العالم

World Cup *n* ka's al-'ālam كأس العالم

worldwide [wə:ld'waid] *adj/adv* 'ālamī عالمي

worm [wə:m] *n* dūda دودة (collective dūd ;دود; *pl* dīdān (ديدان)

worn [wo:n] *see* **wear**

worried ['wʌrid] *adj* qaliq قلق

worry ['wʌri] 1. *n* qalaq قلق 2. *v* aqlaqa أقلق

worse [wə:s] *adj* aswa' أسوأ

worship ['wə:ship] 1. *n* 'ibāda عبادة 2. *v* 'abada عبد (u; 'ibāda (عبادة)

worst [wə:st] *adj* aswa' أسوأ

worth [wə:th] *n* qīma قيمة

worthless ['wə:thlis] *adj* lā qīma lah لا قيمة له

worthwhile [wə:th'wail] *adj* dhū sha'n ذو شأن; dhū qīma ذو قيمة

worthy ['wə:dhi] *adj* fāḍil فاضل (-ūn)

would [wud] *see* **will**

wound [waund] *see* **wind**

wound [wu:nd] 1. *n* jurḥ جرح (jurūḥ جروح) 2. *v* jaraḥa جرح (a; jarḥ (جرح)

wounded ['wu:ndid] *adj* majrūḥ مجروح

wove; woven [wəuv; 'wəuvən] *see* **weave**

wrap [rap] *v* laffa لف (u; laff (لف)

wreck [rek] 1. *n* safina ghāriqa سفينة غارقة 2. *v* kharraba خرب

wrench [rench] *n* miftāḥ rabṭ مفتاح ربط

wrestling ['resling] *n* muṣāra'a مصارعة

wriggle ['rigəl] *v* talawwā تلوى

wrinkles ['ringkəls] *pl* tajā'īd تجاعيد

wrist [rist] *n* mi'ṣam معصم (ma'āsim (معاصم

write [rait] *v* (wrote, written) kataba كتب (u; katb كتب; kitāba (كتابة

writer ['raitə] *n* kātib كاتب (ūn; kuttāb كتاب; kataba (كتبة

writing ['raiting] *n* kitāba كتابة

written ['ritən] *adj* **1.** maktūb مكتوب **2.** *see* **write**

wrong [rong] **1.** *adj* khāṭi' خاطئ؛ **2.** *n* ghalaṭ غلط (aghlāṭ أغلاط) **3.** ẓulm ظلم **4.** *adv* 'alā khaṭa' على خطأ

wrote [rəut] *see* **write**

xenophobia [zenə'fəubya] *n* kurh al-ajānib كره الأجانب

Xmas ['eksməs] *n* 'īd al-mīlād عيد الميلاد

X-ray ['eksrei] **1.** *n* ashi''a أشعة **2.** to take an x-ray akhadha ṣūrat al-ashi''a أخذ صورة الأشعة

yacht [yot] *n* yakht يخت (yukhūt (يخوت

yard [ya:d] *n* **1.** yārda ياردة (-āt) **2.** sāḥa ساحة (-āt) **3.** *(US)* junayna جنينة (āt; janā'in (جنائن

yawn [yo:n] **1.** *n* tathā'ub تثاؤب **2.** *v* tathā'aba تثاءب

year [yiə] *n* **1.** 'ām عام (a'wām أعوام)؛ sana سنة (sanawāt سنوات؛ sinūn سنون) **2. leap year** sana kabīsa سنة كبيسة

yell [yel] **1.** *n* ṣarkha صرخة **2.** *v* ṣarakha صرخ (u; ṣurākh (صراخ

yellow ['yeləu] *adj* aṣfar أصفر

yes [yes] na'am نعم

yesterday ['yestədei] *n/adv* **1.** ams أمس **2. the day before yesterday** awwal ams أول أمس

yet [yet] 1. *adv* ba'd بعد 2. **as yet**
ḥattā 'l-ān حتى الآن; ba'd بعد 3. *conj*
ma'a dhālik مع ذلك

yield [yiːld] *n* maḥṣūl محصول (āt;
maḥāṣil محاصيل)

yoghurt; yogurt ['yogət] *n* laban
zabādī لبن زبادي

you [yuː] *pronoun* 1. anta أنت; anti
أنت; antumā أنتما; antum أنتم;
antunna أنتن 2. -ka ك; -ki ك; -kumā
كما; -kum كم; -kunna كن

young [yʌng] *adj* ṣaghīr (as-sinn)
صغير (السن); shābb شاب

your [yoː] -ka ك; -ki ك; -kumā كما;

-kum كم; -kunna كن

yours [yoːz] laka لك; laki لك;
lakumā لكما; lakum لكم; lakunna
لكن

yourself [yoːˈself] (*pl* **yourselves**)
anfusuka *etc* أنفسك

youth [yuːth] 1. *adj* shābb شاب 2. *n*
shābb شاب (shubbān شبان; shabāb
شباب) 3. **a youth** shabāb شباب;
shabība شبيبة

Yugoslavia [yuːgəuˈslaːvyə] *n*
yūghūslāviya يوغوسلافيا

Yugoslavian [yuːgəuˈslaːvyən] *adj*
yūghūslāvī يوغوسلافي

Z

zero ['ziərəu] *n* ṣifr صفر (aṣfār أصفار)
zip [zip, 'zipə] 1. *n* saḥḥāb سحاب 2.
(US) **zip code** ramz barīdī رمز بريدي
zodiac ['zəudiak] *n* dā'irat al-abrāj
دائرة الأبراج

zone [zəun] *n* minṭaqa منطقة
(manāṭiq مناطق)
zoo [zuː] *n* ḥadīqat al-ḥayawānāt
حديقة الحيوانات

APPENDICES

Days of the week

Monday	(yawm) al-ithnayn	(يوم) الإثنين
Tuesday	(yawm) ath-thalāthā'	(يوم) الثلاثاء
Wednesday	(yawm) al-arba'ā'	(يوم) الاربعاء
Thursday	(yawm) al-khamīs	(يوم) الخميس
Friday	(yawm) al-jum'a	(يوم) الجمعة
Saturday	(yawm) as-sabt	(يوم) السبت
Sunday	(yawm) al-aḥad	(يوم) الأحد

Months

In the right-hand columns are months used in Lebanon, Syria, Jordan & Iraq.

January	yanāyir	يناير	kānūn ath-thānī	كانون الثاني
February	fabrāyir	فبراير	shubāṭ	شباط
March	mārs	مارس	ādhār	آذار
April	abrīl	أبريل	nīsān	نيسان
May	māyū	مايو	nawwār	نوّار
June	yūniyū	يونيو	ḥazīrān	حزيران
July	yūliyū	يوليو	tammūz	تموز
August	aghusṭus	أغسطس	āb	آب
September	sibtambir	سبتمبر	aylūl	أيلول
October	uktūbir	أكتوبر	tishrīn al-awwal	تشرين الأوّل
November	nūfimbir	نوفمبر	tishrīn ath-thānī	تشرين الثاني
December	dīsambir	ديسمبر	kānūn al-awwal	كانون الأوّل

Islamic months

1.	**Muharram**	muḥarram	محرّم
2.	**Safar**	ṣafar	صفر
3.	**Rabi-al-Awwal**	rabīʿ al-awwal	ربيع الأوّل
4.	**Rabi-al-Thani**	rabīʿ ath-thānī	ربيع الثاني
5.	**Jumada-al-Ula**	jumādā 'l-ūlā	جمادى الأولى
6.	**Jumada-al-Akhira**	jumādā 'l-ākhira	جمادى الآخرة
7.	**Rajab**	rajab	رجب
8.	**Shaban**	shaʿbān	شعبان
9.	**Ramadan**	ramaḍān	رمضان
10.	**Shawwal**	shawwāl	شوّال
11.	**Zul-Qida**	dhū 'l-qiʿda	ذو القعدة
12.	**Zul-Hijja**	dhū 'l-ḥijja	ذو الحجّة

Countries

Note that there can be variation in preferred spellings and pronunciations.

Africa	afrīqiyā	أفرقيا
America	amerikā	أميركا
Antartica	antārktīkā	أنتاركتيكا
Arabian (Persian) Gulf	al-khalīj al-'arabī	الخليج العربي
Asia	āsiyā	آسيا
Atlantic Ocean	al-muḥīṭ al-aṭlanṭī	المحيط الأطلنطي
the Caribbean	al-kārīb	الكاريب
the Caucasus	al-qawqāz	القوقاز
Central America	amerikā al-wusṭā	أميركا الوسطى
Central Asia	āsiyā al-wusṭā	آسيا الوسطى
East Africa	sharq afrīqiyā	شرق أفرقيا
River Euphrates	al-furāt	الفرات
Europe	ūrūbā	أوروبا
European Union	al-ittiḥād al-ūrūbī	الإتّحاد الأوروبي
Far East	as-sharq al-aqṣā	الشرق الأقصى
Horn of Africa	al-qarn al-afrīqī	القرن الأفريقي
Indian Ocean	al-muḥīṭ al-hindī	المحيط الهندي
Mediterranean Sea	al-baḥr al-mutawassiṭ	البحر المتوسّط
Middle East	ash-sharq al-awsaṭ	الشرق الأوسط
River Nile	an-nīl	النيل
North Africa	shamāl afrīqiyā	شمال أفريقا
Northwest Africa; the Maghreb	al-maghrib	المغرب
Pacific Ocean	al-muḥīṭ al-hādi'	المحيط الهادئ
Southeast Asia	janūb sharq āsiyā	جنوب شرق آسيا
River Tigris	dijla	دجلة
South America	amrīkā al-janūbīya	أمريكا الجنوبية
United Nations	hay'at al-umam al-muttaḥida	هيئة الأمم المتّحدة
West Africa	gharb afrīqiyā	غرب أفرقيا

Abu Dhabi	abū ẓabī	أبو ظبي
Afghanistan	afghānistān	أفغانستان
Ajman	'ajmān	عجمان
Albania	albāniyā	ألبانيا
Algeria	al-jazā'ir	الجزائر
American Samoa	sāmuwā al-amrīkīya	ساموا الأمريكية
Andorra	andōrā	أندورا
Angola	anghōlā	أنغولا
Anguilla	angwīlā	أنغويلا
Antigua and Barbuda	antīgwā wa bārbūdā	أنتيغوا وباربودا
Argentina	al-arjintīn	الأرجنتين
Armenia	armīniyā	أرمينيا
Australia	usturāliyā	أستراليا
Austria	an-nimsā	النمسا
Azerbaijan	adharbayjān	أذربيجان
the Bahamas	juzur al-bahāmā	جزر البهاما
Bahrain	al-baḥrayn	البحرين
Bangladesh	banglādēsh	بنغلاديش
Barbados	barbēdos	بربادوس
Belarus	bēlārūs	بيلاروس
Belgium	beljīkā	بلجيكا
Belize	belīz	بليز
Benin	benīn	بينين
Bermuda	bermūdā	برمودا
Bhutan	būtān	بوتان
Bolivia	bolīviyā	بوليفيا
Bosnia and Herzegovina	al-bōsna wa 'l-harsak	البوسنة والهرسك
Botswana	bōtsuwānā	بوتسوانا
Brazil	al-brāzīl	البرازيل
Britain	brīṭāniyā	بريطانيا
British Virgin Islands	juzur vīrjīn al-brīṭāniya	جزر فيرجين البريطانية
Brunei Darussalam	brūnay dār as-salām	بروني دار السلام
Bulgaria	bulgāriyā	بلغاريا
Burkina Faso	būrkīnā fāṣū	بوركينا فاصو

Burundi	būrūndī	بوروندي
Cambodia	kambōdiyā	كمبوديا
Cameroon	al-kāmīrūn	الكاميرون
Canada	kanadā	كندا
Cape Verde	ar-ra's al-aḥḍar	الرأس الأخضر
Cayman Islands	juzur kāymān	جزر كايمان
Central African Republic	jumhūrīya afrīqīya al-wusṭā	جمهورية أفريقيا الوسطى
Chad	chād	تشاد
Chechnya	ash-shīshān	الشيشان
Chile	shīlī	شيلي
China	aṣ-ṣīn	الصين
Colombia	kūlūmbiyā	كولومبيا
the Comoros	juzur al-qamar	جزر القمر
the Congo	al-kongo	الكونغو
Democratic Republic of the Congo	jumhūrīyat al-kongo ad-dīmuqrāṭīya	جمهورية الكونغو الديمقراطية
the Cook Islands	juzur kūk	حذر كوك
Costa Rica	kostārīkā	كوستاريكا
Côte d'Ivoire	kōt dīvwār	كوت ديفوار
Croatia	kruwātiyā	كرواتيا
Cuba	kūbā	كوبا
Cyprus	qubruṣ	قبرص
the Czech Republic	al-jumhūrīya al-chīkīya	الجمهورية التشيكية
Denmark	ad-dinmārk	الدنمارك
Djibouti	jībūtī	جيباتي
Dominica	dōmīnīkā	دومينيكا
the Dominican Republic	jumhūrīyat ad-dōmīnīkān	جمهورية الدومينيكان
Dubai	dubai	دبي
Ecuador	ikwādūr	إكوادور
Egypt	miṣr	مصر
El Salvador	elsalvādūr	السلفادور
England	ingilterā	إنكلترا
Equatorial Guinea	gīniyā al-istiwā'īya	غينيا الإستوائية

Eritrea	irītriyā	إريتريا
Estonia	istōniyā	إستونيا
Ethiopia	ithyūpiyā	إثيوبيا
Faeroe Islands	juzur fayruwīya	جزر فيرويه
Falkland Islands (Malvinas)	juzur fālkland (mālvīnas)	جزر فالكلند (مالفينس)
Fiji	fījī	فيجي
Finland	finlandā	فنلندا
France	faransā	فرنسا
French Guiana	gīyānā al-faransīya	غوايانا الفرنسية
French Polynesia	pōlīnīziyā al-faransīya	بولينيزيا الفرنسية
Gabon	gābōn	غابون
the Gambia	gāmbiyā	غامبيا
Georgia	gōrjiyā	جورجيا
Germany	almānīyā	ألمانيا
Ghana	gānā	غانا
Gibraltar	jabal ṭāriq	جبل طارق
Greece	al-yūnān	اليونان
Grenada	grinādā	غرينادا
Guadeloupe	guwādelūp	غواديلوب
Guam	guwām	غوام
Guatemala	guwātemālā	غواتيمالا
Guinea	gīniyā	غينيا
Guinea-Bissau	gīniyā-bīsāw	غينيا – بيساو
Guyana	gayānā	غيانا
Haiti	hāyitī	هايتي
Holy See	al-maqām al-bābāwī	المقام الباباوي
Honduras	hundūrās	هندوراس
Iceland	ayslandā	أيسلندا
Hungary	al-majar	المجر
India	al-hind	الهند
Indonesia	indōnīsiyā	إندونيسيا
Iran	īrān	إيران
Iraq	al-ʿirāq	العراق
Ireland	āyrlandā	آيرلندا

Israel	isrā'īl	إسرائيل
Italy	īṭāliyā	إيطاليا
Jamaica	jāmāykā	جامايكا
Japan	al-yābān	اليابان
Jordan	al-urdunn	الأردن
Kazakhstan	kāzākhstān	كازاخستان
Kenya	kenyā	كينيا
Kiribati	kīrībātī	كيريباتي
North Korea	kōriyā ash-shamālīya	كوريا الشمالية
South Korea	kōriyā al-janūbīya	كوريا الجنوبية
Kuwait	al-kuwayt	الكويت
Kyrgyzstan	qīrghīzistān	قيرغيزستان
Laos	lāwōs	لاوس
Latvia	lātviyā	لاتفيا
Lebanon	lubnān	لبنان
Lesotho	lēsōtō	ليسوتو
Liberia	lībēriyā	ليبريا
Libya	lībīyā	ليبيا
Liechtenstein	likhtinshtāyn	لختنشتاين
Lithuania	lītūwāniyā	ليتوانيا
Luxembourg	luksimburg	لكمبرغ
Madagascar	madagashqar	مدغشقر
Malawi	malāwī	ملاوي
Malaysia	mālayziyā	ماليزيا
Maldives	maldīv	ملديف
Mali	mālī	مالي
the Marshall Islands	juzur mārshāl	جزر مارشال
Malta	mālṭa	مالطة
Martinique	mārtīnīk	مارتينيك
Mauritania	mōrītāniyā	موريتانيا
Mauritius	mōrūshyūs	موريشيوس
Mexico	al-miksīk	المكسيك
Micronesia	mīkrūnīziyā	ميكرونيزيا
Moldova	mōldōvā	مولدوفا
Monaco	mōnākō	موناكو

Mongolia	munghīliyā	منغوليا
Montserrat	mōnsirāṭ	مونسراط
Morocco	al-maghrib	المغرب
Mozambique	mōzāmbīq	موزامبيق
Myanmar (Burma)	mayānmār (būrmā)	ميانمار (بورما)
Nauru	nāwurū	ناورو
Namibia	nāmībiyā	ناميبيا
Nepal	nēpāl	نيبال
the Netherlands	hōlandā	هولندا
Netherlands Antilles	juzur al-antīl al-hōlandīya	جزر الأنتيل الهولندية
New Caledonia	kālīdōniyā al-jadīda	كاليدونيا الجديدة
New Zealand	niyūzīlandā	نيوزيلندا
Nicaragua	nīkārāgwā	نيكاراغوا
the Niger	an-nījer	النيجر
Nigeria	nījēriyā	نيجيريا
Niue	niyuway	نيوي
Northern Ireland	āyrlandā ash-shamālīya	آيرلندا الشمالية
Norway	an-nurwēj	النرويج
Oman	ʿumān	عمان
Pakistan	al-bākistān	الباكستان
Palau	pālāw	بالاو
Palestine	filasṭīn	فلسطين
Panama	panamā	بنما
Papua New Guinea	pāpuwā gīniyā al-jadīda	بابوا غينيا الجديدة
Paraguay	pārāgwāy	باراغواي
Peru	perū	بيرو
the Philippines	filībīn; al-filibīn	فيليبين؛ الفلبين
Poland	pōlandā	بولندا
Portugal	al-burtughāl	البرتغال
Puerto Rico	pōrtōrīkō	بورتوريكو
Qatar	qaṭar	قطر
Ras Al Khaimah	ra's al-khayma	رأس الخيمة
Réunion	reyūniyūn	ريونيون

Romania	rōmāniyā	رومانيا
the Russian Federation	al-ittiḥād ar-rūsī	الإتّحاد الروسي
Rwanda	ruwāndā	رواندا
Saint Helena	sānt helenā	سانت هيلينا
Saint Kitts and Nevis	sēnt kīts wa nēvis	سانت كيتس ونيفس
Saint Lucia	sēnt lūsīya	سانت لوسيا
Saint Pierre and Miquelon	sān pīyer wa mīkelōn	سان بيير وميكلون
Saint Vincent and the Grenadines	sān vinsint wa juzur grenādīn	سانت فنسنت وجزر غرينادين
Samoa	sāmowā	ساموا
San Marino	san mārīnō	سان مارينو
Sao Tome and Principe	sān tōmē wa prinsīpē	ساو تومي وبرنسيبي
Saudi Arabia	al-mamlaka al-ʿarabīya as-saʿūdīya	المملكة العربية السعودية
Scotland	iskotlandā	اسكتلندا
Senegal	as-sinigāl	السنغال
Serbia and Montenegro	ṣirbiyā wa 'l-jabal al-aswad	صربيا والجبل الأسود
Seychelles	as-sayshēl	السيشيل
Sharjah	ash-shāriqa	الشارقة
Sierra Leone	sīrāliyōn	سيراليون
Singapore	singāpōr	سنغافورة
Slovakia	slōvākiyā	سلوفاكيا
Slovenia	slōvīniyā	سلوفينيا
Solomon Islands	juzur sulaymān	جزر سليمان
Somalia	aṣ-ṣūmāl	الصومال
South Africa	dawlat janūb afrīqīyā	دولة جنوب أفريقيا
Spain	isbāniyā	إسبانيا
Sri Lanka	srī lānkā	سري لانكا
the Sudan	as-sūdān	السودان
Suriname	sīrīnām	سورينام
Swaziland	suwāzīland	سوازيلند
Sweden	as-suwīd	السويد
Switzerland	suwīserā	سويسرا
Syria	sūrīya	سوريا؛ سورية
Taiwan	tāywān	تايوان

Tajikistan	ṭājīkistān	طاجيكستان
Tanzania	tanzāniyā	تنزانيا
Thailand	tāyland	تايلند
Macedonia	maqadōniyā	مقدونيا
Timor-Leste	tīmōr leste	تيمور – ليشتي
Togo	tōgō	توغو
Tokelau	juzur tūkelāw	جزر توكيلاو
Tonga	tōngā	تونغا
Trinidad and Tobago	trinidād wa tobēgo	ترينيداد وتوباغو
Tunisia	tūnis	تونس
Turkey	turkīya	تركيا
Turkmenistan	turkministān	تركمنستان
Turks and Caicos Islands	juzur turks wa kaykos	جزر تركس وكايكوس
Tuvalu	tūvālū	توفالو
Uganda	ūgāndā	اوغندا
Ukraine	ūkrāniyā	أوكرانيا
Umm Al Qaiwain	umm al-qaywayn	أمّ القيوين
the United Arab Emirates	dawlat al-imārāt al-ʿarabīya al-muttaḥida	دولة الامارات العربية المتّحدة
the United Kingdom	al-mamlaka al-muttaḥida	المملكة المتّحدة
the United States of America	al-wilāyāt al-muttaḥida al-amrīkīya	الولايات المتّحدة الأمريكية
United States Virgin Islands	juzur vīrjīn at-tābiʿa li 'l-wilāyāt al-muttaḥida	جزر فيرجين التابعة للولايات المتّحدة
Uruguay	ūrūguwāy	أوروغواي
Uzbekistan	ūzbekistān	أوزبكستان
Vanuatu	vānuwātū	فانواتو
the Vatican	al-vātīkān	الفاتيكان
Venezuela	vinizwīlā	فنزويلا
Viet Nam	viyatnām	فيتنام
Wales	muqāṭaʿat waylz	مقاطعة ويلز
Wallis and Futuna Islands	juzur wālīs wa fūtūnā	جزر واليس وفوتونا
Yemen	al-yaman	اليمن
Zambia	zāmbiyā	زامبيا
Zanzibar	zanjibār	زنجبار
Zimbabwe	zimbābway	زمبابوي

Also available from Hippocrene Books . . .

Arabic-English/English-Arabic
Dictionary & Phrasebook
4,500 entries · ISBN 0-7818-0973-8 · $13.95pb

Mastering Arabic 1 with 2 Audio CDs:
The Complete Course for Beginners
ISBN 0-7818-1042-6 · $32.00pb

Mastering Arabic 2 with 2 Audio CDs:
An Intermediate Course
ISBN: 978-0-7818-1254-2 · $29.95pb

Mastering Arabic 1 Activity Book
ISBN 978-0-7818-1269-6 · $16.95pb

Beginner's Iraqi Arabic with 2 Audio CDs
ISBN 0-7818-1098-1 · $29.95pb

English-Arabic/Arabic-English Modern Military Dictionary
11,000 entries · ISBN 0-7818-0243-1 · $16.95p

Pocket Guide to Arabic Script
ISBN 0-7818-1104-X · $6.95pb

Arabic Verbs
155 entries · 6 x 9 · 0-7818-1229-1 · $23.95pb

Basic Arabic Workbook
350 pages · 6 x 9 · 0-7818-1126-0 · $29.95pb

Intermediate Arabic Workbook
171 pages · 6 x 9 · 0-7818-1177-5 · $29.95pb

Hippocrene Children's Illustrated Arabic Dictionary
500 entries · 94 page · 8½ x 11 · 0-7818-0891-0 · $14.95pb

Prices subject to change without prior notice. **To purchase Hippocrene Books** contact your local bookstore, visit www.hippocrenebooks.com, call (212) 685-4373, or write to: HIPPOCRENE BOOKS, 171 Madison Avenue, New York, NY 10016.